אין איינעם
In eynem
The New Yiddish Textbook
Volume 1

AUTHORS AND EDITORS:

Asya Vaisman Schulman

Jordan Brown

CONTRIBUTING AUTHOR:

Mikhl Yashinsky

ייִדיש

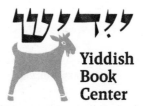

Yiddish
Book
Center

אין איינעם
In eynem
The New Yiddish Textbook

Authors and Editors	Asya Vaisman Schulman Jordan Brown
Contributing Author	Mikhl Yashinsky
Pedagogy Editors	Beatrice (Brukhe) Lang Rebecca (Rivke) Margolis
Language Editors	Yitskhok Niborski Yakov Peretz Blum
Copyeditors	Madeleine Cohen Gregory Lauzon

Project Director	Lisa Newman
Design and Production	Alexander Isley Inc. Christina Holland Yankl Salant
Illustration	Alexander Vaisman Shura Vaisman
Project Managers	Gretchen Fiordalice David Staloch
Project Contributors	Adah Hetko Zeke Levine Jessica Parker Allison Posner Sebastian Schulman Rebecca White Rola Younes
Website Development	Amber Clooney Common Media

Yiddish Book Center Founder and President	Aaron Lansky
Yiddish Book Center Executive Director	Susan Bronson

In eynem published by White Goat Press,
the Yiddish Book Center's imprint
10 9 8 7 6 5 4 3 2 1

Published as two volumes
Library of Congress Cataloging-in-Publication Data available.
Library of Congress Control Number
2020939564
ISBN 978-1-7343872-3-0

The *In eynem* website can be accessed at
http://textbook.yiddishbookcenter.org.

Yiddish Book Center
Amherst, MA 01002
yiddishbookcenter.org
413-256-4900

In eynem is made possible
thanks to the generous support of
Michael G. & Tatiana Reiff

TABLE OF CONTENTS

VOLUME 1

INTRODUCTION

REFERENCE

Volume 1 Reference section follows Unit III: see page x for detail.

VOLUME 2

REFERENCE

For a full list of appendices that appear in the back matter of Volumes 1 and 2, see page TOC1.

1. A NOTE ON AIMS AND APPROACH

WHY A NEW TEXTBOOK?

To study or teach Yiddish today is a vastly different enterprise than it was even a decade ago. The demography and geography of the Yiddish-speaking world continue to change. Textual and archival resources are more widely accessible than ever. Students are more numerous and more diverse and bring different interests, goals, and aspirations to their language studies. Teachers have levels of scholarly and pedagogical training that were rare a generation ago, but often lack the native linguistic and cultural competence that was once taken for granted. All of these developments in the world of Yiddish language instruction must be placed in the context of the broader social and technological changes of recent decades, which continue to profoundly affect language, culture, and education everywhere.

Students and teachers need Yiddish instructional materials designed with these new circumstances in mind, materials that meet contemporary challenges and capitalize on contemporary opportunities. Students have been asking for such materials for some time, and individual teachers—amid the competing demands of academia and other day jobs—have done their best to create them. The authors of this volume are only too familiar with this situation and have long felt the need for new materials for their own classes. When the Yiddish Book Center, with Aaron Lansky's steadfast belief in our vision and thanks to the support of its generous donors, provided the opportunity to create a comprehensive set of materials for the first two semesters of college-level Yiddish instruction, we were able to draw upon the work that we, and so many of our colleagues, had informally begun many times. The result is this full-color, pedagogically rigorous multimedia textbook, a book unlike anything that has been available for Yiddish language learning before.

A COMMUNICATIVE APPROACH

An important development in modern language instruction has been the introduction of a more deliberate and sophisticated pedagogy. For this book we have adopted a *communicative approach*, a teaching style grounded in the idea that the best way to learn a language is to use it to communicate meaningful information to others. We have designed *In eynem* to support this method of teaching and learning both inside and outside the classroom. As such, *In eynem* functions to provide both the *context* for meaningful language use as well as crucial lexical, grammatical, and cultural *content*.

Creating such a context for language learning involves structure and planning at all levels, from focusing the major units of the course on practical themes, to ordering grammatical concepts so each builds logically from the last to the next, to developing reading, writing, listening, and speaking activities requiring precisely modulated levels of active student participation, to composing original texts that introduce practical language in clear, idiomatic contexts. All of these building blocks are brought to life in the classroom with the aid of the comprehensive Teacher's Guide, which offers detailed lesson plans describing activities grounded in communication-based partner and group work.

In eynem guides student and teacher alike through the process of acquiring each new bit of language, from introduction to creative output. As they work through

the exercises, students first learn to make sense of new linguistic material in terms of what they already know and then gradually develop their ability to use the new material actively. Primary sources thematically linked to the topic of each lesson enrich the learning experience, connecting students to the broader cultural context and enabling them to creatively synthesize and actively use new material. By the end of each lesson, students have gone well beyond simply learning a new vocabulary set. Rather, they have assimilated the new words and concepts into their personal lives and developed a sense of the cultural attachments that certain concepts have in the Yiddish-speaking world.

For instance, the section on profession-related vocabulary opens with an illustration of familiar characters at their places of work, described using previously learned and cognate words and phrases. As students progress through the section, they learn to identify people's professions based on their daily activities. As they develop an increasingly active command of new terminology, students begin to express their own opinions in Yiddish, debating the merits and shortcomings of various professions with a classmate. Students then learn the role professions play in Yiddish culture by listening to a folk song about how a potential bridegroom's vocation affects his appeal to a young bride. Creatively engaging with the cultural content, students write a new stanza, drawing on other profession-related terminology they've learned. They then connect the cultural material to their own lives by discussing whether a potential partner's profession factors into their own romantic calculations.

Through a series of ten separate activities and exercises engaging with diverse materials (illustrations, texts, songs, film clips, and more), students do not just commit a set of words to memory but rather build up a network of associations and contexts for them, enabling them to convey their thoughts and relate to others. Each chapter uses this process of building to ever-increasing levels of linguistic and cultural complexity.

AUDIENCE

True to its name, *In eynem* (*Together*) aims to reach the widest possible audience of Yiddish teachers and learners. We believe it is ideal to study Yiddish in a classroom with an expert teacher, but we recognize that many students do not have such an opportunity due to issues of availability or accessibility. We have therefore designed *In eynem* to be used effectively by all students, whether they study in traditional classroom courses, in online courses, in community groups, or independently.

We provide this flexibility by maintaining two paths through the materials. For the independent learner, the textbook assumes the role of teacher, guiding and pacing students in their study; for learners studying collectively (whether in a traditional classroom, online course, or community group), the Teacher Guide describes partner- and groupwork-based activities that make most effective use of communicative learning. For all these learners, the textbook and its associated online resources provide language instruction in all four areas of learning—speaking, writing, reading, and listening—and with multiple learning styles in mind, including visual, auditory, and kinesthetic.

We have also considered the diverse motivations of students, which range from academic to recreational to deeply personal and impact the types of content a

student will find most stimulating and relevant to them. *In eynem* exposes students to a variety of linguistic and cultural texts and contexts, and it focuses on strategies that help students make sense of them, often despite incomplete knowledge, enabling students to take charge of their own studies.

It is worth noting certain choices we have made in consideration of the diversity of students' motivations. First, even though the variety of Yiddish taught in these materials is *klal-shprakh*, or Standard Yiddish, we have included numerous texts and recordings representing other varieties of Yiddish, without editorial modification. This approach exposes students to real Yiddish texts and contexts and helps them develop such skills as understanding different manifestations of the language across time and space, facility with varied writing conventions, and familiarity with important social contexts of language use (e.g., Bundist, Hasidic). We've also incorporated exercises specifically focused on texts well above the student's language level in order to sharpen the information-extraction skills crucial to ongoing language study, where perfect comprehension is never to be expected. At a more fundamental level, we have created opportunities for students to examine exactly why they are studying this language and what place it has in their academic, professional, or personal lives. This is achieved by supporting students in finding space in the language for themselves and finding space in themselves for the language.

PRIMARY SOURCES

In eynem helps students find their way through Yiddish language and culture by drawing on the plethora of primary source documents in archival collections and in the vast corpus of Yiddish literature. We draw on Yiddish sources from different time periods, geographical regions, and positions on religious and political spectra. *In eynem* provides an immersive plunge into Yiddishland in all its variety so students acquire a sense of belonging in that cultural world. Students are prompted in their encounters with these materials to ask searching questions not only about linguistic and cultural concepts but also about deeper critical and philosophical ideas. The linguistic, cultural, demographic, artistic, and personal variety of these texts span Yiddish high culture and vernacular culture alike, and the selections serve as a launching pad for a new generation of Yiddish scholars, artists, and professionals.

Another goal of this book is to prepare students for their eventual entry into an immersive context. Such contexts are rarer and more difficult to find for Yiddish learners than for learners of more commonly taught languages, but Yiddishland still exists in many forms and in many places, and the better a student can recognize and negotiate those spaces, the better they can develop—and keep—their linguistic and cultural competence. It is for this reason that *In eynem* is infused with a suite of characters representative of the broad categories of people who speak and study Yiddish today, preparing students for real-world Yiddish interactions.

We hope this book will help you become the Yiddish teacher or learner you want to be. We know it has helped us in our own never-ending journey—we are, after all, nonnative Yiddish speakers ourselves and perpetual students of the language and culture. That is perhaps the simplest way to explain this book's existence: with it, we hope to guide others along the same path we have walked, both in learning the language ourselves and in teaching it to others.

2. TO THE INSTRUCTOR ❗

The exercises and activities in this book are optimized for use by independent learners. To make the most effective use of these materials in the classroom setting, instructors are encouraged to log on to the teacher portal of the textbook website and download the Teacher Guide, which contains detailed lesson plans for small-group and partner activities that do not appear in the print book. The Teacher Guide also offers step-by-step instructions for presenting new vocabulary using the communicative approach and describes recurring learning activities to use in the classroom. The teacher portal also offers printable game cards and worksheets for classroom use, digital images to accompany vocabulary displays, and a variety of additional resources.

The website can be accessed at **http://textbook.yiddishbookcenter.org**.

(Note that the link to the teacher portal will be sent to you when you register to access the website.)

3. GUIDED TOUR OF *IN EYNEM*

In eynem *is divided into six thematic units* (**טעמעס**)*, with supplementary materials preceding and following the units. Volume 1 contains the front matter, Units I–III, and back matter; Volume 2 contains Units IV–VI and back matter.*

UNITS

The units follow a consistent format:

Unit Overview
This page introduces the unit with a visual representation of the theme[1] and a summary of unit goals[2], as well as a list of the chapters in the unit[3]. Units are numbered with Roman numerals[4].

CHAPTERS

There are three to four chapters (**קאַפּיטלען**) in each unit, each essentially containing the following:

Chapter Overview
This page features the chapter objectives[5] and a list of the chapter's components, divided into Vocabulary (**וואָקאַבולאַר**)[6], Grammar (**גראַמאַטיק**)[7], and Culture (**קולטור**)[8] sections. The culture section is further subdivided by medium: Texts (**טעקסטן**), Audio (**אוידיאָ**), and Video (**ווידעאָ**). Chapters are numbered with Arabic numerals[9].

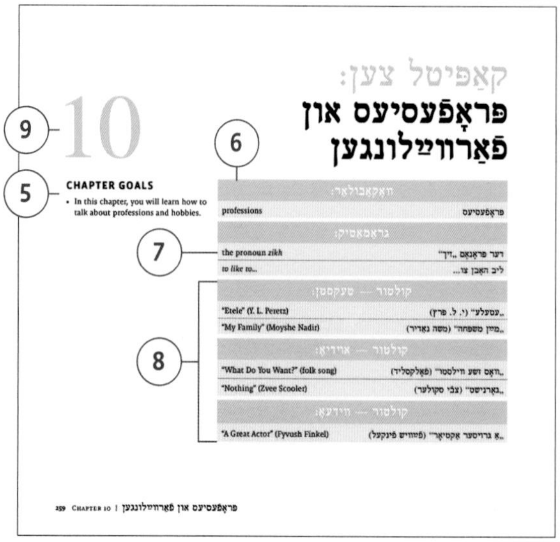

SECTIONS

Each chapter contains one to four sections[10], each of which presents a vocabulary set, a grammatical topic, or a combination of the two. Sections are organized according to letters of the Hebrew alphabet[11].

Visual Introduction and Exercises

Each section begins with an art display[12] accompanied by a variety of exercises[13], guiding students from passive (receptive) to active (productive) usage of the language and incorporating cultural information. Some sections present the new material in stages, with additional art displays appearing mid-section.

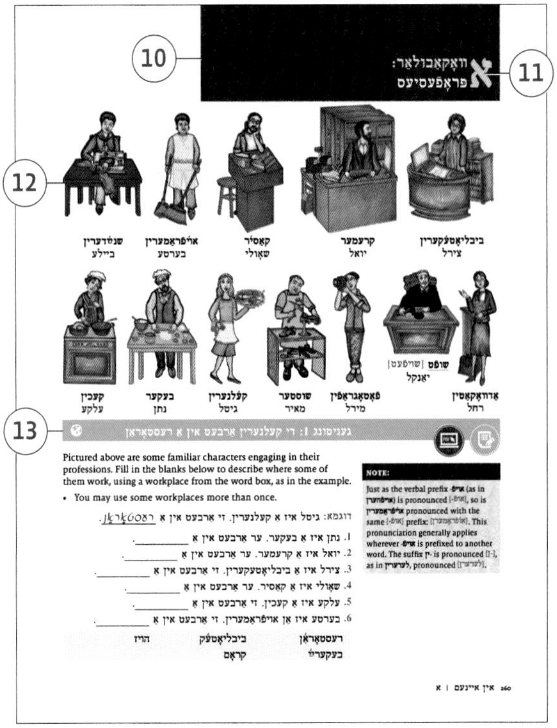

Grammar Presentations

When the section presents a grammatical topic, the art display is accompanied by an exercise that guides students to an understanding of the grammar through a set of inductive questions[14].

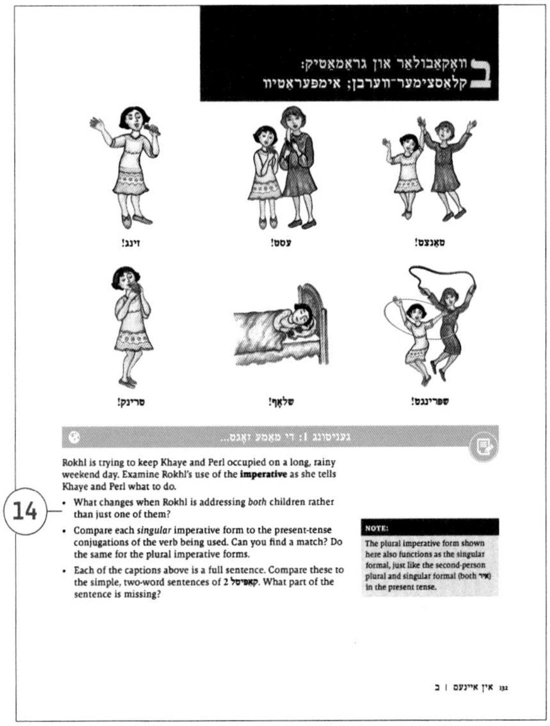

EXERCISES

The sections are made up of a variety of exercises (געניטונגען) practicing vocabulary and grammar and introducing students to authentic texts. Each exercise type is accompanied by an easy-to-recognize icon and color scheme:

green bars for written exercises ( );

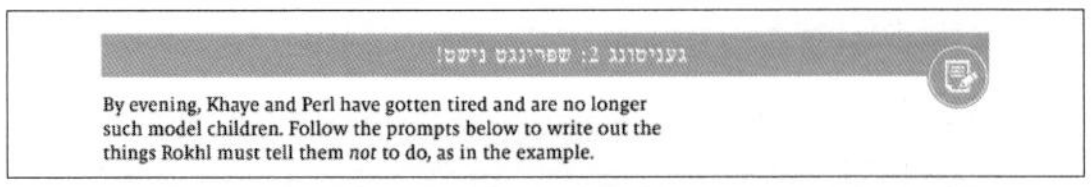

red bars for partner or small-group exercises ( );

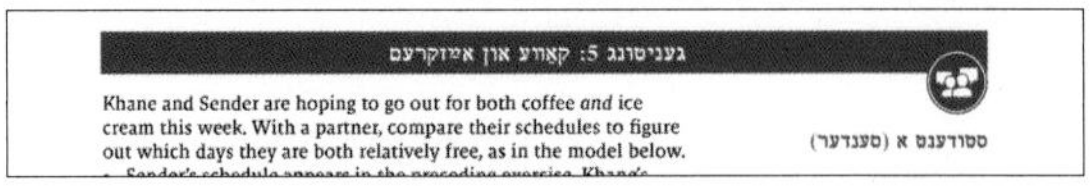

blue bars and shading for video exercises ( );

orange bars and shading for audio exercises ( );

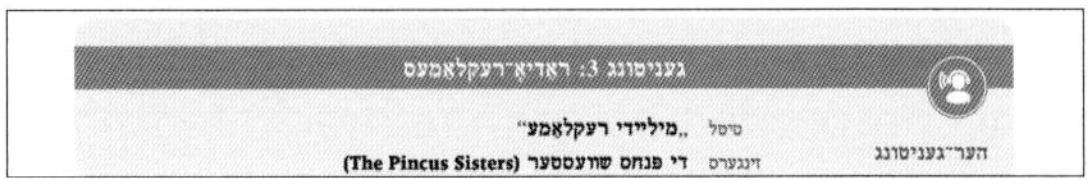

and green shading for exercises based on authentic texts.

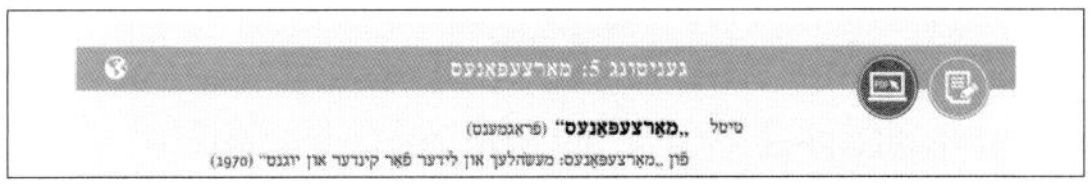

Online icons ( ) direct students to the website, where they can find supplementary resources. PDF icons ( ) indicate that the exercise should be completed in the PDF workbook, which can be found online and printed out.

Small-group exercises often have a homework component, indicated by a green homework (היימאַרבעט) bar, while written exercises sometimes have an in-class component, indicated by a red in-class (אין קלאַס) bar.

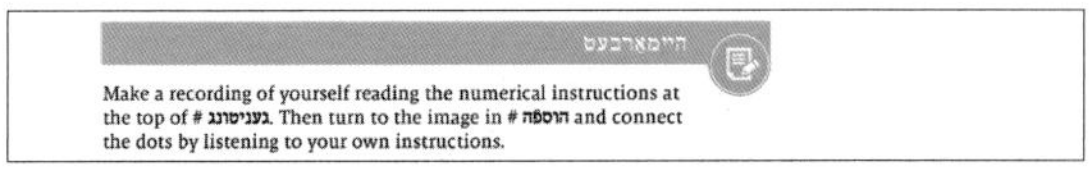

Make a recording of yourself reading the numerical instructions at the top of # געניטונג. Then turn to the image in # הוספה and connect the dots by listening to your own instructions.

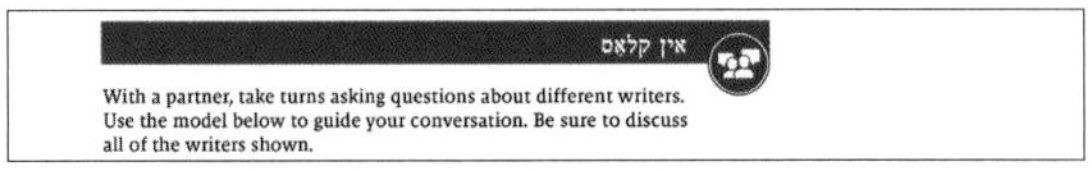

Notes and Glosses

Exercises are accompanied by note boxes and gloss boxes to give students additional guidance. Regular (gray) note boxes[15] usually contain supplementary, clarifying, or supporting information and are not essential to completing the exercise. Red reminder note boxes (!געדענקט)[16] contain key information or reminders about important notes provided earlier.

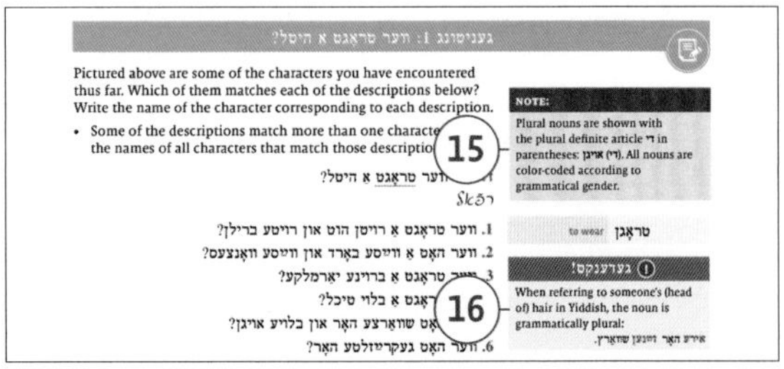

Pictured above are some of the characters you have encountered thus far. Which of them matches each of the descriptions below? Write the name of the character corresponding to each description.
NOTE:
Plural nouns are shown with the plural definite article די in parentheses. All nouns are color-coded according to grammatical gender.
15
16
When referring to someone's (head of) hair in Yiddish, the noun is grammatically plural:

Glosses come in three styles: marginal glosses[17] that aid in comprehending texts or instructions, gloss boxes[18] that provide key vocabulary needed to complete an activity or supplementary vocabulary for understanding a text, and cultural gloss boxes[19], which provide lengthier explanations of cultural concepts encountered in the textbook.

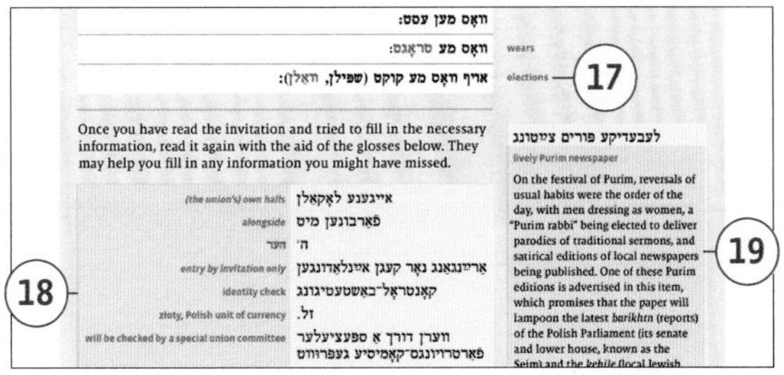

REFERENCE SECTION

The end of each chapter features Vocabulary Overviews (וואָקאַבולאַר־איבערבליק)[20] and Grammar Overviews (גראַמאַטיק־איבערבליק)[21], easily recognized by their purple and yellow shading (respectively).

Vocabulary Overviews are organized as follows:

- Each noun[22] is presented with its gendered definite article and plural ending (in parentheses).
- Nouns are divided into sections[23] by grammatical gender.
- Irregular verbs are provided with conjugated forms[24].
- Words of Hebrew or Aramaic origin are accompanied by orange bracketed phonetic transcriptions[25].
- Words with irregular stress patterns are annotated with an accent over the stressed vowel.
- At the end of each section is a list of words that are cognates[26] in English and Yiddish, on a darker purple background.

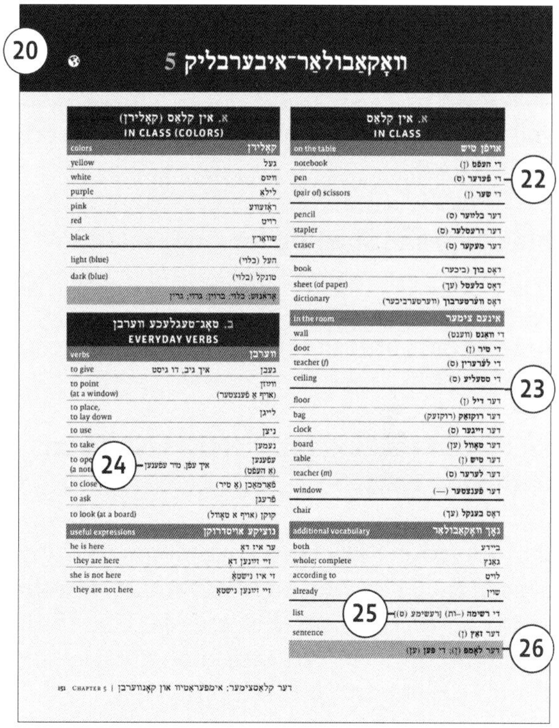

Grammar Overviews provide concise explanations in English of the grammatical concepts introduced in the chapter (with Yiddish examples where relevant) and include summary tables[27] for reference. Red exclamation point icons[28] draw attention to irregular forms.

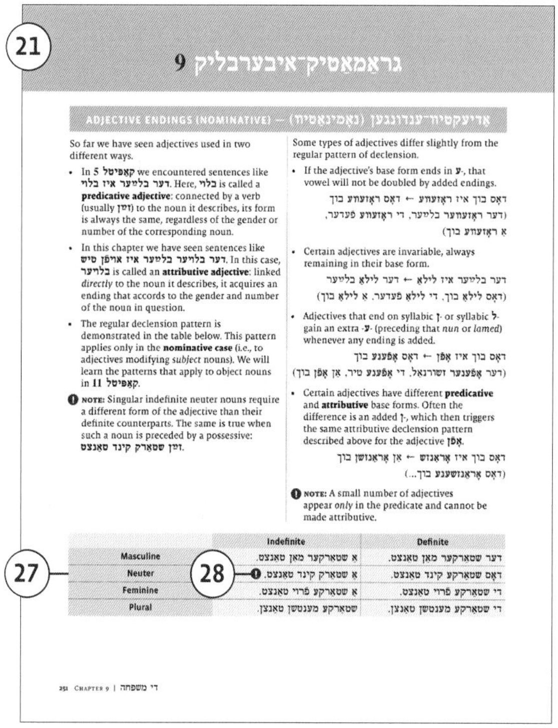

CULTURAL AND REVIEW MATERIAL

Review Section

Each chapter concludes with a review section (איבערחזר־געניטונגען)[29], which synthesizes the vocabulary, grammar, and cultural components in that chapter. These sections always begin with an open-ended writing exercise[30] featuring a *goylem*—a magical being the students invent at the beginning of the course and continue to "flesh out" with each chapter. Many of the remaining exercises in a review section are based on authentic texts, including excerpts from Yiddish literature, film, and song, and feature vocabulary and/or grammatical structures from the chapter.

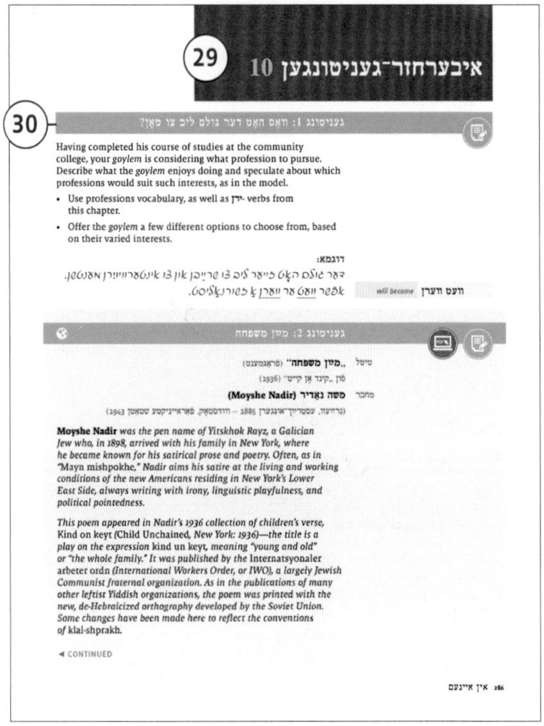
29 איבערחזר־געניטונגען 10

30 געניטונג 1: וואָס האָט דער גולם ליב צו טאָן?

Having completed his course of studies at the community college, your *goylem* is considering what profession to pursue. Describe what the *goylem* enjoys doing and speculate about which professions would suit such interests, as in the model.

- Use professions vocabulary, as well as ־ירן verbs from this chapter.
- Offer the *goylem* a few different options to choose from, based on their varied interests.

דוגמא:

וועט ווערן *will become*

געניטונג 2: מײַן משפּחה

טיטל „מײַן משפּחה" (פֿראַגמענט)
פֿון „קינד און קייט" (1936)

מחבר **משה נאַדיר (Moyshe Nadir)**
(נאַרעווע, עסטרײַך־אונגערן 1885 – וווּדסטאָק, פֿאַראייניקטע שטאַטן 1943)

***Moyshe Nadir** was the pen name of Yitskhok Rayz, a Galician Jew who, in 1898, arrived with his family in New York, where he became known for his satirical prose and poetry. Often, as in "Mayn mishpokhe," Nadir aims his satire at the living and working conditions of the new Americans residing in New York's Lower East Side, always writing with irony, linguistic playfulness, and political pointedness.*

This poem appeared in Nadir's 1936 collection of children's verse, Kind on keyt *(Child Unchained, New York: 1936)—the title is a play on the expression* kind un keyt, *meaning "young and old" or "the whole family." It was published by the* Internatsyonaler arbeter ordn *(International Workers Order, or IWO), a largely Jewish Communist fraternal organization. As in the publications of many other leftist Yiddish organizations, the poem was printed with the new, de-Hebraicized orthography developed by the Soviet Union. Some changes have been made here to reflect the conventions of* klal-shprakh.

◄ CONTINUED

286 אין איינעם

Holiday Chapters

The last chapter in each unit focuses on a Jewish holiday[31], beginning with *shabes* (the Sabbath) and then cycling through the Jewish calendar, from *rosheshone* (Rosh Hashanah) to *shvues* (Shavuos). They open with an illustrated presentation[32] of holiday-related vocabulary and include an overview of the holiday's history and customs, as well as relevant songs, literary passages, and other authentic texts revolving around the holiday.

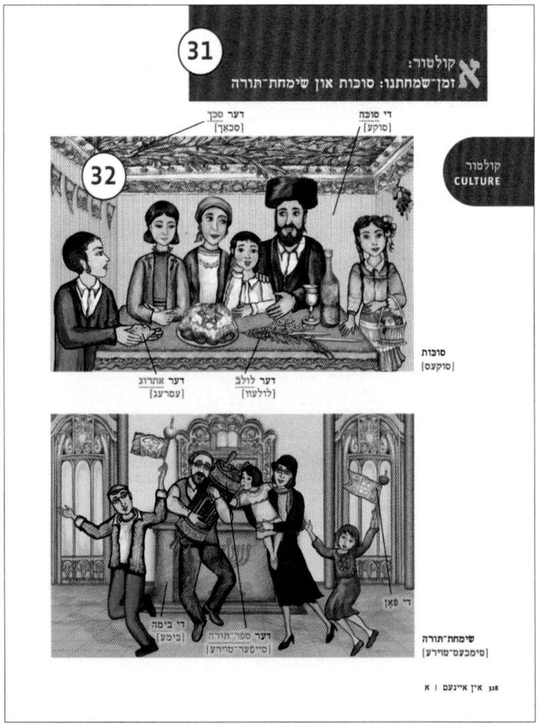

CULTURAL AND REVIEW MATERIAL (continued)

Unit Review

Each unit closes with a unit-wide review section[33] consisting of a free-writing exercise[34] based on a piece of fine art[35], and an exercise based on an archival image, such as an advertisement, poster, or greeting card.

איבערחזר־געניטונגען: טעמע דרײַ

געניטונג 1: באַשרײַבט אַ בילד

טיטל ,,טאַנץ־לעקציע" (1926)

קינסטלער רפֿאל סויער (Raphael Soyer)

(באָריסאָגלעבסק, רוסישע אימפּעריע 1899 – ניו־יאָרק, פֿאַראײניקטע שטאַטן 1987)

Fleeing political upheaval in Czarist Russia, **Raphael Soyer**'s *family immigrated to the Bronx in 1910. He considered his new city his true homeland, and his canvases are filled with depictions of life there; he once said in an interview, "I painted only what I saw in my neighborhood in New York City, which I call my country rather than my city." This painting,* Dancing Lesson, *was completed in the mid-1920s.*

◄ CONTINUED

FRONT AND BACK MATTER

Front Matter (Volume 1)

In the book's front matter, you will find a preface that explains the aims and approach of the textbook, an introduction to the history of the Yiddish language and culture, a description of the characters that populate the book's exercises, a chapter that teaches students to read and write in the Yiddish alphabet, and a list of useful classroom expressions.

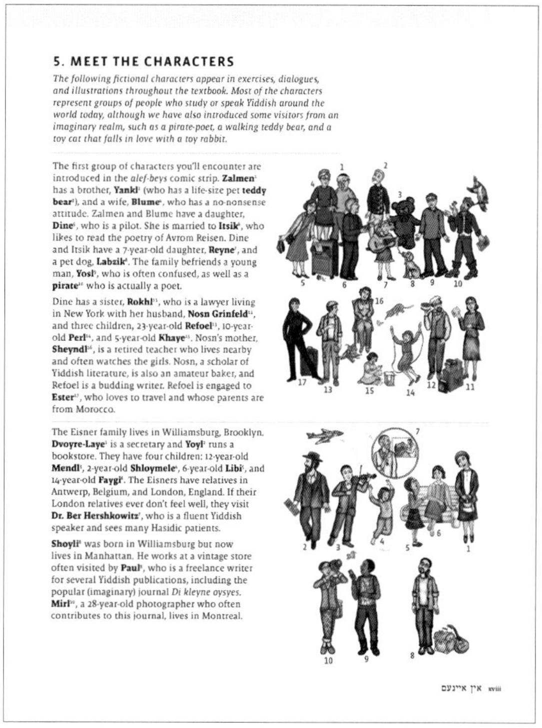
5. MEET THE CHARACTERS

The following fictional characters appear in exercises, dialogues, and illustrations throughout the textbook. Most of the characters represent groups of people who study or speak Yiddish around the world today, although we have also introduced some visitors from an imaginary realm, such as a pirate-poet, a walking teddy bear, and a toy cat that falls in love with a toy rabbit.

The first group of characters you'll encounter are introduced in the *alef-beys* comic strip. **Zalmen**[1] has a brother, **Yankl**[2] (who has a life-size pet **teddy bear**[3]), and a wife, **Blume**[4], who has a no-nonsense attitude. Zalmen and Blume have a daughter, **Dine**[5], who is a pilot. She is married to **Itsik**[6], who likes to read the poetry of Avrom Reisen. Dine and Itsik have a 7-year-old daughter, **Reyne**[7], and a pet dog, **Labzik**[8]. The family befriends a young man, **Yosl**[9], who is often confused, as well as a **pirate**[10] who is actually a poet.

Dine has a sister, **Rokhl**[11], who is a lawyer living in New York with her husband, **Nosn Grinfeld**[12], and three children, 23-year-old **Refoel**[13], 10-year-old **Perl**[14], and 5-year-old **Khaye**[15]. Nosn's mother, **Sheyndl**[16], is a retired teacher who lives nearby and often watches the girls. Nosn, a scholar of Yiddish literature, is also an amateur baker, and Refoel is a budding writer. Refoel is engaged to **Ester**[17], who loves to travel and whose parents are from Morocco.

The Eisner family lives in Williamsburg, Brooklyn. **Dvoyre-Laye**[1] is a secretary and **Yoyl**[2] runs a bookstore. They have four children: 12-year-old **Mendl**[3], 2-year-old **Shloymele**[4], 6-year-old **Libi**[5], and 14-year-old **Faygi**[6]. The Eisners have relatives in Antwerp, Belgium, and London, England. If their London relatives ever don't feel well, they visit **Dr. Ber Hershkowitz**[7], who is a fluent Yiddish speaker and sees many Hasidic patients.

Shoyli[8] was born in Williamsburg but now lives in Manhattan. He works at a vintage store often visited by **Paul**[9], who is a freelance writer for several Yiddish publications, including the popular (imaginary) journal *Di kleyne oysyes*. **Mirl**[10], a 28-year-old photographer who often contributes to this journal, lives in Montreal.

אין איינעם xviii

FRONT AND BACK MATTER (continued)

Back Matter (Volumes 1 and 2)
In the back matter, you will find a supplementary chapter that introduces additional vocabulary sets and grammar topics (Volume 2 only), an appendix with exercise-related worksheets, summary grammar tables and references, a Yiddish-English and English-Yiddish vocabulary, and an index of grammatical, thematic, and cultural topics.

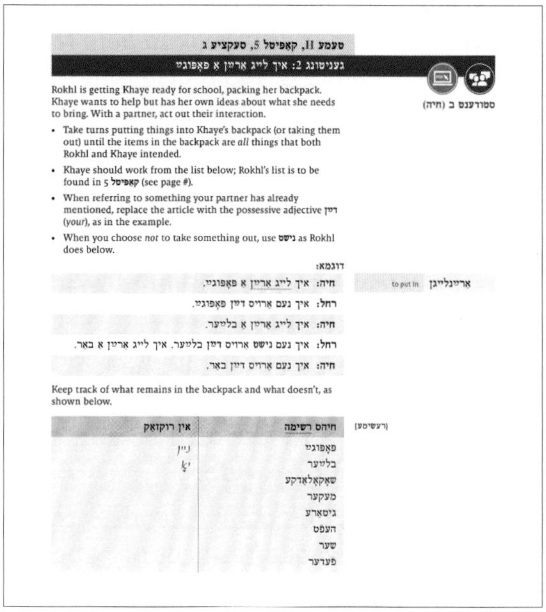
טעמע II, קאַפּיטל 5, סעקציע ג

געניטונג 2: איך לייג אַרײַן אַ פּאַפּוגײַ

סטודענט ב (חיה)

Rokhl is getting Khaye ready for school, packing her backpack. Khaye wants to help but has her own ideas about what she needs to bring. With a partner, act out their interaction.

- Take turns putting things into Khaye's backpack (or taking them out) until the items in the backpack are *all* things that both Rokhl and Khaye intended.
- Khaye should work from the list below; Rokhl's list is to be found in 5 **קאַפּיטל** (see page #).
- When referring to something your partner has already mentioned, replace the article with the possessive adjective דײַן (*your*), as in the example.
- When you choose *not* to take something out, use **נישט** as Rokhl does below.

דוגמא:

אַרײַנלייגן — to put in

חיה: איך לייג אַרײַן אַ פּאַפּוגײַ.

רחל: איך נעם אַרויס דײַן פּאַפּוגײַ.

חיה: איך לייג אַרײַן אַ בלײַער.

רחל: איך נעם נישט אַרויס דײַן בלײַער. איך לייג אַרײַן אַ באַר.

חיה: איך נעם אַרויס דײַן באַר.

Keep track of what remains in the backpack and what doesn't, as shown below.

[רעשימע]

אין רוקזאַק	חיהס רשימה
ניין	פּאַפּוגײַ
יאָ	בלײַער
	שאָקאָלאַדקע
	מעקער
	גיטאַרע
	העפֿט
	שער
	פֿעדער

TEXTBOOK WEBSITE

For Students
The student website accompanying *In eynem* contains the following elements:

- Multimedia materials: audio (dialogues, songs, radio broadcasts, and commercials) and video (clips of Yiddish films, oral histories, and interviews with native speakers).
- Printable PDF workbook.
- Links to full-text sources for texts excerpted in the printed book.
- High-resolution versions of art and authentic images.
- Supplementary resources (such as audio recordings of texts in book).

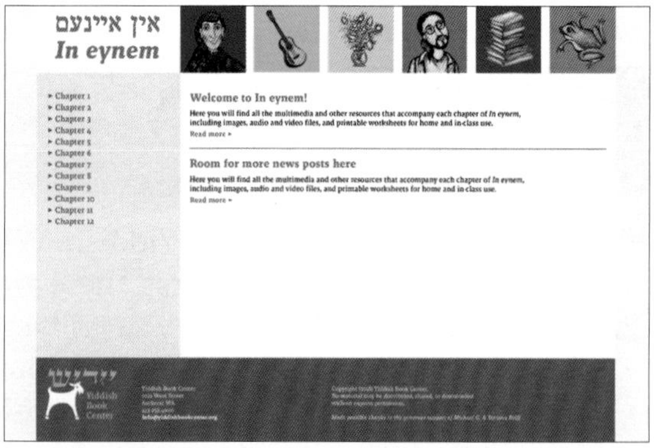

http://textbook.yiddishbookcenter.org

For Teachers
The teacher website includes all of the components of the student website, as well as the following:

- Teacher guide, which helps instructors create lesson plans, suggests additional activities, and provides further cultural and linguistic information to share with students.
- Textbook illustrations to project in class for vocabulary and grammar presentations.
- Activity cards and other printable resources.

4. HOW TO USE THIS BOOK

Below you will find a detailed description of the features used in this book to help facilitate your learning process. You'll also find tips for maximizing the value of your study time.

GETTING STARTED

When you first encounter an exercise, there are several strategies to keep in mind that can help you work through it.

1. Icon. As a first step, check the icon in the top right corner of the exercise to get a general sense of what type of activity you'll be doing—written, small-group, audio, or video.

2. PDF icon. While many exercises can be completed on a separate sheet of paper, some should be done on the specially provided worksheets that you can find as part of a workbook on the textbook website. Whenever an exercise should be done in the workbook, there will be a PDF icon in the top right corner of that exercise in the textbook.

3. Instructions.

- Be sure to read *all* instructions.
- Some instructions will be in Yiddish. While this may seem daunting at first, there are many recurring exercise types, and you will learn to recognize the instructions for each. Note that **Yiddish instructions often serve to remind you of vocabulary or concepts you need to complete the exercise**—they are there to help you!
- Each new Yiddish instruction is translated in italics the first few times it appears. Thereafter, the same instruction may be reused without translation, so it is crucial to *learn* the instructions as you encounter them. Note that a *partial* translation may be provided, when a new phrase is added to the end of a previously encountered instruction.

געניטונג 1: וויפֿל פּאָפּוגײַען?

וויפֿל פּאָפּוגײַען זעט איר אויפֿן בילד? ענטפֿערט אויף די פֿראַגעס אונטן, לויט דער דוגמא.

How many parrots do you see in the picture? Answer the questions below according to the example.

4. Model. Perhaps the best guide to how to complete an exercise is the model provided with it (**דוגמא** in Yiddish)[36]. If you produce language that mimics the structure of the example, you will be on the right track.

5. Notes. Additional helpful information is contained in note boxes[37] in the margins or below the exercise. The red note boxes[38] often contain important reminders of key grammatical points that you will rely on throughout the chapter.

געניטונג 1: ווען לויפֿט מען?

What time of day does one usually go running? Answer the questions below, as in the example.

- Be sure to use all four times of day pictured above.

דוגמא: ווען לויפֿט מען?

(36) געוויינטלעך לויפֿט מען אין דער פֿרי.

1. ווען שלאָפֿט מען?
2. ווען טרינקט מען קאַווע?
3. ווען טרינקט מען ווײַן?
4. ווען אַרבעט מען?

NOTE: The preposition **בײַ** is often pronounced [**בא**]. (37)

געוויינטלעך	usually

גערענקט! When the subject (in this case **מען**) is not the first sentence unit, it appears immediately after the verb. (38)

GUIDE TO SPECIFIC EXERCISE TYPES

Some exercise types that recur throughout the book are outlined and described below.

1. Goylem. In Jewish tradition, a *goylem* is an artificial being made of clay and brought to life by someone learned in mystical Jewish teachings. The *goylem* that you "animate" over the course of your study with these materials will be a testament to your growing language skills. In the review section accompanying each chapter, you will be tasked with using the material learned in that chapter to further develop your *goylem*'s character, whether this means reporting on their latest wardrobe change, bringing us up to date on the status of their family relationships, or filling in their weekend schedule. In this way, you are able to expand your familiarity with personal descriptive language, even for activities or facts that do not strictly apply to you.

Your *goylem* just signed up to take some classes at the local community college. Describe his class schedule Monday–Friday, as in the model.

- Talk about the number of students in each class and the kind (and quantity) of assignments the *goylem* does.

דוגמא:

מאָנטיק גייט דער גולם אויפֿן פּסיכאָלאָגיע־קורס. עס זײַנען דאָ 120 סטודענטן אין קלאַס. ער מאַכט נישט קיין סך היימאַרבעט.

2. Information gap. Information gap exercises generally consist of two worksheets to be used by two people working together. The worksheet for one student will be found in the body of the chapter, while the other worksheet may be found in the appendix. Printable versions of these worksheets may also be found in the PDF workbook on the website. Each worksheet is labeled with a caption in the top right corner (below the header bar) indicating whether it is for **סטודענט א** (Student A) or **סטודענט ב** (Student B).

געניטונג 3: ווער בין איך?

סטודענט א

With a partner, take turns role-playing some of the characters we've met so far. Your partner will work from the corresponding exercise in # **הוספה** (see page #).

Each column in the table below pertains to a separate character. Using the model provided, ask your partner questions to fill in the missing information in columns 1 and 2.

- You will need to ask both open-ended (**פֿון וואַנען קומסטו?**) and yes-or-no questions (**דו ביסט אַ סטודענט?**).

3. Grammar presentation. Whenever a new grammar topic is introduced, it is initially presented in illustrated and contextualized sentences. These sentences are followed by inductive questions, which help the student work out how and why the grammatical forms are used the way they are. It is important to do this inductive stage before looking at the grammar summary at end of the chapter so that you truly integrate and understand the structures rather than simply memorize forms.

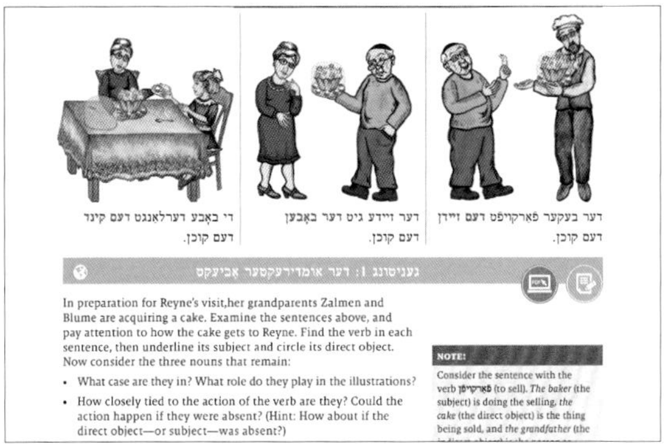

4. Multimedia exercises. Some of the audio and video exercises that are part of these learning materials appear on the website alone, with only a placeholder in the book, directing students to the appropriate webpage.

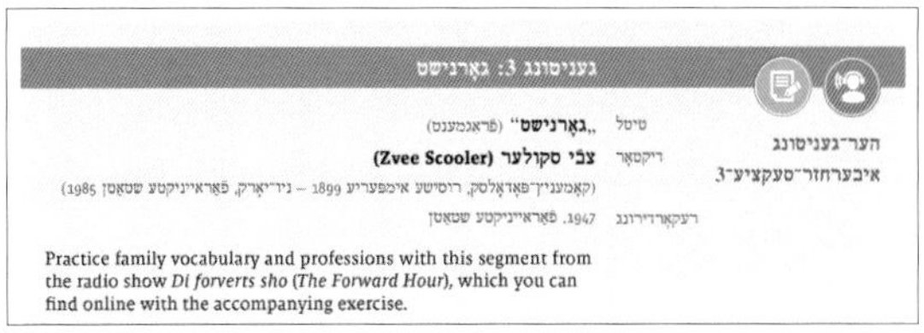

5. Complex texts.

- Certain prose texts presented in the textbook may contain language that is too complex for the student to understand word for word. When you come across one of these texts, **do not try to look up all of the words in the dictionary.** This will not help you complete the exercise. We have taken care to provide you with all the vocabulary you need.
- The skill that you **will** need to exercise is that of inference and educated guesswork. This is an extremely important skill for any language learner to develop: once the learner of a new language leaves the classroom, they will inevitably encounter texts and real-life speech contexts well above their level that they will nevertheless need to be able to understand. It is therefore crucial to prepare for such situations during one's studies.
- The complex exercises in this textbook will provide practice and strategies for managing these situations, helping you develop skills useful in multiple contexts outside of class, such as searching for specific pieces of information in an otherwise perplexing text, listening to an audio recording multiple times while taking notes and capturing more and more of the initially indecipherable content, and using contextual and conceptual clues to infer the structure or function of an unfamiliar document.

SPECIAL MARKINGS

This book employs certain formatting conventions to help you process the Yiddish text more smoothly.

1. Stress markings.

- Word stress in Yiddish is somewhat unpredictable, and the best policy is simply to memorize proper stress patterns alongside a word's meaning and its grammatical gender. However, there is a broad tendency for emphasis to fall on the second-to-last syllable of a multisyllabic word. It is also generally true that the addition of prefixes and suffixes does not shift the stress from one syllable to another.
- When either or both of these rules fully determines the placement of stress in a given word, we have left the stress unmarked. Otherwise, we have indicated the stressed syllable with an accent mark the first time that a word appears in the textbook and in the vocabulary overview. Thus, we mark the accent in **ראָ́זעווע** and **אָראַ́נזש**, but not in **לילאַ**. If, however, **אָראַנזש** is familiar already, then **אָראַנזשענע** is not marked for accent, since its pronunciation is the same as that of the root form. Similarly, neither **עפּל** nor **עפּעלעך** is marked for stress, since the vowel placement in the root is regular and the same vowel is still evident in the derived form.
- Note that some words do change their stress pattern as a result of the addition of suffixes, e.g., **דאָ́קטער** and **דאָקטוי́רים**, or **פּראָפֿע́סאָר** and **פּראָפֿעסאָ́רן**, or any number of *loshn-koydesh*-derived words: **שבת** [שאַ́בעס] and **שבתים** [שאַבאָ́סים]. Some special cases are noted as they appear. For example, all separable prefix verbs are accented on the prefix (**אָ́נהייבן**), and all **-ירן**-verbs carry the accent on the **-יר-** syllable, the final syllable of the root (**שטודי́רן**).

2. Pronunciation guides. When the pronunciation of a Yiddish word differs from its spelling, we provide a bracketed pronunciation guide in orange characters. The word itself will have an orange underline. The largest category of words marked in this manner are words of *loshn-koydesh* (Hebrew and Aramaic) origin.

א: מזל־טובֿ! ווי אַלט ביסטו?	[מאַזל־טאָוו]

3. Glosses.

- When an unfamiliar word appears in Yiddish text, it is generally glossed in the margin of the same line. Both the word being glossed and the English definition appear in blue characters. When a text has many glosses per line, the glossed words are additionally marked with superscript numbers. When an English word or phrase defines a multiword Yiddish phrase, the English definition will be italicized.

> ב: אַ יישר־כּוח[1]!
> אָדער
> ב: ניין, פּרוּוו[2] נאָך אַ מאָל[3].
>
> [1]*well done!* [יאַשער־קויעך]
> [2]try; [3]again

- Sometimes, new words that will be used actively throughout an exercise are glossed in special boxes in the margin. In these cases, the words appear in the body of the exercise with a blue underline.

> | | |
> |---|---|
> | וויפֿל | how many |
> | זען | to see |
> | בילד | picture |
>
> **דוגמא:** וויפֿל פּאָפּוגײַען זעט איר אויפֿן בילד?
> *איך זע דרײַ פּאָפּוגײַען.*
> **1.** וויפֿל בלײַערס זעט איר אויפֿן בילד?

- Some Yiddish texts contain too many unfamiliar words to gloss them all in the margin. In these cases, those words that are not essential to understanding the core meaning of the text are provided in a mini-dictionary following the text.

4. Emphasis. When an exercise requires you to pay special attention to a particular word or phrase, that word or phrase appears in purple characters. This occurs, for example, when the student is called upon to creatively replace one word with another or make grammatical inferences about the relationship between different forms of a verb or adjective.

> איך הייב אָן עסן.
> מיר הייבן אָן עסן.

5. Grammatical genders. When multiple nouns are presented in a vocabulary display, they are color-coded by grammatical gender—feminine nouns are purple, masculine nouns are green, and neuter nouns are blue. In exercises where the student is supposed to figure out the gender of the nouns, they appear in regular black print.

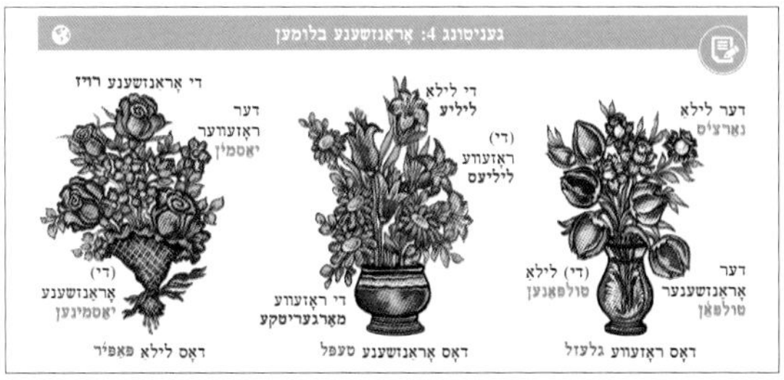

Plural nouns are shown with the plural definite article **די** in parentheses:

(די) ראָזעווע ליליעס.

STRATEGIES FOR THE INDEPENDENT LEARNER

Many students of Yiddish do not have the opportunity to attend regular classes due to issues of availability or accessibility. We have designed these materials so that they may be used effectively by all students, whether or not they have access to a teacher or classroom, with minimal adjustment. However, if you are studying on your own, here are a couple of pointers to keep in mind.

1. Vocabulary. It is important to spend some extra time studying the vocabulary sets over and above the framework of the provided exercises. Some suggestions include making and studying vocabulary flash cards and writing sentences using new words in meaningful contexts. Remember to memorize the gender of each new noun you learn.

2. Exercise types. As an independent learner, you will be able to do all written, audio, and video exercises as they are presented in the book. For the small-group exercises, be sure to read through the exercise as usual (including *all* glosses and notes), and then look for the portion of the exercise beneath the green "homework" bar. For extra practice, adapt the small-group exercises by writing a skit between yourself and an imaginary partner or by acting out both sides of the dialogue yourself.

5. MEET THE CHARACTERS

The following fictional characters appear in exercises, dialogues, and illustrations throughout the textbook. Most of the characters represent groups of people who study or speak Yiddish around the world today, although we have also introduced some visitors from an imaginary realm, such as a pirate-poet, a walking teddy bear, and a toy cat that falls in love with a toy rabbit.

The first group of characters you'll encounter are introduced in the *alef-beys* comic strip. **Zalmen**[1] has a brother, **Yankl**[2] (who has a life-size pet **teddy bear**[3]), and a wife, **Blume**[4], who has a no-nonsense attitude. Zalmen and Blume have a daughter, **Dine**[5], who is a pilot. She is married to **Itsik**[6], who likes to read the poetry of Avrom Reisen. Dine and Itsik have a 7-year-old daughter, **Reyne**[7], and a pet dog, **Labzik**[8]. The family befriends a young man, **Yosl**[9], who is often confused, as well as a **pirate**[10] who is actually a poet.

Dine has a sister, **Rokhl**[11], who is a lawyer living in New York with her husband, **Nosn Grinfeld**[12], and three children, 23-year-old **Refoel**[13], 10-year-old **Perl**[14], and 5-year-old **Khaye**[15]. Nosn's mother, **Sheyndl**[16], is a retired teacher who lives nearby and often watches the girls. Nosn, a scholar of Yiddish literature, is also an amateur baker, and Refoel is a budding writer. Refoel is engaged to **Ester**[17], who loves to travel and whose parents are from Morocco.

The Eisner family lives in Williamsburg, Brooklyn. **Dvoyre-Laye**[1] is a secretary and **Yoyl**[2] runs a bookstore. They have four children: 12-year-old **Mendl**[3], 2-year-old **Shloymele**[4], 6-year-old **Libi**[5], and 14-year-old **Faygi**[6]. The Eisners have relatives in Antwerp, Belgium, and London, England. If their London relatives ever don't feel well, they visit **Dr. Ber Hershkowitz**[7], who is a fluent Yiddish speaker and sees many Hasidic patients.

Shoyli[8] was born in Williamsburg but now lives in Manhattan. He works at a vintage store often visited by **Paul**[9], who is a freelance writer for several Yiddish publications, including the popular (imaginary) journal *Di kleyne oysyes*. **Mirl**[10], a 28-year-old photographer who often contributes to this journal, lives in Montreal.

Mirl's cousin, **Khane**[1], is from New Jersey and studies Yiddish in Lernton, Massachusetts, with **Professor Etl Kluger**[2]. The other students in Khane's class come from all over the world. **Elke**[3] is a student from Poland who likes to cook, and she often spends time with **Avrom**[4], a student from Israel. Their friend **Gitl**[5], who comes from Germany, is a history student. She enjoys going to the dance performances of **Sore**[6], who comes from Argentina. **Moyshe**[7], a student from Russia, shares a dorm room with **Sender**[8], who comes from Philadelphia. **Eydl**[9], who is from Boston, has one sister and three brothers. **Arye-Leyb**[10] is from Toronto. He is good at math and likes to play guitar. **Khave**[11], whose parents are from Ecuador, studies music and volunteers at a farmers' market. **Velvl**[12] is a graduate student and an anarchist. Some of the students also take classes with **Professor Hershl Yoshido**[13], who is on sabbatical from his job teaching Yiddish studies and linguistics in Japan.

Khane and Mirl's grandfather, **Meyer**[1], is retired and lives in Florida. Meyer attends the same Yiddish reading group as **Tsirl**[2], a librarian. **Berte**[3], a former dentist from Moldova who currently lives in New York and makes money cleaning houses, likes to vacation in Florida. Whenever **Shikl**[4], a klezmer violinist, and **Rivke**[5], a Yiddish singer and actress, visit Florida, Meyer, Tsirl, and Berte attend their performances. Sometimes Rivke, who is from Israel, also tours with **John**[6], a Yiddish actor. Whenever she sees one of their plays, Berte calls her sister **Beyle**[7], a seamstress who lives in Germany, to tell her all about it.

6. MEET THE ACTORS

The dialogues in this book are voiced by four native-speaking Yiddish actors. Two of these actors, Paula Teitelbaum and Eli Rosen, also appear in video interviews throughout the book.

VIDEO AND AUDIO ACTORS:

פערל טײטלבױם (Paula Teitelbaum)

(ברעסלע, פּױלן 1954 –)

Paula Teitelbaum is a language instructor who has taught Yiddish as well as Spanish and English to speakers of other languages (ESL) in a variety of settings. Teitelbaum is also a Yiddish singer and song teacher who coproduced the album of Yiddish children's songs Di Grine Katshke *(1997).*

אלי ראָזען (Eli Rosen)

(ניו־יאָרק, פֿאַראײניקטע שטאַטן 1979 –)

Eli Rosen was born and raised in a Hasidic community in the Boro Park neighborhood in Brooklyn, NY, which he left to pursue, in his words, "life, liberty, and a law degree." Rosen is currently an actor, translator, and managing director for the New Yiddish Rep theater company.

AUDIO ACTORS:

עלענאָר ריסאַ (Eleanor Reissa)

(ניו־יאָרק, פֿאַראײניקטע שטאַטן –)

Eleanor Reissa is an award-winning director, singer, actor, and writer in both Yiddish and English. Reissa has helped revitalize Yiddish theater as artistic director of the Folksbiene; adapted Yidl Mitn Fidl *and* Hershele Ostropolyer *for the musical stage; directed Sholem Asch's* Got Fun Nekome*; and co-created/directed Carnegie Hall's* From Shtetl to Stage.

אורן לײב ריקמאַן (Allen Lewis Rickman)

(ניו־יאָרק, פֿאַראײניקטע שטאַטן 1960 –)

Allen Lewis Rickman is an actor, writer, and director for theater, television, and film. Rickman translated Yiddish dialogue for and played Velvl in the Coen brothers' A Serious Man *(2009), and he is an internationally produced playwright whose work has been presented in six languages.*

7. ACKNOWLEDGMENTS

FROM THE AUTHORS:

It takes a shtetl to create a textbook, and the authors extend our deepest gratitude to everyone who worked so hard to bring this project to fruition.

First, we'd like to extend our heartfelt thanks to Michael and Tatiana Reiff, whose gracious and generous support made our work possible.

Our thanks to our colleagues (past and present) at the Yiddish Book Center for their tireless work on numerous aspects of the project. Thanks in particular to Aaron Lansky and Susan Bronson for believing in the importance of this work, and to Lisa Newman for her expertise and guidance in getting us from manuscript to publication. We are indebted to Gretchen Fiordalice for her help with the logistics and coordination of the project and for her constant encouragement and support. We are grateful to Amber Clooney and Common Media for developing the textbook's website, and to Tristan Chambers, Jessica Parker, and Raphi Halff for their work on the online materials. Special thanks to Adah Hetko and Rebecca White for researching and compiling the geographical information and working on online content. Allison Posner and Rola Younes helped in the very early stages of planning the book's structure and contributed delightful and humorous exercises. Our gratitude to Mindl Cohen and Sebastian Schulman for editing the historical and biographical digests accompanying the cultural material. We are also grateful to Sebastian for the comprehensive history of Yiddish in the book's introduction. Many of our co-workers provided moral and practical support, such as research, editing, and exercise testing. We'd like especially to thank Josh Lambert, Zeke Levine, Michael Reid, Sylvia Peterson, Sarah Bleichfeld, Phoenix Wyatt, Megan Kroll, Sadie Gold-Shapiro, and Diana Clarke.

We gratefully acknowledge our debt to our all-star team of pedagogy and language editors, whose expertise, enthusiasm, and endless dedication contributed immeasurably to our work. The inspiration to create a communicative Yiddish textbook came from Brukhe (Beatrice) Lang, who modeled this approach in her classrooms and her teaching materials for many years leading up to the writing of this book. We have been immensely fortunate to work with Brukhe on this project and are grateful for her encouragement and exceptionally detailed feedback on nearly every exercise that we have written. We are indebted to Rebecca Margolis for showing us what impeccable classroom instruction looks like and for always reminding us to keep our materials relevant, manageable, and accessible to our students. We are grateful to Yankl-Peretz Blum for reading every word of the book (multiple times) and for providing thoughtful, thorough comments and explanations on numerous aspects of Yiddish grammar and usage. Many thanks to Gregory Lauzon for copyediting the English text and cheerfully answering numerous stylistic questions. Any remaining errors are of course our own.

עס איז שווער צו באַשרײַבן וויפֿל מיר שאַצן אָפּ די אויסבעסערונגען וואָס מיר האָבן באַקומען פֿון יצחק ניבאָרסקין. זײַנע בריוו מיט אָפּרופֿן אויף אונדזערע קאַפּיטלען האָבן אין זיך כּולל געווען אַ גאַנצן אַוואַנסירטן קורס פֿון גראַמאַטיק און באַנוץ. מיר זײַנען ספּעציעל דאַנקבאַר אַז ער האָט אונדז געצוווּנגען נישט אַרײַנצופּאַקן אונדזער לשון אין גראַמאַטישע סדום־בעטלעך, נאָר צו שרײַבן שטענדיק אידיאָמאַטיש.

One of the most distinctive features of this book is the art that adorns nearly every page. We offer our heartfelt thanks to Alexander Vaisman, who created all of the characters and settings in an original style firmly rooted in Yiddish culture, and to Shura Vaisman, who brought them to life and modified them to support the learning process.

We would also like to express our gratitude to the design and production team who crafted the beautifully laid out pages of the book. Our thanks to Alexander Isley and his crew at Alexander Isley Inc., and especially to designer Christina Holland, who worked closely and painstakingly with us to optimize every element of every exercise for the student's ease of use, making the pages look exactly as we envisioned them. We are grateful to Yankl Salant for setting the Yiddish text on our vocabulary presentations, for working on the index and table of contents, and for helping with many tasks related to converting our manuscripts to publishable pages. At the very early stages of this work, we benefited immensely from the textbook-production experience of David Staloch and Sally Steele.

It was a pleasure to work with a world-class group of native Yiddish-speaking actors on recording the scripted dialogues in the book. Special thanks go to Eleanor Reissa, Allen Lewis Rickman, Eli Rosen, and Paula Teitelbaum for their expert and spirited voicing of our characters. Thanks also to Sasha Lurje, Craig Judelman, and Ilya Shneyveys for their beautiful recordings of three songs for the textbook's earliest chapters.

It has been a privilege to have our materials tested by members of the Yiddish-teaching profession, who used earlier versions of the book in their classrooms and provided valuable feedback on their students' experience. We are grateful to the first-year cohort of the Yiddish Pedagogy Program: Jessica Kirzane, Elena Luchina, Sara Feldman, Marianne Tatom, David Schlitt, Rachelle Grossman, Gabe Miner, Moishele Mario Alfonso, Agnieszka Ilwicka-Karuna, Josh Price, Meyer Weinshel, Zushe Wiener, Erin Faigin, Adi Mahalel, and Sonia Gollance; and to the second-year cohort: Miriam Borden, Zisl Chloe Piazza, Nancy Sculnik, Sandra Chiritescu, Sasha Berenstein, Linda Motzkin, Naftali Ejdelman, and LeiAnna Hamel. We also thank our friends and colleagues in the global community of Yiddish creators and scholars who have provided valuable insight and suggestions both online and in person.

We extend our thanks to all of our students (in the Yiddish Book Center's Steiner Summer Yiddish Program, the Center's annual YiddishSchool, and the Five College Yiddish courses) for putting their hearts and souls into learning with us these past several years. This book has as much of them in it as it does of us.

ASYA VAISMAN SCHULMAN:

I dedicate the work I have put into this book to my family.

I am grateful to my parents, Iosif and Shura Vaisman, for instilling in me a deep love for Yiddish language and culture, for always supporting and encouraging me, and for being an inexhaustible source of advice and help. I also thank my mother for the countless hours spent skillfully crafting the book's illustrations and adjusting and readjusting them throughout the editing process. The choice of artist for the book was an obvious one—I knew from the start that my uncle Alexander Vaisman's deeply Yiddish style was the perfect fit for the book's characters and settings, and I thank him for making the book a visual delight. Thanks also to my aunt

Mila Vaisman for scanning, printing, and emailing these pictures at all kinds of odd hours across multiple time zones. I would also like to thank my grandparents, Faina and Maksim Yakobzon and Genia and Ilya (*z"l*) Vaisman, for singing to me in Yiddish before I could even speak, and for cheering me on, motivating me, and inspiring me; I hope that they *shep* much *nakhes* from my work.

For being a constant source of joy and wonder, I thank my daughter, Tzina Chaya, who thinks the *klal-shprakh* that my students and I speak is hilarious, probably because her native *tote-lushn* is so much richer and more delightful. The credit for that goes to my partner, Sebastian Schulman, who embodies Yiddish cultural and linguistic transmission by speaking Yiddish to Tzina every single day. In addition to suffusing our home with Yiddish, Seb has supported me throughout the many years of this project with his selfless love, editorial prowess, and historical acumen. *Azoy vi di, gefint men nisht, az me zol di velt oysfurn.*

I have been extremely fortunate to study Yiddish language and culture with the finest teachers in the United States and abroad. As a high school student, I began learning Yiddish with Sheva Zucker, whose passion for Yiddish and expert pedagogy were equally inspirational. In college, my growing love of Yiddish was nurtured by Miriam Hoffman, who showed me how much can be learned through song, and Mordkhe Schaechter (*z"l*), who was always ready to patiently answer my myriad questions. My role model for giving feedback on written assignments was Yitskhok Niborski, whose thoughtful and instructive comments were often longer than my original compositions. I learned about teaching with authentic texts from Eugene Orenstein and Khayele Beer, who balanced literary analysis with language study. In graduate school, I delved into the *kleyne oysyes* with David Braun, whose knowledge of the finer points of Yiddish linguistics was boundless. It was then that I also observed Brukhe Lang's classroom teaching and began learning from her how to apply what I loved as a language student to becoming a language teacher. I am endlessly grateful to her for being a mentor, friend, and inspiration for the past 20 years. I am indebted to my graduate advisor, Ruth Wisse, for providing me with an intellectual framework that informs how I teach Yiddish culture, and for supporting my research on the Yiddish songs of Hasidic women. I have also been privileged to study Yiddish culture and history with Pesakh Fiszman (*z"l*), Jeremy Dauber, David Roskies, David Fishman, Avrom Nowersztern, and Hershl Glasser.

There are many people deserving of my personal thanks who have already been recognized in the authors' acknowledgments above. In the interest of concision, I won't mention them here again, but know that my gratitude is no less heartfelt for all their hard work and support.

At the Yiddish Book Center, I have had the pleasure of working with a series of talented young people in the fellowship program. I thank especially Allison Posner, Rola Younes, Martina Ravagnan, Adah Hetko, and Rebecca White for their assistance and camaraderie.

I am deeply grateful to Mikhl Yashinsky for searching far and wide to find just the right text for every chapter and for bringing his wit and ingenuity to crafting the exercises that go along with those texts.

It has been my privilege to write this book with Jordan Brown, whose dedication, spirited creativity, and profound intellectual curiosity have been truly inspiring. This book only exists because it has been a *tsuzamenarbet* that was the very definition of *in eynem*.

JORDAN BROWN:

To Mom, for imparting to me *The Joys of Yiddish*. She knew not what she wrought. To Dad for imparting to me *The 2000 Year Old Man*. He knew *exactly* what he was doing. To Sadie Espar for giving me her copy of *The Yiddish Teacher*. To the Palo Alto Yiddish Club and the KlezCalifornia Flisik Salon. To my mentors and adoptive Yiddish *mishpokhe*, Rosie, Evie, Arje, Gerry, and Adina. To my family—especially Nana, Gramps, Addie, Marty, and Grandma Ruth—for the fundamentals.

צו ריווען, פֿאַרן שטענדיקן דערמאָנען מיר אַז „ס׳איז די זעלביקע משוגענע וועלט“ ווי תּמיד, און אַז מע דאַרף כאָטש גוט אַ לעב טאָן דערינען — זאָל זי מיר זײַן געזונט און פֿריילעך ביז 120 יאָר, אָמן!

To all my Yiddish tutors and teachers, in rough chronological order: Amy Blau, Natalia Krynicka, Delphine Bechtel, Itay Zutra, Rebecca Margolis, Sebastian Schulman, Sharon Bar-Kochva, Beatrice Lang, Yankl-Peretz Blum, and Yitskhok Niborski. To Gabriella Safran, both for making the mighty Yiddish *vinkl* at Stanford what it is and for encouraging my earliest attempts at teaching.

To all my dear Steiner Summer Yiddish Program *khevre*, with whom it is never a question which language to speak, the answer being . . . *all* of them! To my co-fellows: Tanya, Elissa, Sadie, Alexis, Zeke, Raphi, Miranda, and thrice Mikhl. I am so blessed to have spent so much time separated from all of your expertise, silliness, and Yiddish by mere cubicle walls. To Mikhl, my nearest and dearest cubicle brother: I owe you three years of very delightful and crucial companionship amid mountains of work. To Jes and Sylvia, for after-hours companionship. To Ollie, for knowing *exactly* what "after-hours" really meant. And to all of the unsung lexicographers, grammarians, and just plain folks who have seen fit to write down what they knew about Yiddish. We would be lost without you.

Most of all, to Asya, my dear friend and teacher in so many things—it has been my unbelievable luck and joy to join you in this endeavor.

MIKHL YASHINSKY:

With deep feeling, I thank the Yiddish speakers who have come before me, both my own ancestors and all those who have preserved this language and lore so that their treasures could be received by those of my generation. And to all the coming generations of Yiddish learners, to whom we pass such treasures on in this volume: may they add to them from their own stores of creativity, remembering that the spirit and lessons of past generations remain vivid as long as their language is still spoken, their customs studied, and the songs of their poets still allowed to resound.

8. A SHORT INTRODUCTION TO YIDDISH LANGUAGE AND CULTURE

The vernacular language of Eastern European Jews and their descendants the world over, Yiddish is, in terms of numbers of speakers and geographic spread, one of the most widely spoken Jewish languages in history. As such, an understanding of Yiddish and its development is crucial to understanding modern Ashkenazi culture and history and illuminates numerous fields of study, professional domains, and contemporary cultural endeavors. The following overview of the Yiddish language as a linguistic, cultural, and historical phenomenon is a broad introduction. Students are encouraged to further explore any topics and issues that pique their interest.

WHAT IS YIDDISH?

The renowned linguist and scholar Max Weinreich (1884–1969) famously categorized Yiddish as a "fusion language," pointing to the wide variety of linguistic components brought together in its vocabulary, grammar, syntax, and more. At its base, Yiddish is, like English, a Germanic language. Yet it also incorporates a large number of lexical borrowings and grammatical formations from other language families, including Semitic languages (specifically Hebrew and Aramaic—the languages of Jewish liturgy, prayer, and traditional text study), Slavic languages (especially Polish, Ukrainian, and Belarusian), and to a lesser extent Romance languages. The long history of Ashkenazi Jews and their migrations across the Middle East into western Europe, and further east across German and Slavic-speaking lands, is imprinted in the language itself.

This amazing diversity may be evidenced in even the simplest phrases. Take, for example, the sentence *Di bobe makht tsholnt af shabes* ("The grandmother makes cholent [a slow-cooked stew] for the Sabbath"). It contains all of Yiddish's major linguistic elements. While the basic grammar of the sentence and its verb (*makhn*, "to make") is Germanic, the nouns all derive from different language families: *bobe* (grandmother) from Slavic; *tsholnt* (cholent) from Romance; and *shabes* (Saturday/the Sabbath) from Semitic.

Weinreich characterized language use among Eastern European Jews as defined by a system of "external and internal bilingualism." External bilingualism refers to Yiddish speakers' knowledge of their own vernacular and the language(s) of the non-Jewish peoples who lived among and around them. Internal bilingualism refers to Eastern European Jewry's knowledge of their communal languages, meaning both the Yiddish of everyday life and *loshn-koydesh*, the "Holy Tongue" of Hebrew/Aramaic, used in the synagogue, study house, and other contexts. *Loshn-koydesh* was traditionally considered prestigious and the purview of a learned male elite, used for high-status functions such as writing, rhetoric, and official correspondence. Yiddish was used in the domestic sphere, coded as feminine and as a low-status way of talking about mundane matters. Languages were in constant contact in Eastern European Jewish life. Understanding the complexity, friction, and playfulness between these various cultural layers is an essential part of learning Yiddish.

As Yiddish spread across Europe, several regional dialects developed; these can be grouped into two principal forms: Western Yiddish and Eastern Yiddish. Western Yiddish, once spoken in what is today the Netherlands, Alsace-Lorraine, Switzerland, and northern Germany, had fallen largely out of use by the end of the 19th century.

Eastern Yiddish became what is generally referred to as Yiddish today and can, in turn, be divided into three main dialects: Northeastern (*litvish*, or Lithuanian, corresponding to present-day Belarus, Lithuania, parts of Poland, and other neighboring regions), Central or Mideastern (*poylish*, or Polish, corresponding to much of present-day Poland, Hungary, and parts of Romania and Ukraine), and Southeastern (*ukrainish*, or Ukrainian, corresponding to much of present-day Ukraine, Moldova, and Romania). The most telling difference between these dialects is the pronunciation of stressed vowels within a word, although other points of divergence in both lexicon and grammar abound. Yiddish speakers sometimes refer to these dialects by witty shorthand phrases that highlight the most distinctive features of a given subgroup's speech. For instance, the phrase *tote-mome lushn* (as opposed to the more standard *tate-mame loshn*, literally "father-mother tongue") is sometimes used to refer to various Southeastern subdialects, highlighting their typical vowel shifts. Similarly, the phrase *sabesdike losn* (as opposed to the more standard *shabesdike loshn*, literally "sabbath language") is a codeword for Lithuanian Yiddish, emphasizing the dialect's characteristic merging of sibilants that other dialects distinguish. Dialects also often mark subtle cultural differences between groups of Yiddish speakers and can be the subject of humor and stereotyping. Speakers of Lithuanian Yiddish, or *litvaks*, for example, have been said to be overly rational, dour, and egg-headed, while *galitsyaners*, as Polish Yiddish speakers may be called, have been thought to be more frivolous and ignorant. Yiddish dialects are also markers of distinct traditions within Ashkenazi cuisine.

Several additional varieties of Yiddish have arisen in specific social contexts. For a time, Yiddish theaters across Eastern Europe and elsewhere used a distinct *teater-lushn* ("language of the theater"), based on a somewhat standardized version of Southeastern Yiddish. Contemporary Hasidic Yiddish, the language spoken by most of today's native Yiddish speakers, is based primarily on the Polish and Hungarian dialects of Mideastern Yiddish. This book teaches *klal-shprakh*, or Standard Yiddish, a linguistic construction that incorporates elements from all major dialects with a pronunciation that most closely resembles Northeastern Yiddish; it is used by most literary and academic establishments.

ORIGINS AND EARLY DEVELOPMENT

Although the exact origins of the Yiddish language are still a matter of some debate, a consensus pinpoints its genesis at about a thousand years ago. Leading theories say Yiddish developed as a distinct vernacular in German-speaking borderlands, either in the Rhineland cities of Speyer, Mainz, and Worms or farther east, in centers such as Regensburg, Nuremberg, and Rothenburg. Although direct comparisons are sometimes difficult to make, Yiddish can be considered as old as many other contemporary European vernaculars, such as French, German, or English.

The earliest known extant Yiddish text dates from 1272. Nestled in the hollows of an illuminated Hebrew word in the famed Worms Mahzor, the text is a simple sentence in Old Yiddish: *Gut im betage / s'ver dis makhzor in bes hakneses trage*, or, as scholar Jeffrey Shandler has translated it, "A good day is given to the man who bears / into the synagogue this Book of Prayers." The text itself, written as a rhyming couplet, suggests that Yiddish, even at this early stage, was considered a language capable of creative, playful expression. The text's placement inside a Hebrew word and, in turn, inside a prayer book underscores the depth of the relationship between the Yiddish vernacular and its holy Hebraic counterpart.

Other early texts in Yiddish include translations and adaptations of medieval European courtly romances, such as the famed *Bove-bukh* (*The Book of Bovo*, first printed in 1541) by Elye Bokher (c. 1469–1549), considered by some to be the first nonreligious book printed in Yiddish. In this early period, Yiddish was also often used to translate or adapt traditional Jewish texts of liturgy and learning originally composed in Hebrew or Aramaic, making them accessible to a wider audience. One of the most enduring such adaptations is the *Tsene-rene* by Yankev ben Yitskhok Ashkenazi of Janów. Often considered a kind of women's Bible, it contains explanations and commentary of the weekly portion of the Torah, all written in Yiddish. Written with a similar audience in mind, *Tkhines* ("supplications") were prayers, devotional texts, and inventive ritual scripts written in Yiddish, often by female authors, and published in short books or pamphlets for use primarily by women. Of a very different nature and genre, *Memoirs of Gluckl of Hameln* by its eponymous author (1645–1724) is another important early Yiddish text, studied and read to this day. The text details the social and spiritual worlds of a Jewish businesswoman and her family in German-speaking lands in the late 17th and early 18th centuries.

YIDDISH IN EASTERN EUROPE AND AROUND THE WORLD

Records suggest that Jews settled in large numbers in Slavic-speaking territories beginning in the 12th–14th centuries. This movement was likely driven by a combination of factors, including expulsions from German states and the expansion of opportunities farther east in the Polish-Lithuanian commonwealth. Documents record significant Jewish involvement in commerce and trade, as local nobility often gave Jews special political privileges and residency rights in exchange for their perceived critical role in local economic affairs. Within these territories, Jews tended to settle in urban areas and towns rather than in the countryside.

From Polish lands, Yiddish-speaking Jews moved throughout Eastern Europe. The archetypical Yiddish town was the *shtetl*, a market town with a significant Jewish population. Such *shtetlekh*, as they were called, existed throughout the region. Contrary to popular imagination, *shtetlekh* were not isolated "ghettos" closed off to the outside world. Rather, Jewish life in these towns, even towns with majority Jewish populations, was marked by constant cultural and economic interchange with other peoples both within and outside the confines of the immediate geographic area. Yiddish speakers were also a part of the fabric of many Eastern European cities, where they often constituted a large proportion of the population. In smaller numbers, Yiddish-speaking Jews could also be found in more rural locales, such as the largely agrarian region of Bessarabia or in small villages and farming communities throughout Eastern Europe.

Beginning in the late 19th century, as Eastern European Jews emigrated across the world, Yiddish became a global language. By the early 20th century, Yiddish could be heard in cities across Western Europe, such as Berlin, London, and Paris, throughout Canada and the United States, and in Latin America, South Africa, and Australia. In these new geographies, Yiddish collided with new cultures. As in Eastern Europe, Yiddish incorporated elements of new languages into itself while simultaneously influencing the surrounding cultures. Away from the Eastern European heartland of Yiddish and often struggling to make ends meet in their new homes, these Jewish immigrants often faced intense pressure to assimilate. For many immigrants, maintaining Yiddish thus became a much more self-conscious choice.

Despite the wide geographic spread of their communities, Yiddish speakers maintained a unified, if increasingly diverse, culture. Although separated by thousands of miles, educated Yiddish speakers would be familiar with the same canon of literary texts and might even read the same books and newspapers, hear the same music, and see the same plays on their hometown stages, in addition to the works of their own local literary stars.

THE BIRTH OF MODERN YIDDISH CULTURE

For much of its early history, Yiddish was considered a *zhargon*, a "jargon" derided by many of its speakers and outsiders alike. In the 19th and 20th centuries, when dramatic social, economic, and political shifts occurred in Eastern European Jewish life and in the larger region, this view became hotly contested.

In the religious sphere, the early Hasidic movement elevated Yiddish to an almost holy stature. Emerging in the latter half of the 18th century, the Hasidic movement recentered more accessible forms of worship, such as ecstatic singing and the telling of moralistic tales, over the more restricted rigors of Torah scholarship. At the center of Hasidic practice was the rebbe, a new kind of spiritual leader who derived his authority not from his erudition, as Jewish leaders traditionally did, but rather from the force of his own charisma. As the spoken language of both rebbes and the Ashkenazi layperson, Yiddish thus took on a special meaning among Hasidim, a tongue to be revered and respected in its own right. The texts that emerged from this milieu emphasized orality, putting a Yiddish on the printed page that resembled something like its spoken form for the first time. The tradition of the Hasidic tale continues to influence Yiddish literature and storytelling. Perhaps the most famous examples in this genre are the deeply mystical, symbolist stories of the enigmatic Rebbe Nakhmen of Bratslav (1772–1881). First published in Yiddish and Hebrew around 1815, they have captured the imagination of readers, writers, and other artists, both religious and secular, for generations.

The Haskalah, or Jewish Enlightenment, also had a great influence on the devleopment of Yiddish. Beginning in Berlin and other German-speaking cities in the late 18th century and spreading into Eastern Europe by the middle of the 19th century, the Haskalah can be seen as an attempt by certain Jewish elites to bring their community's life and thought in line with broader modern European trends toward philosophical rationality, economic utilitarianism, and urban civility. For maskilim, as the movement's adherents were known, Yiddish, in its supposedly mongrel nature, was a symbol of Jewish backwardness and impurity. And yet in their attempt to enlighten the largest number of Jewish readers, maskilic writers ironically resorted to writing in Yiddish to reach the Jewish masses, in many respects creating the conditions for the spread of modern Yiddish literature and the popular press. This duality of Yiddish as both an object of derision and a necessary tool of communication remained a critical part of Jewish thought well into the 20th century.

Modern Yiddish literature is said to have *dray klasiker*, or three "classic" writers: Mendele Moykher Sforim (pseudonym of Sholem-Yankev Abramovitsh, 1835–1917), Sholem Aleichem (pseudonym of Sholem Rabinovitsh, 1859–1916), and Yitskhok Leybush Peretz (1852–1915). Employing satire, humor, and pathos, these writers solidified Yiddish's literary norms and lent its literary tradition a sense of self-worth and prestige. These writers laid the foundation for an expansive literary edifice, a republic of letters that spans every genre and style with countless writers, poets, and playwrights. At once a record of the Jewish people and their distinctive experience

in the modern world, Yiddish literature also addresses universal questions, conflicts, and emotions. Whether written on the streets of Warsaw, the fields of South Africa, or the pampas of Argentina, Yiddish literature is not only *of* the world but *for* the world. Much of its riches remain insufficiently read, studied, or translated, a task for new students, speakers, and readers of Yiddish to plunge into.

Parallel to the rise of modern Yiddish literature was the spread of modern Yiddish theater. While Yiddish literature, including its *dray klasiker*, first rose in the Tsarist Empire, Yiddish theater flowered in Romania. The impresario, actor, playwright, and songwriter Avrom Goldfaden (1840–1908) is considered the father of modern Yiddish theater. By incorporating European aesthetics and genres such as operetta into distinctly Jewish traditions and forms, Goldfaden professionalized the theater for an Eastern European Jewish public. The international success of the *Vilner trupe* (Vilna Troupe), which began as a professional Yiddish theater company in interwar Poland and grew into a global phenomenon, indicates the importance and popularity of the dramatic arts for the Yiddish-speaking world. Today Yiddish theater thrives in New York, Montreal, Tel Aviv, Paris, Strasbourg, Bucharest, and elsewhere.

THE POLITICS OF YIDDISH

Public discourse in late-19th-century Eastern Europe was often dominated by the "Jewish question": In the face of increasing ethnic violence against Jews, politicians and thinkers both within and outside the Jewish community asked how to best integrate Jews and what rights they should have in modern society. Within the Jewish community, answers came from a range of political ideologies and often took on a linguistic character. Should Jews assimilate the languages of the states in which they lived? Should they adopt another, more prestigious foreign language? Or should they use one of their own internal languages to fight for their rights?

As the language of the Jewish working class, Yiddish was the language of choice for many Jewish political groups on the left, including socialists, communists, anarchists, and others. One of the most significant forces in Eastern European Jewish politics, and a major proponent of Yiddish language and culture, was the Bund (*Der algemeyner yidisher arbeter bund in lite, poyln un rusland*, or the General Jewish Workers Union in Lithuania, Poland, and Russia). Founded in Vilnius (then in the Tsarist Empire) in 1897, the Bund was a Jewish socialist party that sought to educate and radicalize Jewish laborers, fighting to improve their working conditions and win equal political and economic rights. While Yiddish was generally condemned by the Zionist movement in favor of the newly constructed and "revived" form of Hebrew, many left-wing Labor Zionist groups considered the promotion of Yiddish alongside Modern Hebrew as an essential part of their program.

A critical moment in the development of Yiddishist politics was the 1908 Jewish Language Conference that took place in Czernowitz, then the capital of Bukovina in the Austro-Hungarian Empire, now called Chernivtsi, in present-day Ukraine. Bringing together delegates from across ideological divides and from different linguistic camps, the conference was organized around an ambitious agenda related to practical policies on the use and support of Yiddish, but these plans were subsumed by an intense and most symbolic debate over the status of Yiddish. Eventually, a resolution was adopted that certified Yiddish to be "*a* national language of the Jewish people," rather than a declaration of Yiddish as "*the* national language" that many had hoped for.

A crowning achievement of the Yiddishist camp in the interwar period was the establishment of the YIVO in Vilnius in 1925 (*Der yidisher visnshaftlekher institut*, literally the Yiddish Scientific Institute, now known as the YIVO Institute for Jewish Research). The result of a collaboration between some of the greatest Jewish scholars of its day, the YIVO aimed to be an all-purpose research institute and archive for Eastern European Jewish language, economic life, and culture, both past and present. Under the direction of Max Weinreich and in line with many similar projects of national revival in Eastern Europe at the time, the YIVO promoted a standardized Yiddish to ease communication, printing, and education. The *klal-shprakh* that emerged from this work is the Standard Yiddish in use in academic and literary circles today. The YIVO is currently based in New York, with smaller branches in Buenos Aires and Chicago.

In the interwar period, Yiddish also enjoyed full recognition and support from the Soviet Union. Thanks in part to the efforts of Soviet Jewish activists, including many former Bundists such as Ester Frumkin (née Khaye Malke Lifshits, 1880–1943), the USSR built an entire infrastructure of educational, cultural, and literary initiatives in Yiddish designed to create a culture that conformed to state ideology and induced loyalty in the new country's Jewish citizens. Soviet Yiddish philologists reformed and standardized Yiddish according to Communist principles, removing its "religious element" by phonetically respelling words of Hebrew/Aramaic origin. Although Yiddish culture enjoyed the state's approval for much of the interwar period, the Yiddish-speaking intelligentsia fell victim, as did so many others, to the purges of the late 1930s and in the specifically antisemitic attacks against Jewish intellectuals and Yiddish cultural figures in 1952. After Stalin's death, Yiddish again received state support, albeit in a minimal fashion, with the publication of *Sovetish heymland* (*Soviet Homeland*), a major Yiddish literary journal into the 1990s. Yiddish was maintained as a vernacular by some Soviet Jews after the war, especially in those parts of the country, such as Moldova, western Ukraine, and the Baltic States, where they lived in relative isolation and dense concentrations.

THE HOLOCAUST AND ITS AFTERMATH

The Holocaust had a devasting impact on Yiddish, as it was the language of most of its victims. While many Yiddish speakers remained in Eastern Europe in the wake of the Nazi genocide, by 1945 the language and its community had been decimated. An understanding of Yiddish is crucial in order to fully comprehend the loss the Holocaust represents and the deep trauma it has left on Jewish culture as a whole. As a language of testimony, Yiddish provides unique and direct insight into the lives of Holocaust victims and survivors—a record of tragedy, resistance, bravery, and sorrow.

In Yiddish, the Holocaust is known as *der khurbn* ("the destruction"). This *loshn-koydesh* word directly connects World War II to previous Jewish catastrophes, chiefly *khurbn-bais-rishn* and *khurbn-bais-sheyni*, the destruction of the First and Second Temples respectively, and to other moments of violence, such as the pogroms of the 19th century and the ravages of World War I. By calling this event "*khurbn*," it becomes part of a culturally understood cycle of persecution and perseverance, an extreme event with both historical antecedents and a future beyond it. This is in contrast to the English term *Holocaust* and the Modern Hebrew term *Shoah* ("calamity"), which both single out the event as an exceptional moment in time without parallel, precedent, or comparison.

After the war, the number of Yiddish speakers continued to decline. In the new state of Israel, where Zionist ideology was often hostile to Yiddish and other markers of diaspora life, Modern Hebrew was declared the national language. In the United States, economic and cultural pressures encouraged the rapid assimilation of Yiddish speakers into the English mainstream. In the Soviet Union, new opportunities and widespread antisemitism pushed Eastern European Jews toward Russian. The postwar period was not simply a period of straightforward decline, however. Despite the radical changes wrought by war, genocide, nationalism, and assimilation, this was also a time of continuity and accomplishment. Yiddish culture received international acclaim and recognition when Isaac Bashevis Singer (1902–1991) was awarded the Nobel Prize for Literature in 1978.

YIDDISH IN THE 21ST CENTURY

Yiddish today is used by a diverse and rapidly growing transnational community. Although modern Yiddish is starkly different from what it was before World War II, it is still a language where traditions are passed down and culture expands and thrives. Speaking broadly, Yiddish speakers today can be loosely divided into two groups: "secular" Yiddishists and Hasidic speakers of Yiddish.

In Yiddish culture, which is steeped in Judaic concepts, there is no clearly defined boundary between the secular and the religious. The Yiddish word commonly translated as "secular" is *veltlekh*, which means "worldly" and connotes a perspective that is open to outside influences rather than a strictly *frum*, or pious, inward-looking worldview. Among so-called secular Yiddishists, therefore, are many religious people.

"Secular" Yiddish speakers today are primarily those who have consciously decided to speak, use, study, and cultivate the language and its culture. These Yiddishists, as they are sometimes called, are often attracted to Yiddish as an alternative form of Jewish identity or as a form of artistic and political expression. This global community of native speakers and second-language learners is incredibly diverse, bringing together all sorts of people: Jews, non-Jews, young and old, religious and secular, queer and straight. Without a single center, the community comes together at international klezmer festivals, summer language programs, academic conferences, and other venues happening on virtually every continent, wherever Yiddish language and art are being studied and transmitted to new generations. This part of the Yiddish world embodies an ethos of openness and eagerly shares its riches with others, mounting concerts and shows to great outside acclaim, translating its literature for a world of readers, and creating increasingly accessible cultural spaces. As a growing phenomenon, this Yiddish cultural community is becoming increasingly visible to the mainstream Jewish community and is achieving broader recognition from the culturally curious at large.

The second group of contemporary Yiddish speakers, and the largest group overall, are Hasidic communities of ultra-Orthodox Jews in densely populated neighborhoods or towns in and around New York, Montreal, Antwerp, Jerusalem, and elsewhere. These people maintain Yiddish as a vernacular, everyday language. Alongside this community's distinctive dress and its especially strict interpretation of Jewish religious law, a Yiddish vernacular functions as a way to maintain communal insularity and counter the perceived negative influences of the outside world. An incredibly fast-growing community, where families have on average

upward of 10 children, Hasidic society produces a vast and constantly expanding array of Yiddish cultural products, including literature, newspapers, theatrical productions, music, films, children's games, and more. Contrary to their own internal pronouncements, Hasidim are also active in creating in Yiddish online, particularly in community-based forums and chat sites. For all their efforts to remain closed off, Hasidic communities are often more open than may be expected, especially if interlocutors respect their language and customs.

At first glance, it may appear that these two groups of contemporary Yiddish speakers—Yiddishists and ultra-Orthodox—have little to do with one another. While the border between them is real, it is also quite porous, and exchange and interaction are increasingly common. Moreover, there are many Yiddish speakers today who do not adhere to either of these groups, instead belonging to the large number of heritage speakers or curious learners who are drawn to the language for a host of other reasons. What remains constant in Yiddish culture today is the language's nature as inherently transnational and extraterritorial, a powerful force that connects its users to a rich history and an ever-evolving future.

Sebastian Schulman
Montréal, Québec

9. A NOTE FROM AARON LANSKY, PRESIDENT OF THE YIDDISH BOOK CENTER

When, in the summer of 1980, we first set out to save the world's Yiddish books, we couldn't have imagined that four decades later we'd be releasing a new Yiddish textbook. Back then, most Yiddish readers were native speakers who had no need of a textbook, and the relatively small number of young people determined to learn the language were well served by *College Yiddish*, which first appeared in 1947. We for our part focused on a more pressing priority: to save physical Yiddish books before it was too late.

Why Yiddish books needed saving is a story unto itself. Yiddish was spoken by more Jews in more places for a longer time than any other Jewish language. Beginning in the 19th century, as the Enlightenment made its way into Jewish communities in Eastern Europe, Yiddish gave rise to what Ruth Wisse has called "a mighty literature": 40,000 titles and 3,000 separate newspapers, journals, and magazines that together provided a chronicle of traditional Jewish life and probed the possibilities of Jewish identity in the modern world.

Literature takes on greater urgency in times of social change, and Yiddish readers proved more voracious than they themselves sometimes realized. Before we began collecting Yiddish books, we met with Yiddish scholars to ask how many we could expect to find. They estimated 70,000—a number we surpassed in the first six months. Today, four decades later, we've recovered 1.5 *million* volumes, and more continue to arrive every day.

The fact that respected scholars got the number so wrong reflects a deep pessimism that suffused much of the Yiddish world back then, and for good reason. Half of the 11 million Jews who spoke Yiddish in 1939 were murdered in the Holocaust. Persecution in the Soviet Union culminated on August 12, 1952, when Stalin ordered the execution of his country's leading Yiddish writers on a single night. The leaders of the new State of Israel opted for Hebrew—a language that hadn't been spoken for two thousand years—over their native Yiddish. In America, Jewish immigrants found freedom of religion but little tolerance for differences of language and culture. They responded by redefining what had been a complex civilization as a religion alone, divorced from culture. Yiddish, like everything else that made Jews different, was trivialized, disparaged, swept under the rug, hidden from the kids, and eventually forgotten. Is it any wonder, given the depredations and displacement of the past century, that downhearted Yiddish scholars underestimated the number of books that remained?

Scholars weren't the only ones ready to say kaddish for Yiddish. When we began saving books, leaders of the established Jewish community were so disdainful they left it to us, scruffy students in our twenties, to take possession of an irreplaceable cultural treasure. Often, as we hauled boxes out to the truck, we looked over our shoulders, wondering when the grown-ups would show up and take over. They never came. When we reached out to them, they couldn't get rid of us fast enough.

"Don't you know that Yiddish is dead?" one executive demanded.

"Yiddish?!" sputtered another. "That's exactly the part of Jewish life we're trying to forget!"

"Even if you can manage to save Yiddish books," challenged a third, "who in the world is going to read them?"

At the time all I could answer was that Yiddish books had enormous intrinsic value, and we needed to save them while there was still time. As for readers, I was confident they'd come, but I had no idea when.

Fortunately, the world changed in the ensuing years. Growing appreciation of diversity and an academic shift to social and cultural history led to a dramatic increase in demand for Yiddish books. In 1998 we digitized most of the titles in our collection, and ten years later we made them freely available online. At last count, they have been downloaded an astonishing four million times. New software allows visitors to our website to find any word, phrase, name, or place-name in millions of pages of Yiddish literature in a matter of seconds. We're now working with other institutions to create a *Universal* Yiddish Library that will pool online resources and make Yiddish—once in danger of extinction—the most accessible literature on the planet.

We didn't forget those who can't read Yiddish in the original. With 98 percent of Yiddish titles yet to be translated into English, we cosponsored a translation series at Yale University Press and then launched an initiative to train, mentor, and publish a new generation of Yiddish translators. We began a far-reaching oral history project to capture Jews' personal stories (a quarter of them in Yiddish). We offer educational opportunities for high school, college, and graduate students, twentysomethings, teachers, writers, and adult learners. And we sponsor exhibits and public programs, including Yidstock, our annual festival of new Jewish music.

The more successful we are at bringing Yiddish to a wider audience, the more eager people are to learn Yiddish for themselves. In 2012 we established a Yiddish Language Institute and hired a young scholar named Asya Vaisman Schulman as its first director. She was born for the job. A native of Czernowitz (now Chernivtsi), the city where Yiddish was once declared "a national language of the Jewish people," Asya immigrated to the United States at age 7 and promptly learned English and Yiddish. She developed an online Yiddish dictionary for her bas mitzvah project and raced through Barnard in three years before completing a doctorate in Yiddish at Harvard, also in record time. If she was in a rush, it was because she was so clear about her goal: to teach Yiddish—and to teach teachers how to teach Yiddish—using a "communicative" approach consistent with the latest innovations in language pedagogy. At the Center she launched YiddishSchool, a week-long program for adults. She took charge of our Steiner Summer Yiddish Program for college students. And she spent seven years working with talented Yiddish teachers around the world to develop *In eynem*, the lively, state-of-the-art Yiddish textbook you're holding in your hands. Learning Yiddish is about to become a lot quicker, easier, and more fun, and the Yiddish books we've saved are about to find even more of the readers they so richly deserve.

Aaron Lansky
President
Yiddish Book Center

UNIT TABLE OF CONTENTS

טעמע I: שלום־עליכם!

UNIT I: HELLO!

טעמע II: אין קלאַס

UNIT II: IN CLASS

טעמע III: עס בלײַבט אין דער משפּחה

UNIT III: ALL IN THE FAMILY

טעמע IV: אַרום דעם טיש

UNIT IV: AROUND THE TABLE

טעמע V: פֿאַרברענגען אין שטאָט

CHAPTER 16 | קאַפּיטל 16

UNIT V: OUT ON THE TOWN

טעמע VI: פֿלענער און וואַקאַציעס

UNIT VI: PLANS AND VACATIONS

SUPPLEMENTARY CHAPTER — צוגאָב־קאַפּיטל

אַלף־בית־קאַפּיטל

CHAPTER GOALS

- In this chapter, you will learn how to read and write in the Yiddish alphabet. You will learn both the print and the cursive forms of letters.

וואָקאַבולאַר:	
the alphabet	דער אַלף־בית
גראַמאַטיק:	
pronunciation	אַרויסרעד
orthography	אויסלייג
קולטור — אוידיאָ:	
"The Alphabet" (Asya Vaisman Schulman)	„דער אַלף־בית“ (אַסיאַ ווײַסמאַן שולמאַן)
"All Together" (folk song)	„לאָמיר אַלע אין איינעם“ (פֿאָלקסליד)

ד ד **d**aled CONSONANT	ג ג **g**iml/ as in **g**irl CONSONANT	בֿ בֿ **v**eys HEBREW ONLY	ב ב **b**eys CONSONANT	אָ אָ k**o**mets alef/ as in l**aw**yer VOWEL	אַ אַ p**a**sekh alef/ as in ah**a** VOWEL	א א shtumer alef/ silent SILENT
ח ח **kh**es/ as in Scottish Gaelic lo**ch** HEBREW ONLY	ז ז **z**ayen CONSONANT	וי וי vov yud/ as in b**oy** DIPHTHONG	וו וו tsvey **v**ovn CONSONANT	וּ וּ melupm vov/ as in b**oo**t VOWEL	ו ו vov/ as in b**oo**t VOWEL	ה ה **h**ey CONSONANT
כ כ **kh**of/ as in Scottish Gaelic lo**ch** CONSONANT	כּ כּ **k**of HEBREW ONLY	ײַ ײַ pasekh tsvey yudn/ as in ch**ai** DIPTHONG	ײ ײ tsvey yudn/ as in w**ei**gh DIPHTHONG	יִ יִ khirek yud/ as in f**i**sh VOWEL	י י **y**ud/ as in **y**es, or as in f**i**sh CONSONANT/VOWEL	ט ט **t**es CONSONANT
ס ס **s**amekh CONSONANT	ן ן langer **n**un FINAL FORM	נ נ **n**un CONSONANT	ם ם shlos **m**em FINAL FORM	מ מ **m**em CONSONANT	ל ל **l**amed CONSONANT	ך ך langer **kh**of/ as in Scottish Gaelic lo**ch** FINAL FORM
ק ק **k**uf CONSONANT	ץ ץ langer **ts**adek FINAL FORM	צ צ **ts**adek CONSONANT	ף ף langer **f**ey FINAL FORM	פֿ פֿ **f**ey CONSONANT	פּ פּ **p**ey CONSONANT	ע ע ayen/ as in b**e**t VOWEL
		ת ת **s**of HEBREW ONLY	תּ תּ **t**of HEBREW ONLY	שׂ שׂ **s**in HEBREW ONLY	ש ש **sh**in CONSONANT	ר ר **r**eysh (rolled or guttural) CONSONANT
				טש טש tes shin/ as in **ch**eese CONSONANT	זש זש zayen shin/ as in bei**g**e CONSONANT	דזש דזש daled zayen shin/ as in **j**ar CONSONANT

Silent; used at beginning of word before most vowels

Vowel

Diphthong

Consonant / consonant cluster

Final form; only appears at end of word

Hebrew only; only appears in words of Hebrew origin

גענִיטונג 1: דער אַלף־בית

.n this chapter, you will begin to learn how to read and write in Yiddish. Yiddish is written in the Hebrew alphabet, and for these lessons, we will be using standard YIVO orthography. The full Yiddish alphabet can be found in the chart on the preceding page. As you examine the letters, keep in mind the following:

- The Yiddish alphabet is written from right to left (and the chart should be read right to left as well).
- The cursive form of a letter is sometimes quite different from its print form. You will learn to read print letters and to both read and write cursive letters. In the chart, the print form appears at the top of each cell, while the cursive form is immediately below it.
- The name of each letter, as well as an approximation of the sound the letter makes, appears below the cursive form.
- On the website, you will find audio recordings of the sounds all of the letters make. The best strategy for learning to produce and distinguish Yiddish sounds is to listen carefully and imitate often, since many of these sounds do not correspond exactly to English sounds and also vary depending on phonological context. However, we do provide advice on pronunciation in the pronunciation guide at the end of this chapter (pages 14–16). The chart on page 2 is not meant to be a detailed guide to precise pronunciation.
- Yiddish has a mostly phonetic writing system—that is, there is usually a direct relationship between the spelling of a letter and its sound. Words of Hebrew and Aramaic origin, however, are the exceptions, retaining the spelling used in those languages, which differs from Yiddish spelling and pronunciation conventions.
- There are six letters that appear only in words deriving from Hebrew and Aramaic. Each of these letters has the same sound as another letter in the alphabet. These letters have the "Hebrew Only" label in the chart.
- Five letters have a different form when they appear at the end of a word. (For example, *langer khof* (ך) appears only at the end of a word, whereas *khof* (כ) appears anywhere else.) These letters have the "Final Form" label in the chart.
- The letter *yud* (י) can be either a vowel or a consonant, much like the English letter "y."
- The letter *reysh* (ר) is pronounced as a trill with the tip of the tongue (like the Spanish *arroyo*) or as a trill with the uvula (like the French *Renoir*). Both pronunciations are equally admissible.
- The vowels ו and י, as well as the diphthongs (vowel combinations) יי, ײַ, and וי, cannot appear at the beginning of a word. They are always preceded by a *shtumer alef* (א) at the beginning of a word.

As you examine the chart, look for the answers to the questions below.

1. Can you find the five letters that have a different form when they appear at the end of a word? What are they?

2. Which pairs or groups of letters sound the same?

געניטונג 2: די אותיות

ווידעאָ־געניטונג א־2

א אַ אָ ב בֿ ג ד

ה ו וּ וו וי ז ח

Practice reading and writing Yiddish letters with this video, which you can find online with its accompanying exercise. As you learn to write in cursive, follow the motions in the video to form the letters correctly.

Use the worksheet on the following page as a guide. The cursive letters on it are adapted from David Bridger's 1947 primer *Der onheyber,* which was published in New York for use in Yiddish schools.

- Note that as with all handwriting, there is considerable variability in the forms of Yiddish cursive letters. In cases when a given letter has more than one widespread form, an alternate form has been supplied in parentheses.
- The numbered arrows indicate the steps to follow to form the letters correctly. Remember to write from right to left.

1.	א	18.	יי	35.	ק
2.	אַ	19.	ײַ	36.	ר
3.	אָ	20.	כּ	37.	ש
4.	ב	21.	כ	38.	שׂ
5.	בֿ	22.	ך	39.	תּ
6.	ג	23.	ל	40.	ת
7.	ד	24.	מ		
8.	ה	25.	ם		
9.	ו	26.	נ		
10.	וּ	27.	ן		
11.	וו	28.	ס		
12.	וי	29.	ע		
13.	ז	30.	פּ		
14.	ח	31.	פֿ		
15.	ט	32.	ף		
16.	י	33.	צ		
17.	יִ	34.	ץ		

געניטונג 3: דער אַלף־בית איז זייער שיין

הער־געניטונג א־3

טיטל	♫ „דער אַלף־בית איז זייער שיין“
אַראַנזשירער	**אַסיאַ ווײַסמאַן שולמאַן (Asya Vaisman Schulman)** (טשערנאָוויץ, ראַטן־פֿאַרבאַנד 1983 –)
זינגער	**סאַשאַ לוריע (Sasha Lurje)** (ריגע, ראַטן־פֿאַרבאַנד 1985 –)
רעקאָרדירונג	2019, פֿאַראייניקטע שטאַטן

Asya Vaisman Schulman *set the* alef-beys *to* "Moyshe emes" *(משה אמת), a traditional Hasidic melody. Here it is sung by* **Sasha Lurje***, a Berlin-based Yiddish vocalist who specializes in traditional Yiddish song and brings historically informed performance of Yiddish song to theater, modern classical music, and even rock. She is accompanied by* **Craig Judelman** *and* **Ilya Shneyveys***.*

This song will help you learn the names of all of the letters, as well as their sequence in the alphabet. You'll notice that the alphabet has been divided into five groups in the song, with the letters in each group repeated twice. Follow along with the transcription below as you listen to the recording.

alef, beys, veys, giml, dalet, hey, vov, zayen, khes, tes, yud.
alef, beys, veys, giml, dalet, hey, vov, zayen, khes, tes, yud.

kof, khof, langer khof, lamed, mem, shlos mem.
kof, khof, langer khof, lamed, mem, shlos mem.

nun, langer nun, samekh, ayen.
nun, langer nun, samekh, ayen.

pey, fey, langer fey, tsadek, langer tsadek.
pey, fey, langer fey, tsadek, langer tsadek.

kuf, reysh, shin, sin, tof, sof.
kuf, reysh, shin, sin, tof, sof.

der alef-beys iz zeyer sheyn,
zingt im itst far zikh aleyn.

der alef-beys iz zeyer sheyn,
zingt im itst far zikh aleyn.

NOTE:

The biographical information about authors, performers, artists, and directors that accompanies the authentic texts in this book supplies the place names in Yiddish where each person was born and died, along with the name of the country each city or town was in at the time. Appendix D (alphabetical by Yiddish name, starting on page D1 in Volume 2) provides the current English names of these cities, as well as the present-day countries where they are located.

זייער שיין	*very nice*
אים	*it*
איצט	*now*
פֿאַר זיך אַליין	*for yourself*

Now write out each line of the song with the Yiddish letters themselves.

געניטונג 4: די וואָקאַלן

Match the Yiddish vowel in the left column to its name and pronunciation in the right.

ו 7	1. *komets alef* (**aw** as in l**aw**yer)
אָ ___	2. *vov yud* (**oy** as in b**oy**)
וי ___	3. *tsvey yudn* (**ei** as in w**ei**gh)
י ___	4. *ayen* (**e** as in b**e**t)
יי ___	5. *pasekh tsvey yudn* (**ai** as in ch**ai**)
ע ___	6. *pasekh alef* (**a** as in ah**a**)
ײַ ___	7. *vov* (**oo** as in b**oo**t)
אַ ___	8. *yud* (**i** as in f**i**sh)

The letter *yud* (י) can sometimes be a consonant (pronounced "y" as in "yes") and sometimes a vowel (pronounced "i" as in "fish"). The *khirek* (a dot below the *yud*: יִ) helps differentiate the two.

- When *yud* appears at the beginning of a word (not preceded by a *shtumer alef*) or next to a vowel, it is read as a consonant (for example, **יאָ** = *yo* and **פּיאַנע** = *pyane*).
- When *yud* appears between two consonants or after a *shtumer alef*, it is read as a vowel (for example, **ליפּ** = *lip* and **אין** = *in*).
- The *yud* is spelled with *khirek* when it appears next to a vowel and should be read as a vowel, not a consonant (for example, **העברעיִש** = *hebreish*).
- The *khirek* also appears under a *yud* being used as a vowel when it follows a *yud* being used as a consonant (for example, **ייִדיש** = *yidish*) or a *vov* being used as a vowel (for example, **רויִנען** = *ruinen*), to distinguish the letter combinations from the diphthongs *tsvey yudn* and *vov yud*, respectively.
- Note that two consecutive unmarked *yudn* spell the diphthong *tsvey yudn* (יי), pronounced like the English "ei" in the word "weigh." Two *yudn* with a *pasekh* underneath them spell the diphthong *pasekh tsvey yudn* (ײַ), pronounced like the English "aye."

The letter *vov* also has two forms: *vov* and *melupm vov*.

- The vowel *vov* (ו) is spelled with a *melupm* (a dot in the center of the letter: וּ) when it appears before or after the consonant *tsvey vovn* (וו) (for example, **װוּנדער** = *vunder*).
- A *melupm* is also added to the first *vov* of two consecutive *vovn* when both letters are vowels (for example, **טוּונג** = *tuung*).
- Note that two consecutive unmarked *vovn* spell the consonant *tsvey vovn* (וו), pronounced like the English "v."

געניטונג 5: ענלעכע אותיות

Some Yiddish letters look very similar. Circle the Yiddish letter in each pair that corresponds to the name above it.

- Pay special attention to variations around the corners and edges of the letters.

samekh		*nun*	
ם	ס	ג	נ
hey		*beys*	
ה	ח	ב	כ
vov		*reysh*	
ז	ו	ר	ד
fey		*shin*	
פֿ	פּ	שׂ	ש

געניטונג 6: סוף־אותיות

Match each Yiddish letter in the right column to its final form in the left.

ף 4	1. כ
ך ___	2. מ
ם ___	3. נ
ץ ___	4. פֿ
ן ___	5. צ

געניטונג 7: אותיות אין לשון־קודש־שטאַמיקע ווערטער

The letters in the left column below appear only in Yiddish words of Hebrew or Aramaic origin. Can you find the letter in the right column that is pronounced the same way as the one on the left?

בֿ 6	1. ס
ח ___	2. ט
שׂ ___	3. כ
כּ ___	4. ס
תּ ___	5. ק
ת ___	6. וו

געניטונג 8: וויטער לייענען

The comic strip found at the end of this chapter on pages 17–30 serves as reading practice and establishes familiarity with Yiddish consonants by focusing on them one at a time. For example, the second panel only includes words with vowels and the consonant *dalet*. The third and fourth panels contain words made up of vowels and the consonants *dalet* and *yud*. The fifth and sixth panels have words with *dalet*, *yud*, and *zayen*, and so on. You will be able to understand the meaning of the words from the pictures and the glosses appearing below each panel.

Once you feel comfortable with reading the print letters, focus on practicing your cursive by writing out the comic text in cursive letters.

NOTE:

Remember that Yiddish comics, like all Yiddish texts, are read right to left. The speech bubbles in each panel should be read top to bottom. When there are two or more bubbles at the same height, they should be read right to left.

געניטונג 9: ייִדישע שרײַבערס

הער־געניטונג א־9

On this recording, you will hear the first and last names of ten prominent Yiddish writers. As you listen, match up the first name in the right column to the last name in the left column below.

ה 1. איציק	א. דריז
___ 2. קאַדיע	ב. לעמפּל
___ 3. לייב	ג. שאַגאַל
___ 4. ציליע	ד. עסעלין
___ 5. בעלאַ	ה. מאַנגער
___ 6. יאָסל	ו. מאַש
___ 7. שיקע	ז. מאָלאָדאָווסקי
___ 8. אַלטער	ח. קאָטלער
___ 9. בלומע	ט. דראָפּקין
___ 10. יענטע	י. קוויטקאָ

גענישונג 10: שרײַבט די ווערטער

הער־געניטונג א־10

On this recording, you will hear the names of the ten common objects pictured below. Write down each word as you hear it. Then label each picture with the appropriate word.

NOTE:

All of the words in this exercise have English **cognates**—that is, their English equivalents sound very similar and have the same etymological origin.

גענישונג 11: די שטאַטן

Read aloud the 16 state names below. Write each state name in English underneath its Yiddish spelling.

1. לויִזיאַנע	2. וואַשינגטאָן	3. מישיגען	4. ניו־דזשערסי
5. ווירדזשיניע	6. אײַדאַהאָ	7. אינדיאַנע	8. מיין
9. אילינוי	10. דזשאָרדזשיע	11. מאַסאַטשוסעטס	12. ניו־יאָרק
13. ווײַאָמינג	14. אָהײַאָ	15. קאַליפֿאָרניע	16. אײַאָווע

געניטונג 12: פּאַראַלעלן

There are certain patterns you can learn that will help you recognize more Yiddish words that share etymological origins with English words. Note that all of the patterns listed below represent historical correspondences but not sound equivalencies.

1. The Yiddish letter **כ** (*khof*) often corresponds to the English letter combination "gh." For example, the English word "light" is **ליכט** in Yiddish. With that in mind, can you guess what the following Yiddish words mean?

רעכט ________ לאַך ________ נאַכט ________

2. The Yiddish letter **ז** (*zayen*) often corresponds to the English letter "s." For example, the English word "sack" is **זאַק** in Yiddish. What do you think the following Yiddish words mean?

זינג ________ זאָק ________ זופּ ________

3. The Yiddish letter **ש** (*shin*) often corresponds to the English letter "s." For example, the English word "state" is **שטאַט** in Yiddish. What do you think the following Yiddish words mean?

שמיר ________ שלײַם ________ שטאָל ________

4. The Yiddish letter **פֿ** (*fey*) often corresponds to the English letter "p." For example, the English word "sharp" is **שאַרף** in Yiddish. What do you think the following Yiddish words mean?

שיף ________ פֿעפֿער ________ האַרף ________

5. The Yiddish letter **ט** (*tes*) often corresponds to the English letter "d." For example, the English word "bed" is **בעט** in Yiddish. What do you think the following Yiddish words mean?

האַנט ________ טרינק ________ גוט ________

6. The Yiddish letter **ד** (*daled*) often corresponds to the English letter combination "th." For example, the English word "thin" is **דין** in Yiddish. What do you think the following Yiddish words mean?

לעדער ________ דערפֿאַר ________ פֿעדער ________

געניטונג 13: לאָמיר אַלע אין איינעם

הער־געניטונג א־13

טיטל	♫ **„לאָמיר אַלע אין איינעם“** פֿאָלקסליד
זינגער	**סאַשאַ לוריע (Sasha Lurje)** (ריגע, ראַטן־פֿאַרבאַנד 1985 –)
רעקאָרדירונג	2019, פֿאַראייניקטע שטאַטן

This popular folk song is traditionally sung at celebrations and gatherings as a way to welcome honored guests. This recording was made especially for this textbook as a way to welcome you, the learner, to the study of Yiddish! **Sasha Lurje** *sings, accompanied by* **Craig Judelman** *and* **Ilya Shneyveys**.

Read the questions below before you listen to the song. They will help you understand the text.

1. Each stanza of the song suggests welcoming someone. To whom is the welcome extended in each stanza?
2. With what beverage are the guests welcomed?

Listen to the song, but don't look at the text. Answer the questions above. Now listen again and follow along with the text below.

לאָמיר אַלע אין איינעם, אין איינעם
ייִדיש מקבל־פּנים זײַן.] 2 מאָל
לאָמיר אַלע אין איינעם,
לאָמיר אַלע אין איינעם,] 2 מאָל
טרינקען אַ גלעזעלע ווײַן.

לאָמיר אַלע אין איינעם, אין איינעם
סטודענטן מקבל־פּנים זײַן.] 2 מאָל
לאָמיר אַלע אין איינעם,
לאָמיר אַלע אין איינעם,] 2 מאָל
טרינקען אַ גלעזעלע ווײַן.

לאָמיר אַלע אין איינעם, אין איינעם
לערערס מקבל־פּנים זײַן.] 2 מאָל
לאָמיר אַלע אין איינעם,
לאָמיר אַלע אין איינעם,] 2 מאָל
טרינקען אַ גלעזעלע ווײַן.

לאָמיר	let's
אַלע	all
אין איינעם	*together*
מקבל־פּנים זײַן [מעקאַבל־פּאָנעם]	*welcome*
לערערס	teachers

! געדענקט!

In this textbook, whenever a word of *loshn-koydesh* origin is used for the first time, it will be followed by brackets containing a phonetic spelling in Yiddish characters, indicating its pronunciation (as with *mekabl-ponem* above).

דער אַלף־בית
THE ALPHABET

lake		די **אָזערע** (ס)
pear		די **באַר** (ן)
tree		דער **בוים** (ביימער)
pencil		דער **בלײַער** (ס)
coat		דער **מאַנטל** (ען)
parrot		דער **פּאָפּוגײַ** (ען)
poem; song		דאָס **ליד** (ער)
girl		דאָס **מיידל** (עך)
outside		אין דרויסן
to work	איך אַרבעט, ער אַרבעט	אַרבעטן
all; everyone		אַלע
everything		אַלץ

די **אידעע** (ס); דער **באַל** (ן); די **באַנאַנע** (ס); דאָס **בוך** (ביכער); די **בלום** (ען); דאָס **בעט** (ן); דער **בער** (ן); די **גיטאַרע** (ס); דער **הונט** (הינט); דאָס **וואַסער** (ן); די **טיי** (ען); דער **עפּל** (—); דער **פּאָעט** (ן); דער **פּאַרק** (ן); די **קאַווע**; דער **קאָנצערט** (ן); די **קאַץ** (קעץ)

גראַמאַטיק־איבערבליק א־ב

PRONUNCIATION GUIDE

One of the crucial tasks in learning Yiddish, or any spoken language, is learning how to distinguish and produce the particular range of sounds that form its phonological basis. Every language has its own set of sounds, or *phonemes*, and its own rules about the differences between phonemes that carry meaning. For example, in English "dock" and "tock" are distinguished only by voicing or unvoicing the first consonant, while in other languages that difference may not register as meaningful (more on voiced and unvoiced sounds below). The best strategy for learning to produce and distinguish Yiddish sounds, as with so much else in language study, is to listen carefully and imitate often. However, we also provide notes and advice on pronunciation throughout the text. The following guide is an introduction to those notes and an expansion on certain points we felt deserved additional coverage. This is *not* an exhaustive, formal linguistic treatment of Yiddish phonology. If you would like to investigate these topics further, please consult the Further Reading section below.

We have tried to avoid dense linguistic terminology below, and to explain necessary terms when they are used, but one distinction is worth keeping in mind: that between **voiced** and **unvoiced** sounds. The difference is whether or not the speaker's vocal folds vibrate when producing a given sound. For example, the *s* in *sue* is unvoiced, while the *z* in *zoo* is voiced. Try saying both words in succession, dragging out the first consonant of each while holding a couple of fingers against your voice box. Your vocal cords vibrate while producing the voiced *z* but not while producing the *s*. (They do start vibrating, however, to produce the subsequent vowels.) Many languages, including Yiddish and English, use this distinction between voiced and unvoiced sounds to differentiate one word from another. As a result, there are many voiced/unvoiced pairs of sounds in both languages.

VOWELS

Yiddish vowels differ according to dialect, and there is a certain degree of variability even within Standard Yiddish. However, at base, most Yiddish vowels have close equivalents in English. For the in-between sounds below (אָ, ו, and י), our advice is—as above—to listen and imitate!

- *Pasekh alef* (אַ) sounds like the *a* in *aha*.
- *Komets alef* (אָ) lies somewhere between the *aw* in *lawyer* and the *o* in *done*.
- *Vov* (ו) lies between the *u* in *put* and the *oo* in *boot*.
- *Yud* (י) lies between the *i* in *fish* and the *ee* in *feet*.
- *Ayen* (ע) sounds like the *e* in *bet*.
- *Vov-yud* (וי) sounds like the *oy* in *boy*, but shorter.
- *Tsvey-yudn* (יי) sounds like the *ei* in *weigh*, but shorter.
- *Pasekh tsvey-yudn* (ײַ) sounds like the *ai* in *chai*, but shorter.

גראַמאַטיק־איבערבליק א־ב

CONSONANTS

Many Yiddish consonants also have near-English equivalents. Since they are more numerous than the vowels, they are listed here without comment, each followed by an English word beginning with the same sound. (Letters that appear only in words derived from Hebrew and Aramaic are omitted—please consult the *alef-beys* chapter for details.)

- These near-English consonants are as follows: ב (***b**all*), ג (***g**ill*), ד (***d**am*), ה (***h**op*), וו (***v**erve*), ז (***z**oo*), י (***y**ell*), מ (***m**ap*), נ (***n**ap*), ס (***s**ap*), פֿ (***f**ake*), ש (***sh**op*).

A number of Yiddish consonant sounds, however, *do* differ markedly from English.

- Some are almost entirely absent in English:
  - כ is similar to *ch* in German *Bach*. This sound may be practiced by placing your tongue as you would if you were about to say *cut* and then exhaling forcefully (as if trying to dislodge phlegm) while keeping your tongue tense so that it vibrates against your palate.
  - ר is either a lingual trill or flap—like *rr* in Spanish *arroyo* or *dd* in English *udder*, respectively—or a uvular trill or flap, similar to the *r* in French *rendez-vous* and not unlike the sound one makes while gargling.
- Other sounds exist in English but differ somewhat in their use or ubiquity:
  - Some sounds are written with one letter in Yiddish but multiple letters in English, such as צ (*ts* in *ca**ts***). Other sounds are represented with multiple letters both in Yiddish and in English, for example: דז (*ds* in *fa**ds***), טש (*ch* in ***ch**ild*), שטש (*sh ch* in *fre**sh** **ch**eese*). Still other sounds are represented with multiple letters in Yiddish and one letter in English, such as זש (*s* in *mea**s**ure*) and דזש (*j* in ***j**ar*).
  - In many varieties of Yiddish, ל exhibits two shades: "dark" and "light" (i.e., palatalized). These can be approximated by comparing the *l* in *luck* and the *l* in *leap*—hold the *l* sound for a second or two, noticing the higher position of the back of the tongue when preparing to say *leap*. Hear the difference?
    - This distinction between the dark and light ל is rarely crucial in distinguishing one word from another, and many native Yiddish speakers do not produce this distinction in their speech. Speakers of certain varieties of Yiddish, however, do consistently make this contrast.
  - Both ל and נ may be **syllabic**. That is, they may form a syllable unto themselves without needing a supporting vowel. In this role, they sound much like the *le* in *riddle* and the *en* in *written*. Notice that if you say these words at a natural speaking pace, you do not open your mouth to make a separate vowel sound before pronouncing the *l* or *n* sound. The same is true in Yiddish—adding in an extra vowel would be incorrect!
  - The letters ט, פּ, and ק sound much like English *t*, *p*, and *k* but with one important difference: they are unaspirated. That is, they sound like the middle consonants in *stop*, *spot*, and *scotch*; compare these to the first consonants in *top*, *pot*, and *cot*.
    - Hold your hand an inch or so from your lips as you say the first set of words (*stop*, *spot*, *scotch*). Then say the second set (*top*, *pot*, *cot*)—do you feel the puff of air against your hand? That is called **aspiration**, meaning that an extra release of air follows the consonant's pronunciation.
    - Generally speaking, Yiddish ט, פּ, and ק are unaspirated whether they fall in the beginning, middle, or end of a word. As in many aspects of Yiddish language, however, there is variation between different speech communities on this point. Again, listen and imitate!

גראַמאַטיק־איבערבליק א־ב

COMBINATIONS OF SOUNDS

- When נ precedes ג or ק (like in פֿרילינג [*spring*] or דאַנק [*thank*]), it becomes the sound *ŋ* (the phonetic symbol equivalent to *ng* in *sing*), but the subsequent ג or ק is still pronounced (as in *linger* or *sink* but unlike *singer*).
- When a syllabic נ follows ב or פּ (like in האָבן [*have*] or ליפּן [*lips*]), it is pronounced as an *m* sound—one merely keeps one's lips closed (as they were for the preceding ב or פּ) and continues to pronounce the nasal sound. There is no break between the two sounds to expel air through the mouth; air is released only through the nose.
- When a syllabic נ *follows* ג or ק (like in זאָגן [*say*] or זאָקן [*socks*]), it also becomes *ŋ*. Again, there is no break between the two sounds, and no extra vowel is pronounced. Air is released only through the nose.
- Yiddish exhibits "regressive voicing assimilation," in which two adjacent sounds assimilate to either both voiced or both unvoiced, depending on the latter sound. Thus, זאָגט (*says*) is pronounced [זאָקט] (both consonants become unvoiced) and עקדיש (*scorpion*) is pronounced [עגדיש] (both consonants become voiced).
  - This appears quite commonly when conjugating verbs, for example: איך רעד (*I speak*) is pronounced as written, but דו רעדסט (*you speak*) becomes [רעטסט].

SPELLING

The details of Yiddish spelling are covered in the *alef-beys* chapter, but a few notes are in order regarding departures from phonetic spelling rules.

- Generally speaking, Yiddish words are spelled phonetically (except for the changes in pronunciation caused by the combinations of sounds mentioned above, which are not reflected in the spelling). (This does not include words from Hebrew and Aramaic, which retain their traditional spellings derived from the source languages.)
- A few non-Hebraic words, however, are realized in "historical" spellings, including:
  - אויף, which is pronounced [אַף] when it is the preposition *on* and [אוף] when it plays the role of a verbal complement.
  - בײַ is pronounced [באַ], and its contraction with the definite article (דעם)—spelled בײַם—is pronounced [באַם].
- A small number of other such cases exist; we have noted them where they appear.
- Note that many native speakers do, in fact, pronounce such words as they are spelled, especially when reading. Such phenomena—known as "spelling pronunciations"—may herald a shift in the language. After all, there was a time when the *t* in English *often* was never pronounced.

FURTHER READING

In English:

Jacobs, Neil G. *Yiddish: A Linguistic Introduction*. Cambridge University Press, 2005, pp. 90–121.

Weinreich, Uriel. *College Yiddish*. 6th ed., YIVO Institute for Jewish Research, 2006, pp. 19–24.

In Yiddish:

Mark, Yudel. *Gramatik fun der yidisher klal-shprakh*. Alveltlekher yidisher kultur-kongres (World Congress for Jewish Culture), 1978, pp. 15–31.

Schaechter, Mordkhe. *Yidish tsvey*. Yiddish Language Resource Center, 1995, pp. 418–30.

לאָמיר לייענען!

yes יאָ

see זע

here דאָ

grandfather זיידע

זי she

באָבע grandmother

בייז angry

אַז if

ער he

זייער very

אָבער but

דער ברודער
איז דאָ!

ברודער brother

ער איז דער ברודער
אָדער דער זיידע?
ער איז דער
ברודער.

אָדער or

זע! אַ באַר!

די באַר
איז זויער?
זי איז
זייער זויער.

זויער sour

דער בער איז זויער
אָדער די באַר איז זויער?

ער איז אַ נאַר.
נ

נאַר fool

נאָר only

אָזערע lake

ריין clean

רעדן are talking

עס איז דאָ there is

זיס sweet

אין דרויסן outside

לילאַ purple

טאַטע father

אַרבעט works

זאָלסט you should

דאָרטן (over) there

לייענט reads

אַליין alone

ווײַס white

לידער poems

זײַט are

איר you

וווינט live

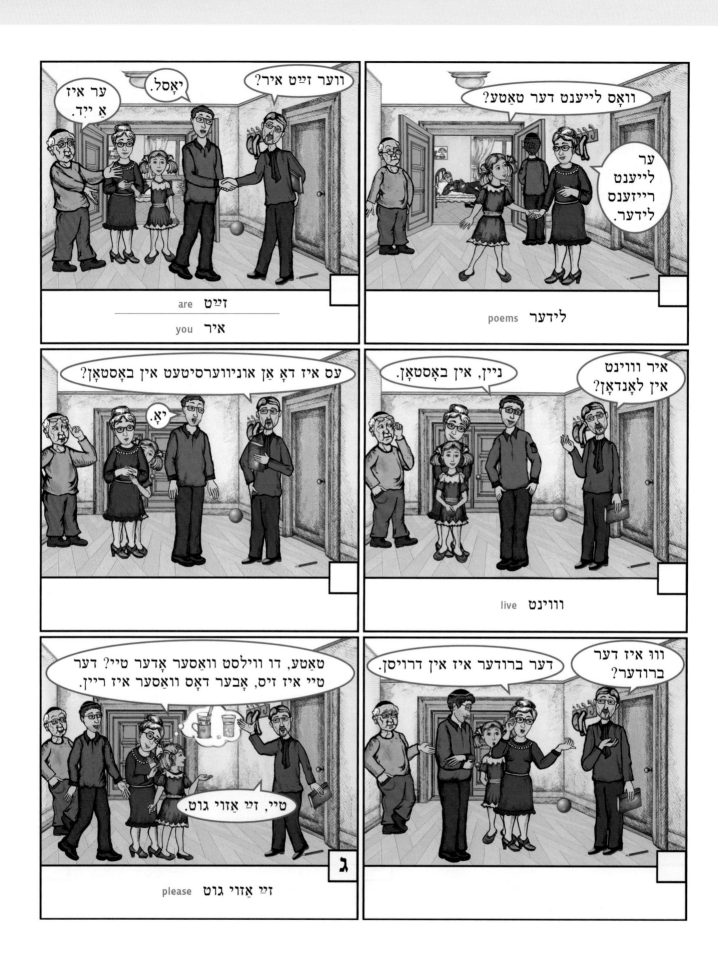

זײַ אַזוי גוט please

דער טיי איז גרין.
זייער גוט.
זיידע, ווו איז דײַן גיטאַרע?
ריינע, ברענג די גיטאַרע.
די גיטאַרע איז אין גאָרטן. דו ווילסט זינגען?
די גיטאַרע איז גרויס!
זינג, ריינע!
גרויס big
אײַ־ליו־ליו, אײַ־ליו־ליו...
דאָס איז אַ וויגליד.
וויגליד lullaby
אײַ־ליו־ליו, אײַ־ליו־ליו...
אײַ־ליו־ליו, אײַ־ליו־ליו...
ער איז זייער מיד...
מ
מיד tired

מיידל girl

מאַנטל coat

איז געוועזן was שיין beautiful

בוים tree

טיש table

שטייט stands

ריינע, זײַ אַזוי גוט און ברענג דעם טיש.
אָבער ער איז אַזוי שווער!
שווער heavy
טאַטע, ברענג דעם טיש מיט ריינען.
דער טיש איז ריין!
מאַמע, דאָס איז יאָסל.
זייער אײַנגענעם!
זייער אײַנגענעם!
זייער אײַנגענעם! Very pleased to meet you!
דאָס קינד קען זינגען!
זי איז קליין אָבער קלוג!
ק
קינד child
קלוג smart
קליין small

יאָסל, איר ווילט קאַווע?
יאָ, אַ דאַנק.

אַ דאַנק thanks

נישט not

ווי than

יאָסל טרינקט קאַווע אָבער דער טאַטע טרינקט טיי!

מיר זײַנען הונגעריק.
לאָמיר גיין עסן הערינג!

ה

לאָמיר let's

גיין go

דער הונט איז אין דער היים!

היים home

ער הייסט לאַבזיק. קום אַהער, לאַבזיק!

ער הייסט his name is

loves האָט ליב

take נעם

jump שפּרינג

parrot פּאָפּוגײַ

but נאָר

daughter טאָכטער	laughs לאַכט
thinks טראַכט	bad שלעכט

וואָס מאַכסטו? How are you?

דאַרפֿן need to

מע one

זיצן sit

װוּ איז לאַבזיק?
ער איז נישטאָ...
אָבער אָט איז אַ קאַץ!
די קאַץ
איז שוואַרץ.
ז
שוואַרץ black
טאַטע! מאַמע! יאָסל!
אָט איז מײַן קאַץ!

CLASSROOM EXPRESSIONS
אויסדרוקן פֿאַרן קלאַסצימער

THE TEACHER SAYS...	...דער לערער זאָגט
feedback	**אָפּרופֿן**
very good / very nice	זייער גוט / זייער שיין
extraordinary / excellent	אויסערגעוויינטלעך / אויסגעצייכנט
correct	ריכטיק
exactly	פּונקט אַזוי́
of course	פֿאַרשטײ́ט זיך
almost	כמעט [קימאַ́ט]
really?	טאַקע?
is that true?	דאָס איז אמת? [עמעס]
try again	פּרוּווט נאָך אַ מאָל
instructions	**אָנווײַזונגען**
listen	הערט זיך צו
repeat	חזרט איבער [כאַזערט] / זאָגט נאָך
stand up	שטייט אויף [אוף]
sit down	זעצט זיך אַװע́ק
give me the homework	גיט מיר די הײ́מאַרבעט
open your books	עפֿנט די ביכער
close your books	פֿאַרמאַ́כט די ביכער
look at page...	קוקט אויף זײַט ... [אַף]
look at the picture	קוקט אויפֿן בילד
write on the board	שרײַבט אויפֿן טאָוול [אַפֿן]
read aloud	לייענט אויף אַ קול [קאָל]
read one sentence / line / stanza	לייענט איין זאַץ / שורה [שורע] / סטראָפֿע
answer out loud	ענטפֿערט אויף אַ קול [קאָל]
work with a partner	אַרבעט מיט אַ חבֿר [כאַווער]
look in the appendix	קוקט אין הוספֿה [העסאָפֿע]
ask and answer according to the example	פֿרעגט און ענטפֿערט לויט דער דוגמא [דוגמע]
find a person who...	...געפֿי́נט אַ מענטש וואָס
make a list	מאַכט אַ רשימה [רעשימע]
take a look	גיט אַ קוק

CLASSROOM EXPRESSIONS
אויסדרוקן פֿאַרן קלאַסצימער

THE TEACHER SAYS...	...דער לערער זאָגט
questions	**פֿראַגעס**
who knows?	?ווער ווייסט
questions?	?פֿראַגעס
is everything clear?	?אַלץ איז קלאָר
are you ready?	?איר זײַט גרייט
have you finished?	?איר האָט געענדיקט
do you agree?	[מאַסקעם] ?איר זײַט מסכּים
useful phrases	**נוציקע אויסדרוקן**
so...	...איז
please	זײַט אַזוי גוט
again	נאָך אַ מאָל
together	צוזאַמען
let's...	...לאָמיר
in Yiddish	אויף ייִדיש
for example	[לעמאָשל] למשל
that's all!	!שוין
hooray!	!הוראַ
too bad	אַ שאָד
when someone sneezes...	**...אַז מע ניסט**
to health! (after sneeze)	!צו געזונט
to life! (after second sneeze)	!צום לעבן
to long years! (after third sneeze)	!צו לאַנגע יאָר

טעמע I:
שלום־עליכם!

UNIT GOALS

- In this unit, you will learn everything you need to make new acquaintances, from greetings, introductions, and courtesies to geography, days of the week, numbers, and basic activity verbs.
- This unit will introduce the traditions and rituals of Shabbos, the day of rest.

אינהאַלט:

1

קאַפּיטל איינס:
באַקענען זיך און געאָגראַפֿיע

CHAPTER GOALS

- In this chapter, you will learn how to introduce yourself to someone new and how to talk about geography.

	וואָקאַבולאַר:
getting acquainted	באַקענען זיך
classroom phrases	קלאַסצימער־אויסדרוקן
geography	געאָגראַפֿיע

	גראַמאַטיק:
nouns (grammatical gender; articles)	סובסטאַנטיוון (גראַמאַטישער מין; אַרטיקלען)
word order (asking questions; verb second)	ווערטער־סדר (פֿרעגן פֿראַגעס; ווערב־צווייי)
pronouns	פּראָנאָמען

א וואָקאַבולאַר און גראַמאַטיק: באַקענען זיך; ווערבן און סובסטאַנטיוון

hello (*to a new acquaintance*) שלום־עליכם
[שאָלעם־אַלייכעם]

also אויך
but אָבער

no ניין

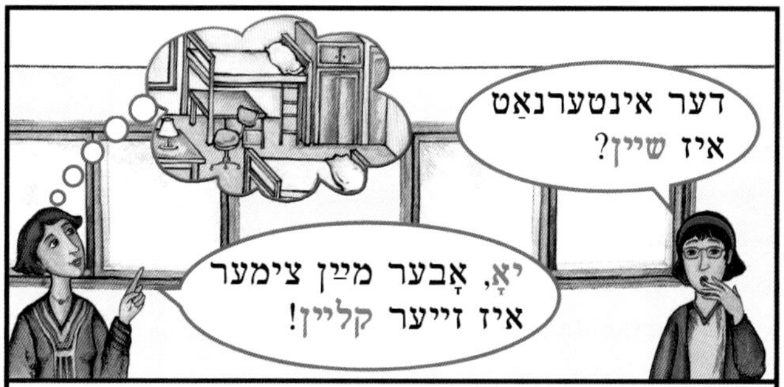

yes יאָ
nice שיין
small קליין

I know about איך ווייס פֿון
from where פֿון וואַנען

speak רעדסט
[רעטסט]

גענִיטונג 1: אַ נײַע סטודענטקע

It is the first day of Yiddish class, and Elke is the first student to arrive. Read the dialogue for comprehension.

[אַף] ענטפֿערט אויף די פֿראַגעס: יאָ אָדער ניין.

Answer the questions: **יאָ** *or* **ניין**.

1. די סטודענטקע הייסט גיטל?
2. פּראָפֿעסאָר קלוגער וווינט אין מאַסאַטשוסעטס?
3. עלקע וווינט אין ניו־יאָרק?
4. דער אינטערנאַט איז אין לערנטאָן־קאַלעדזש?
5. עלקע וווינט אין אַ קליינעם צימער?
6. פּראָפֿעסאָר קלוגער וווינט אין אַן אינטערנאַט?
7. פּראָפֿעסאָר קלוגער קומט פֿון ניו־יאָרק?
8. עלקע רעדט פֿראַנצייזיש? [רעט]

גערעדנקט!

Stress usually falls on the second-to-last syllable of a multisyllabic word. Nonpenultimate stress will be indicated when a word first appears, as well as in the appropriate vocabulary overview.

NOTE:

Professor Kluger addresses Elke using the **informal** pronoun **דו**. The equivalent **formal** pronoun is **איר**, which requires a different verb ending:

וװי הייסט איר? וווּ וווינט איר? פֿון וואַנען קומט איר? וואָסערע שפּראַכן רעדט איר?

We will learn more about formal and informal speech in **קאַפּיטל 2**.

גענִיטונג 2: צוויי סטודענטן באַקענען זיך

Avrom walks into class, and Elke greets him. Listen to the dialogue and follow along with the text below.

הער־גענִיטונג א־2

עלקע:	שלום־עליכם!
אַבֿרהם:	עליכם־שלום! ווי הייסטו?
עלקע:	איך הייס עלקע. און ווי הייסט דו?
אַבֿרהם:	איך הייס אַבֿרהם.
עלקע:	זייער אײַנגענעם!
אַבֿרהם:	זייער אײַנגענעם!

[אַוורָאָם]

NOTE:

The word **הייסטו** is a contraction, combining the verb **הייסט** and the unstressed pronoun **דו**. When the pronoun is stressed for purposes of emphasis or contrast—as in Elke's second line—no contraction occurs. This spelling convention reflects actual speech patterns and applies in both formal and informal writing.

Now take Avrom's role in the conversation, speaking during the pauses between Elke's lines. When Elke asks your name, answer with your own name instead of Avrom's.

גענײטונג 3: ער הייסט אַבֿרהם!

פּראָפֿעסאָר קלוגער רעדט מיט די סטודענטן. לייענט דעם דיאַלאָג אונטן.

Read the dialogue below.

[דוגמע] ענטפֿערט אויף די פֿראַגעס לויט דער דוגמא.

Answer the questions according to the example.

- Be sure to use the appropriate third-person pronoun, as in the dialogue.

דוגמא: ווי הייסט די פּראָפֿעסאָרשע?
זי הייסט עטל קלוגער.

1. ווי הייסט דער סטודענט?
2. ווי הייסט די סטודענטקע?

◀ CONTINUED

דוגמא	example, model

NOTE:

The suffixes **קע-** and **שע-** are added to certain nouns to create feminine forms, such as **די סטודענטקע** and **די פּראָפֿעסאָרשע.**

CONTINUED

Look at the declarative (nonquestion) sentences in the first, third, and fourth cells of the dialogue. The verb appears in two different forms in these sentences.

- What word appears in front of הייס?
- What words appear in front of הייסט?

These words are all **subject pronouns**, referring to the main noun in the sentence.

Now look at the question in the first cell.

- What is the first word in this sentence?
- Where does the subject pronoun appear?

Write down a rule for word order in declarative sentences and another for word order in questions. Based on this second rule, think about the question ווי הייסטו.

- Try taking apart the contraction הייסטו. Though the pronoun here (דו) is hidden by contraction with the verb, it still follows the verb, as expected.
- Write a declarative sentence corresponding to the question ווי הייסטו (like ער הייסט אַבֿרהם matches ווי הייסט ער).

NOTE:

The sentence in the second cell begins with the conjunction און, which is always followed by regular word order (which you have just established here). This is the case with all conjunctions.

געניטונג 4: ווּ ווױנסטו?

הער־געניטונג א־4

! געדענקט!

Yiddish has three grammatical genders: masculine, neuter, and feminine. For each gender, the definite article (*the*) changes:

Feminine	Neuter	Masculine
די	דאָס	דער

In the plural, the definite article always takes the form **די**, no matter the intrinsic grammatical gender of the noun it refers to:

דער סטודענט ← די סטודענטן

פּראָפֿעסאָר קלוגער און אַבֿרהם רעדן וועגן ווּ עלקע וווינט און ווּ זיי וווינען. לייענט איבער די פֿראַגעס אונטן אײדער איר הערט זיך צו צום דיאַלאָג. זיי וועלן אײַך העלפֿן פֿאַרשטיין דעם טעקסט. — about

Read the questions below before you listen to the dialogue. They will help you understand the text.

1. עלקע וווינט אין אַ הויז, אָדער אין אַן אינטערנאַט? — אָדער or
2. ווּ וווינט אַבֿרהם?
3. פּראָפֿעסאָר קלוגער וווינט אויף סאָסנע־גאַס, אָדער אויף קלינינע־גאַס?

◀ CONTINUED

CONTINUED

[אַפֿן] הערט זיך צו צום דיאַלאָג, נאָר קוקט נישט אויפֿן טעקסט. ענטפֿערט אויף די פֿראַגעס אויבן.

Listen to the recording, but don't look at the text. Answer the questions above. Now listen again, and fill in the blanks in the text below.

אַבֿרהם:	ווו ווינט עלקע?
פּראָפֿעסאָר:	זי ווינט אין לערנטאָן, אין ___ __________. און דו?
אַבֿרהם:	איך ווין אויך אין ____________, אויף סאָסנע־גאַס.
פּראָפֿעסאָר:	איך ____________ אויף קלינינע־גאַס!
אַבֿרהם:	זייער נאָענט!
פּראָפֿעסאָר:	דו ווינסט אין ___ ____________?
אַבֿרהם:	ניין, איך ווין אין ___ ____________.

!גערעדנקט

The preposition **אין** (*in*) applies to dwellings and cities, towns, etc. The preposition **אויף** (*on*) applies to streets in this case and is typically pronounced [אַף].

near	**נאָענט**
far	**ווײַט**

Look at the question Avrom asks in the first line of the dialogue.

- What is the first word in this sentence?
- Where does the subject appear?

Look for the pronouns **איך**, **דו**, and **זי** in the dialogue.

- Write down the verb following each one, exactly as written in the dialogue.
- How do these verb forms differ from one another?
- Write a rule for constructing each verb form, starting from the one for **איך**.
- How do these forms compare to those of the verb you saw in **3 געניטונג**?
- Can you spot the one usage of a verb in the above dialogue *not* connected to a pronoun? Why do you think this verb has the ending it does? What is its subject?

NOTE:

The **איך** form of the verb is the same as the **verb stem**. This stem is the core of the verb, to which endings for different conjugations are then attached.

איך הייס ← זי הייסט

Take Avrom's role in the conversation, speaking during the pauses between Professor Kluger's lines. Now take part in the dialogue again, this time responding as yourself.

- Substitute information about your own living situation where appropriate (i.e., instead of any purple or filled-in words).
- Since you don't live in Lernton, omit the word **אויך** from the third line.

◀ CONTINUED

אין קלאַס

מיט אַ חבֿר, חזרט איבער דעם דיאַלאָג אויבן. [כאַזערט]; [כאַווער]

With a partner, repeat the dialogue above, substituting information about your *own* living situation where appropriate (i.e., instead of any purple or filled-in words). Find another partner and repeat the exercise. Then find another pair of students and tell them where your partner lives.

- Focus on speaking as quickly and smoothly as possible.

! גערענקט!

♂ ער וווינט אין ____________ אויף ____________.

♀ זי וווינט אין ____________ אויף ____________.

ב וואָקאַבולאַר: געאָגראַפֿיע

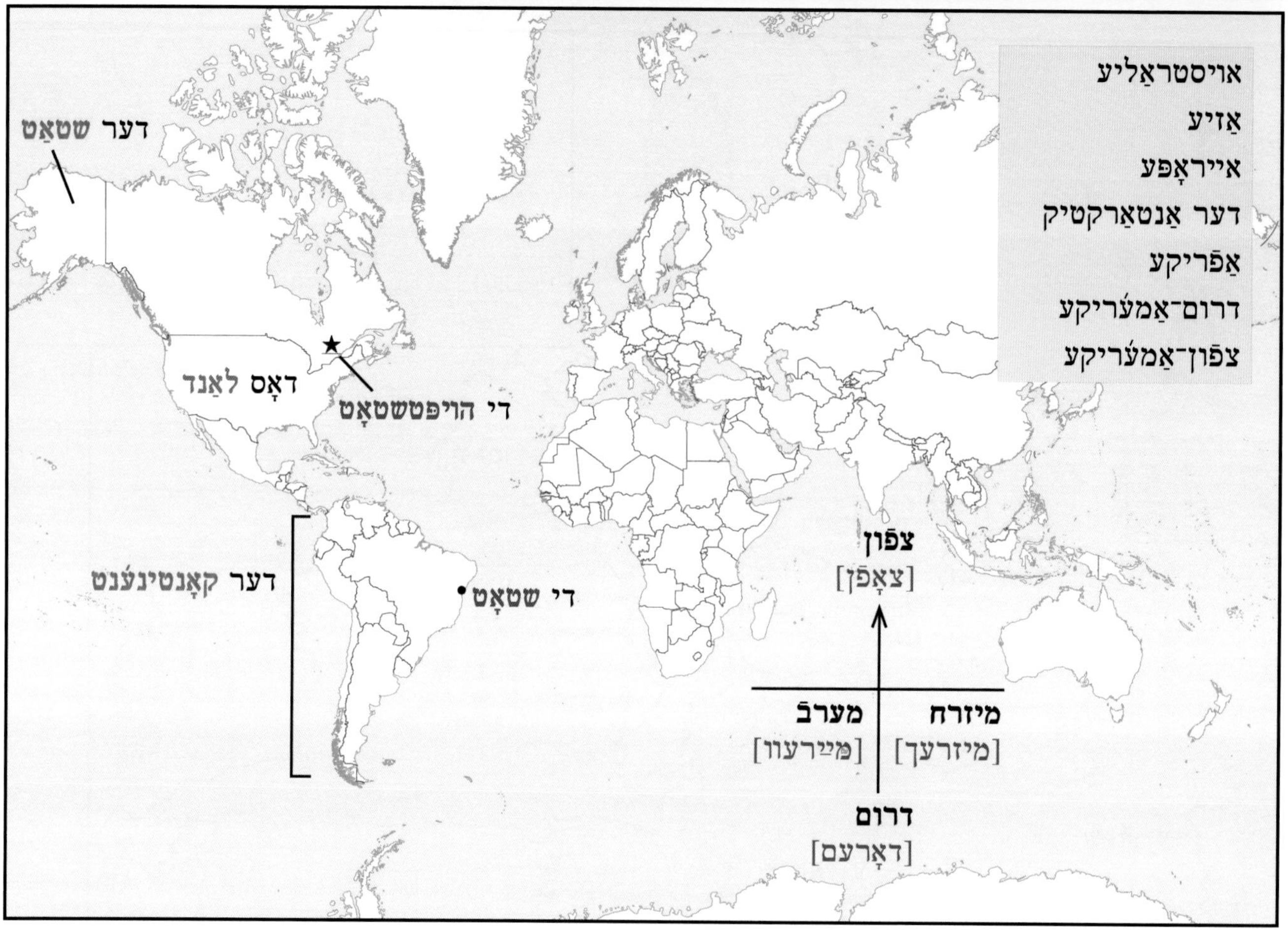

געניטונג 1: פֿלאָרידע איז אַ שטאָט

Examine the geographical terms on the map above, and match each of the place-names below with the corresponding geographical term.

1. פֿלאָרידע ב		א. הויפּטשטאָט
2. קאַליפֿאָרניע ___		ב. שטאַט
3. מאַדריד ___		ג. לאַנד
4. קאַנאַדע ___		ד. קאָנטינענט
5. אָסטין ___		ה. לאַנד
6. אַפֿריקע ___		ו. שטאָט
7. די פֿאַראייניקטע שטאַטן ___		ז. שטאַט

די פֿאַראייניקטע שטאַטן	The United States

Label each continent pictured above with its Yiddish name from the word box on the map.

Examine the countries labeled on the map above. Fill in the blanks in the statements below using the compass directions appearing on the map on page 43.

[דוגמע] **דוגמא:** רוסלאַנד איז ___מיזרח___ פֿון ווײַסרוסלאַנד.

1. איטאַליע איז ________ פֿון דײַטשלאַנד.
2. ליטע איז ________ פֿון רומעניע.
3. יאַפּאַן איז ________ פֿון כינע.
4. ענגלאַנד איז ________ פֿון פּוילן.

NOTE:

Certain Yiddish place-names carry stress on a different syllable than their English cognates do (**איטאַליע, ישׂראל**). Others are stressed on the *same* syllable as their English cognates, which sometimes results in irregular, non-penultimate stress (**יאַפּאַן, אונגערן**).

גענישטונג 3: ווו רעדט מען פֿראַנצייזיש?

The table below lists some of the languages that are spoken in the countries labeled on the map in **גענישטונג 2**. Like Yiddish, many languages are spoken in more than one country. For the purposes of this exercise, write below each language the name of the country where it is most widely spoken.

פֿראַנצייזיש פֿראַנקרײַך	רומעניש ________	שפּאַניש ________	פּויליש ________
דײַטש ________	ליטוויש ________	אַראַביש ________	רוסיש ________
כינעזיש ________	יאַפּאַניש ________	אוקראַיִניש ________	אוּנגעריש ________
איטאַליעניש ________	ווײַסרוסיש ________	ענגליש ________	העברעיִש ________

NOTE: Be sure to familiarize yourself with the place names and languages that are personally relevant to you. A more extensive list appears in Appendix C.

אין קלאַס

Ask a partner questions about the languages in the table above according to the following model.

דוגמא:

א: ווו רעדט מען פֿראַנצייזיש?

ב: פֿראַנצייזיש רעדט מען אין פֿראַנקרײַך. און ווו רעדט מען דײַטש?

א: דײַטש רעדט מען אין דײַטשלאַנד.

גערעדנקט!

Look at the second line of the model provided, concentrating on word order. The first element of this sentence is the **object** of the verb (the language being spoken). The verb (**רעדט**) comes next—in second position, as usual. The subject (**מען**) follows the verb, in third position.

- In a declarative sentence, the subject usually comes first. Starting with another element (like the object) is a stylistic decision, often serving to emphasize that element.
- Remember that a conjunction (such as **און**) is not counted as a sentence unit.

גערעדנקט!

The verb **רעדן** means *to speak*.

NOTE:

The pronoun **מען** in these sentences functions like the passive construction in English. It may also be equivalent to the pronoun *one* or the impersonal *they*.

ווו **רעדט** מען פֿראַנצייזיש?

Where **is** French **spoken**?

Verb conjugations for **מען** are the same as for other third-person-singular pronouns (**ער/זי/עס**).

געניטונג 4: פֿון וואַנען קומסטו? וואָסערע שפּראַכן רעדסטו?

עלקע און אַבֿרהם רעדן וועגן שפּראַכן, שטעט און לענדער. לייענט דעם דיאַלאָג אונטן.

languages

עלקע: איך קום פֿון פּוילן. פֿון וואַנען קומסט דו? *from where*

אַבֿרהם: איך קום פֿון ירושלים. [יערושאָלאַיִם]

עלקע: דו רעדסט העברעיִש?

אַבֿרהם: יאָ. איך רעד העברעיִש, אַראַביש, און ענגליש. וואָסערע שפּראַכן רעדסט דו? what

עלקע: איך רעד פּויליש, ענגליש, פֿראַנצייזיש און אַ ביסל ייִדיש!

Look at the questions that end the first and fourth lines of the dialogue.

- What is the verb in each of these sentences?
- What is the subject?
- How many words precede the verb? How does this compare to the usage of **ווי** and **ווו**?

Though they are composed of more than one word, these question phrases still act as a single unit. Until now, the verb had always been the second word in the sentence. Now we must revise our rule: the verb is always the second **unit** of the sentence. We will explore this notion of **sentence unit** further in **2** קאַפּיטל.

NOTE:

The question word **וואָסערע** is used with plural nouns (**שפּראַכן**). With singular nouns, **וואָסער** is used:
וואָסער שפּראַך רעדסטו אין אינטערנאַט?

געניטונג 5: זייער אײַנגענעם!

Practice introductions with this video interview, which you can find online with its accompanying exercise.

ווידעאָ־געניטונג ב־5

געניטונג 6: איך קום פֿון...

Now Elke wants to get to know *you*! Fill in the dialogue below with information about yourself. Use complete sentences.

עלקע: איך קום פֿון פּוילן. פֿון וואַנען קומסט דו?

סטודענט: ____________________.

עלקע: איך רעד פּויליש, ענגליש, פֿראַנצייזיש, און אַ ביסל ייִדיש! וואָסערע שפּראַכן רעדסט דו?

סטודענט: ____________________.

געניטונג 7: אין קלאַס

Introduce yourself to a new partner. Greet one another, and then ask questions to learn each other's names, where each of you comes from, what languages you speak, and where you each live now, as in the model. Write down your partner's responses on a separate sheet of paper.

דוגמא:

א: שלום־עליכם!

ב: עליכם־שלום!

א: ווי הייסטו?

ב: איך הייס מערי, און דו?

א: איך הייס דזשאָן.

ב: ווו וווינסטו?

א: איך וווין אין באָסטאָן, אין אַ הויז אויף מיין־גאַס. און דו?

ב: איך וווין אין ניוטאָן, אין אַ דירה אויף מיל־גאַס.

א: פֿון וואַנען קומסטו?

ב: איך קום פֿון קאַליפֿאָרניע. און דו?

א: איך קום פֿון אַלאַבאַמע.

ב: וואָסערע שפּראַכן רעדסטו?

א: איך רעד ענגליש און אַ ביסל שפּאַניש. און דו?

ב: איך רעד אויך ענגליש און שפּאַניש!

Now that you and your partner are well-acquainted, introduce your partner to the class. Be sure to include all the information you have learned.

געדענקט!

When introducing someone you already know to another person, remember to use a third-person pronoun, like **ער** or **זי**.

געניטונג 8: איך וויל עפּעס פֿרעגן

גיטל און וועלוול רעדן אין קלאַס.

Read the following questions, and then use them as a guide as you read the dialogue.

1. ווּ וווינט וועלוול? ווּ וווינט גיטל?
2. וואָסער וואָרט[1] פֿאַרשטייט גיטל נישט[2]?
3. וואָסער וואָרט האָט וועלוול פֿאַרגעסן[3]?

[1]word; [2]*doesn't ... understand*
[3]*did ... forget*

Read the dialogue once through for comprehension and answer the questions above. Now read the dialogue again, this time paying close attention to the glossed clarifying phrases that both Gitl and Velvl use in conversing with one another.

גיטל:	איך וויל עפּעס פֿרעגן: ווּ וווינסטו?	*I have a question*
וועלוול:	איך וווין אין אַ דירה אויף סאָסנע־גאַס.	
גיטל:	איך פֿאַרשטיי נישט. וואָס מיינט „דירה“?	*I don't understand. What does... mean?*
וועלוול:	„דירה“ מיינט “apartment”.	
גיטל:	אָ! ווי שרײַבט מען דאָס?	*How does one write that?*
וועלוול:	דלת, יוד, ריש, הא. און ווּ וווינסט דו?	[דאַלעט]; [רייש]; [היי]
גיטל:	ע... ווי זאָגט מען “house” אויף ייִדיש?	*How does one say... in Yiddish?*
וועלוול:	איך געדענק נישט... האָ... האָ...	*I don't remember*
גיטל:	הויז?	
וועלוול:	יאָ!	
גיטל:	איך וווין אין אַ **הויז** אויף צענטער־גאַס!	
וועלוול:	צענטער־גאַס איז נאָענט צו סאָסנע־גאַס?	
גיטל:	איך ווייס נישט...	*I don't know*

Write down the seven expressions of clarification demonstrated above. Then rewrite the dialogue, replacing "**ווּ וווינסטו**" with a different question you've learned in this chapter. Adjust the rest of the script accordingly.

NOTE:

The English phrase *I have a question* has no word-for-word translation in Yiddish. Instead, the equivalent classroom phrase is **איך וויל עפּעס פֿרעגן** (lit. *I want to ask something*).

וואָקאַבולאַר־איבערבליק 1

א. באַקענען זיך
GETTING ACQUAINTED

expressions	אויסדרוקן
hello (*to a new acquaintance*)	שלום־עליכם [שאָלעם־אַלייכעם]
hello (*response to* **שלום־עליכם**)	עליכם־שלום
what's your name? (*informal*) (*formal*)	ווי הייסטו? ווי הייסט איר?
my name is...	איך הייס...
where do you live?	ווו וווינסטו? ווו וווינט איר?
I live in... (on...)	איך וווין אין... (אויף...) [אַף]
where do you come from?	פֿון וואַנען קומסטו? פֿון וואַנען קומט איר?
I come from...	איך קום פֿון...
what languages do you speak?	וואָסערע שפּראַכן רעדסטו? וואָסערע שפּראַכן רעדט איר?
I speak...	איך רעד...
very pleased (to meet you)	זייער אײַנגענעם

verbs	ווערבן
to be called, named	הייסן
to live, reside	וווינען
to say	זאָגן
to answer	ענטפֿערן
to come	קומען
to speak	רעדן
to write	שרײַבן

pronouns	פּראָנאָמען
I	איך
you	דו
he	ער
she	זי

א. באַקענען זיך
GETTING ACQUAINTED (continued)

places of residence	וווינערטער
street	**די גאַס** (ן)
apartment	**די דירה** (–ות) [דירע(ס)]
dormitory	**דער אינטערנאַט** (ן)
room	**דער צימער** (ן)
house	**דאָס הויז** (הײַזער)

adjectives	אַדיעקטיוון
near	נאָענט
far	ווײַט

question words	פֿרעגווערטער
what	וואָס
which	וואָסער (וואָסערע)
where	ווו
how	ווי
who	ווער
from where	פֿון וואַנען

useful expressions	נוציקע אויסדרוקן
example, model	**די דוגמא** (–ות) [דוגמע(ס)]
I don't remember	איך געדענק נישט
I forgot	איך האָב פֿאַרגעסן
I don't know	איך ווייס נישט
I have a question (*lit.* I want to ask something)	איך וויל עפּעס פֿרעגן
I don't understand	איך פֿאַרשטיי נישט
what does ... mean?	וואָס מיינט ... ?
how does one say ... in Yiddish?	ווי זאָגט מען ... אויף ייִדיש?
how is that written?	ווי שרײַבט מען דאָס?

1 וואָקאַבולאַר־איבערבליק

א. באַקענען זיך
GETTING ACQUAINTED (continued)

little words	קלײנע װערטערלעך
or	אָדער
yes	יאָ
no	ניין
prepositions	**פּרעפּאָזיציעס**
on	אויף
in	אין
from; of	פֿון
about	וועגן

די אוניווערסיטעט (ן); **די סטודענטקע** (ס); **דער סטודענט** (ן);
דער פּראָפֿעסאָר (ן); **די פּראָפֿעסאָרשע** (ס); **דער קאַלעדזש** (ן)

ב. געאָגראַפֿיע
GEOGRAPHY

general terms	אַלגעמיינע טערמינען
capital city	**די הויפּטשטאָט** (...שטעט)
city	**די שטאָט** (שטעט)
language	**די שפּראַך** (ן)
state	**דער שטאַט** (ן)
country	**דאָס לאַנד** (לענדער)
on the compass	**אויפֿן קאָמפּאַס**
south	**דרום** [דאָרעם]
east	**מיזרח** [מיזרעך]
west	**מערבֿ** [מײַרעוו]
north	**צפֿון** [צאָפֿן]

! געדענקט

On these vocabulary pages, nouns are provided with their definite articles and plural endings. When the plural form of a noun is the same as the singular form, the word will be followed by a long dash in parentheses: (—). A shorter dash preceding a plural ending means that the last letter of the stem is dropped before adding the plural ending; thus, **דירה** (–ות) indicates that the plural of **דירה** is דירות.

ב. געאָגראַפֿיע
GEOGRAPHY (continued)

countries	לענדער
Hungary	אונגערן
Germany	דײַטשלאַנד
Belarus	ווײַסרוסלאַנד
Japan	יאַפּאַן
Israel	ישׂראל [ייִסראָעל]
China	כינע
Lithuania	ליטע
Poland	פּוילן
The United States	די פֿאַראייניקטע שטאַטן
France	פֿראַנקרײַך
Russia	רוסלאַנד
Spain	שפּאַניע
languages	**שפּראַכן**
Hungarian	אונגעריש
German	דײַטש
Belarussian	ווײַסרוסיש
Japanese	יאַפּאַניש
Chinese	כינעזיש
Lithuanian	ליטוויש
French	פֿראַנצייזיש
Romanian	רומעניש
Russian	רוסיש

דער קאָנטינענט (ן)
אויסטראַליע; אַזיע; אייראָפּע; דער אַנטאַרקטיק; אַפֿריקע;
דרום־אַמעריקע; צפֿון־אַמעריקע
אוקראַיִנע; איטאַליע; אַלזשיריע; טערקײַ; מאַראָקאָ;
סאַוד־אַראַביע; ענגלאַנד; רומעניע
אוקראַיִניש; איטאַליעניש; אַראַביש; העברעיִש; ענגליש;
פּויליש; שפּאַניש

NOTE:

See Appendix C for more geographical terms.

1 גראַמאַטיק־איבערבליק

NOUNS — סובסטאַנטיוון

GENDER

- Every noun has a **grammatical gender**—feminine, neuter, or masculine.
- The gender of a noun cannot always be determined based on the structure of the noun itself, and it sometimes differs even from the apparent biological gender of the noun.
- A noun's gender affects other elements of the noun phrase, such as definite articles and adjectives.
- Third-person-singular pronouns generally match the gender of the noun to which they refer.

NOTE: As you learn new nouns, be sure to memorize the word's gender along with its meaning. In **11 קאַפּיטל**, we will learn some techniques for guessing a noun's gender based on its structure, but these are only guidelines, not firm rules.

NUMBER

- Most nouns have distinct forms for singular and plural **number**.

  Number may also affect other elements of the noun phrase. We will learn more about grammatical number in **5 קאַפּיטל**.

CASE

- Depending on its grammatical role in a given phrase, a noun is assigned one of three **cases**—nominative, accusative, or dative.
- Case may also affect other elements of the noun phrase. We will learn more about cases in **9 קאַפּיטל** and **11 קאַפּיטל**.

ARTICLES

- Nouns usually appear with an **article**, which can be definite (often when referring to things previously mentioned or otherwise known to the listener) or indefinite (when referring to something for the first time or without a specific instance of it in mind).
- **The definite article** changes form depending on the gender of the noun it accompanies.

Masculine	Neuter	Feminine
דער אינטערנאַט	דאָס הויז	די גאַס

  These are the nominative forms of the definite article. We will learn the accusative and dative forms in **11 קאַפּיטל** and **13 קאַפּיטל**.

- For plural nouns, the definite article is always **די**, regardless of gender or case.

די אינטערנאַטן	די הײַזער	די גאַסן

- The **indefinite article** is **אַ** for all cases and genders (or **אַן** when the following word begins with a vowel). The indefinite article disappears in the plural.

Singular	אַן אינטערנאַט	אַ הויז	אַ גאַס
Plural	אינטערנאַטן	הײַזער	גאַסן

1 גראַמאַטיק־איבערבליק

VERBS — ווערבן

REGULAR VERBS

The verbs we have learned so far are all considered **regular verbs** and follow a uniform pattern of conjugation (exemplified by **רעדן** below), with minor variations in spelling and pronunciation. Two such variations are:

- The third-person singular of **רעדן** is written **רעדט** but pronounced simply as [רעט].
- The second-person singular of **הייסן** is written **הייסט**, with a single **ס**, as opposed to the two that would result from simply adding the ending **סט**- to the stem **-הייס**.

❗ **NOTE:** The stem of a verb is generally equivalent to its first person singular (**איך**) form.

First-person singular	איך הייס	איך רעד
Second person singular	דו הייסט ❗	דו רעדסט
Third person singular	ער/זי/עס הייסט	ער/זי/עס רעדט

PRESENT TENSE

English has three different present tense forms—e.g., she speaks, she **is** speak**ing**, **does** she speak?—each serving a different grammatical purpose. All three forms are rendered in Yiddish with a single form: **זי רעדט**.

She speaks Yiddish.	זי רעדט ייִדיש.
She is speaking Yiddish.	זי רעדט ייִדיש.
Does she speak Yiddish?	זי רעדט ייִדיש?

1 גראַמאַטיק־איבערבליק

WORD ORDER — ווערטער־סדר

SENTENCE UNITS

- Yiddish word order is organized in terms of **sentence units.**
- A sentence unit may consist of a word, a phrase, or even an entire clause.
- Some words do not count as sentence units (e.g. **ניין, יאָ, און, אויך, אָדער, אָבער**).
- To identify a sentence unit, ask yourself if it answers a single specific question, such as *Who? What? Where? When? Why? How? For whom? With what?*

Who?	ער 1	הייסט 2	אַבֿרהם. 3	
Where?	אין אַ קליין הויז 1	וווינט 2	דער סטודענט. 3	
When?	ווען זי איז הונגעריק, 1	עסט 2	זי 3	אַן עפּל. 4

VERB PLACEMENT

- The single most important rule of Yiddish word order is the following:

The conjugated verb is the second unit in the sentence.

- This rule can be seen in the example sentences in the preceding table, in which each of the three verbs (**הייסט, וווינט**, and **עסט**) appears in second position.
- As with many rules, this one is sometimes broken—but never without good cause. Some of the more common exceptions occur due to **consecutive word order** (see page 677), the **imperative** (see page 155), and **question inversion** (see page 610).

NOTE: In the last two example sentences, the verb precedes the subject noun, while the first sentence has the reverse. Yiddish word order is flexible and is often manipulated for style or emphasis. We will learn more about word order in **קאַפּיטל 2**.

QUESTIONS

- Some questions are indicated by a shift in intonation alone:

דו רעדסט העברעיִש?

- Others begin with interrogative pronouns:

וווּ וווינסטו? וואָסערע שפּראַכן רעדסטו?

- If the interrogative element consists of more than one word, the *entire* phrase must precede the verb (unlike in English):

Where do you come from?	פֿון וואַנען קומסטו?

- In questions with an interrogative in first position, the subject comes *after* the verb.
- In the case of the pronoun **דו**, this "inversion" results in a contraction (**-סטו**):

פֿון וואַנען קומסט + דו? = פֿון וואַנען קומסטו?

NOTE: No contraction occurs when **דו** is stressed (e.g., for contrast or emphasis). In such cases, the verb and pronoun remain separate. Otherwise, contraction is obligatory.

איבערחזור־געניטונגען 1

געניטונג 1: די גולמס באַקענען זיך

It's time to begin creating your *goylem* (**גולם**)! Answer the following questions about your *goylem*. Be creative!

דוגמא: ווי הייסט דער גולם?

ער הייסט לייבער.

1. ווי הייסט דער גולם?
2. ווּ וווינט דער גולם?
3. פֿון וואַנען קומט דער גולם?
4. וואָסערע שפּראַכן רעדט דער גולם?

NOTE:

The *goylem* in the example is referred to as **ער**. In your responses, use whichever pronoun fits the gender you have chosen for your *goylem*.

אין קלאַס

Find a partner and introduce your *goylems* to each other by asking and answering questions, as you would when meeting someone for the first time. Make sure to learn as much about your partner's *goylem* as you know about yours!

געניטונג 2: ייִדישע שרײַבערס און דיאַלעקטן

The map provided on the next page shows the territorial divisions of the three major dialects of Eastern Yiddish, as well as the birthplaces (and sites of later literary activity) of six important early Yiddish writers.

NOTE:

Refer to pages xxxv–xxxvi in the front matter for more information on the various dialects of Yiddish.

Describe each writer as in the model below.

דוגמא:

שלמה עטינגער קומט פֿון וואַרשע. אין וואַרשע רעדט מען פּויליש ייִדיש. שפּעטער וווינט עטינגער אין זאַמאָשטש.

◀ CONTINUED

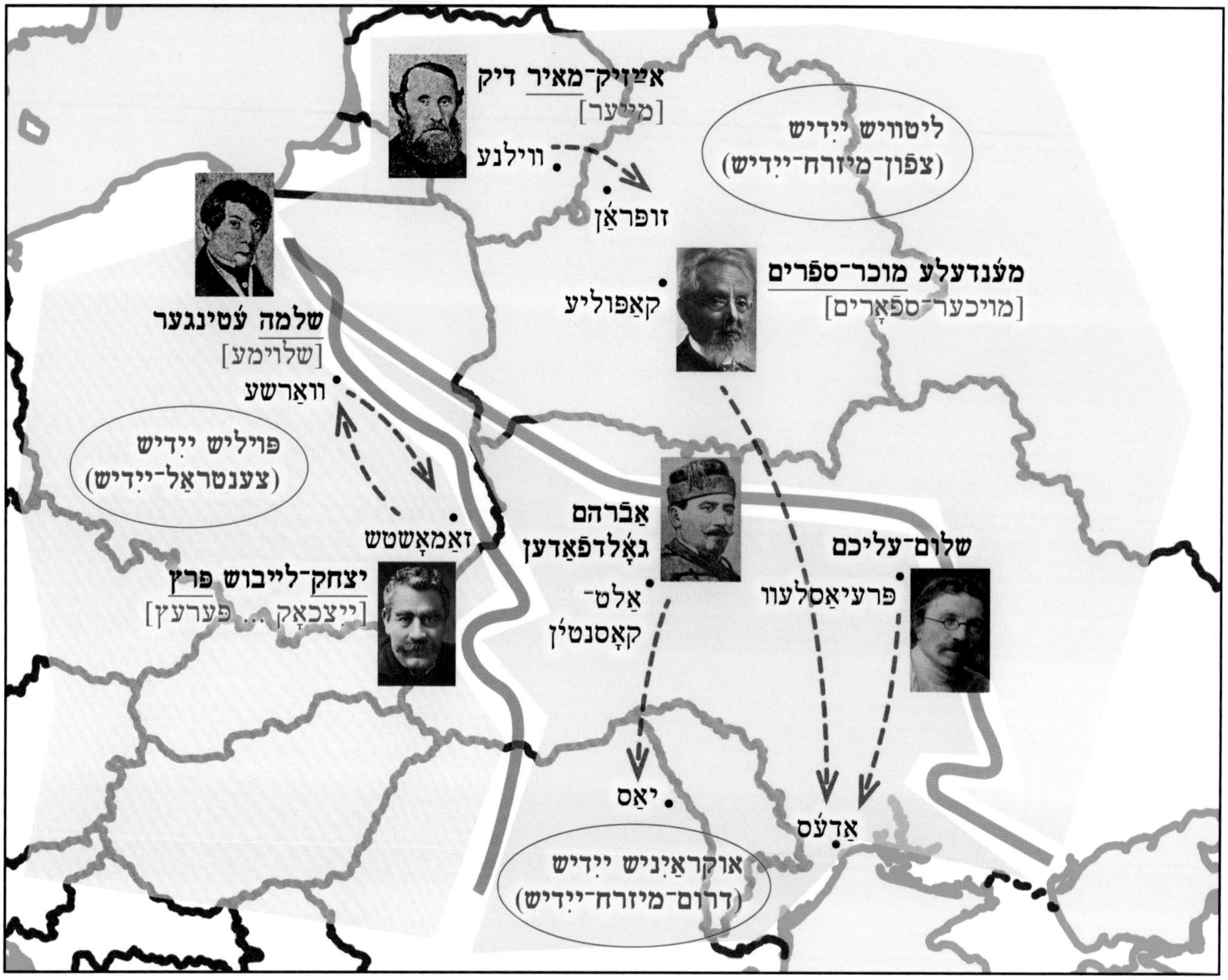

אין קלאַס

With a partner, take turns asking questions about different writers. Use the model below to guide your conversation. Be sure to discuss all of the writers shown.

דוגמאַ:

א: פֿון וואַנען קומט שלמה עטינגער?

ב: ער קומט פֿון וואַרשע. וואָסער ייִדיש רעדט מען אין וואַרשע?

א: אין וואַרשע רעדט מען פּויליש ייִדיש. וווּ וווינט עטינגער שפּעטער?

later

ב: שפּעטער וווינט ער אין זאַמאָשטש.

2

קאַפּיטל צוויי:

גרונטיקע ווערבן און באַגריסונגען

CHAPTER GOALS

- In this chapter, you will learn how to use common verbs in the present tense, as well as how to greet people and ask after their well-being. You will also learn the days of the week and how to discuss the time of day.

וואָקאַבולאַר:	
basic verbs	גרונטיקע ווערבן
times of day	צײַטן פֿון טאָג
days of the week	טעג פֿון וואָך
greetings	באַגריסונגען
גראַמאַטיק:	
more pronouns	נאָך פּראָנאָמען
verbs (present tense)	ווערבן (איצטיקע צײַט)
קולטור — אוידיאָ:	
"Potatoes" (folk song)	„בולבע" (פֿאָלקסליד)
"Where Do You Come From?" (folk song)	„פֿון וואַנען קומט אַ ייִד?" (פֿאָלקסליד)
קולטור — ווידעאָ:	
Green Fields (Jacob Ben-Ami and Edgar Ulmer)	„גרינע פֿעלדער" (יעקבֿ בן־עמי און עדגאַר אולמער)

א וואָקאַבולאַר און גראַמאַטיק: ווערבן; פּראָנאָמען

1. אין דער רעדאַקציע

2. אויף אַ קאָנצערט

3. אין פּאַרק

NOTE:

The Hasidic names **ליבי** and **פֿייגי** are equivalent to the names **ליבע** and **פֿייגע** in *klal-shprakh*. Bracketed pronunciations of the names of Hasidic characters are provided in the character's dialect, when the pronunciation differs from *klal-shprakh*.

געניטונג 1: חנה טאַנצט אויף אַ קאָנצערט

It's a busy afternoon in *yidishland*: there's a meeting of the editorial board of a Yiddish journal in Manhattan, a klezmer concert in Florida, and an outing to a park in Brooklyn. Use the words and phrases in the word box provided to write more detailed sentences about what some of the characters on page 58 are doing, as in the model.

דוגמא: חנה טאַנצט אויף אַ קאָנצערט.

אַ בוך	מוזיק	אין פּאַרק
אַן עפּל	טיי	אויף אַ קאָנצערט
פֿידל		

NOTE:
Some of the vocabulary used here is drawn from the **אַלף־בית קאַפּיטל**. Refer to page 13 for review.

אין קלאַס

With a partner, take turns pointing out characters in the snapshots on page 58 and asking questions about them, as in the model.

- In your answers, be sure to replace the character's name with the correct pronoun (**ער** or **זי**).

דוגמא:

א: וואָס טוט שלמהלע? *What's Shloymele doing?*

ב: ער שפּרינגט.

! גערדענקט!
As in the example, your answer should not contain the word **טוט** (*is doing*), even though the question itself does.

געניטונג 2: איך הער...

In each of the pictures on page 58, one character is talking to another and describing what they see. Write a sentence for each prompt, where the first person listed is **איך**, the second is **דו**, and the third is **ער** or **זי**, as in the example below.

- Note the use of the conjunctions **אָבער** and **און** in the example. Use these in your answers as well, making sure to keep the word order the same as shown below.
- Depending on the pronoun that precedes it, conjugate each verb correctly, as in the example.

דוגמא: צירל (חנה, מאיר)
צירל: איך הער, אָבער דו טאַנצסט, און מאיר שלאָפֿט.

1. דזשאָן (הערשל, מירל)
2. ליבי (שלמהלע, מענדל)

! גערדענקט!
The first-person (**איך**) form of a verb is identical to the stem of that verb. The verbs in this section are presented in the third person, so you will have to uncover their stems by removing the third-person ending (**ט**-). Then add the appropriate endings for second person (**דו ...סט**) and third person (**ער/זי ...ט**).

גענייטונג 3: מיר און זיי

הערשל און <u>נתן</u> רעדן וועגן וואָס זיי טוען. לייענט דעם דיאַלאָג אונטן. [נאָסן]; about

Hershl and Nosn are talking about what they're doing. Read the dialogue below.

- Pay special attention to the words highlighted in purple.

הערשל: איך שרײַב, און דו שרײַבסט אויך, נתן.

נתן: יאָ, מיר שרײַבן, אָבער חנה שרײַבט נישט.

הערשל: ניין, זי לויפֿט. און <u>משה</u> לויפֿט אויך. [מוישע]

נתן: יאָ, זיי לויפֿן.

What new pronouns do you see? How many people are they describing? Are they first, second, or third person? What ending appears on the verb when it is conjugated for these pronouns?

Now look at the remaining purple words, **אויך** (*also*) and **נישט** (*not*). Where do they appear relative to the conjugated verb? We will learn more about negation in **קאַפּיטל 6**, but for now remember that **נישט** comes *after* the conjugated verb.

Now, in the dialogue above, replace the verb stems **-שרײַב** and **-לויפֿ** with **-עס** and **-שלאָפֿ**. Be sure to apply the appropriate endings to all verbs, so that they fit the pronoun used.

! געדענקט!

When a verb stem ends on a **ס**, the **דו** ending is just **-ט** (instead of **-סט**) so as to avoid doubled letters:

איך עס ← דו עסט.

געניטונג 4: מיר טרינקען

מירל און פּאָל רעדן. לייענט דעם דיאַלאָג אונטן.

- Pay special attention to the words highlighted in purple.

מירל: איך טרינק, און דו טרינקסט אויך, פּאָל.

פּאָל: יאָ, מיר טרינקען, אָבער גיטל טרינקט נישט.

מירל: ניין, זי גייט. און עלקע גייט אויך.

פּאָל: יאָ, זיי גייען.

What is different about the endings of the purple verbs, compared to those shown in the previous exercise?

The **מיר** and **זיי** forms of most verbs are spelled by adding a **ן**- ending. However, depending on the final sound of a given verb stem, that verb may require an additional -**ע**-, resulting in the ending **ען**-. This mirrors the pronunciation of the word as it is actually spoken.

- Some examples of verb stems that trigger this phenomenon are those ending in **מ**- (**קומען**), **נ**- (**וויינען**), **נג**- (**זינגען**), **נק**- (**טרינקען**), a stressed vowel or diphthong (**גייען**), or a syllabic **ל**- (**שמייכלען**, *to smile*).

Now, in the dialogue above, replace the verb stems -**טרינק** and -**גיי** with the stems -**וויינ** and -**שפּרינג**. Be sure to apply the appropriate endings to all verbs so that they fit their pronouns. Use the ending **ען**- where necessary.

געניטונג 5: ווּ לייענט מען?

עלקע און אַבֿרהם רעדן וועגן ווּ זיי לייענען. לייענט דעם דיאַלאָג.

עלקע: ווּ לייענסטו געוויינטלעך? usually

אַבֿרהם: איך לייען געוויינטלעך אין קלאַס.

עלקע: דו לייענסט אין קלאַס?! איך לייען אויך אין קלאַס!

אַבֿרהם: הוראַ! מיר לייענען אין קלאַס! ווּ לייענט איידל ?

עלקע: זי לייענט נישט אין קלאַס — זי לייענט אין פּאַרק.

אַבֿרהם: אָט גייען סענדער און חנה . זיי לייענען אין פּאַרק? there

עלקע: סענדער ! חנה ! איר לייענט אין פּאַרק?!

Look at the last sentence of the dialogue. What new pronoun do you see? How many people does it describe? Is it first, second, or third person? What ending appears on the verb when it is conjugated for this pronoun?

Now rewrite the dialogue, replacing the verb (highlighted in purple) with another verb you learned in this section, conjugating appropriately.

- You may also replace the underlined names with the names of your friends.
- Remember to use the appropriate third-person pronoun in the fifth line.

אין קלאַס

מיט אַ חבֿר, חזרט איבער דעם דיאַלאָג איבער עטלעכע מאָל. רעדט אַזוי גיך און פֿליסיק ווי מעגלעך.

With a partner, repeat the dialogue above several times. Speak as quickly and fluently as possible.

Now repeat the dialogue, making the substitutions described above.

גע׳ניטונג 6: דו און איר

Whether at home, at the store, or in the synagogue, the Yiddish-speakers pictured below have some questions to ask one another. Read the dialogues, and pay attention to the social relationships between the characters shown and the pronouns they use with one another.

דבֿורה־לאה [דווירע־לײַע]

נאָך בעסער even better

פֿאַר וואָס why

שאָולי [שוילי]

שׂרה [סאָרע]

אַזוי שיין so beautifully

רבונו־של־עולם [רעבוי́נע־שעלוילעם]

יואל [יויל]

Consider the usage of the pronoun **איר** in the dialogues above.

- Is it used the same way as in **גע׳ניטונג 5**? How many people does it refer to here?
- Are associated verbs conjugated the same or differently?

Compare the usage of the two pronouns **דו** and **איר**.

- Who uses which pronoun with whom?
- What sorts of social relationships seem to require one pronoun or the other?

NOTE:

In addressing God, the phrase **רבונו־של־עולם** (lit. *master of the universe*) expresses more intimacy than other more general or scholarly religious terms.

געניטונג 7: דו אָדער איר?

In each of the scenes below, only one character is speaking. Determine whether that character is using **דו** or **איר**.

.1

.2

.3

.4

.5

.6

In each image above, one character is asking the other(s) what they're doing. Write one question for each speech bubble above, as in the example.

- Use either **דו** or **איר**, according to the relationship between the two characters, and one of the verbs from the word box.
- Note that only the stems of the verbs appear below, so be sure to conjugate correctly for whichever pronoun you use.

דוגמא:

.1 דו הערסט?

טרינק-	לאַכ-	שלאָפֿ-
שפּיל-	לייענ-	הער-

געניטונג 8: וואָס טו איך?

With a partner, take turns acting out some of the verbs we have learned in this section and describing your partner's action, as in the example below.

דוגמא:

דו שלאָפֿסט!

Now repeat the exercise, role-playing the character pairs below. Be sure to use the appropriate pronoun in each case.

סטודענט א	סטודענט ב
קינד	קינד
פּראָפֿעסאָר	סעקרעטאַרשע
סטודענט	סטודענטקע
קינד	לערער
פּילאָט	פּאַסאַזשיר

דאָס קינד child

teacher

געניטונג 9: וואָס טוסטו אין הויז?

What do you do in each of the places asked about below? Answer the questions according to the model.

דוגמא: וואָס טוסטו אין הויז?

אין הויז שלאָף איך.

1. וואָס טוסטו אין הויז?
2. וואָס טוסטו אין קלאַס?
3. וואָס טוסטו אין פּאַרק?

NOTE:

Pay careful attention to the placement of the verb and subject in the model. Make sure your sentences follow this word order.

! Look at the example above. The first unit of the sentence (אין הויז**) answers the question "Where?" Because this **sentence unit** occupies the first position in the sentence, the subject (**איך**) appears in the third position, after the conjugated verb. The verb, as always, appears in the second position.

! געדענקט!

The answer given in the example above does not contain the verb *to do* (stem: **-טו**), even though the question itself does. Be sure that your answers follow this pattern.

גענײטונג 10: אין דער אונטערבאַן

הער־גענײטונג א־10

Avrom is visiting New York for the weekend. On the subway, his copy of the *Forverts* attracts the attention of Rokhl and Nosn, who happen to be in the same car.

לײענט די פֿראַגעס אונטן אײדער איר הערט זיך צו צום דיאַלאָג. זײ װעלן אײַך העלפֿן פֿאַרשטײן דעם טעקסט.

Read the questions below before you listen to the dialogue. They will help you understand the text.

1. װאָסערע שפּראַכן רעדן רחל, נתן, און אַבֿרהם?
2. װוּ װױנען זײ?
3. פֿון װאַנען קומען זײ?

הערט זיך צו צום דיאַלאָג, נאָר קוקט נישט אױפֿן טעקסט. ענטפֿערט אױף די פֿראַגעס אױבן.

Listen to the dialogue, but don't look at the text. Answer the questions above. Now listen again and fill in the blanks in the transcript below.

נתן, רחל:	שלום־עליכם!	
אַבֿרהם:	עליכם־שלום! ______ רעדט ייִדיש?	
נתן:	אַװדאי רעדן מיר ייִדיש! און דו?	of course [אַװאַדע]
אַבֿרהם:	אַװדאי! װי הײסט ______?	
נתן:	איך ______ נתן.	
רחל:	און איך הײס רחל. װי ______ ______?	
אַבֿרהם:	איך הײס אַבֿרהם. פֿון װאַנען ______ איר?	
רחל:	______ קומען בײדע פֿון ניו־יאָרק. און פֿון װאַנען קומסט דו?	both
אַבֿרהם:	איך ______ פֿון ישׂראל, אָבער איך װױן אין לערנטאָן, מאַסאַטשוסעטס. איר ______ דאָ אין ניו־יאָרק?	here
נתן:	יאָ, מיר ______ טאַקע אין ניו־יאָרק! די עלטערן װױנען נאָך אין ישׂראל?	indeed; *(your)* parents still
אַבֿרהם:	יאָ. זײ ______ אין ירושלים.	
רחל:	װאָס טוען זײ דאָרטן?	do; there
אַבֿרהם:	______ שרײַבן אַרטיקלען פֿאַר אַ העברעיִשער צײַטונג.	articles; newspaper
נתן:	זײ ______ אױך ייִדיש?	
אַבֿרהם:	נײן, נאָר ______ און די באָבע!	only

◄ CONTINUED

CONTINUED

NOTE:

The greeting **שלום־עליכם** is typically reserved for guests and new or long-absent acquaintances.

Welcome! *or* Good to meet/see you!	א: שלום־עליכם!
Thank you! *or* Good to meet/see you!	ב: עליכם־שלום!

We will learn more about greetings in the next section.

Answer the following questions about the dialogue in complete sentences, using the model below.

- When answering a question with **ניין** (as in the example), be sure to write out the correct answer as well, replacing the purple word from the original question to make the statement true.

דוגמא: רחל און נתן רעדן מיט עלקען?
ניין! רחל און נתן רעדן מיט אַבֿרהאמען.

1. רחל און נתן אירצן אַבֿרהמען?
2. אַבֿרהם קומט פֿון ניו־יאָרק?
3. רחל און נתן רעדן ייִדיש?
4. אַבֿרהמס עלטערן ווױנען אין אַרגענטינע?
5. רחל און נתן קומען פֿון רוסלאַנד?
6. אַבֿרהמס עלטערן שרײַבן אויף ייִדיש?
7. אַבֿרהמס באָבע רעדט ייִדיש?

NOTE:

For the purposes of verb conjugation, the compound subject **רחל און נתן** behaves just like the pronoun **זיי**. So: **רחל און נתן (זיי) רעדן**.

NOTE:

The suffix **ן(ע)**- at the end of a person's name indicates the accusative or dative case. We will learn more about cases in **11 קאַפּיטל**.

to address with איר	אירצן
to address with דו	דוצן

NOTE:

One way to form the possessive in Yiddish is to add the suffix **ס**- to the end of the possessor's name.

ב וואָקאַבולאַר:
טעג פֿון וואָך און באַגריסונגען

אין דער פֿרי

בײַ טאָג

אין אָוונט

בײַ נאַכט

געניטונג 1: ווען לויפֿט מען?

What time of day does one usually go running? Answer the questions below, as in the example.

- Be sure to use all four times of day pictured above.

דוגמא: ווען לויפֿט מען?

<u>געוויינטלעך</u> לויפֿט מען אין דער פֿרי.

1. ווען שלאָפֿט מען?
2. ווען טרינקט מען קאַווע?
3. ווען טרינקט מען ווײַן?
4. ווען אַרבעט מען?

NOTE:

The preposition **בײַ** is often pronounced **[באַ]**.

געוויינטלעך	usually

! געדענקט!

When the subject (in this case **מען**) is not the first sentence unit, it appears immediately after the verb.

אין קלאַס

What do *you* typically do at different times of day? With a partner, take turns asking and answering questions, as in the model below.

דוגמא:

א: וואָס טוסטו אין דער פֿרי?

ב: געוויינטלעך לויף איך אין דער פֿרי.

גענִיטונג 2: וואָס טוט עלקע?

שבת [שאַבעס]   פֿרײַטיק   דאָנערשטיק   מיטוואָך   דינסטיק   מאָנטיק   זונטיק

The calendar above describes some of the broad strokes of Elke's busy weekly schedule.

ענטפֿערט אויף די פֿראַגעס אונטן, לויט דער דוגמא.

דוגמא: ווען זינגט עלקע?

מיטוואָך אין אָוונט זינגט זי.

1. ווען לויפֿט עלקע?
2. ווען טאַנצט עלקע?
3. ווען לייענט עלקע?
4. ווען שלאָפֿט עלקע?

> **! גערעדנקט!**
>
> You can recognize a sentence unit by whether it answers a question such as "Where?" or "When?" Thus, a phrase like **מיטוואָך אין אָוונט** constitutes a single sentence unit.

> **! גערעדנקט!**
>
> The English phrase on *Wednesday* is translated by the single word **מיטוואָך**, with no preposition. Such one-word adverbs of time are common in Yiddish: the names of days, months, seasons, and holidays also function this way.

פֿילט אויס די טאַבעלע אונטן.

Fill in the table below with activities you usually do on each day of the week.

שבת	פֿרײַטיק	דאָנערשטיק	מיטוואָך	דינסטיק	מאָנטיק	זונטיק
						איך שלאָף

Now compare your schedule to Elke's. Write four sentences based on the model below.

- Pay special attention to the placement of **נישט**: make sure that your sentences match the model in this respect.

דוגמא:

זונטיק טאַנץ איך נישט. זונטיק שלאָף איך.

> **NOTE:**
>
> When the subject follows the verb, **נישט** is placed after the subject.

געניטונג 3: בולבע!

הער־געניטונג ב־3

טיטל ♫ „**בולבע**“ (פֿראַגמענט)
פֿאָלקסליד

זינגער **מאַרק אָלף (Mark Olf)**
(באַלסק, רוסישע אימפּעריע 1905 – ניו־יאָרק, פֿאַראייניקטע שטאַטן 1987)

רעקאָרדירונג 1951, פֿאַראייניקטע שטאַטן

This well-known Yiddish folk song makes light of the poverty of the shtetl. The song repeats in a tedious two-note refrain that all there is to eat each day of the week is a meager meal of potatoes. On Shabbos, ironic excitement greets a potato kugel (a sort of casserole made by grating potato together with onion and adding egg, flour, and salt and pepper). ***Mark Olf****, the singer and guitarist on this recording, immigrated to the United States with his family in the early twentieth century and made a living in automobile repairs before eventually embarking on a second career as a folksinger and teacher of the guitar.*

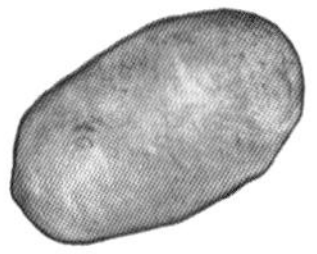
די בולבע

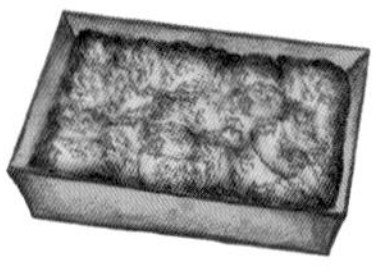
דער קוגל

דאָס ברויט

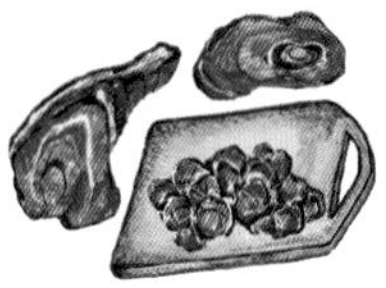
דאָס פֿלייש

לייענט די פֿראַגעס אונטן אײדער איר הערט זיך צו צום ליד. זיי וועלן אײַך העלפֿן פֿאַרשטיין דעם טעקסט.

Read the questions below before you listen to the song. They will help you understand the text.

1. וואָסערע טעג עסט מען בולבעס? — days
2. וואָסער טאָג עסט מען אַ קוגל?
3. וואָס פֿאַר אַ קוגל עסט מען? — *what kind of*
4. מיט וואָסערע מינים עסנוואַרג עסט מען בולבעס? — with; *types (of) food*
5. צו וואָסערע מאָלצײַטן עסט מען בולבעס? — at; meals

! גערעדנקט!

The pronoun **מען** has two forms: **מע** and **מען**. It is always **מען** when it follows the verb (in third position). Before the verb (in first position), it is usually **מע** unless the verb begins with a vowel, in which case the form **מען** is used (**מע רעדט** versus **מען עסט**).

◀ CONTINUED

CONTINUED

הערט זיך צו צום ליד, נאָר קוקט נישט אויפֿן טעקסט. ענטפֿערט אויף די פֿראַגעס אויבן.

Listen to the song, but don't look at the text. Answer the questions above. Now listen again and fill in the blanks in the text below.

	זונטיק — בולבע,	
	________ — בולבע,	
	דינסטיק און ________ — בולבע,	
	________ און פֿרײַטיק — ________,	
2 מאָל	שבת אין אַ נאָווענע — אַ בולבע־קוגעלע!	for a change
	________ — ווײַטער בולבע.	again
	ברויט מיט בולבע,	
	פֿלייש מיט ________,	
	וואַרעמעס און וועטשערע — בולבע,	lunch; dinner
	אָבער און ווידער — בולבע,	again and again
2 מאָל	איין מאָל אין אַ נאָווענע — אַ בולבע־___!	once in a long while
	זונטיק ________ בולבע.	

NOTE:

The word **בולבע** as used in the song refers not to a single potato but instead to many, all grouped together as one mass of potato. When describing a finite number of potatoes, the plural form **בולבעס** is used. Another widespread Yiddish word for *potato* is **קאַרטאָפֿל**. The word **בולבע** is characteristic of Northeastern Yiddish.

געניטונג 4: וואָס מאַכסטו?

זונטיק

פֿריידל: וואָס מאַכסטו, מאָטל?

מאָטל: (זייער) גוט!

פֿריידל: ______________

מאָנטיק

פֿריידל: וואָס מאַכסטו, מאָטל?

מאָטל: זייער שלעכט! / נישט אַזוי' אײַ־אײַ־אײַ!

פֿריידל: ______________

דינסטיק

פֿריידל: וואָס מאַכסטו, מאָטל?

מאָטל: נישקשה. [נישקאָשע]

פֿריידל: ______________

Motl and Freydl meet up for coffee every day. On each of the three days depicted above, Freydl asks Motl **וואָס מאַכסטו**—*how are you*, and each day he gives a different response. Look at the list of possible reactions provided below, and determine which phrase Freydl uses each day to react to Motl's utterance.

קיין עין־הרע!	*No evil eye!* [קיינײנאָרע]
אוי־ווי'! נעבעך!	*Oh dear! Poor thing!*
נו, גוט.	*Well, all right.*

NOTE:

Yiddish is full of expressions that seek to block the interference of the **עין־הרע** (*evil eye* [אײנאָרע]) in daily life. Whether thought of as a maleficent spirit or, more simply, as the manifestation of bad luck itself, the **עין־הרע** is usually invited into a situation by an individual's slip of the tongue or through a stranger's envious glance. Verbal talismans like **קיין עין־הרע** are so ubiquitous in Yiddish speech that they are commonly employed regardless of the individual speaker's feelings about such superstition.

NOTE:

The expression **נישקשה** (*not bad*) is the result of the etymologically-Germanic word **נישט** (*not*) melding with the etymologically-Hebraic word **קשה** [קאָשע] (*difficult*) to form a uniquely Yiddish word with its own distinct meaning.

NOTE:

Motl is being addressed informally here. The formal version of this phrase is **וואָס מאַכט איר**.

געניטונג 5: שאָקאָלאַד, ברוך־השם!

Sore has just sat down next to Moyshe in the cafeteria and is asking how he is doing. Read the dialogue below and observe how Moyshe and Sore feel about what they are eating.

שׂרה: וואָס מאַכסטו?

משה: זייער גוט, ברוך־השם! איך עס שאָקאָלאַד! [באָרעכאַשעם]

שׂרה: קיין עין־הרע!

משה: און דו?

שׂרה: נישט אַזוי איַ־איַ־איַ! איך עס הערינג.

משה: אוי־וויי! נעבעך!

Rewrite the dialogue, replacing the underlined food words with other foods from the word box below and—in place of the purple phrases—substitute appropriate emotional reactions and responses.

אַ בייגל *(m)*	מצה [מאַצע] *(f)*	געפֿילטע פֿיש *(pl)*
אַ באַנאַנע *(f)*	אַן עפּל *(m)*	אײַזקרעם *(m)*

NOTE:

The phrase **ברוך־השם** (lit. *blessed is God*) is used to recognize a bit of good fortune. It is often added as an interjection when expressing one's state of health or well-being. It can also stand alone as a one-phrase response meaning *fine* or well. The phrase is used by both religious and secular speakers, falling into the same broad category as **קיין עין־הרע**—that of common idiomatic phrases acknowledging the influence of supernatural forces on human affairs, and appealing to their aid or mercy.

NOTE:

Some of the words provided here are accompanied by an article, while others are not. This reflects a distinction between two different types of Yiddish nouns: nouns for things that can be counted (**באַנאַנעס**) and nouns for things that cannot (**שאָקאָלאַד**). We will learn more about these two types of nouns in **קאַפּיטל 5**. For now, use the forms as they are provided in the word box.

אין קלאַס

מיט אַ חבֿר, חזרט איבער דעם דיאַלאָג איבן עטלעכע מאָל. רעדט אַזוי גיך און פֿליסיק ווי מעגלעך.

With a partner, repeat the dialogue above several times. Speak as quickly and fluently as possible.

Now repeat the dialogue, making the substitutions described above.

- Make sure that your partner's responses match your reactions, as in the model.

געניטונג 6: איך בין מיד...

מיטוואָך

מאָטל: וואָס מאַכסטו, פֿריידל?

פֿריידל: איך בין (זייער) מיד!

מאָטל: ______________

דאָנערשטיק

מאָטל: וואָס מאַכסטו, פֿריידל?

פֿריידל: איך בין (זייער) קראַנק!

מאָטל: ______________

פֿרײַטיק

מאָטל: וואָס מאַכסטו, פֿריידל?

פֿריידל: איך בין (ברוך־השם) געזונט!

מאָטל: ______________

As the week progresses, Motl is now asking Freydl how she is, and Freydl is responding. Determine which phrase from the list below Motl should use on each day to react to each of Freydl's utterances.

נעבעך! אַ רפֿואה־שלמה! — *(May you have) a complete recovery!* [רעפֿוע־שליימע]

קיין עין־הרע! ביז הונדערט און צוואַנציק! — *(May you so live) until 120!*

נו, טרינק קאַווע.

Now it's your turn to have a conversation with Freydl. Write out what you say to each other, making sure to include your reaction to how Freydl is doing, and her reaction to how you're doing.

- Be sure to include how you feel as well, and Freydl's response.

דוגמאַ:

סטודענט: וואָס מאַכסטו?

פֿריידל: איך בין קראַנק.

סטודענט: נעבעך! אַ רפֿואה־שלמה!

! געדענקט!

Motl and Freydl's responses to the question *how are you* differ in that Motl's are single phrases that stand alone, while Freydl's all begin with **איך בין** (*I am*). Motl's responses *cannot* begin with this phrase.

!גענִיטונג 7: גוט־מאָרגן

Professor Kluger's students encounter each other at different times of day and have short conversations. Read the dialogues below and pay special attention to the different greeting and parting phrases being used.

װעלװל: גוט־מאָרגן!
גיטל: גוט־מאָרגן, גוט־יאָר!
װעלװל: װאָס מאַכסטו?
גיטל: זייער גוט, און דו?
װעלװל: נישקשה.
גיטל: נו, גוט. אַ גוטן טאָג!
װעלװל: אַ גוט יאָר!

משה: גוטן־אָװנט!
שׂרה: גוטן־אָװנט, גוט־יאָר!
משה: װאָס מאַכסטו?
שׂרה: נישקשה, און דו?
משה: איך בין מיד.
שׂרה: נו, גיי שלאָפֿן. אַ גוטע נאַכט!
משה: אַ גוט יאָר!

How do the greeting phrases differ from the parting phrases? How is the responder's greeting or parting phrase different from the first speaker's? What is added or changed?

Fill in the table below.

- Use the appropriate greetings and farewells for each time of day.

		אַ גאַנצן טאָג	אין דער פֿרי און בײַ טאָג	אין אָװנט
←→ באַגריסן זיך	א:		גוט־מאָרגן	______
	ב:		______	______
→← געזעגענען זיך	א:	______	______	______
	ב:	זײַ(ט) געזונט	______	______

!גערענקט ⓘ

Yiddish greetings often take a call-and-response form. The call must precede the response.

NOTE:

In response to farewell phrases like **אַ גוטן טאָג** (*a good day*), the response **אַ גוט יאָר** (*a good year*) serves to augment the first speaker's wish of good fortune: "A good day to you!" "And to you a good year!" The phrase **גוט־יאָר** serves the same purpose in response to a greeting.

!גערענקט ⓘ

Instead of the farewell phrases above, the wish **זײַ געזונט** (*be well*) may also be used. This is the informal (**דו**) form. The corresponding formal (**איר**) version is **זײַט געזונט**.

◀ CONTINUED

CONTINUED

Write short dialogues to accompany the illustrations below, based on the dialogues modeled above. Be sure to include greeting, parting, and how-are-you phrases and responses appropriate to the illustrations.

NOTE:

The greeting **גוט־מאָרגן** is typically used throughout the day, until evening. Southeastern Yiddish *does* have an afternoon-specific greeting: **גוטהעלף**. Other speakers extend **גוטן־אָוונט** back into the afternoon instead. Here we present only one greeting for each time of day, but there are more.

אַבֿרהם   עלקע

אַריה־לייב   איידל

געניטונג 8: רעדן שיין

Khane has forgotten Arye-Leyb's name and is politely asking for a reminder. Read the following questions, and then use them as a guide as you read the dialogue.

1. חנה האָט עפּעס פֿאַרגעסן. וואָס איז עס? — *forgot something*
2. וואָס איז אַריה־לייבס פֿאַמיליע־נאָמען? — [אַריע]
3. ס׳איז בײַ טאָג אָדער אין אָוונט?

◀ CONTINUED

CONTINUED

Read the dialogue once through for comprehension and answer the questions above. Now read the dialogue again, this time paying close attention to the purple phrases of politeness that both Khane and Arye-Leyb use in conversing with one another.

חנה: גוט־מאָרגן!

אַריה־לייב: גוט־מאָרגן, גוט־יאָר, חנה.

חנה: זײַ מיר מוחל, איך געדענק נישט דײַן נאָמען! זײַ אַזוי גוט און זאָג מיר ווי דו הייסט.

I'm sorry [מויכל]; *please* (lit. *be so kind*)
tell me

אַריה־לייב: מיטן גרעסטן פֿאַרגעניגן! איך הייס אַריה־לייב קאַץ, אָדער סתּם לייב.

with the greatest pleasure
just [סטאָם]

חנה: אַ דאַנק!

thanks

אַריה־לייב: נישטאָ פֿאַר וואָס. אַ גוטן טאָג, חנה.

you're welcome (alt. *no problem*)

חנה: אַ גוטן, לייב!

NOTE:

The phrase **זײַ אַזוי גוט** (please) typically appears with a command (e.g., **זאָג מיר ווי דו הייסט**). It is generally placed either before the command, with the conjunction **און** in between (as in the dialogue), or *after* the command, separated by a comma: **זאָג מיר ווי דו הייסט, זײַ אַזוי גוט**.

NOTE:

The formal versions of the imperative phrases used in the dialogue are **זײַט אַזוי גוט** and **זײַט מיר מוחל** (marked by the presence of **ט**- at the end of the verb). Khane and Arye-Leyb are on familiar terms.

Write down the five expressions of courtesy demonstrated above and use them to fill in the blanks in the following dialogue. Use each expression only once.

סענדער: חנה, דו עסט מײַן עפּל.

my

חנה: אוי־וויי! ________! איך האָב אַ באַנאַנע. ________ און עס די באַנאַנע.

סענדער: ________! איך האָב ליב באַנאַנעס.

love

חנה: נאַ!

here (you go)!

סענדער: ________!

חנה: ________.

2 וואָקאַבולאַר־איבערבליק

א. וואָס טוען זיי?
WHAT ARE THEY DOING?

basic verbs		גרונטיקע ווערבן
to go (by foot)	איך גיי, מיר גייען	גיין
to hear		הערן
to cry		וויינען
to sit		זיצן
to do	איך טו, מיר טוען	טאָן
to drink		טרינקען
to laugh		לאַכן
to run		לויפֿן
to read		לייענען
to eat		עסן
to stand	איך שטיי, מיר שטייען	שטיין
to sleep		שלאָפֿן
to play		שפּילן
to jump		שפּרינגען
to write		שרײַבן [שרײַבם]

pronouns	פּראָנאָמען
I	איך
you (*sg informal*)	דו
he; it (*m*)	ער
she; it (*f*)	זי
it (*n*)	עס
one (*indefinite*)	מען (מע)
we	מיר
you (*pl; sg formal*)	איר
they	זיי

זינגען; טאַנצן

א. וואָס טוען זיי?
WHAT ARE THEY DOING? (continued)

little words	קלײנע ווערטערלעך
but	אָבער
also	אויך
and	און
now	איצט
better; rather	בעסער
not	נישט

additional vocabulary	נאָך וואָקאַבולאַר
to address someone with **איר**	אירצן
to address someone with **דו**	דוצן
there (goes)	אָט (גייט)
usually	געוויינטלעך
editorial office	**די רעדאַקציע** (ס)
friend	דער **חבֿר** (ים) [כאַווער (כאַווײרים)]
teacher	דער **לערער** (ס)
song; poem	דאָס **ליד** (ער)
child	דאָס **קינד** (ער)

די סעקרעטאַרשע (ס); דער **פּאַסאַזשיר** (ן); דער **פּאַרק** (ן); דער **פּילאָט** (ן); דער **פֿידל** (ען); דער **קאָנצערט** (ן); דער **קלאַס** (ן)

ב. באַגריסן זיך
GREETING ONE ANOTHER

days of the week	טעג פֿון וואָך
Sunday	זונטיק
Monday	מאָנטיק
Tuesday	דינסטיק
Wednesday	מיטוואָך
Thursday	דאָנערשטיק
Friday	פֿרײַטיק
Saturday	שבת [שאַבעס]

2 וואָקאַבולאַר־איבערבליק

ב. באַגריסן זיך
GREETING ONE ANOTHER (continued)

times of day	צײַטן פֿון טאָג
in the morning	אין דער פֿרי
during the day	בײַ טאָג
in the evening	אין אָוונט
at night	בײַ נאַכט

asking how someone's doing	פֿרעגן וואָס מע מאַכט
how are you? (*informal*) (*lit.* what are you doing?)	וואָס מאַכסטו?
(*formal*)	וואָס מאַכט איר?
fine (*lit.* blessed be God)	ברוך־השם [באָרעכאַשעׂם]
(very) good/well	(זייער) גוט
not so great	נישט אַזוי׳ אײַ־אײַ־אײַ
not bad	נישקשה [נישקאָשע]
(very) bad/badly	(זייער) שלעכט
(I'm) healthy	(איך בין) געזוׄנט
(I'm) tired	(איך בין) מיד
(I'm) sick	(איך בין) קראַנק
(may you have) a complete recovery!	אַ רפֿואה־שלמה! [רעפֿוע־שליימע]
oh dear!	אוי־ווײ׳!
(may you so live) until 120!	ביז הונדערט און צוואַנציק!
well, all right	נו, גוט
poor thing!	נעבעך!
no evil eye!	קיין עין־הרע! [קיינײנאָרע]

greetings	ענטפֿערס	באַגריסונגען
nice to meet/see you	עליכם־שלום	שלום־עליכם
good morning/afternoon	גוט־מאָרגן, גוט־יאָר	גוט־מאָרגן
good evening	גוטן־אָוונט, גוט־יאָר	גוטן־אָוונט

farewells	ענטפֿערס	געזעגענונגען
(have a) good day	אַ גוט יאָר	אַ גוטן טאָג
good night	אַ גוט יאָר	אַ גוטע נאַכט
good-bye (*formal/informal*) (*lit.* be well)		זײַ(ט) געזוׄנט

ב. באַגריסן זיך
GREETING ONE ANOTHER (continued)

speaking politely	רעדן שיין
please (*formal/informal*) (sing) (*lit.* be so good [and sing])	זײַ(ט) אַזוי גוט (און זינג[ט])
with the greatest pleasure	מיטן גרעסטן פֿאַרגעניגן
thank you	אַ דאַנק
you're welcome; no problem	נישטאָ פֿאַר וואָס
(I'm) sorry; excuse me	זײַ(ט) (מיר) מוחל [מויכל]

additional vocabulary	נאָך וואָקאַבולאַר
with	מיט
potato	**די בולבע** (ס)
matzo	**די מצה** (–ות) [מאַצע(ס)]
noodle or potato casserole, usually eaten on Shabbos	**דער קוגל** (ען)
meat	**דאָס פֿלייש** (ן)

דער אײַזקרעם; **דער בייגל** (—); **די געפֿילטע פֿיש**;
דער הערינג (—); **דער שאָקאָלאַד** (ן)

2 גראַמאַטיק־איבערבליק

VERBS — ווערבן

REGULAR VERBS

- Verbs like **שלאָפֿן** constitute the most common class of regular verbs. To form the present tense, the stem of the verb (-**שלאָפֿ**) combines with the endings shown in **bold** below.
- Verbs with stems ending in **ס**- (e.g., **עסן**) have a special conjugation for **דו**, adding only **ט**- (rather than **סט**-) in order to avoid doubling the **ס**.
- Similarly, verbs with stems ending in **ט**- (e.g., **אַרבעטן**) omit the usual third-person singular and second-person-plural/formal endings in order to avoid doubling the final **ט**.
- Verbs with stems ending in **מ**-, **נ**-, **נג**-, **נק**-, an accented vowel, or a syllabic **ל**- have a special ending in the first- and third-person plural: **ען**- (instead of **ן**- alone). For example:

מיר ווינען, זינגען, טרינקען, פֿליִען *(fly)*, קומען, שמייכלען *(smile)*

These usually form the infinitive too (with some exceptions, such as **גיין ← מיר גייען**).

Infinitive	קומען (!)	אַרבעטן	עסן	שלאָפֿן	
First-person singular	קום	אַרבעט	עס	שלאָף	**איך**
Second person singular (*informal*)	קומסט	אַרבעטסט	עסט (!)	שלאָפֿסט	**דו**
Third-person singular	קומט	אַרבעט (!)	עסט	שלאָפֿט	**ער/זי/עס**
First-person plural	קומען (!)	אַרבעטן	עסן	שלאָפֿן	**מיר**
Second person plural (and *singular formal*)	קומט	אַרבעט (!)	עסט	שלאָפֿט	**איר**
Third-person plural	קומען (!)	אַרבעטן	עסן	שלאָפֿן	**זיי**

(!) **NOTE:** After the consonants **ב** and **פּ**, a syllabic **נ** (as in **שרײַבן**) is pronounced as a **מ**, thus [שרײַבם]. There is no vowel between the two consonants—the lips remain closed and air is expelled through the nose with the **מ** sound. This pronunciation is obligatory.

NEGATION

- Verbs are negated using the word **נישט**, which is generally placed somewhere after the verb. In simple sentences, it follows the verb directly: **ער שלאָפֿט נישט**.

WORD ORDER

- When the first unit of the sentence is *not* the subject, the subject appears after the verb: **אין הויז שלאָף איך**.
- If the subject is a pronoun, then it will also *precede* any adverbs (including **נישט**):

אין הויז שלאָף איך נישט / העברעיִש רעדט מען אויך.

גראַמאַטיק־איבערבליק 2

PRONOUNS — פּראָנאָמען

GENDERED PRONOUNS

- After a noun is first mentioned, it is often referred to with a pronoun.
- The pronoun used matches the gender of the noun to which it refers.

דער צימער איז גרויס. ← **ער** איז גרויס.
דאָס הויז איז ווײַט. ← **עס** איז ווײַט.
די שטאָט איז אין פֿראַנקרײַך. ← **זי** איז אין פֿראַנקרײַך.

There are exceptions to this rule, most notably in connection with nouns referring to *people*, where some native speakers tend to use the pronoun corresponding to the gender identity of the person in question, rather than the grammatical gender of the word itself.

דאָס קינד איז קיין עין־הרע געזונט. ← **זי** איז קיין עין־הרע געזונט. (אָדער: **עס** איז קיין עין־הרע געזונט.)

- Plural nouns are always referred to using the pronoun **זיי**.

דו AND איר

Yiddish has two second-person pronouns, **דו** and **איר**, where standard English has only one: *you*. When addressing a group of two or more people, only **איר** is used. In the singular, however, the speaker must choose the appropriate pronoun, depending on various social considerations.

Singular (*informal*)	דו
(*formal*)	איר
Plural	איר

The following are some general patterns regarding the use of formal and informal pronouns:

- A child is always addressed as **דו**.
- Young people generally use **דו** with one another in informal settings.
- Closely related family members generally use **דו** with one another, but pronoun usage varies: in some families, elders and more distant relatives are addressed as **איר**.

דו AND איר (CONTINUED)

- Close friends of the same generation, whether young or old, address one another as **דו**.
- A child or young person will address an unfamiliar older adult as **איר**.
- An adult will address a stranger as **איר** (unless it is a child).
- Adults typically address one another as **איר** when linked by a formal relationship—e.g., employer-employee, shopkeeper-customer, doctor-patient—or in a formal setting, such as a meeting or conference.
- In addressing college-aged students, professors differ as to which pronouns they employ. In the United States, many professors use **דו**, as Professor Kluger does.

NOTE: Conventions about the use of **דו** and **איר** depend on social, geographical, religious, and generational factors. When speaking to an adult, it is best to default to **איר**, and switch to **דו** only if they ask you to do so, or if there is another clear social indication that **דו** is appropriate.

מען

- The third-person pronoun **מען** conveys that the subject is indeterminate or general and may also play the role of the passive voice in English.

אין פֿראַנקרײַך רעדט מען פֿראַנצייזיש.

In France, **they speak** French.
In France, **one speaks** French.
In France, French **is spoken**.

When this pronoun precedes a verb beginning with a consonant, it takes the shortened form **מע**: **מע שרײַבט אַ בוך**. (Still, native speakers sometimes use **מען** in such situations.)

- When **מען** follows the verb, it can only appear in its full form.

איבערחזר־געניטונגען 2

געניטונג 1: אַ גולם איז נישט פֿויל!

Using activity verbs (see page 58) and combining them with the time and location phrases provided below, write four sentences describing some of your *goylem*'s activities.

ווען?	ווו?
אין אָוונט	אין אינטערנאַט
אין דער פֿרי	אין גאַס
בײַ טאָג	אין הויז
בײַ נאַכט	אין פּאַרק

דוגמא:

בײַ טאָג שלאָפֿט דער גולם אין הויז.

געדענקט!

As in the example provided, adverbs of time (**בײַ טאָג**) are often the first unit of a sentence. Since the verb (**שלאָפֿט**) must remain in second position, the subject (**דער גולם**) follows the verb.

אין קלאַס

With a partner, role-play four short conversations between your *goylems* (based on the sentences you composed above), each one performed as though taking place at a different time of day. Be sure to use the appropriate greetings and farewells each time, as demonstrated in the model below.

דוגמא:

א: גוט־מאָרגן!

ב: גוט־מאָרגן, גוט־יאָר! וואָס מאַכסטו?

א: נישקשה. און דו?

ב: ברוך־השם. וואָס טוסטו?

א: **איצט** שפּיל איך אין גאַס. וואָס טוסט דו? (now)

ב: איך שלאָף אין הויז. אַ גוטן טאָג!

א: אַ גוט יאָר!

געניטונג 2: פֿון וואַנען קומט אַ ייִד?

הער־געניטונג
איבערחזר־סעקציע־2

טיטל ♫ **„שלום־עליכם“**
פֿאָלקסליד

זינגער **רות רובין (Ruth Rubin)**
(כעטין, רוסישע אימפּעריע 1906 – מאַמאַראָנעק, פֿאַראייניקטע שטאַטן 2000)

רעקאָרדירונג 1956, פֿאַראייניקטע שטאַטן

Ruth Rubin *was a folklorist and singer of Yiddish folk song. In 1945, she began traveling to the homes of immigrants across North America, collecting thousands of their songs. In this recording, she herself sings a humorous folk song about Kasrilevke, a fictional town invented by the author Sholem Aleichem. An earlier variant of the song was about Lyubavitsh, the birthplace of the Lubavitcher Hasidic dynasty, and was likely intended as a satire on the allegedly excessive drinking habits of Hasidim.*

Listen to the excerpt once with your book closed. Now play the recording again and follow along with the text below.

	— שלום־עליכם!	3 מאָל
	— עליכם־שלום!	2 מאָל
[1]*here:* איר (lit. *a Jew*)	— פֿון וואַנען קומט אַ ייִד[1]?	3 מאָל
[קאַסרילעווקע]	— פֿון כּתרילעווקע.	2 מאָל
[2]*what's new...?*	— וואָס הערט זיך אין כּתרילעווקע	3 מאָל
	עפּעס נײַעס[2]?	2 מאָל
[3]brandy; [4]make merry	— מע טרינקט בראָנפֿן[3] און מע הוליעט[4]	7 מאָל
[5]circle dance	און מע גייט אַ קאַראַהאָד[5].	

NOTE:
The phrase **אַ ייִד** functions here as a second-person pronoun, roughly equivalent to **איר**. Though similarly neutral and respectful in tone, the two are not interchangeable: **אַ ייִד** is used in in-group contexts where Jewish identity is assumed and traditionally applies only to men. As a result, **אַ ייִד** would be out of place in many contexts in which **איר** is used.

Yosl heard this song from his grandfather, but he seems to misremember it somewhat. Find the errors in his statements below and correct them.

דוגמא: דאָס איז אַ ליד **וועגן** אַ פּיראַט. — about

ניין, דאָס איז אַ ליד וועגן אַ ייִד פֿון כּתרילעווקע.

ערנסט	serious
קאָמיש	funny

1. דאָס ליד איז זייער ערנסט.
2. דער ייִד קומט פֿון לאָנדאָן.
3. אין כּתרילעווקע טרינקט מען קאַווע.
4. אין כּתרילעווקע טאַנצט מען אַ פֿאָקסטראָט.
5. אין כּתרילעווקע אַרבעט מען **שטענדיק**. — always

געניטונג 3: גרינע פֿעלדער

טיטל „גרינע פֿעלדער“ (1937) (פֿראַגמענט)

רעזשיסאָרן (directors) **יעקבֿ בן־עמי (Jacob Ben-Ami)** [יאַנקעוו בען־אַמי]

(מינסק, רוסישע אימפּעריע 1890 – ניו־יאָרק, פֿאַראייניקטע שטאַטן 1977)

עדגאַר אולמער (Edgar Ulmer)

(אָלמיצע, עסטרײַך 1904 – לאָס־אַנדזשעלעס, פֿאַראייניקטע שטאַטן 1972)

ווידעאָ־געניטונג

איבערחזר־סעקציע־3

Practice greetings with this excerpt from the film *Grine felder,* which you can find online with its accompanying exercise.

3

קאַפּיטל דרײַ:

צאָלווערטער, האָבן און זײַן

CHAPTER GOALS

- In this chapter, you will learn how to count and to conjugate the verbs **האָבן** and **זײַן**.

וואָקאַבולאַר:	
numerals	צאָלווערטער

גראַמאַטיק:	
verbs (**האָבן** and **זײַן**)	ווערבן (האָבן און זײַן)

קולטור — טעקסט:	
"What Does Your Dad Do?" *(Grininke beymelekh)*	„וואָס טוט דער טאַטע?“ (גרינינקע ביימעלעך)

קולטור — אווידיאָ:	
"In What Country Does the Public Go to the Movies Most?" (Celia Silver and Zalmen Zylbercweig)	„אין וועלכן לאַנד גייט דער עולם אַממערסטן אין די מוּוויס?“ (צילִיע זילבער און זלמן זילבערצווײַג)

א וואָקאַבולאַר און גראַמאַטיק: צאָלווערטער; האָבן

איין בער

צוויי גיטאַרעס

דרײַ פּאָפּוגײַען

פֿיר באַלן

פֿינף באַרן

זעקס עפּל

זיבן ביכער

אַכט בלײַערס

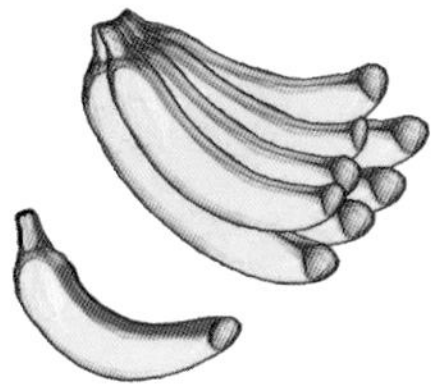
נײַן באַנאַנעס

צען בלומען

געניטונג 1: וויפֿל פּאָפּוגײַען?

וויפֿל פּאָפּוגײַען זעט איר אויפֿן בילד? ענטפֿערט אויף די פֿראַגעס אונטן, לויט דער דוגמא.

How many parrots do you see in the picture? Answer the questions below according to the example.

דוגמא: וויפֿל פּאָפּוגײַען זעט איר אויפֿן בילד?
איך זע דרײַ פּאָפּוגײַען.

1. וויפֿל בלײַערס זעט איר אויפֿן בילד?
2. וויפֿל בלומען זעט איר אויפֿן בילד?
3. וויפֿל גיטאַרעס זעט איר אויפֿן בילד?
4. וויפֿל באַלן זעט איר אויפֿן בילד?
5. וויפֿל באַנאַנעס זעט איר אויפֿן בילד?
6. וויפֿל באַרן זעט איר אויפֿן בילד?

וויפֿל	how many
זען	to see
דאָס בילד	picture

NOTE:

Since the final (syllabic) נ in **זיבן** is preceded by a **ב**, the word must be pronounced [זיבם]. See page 16 for a more detailed explanation of this phenomenon.

געניטונג 2: נישט איינס...

With a partner, count the students in your class using the model below.

דוגמא:

א: נישט איינס...

ב: נישט צוויי...

א: נישט דרײַ...

NOTE: According to custom, to avoid drawing the attention of the **עין־הרע**, one should not count people in the same way one counts objects lest the evil eye seek to reduce that number. Instead, one counts the number of people not there (**נישט איינס, נישט צוויי, נישט דרײַ...**) in order to deceive the evil spirit.

גערעדנקט!

When counting, the number 1 is **איינס**. However, when one modifies a noun, it becomes **איין**:

איינס, צוויי, דרײַ...

איין **בער**

געניטונג 3: מאַטעמאַטיק

Write down five simple mathematical problems using the numbers 1–10. Read each problem aloud so that your partner can answer, and then move on to the next question.

- Once you have asked all of yours, answer your partner's five questions.

דוגמא:

א: וויפֿל איז דרײַ <u>פּלוס</u> דרײַ?

ב: דרײַ פּלוס דרײַ איז זעקס. וויפֿל איז נײַן <u>מינוס</u> צוויי?

א: נײַן מינוס צוויי איז זיבן.

how much

+	פּלוס
−	מינוס
×	מאָל
÷	געטיילט אויף

היימאַרבעט

Write out five mathematical problems with their solutions, as in the example below.

- Use numbers 1–10.
- Write out all the numbers; do not use numerals.

דוגמא:

נײַן מינוס צוויי איז זיבן.

געניטונג 4: וואָס איז דײַן טעלעפֿאָן־נומער?

Professor Kluger's students need each other's phone numbers so that they can plan their study group.

לייענט דעם דיאַלאָג אונטן.

עלקע: וואָס איז דײַן טעלעפֿאָן־נומער? — your

אַבֿרהם: פֿיר־צוויי־איינס, פֿינף־צוויי־זעקס, זיבן־פֿיר־פֿיר־נײַן.
און דײַנער? — yours

עלקע: פֿיר־צוויי־איינס, זיבן־צוויי־צוויי, איינס־דרײַ־אַכט־דרײַ.

שרײַבט אויס די טעלעפֿאָן־נומערן.

Write out the phone numbers that Avrom and Elke give each other. Use numerals.

Now write out your own phone number and the numbers of a few friends. Write in Yiddish letters, *not* numerals.

נול — zero

געניטונג 5: ווו איז דער דאָקטער?

Upon returning to work after a few days of vacation, Dr. Hershkowitz finds his voice mail full of messages from his patients. Help Dr. Hershkowitz make a list of calls he needs to return.

הער־געניטונג א־5

טעלעפֿאָן־נומער	פֿאַמיליע	נאָמען
		סימי
	טייטלבוים	
020-8800-4321		

די פֿאַמיליע — surname (*lit.* family)

גענײטונג 6: וויפֿל באַרן האָסטו?

Reyne and Yosl are on their way to a picnic and are discussing what they're bringing. Read the following dialogue and pay close attention to the varying forms of the verb **האָבן** (*to have*).

- Compare these forms to those of the regular verbs you have learned so far. What differences do you notice?

ריינע: גוטן־אָוונט! דו האָסט באַרן?

יאָסל: יאָ, איך האָב דרײַ באַרן. וויפֿל באַרן האָסט דו?

ריינע: איך האָב איין באַר. צוזאַמען האָבן מיר פֿיר באַרן!

יאָסל: אָט גייט יאַנקל. ער האָט אַ באַר?

ריינע: ניין, ער האָט אַ בער, און דער בער האָט אַ גיטאַרע.

יאָסל: יאַנקל האָט אויך אַ גיטאַרע. צוזאַמען האָבן זיי צוויי גיטאַרעס.

ריינע: יאַנקל! בער! איר האָט צוויי גיטאַרעס! איר שפּילט אַ סאָנאַטע?

וויפֿל	how many
צוזאַמען	together
אָט	there

NOTE:

Since the final (syllabic) **נ** in **האָבן** is preceded by a **ב**, the word must be pronounced [האָבם]. See page 16 for a more detailed explanation of this phenomenon.

NOTE:

In these sentences (with the verb **האָבן**, *to have*), there is both a *subject* noun (the person who *has* something) and a second noun called the *object* (the thing being *had*). When the subject comes first, it is followed by the verb, then the object. When a different element (e.g., **צוזאַמען**) begins the sentence, the verb still comes second, followed directly by the subject and finally the object. We will learn more about these patterns later.

Now rewrite the dialogue, choosing other nouns to replace **באַרן** and **גיטאַרעס** above. You may also change the number of things that each person has.

- Change the question at the end to suit the new nouns.

פֿילט אויס די טאַבעלע אונטן.

- Use the conjugations of **האָבן** shown in the dialogue.

איך	________	מיר	________
דו	________	איר	________
ער/זי/עס	________	זיי	________

אין קלאַס

מיט אַ חבֿר, חזרט איבער דעם דיאַלאָג אויבן עטלעכע מאָל. רעדט אַזוי גיך און פֿליסיק ווי מעגלעך.

Now repeat the dialogue, making the substitutions described above.

געניטונג 7: וואָס האָבן זיי?

After the picnic, Yosl and Reyne return to Reyne's house, where Yosl asks about the various family members' possessions.

> **NOTE:**
> Some of the vocabulary used here is drawn from the **אַלף־בית קאַפּיטל**. Refer to page 13 for review.

א____ 1. **יאָסל:** דער טאַטע האָט אַ בוך?
ריינע: יאָ, ער האָט אַ בוך.

____ 2. **יאָסל:** איך ________ אַ טעפּל קאַווע?
ריינע: יאָ, איר ________ אַ טעפּל קאַווע.

____ 3. **יאָסל:** די מאַמע ________ אַ מאַנטל?
ריינע: יאָ, זי ________ אַ מאַנטל.

____ 4. **יאָסל:** ריינע, דו ________ אַ באַל?
ריינע: יאָ, איך ________ אַ באַל.

____ 5. **יאָסל:** איר ________ אַ הונט?
ריינע: יאָ, מיר ________ אַ הונט.

____ 6. **יאָסל:** זיי ________ אַ בעט?
ריינע: יאָ, זיי ________ אַ בעט.

Now match each image below with the appropriate pair of sentences above, and write the corresponding letter in the blank provided next to the sentences.

א.

ב.

ג.

ד.

ה.

ו.

געניטונג 8: עסן בולבעס

The anonymous composer of "בולבע" was inspired to sing of the weekly redundancy of their diet.
In this spirit, choose an aspect of your own weekly routine to immortalize in song!

- From the table below, pick one verb and one noun. Write two sentences, as in the example, using both singular and plural forms of the noun.
- Plural endings of all nouns below are in parentheses.
- Remember that the indefinite article **אַ** has no plural form.

דוגמא:

איך עס אַ בולבע.
איך עס בולבעס.

> **(!) געדענקט!**
> The regular, finite plural form of **בולבע** is **בולבעס**.

סובסטאַנטיוון	ווערבן	
בולבע (ס)	הערן	
בוך (ביכער)	זינגען	
בליצבריוו (–)	טאַנצן	e-mail
האָרע (ס)	טרינקען	hora (dance)
טאַנגאָ (ס)	לייענען	
ליד (ער)	עסן	
	שרײַבן	

Now write a song or poem in the form demonstrated below.

(!) Pay special attention to the change in word order.

- Use counting to intensify your ode to repetition. The numbers needn't be in order.
- Be creative: come up with your own phrase to follow **שבת אין אַ נאָווענע**.

דוגמא:

זונטיק עס איך איין בולבע,
מאָנטיק עס איך צוויי בולבעס,
...
שבת אין אַ נאָווענע זינג איך זעקס לידער,
און זונטיק עס איך ווײַטער בולבעס.

> **NOTE:**
> In the last line of the example, **בולבעס** appears in the plural. Use this form for any other noun you insert here. (As you saw in Mark Olf's recording of "**בולבע**," the unsuffixed collective form could also be used in this context. This is a special characteristic of certain nouns.)

(!) **NOTE:** The verbs listed above can be used either with a subject alone (**איך עס**) or with both a subject and an object (**איך עס אַ באַנאַנע**).

ב וואָקאַבולאַר און גראַמאַטיק:
ווײַטערדיקע צאָלווערטער; זײַן

0 = נול	10 = צען	
1 = איינס	11 = עלף	
2 = צוויי	12 = צוועלף	20 = צוואַנציק
3 = דרײַ	13 = דרײַצן	30 = דרײַסיק
4 = פֿיר	14 = פֿערצן	40 = פֿערציק
5 = פֿינף	15 = פֿופֿצן	50 = פֿופֿציק
6 = זעקס	16 = זעכצן	60 = זעכציק
7 = זיבן	17 = זי́בעצן	70 = זי́בעציק
8 = אַכט	18 = אַכצן	80 = אַכציק
9 = נײַן	19 = נײַנצן	90 = נײַנציק

געניטונג 1: ווײַטער ציילן

As you study the table above, compare the numbers under ten with the teens and multiples of ten. How are they similar? How are they different?

- What do all the teens have in common?
- What do all the multiples of ten have in common?

Answer the arithmetic questions below.

דוגמא: וויפֿל איז נײַן פלוס פֿיר?
נײַן פּלוס פֿיר איז דרײַצן.

1. וויפֿל איז אַכצן מינוס זיבן?
2. וויפֿל איז דרײַסיק פלוס פֿערציק?
3. וויפֿל איז זיבעצן פלוס דרײַ?
4. וויפֿל איז זעכצן מינוס פֿיר?
5. וויפֿל איז דרײַסיק מינוס זעכצן?
6. וויפֿל איז דרײַ מאָל פֿינף?
7. וויפֿל איז צען מאָל זעקס?

! געדענקט!

Suffixes (excluding some from *loshn-koydesh*) are generally ignored when determining stress placement, which remains the same as in the word or stem from which the suffixed form derives:

זי́בן ← זי́בעצן, זי́בעציק

געניטונג 2: איין און צוואַנציק

Examine the compound numbers below. What do you notice about how they are formed?

20 = צוואַנציק	100 = הונדערט
21 = איין און צוואַנציק	1000 = טויזנט
22 = צוויי און צוואַנציק	2439 = צוויי טויזנט פֿיר הונדערט נײַן און דרײַסיק
23 = דרײַ און צוואַנציק	
24 = פֿיר און צוואַנציק	
25 = פֿינף און צוואַנציק	
26 = זעקס און צוואַנציק	
27 = זיבן און צוואַנציק	
28 = אַכט און צוואַנציק	
29 = נײַן און צוואַנציק	

NOTE: In all compound numbers (e.g., 21, 34, 87), the units digit is said before the tens digit, and joined to it by the conjunction **און** (and):

23 = דרײַ און צוואַנציק

Remember that when counting, the number 1 is **איינס**. However, when *one* modifies a noun or is used in the twenties, thirties, and so on, it becomes **איין**:

1 = איינס

51 = איין און פֿופֿציק

איין סטודענט

NOTE:

The phrase *a hundred* (i.e., *one hundred*) is translated simply as **הונדערט**: ***a hundred*** *students live in the dormitory* =
אין אינטערנאַט וווינען הונדערט סטודענטן
Adding the indefinite article **אַ** makes the number approximate: ***about a hundred*** *students live in the dormitory* =
אין אינטערנאַט וווינען אַ הונדערט סטודענטן

געניטונג 3: וואָס איז דאָס?

Help your partner connect the dots in the image provided (see page A1) by reciting the text below.

סטודענט א

> **NOTE:**
> Information gap exercises such as this one will be used throughout the textbook in order to allow you to practice sharing information with a partner. In each such activity, one student will work from the exercise itself and the other will work from the corresponding page in Appendix A.

begin with הייב אָן מיט 1. גיי צו 25, צו 14, צו 44, צו 58, צו 77,
צו 63, צו 37, צו 18, צו 41, צו 82, צו 93, צו 20, צו
33, צו 55, צו 6, צו 11, צו 51, צו 31, צו 87, צו 68, צו
4, צו 16, צו 30, צו 47, צו 95, צו 65, צו 28, צו 10, צו
61, צו 84, צו 39, צו 8, צו 72, צו 90, צו 49, צו 98 , צו
19, צו 23, צו 35, צו 57, צו 78, צו 12, צו 92, און
finally [סאָף] צום סוף צו 45. דאָס איז אַ פּאַווע!

Now follow your partner's instructions to connect the dots in the image below.

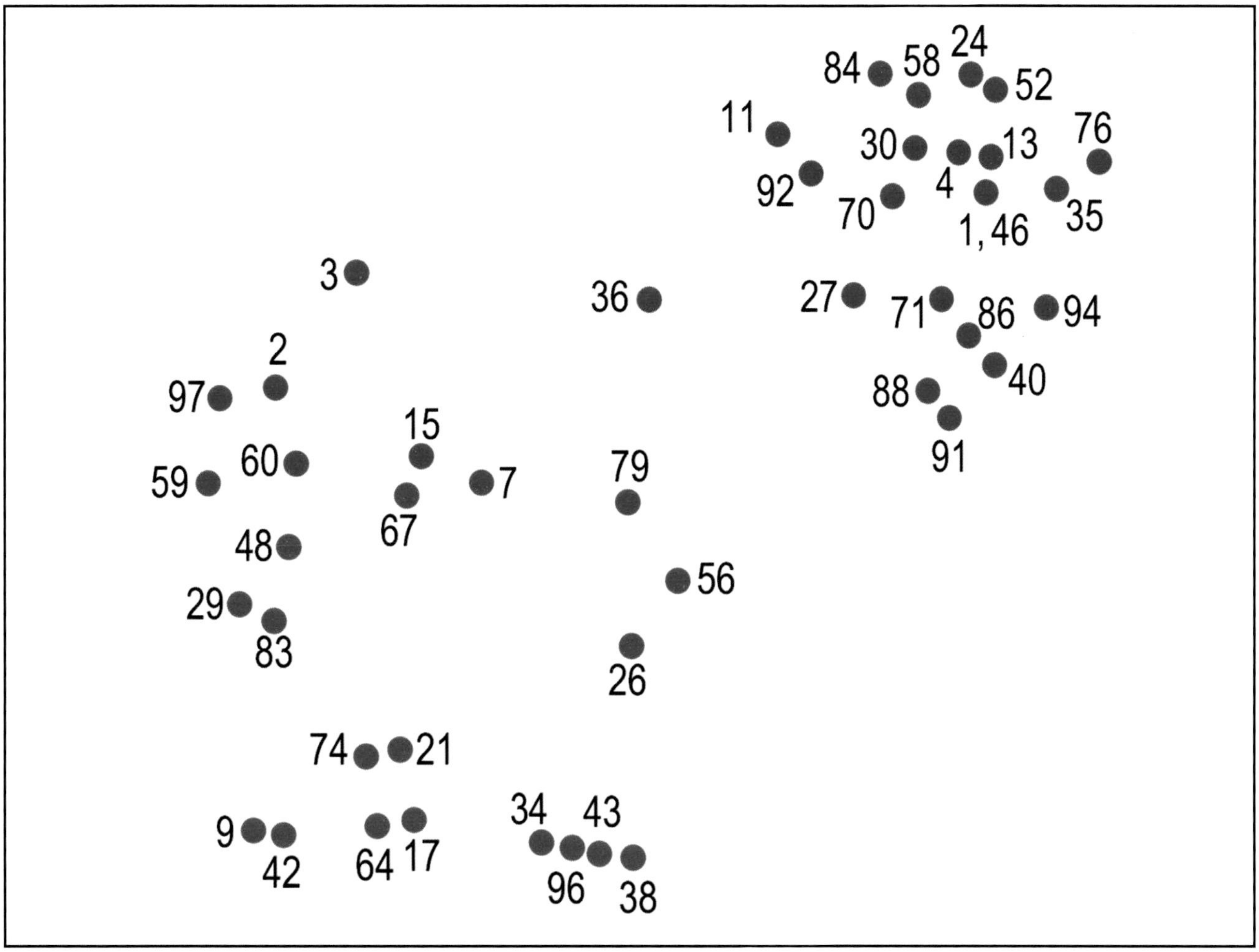

◀ CONTINUED

CONTINUED

הײמאַרבעט

Make a recording of yourself reading the numerical instructions at the top of 3 **געניטונג**. Then turn to the image on page A1 and connect the dots by listening to your own instructions.

געניטונג 4: בינגאָ!

הער־געניטונג ב־4

די סטודענטן אין פּראָפֿעסאָר קלוגערס קלאַס שפּילן בינגאָ מיט נומערן פֿון 10 ביז 1000. שרײַבט אויס די נומערן וואָס פּראָפֿעסאָר קלוגער זאָגט.

Write down the numbers that Professor Kluger says.

NOTE: The professor sometimes repeats numbers as she speaks.

let's	לאָמיר
find (imperative)	געפֿינט
on your pages	אויף אײַערע בלעטלעך
further	װײַטער
I won	איך האָב געוווּנען
row	ריי

מיט וואָסערע נומערן געווינט עלקע? שרײַבט זיי אויס.

גענִיטונג 5: ער איז אַ פּאָעט!

Yosl is very confused when he sees that a pirate has followed Reyne home. Read the dialogues below and pay attention to the forms of the verb **זײַן** (*to be*) that appear in the text.

יאָסל: ריינע, דו ביסט דאָ מיט אַ פּיראַט!
פּיראַט: איך בין אַ פּאָעט.
יאָסל: איר זײַט אַ פּילאָט?
פּיראַט: איך בין אַ פּאָעט!
יאָסל: ער איז אַ פּראָפֿעסאָר?
פּיראַט: ניין! איך בין אַ פּאָעט!
ריינע: מיר זײַנען מיד.
יאָסל: זיי זײַנען מאָדנע! strange

פֿילט אויס די טאַבעלע אונטן.

- Use the conjugations of **זײַן** shown in the dialogue.

איך	____________	**מיר**	____________
דו	____________	**איר**	____________
ער/זי/עס	____________	**זיי**	____________

געניטונג 6: ווי אַלט ביסטו?

Imagine that it's your partner's birthday. Ask them how old they are, and react to their answer as in the model provided. Then switch roles.

א: מזל־טובֿ! ווי אַלט ביסטו? [מאַזל־טאָוו]

ב: איך בין אַלט ___צוואַנציק___ יאָר, קיין עין־הרע. [קיינײנאָרע]

א: ביז הונדערט און צוואַנציק!

היימאַרבעט

Try to guess the ages of the characters pictured below. Structure your answer as in the example provided.

דוגמא: ווי אַלט איז גיטל?

זי איז אַלט צוואַנציק יאָר.

1. ווי אַלט איז בער?

2. ווי אַלט איז וועלוול?

3. ווי אַלט איז דער פּיראַט?

4. ווי אַלט איז דבֿורה־לאה?

5. ווי אַלט ביסט דו?

גענִיטונג 7: די באָבע יערט זיך...

Khaye wants to know how old Grandma Sheyndl is, and Sheyndl is making her guess.

לייענט דעם דיאַלאָג.

[כּײַע]	**חיה:**	באָבע שיינדל, ווי אַלט ביסטו?
Can you guess?	**שיינדל:**	קענסט טרעפֿן?
	חיה:	ביסט אַלט דרײַסיק יאָר?
	שיינדל:	ניין, איך בין, קיין עין־הרע, עלטער פֿון דרײַסיק!
	חיה:	ביסט נײַנציק יאָר?
	שיינדל:	ניין, איך בין ייִנגער פֿון נײַנציק!
	חיה:	ביסט זיבעציק יאָר?
a little	**שיינדל:**	ניין, איך בין אַ ביסל עלטער פֿון זיבעציק.
	חיה:	ביסט פֿיר און זיבעציק יאָר?
exactly	**שיינדל:**	יאָ! פּונקט פֿיר און זיבעציק!
	חיה:	ביז הונדערט און צוואַנציק!

ייִנגער (פֿון...)	younger (than...)
עלטער (פֿון...)	older (than...)

NOTE:

Particularly in colloquial speech, the pronoun **דו** is often omitted:
דו ביסט אַלט דרײַסיק יאָר? ←
ביסט אַלט דרײַסיק יאָר?

NOTE:

After the first time Khaye asks Sheyndl how old she is, she omits the word **אַלט** from the question. This is simply to avoid repetition. Due to the context, Sheyndl knows what is being asked.

Write down (as numerals) the numbers that Khaye guesses.

אין קלאַס

With a partner, play the roles of grandmother and grandchild, as in the dialogue above. The "grandmother" decides what age she is, and the "child" must guess. Once you've guessed correctly, switch roles.

געניטונג 8: מיר זײַנען פּאָעטן

יאָסל און דער פּיראַט רעדן וועגן פּאָעטן. לייענט דעם דיאַלאָג אונטן.

יאָסל: אָט גייען יאַנקל און איציק.

פּיראַט: איציק איז אַ __פּאָעט__, ווי איך.

יאָסל: זיי זײַנען ביידע __פּאָעטן__. איר זײַט אַלע __פּאָעטן__!

פּיראַט: איציק! יאַנקל! מיר זײַנען אַלע __פּאָעטן__!

Now rewrite the dialogue, replacing the underlined noun with another noun from the word box below, using the correct singular or plural form where needed.

זינגער (ס)	טענצער (ס)	פּיראַט (ן)
פּילאָט (ן)	שרײַבער (ס)	אַסטראָנױט (ן)

אין קלאַס

מיט אַ חבֿר, חזרט איבער דעם דיאַלאָג אויבן עטלעכע מאָל. רעדט אַזוי גיך און פֿליסיק ווי מעגלעך.

Now repeat the dialogue, making the substitutions described above.

געניטונג 9: פּיראַטן און פּאָעטן

Write a dialogue between a pirate and a pilot who both turn out to be poets.

- Use as many numbers and conjugations of the verbs **זײַן** and **האָבן** as you can.
- Mention the characters' ages, parents, grandparents, things they have in various quantities, and activities they engage in, as in the model.

דוגמא:

פּיראַט: מײַן באָבע און מײַן זיידע זײַנען אויך פּיראַטן.

פּילאָט: איר זײַט אַלע פּיראַטן! ווי אַלט איז די באָבע?

3 וואָקאַבולאַר־איבערבליק

NOTE: Plural forms of nouns taught in the *alef-beys* chapter are listed in the vocabulary overview following that chapter.

א. צאָלווערטער
NUMERALS

verbs		ווערבן
to have	איך האָב, דו האָסט	האָבן [האָבם]
to see	איך זע, מיר זעען	זען

numerals	צאָלווערטער
zero	נול
one	איינס (איין)
two	צוויי
three	דרײַ
four	פֿיר
five	פֿינף
six	זעקס
seven	זיבן [זיבם]
eight	אַכט
nine	נײַן
ten	צען

א. צאָלווערטער (נאָך וואָקאַבולאַר)
NUMBERS (Additional Vocabulary)

mathematics		מאַטעמאַטיק
plus		פלוס
minus		מינוס
times		מאָל
divided by		געטײלט אויף
how many; how much		וויפֿל
together		צוזאַמען

meeting up		טרעפֿן זיך
cell phone		די **מאָבילקע** (ס)
surname	*lit.* family	די **פֿאַמיליע** (ס)
name		דער **נאָמען** (נעמען)
your		דײַן
my		מײַן

דער **אַדרעס** (ן); דער **טעלעפֿאָן־נומער** (ן)

ב. ווײַטערדיקע צאָלווערטער
MORE NUMBERS

numerals		צאָלווערטער
eleven		עלף
twelve		צוועלף
thirteen		דרײַצן
fourteen		פֿערצן
fifteen		פֿופֿצן
sixteen		זעכצן
seventeen		זיבעצן
eighteen		אַכצן
nineteen		נײַנצן
twenty		צוואַנציק
thirty		דרײַסיק
forty		פֿערציק
fifty		פֿופֿציק
sixty		זעכציק
seventy		זיבעציק
eighty		אַכציק
ninety		נײַנציק
(a) hundred	*alt.* one hundred	הונדערט
(a) thousand	*alt.* one thousand	טויזנט

verbs	ווערבן
to be	זײַן

additional vocabulary	נאָך וואָקאַבולאַר
let's	לאָמיר

age	עלטער
how old are you? *(informal)*	ווי אַלט ביסטו?
(formal)	ווי אַלט זײַט איר?
I am ... years old	איך בין אַלט ... יאָר
younger (than)	ייִנגער (פֿון)
older (than)	עלטער (פֿון)
exactly	פּונקט
dancer	דער **טענצער** (ס)
writer	דער **שרײַבער** (ס)

דער **אַסטראָנאָווט** (ן); דער **זינגער** (ס)

3 גראַמאַטיק־איבערבליק

האָבן AND זײַן

- In this chapter, we learned two very useful irregular verbs (conjugated below).
- Irregular forms of **האָבן** are followed by an exclamation point. These forms omit the **ב**- from the stem, so they are conjugated as though the stem were just -**האָ**.

	האָבן	זײַן
איך	האָב	בין
דו	האָסט !	ביסט
ער/זי/עס	האָט !	איז
מיר	האָבן	זײַנען
איר	האָט !	זײַט
זיי	האָבן	זײַנען

WORD ORDER

- When a sentence includes an **object** noun, word order rules become more complex.
- Basic sentence order is subject-verb-object: **די סטודענטקע לייענט אַ בוך**.
- If the first sentence unit is something other than the subject, then the subject appears directly after the verb, *before* the object: **אין הויז לייענט די סטודענטקע אַ בוך**.

! **NOTE:** If an adverb or nonsubject *pronoun* is present in the sentence, this order may change.

COUNTING

- Numbers from 20 to 100 are formed as follows, using the connector **און**:

40 = פֿערציק
41 = איין און פֿערציק
42 = צוויי און פֿערציק

! **NOTE:** When the units digit is 1, the form **איין** is used.

- Numbers from 100 to 1,000 are formed as follows, with the order of units and tens intact:

101 = הונדערט איינס
300 = דרײַ הונדערט
341 = דרײַ הונדערט איין און פֿערציק

! **NOTE:** When the units digit is 1 *and the tens digit is 0*, **איינס** is used.

- Numbers 1,000 and above keep intact the order of all subgroups marked off by a comma:

1,001 = טויזנט איינס
19,000 = נײַנצן טויזנט
19,341 = נײַנצן טויזנט דרײַ הונדערט איין און פֿערציק

! **NOTE:** One hundred and one thousand are simply **הונדערט** and **טויזנט**.

- Names of years from 1100 to 2000 are often rendered differently:

1272 = צוועלף (הונדערט) צוויי און זיבעציק
1600 = זעכצן הונדערט
1860 = אַכצן (הונדערט) זעכציק

! **NOTE:** Some speakers would render these years in the same way as any other number.

איבערחזר־געניטונגען 3

געניטונג 1: וואָס איז דײַן אַדרעס?

Your *goylem* is filling out a scholarship application and must provide the personal information indicated in the table below. Fill out the table and practice saying the numbers aloud as you write them.

נאָמען:	עלטער:
אַדרעס:	שטאָט:
שטאַט/פּראָווינץ:	לאַנד:
טעלעפֿאָן־נומער:	
קרעדיט־קאַרטל־נומער:	
סאָציאַל־פֿאַרזיכערונג־נומער:	
יערלעכע הכנסה:	

age

security

income [האַכנאָסע]

אין קלאַס

Now that you have spent all this time filling out the whole form, it turns out that the financial aid office would rather have the information conveyed over the phone. Find a partner and take turns playing the role of the financial aid officer and one of the *goylem* applicants.

- While playing the role of the aid officer, ask questions to obtain all of the necessary information about your partner's *goylem*.
- Be sure to use appropriate phrases of politeness.

NOTE: When two people greet each other on the phone in Yiddish, each says simply **האַלאָ**. In this way, phone greetings differ from in-person greetings (see **קאַפּיטל 2**).

דוגמא:

א: וואָס איז דײַן אַדרעס?

ב: מײַן אַדרעס איז 15 מיין־גאַס, לערנטאָן, מאַסאַטשוסעטס,
די פֿאַראייניקטע שטאַטן.

געניטונג 2: וואָס טוט דער טאַטע?

טיטל „וואָס טוט דער טאַטע?“
צײַטשריפֿט גרינינקע ביימעלעך

This humorous dialogue originally appeared in the periodical Grininke beymelekh *and was later reprinted in the second volume of the schoolbook* Yidishe kinder*, published by the Workmen's Circle in 1961.* Grininke beymelekh *(Little Green Trees) was one of the first regularly published children's periodicals in Yiddish. First published in Vilnius in 1914, new issues were released until the beginning of the Second World War. The magazine featured poetry and short stories from Yiddish authors, as well as riddles, puzzles, and contributions from young readers.*

Use the word box below to guess which questions the teacher asked to elicit the boy's responses in the following dialogue. Note that some questions may be used more than once.

אַ ייִנגעלע איז געקומען צום ערשטן מאָל אין שול, און דער לערער האָט אים געפֿרעגט:

A little boy came to school for the first time, and the teacher asked him:

— ____________, ייִנגעלע?	
— בערעלע.	
— ________?	
— זיבן יאָר.	
— ________?	
— מײַן טאַטע איז קראַנק.	
— ניין, נישט דאָס מיין איך. איך פֿרעג: ____________?	*that's not what I mean*
— ער הוסט.	coughs
— ניין, נישט דאָס מיין איך. איך וויל וויסן ____________ ווען ער איז געזונט.	*want to know*
— ווען ער איז געזונט, הוסט ער נישט.	
— נאַרעלע, דו פֿאַרשטייסט נישט וואָס מע רעדט צו דיר.	silly; you (*dative*)
זאָג מיר: ____________, ווען ער איז נישט קראַנק, און ער הוסט נישט?	*tell me*
— ווען דער טאַטע איז נישט קראַנק און ער הוסט נישט, — טוט ער זיך אָן און גייט צו דער אַרבעט...	*he gets dressed*

וואָס טוט דײַן טאַטע   ווי אַלט ביסטו   ווי הייסטו

גענײטונג 3: ווער בין איך?

סטודענט א

With a partner, take turns role-playing some of the characters we've met so far. Your partner will work from the corresponding exercise in Appendix A (see page A2).

Each column in the table below pertains to a separate character. Using the model provided, ask your partner questions to fill in the missing information in columns 1 and 2.

- You will need to ask both open-ended (**?פֿון וואַנען קומסטו**) and yes-or-no questions (**?דו ביסט אַ סטודענט**).
- Once your table is complete, answer your partner's questions according to the information in columns 3 and 4.
- Be sure to use the pronoun provided at the top of each column when asking or answering the corresponding questions.

דוגמא:

א: דו ביסט אַ סטודענטקע?

ב: ניין, איך בין אַ סטודענט.

א: פֿון וואַנען קומסטו?

ב: איך קום פֿון ישׂראל.

[...]

א: דו הייסט ________!

ב: אַ יישר־כּוח[1]!

אָדער

ב: ניין, פּרוּוו[2] נאָך אַ מאָל[3].

[1] *well done!* [יאַשער־קויעך]

[2] try; [3] *again*

	1. (דו)	2. (איר)	3. (מיר)	4. (איך)
זײַן	אַ סטודענט		קינדער	אַ סטודענטקע
קומען	פֿון ישׂראל		פֿון די פֿאַראייניקטע שטאַטן	פֿון פּוילן
רעדן			ייִדיש און ענגליש	ענגליש, פּויליש, און פֿראַנצייזיש
וווינען			אין ניו־יאָרק	אין לערנטאָן
האָבן			אַ צימער אין אַ דירה	אַ צימער אין אינטערנאַט
זײַן			5 און 10 יאָר אַלט	23 יאָר אַלט
הייסן			חיה און פּערל	עלקע

געניטונג 4: אין וועלכן לאַנד גייט דער עולם אַמערסטן אין „די מוּוויס“?

הער־געניטונג
איבערחזר־סעקציע־4

טיטל — **„די ייִדישע שטונדע“** (פֿראַגמענט)

דיקטאָרן (announcers) — **ציליע זילבער (Celia Zuckerberg Silver)**

(כעלעם, רוסישע אימפּעריע 1905 – לאָס־אַנדזשעלעס, פֿאַראייניקטע שטאַטן 1997)

זלמן זילבערצווײַג (Zalmen Zylbercweig)

(אָזערקעוו, רוסישע אימפּעריע 1894 – לאָס־אַנדזשעלעס, פֿאַראייניקטע שטאַטן 1972)

רעקאָרדירונג — 1969, פֿאַראייניקטע שטאַטן

Practice numbers with this excerpt from the radio show *Di yidishe shtunde,* which you can find online with its accompanying exercise.

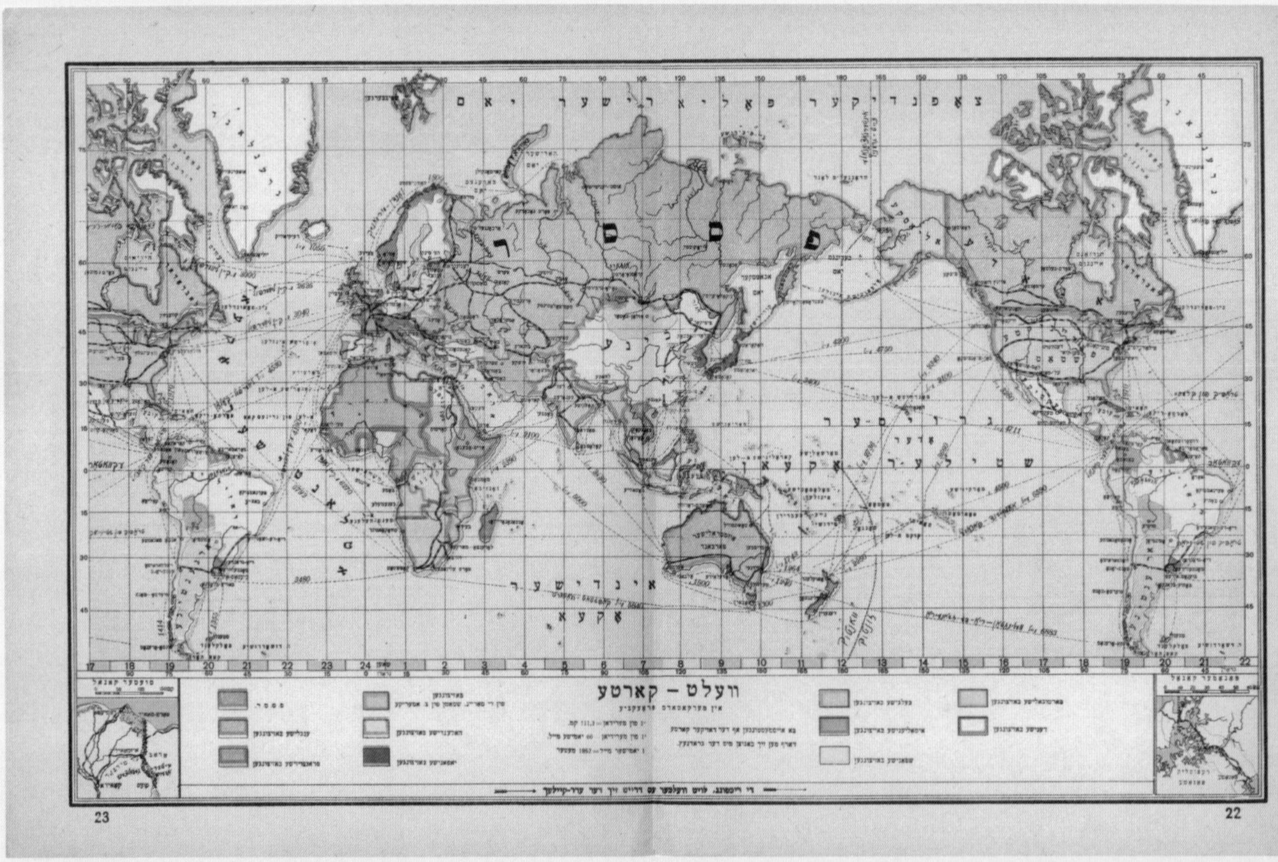

(פֿון „געאָגראַפֿישער אַטלאַס“, 1928)

4

קאַפּיטל פּיר:
שבת

CHAPTER GOALS

- In this chapter, you will learn how to talk about Shabbos.

װאָקאַבולאַר:	
Shabbos	שבת

קולטור — אױדיאָ:	
"Sholem-aleykhem" (Sholem Berenstein)	„שלום־עליכם" (שלום בערנשטײן)
"*Melave-malke* Song" (folk song)	„מלװה־מלכּה־ליד" (פֿאָלקסליד)

איבערחזר־געניטונגען:

קולטור — טעקסט:	
"Sholem Aleichem" *(Argentiner beymelekh)*	„שלום־עליכם" (אַרגענטינער בײמעלעך)

קולטור — בילד:	
Friday Night (Isidor Kaufmann)	„דאָס שטילע געבעט אָדער פֿרײַטיק אין אָװנט" (איסידאָר קאַופֿמאַן)

א קולטור: שבת

קולטור
CULTURE

__1__ הײַנט איז שבת, אַ טאָג פֿון רו. — today; day; rest

____ די שבת־ליכט ברענען.

____ נאָך שבת מאַכט מען הבֿדלה. — after; [האַוודאָלע]

____ הײַנט אַרבעט מען נישט!

____ מען עסט אַ גרויסע סעודה — [סודע]
מיט פֿלייש און פֿיש און — [כאַלע]
געשמאַקע מאכלים. — delicious dishes [מײַכאָלים]

____ מע וואַשט זיך די הענט און
מען עסט חלה.

____ מע מאַכט קידוש אויף װײַן. — [קידעש]

געניטונג 1: שבת — אַ טאָג פֿון רו

Perl talks about Shabbos—the day of rest. Listen to the recording and number the sentences on the preceding page from 1 to 7 in the order you hear them spoken.

- Pay special attention to the words highlighted in purple. You will be able to determine their meanings by looking at the illustrations.

הער־געניטונג א־1

קולטור
CULTURE

! גערעדנקט!

The word **שבת** is both a noun (*Shabbos; Saturday*) and an adverb (*on Shabbos; on Saturday*).

געניטונג 2: שבת אין דער אַלטער היים

It's *shabes* in the *shtetl*. Based on the images above, match each person below with the action they are performing.

1. דער טאַטע ___ב___
2. דאָס מיידל ___
3. דאָס ייִנגל ___
4. די משפּחה ___
5. די מאַמע ___

א. עסט חלה.
ב. מאַכט קידוש.
ג. וואַשט זיך.
ד. בענטשט ליכט.
ה. עסט די סעודה.

דאָס ייִנגל		boy
די משפּחה	[מישפּאָכע]	family
בענטשן		to bless

געניטונג 3: שלום־עליכם

הער־געניטונג א־3

קולטור
CULTURE

טיטל	♫ **„שלום־עליכם“** (פֿראַגמענט) פֿון „מאַגאַזין פֿון יודישע לידער פֿאַר דעם יודישען פֿאָלק“ (1869)
פּאָעט	**שלום בערנשטיין (Sholem Berenstein)** (קאָמעניץ־פּאָדאָלסק, רוסישע אימפּעריע ? – ?)
קאָמפּאָזיטאָר	**מיכל געלבאַרט (Mikhl Gelbart)** (אָזערקעוו, רוסישע אימפּעריע 1889 – ניו־יאָרק, פֿאַראייניקטע שטאַטן 1962)
זינגער	**אַרקאַדי גענדלער (Arkady Gendler)** (סאָראָקע, רומעניע 1921 – זאַפּאָראָזשע, אוקראַיִנע 2017)
רעקאָרדירונג	2001, אוקראַיִנע

"Sholem-aleykhem" *takes its name (though not its text) from a Hebrew song traditionally sung on Shabbos before the Friday night meal. Both songs draw on the belief that a person returning home from synagogue on Friday night is accompanied by two angels, who must be received with proper ceremony.*

The text was published in 1869 by Yiddish poet **Sholem Berenstein**. *The music was written by* **Mikhl Gelbart**, *a prolific composer and arranger of Yiddish songs. Upon settling in the United States, Gelbart also served as a voice teacher at the Workmen's Circle.*

In this recording, we hear the voice of Yiddish folksinger **Arkady Gendler**. *A native of Bessarabia (present-day Moldova), Gendler performed in the folk idiom of his childhood and innovated within the same tradition in crafting his own compositions.*

לייענט די פֿראַגעס אונטן איידער איר הערט זיך צו צום ליד. זיי וועלן אײַך העלפֿן פֿאַרשטיין דעם טעקסט.

Read the questions below before you listen to the song. They will help you understand the text.

1. וועמען באַגריסט מען אין דעם ליד? — *who is greeted*
2. וואָסער טאָג איז הײַנט? — today

הערט זיך צו צום ליד, נאָר קוקט נישט אויפֿן טעקסט. ענטפֿערט אויף די פֿראַגעס אויבן.

Listen to the recording, but don't look at the text. Answer the questions above. Now play the recording again and follow along with the text.

שלום־עליכם, מלאָכים מײַנע,	*angels mine* [מאַלאָכים]
שלום־עליכם, מלאָכים פֿײַנע!	
שלום־עליכם, ווײַב און קינד,	wife
שבת קודש איז אַצינד.	*(the) holy Shabbos* [קוידעש]; now
שלום־עליכם, גוטע פֿרײַנד,	
שבת קודש איז דאָך הײַנט!	
שלום־עליכם, זיידעס, באָבעס,	
שלום־עליכם, אַ גוטן שבת!	

געניטונג 4: אַ גוטע וואָך

הער־געניטונג א־4

טיטל	♫ „מלווה־מלכּה־ליד“ (פֿראַגמענט)
	פֿאָלקסליד
קאָמפּאָזיטאָר	**גרשון איַיזנבערג (Gershon Eisenberg)** [גערשן]
זינגער	**לאָרין סקלאַמבערג (Lorin Sklamberg)**
	(לאָס־אַנדזשעלעס, פֿאַראייניקטע שטאַטן 1956 –)
רעקאָרדירונג	2002, פֿאַראייניקטע שטאַטן

קולטור
CULTURE

This folk song is traditionally sung at **מלווה־מלכּה** *(lit. escorting the queen [מעלאַווע־מאַלקע]), the ceremonial feast held on Saturday evening (chiefly among Hasidim) to mark the departure of the queenly Shabbos. As the text of "A gute vokh" suggests,* **מלווה־מלכּה** *is a lively event, often accompanied by song and dance.*

This recording features **Lorin Sklamberg**, *a Yiddish singer, instrumentalist, and cofounder of The Klezmatics, a Grammy Award–winning American klezmer group, performing an arrangement by* **Gershon Eisenberg**.

Listen to the excerpt once with your book closed. Now play the recording again and follow along with the text below.

אַ גוטע וואָך, אַ געזונטע וואָך	
אוי, ווינטשן מיר צו אַלע ייִדן	wish
און צו אַלע פֿײַנע, גוטע חסידים	Hasidim [כסידים] (*pl*)
וועלכע זײַנען אַלע דאָ.	which; here
געזונט זאָלן מיר זײַן	may
טרינקען וועלן מיר ווײַן (2 מאָל)	will
ביז אין ווײַסן טאָג אַרײַן.	*until dawn* (lit. *until the white day*)

ריכטיק אָדער פֿאַלש?

1. מע זינגט אַזאַ ליד נאָך הבֿדלה.	such a
2. מע זינגט וועגן טרינקען קאַווע.	about
3. די פֿײַנע, גוטע חסידים זײַנען דאָ.	
4. מע זאָל נישט זײַן קראַנק.	
5. מע טרינקט ביז אָוונט.	*until evening*

4 וואָקאַבולאַר־איבערבליק

שבת
SHABBOS

to work	**אַרבעטן**
to bless	**בענטשן**
today	**הײַנט**
during Shabbos; on Saturday	**שבת**
Havdalah	די **הבֿדלה** (–ות) [האַוודאָלע(ס)]
week	די **וואָך** (ן)
challah	די **חלה** (–ות) [כאַלע(ס)]
family	די **משפּחה** (–ות) [מישפּאָכע(ס)]
festive meal; feast	די **סעודה** (–ות) [סודע(ס)]
rest	די **רו**
wine	דער **ווײַן** (ען)
kiddush	דער **קידוש**
Shabbos	דער **שבת** (ים) [שאַבעס (שאַבאָסים)]
boy	דאָס **ייִנגל** (עך)
girl	דאָס **מיידל** (עך)
Shabbos candle	דאָס **שבת־ליכט** (—)

greetings	ענטפֿערס	באַגריסונגען
good Shabbos	גוט־שבת, גוט־יאָר	גוט־שבת
good evening (*after Havdalah*)	גוט־וואָך, גוט־יאָר	גוט־וואָך

farewells	ענטפֿערס	געזעגענונגען
(have a) good Shabbos	אַ גוט יאָר	אַ גוטן שבת
(have a) good week	אַ גוט יאָר	אַ גוטע וואָך

איבערחזר־געניטונגען: טעמע איינס

געניטונג 1: באַשרײַבט די בילדער

טיטל ,,דאָס שטילע געבעט אָדער פֿרײַטיק אין אָוונט‘‘ (1897–1898)

קינסטלער (artist) **איסידאָר קאַופֿמאַן (Isidor Kaufmann)**

(אַראַד, אונגערן 1853 – ווין, עסטרײַך 1921)

The paintings of **Isidor Kaufmann** *were widely popular among the bourgeoisie of fin-de-siècle Vienna. In his work, Kaufmann fashioned an idealized image of the* Ostjuden*—the Yiddish-speaking Jews of Eastern Europe—whose lives were depicted as simple and suffused with religious piety and tradition. Kaufmann also designed a "Sabbath room" for Vienna's Jewish Museum in 1899, filling it with religious artifacts that he had collected on his travels throughout the region.*

Spend two minutes writing as many sentences as you can about the painting above. Write about what the woman is doing and what possessions she has (look on the table). Invent some details about her life: her name, how old she is, where she comes from, etc.

- Use Shabbos vocabulary from the previous chapter, as well as verbs presented in **קאַפּיטל 2**.

דוגמא: די פֿרוי איז אַלט זיבן און דרײַסיק יאָר. זי אַרבעט נישט און זי איז זייער מיד.

גענ׳יטונג 2: פֿון אַרכיוו

טיטל	„שלום־עליכם: אילוסטרירטע ביאָגראַפֿיע“
צײַטשריפֿט	**אַרגענטינער בײמעלעך**
	(בוענאָס אײַרעס, מאַרץ־אַפּריל 1959)

Argentiner beymelekh, *or, as it was known in Spanish,* Arbolitos argentinos, *was an illustrated children's monthly published in Buenos Aires and read by Yiddish-speaking children the world over. This pictorial timeline of the life of preeminent Yiddish writer Sholem Aleichem appears in an issue of the magazine dedicated to him.*

ארגענטינער ביימעלעך — זייט 5

שלום עליכם — אילוסטרירטע ביאָגראַפיע

שלום עליכם איז געבוירן געוואָרן דעם 18־טן פעברואַר 1859, אין פּע־רעיאַסלעוו, אוקראַינע. זיינע קינדער יאָרן האָט ער פאַרבראַכט אין דעם שטעטל וואָראָנקע.

אין 1876 האָט ער פאַרענדיקט די רוסישע שול און געגעבן רוסישע לעקציעס. אין 1879 האָט ער אָנגע־הויבן צו שרייבן אין אַ העברעי־שער צייטונג.

אין 1883 האָט ער חתונה געהאַט. אין 1884 האָט ער אָנגעשריבן זיין ערשטע קינדער־דערציילונג „דאָס מעסערל". פון דאַן האָט ער אַלץ געשריבן אויף יידיש.

אין 1903 האָט ער זיך פאַרבונדן מיט די באַרימטע רוסישע שרייבער גאָרקי, טאָלסטאָי און אַנדערע וועגן דעם זאַמלבוך „הילף" פאַר די פּאָ־גראָמירטע יידן.

אין 1906 איז ער געקומען דאָס ערשטע מאָל קיין אַמעריקע. דאָן האָט ער אָנגעשריבן זיינע ערשטע מעשיות פון „מאָטל פּייסי דעם חזנס".

אין 1908 איז איבער דער גאַנצער וועלט געפייערט געוואָרן זיין 25־יאָ־ריקער ליטעראַרישער יובילײ.

פון 1908 ביז 1912 האָט ער צר־ליב זיין געזונט געוווינט אין נערווי, איטאַליע, און אין פאַרשיידענע סאַ־נאַטאָריומס אין אַנדערע לענדער.

אין 1914 באַזעצט ער זיך אין ניו־יאָרק. אין 1916 ווערט ער זייער קראַנק. ליגנדיק אין בעט שרייבט ער „פונעם יאַריד". ער איז געשטאָרבן דעם 13־טן מאַי.

איצט פייערט די גאַנצע וועלט זיין 100־סטן געבורטסטאָג. יידישע קינ־דער אין יידישע שולן איבער דער גאַנצער וועלט לייענען אים און פרייען זיך מיט אים.

NOTE:

The past tense—used repeatedly in this biography—is composed of two parts:

פֿון דאַן האָט ער אַלץ געשריבן אויף ייִדיש.

אין 1906 איז ער געקומען דאָס ערשטע מאָל קיין אַמעריקע.

The first part is a **helping verb**, which functions only to signal the past tense. The second part, which carries the *meaning* of the verb, is called the **past participle**. Remove the prefix **-גע**: do you recognize the underlying verb? Can you find any other familiar verbs hiding in past participles in the text? We will learn more about the past tense in **17 קאַפּיטל**.

NOTE:

A higher-resolution copy of this image may be found on the textbook website. If you find the font here to be too small, please refer to the online version.

◀ CONTINUED

CONTINUED

Read the biography while looking at the pictures. As you read the text, underline any familiar words.

- Don't worry about words (or even entire sentences) that you don't understand. You will still be able to complete the exercise.
- Note that the events of the timeline proceed from right to left.

Now read the list of statements about Sholem Aleichem's life below. Number them according to the order in which the events took place, based on what you learned from the biography.

- Look for keywords in the biography that match words in the sentences below.

שלום־עליכם האָט חתונה.	____	*marries* [כאַסענע]
ער אַרבעט מיט רוסישע שרײַבער: גאָרקי, טאָלסטאָי, און אַנדערע.	____	others
ער אַרבעט ווי אַ לערער פֿון רוסיש.	____	
ער שרײַבט, אויף ייִדיש, אַ קינדער־דערציילונג („דאָס מעסערל“).	____	story; little knife
שלום־עליכם ווערט געבוירן אין פֿעברואַר אין פּערעיאַסלעוו, אוקראַיִנע.	1	*is born*
ער איז זייער קראַנק. ער ליגט אין בעט און שרײַבט „פֿונעם יאַריד“. ער שטאַרבט אין מאַי.	____	*from the fair* / dies
ער קומט קיין אַמעריקע און שרײַבט „מאָטל פּייסי דעם חזנס“.	____	*Peysi the cantor's (son)* [כאַזנס]
עס איז שלום־עליכמס הונדערטסטער געבורטסטאָג.	____	birthday
עס איז פֿינף און צוואַנציק יאָר זינט שלום־עליכמס ליטעראַרישן דעביוט.	____	
ער וווינט אין איטאַליע און אין סאַנאַטאָריומס אין אַנדערע לענדער.	____	
ער שרײַבט אין אַ העברעיִשער צײַטונג.	____	newspaper
ער וווינט אין ניו־יאָרק.	____	

Determine which year each event took place, based on the text.

- Write out the year in Yiddish characters next to the sentence it corresponds to.

(from... until...) (פֿון... ביז...)

דוגמא: שלום־עליכם ווערט געבוירן אין פֿעברואַר אין פּערעיאַסלעוו, אוקראַיִנע.

טויזנט אַכט הונדערט נײַן און פֿופֿציק.

איצט, ענטפֿערט אויף די פֿראַגעס אונטן.

- Every answer should contain a number in it, fully written out.

1. ווי אַלט איז שלום־עליכם ווען ער האָט חתונה?
2. ווען שרײַבט שלום־עליכם די ווערטער „אַ מענטש איז דאָס וואָס ער וויל זײַן“? — person; wants
3. פֿאַר וואָס פּובליקירט מען אַ נומער „אַרגענטינער ביימעלעך“ לכּבוד שלום־עליכם גראָד אין 1959? — issue; in honor of [לעקאָוועד]; precisely

טעמע II:
אין קלאַס

UNIT GOALS

- In this unit, you will learn to talk about the classroom: both the objects that can be found within it and the activities that take place there.
- The holidays covered in this unit are the *yomim-neroim,* or High Holy Days (Rosh Hashanah, Yom Kippur, and the days between).

אינהאַלט:

קאַפּיטל פֿינף:
דער קלאַסצימער; אימפּעראַטיוו און קאָנווערבן

5

CHAPTER GOALS

- In this chapter, you will learn how to talk about your classroom and the objects in it (and their colors), and how to give commands; you will also learn verbs commonly used in the classroom.

וואָקאַבולאַר:	
classroom objects	קלאַסצימער־אָביעקטן
colors	קאָלירן
everyday verbs	טאָג־טעגלעכע ווערבן

גראַמאַטיק:	
the diminutive	דימינוטיוו
nouns (plurals)	סובסטאַנטיוון (מערצאָל)
commands (the imperative)	באַפֿעלן (אימפּעראַטיוו)
verbs with separable prefixes	ווערבן מיט קאָנווערבן

קולטור — ווידעאָ:	
“Snow and Herring” (Benjamin Harshav)	„שניי און הערינג“ (בנימין הרשב)

א וואָקאַבולאַר:
דער קלאַסצימער און קאָלירן

גענִיטונג 1: וואָס איז דאָס?

Examine the labeled classroom objects and features of Professor Kluger's classroom in the picture above. Write a few sentences about the size of the objects, as in the example.

- Be sure to use the correct definite article.

דוגמא: *די העפֿט איז קליין.*

גרויס	big
קליין	small

געדענקט!

The font color of each noun in the illustration corresponds to the noun's grammatical gender. Feminine nouns are purple, masculine nouns are green, and neuter nouns are blue.

אין קלאַס

Take turns pointing at different objects in your own classroom, and ask your partner questions based on the model below.

- Be sure to use the correct definite article for each noun, according to the image above.

דוגמא:

א: וואָס איז דאָס?

ב: דאָס איז אַ העפֿט!

א: די העפֿט איז קליין.

געדענקט!

Though the article preceding each *noun* may differ, the phrases **דאָס איז** and **וואָס איז דאָס** always use the neutral **דאָס**. In these phrases, **דאָס** functions as a **demonstrative pronoun** (e.g., *this, that*), referring to the unidentified item that is about to be named.

געניטונג 2: מיט וואָס שרײַבט מען?

ענטפֿערט אויף די פֿראַגעס אונטן. שרײַבט גאַנצע זאַצן. ניצט דעם אומבאַשטימטן אַרטיקל.

Write full sentences. Use the indefinite article.

- For questions 1–4, your answers will begin with the pronoun **מע**.
- For questions 5 and 6, use the subject nouns **דער לערער** and **די סטודענטן** instead.

דוגמא: מיט וואָס שרײַבט מען?

מע שרײַבט מיט אַ בלײַער.

1. מיט וואָס שרײַבט מען? (צוויי ענטפֿערס).
2. וואָס לייענט מען? (צוויי ענטפֿערס).
3. אויף וואָס זיצט מען?
4. אויף וואָס שטייט מען?
5. אויף וואָס שרײַבט דער לערער?
6. אויף וואָס אָדער אין וואָס שרײַבן די סטודענטן? (צוויי ענטפֿערס)

NOTE:

The preposition **מיט** (*with*) appears as part of the question phrase **מיט וואָס** (*with what*) at the beginning of the question. In the answer, **מיט** appears in the middle, in the prepositional phrase **מיט אַ בלײַער** (*with a pencil*). The same applies to the prepositions **אויף** and **אין** in questions 3–6.

געניטונג 3: וואָסער קאָליר?

לייענט די נעמען פֿון די קאָלירן אויפֿן בילד און ענטפֿערט אויף די פֿראַגעס אונטן. שרײַבט גאַנצע זאַצן. פֿאַרגעסט נישט צו ניצן דעם ריכטיקן אַרטיקל.

Don't forget to use the correct article.

דוגמא: וואָס איז בלוי?

דאָס בענקל איז בלוי.

1. וואָס איז ווײַס?
2. וואָס איז לילאַ?
3. וואָס איז אָראַנזש?
4. וואָס איז ראָזעווע?

דוגמא: וואָסער קאָליר האָט די פֿעדער?

די פֿעדער איז שוואַרץ.

5. וואָסער קאָליר האָט דאָס בוך?
6. וואָסער קאָליר האָט די טיר?
7. וואָסער קאָליר האָט דער בלײַער?
8. וואָסער קאָליר האָט דער טיש?

NOTE:

The question ...וואָסער קאָליר האָט is an example of idiomatic phrasing: there is no simple way to predict that the verb here will be האָבן. Note also that the *response* uses a different verb than the question does: די פֿעדער איז שוואַרץ.

געניטונג 4: אַ שניימענטש איז ווײַס

דוגמא. ____________

1. ____________

2. ____________

3. ____________

4. ____________

5. ____________

וואָסער קאָליר האָבן די אָביעקטן אויבן? ענטפֿערט אויף די פֿראַגעס אונטן, לויט דער דוגמא.

דוגמא: אַ שניימענטש איז בלוי?

ניין, אַ שניימענטש איז נישט בלוי.

אַ שניימענטש איז ווײַס.

1. אַן עפּל איז לילאַ?
2. אַ רויז איז שוואַרץ?
3. די זון איז גרין?
4. בלעטלעך זײַנען ווײַס? leaves
5. וואַסער איז רויט?

NOTE:

So far, we have negated only verbs (**איך לויף נישט**). Adjectival statements are negated in much the same way, by adding **נישט** after the verb: **דאָס איז נישט בלוי.**

NOTE:

The definite article is used when referring to a specific entity (e.g., *the* sun); an indefinite article is used when the reference is general (e.g., *an* apple ~ any apple). The indefinite article is sometimes “invisible”: in the plural (**בלעטלעך**) or before an uncountable noun (**וואַסער**).

געניטונג 5: דער לאָמפּ איז געל

וואָס איז דאָס?

- ענטפֿערט לויט דער דוגמא.

דוגמא: דאָס איז אַ לאָמפּ.

.1 ______

.2 ______

.3 ______

.4 ______

.5 ______

.6 ______

וואָסער קאָליר האָבן די קלאַסצימער־אָביעקטן?

- שרײַבט אָן איין פֿראַגע וועגן יעדער אָביעקט אויבן, לויט דער דוגמא. ניצט דעם פּאַסיקן באַשטימטן אַרטיקל.
- *Write one question about each object above, according to the example. Use the appropriate definite article.*

דוגמא:

וואָסער קאָליר האָט דער לאָמפּ?

ענטפֿערט אויף די פֿראַגעס, לויט דער דוגמא.

- ניצט דעם פּאַסיקן פּראָנאָם פֿאַר יעדער סובסטאַנטיוו, לויט זײַן גראַמאַטישן מין.
- *Use the appropriate pronoun for each noun, according to its grammatical gender.*

דוגמא:

וואָסער קאָליר האָט דער לאָמפּ?

ער איז געל.

! געדענקט!

The personal pronouns **ער**, **זי**, and **עס** reflect the gender of the nouns they replace. For example, **ער** refers to **דער לאָמפּ** because the grammatical gender of **לאָמפּ** is masculine.

געניטונג 6: וואָס ווילסטו?

רחל און פּערל זײַנען אין אַ קראָם. store

Perl doesn't want to buy what her mother suggests.

- For each of Rokhl's suggestions, write Perl's negative response, using the color provided in parentheses. Be sure to use the appropriate pronoun and verb for each noun.
- Then add Rokhl's exasperated restatement of her daughter's desires, as in the example.

NOTE:

In her questions, Rokhl uses **די** and **דאָס** as **demonstrative articles**:

Do you want *this* watch?
ווילסט דאָס זייגערל?

In writing, it is often only the context that distinguishes demonstrative articles from plain definite articles (which are spelled identically). In speech, you can tell the difference by listening to intonation: demonstrative articles are emphasized, while definite articles are not.

דוגמא:

רחל: ווילסט דאָס זייגערל? (רויט)

פּערל: ניין, עס איז נישט רויט.

רחל: ווילסט אַ זייגערל וואָס איז רויט.

1. **רחל:** ווילסט די העפּט? (שוואַרץ)
2. **רחל:** ווילסט דאָס בוך? (גרין)
3. **רחל:** ווילסט די מעקערס? (ווײַס)
4. **רחל:** ווילסט די בלײַערס? (געל)
5. **רחל:** ווילסט די בלעטלעך? (ראָזעווע)

וואָס איז	that is
וואָס זײַנען	that are

געניטונג 7: בערעלע, בערל, בער

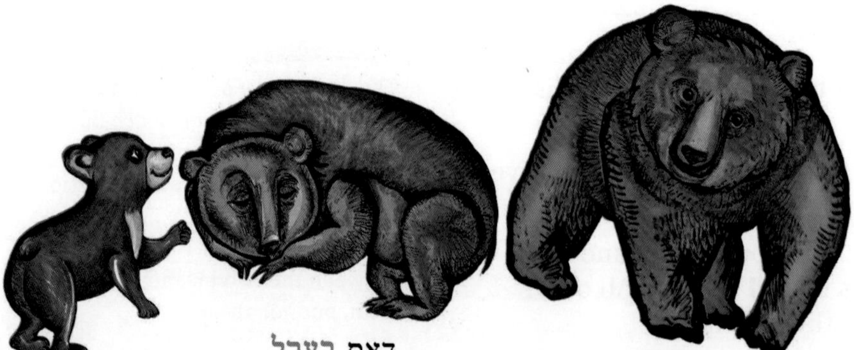

דאָס בערעלע
דאָס בערל
דער בער

אין אַ הויז נישט ווײַט פֿון לערנטאָן וווינט אַ משפּחה בערן: טאַטע־בער, מאַמע־בער, און צוויי קינדער: בערל און בערעלע.

family [מישפּאָכע]

◀ CONTINUED

CONTINUED

בערל גייט אין קינדער־גאָרטן. וואָס ברענגט ער מיט? along

Since Berl is a young bear, his school supplies are miniature. There is a special grammatical form for this, called the **diminutive**. Match each word with the image to which it corresponds.

- Each word below is the diminutive form of a word you know.

א. דאָס רוקזעקל
ב. דאָס שערל
ג. דאָס העפֿטל
ד. דאָס ביכל
ה. דאָס באַרל

1. __________

2. __________

3. __________

4. __________

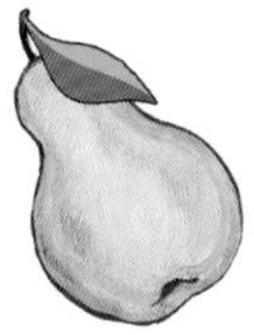
5. __________

Berl, ever the helpful son, spends the morning filling his mom's work bag with grown-up-sized versions of the school supplies listed above. Write a list of these nondiminutive nouns, as in the example below.

דוגמא: דער רוקזאַק

Compare the two sets of words, diminutive and nondiminutive.

- What is the most consistent difference between a diminutive and its nondiminutive root? Are there other shifts?
- What about the definite article? Is it the same for both forms? What does this tell us about the grammatical gender of diminutives?

In the right column below, Berl is imagining what his mom must be doing at work. In the left column he describes what he is doing at school.

Complete the sentences in the left column with the diminutive forms of the nouns in the right column, as in the model.

- Note the words **באַנק** and **בלאַט** below: you already know their (irregular) diminutive forms from **1 געניטונג**. All other diminutives here are regular, like the example.

דוגמא:

די מאַמע עסט אַ באַר.	איך עס אַ בערל.
1. זי עפֿנט די טיר. (opens)	1. איך עפֿן דאָס __________.
2. זי זינגט אַ ליד.	2. איך זינג אַ __________.
3. זי זיצט אויף אַ באַנק. (bench)	3. איך זיץ אויף אַ __________.
4. זי אַרבעט בײַ אַ טיש.	4. איך אַרבעט בײַ אַ __________.
5. זי שרײַבט אויף אַ בלאַט.	5. איך שרײַב אויף אַ __________.
6. זי שלאָפֿט אין אַ בעט.	6. איך שלאָף אין אַ __________.

NOTE:

Sometimes the diminutive form may have a different vowel sound than the root word. The shifts present in the above forms are the following:
אַ ← ע (רוקזאַק ← רוקזעקל; קאַץ ← קעצל)
ו ← י (בוך ← ביכל; הונט ← הינטל)

These are just common patterns, *not rules*. For example, **באַר** retains its vowel and becomes **באַרל**.

NOTE:

The diminutive of **באַנק** (**בענקל**) means not only *small bench* but also has the distinct meaning of *chair*. Diminutives often acquire additional meanings this way (e.g., **קאַץ → קעצל**, *small cat* or *kitten*). The connection between the two meanings is usually clear, but not always.

געניטונג 8: דער אימינוטיוו

Berl and his little brother, Berele, have mixed up their school supplies. Berele is in preschool, where everything is even tinier than at kindergarten, so the things that belong to him will be in the **iminutive**, another diminutive form (modeled below) that expresses yet another degree of smallness.

Help Berl and Berele's dad sort out whose supplies are whose. Label all of Berele's things with the appropriate iminutive form, as in the example.

- Be sure to preserve all vowel changes already present in the diminutive.
- All diminutives (iminutives included) are neuter. Here, this means they take the article **דאָס**.

NOTE:

Some nouns have only one diminutive form. Depending on the form of the base noun itself, this lone diminutive may end either with **ל–** or **עלע–**. For example:

דער טאָוול ← דאָס טעוועלע

דער בלײַער ← דאָס בלײַערל

Note that not all nouns that end in a syllabic lamed are diminutive (e.g., **טאָוול**).

NOTE:

Though we are using the diminutive here purely as a descriptor of relative size, it has other uses and meanings: it can express endearment, triviality or cuteness, or even scorn.

דאָס רוקזעקעלע

געניטונג 9: מערצאָל

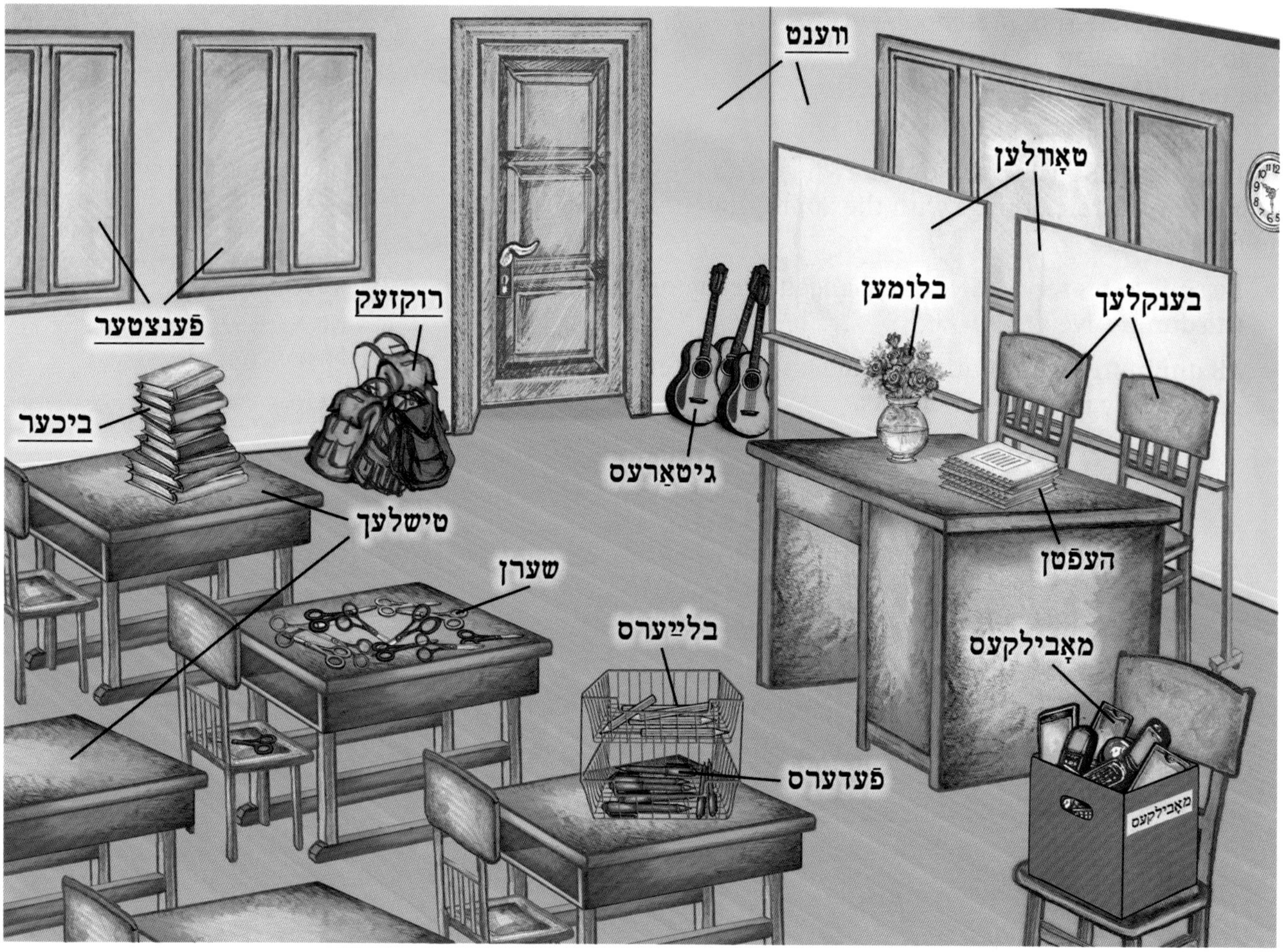

picture ענטפֿערט אויף די פֿראַגעס אונטן, לויטן בילד.

- Your answers to questions 1–5 should all begin with **זיי זײַנען**.

דוגמא:

וואָסער קאָליר האָבן די העפֿטן?

זיי זײַנען גרין, בלוי, און געל.

1. וואָסער קאָליר האָבן די טאָוולען?
2. וואָסער קאָליר האָבן די גיטאַרעס?
3. וואָסער קאָליר האָבן די בלײַערס?
4. וואָסער קאָליר האָבן די בענקלעך?
5. וואָסער קאָליר האָבן די ווענט?

דוגמא:

וואָס **איז דאָ** אונטער די בלײַערס? *is there*

די פֿעדערס.

6. וואָס איז דאָ בײַ דער טיר?
7. וואָס איז דאָ אויפֿן בענקל?
8. וואָס איז דאָ אויפֿן טישל?
9. וואָס איז דאָ אויפֿן לערערס טיש?
10. וואָס איז דאָ אין די ווענט?

NOTE:

Just as the preposition **אויף** is pronounced [אַף], so is the contraction **אויפֿן** (= **אויף + דעם**) pronounced [אַפֿן].

◀ CONTINUED

CONTINUED

Ignore, for the moment, the four underlined nouns. Focusing on the other nouns, answer the following questions.

- How do the words for these objects change in the plural? What patterns can you find?
- How does the definite article change between singular and plural? (You can find plural nouns with their definite articles in questions 1–5.)
- When one of these plural nouns is replaced by a pronoun, what pronoun is it?

The endings ן- and ען- are alternate forms of the same plural suffix (the default suffix used when no other special pattern applies). The ען- form appears when the singular form of the noun meets one of the following criteria:

- Ends in נג- or נק-.
- Ends in a syllabic ל- and is *not* a diminutive.
- Carries stress on its final syllable and ends in ם-, ן-, or a vowel or diphthong.

Among the words you already know, find at least one belonging to each of these three categories.

NOTE:

If a vowel change occurs in the *plural* form of a noun, the same change will—with very few exceptions—also be present in the diminutive (ביכער → ביכל). The reverse is not always true (בלימל but בלומען).

Now consider the four underlined plural nouns in the illustration.

- How do they differ from their singular counterparts? Describe each difference.
- What patterns do you notice? Divide the words into two or three categories.

The sentences below differ in the type of article used: definite or indefinite, singular or plural. How does the use of one or another type of article affect the meaning of the sentence?

	Plural	Singular
Indefinite	מענדעלע שרײַבט ביכער.	דו ברענגסט אַן עפּעלע.
Definite	איך לייען די ביכער וואָס מענדעלע שרײַבט.	איך עס דאָס עפּעלע וואָס דו ברענגסט.

We know the definite article always becomes די in the plural. What happens to the *indefinite* article in the plural?

געניטונג 10: דאָס זײַנען לאָמפּן

The stationery store pictured above sells some unusual items. Ask your partner questions about the items, according to the model. Label the picture with their responses.

- Since these are indefinite plural nouns, they appear *without* articles.

דוגמא:

א: וואָס איז דאָס?

ב: <u>דאָס זײַנען</u> לאָמפּן.

דאָס זײַנען... those are...

היימאַרבעט

שרײַבט אָן עטלעכע זאַצן, לויט דער דוגמא.

Write several sentences, according to the example.

דוגמא:

די לאָמפּן זײַנען אָראַנזש.

ב וואָקאַבולאַר און גראַמאַטיק:
קלאַסצימער־ווערבן; אימפּעראַטיוו

טאַנצט!

עסט!

זינג!

שפּרינגט!

שלאָף!

טרינק!

געניטונג 1: די מאַמע זאָגט...

Rokhl is trying to keep Khaye and Perl occupied on a long, rainy weekend day. Examine Rokhl's use of the **imperative** as she tells Khaye and Perl what to do.

- What changes when Rokhl is addressing *both* children rather than just one of them?
- Compare each *singular* imperative form to the present-tense conjugations of the verb being used. Can you find a match? Do the same for the plural imperative forms.
- Each of the captions above is a full sentence. Compare these to the simple, two-word sentences of **קאַפּיטל 2**. What part of the sentence is missing?

NOTE:

The plural imperative form shown here also functions as the singular formal, just like the second-person plural and singular formal (both **איר**) in the present tense.

געניטונג 2: שפּרינגט נישט!

By evening, Khaye and Perl have gotten tired and are no longer such model children. Follow the prompts below to write out the things Rokhl must tell them *not* to do, as in the example.

- Use verbs from the word box provided, conjugated for the imperative.
- Note the placement of **נישט** in the example.
- Be sure you know why you are using the singular or plural form.
- Remember: these sentences will lack a grammatical subject.

דוגמא: (אויפֿן בעט)

שפּרינגט נישט!

1. (אויפֿן טיש)
2. (אין הויז)
3. (אויפֿן דיל)
4. (אויף דער וואַנט)
5. (ווען דו עסט)

שפּרינגען	שלאָפֿן	זינגען
שרײַבן	זיצן	לויפֿן

געניטונג 3: וואָס טוען זיי?

וואָס טוען די סטודענטן? ענטפֿערט אויף די פֿראַגעס אונטן, לויטן בילד.

- Use the third-person form of each verb, as in the example. All verbs here are regular.
- Use only the indefinite article, and make sure to use **אויף** where necessary.

דוגמא: וואָס טוט משה?
ער עפֿנט אַ העפֿט.

1. וואָס טוט אַבֿרהם?
2. וואָס טוט עלקע?
3. וואָס טוט חווה?
4. וואָס טוט װעלוול?
5. וואָס טוט גיטל?
6. וואָס טוט שׂרה?

גענימונג 4: איך עפֿן, מיר עפֿענען

The verbs in the preceding exercise are all regular in conjugation (with one variation, noted below). To refresh your verb-conjugating abilities, fill in the table below.

- Begin with two verbs of your choice in the right and middle columns. Then fill in the missing forms for the verb on the left, taking note of its irregular **מיר** and **זיי** forms.
- The "supporting" -**ע**- appears only in the **מיר/זיי** forms of **עפֿענען**. The other forms of this verb are built on the stem -**עפֿנ**. No other verbs taught here have this irregularity.

איך ______ ______	איך ______ ______	איך עפֿן אַ בוך
דו ______ ______	דו ______ ______	דו ______ ______
ער / זי / עס ______ ______	ער / זי / עס ______ ______	ער / זי / עס ______ ______
מיר ______ ______	מיר ______ ______	מיר עפֿענען ______
איר ______ ______	איר ______ ______	איר ______ ______
זיי ______ ______	זיי ______ ______	זיי עפֿענען ______

גענימונג 5: עלקע פֿאַרמאַכט די טיר

The students are getting ready for a study session, as Moyshe narrates what each person is doing.

- Use various forms of the verbs you learned in **גענימונג 3** to complete Moyshe's description below. Use each verb at least once.

משה: עלקע פֿאַרמאַכט די טיר. מיר ______ די העפֿטן. וועלוול
______, „ווּ איז אַ בלײַער?“ עלקע און אַבֿרהם ______
אויף אַ בלײַער. חווה און שׂרה ______ די ביכער אויפֿן
טיש. אַבֿרהם און גיטל ______ אויף די מאָבילקעס. איך ______
אַ בלײַער און שרײַב.

געניטונג 6: לעבן הייסט געבן

After their study session, the students meet the rest of their class for dinner. However, splitting the check has proven to be a complicated affair. Moyshe has a credit card, but how much does everyone actually owe him? Arye-Leyb and Khane are nominated to work out the calculations.

- Read through the dialogue and record all forms of the verb **געבן**. Note the similarities between its conjugation pattern and that of **האָבן**.

אַריה־לייב: איך האָב דרײַצן __דאָלאַר__. איך גיב משהן צען __דאָלאַר__.

חנה: דו גיסט משהן צען __דאָלאַר__, אָבער דו האָסט דרײַצן?

אַריה־לייב: יאָ, דרײַ גיב איך סענדערן. אַזוי האָט סענדער צען __דאָלאַר__, און ער גיט משהן די גאַנצע צען.

חנה: איז, איר ביידע גיט משהן צוואַנציק __דאָלאַר__, און איך גיב אַכט.

אַריה־לייב: צוזאַמען גיבן מיר אַכט און צוואַנציק __דאָלאַר__. אוי, דאָס איז נישט גענוג!

חנה: ניין, ס׳איז גוט — גיטל און שׂרה האָבן אַכצן __דאָלאַר__, און זיי גיבן משהן די גאַנצע אַכצן.

that way (אַזוי)

both (ביידע)

together (צוזאַמען)

enough (גענוג)

שרײַבט איבער דעם דיאַלאָג מיט אַן אַנדער סובסטאַנטיוו (אויך אין מערצאָל) אַנשטאָט **דאָלאַר**.

Rewrite the dialogue with a different noun (also in the plural) instead of **דאָלאַר**.

NOTE:

When a person's name is the object of a verb, the name takes the ending ן- (or ען-, if the name ends on, ם-, ן-, or a syllabic ל). We will learn more about this in **10 קאַפּיטל**.

NOTE:

The word **דאָלאַר** does not change, whether there is one or many:

דער מאַנטל קאָסט צוויי הונדערט דאָלאַר.

איך האָב איין דאָלאַר.

געניטונג 7: נאָך אימפּעראַטיוון

Work out the imperative forms of the new verbs you have encountered in the preceding exercises and use them to fill in the table below, as shown.

- Even irregular verbs generally have predictable imperatives so long as you know their present-tense **איך** and **איר** forms.

Infinitive	נעמען	פֿאַרמאַכן	געבן	עפֿענען
Singular				עפֿן אַ בוך!
Plural				עפֿנט די העפֿטן!

געניטונג 8: פֿרעגט די באָבע!

Rokhl is desperately trying to finish a journal article, and Khaye and Perl will not leave her alone. Fill in the appropriate imperative verb forms (from this section) in the dialogue below.

- Be careful to use singular and plural forms when appropriate.

1. **חיה:** עס איז הייס אין הויז!

רחל: נו, עפֿן אַ פֿענצטער.

2. **פערל:** איך זינג מיט רבֿקהן זונטיק?

רחל: איך געדענק נישט. ________ אויף דײַן קאַלענדאַר.

3. **חיה:** איך גיי קוקן אויף טעלעוויזיע.

רחל: נישקשה, אָבער ________ די טיר!

4. **חיה און פערל:** וויפֿל איז דרײַצן מאָל אַכצן?

רחל: ________ די באָבע.

5. **פערל:** איך שרײַב אַן עסיי, אָבער איך ווייס נישט ווו מײַן פֿעדער איז...

רחל: נישקשה, ________ מײַן פֿעדער.

6. **חיה:** איך האָב פֿינף עפּל — דאָס איז **צו פֿיל**! *too many*

רחל: ________ פערלען אַן עפּל אָדער צוויי. זי עסט אויך עפּל!

7. **חיה און פערל:** מיר לייענען אַ ליד פֿון קאַדיע מאָלאָדאָווסקי, אָבער מיר פֿאַרשטייען נישט אַלע **ווערטער**. *words*

רחל: אוי, וואָס קען מען טאָן... נו, ________ אויף די ווערטער וואָס איר פֿאַרשטייט נישט.

געניטונג 9: אַ קלאַס מיט קלאַסיקער

Professor Kluger is dreaming, and yet she cannot escape her classroom. However, in her dream, her classroom is full of her favorite Yiddish personalities!

Looking at her roll sheet, Prof. Kluger sees that even *more* notables were supposed to attend, but some are absent. Take attendance according to the image above, and record who's there and who isn't by checking one box or the other in the table below.

	נאָמען	דאָ	ניִשטאָ
	ציליע אַדלער	☐	☐
	מרים אולינאָווער	☐	☐
	ש. אַנ־סקי	☐	☐
	מערנאַ און קלייר בערי	☐	☐
[יאַנקעוו]	יעקבֿ גלאַטשטיין	☐	☐
	מאַקס ווײַנרײַך	☐	☐
	דייוו טאַראַס	☐	☐
	קאַדיע מאָלאָדאָווסקי	☐	☐
	איציק מאַנגער	☐	☐
[מױכער־ספֿאָרים]	מענדעלע מוכר־ספֿרים	☐	☐
	שלמה מיכאָעלס	☐	☐
	יאָסל און חנה מלאָטעק	☐	☐
	מאָלי פּיקאָן	☐	☐
[פּערעץ]	י. ל. פּרץ	☐	☐
	שלום־עליכם	☐	☐

◀ CONTINUED

CONTINUED

Now write one sentence about each person on the attendance list, as in the example below.

- If the person is indeed *present*, then write a second sentence about what that person is doing in the picture, using the classroom verbs you've just learned when possible.
- Use the indefinite article (or no article) for any noun that is the object of a verb.

דוגמא:

דייוו טאַראַס איז דאָ. ער שפּילט קלאַרנעט.

דאָ	here
נישטאָ	not here

Now that you know who's there and who isn't, give some of those who *are* present commands (in the imperative, using classroom verbs). Use the second-person *formal*, as in the example.

דוגמא:

הער טאַראַס, עפֿנט אַ פֿענצטער!

הער	Mr.
פֿרוי	Ms.

געניטונג 10: שניי און הערינג

ווידעאָ־געניטונג

ב־10

דערציילער: **בנימין הרשבֿ (Benjamin Harshav)** [בעניאָמען האַרשאַוו] (פֿראַגמענט)

(ווילנע, פּוילן 1928 – ניו הייווען, קאָנעטיקעט, שטאַטן 2015)

אַרכיוו: Wexler Oral History Project (2013)

Practice classroom vocabulary with this excerpt from an oral history interview with scholar Benjamin Harshav, which you can find online with its accompanying exercise.

ג וואָקאַבולאַר און גראַמאַטיק:
קאָנוווערבן און אינפֿיניטיוון

בערל: איך לייג אַוועק מײַן רוקזאַק.
שמערל לייגט אַוועק זײַן רוקזאַק.

בערל: איך נעם אַרויס אַ העפֿט.
שמערל נעמט אַרויס אַ העפֿט.

his

בערל: איך גיי אַרויס.
שמערל גייט אויך אַרויס.

בערל: איך קום צוריק.
שמערל קומט נישט צוריק.

back

געניטונג 1: קאָנוווערבן

Berl, Shmerl, and Hershl are at school. Look at the pictures taken at different points during the school day and read what Berl says about what he and Shmerl are doing. In each caption, circle the subject and box the object (if there is one). Ignore the adverbs **אויך** and **נישט**. What remains is the verb.

- What is different about these verbs than others you have seen so far? How many *parts* does each verb have?
- Compare the first-person sentences about Berl to the third-person ones about Shmerl. Which part of the verb changes?

! געדענקט!

The verbs taught in this section are called **separable-prefix verbs**.

ענטפֿערט אויף די פֿראַגעס אונטן, לויט די בילדער. — pictures

דוגמא: וואָס לייגן בערל און שמערל אַוועק?

זיי לייגן אַוועק די רוקזעק.

1. וואָס נעמען זיי אַרויס?
2. ווער גייט אַרויס? — ווער: who
3. ווער גייט נישט אַרויס?
4. פֿאַר וואָס גייט ער נישט אַרויס? — why
5. ווער קומט צוריק?
6. ווער קומט נישט צוריק?

Now examine the question-sentences themselves.

- In question 1: What word represents the subject? Is the subject the first sentence unit? What is the function of the two words on either side of the subject?
- In questions 3 and 6: Where does **נישט** appear? How is this similar to the placement of **נישט** for other verbs we have seen up to this point? How is it different?
- In question 4: What do you notice about the relative order of the subject and **נישט**?

After reporting what he and Shmerl are doing, Berl wants to know what Hershl is up to. For each of the pictures on the preceding page, write Berl's question and Hershl's answer, as in the example below.

דוגמא:

בערל: דו לייגסט אַוועק דײַן רוקזאַק, הערשל?

הערשל: ניין, איך לייג אַוועק מײַן גיטאַרע!

געניטונג 2: איך לייג אַרײַן אַ פּאַפּוגײַ

סטודענט א (רחל)

Rokhl is getting Khaye ready for school, packing her backpack. Khaye wants to help but has her own ideas about what she needs to bring. With a partner, act out their interaction.

- Take turns putting things into Khaye's backpack (or taking them out) until the items in the backpack are *all* things that both Rokhl and Khaye intended.
- Rokhl should work from the list below; Khaye's list is to be found on page A3.
- When referring to something your partner has already mentioned, replace the article with the possessive adjective **דײַן** (*your*), as in the example.
- When you choose *not* to take something out, use **נישט** as Rokhl does below.

דוגמא:

חיה: איך לייג אַרײַן אַ פּאַפּוגײַ.

רחל: איך נעם אַרויס דײַן פּאַפּוגײַ.

חיה: איך לייג אַרײַן אַ בלײַער.

רחל: איך נעם נישט אַרויס דײַן בלײַער. איך לייג אַרײַן אַ באַר.

חיה: איך נעם אַרויס דײַן באַר.

אַרײַנלייגן — to put in

Keep track of what remains in the backpack and what doesn't, as shown below.

רחלס רשימה	אין רוקזאַק
באַר	ניין
בלײַער	יאָ
העפֿט	
ביכל	
מעקער	
פֿעדער	
סענדוויטש	
ווערטערבוך	

[רעשימע]

◀ CONTINUED

היימאַרבעט

Under cover of breakfast, Rokhl has repacked Khaye's backpack according to her initial plan. Khaye has discovered this and takes the opportunity to reverse the operation.

- Consult Khaye's list (page A3) and describe what Khaye does in order to make the contents of the backpack resemble *her* list, not Rokhl's.

her	איר
Rokhl's	רחלס

דוגמא:

חיה לייגט אַרײַן <u>איר</u> פּאָפּוגײַ און נעמט אַרויס <u>רחלס</u> בער.

געניטונג 3: נעם אַרויס דײַן פּאָפּוגײַ!

רחל: חיה, נעם אַרויס דײַן פּאָפּוגײַ!

חיה: מאַמע, לייג אַרײַן מײַן העפֿט!

Above are a couple of scenes from Rokhl and Khaye's packing interaction, where they use the singular imperative forms **לייג אַרײַן** and **נעם אַרויס**. Fill in the table below with corresponding plural imperative and infinitive forms, as well as imperative forms of **אַרויסגיין** and **צוריקקומען**.

Infinitive			אַרויסגיין	צוריקקומען
Singular Imperative	נעם אַרויס אַ בוך!	לייג אַרײַן אַ בער!		
Plural Imperative				

גענִיטונג 4: אַ ביסל ביאָלאָגיע...

Perl and her cousin Reyne are in science class, and their experiment has gone wrong... Read the dialogue. Then label each frame in the illustration below with lines from the dialogue that correspond to that image.

ריינע: נעם אַרויס אַ __פּישעלע__ פֿון פֿלעשעלע, פּערל!	vial
פּערל: גוט. גיב מיר אַ __פּיפּעטקע__ — אוי, דאָס שמעקט נישט גוט...	smells
ריינע: אוי־אוי, __חבֿרים__, עפֿנט אַ __פֿענצטער__ !	[כאַווײרים]
פּערל: אוי־ווײ, איך גיי שוין אַרויס פֿון צימער!	already
ריינע: גיי נישט אַרויס! פֿאַרמאַך דאָס פֿלעשעלע!	
פּערל: שוין! איך לייג עס אַוועק. און איצט?	done!; now
ריינע: נו, פֿרעג די לערערין.	
פּערל: לערערין! קוקט אויף אונדזער __פּישעלע__ , זײַט אַזוי גוט.	our
ריינע: פּערל, ווײַז אונדזער __באַנאַנע__ אויך!	

Now replace the underlined nouns with other nouns you know.

- Be sure to use only indefinite articles (and the possessive adjective **אונדזער**), as above.

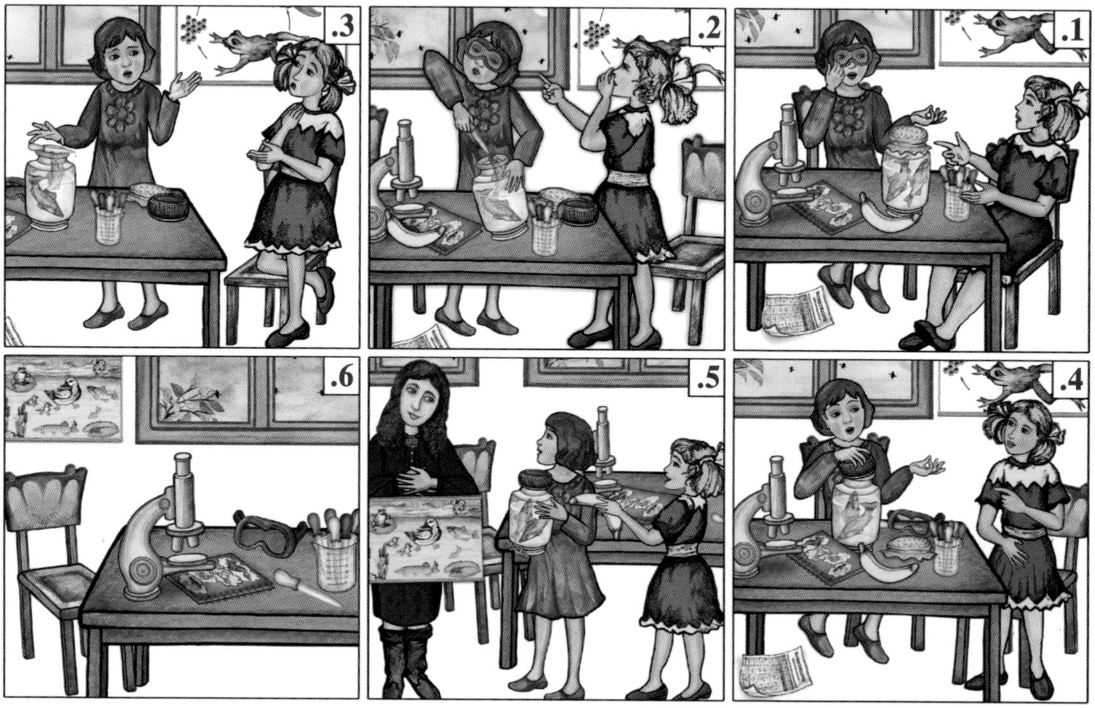

◀ CONTINUED

CONTINUED

אין קלאַס

מיט אַ חבֿר, חזרט איבער דעם דיאַלאָג איבן עטלעכע מאָל. רעדט אַזוי גיך און פֿליסיק ווי מעגלעך.

Now repeat the dialogue, making the substitutions described above.

געניטונג 5: לייג אַוועק דײַן מאָבילקע

Perl and Reyne's teacher is giving commands, sometimes to one and sometimes to both students. Write out the teacher's commands based on the prompts below, as in the example.

- Use separable-prefix verbs.
- Use the words **דײַן** (for a singular object) and **די** (for a plural object), as in the example.

דוגמא:

(פערל) מאָבילקע

פערל, לייג אַוועק דײַן מאָבילקע.

אָדער

(פערל און ריינע) העפֿטן

פערל, ריינע, נעמט אַרויס די העפֿטן.

1. (פערל און ריינע) מאַנטלען
2. (ריינע) סענדוויטש
3. (פערל און ריינע) פֿעדערס
4. (פערל) ביכל
5. (פערל און ריינע) פֿון קלאַסצימער
6. (ריינע) עפּל
7. (פערל) אין קלאַסצימער
8. (פערל) בולבע

אַרויסגיין פֿון...	to go out of the...
צוריקקומען אין...	to come back into the...

געניטונג 6: שׂרה הייבט אָן עסן

גיטל און אַבֿרהם הייבן אָן שרײַבן.

גיטל און אַבֿרהם שרײַבן.

גיטל און אַבֿרהם הערן אויף שרײַבן.

שׂרה הייבט אָן עסן.

שׂרה עסט.

שׂרה הערט אויף עסן.

Examine the pictures above.

- What are Gitl and Avrom doing? What is Sore doing?
- What words describe these two actions? Circle each time these words appear in the captions.

Consider the purple verbs in the first and third pictures of each row.

- Since each row shows a chronological progression, what might each of these verbs mean?
- What kinds of verbs are these? (How many parts does each one have? Which part is conjugated?)

Compare the captions in the bottom row. What verb appears in all three? Does it always appear in the same form? (Read on for an explanation of this phenomenon.)

◀ CONTINUED

CONTINUED

In the first and third captions of each row, the verbs **עסן** and **שרײַבן** appear in the **infinitive**.

- The infinitive is used when one verb is modified by another (as above) or when using the verb to refer to a general concept (e.g., **לאַכן איז געזונט**).
- Infinitives are unconjugated and remain the same regardless of the subject of the sentence.

איך הייב אָן עסן.

מיר הייבן אָן עסן.

(The verb that *modifies* the infinitive *is* conjugated to match its subject.)

- The infinitive form of a verb is usually the same as its **מיר/זיי** form, but not always.

Infinitives of complemented verbs are written as a single word, and the unconjugated portion *precedes* the verb stem:

אַוועקלייגן	**אַרויסגיין**	**אָנהייבן**
אַרויסנעמען	**צוריקקומען**	**אויפֿהערן**

גערענקט!

Some irregular infinitives we have encountered so far are the following:

שטיין	**געבן**
גיין	**זײַן**
פֿאַרשטיין	**טאָן**

NOTE:

Though both parts of the verb **אויפֿהערן** look familiar, it is related neither to the verb **הערן** nor to the preposition **אויף**. In fact, the **-אויפֿ** in **אויפֿהערן** is usually pronounced [אוף].

געניטונג 7: רבֿקה הייבט אָן זינגען

Now that you know how to describe the beginnings and endings of actions, use this knowledge to turn the **אויף אַ קאָנצערט** picture on page 58 into a compelling narrative description, as in the model below, which describes the **אין דער רעדאַקציע** picture.

- Remember that the second verb in each phrase should be in the **infinitive**, *not* conjugated.

דוגמא:

דזשאָן הייבט אָן רעדן. הערשל און רחל הייבן אָן שרײַבן. מירל הייבט אָן עסן. הערשל הערט אויף שרײַבן און הייבט אָן טרינקען.

The imperative forms of the verbs **אָנהייבן** and **אויפֿהערן** are created just like those of the other separable-prefix verbs you learned above. Work out these forms and fill them in below.

Infinitive	אָנהייבן	אויפֿהערן
Singular Imperative		
Plural Imperative		

Now transform the **אין דער רעדאַקציע** picture by giving various characters different commands.

- If you like, these may be from one character to another, as in the example below.
- Make sure that some of your commands apply to one person only and others to more than one. Remember to use the second-person *formal* form too, if appropriate.
- After writing out all of your commands, redraw the scene as you have caused it to be.

דוגמא:

פּאָל: דזשאָן, הערט אויף לאַכן!

געניטונג 8: אָנהייבן און אויפֿהערן

Khane is on the phone with her grandfather Meyer, describing what went on in Yiddish class yesterday. Fill in each pair of blanks with the appropriately conjugated form of either **אָנהייבן** or **אויפֿהערן**.

- You will need to use both present-tense and imperative forms.

NOTE:

Khane speaks in the present tense, even though she is relating past events. This narrative style is called the **narrative past tense**, and is common in spoken and written Yiddish.

עס איז זייער **פֿרי**, און איך זיץ **שוין** אין קלאַסצימער. איך בין זייער מיד, שלאָף איך אַ ביסל.

early; already

פּלוצלינג זאָגט פּראָפֿעסאָר קלוגער: „גוט־מאָרגן, סטודענטן! עפֿנט די ביכער, און הייבט אָן ענטפֿערן אויף די פֿראַגעס אויף זײַט 81.“

suddenly

איך ______ ____ שלאָפֿן און ______ ____ אַרבעטן. אַבֿרהם ______ ____ שפּילן אין **קאָרטן** און ______ ____ **זוכן** דאָס לערנבוך.

cards; looking (for)

אַ ביסל **שפּעטער** זאָגט פּראָפֿעסאָר קלוגער: „איר האָט אַן **אויספֿרעג**!“

later; quiz

די סטודענטן ______ ____ שרײַבן און ______ ____ רעדן **צווישן זיך**. װעלוול ______ ____ לייענען אַ **צײַטונג** און ______ ____ פּראָטעסטירן: „**נאָך אַן** אויספֿרעג! **פֿאַר וואָס**?“

among themselves; newspaper

another; why

צען מינוט שפּעטער — שוין אין **מיטן** אויספֿרעג — זאָגט פּראָפֿעסאָר קלוגער: „װעלוול, ______ ____ **נאָכשרײַבן** שׂרהן!“ שׂרה ______ ____ לאַכן.

(the) middle (of)

copying

צוואַנציק מינוט שפּעטער זאָגט פּראָפֿעסאָר קלוגער: „**שוין!** ס׳איז שוין דער **סוף** פֿונעם אויספֿרעג. ______ ____ שרײַבן!“

that's it!

end [סאָף]

די סטודענטן אָבער ______ ____ שרײַבן **נאָך גיכער**.

even faster

געניטונג 9: סענדער, שרײַב אַן עסיי!

Professor Kluger wants Sender to write an assignment in his notebook and is giving him extremely detailed instructions on how to do so. Write the professor's command corresponding to each picture, providing as much detail as possible.

- Use the possessive pronoun **דײַן** when referring to Sender's notebook and pen.

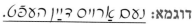

דוגמא: נעם אַרויס דײַן העפֿט.

.1 ______________________

.2 ______________________

.3 ______________________

.4 ______________________

.5 ______________________

5 וואָקאַבולאַר־איבערבליק

א. אין קלאַס
IN CLASS

on the table	אויפֿן טיש
notebook	די העפֿט (ן)
pen	די פֿעדער (ס)
(pair of) scissors	די שער (ן)
pencil	דער בלײַער (ס)
stapler	דער דרעטלער (ס)
eraser	דער מעקער (ס)
book	דאָס בוך (ביכער)
sheet (of paper)	דאָס בלעטל (עך)
dictionary	דאָס ווערטערבוך (ווערטערביכער)

in the room	אינעם צימער
wall	די וואַנט (ווענט)
door	די טיר (ן)
teacher (*f*)	די לערערין (ס)
ceiling	די סטעליע (ס)
floor	דער דיל (ן)
clock	דער זייגער (ס)
board	דער טאָוול (ען)
table	דער טיש (ן)
teacher (*m*)	דער לערער (ס)
window	דער פֿענצטער (—)
backpack	דער רוקזאַק (רוקזעק)
chair	דאָס בענקל (עך)

additional vocabulary	נאָך וואָקאַבולאַר
both	ביידע
whole; complete	גאַנץ
according to	לויט
already	שוין
list	די רשימה (–ות) [רעשימע (ס)]
sentence	דער זאַץ (ן)

דער לאָמפּ (ן); די פּען (ען)

א. אין קלאַס (קאָלירן)
IN CLASS (COLORS)

colors	קאָלירן
yellow	געל
white	ווײַס
purple	לילאַ
pink	ראָזעווע
red	רויט
black	שוואַרץ
light (blue)	העל (בלוי)
dark (blue)	טונקל (בלוי)

אָראַנזש; בלוי; ברוין; גרוי; גרין

ב. טאָג־טעגלעכע ווערבן
EVERYDAY VERBS

verbs		ווערבן
to give	איך גיב, דו גיסט	געבן
to point (at a window)		ווײַזן (אויף אַ פֿענצטער)
to place, to lay down		לייגן
to use		ניצן
to take		נעמען
to open (a notebook)	איך עפֿן, מיר עפֿענען	עפֿענען (אַ העפֿט)
to close (a door)		פֿאַרמאַכן (אַ טיר)
to ask		פֿרעגן
to look (at a board)		קוקן (אויף א טאָוול)

useful expressions	נוציקע אויסדרוקן
he is here	ער איז דאָ
they are here	זיי זײַנען דאָ
she is not here	זי איז נישטאָ
they are not here	זיי זײַנען נישטאָ
why	פֿאַר וואָס

ג. ווערבן מיט קאָנווערבן
VERBS WITH SEPARABLE PREFIXES

אַוועׂקלייגן	איך לייג אַוועׂק, מיר לייגן אַוועק	to put away, put down
אויפֿהערן (שרײַבן)	איך הער אויף, מיר הערן אויף	to stop (writing)
אָנהייבן (לייענען)	איך הייב אָן, מיר הייבן אָן	to start (reading)
אַרויסגיין (פֿון קלאַס)	איך גיי אַרוׂיס, מיר גייען אַרויס	to go out (from class)
אַרוׂיסנעמען (פֿון רוקזאַק)	איך נעם אַרויס, מיר נעמען אַרויס	to take out (from the backpack)
אַרײַׂנלייגן (אין רוקזאַק)	איך לייג אַרײַׂן, מיר לייגן אַרײַן	to put in (into the backpack)
צוריׂקקומען (אין קלאַס)	איך קום צוריׂק, מיר קומען צוריק	to come back (to class)

גראַמאַטיק־איבערבליק 5א

DIMINUTIVE — דימינוטיוו

The suffixes **ל**- and **עלע**- mark the **diminutive** and **iminutive** forms of nouns. Diminutives formed with these suffixes are always neuter in gender.

Iminutive	Diminutive	Base Noun
דאָס טירעלע	דאָס טירל	די טיר

- The diminutive may indicate physical smallness, youth, cuteness, dearness, triviality, or even scorn. (The iminutive expresses a more extreme version of these same qualities.)

For many nouns, there is also a vowel change between the base and diminutive forms.

Iminutive	Diminutive	Base Noun
דאָס ביכעלע	דאָס ביכל	דאָס בוך
דאָס בענקעלע	דאָס בענקל	די באַנק

Some nouns have only one diminutive. (The suffix used depends on the form of the base noun.)

Diminutive	Base Noun
דאָס בלײַערל	דער בלײַער
דאָס טעוועלע	דער טאָוול

- As you see here, words that are not diminutives may still end with **ל**- (or even **עלע**-).
- Some nouns require different forms of the suffixes above (or different suffixes entirely), but these are much less common.

PLURAL — מערצאָל

There are a number of ways to form plural nouns. Generally, this involves a suffix, a vowel change, or both. We have seen four major patterns so far:

(1) Most nouns form their plurals with the suffix **ן**-. (די העפֿט ← די העפֿטן)

- This suffix becomes **ען**- in three cases: when the base noun ends in **נג**- or **נק**-; when the base noun ends in a syllabic **ל**- and is *not* a diminutive; or when the base noun ends in a stressed syllable terminating with **ן**-, **ם**-, or a vowel or diphthong.

  די גענײטונג ← די גענײטונגען

  דער טאָוול ← די טאָוולען

  די בלום ← די בלומען

  דער פּאָפּוגײַ ← די פּאָפּוגײַען

  If a word ends in **ם**- or **ן**- but the last syllable is *not* emphasized, then the plural ending is **ס**-. For example, **לערערין** becomes **לערערינס**, and **גולם** becomes **גולמס**.

(2) Nouns ending in an unstressed **ע**- form their plurals with the suffix **ס**-. (די מאַבילקע ← די מאַבילקעס)

- This group includes nouns from *loshn-koydesh* that are spelled differently but still end in an [**ע**] sound. Their plurals are also spelled differently but still end in a [**ס**] sound. (די דירה ← די דירות)
- Family names are also pluralized with **ס**-, like **די גרינפֿעלדס**.

(3) Nouns ending in unstressed **ער**- also commonly form their plurals with **ס**-. (דער בלײַער ← די בלײַערס)

- There are numerous exceptions to this pattern (e.g., **פֿענצטער**, which is the same in singular and plural), but it is still a good rule of thumb.
- In our usage, agent nouns like **שרײַבער** and **זינגער** all take **ס**- in the plural. However, many of these nouns also have alternative plural forms without any suffix at all (like **פֿענצטער**).
- Nouns that end in a *stressed* **ער**- do *not* form their plurals this way. (די שער ← די שערן)

(4) Diminutive nouns form plurals with עך-. (דאָס בענקל ← די בענקלעך)

- Iminutive nouns form plurals with ך- alone. (דאָס בענקעלע ← די בענקעלעך)

Beyond these rules, there are many unpredictable irregular plurals that must simply be memorized along with the noun itself. Here are some irregular plurals that you know already:

דאָס בוך ← די ביכער

דער רוקזאַק ← די רוקזעק

דער פֿענצטער ← די פֿענצטער

The first form above is a combination of vowel change and suffix. The second is by vowel change only, and the third shows no change at all.

- It is unpredictable *which* nouns will be irregular, but there are patterns, especially in the vowel changes. So far, we have seen ו become י and אָ become ע.

NOTE: If a vowel change occurs in the *plural* form of a noun, the same change will—with very few exceptions—also be present in the diminutive (**ביכער** → **ביכל**). The reverse is not always true (**בלימל** but **בלומען**).

Many nouns from *loshn-koydesh* adhere to their own particular pluralization pattern, where the suffix **ים**- is added and the stressed syllable changes: **שבת** [שאַבעס] becomes **שבתים** [שאַבאָסים].

- A similar pattern exists for some nouns *not* from *loshn-koydesh*. For example, **דאָקטער** becomes **דאָקטוירים**.

Some words have multiple plural forms, sometimes with different meanings, sometimes not.

פֿעדער (pen; feather)	פֿעדערס (pens) פֿעדערן (feathers)
גולם (golem)	גולמס (golems) גולמים [גוילאָמים] (same meaning)

The plural definite article is always **די**, and the plural *indefinite* article is always **null**—that is, there isn't one.

notebooks	העפֿטן
the notebooks	די העפֿטן

The plural forms of **uncountable nouns** (e.g., **ווײַן**) are used differently (and less often) than plurals of **countable nouns.**

- In phrases such as **אַ סך ווײַן** (*a lot of wine*), the singular form is used (as opposed to **אַ סך בלומען**, where the plural form of the countable noun **בלום** is used).
- When the plural of an uncountable noun *is* used, it generally refers to a sense of *variety*, rather than just quantity: אַ סך ווײַנען, *many **types of** wine.*

דעמאָנסטראַטיווע אַרטיקלען און פּראָנאָמען — DEMONSTRATIVE ARTICLES AND PRONOUNS

The same forms that function as definite articles (e.g., **דער**, **די**, **דאָס**) may also serve as **demonstrative articles**. This usage is distinguished by intonation: demonstrative articles are stressed, while other types of articles generally are not.

My house is small.	מײַן הויז איז קליין.
This house, however, is very large.	דאָס הויז איז אָבער זייער גרויס.

- As usual, the article matches the gender of the noun it precedes.
- Depending on context, such articles may be translatable into English as either *this* or *that.*

The word **דאָס** is also often used as a demonstrative *pronoun.*

What is that?	וואָס איז דאָס?
That is a dinosaur.	דאָס איז אַ דינאָזאַווער.

- Note that **דאָס**, in this usage, may pair with both singular and plural verbs: **דאָס זײַנען בערן**.
- The masculine and feminine articles may also function as pronouns in a similar way, but only if the noun they refer to is already clear from context.

גראַמאַטיק־איבערבליק 5ב

עפֿענען און געבן — TO OPEN AND TO GIVE

The verb **עפֿענען** represents a special type of regular verb, one that requires a special spelling—and matching pronunciation—in the infinitive and first- and third-person plural.

- The ending **-ען** is nothing new, shared by all verbs with stems ending in *nun* (e.g., **ווײַנען**).
- The stem in question here, however, ends with a **syllabic** *nun* (**-עפֿנ**), requiring yet another supporting *ayin* (preceding this *nun*). This rule applies widely to verbs with stems ending in a syllabic *nun*.

עפֿענען (!)	Plural	Singular
First Person	(!) מיר עפֿענען	איך עפֿן
Second Person	איר עפֿנט	דו עפֿנסט
Third Person	(!) זיי עפֿענען	ער/זי/עס עפֿנט

The verb **געבן** has a conjugation pattern similar to that of **האָבן** in that it can be viewed as based on a stem (**-גיב**) from which the final **-ב** is deleted in the third-person singular and both second-person conjugations.

- **געבן** differs from **האָבן** in having an irregular infinitive, which does not match its first- and third-person-plural forms.

געבן (!)	Plural	Singular
First Person	מיר גיבן	איך גיב
Second Person	(!) איר גיט	(!) דו גיסט
Third Person	זיי גיבן	(!) ער/זי/עס גיט

פֿאַרניינונג פֿון אַדיעקטיוון — NEGATION OF ADJECTIVES

When negating a predicate adjective, **נישט** follows the verb (usually **זײַן**) directly:

דער מענטש איז מיד. ← דער מענטש איז נישט מיד.

If, however, the subject is displaced from first position, it may come between the verb and **נישט**:

פֿרײַטיק איז דער מענטש מיד. ←

זונטיק איז דער מענטש נישט מיד.

IMPERATIVE — אימפּעראַטיוו

The imperative form is used to express commands, give instructions, and make polite requests.

- The informal, singular (**דו**) imperative is the same form as the first-person singular (**איך**) present-tense conjugation, but without a subject noun. (איך שרײַב ← שרײַב!)
- The formal or plural (**איר**) imperative is the same form as the second-person plural (also **איר**) present-tense conjugation, again minus the subject. (איר שרײַבט ← שרײַבט!)

Even irregular verbs follow these patterns. (איך גיב משהן אַ העפֿט ← גיב משהן אַ העפֿט!)

- The verb **זײַן** is the only important exception to this rule. (איך בין ← זײַ! / איר זײַט ← זײַט!)

The imperative is negated by adding **נישט** directly after the verb. (שרײַב נישט!)

גראַמאַטיק־איבערבליק 5ג

ווערבן מיט קאָנווערבן — VERBS WITH SEPARABLE PREFIXES

There is a category of verbs called **separable-prefix verbs** (e.g., **אָנהייבן** or **אַרויסגיין**, with prefixes -**אָנ** and -**אַרויס**); these have certain special characteristics.

- So far we've seen mostly simple verbs, consisting only of a verb stem without any extra elements other than endings to form the present tense (e.g., **אַרבעטן**, **לייענען**).
- For these sorts of simple verbs, there are no dramatic differences between the **infinitive** form of the verb (the form found in dictionaries) and the conjugated present tense.

Infinitive	לאַכן איז געזונט.
Present Tense	איך לאַך.

- Separable-prefix verbs, however, *do* show major differences between these forms.

Infinitive	אָנהייבן שטודירן אַ נײַע שפּראַך איז אינטערעסאַנט.
Present Tense	איך הייב אָן שטודירן אַ נײַע שפּראַך.

- The prefix (**אָן**) that begins the infinitive *separates* from the verb stem (**הייבן**) and ends up *following* the conjugated stem. Only the stem conjugates; the "prefix" never varies:

איך הייב אָן
דו הייבסט אָן   די היימאַרבעט.
זי הייבט אָן

- The separated prefix does not always *directly* follow the conjugated verb stem. Other elements of the sentence (e.g., subject nouns, adverbs, pronouns) may intervene, bracketed by the verb stem on one side and the prefix on the other.

זי נעמט עס נישט אַרויס.

זונטיק הייבט די סטודענטקע אָן די היימאַרבעט.

- The prefix is always stressed: **אַרוי́סגיין** and **אָ́נהייבן**; **איך גיי אַרוי́ס** and **איך הייב אָ́ן**.

Some prefixes consistently add a clear meaning to the stem of the verb (e.g., **אַרויס**, *out*, or **אַוועק**, *away*). Others generally do not, or they vary depending on the stem to which they are attached.

- When the prefix **אויף** is linked with the stem **הערן**, it creates a brand new verb (**אויפֿהערן**), whose meaning could not be predicted on the basis of its parts. (In other instances, however, the same prefix *does* modify the verb stem in a predictable way.)

דער אינפֿיניטיוו — THE INFINITIVE

- As you have seen in this chapter—with **אָנהייבן** and **אויפֿהערן** —one verb may modify another. The second verb in such a construction is in the **infinitive** form.

איך הייב אָן שרײַבן מײַנע מעמואַרן.

- The infinitive is often accompanied by the particle **צו**, though this depends on the specific construction in question. (In the cases of **אָנהייבן** and **אויפֿהערן**, both usages are equally acceptable: איך הייב אָן צו שרײַבן מײַנע מעמואַרן.)
- The infinitive usually has the same form as the **מיר/זיי** form of the verb in the present tense, with some exceptions, such as the common ones below.

First-/Third-Person Plural	Infinitive
מיר/זיי גייען	גיין
מיר/זיי שטייען	שטיין
מיר/זיי זעען	זען
מיר/זיי זײַנען	זײַן
מיר/זיי גיבן	געבן
מיר/זיי טוען	טאָן

- Note the marked difference between the present-tense conjugation of any **separable-prefix verb** and its infinitive (see above).

איבערחזר־געניטונגען 5

געניטונג 1: דער גולם העלפֿט

Your *goylem* has agreed to help you clean your messy dorm room but needs to know where things go. Tell your *goylem* to put each set of items either into your backpack or on the table, depending on whether you want to bring them to class or keep them at home.

- Use the imperative and the appropriate plural forms of the nouns pictured.

אין רוקזאַק אָדער אויפֿן טיש?

דוגמא:

לייג אַרײַן די פֿעדערס אין רוקזאַק. לייג די ביכער אויפֿן טיש.

געניטונג 2: אַ געניטונג אין קלאַס

הער־געניטונג
איבערחזר־סעקציע־2

סענדער און חנה זיצן צוזאַמען אין פּראָפֿעסאָר קלוגערס קלאַס. הערט זיך צו צום דיאַלאָג און שרײַבט אַרײַן די פֿעלנדיקע ווערטער אינעם טעקסט אונטן.

Listen to the dialogue and write in the missing words in the text below.

פּראָפֿעסאָר: סטודענטן, עפֿנט די ________ און ענטפֿערט אויף די פֿראַגעס אויף **זײַט** ________.

page

חנה: אָבער איך האָב נישט קיין ________...

פּראָפֿעסאָר: סענדער, ________ חנהן דײַן ________.

סענדער: מיטן גרעסטן פֿאַרגעניגן!

חנה: ________!

פּראָפֿעסאָר: סענדער, ________ ________ דײַן מאָבילקע.

סענדער: זײַט מיר מוחל!

פּראָפֿעסאָר: נו, גוט. סטודענטן, ________ ________ שרײַבן.

חנה: סענדער, ________ דײַן בוך!

סענדער: מיטן גרעסטן ________!

ענטפֿערט אויף די פֿראַגעס וועגן דעם דיאַלאָג. שרײַבט גאַנצע זאַצן.

1. ווי הייסן די צוויי סטודענטן?
2. אויף וואָסער זײַט זײַנען די פֿראַגעס?
3. וואָס גיט סענדער חנהן?
4. סענדער טוט **עפּעס** שלעכטס. אויף וואָס קוקט ער?

something

6

קאַפּיטל זעקס:

לימודים; פֿאַרניינונג און „עס איז דאָ“

CHAPTER GOALS

- In this chapter, you will learn how to talk about your studies, how to describe your schoolwork, and how to discuss presence, absence, and existence.

וואָקאַבולאַר:	
studies	לימודים
גראַמאַטיק:	
negation	פֿאַרניינונג
there is	עס איז דאָ
קולטור — אוידיאָ:	
"Yesterday's Already Gone" (folk song)	„שוין אַוועק דער נעכטן“ (פֿאָלקסליד)

א וואָקאַבולאַר: לימודים און שולאַרבעט־טערמינען

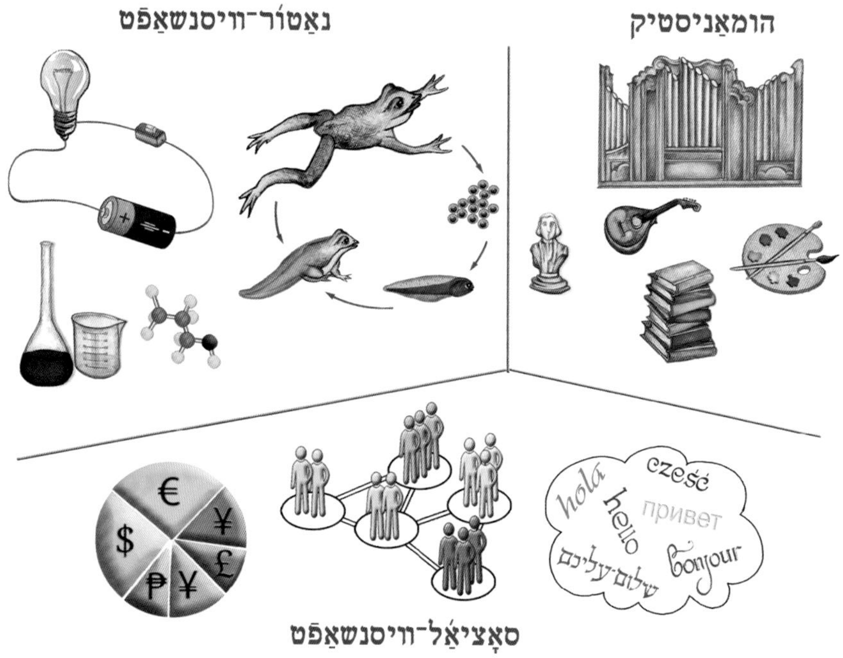

געניטונג 1: לימודים

In order to graduate, Sender needs to take two classes in each category of academic study: humanities, natural sciences, and social sciences. Help him choose his courses by sorting the disciplines from the word box below into the three categories provided in the table.

סאָציאַל־וויסנשאַפֿט	נאַטור־וויסנשאַפֿט	הומאַניסטיק
		מוזיק

NOTE:

The terms presented here are feminine nouns, with one exception: **ייִדישע לימודים** is based on a masculine noun (**לימוד**) but is used only in the plural.

פֿילאָסאָפֿיע	עקאָנאָמיק	מוזיק	
אַנטראָפּאָלאָגיע	מאַטעמאַטיק	געשיכטע	history
פּסיכאָלאָגיע	סאָציאָלאָגיע	פּאָליטיק	
כעמיע	ביאָלאָגיע	ייִדישע לימודים	studies
ליטעראַטור	געאָגראַפֿיע	אינזשעניריע	
קאָמפּיוטער־וויסנשאַפֿט	קונסט־געשיכטע	קונסט	art
פֿיזיק	לינגוויסטיק	דראַמאַטורגיע	theater arts
		רעליגיע	

◄ CONTINUED

CONTINUED

אין קלאַס

Discuss your choices with a partner, as in the model provided.

דוגמא:

א: איך מיין אַז עקאָנאָמיק איז אַ טייל פֿון הומאַניסטיק. part

ב: איך בין מסכּים.

אָדער

ב: איך בין נישט מסכּים. עקאָנאָמיק איז אַ טייל פֿון סאָציאַל־וויסנשאַפֿט.

I think that...	איך מיין אַז...
I agree [מאַסקעם]	איך בין מסכּים
I don't agree	איך בין נישט מסכּים

NOTE:

Since **אַז** is a conjunction (like **און**), it "resets" the sentence unit count to zero. Hence, it is followed by normal subject-verb word order (**...עקאָנאָמיק איז**).

NOTE:

The verb **מסכּים זײַן** is a **periphrastic verb**, a verb made up of more than one word. One element is the verb **זײַן**, which conjugates as usual. However, **מסכּים** is the component that carries *meaning*, and it is *not* conjugated. Note that **נישט** separates these two elements in the negative sentence above. We will learn more about periphrastic verbs in **10 קאַפּיטל**.

געניטונג 2: דו שטודירסט פּסיכאָלאָגיע?

Mirl comes to visit Khane in Lernton, and Khane introduces her to Sender.

הער־געניטונג א־2

לייענט די פֿראַגעס איידער איר הערט זיך צו צום דיאַלאָג. זיי וועלן אײַך העלפֿן פֿאַרשטיין דעם טעקסט. before

1. פֿון וואַנען קומט מירל?
2. ווו שטודירט סענדער?
3. וואָס שטודירט סענדער?
4. וואָס שטודירט חנה?

הערט זיך צו צום דיאַלאָג, נאָר קוקט נישט אויפֿן טעקסט. ענטפֿערט אויף די פֿראַגעס אויבן. but

◀ CONTINUED

CONTINUED

הערט נאָך אַ מאָל, און שרײַבט אַרײַן די פֿעלנדיקע ווערטער אינעם טעקסט אונטן.

Listen again, and write in the missing words in the text below.

מירל: איך __________ מירל — איך בין חנהס שוועסטערקינד.

סענדער: זייער __________! פֿון וואַנען __________, מירל?

מירל: איך קום פֿון מאָנטרעאָל. און דו?

סענדער: איך __________ פֿון פֿילאַדעלפֿיע, אָבער איך שטודיר דאָ, אין לערנטאָן־קאָלעדזש.

מירל: דו שטודירסט __________, אַזוי ווי חנה?

סענדער: ניין, איך שטודיר געשיכטע.

cousin

like

Take Sender's role in the conversation, speaking during the pauses between Mirl's lines. Now take part in the dialogue again, this time responding as yourself.

- Substitute information about your *own* studies in place of the purple words above.

אין קלאַס

און וואָס שטודירט איר? מיט אַ חבֿר, רעדט וועגן די לימודים.

Replace the purple words in the example below with information about your own studies.

דוגמא:

א: ווו שטודירסטו?

ב: איך שטודיר אין לערנטאָן־קאָלעדזש. און דו?

א: איך שטודיר אין וויסנבערג־אוניווערסיטעט.
וואָס שטודירסטו?

ב: איך שטודיר פּסיכאָלאָגיע. און דו?

א: איך שטודיר געשיכטע.

Repeat the dialogue with a few other classmates, taking notes on what each one studies.

געניטונג 3: גיטל שרײַבט אַן עסיי

פּראָפֿעסאָר קלוגערס סטודענטן רעדן וועגן שולאַרבעט.

Based on what each student says, choose which of the two descriptions (**א** or **ב**) best describes their work.

1. **משה:** איך מאַך היימאַרבעט.
   א. ער מאַכט אַ געניטונג אין קאַפּיטל זעקס. **ב.** ער הערט אַ לעקציע וועגן אַדיעקטיוון. — about

2. **סענדער:** איך האַלט אַ רעפֿעראַט. — presentation
   א. ער מאַכט צוויי געניטונגען אויף זײַט 34. **ב.** ער רעדט וועגן דעם שרײַבער משה קולבאַק.

3. **חנה:** איך האַלט אַן אויספֿרעג. — quiz
   א. זי שרײַבט אַן עסיי וועגן ייִדיש־רעדערס אין אונגערן. **ב.** זי ענטפֿערט אויף 20 פֿראַגעס אין קלאַס.

4. **גיטל:** איך שרײַב אַן עסיי.
   א. זי האַלט אַן עקזאַמען אויף קאַפּיטל פֿיר. **ב.** זי שרײַבט דרײַ זײַטלעך וועגן פֿאָלקסלידער.

Each of the schoolwork nouns above pairs with a specific verb. Complete the sentences in the list below using **מע** and the appropriate verb for each noun, as in the example.

- Use indefinite articles. The noun **היימאַרבעט** is (fittingly) uncountable, so it appears *without* an article.

דוגמא: היימאַרבעט

מע מאַכט היימאַרבעט.

1. אַ געניטונג
2. אַ לעקציע
3. אַ רעפֿעראַט
4. אַן אויספֿרעג
5. אַן עסיי
6. אַן עקזאַמען

NOTE:
The first- and third-person-singular forms of the verb **האַלטן** are the same: **איך האַלט ← משה האַלט.**

Determine the plural forms of the nouns listed above (except the uncountable noun **היימאַרבעט**). Use the patterns outlined in the grammar overview following **קאַפּיטל 5**.

געניטונג 4: די היימאַרבעט איז נודנע

How do you feel about the following types of assignments? Fill in the statements below with one of the adjectives provided.

- Note the grammatical gender of each noun, as indicated by the corresponding definite article (shown in purple below).

נודנע	boring
אינטערעסאַנט	interesting

דוגמא: היימאַרבעט וועגן טאָג־טעגלעכע ווערבן

די היימאַרבעט איז נודנע.

1. אַ געניטונג וועגן אַדיעקטיוון
די געניטונג איז __________.
2. אַ לעקציע וועגן פֿילאָסאָפֿיע
די לעקציע איז __________.
3. אַ רעפֿעראַט וועגן מוזיק
דער רעפֿעראַט איז __________.
4. אַן אויספֿרעג אויף פּסיכאָלאָגיע
דער אויספֿרעג איז __________.
5. אַן עסיי וועגן ליטעראַטור
דער עסיי איז __________.
6. אַן עקזאַמען אויף לינגוויסטיק
דער עקזאַמען איז __________.

געניטונג 5: אַ רעפֿעראַט וועגן פֿראַנצייזישער פֿילאָסאָפֿיע

You're designing an independent study on a topic of your choosing. Write a syllabus describing at least four assignments that you'll do for the class.

- Use the preposition **וועגן** (*about*) to combine words from each of the columns below, as in the example.
- Use only indefinite articles and the appropriate infinitive forms of verbs.

דוגמא: -האַלטן אַ רעפֿעראַט וועגן פֿראַנצייזישער פֿילאָסאָפֿיע

אַרבעט	אַדיעקטיוו	לימוד
עסיי	פֿראַנצייזישער	געשיכטע
רעפֿעראַט	מאָדערנער	קונסט
לעקציע	אַמעריקאַנער	פּסיכאָלאָגיע
אויספֿרעג	אַבסטראַקטער	עקאָנאָמיק
	רוסישער	פֿילאָסאָפֿיע
	טעאָרעטישער	

NOTE:

The adjectives in the middle column here all end with the suffix **ער-**. This suffix is one of a few that may attach to an adjective that modifies a noun directly. We will learn more about these adjective endings in **11-9 קאַפּיטלען**. For now, simply use the forms provided.

גענִיטונג 6: וואָס לערנט פּראָפֿעסאָר קלוגער?

סטודענט א

Among the characters we've met so far, there are many part-time and full-time teachers. With a partner, take turns asking questions to find out who teaches what and then fill in the table below.

- Your partner will work from the table on page A4.
- Model your dialogue on the example below.

NOTE:

The verb **לערנען** means *to teach* (though it does also have other meanings, depending on context).

דוגמא:

ב: וואָס לערנט פּראָפֿעסאָר קלוגער?

א: פּראָפֿעסאָר קלוגער לערנט ייִדיש.

נאָמען:	פּראָפֿעסאָר קלוגער	הערשל	נתן	רחל	צירל	פּאָל
לימוד:	ייִדיש	לינגוויסטיק			ליטעראַטור	

היימאַרבעט

Choose two of the teachers above and describe the work they assign their students.

דוגמא: הערשל לערנט לינגוויסטיק. הערשלס סטודענטן האַלטן מאָנטיק און דאָנערשטיק עקזאַמענס.

גענִיטונג 7: ווען איז דער אויספֿרעג?

סטודענט א

With a partner, fill in the missing information about Elke's schoolwork in the schedule below. Structure your conversation as in the model provided.

- Your partner will work from the corresponding exercise on page A4.
- Be sure to use the appropriate verb for each schoolwork noun. Refer to the list you made in **גענִיטונג** **3** for a reminder.

דוגמא:

א: עלקע האַלט פֿרײַטיק אַן עקזאַמען?

ב: יאָ, פֿרײַטיק האַלט זי אַן עקזאַמען אויף קאַפּיטל 2. זי האָט זונטיק אַן אויספֿרעג?

א: ניין, זונטיק מאַכט זי גענִיטונג 3 אין קאַפּיטל 2.

זונטיק	מאָנטיק	דינסטיק	מיטוואָך	דאָנערשטיק	פֿרײַטיק
גענִיטונג 3 אין קאַפּיטל 2		עסיי וועגן מענדעלע מוכר־ספֿרים	אויספֿרעג וועגן אימפּעראַטיוו		

געניטונג 8: אַ סך קאַווע

משה טרינקט אַ סך קאַווע. [סאַך]
שׂרה טרינקט אַ ביסל קאַווע.

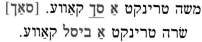

משה האָט אַ סך היימאַרבעט.
שׂרה האָט אַ ביסל היימאַרבעט.

משה טרינקט מער קאַווע ווי שׂרה.

שׂרה האָט ווייניקער היימאַרבעט ווי משה.

Compare the sentences accompanying each pair of images.

- Which phrases describe the amount of coffee or homework shown?
- What pairs of words are used to make comparisons between the two students?

Label the following images with the same phrases you saw above. Then write two comparative sentences using the phrases **מער... ווי** and **ווייניקער... ווי**.

1. חנה ______________.

2. סענדער ______________.

NOTE:

Quantitative phrases like **אַ סך היימאַרבעט** are composed of two elements: a noun describing the *stuff* being quantified (**היימאַרבעט**) and a quantifier (**אַ סך**) telling us *how much* of that stuff there is. Note that there is no preposition between the two elements, unlike in English: *a lot **of** homework*. We will learn more about quantitative constructions in **קאַפּיטל 13**.

NOTE:

The comparative phrases **מער... ווי** and **ווייניקער... ווי** are used to compare two quantities (or qualities, if used with adjectives or adverbs). The conjunction **ווי** works like the English *than*.

איך האָב מער פּאָפּוגײַען ווי בערן.
איך האָב מער פּאָפּוגײַען ווי משה (האָט).
איך בין מער אָפּטימיסטיש ווי רעליגיעז.
איך בין מער אָפּטימיסטיש ווי משה (איז).

Since **ווי** is a conjunction (like **און**), it "resets" the sentence unit count to zero. Hence, it is followed by normal subject-verb word order.

געניטונג 9: אַוודאי, מסתּמא, אפֿשר

וועלוול איז אין קלאַס?

The sentences below describe some activities that Velvl does throughout the week. For each, say how likely you think it is that he is in class, based on the scenario described.

- Each of your responses should begin with either **אַוודאי**, **מסתּמא**, or **אפֿשר**, followed by the verb, as in the example.

דוגמא: ער לייענט אַ בוך.

אפֿשר איז ער אין קלאַס.

1. ער קוקט אויפֿן טאָוול.
2. ער ענטפֿערט אויף פּראָפֿעסאָר קלוגערס פֿראַגע.
3. ער נעמט אַרויס זײַן היימאַרבעט.
4. ער הערט אַ לעקציע וועגן קאַדיע מאָלאָדאָווסקין.
5. ער האַלט אַן עקזאַמען.

אַוודאי	of course [אַוואַדע]
מסתּמא	probably [מיסטאָמע]
אפֿשר	maybe [עפּשער]

! גערעדנקט!

Adverbs (like **אַוודאי**, **מסתּמא**, and **אפֿשר**) generally count as sentence units; if such an adverb begins a sentence, it is then followed by the verb.

געניטונג 10: וואָס מיינסטו?

Elke and Gitl are comparing how much work they and their classmates do for their courses. Read the dialogue below. Underline any quantifiers, comparatives, or probability adverbs that you recognize (see **9–8 געניטונגען**).

עלקע: משה שטודירט פֿיזיק. מסתּמא האָט ער נאָר אַ ביסל היימאַרבעט.

גיטל: נאָר אַ ביסל היימאַרבעט?! אָבער דער לימוד איז אַזוי שווער — אַוודאי האָט ער אַ סך!

[לימעד]; so

עלקע: איך מיין אַז נישט. אפֿשר האָט ער אַ סך עקזאַמענס... אָבער נאָר אַ ביסל היימאַרבעט.

גיטל: אוי, אויף מיר געזאָגט! איך שטודיר כעמיע, און איך האָב זייער אַ סך היימאַרבעט.

I should be so lucky

עלקע: מער ווי משה?

גיטל: אַוודאי מער ווי משה, און אפֿשר נישט ווייניקער עקזאַמענס!

Write a skit where two students speculate about the amount and type of schoolwork their classmates do. Use the dialogue above as a model.

- Be creative—you needn't stick to purely logical guesses about each student's workload.
- Use as many quantity and probability expressions as you can, as well as words for schoolwork and academic disciplines.

נאָר	only
לײַכט	easy
שווער	difficult
איך מיין אַז יאָ	I believe so
איך מיין אַז נישט	I don't believe so

ב גראַמאַטיק: פּאַרניינונג

געניטונג 1: ווער איז דאָס?

Khaye and Perl are waiting at the airport with the people pictured above. To pass the time, the two sisters are playing a guessing game.

פּערל: דער מענטש איז אַ פּילאָט?

חיה: ניין, ער איז נישט קיין פּילאָט.

פּערל: דער מענטש עסט אַ באַר?

חיה: ניין, ער עסט נישט קיין באַר.

פּערל: דער מענטש טרינקט קאַווע?

חיה: ניין, ער טרינקט נישט קיין קאַווע.

פּערל: דער מענטש האָט ביכער?

חיה: ניין, ער האָט נישט קיין ביכער.

פּערל: דער מענטש לייגט אַוועק אַ העפֿט?

חיה: ניין, ער לייגט נישט אַוועק קיין העפֿט.

דער מענטש person

ווער איז דאָס?

Who is it? Can you guess whom Khaye is thinking of?

◀ CONTINUED

CONTINUED

Now consider the sentences in the dialogue.

- Are they the same as other negative statements that you have seen before? If not, how are they different? What word have you not seen before?
- Compare the first two negative sentences to the questions they answer. What word from the question-sentence does **קיין** replace?
- Why is there no article in either the third or fourth question? How does this explain the presence of **קיין** in the answer?
- What is unique about the answer to the last question? Is **נישט** where you expect to find it? Can you explain why **קיין** precedes the noun (and is split from **נישט**)?

Write five negative sentences (one of each type encountered in the dialogue) about the people pictured above, as in the example.

דוגמא:

אסתּר איז נישט קיין דאָקטער.

NOTE:

Just as a verbal prefix (e.g., **אַרויס**) may come between **נישט** and **קיין**, so may a preposition:

א: דו וווינסט אין אַ דירה?

ב: ניין, איך וווין נישט אין קיין דירה.

The two phenomena (separable prefix and preposition) may also occur together:

איך גיי נישט אַרויס פֿון קיין דירה.

(!) Remember that **קיין** is just the negative version of the indefinite article, and you will always know where it goes.

אין קלאַס

With a partner, continue Khaye and Perl's game: take turns asking and answering questions until you can guess the person your partner is thinking of, as in the dialogue above.

- Be sure to use the negative article **קיין** in each negative response, and be careful to split **נישט** and **קיין** when negating a separable-prefix verb.

געניטונג 2: וואָס איז דאָס?

silly נתן שטעלט נאַרישע פֿראַגעס, און חיה ענטפֿערט.

Answer the questions, as in the example. Write complete sentences.

דוגמא: דאָס איז אַ טאָוול?

ניין, דאָס איז נישט קיין טאָוול. דאָס איז אַ שער.

1. דאָס איז אַ בענקל?

2. דאָס איז אַ לאָמפּ?

3. דאָס איז אַ זייגער?

4. דאָס זײַנען טישן?

5. דאָס איז אַ טיר?

6. דאָס זײַנען העפֿטן?

7. דאָס איז אַ סטודענטקע?

8. דאָס איז אַ פֿענצטער?

געניטונג 3: זינגט אַ פּיראַט...

Reyne is reading the newspaper to Yosl and comes across the following headline:

דאָס נײַע ביכל „זינגט און טאַנצט מיט אַ פּיראַט און אַ פּאָפּוגײַ“
לייענט יעדער פּאָעט. every

The image below right is the picture that accompanies the article. However, Yosl is confused by the wording of the headline and imagines the very different picture on the left.

Yosl can hardly believe the image he has conjured, so he asks Reyne some clarifying questions. Answer each of Yosl's questions according to the *actual* picture, as in the example.

דוגמא:

יאָסל: דער פּאָפּוגײַ זיצט אויף אַ טיש?

ריינע: ניין, דער פּאָפּוגײַ זיצט נישט אויף קיין טיש.

1. דאָס ביכל זינגט לידער?
2. דער פּיראַט טאַנצט אַ וואַלס?
3. דער פּאָפּוגײַ נעמט אַרויס אַ פֿעדער?
4. דער פּאָפּוגײַ איז אַ פּאָעט?
5. דער פּאָפּוגײַ לייענט ביכער?

גענײטונג 4: נישט קיין סך

זונטיק

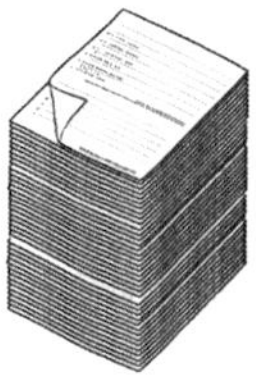

מאָנטיק

דינסטיק

מיטוואָך

דאָנערשטיק

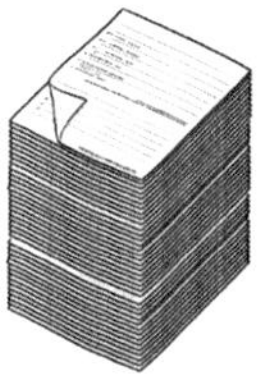

פֿרײַטיק

Above is Sender's homework for the week. Describe his workload each night, as in the model below. Remember to place the verb in second position.

- Note that **אַ סך** is negated just like any other singular indefinite noun, with **קיין** replacing the indefinite article **אַ**.

דוגמא:

זונטיק האָט סענדער אַ סך היימאַרבעט. מאָנטיק האָט ער נישט קיין סך היימאַרבעט.

גענײטונג 5: קאַווע און אײַזקרעם

סטודענט א (סענדער)

Khane and Sender are hoping to go out for both coffee *and* ice cream this week. With a partner, compare their schedules to figure out which days they are both relatively free, as in the model below.

- Sender's schedule appears in the preceding exercise. Khane's may be found in on page A5.

דוגמא:

חנה: זונטיק האָב איך נישט קיין סך היימאַרבעט. וויפֿל היימאַרבעט האָסט דו זונטיק?

סענדער: איך האָב אַ סך היימאַרבעט זונטיק, אָבער מאָנטיק האָב איך נישט קיין סך היימאַרבעט.

היימאַרבעט

Now that you know which days Sender and Khane are both free, choose one day for a coffee outing and the other for an ice cream excursion, then write sentences as follows.

דוגמא:

זונטיק האָבן מיר <u>ביידע</u> נישט קיין סך היימאַרבעט... <u>לאָמיר</u> גיין עסן אײַזקרעם <u>צוזאַמען</u>!

ביידע	both
לאָמיר (גיין)	let's (go)
צוזאַמען	together

געניטונג 6: דאָס איז נישט די לערערין

עלקע: דאָס איז די לערערין?

משה: ניין, דאָס איז נישט די לערערין, דאָס איז די סעקרעטאַרשע.

חנה: זינגסט דאָס ליד פֿון איציק מאַנגער?

סענדער: ניין, איך זינג נישט דאָס ליד פֿון איציק מאַנגער, איך זינג דאָס ליד פֿון לענאַרד <u>כּהן</u>. [קויען]

גיטל: דו נעמסט אַרויס דאָס בוך?

שׂרה: ניין, איך נעם נישט אַרויס דאָס בוך, איך נעם אַרויס די העפֿט.

It's morning in Lernton, and Professor Kluger's students are chatting in class. Read the short dialogues above.

- How do the negative statements here differ from those in **געניטונג 1**?
- Which elements are missing or different? Which elements stay the same?
- How do the nouns here differ from those in **געניטונג 1**? (Hint: Look at the articles.)

NOTE:

Just as the verbal prefix **אַרויס** comes between **נישט** and the negated noun, so may a preposition, such as **אין** in the following sentence:

איך לויף נישט אין דעם פּאַרק.

The two phenomena (separable prefix and preposition) may also occur together:

איך גיי נישט אַרויס פֿון דעם הויז.

געניטונג 7: ווער איז דער פֿידלער?

Rivke and Shikl's band have just done a photoshoot, and they've already gotten a call from a journalist who is confused about who plays what instrument. Answer the journalist's questions below according to the photo, being sure to use proper negation.

דוגמא: ריינע איז די קלאַרנעט־שפּילערין?

ניין, ריינע איז נישט די קלאַרנעט־שפּילערין. ריינע שפּילט גיטאַרע.

1. מירל איז די זינגערין?
2. רבֿקה איז די גיטאַרע־שפּילערין?
3. רפֿאל איז דער באַס־שפּילער?
4. פּאָל איז דער פֿידל־שפּילער?
5. שיקל איז דער פּיאַנע־שפּילער?

ג גראַמאַטיק:
עס איז דאָ

עס איז דאָ אַ <u>טיש</u> אין קלאַס. עס איז נישטאָ קיין <u>בענקל</u> אין קלאַס.
עס איז דאָ אַ <u>בוך</u> אויפֿן טיש. עס איז נישטאָ קיין <u>דרעטלער</u> אויפֿן טיש.

געניטונג 1: עס איז דאָ

The sentences above describe what is and isn't in the classroom and on the table. What difference do you notice between the forms for *there is* and *there isn't*?

- What are the different elements that make up each of these phrases?
- What is added or changed when either phrase is negated?

NOTE:

The word **דאָ** generally means *here*. In these sentences, however, it does not have any independent meaning—only as part of the verbal phrase **איז / זײַנען דאָ**, which expresses *existence* (not "here-ness"). In order to say "There is a book **here**," a second **דאָ** is needed: **עס איז דאָ אַ בוך דאָ**. The same goes for **נישטאָ** —though it arises from a contraction of **נישט** and **דאָ**, it really has to do with *nonexistence* (not "elsewhere-ness"). "There is no book **here**" is **עס איז נישטאָ קיין בוך דאָ**.

געניטונג 2: וואָסער בילד

.1

.2

.3

.4

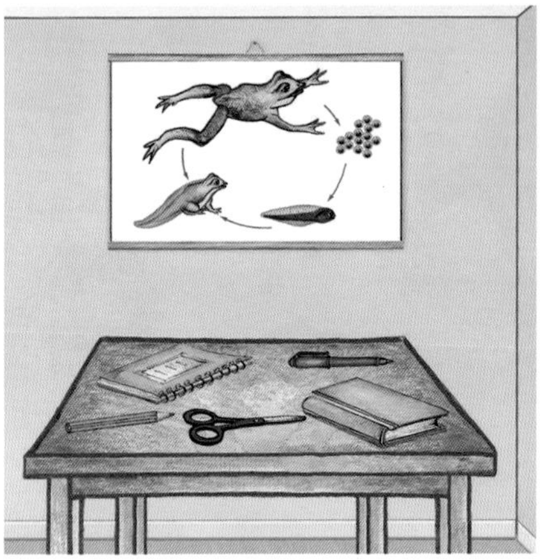

.5

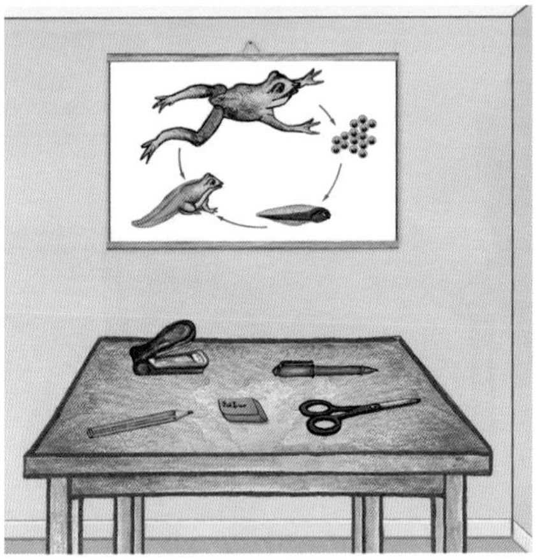

.6

פֿון וואָסער בילד טראַכט איך?

What picture am I thinking of? Figure out which image your partner has in mind by asking questions about what is in the picture. Once you have guessed correctly, switch roles.

דוגמא:

א: עס איז דאָ אַ דרעטלער אויפֿן טיש?

ב: ניין, עס איז נישטאָ קיין דרעטלער אויפֿן טיש.

א: ס׳איז בילד נומער צוויי?

ב: יאָ.

א: הוראַ!

NOTE:

The phrase **עס איז** is often contracted to **ס׳איז**.

היימאַרבעט

Describe one of the pictures above, noting both what is and is *not* in the classroom and on the table. Use the phrases **אין קלאַס** and **אויפֿן טיש**. Structure your sentences like the ones on page 176.

געניטונג 3: וויפֿל?

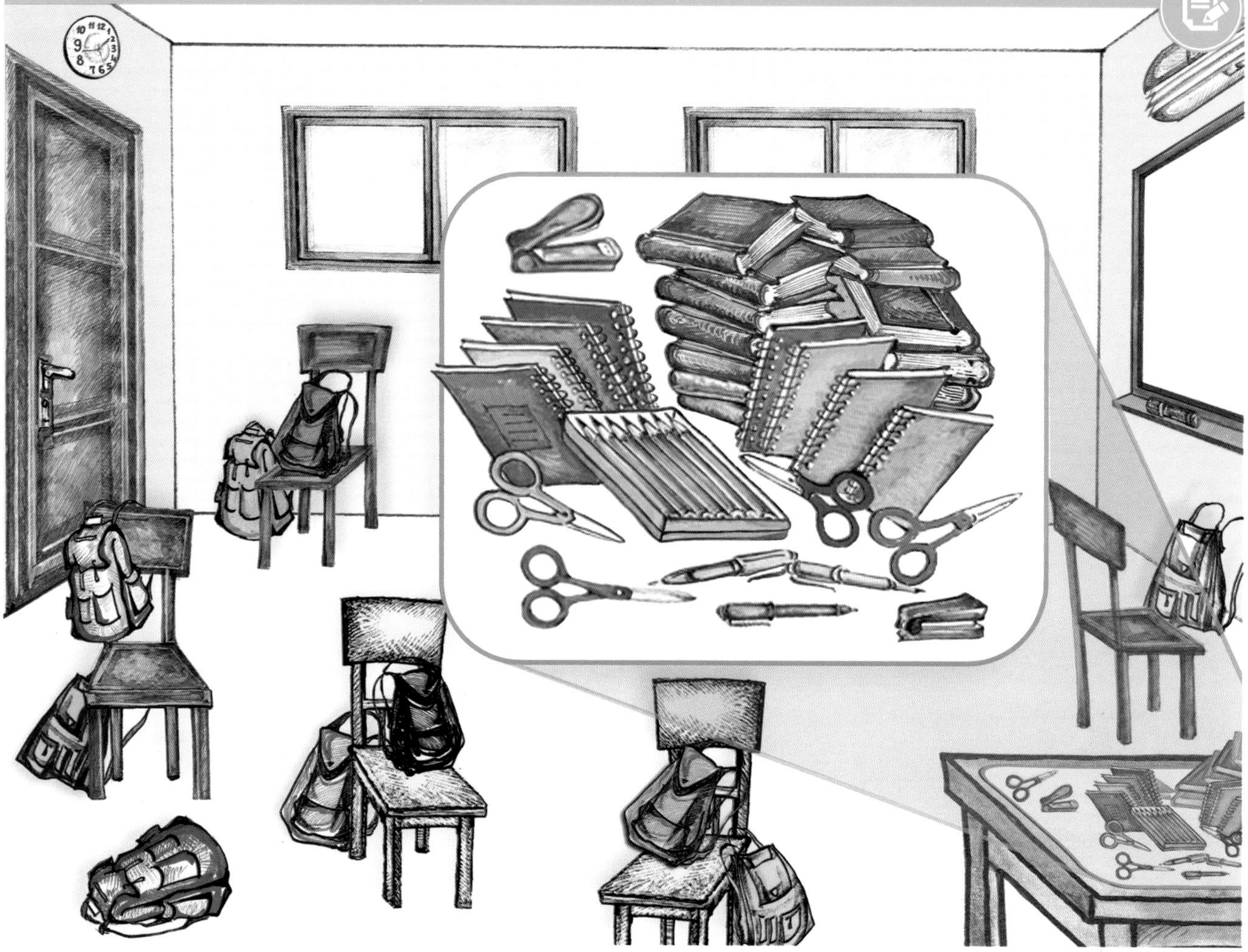

After a study session, Professor Kluger's classroom is a mess! Elke calls Avrom to complain, and he asks her for details about what items are there. Read the dialogue.

אַבֿרהם: וויפֿל <u>רוקזעק</u> זײַנען דאָ אין קלאַס? — how many

עלקע: עס זײַנען דאָ <u>צען רוקזעק</u> אין קלאַס.

אַבֿרהם: וויפֿל <u>ביכער</u> זײַנען דאָ אין קלאַס?

עלקע: עס זײַנען דאָ <u>אַ סך ביכער</u> אין קלאַס!

אַבֿרהם: וויפֿל <u>סטודענטן</u> זײַנען דאָ אין קלאַס?

עלקע: עס זײַנען נישטאָ קיין <u>סטודענטן</u> אין קלאַס!

What difference do you notice between the forms for *there is* (in **געניטונג 1**) and *there are* (shown here)? Which word changes when there are *many* items, as opposed to just one?

Write a few sentences about the picture above, noting which objects are and are *not* in the classroom. Model your sentences on Elke's lines in the dialogue.

גענײטונג 4: אין קלאַס און אין הויז

סטודענט א (אין קלאַס)

Professor Kluger is at the stationery store shopping for school supplies, but she has forgotten to check which items she already owns.

- Help Professor Kluger check what's already in her classroom (see below) while your partner checks her house (see page A6).
- Ask your partner about each item listed below, as in the model provided, and write down (in the corresponding blank) how many of that item Professor Kluger owns.

דרעטלערס _____	שערן _____	בלעטלעך _____	מעקערס _1_	זייגערס _____
לאָמפּן _____	ביכער _____	העפֿטן _____	בלײַערס _____	פֿעדערס _____

אין קלאַס

דוגמא:

א: װיפֿל מעקערס זײַנען דאָ אין הויז?

ב: עס איז דאָ איין מעקער אין הויז. װיפֿל מעקערס זײַנען דאָ אין קלאַס?

א: עס זײַנען נישטאָ קיין מעקערס אין קלאַס. אין גאַנצן איז דאָ איין מעקער.

NOTE:

The question **װיפֿל מעקערס זײַנען דאָ** (and others like it) are asked in the plural (**מעקערס זײַנען**). However, the answer may be either in the plural or in the singular, depending on the number of items actually present: **עס איז דאָ איין מעקער** or **עס זײַנען דאָ פֿינף מעקערס.**
If there are *no* items present at all, the answer may be either plural or singular: **עס זײַנען נישטאָ קיין מעקערס** or **עס איז נישטאָ קיין מעקער.**

אין גאַנצן — in total

היימאַרבעט

Write out how many of each item there are in the classroom and in the house, and list which items aren't there at all.

- Refer to both the picture above and the one on page A6.
- When an object appears in both places, mention whether there are more or fewer of that object in class, as in the model below.

דוגמא:

עס זײַנען דאָ פֿינף בלײַערס אין הויז. עס זײַנען דאָ װייניקער בלײַערס אין קלאַס - נאָר דרײַ. עס זײַנען נישטאָ קיין בלעטלעך אין הויז, און אויך נישט אין קלאַס.

געניטונג 5: לויט מײַן דערפֿאַרונג...

עלקע: וויפֿל פֿענצטער זײַנען דאָ אין דײַן דירה?

אַבֿרהם: אין מײַן דירה זײַנען דאָ צוויי פֿענצטער.

Elke and Avrom are chatting after class. Examine the short dialogue above.

- What phrase is the first sentence unit (preceding the verb) in each sentence?
- Until now, what word have we usually seen before the verb phrase **זײַנען דאָ**?
- Is any meaning lost as a result of omitting this word?

The **עס** that we have seen in the phrases **עס איז/זײַנען דאָ** is in fact a sort of placeholder subject—it does not contribute any meaning to the sentence on its own. Instead, its job is to make the grammar work by occupying the space in front of the verb so that the verb still comes second. As soon as some other sentence element takes over that job (in this case, a prepositional phrase of location), then **עס** is no longer needed and disappears.

Answer the questions below as in the dialogue above.

- Be sure to make **עס** disappear by placing the location phrase in first position.
- In your answers, use **מײַן** instead of the question's **דײַן** where appropriate.

מײַן my

1. וויפֿל פֿענצטער זײַנען דאָ אין דײַן דירה?
2. וויפֿל ביכער זײַנען דאָ אין דײַן רוקזאַק?
3. וויפֿל זייגערס זײַנען דאָ אויף דײַן וואַנט?
4. וויפֿל פֿעדערס זײַנען דאָ אויף דײַן טיש?
5. וויפֿל בלעטלעך זײַנען דאָ אין דײַן העפֿט?
6. וויפֿל שטאַטן זײַנען דאָ אין די פֿאַראייניקטע שטאַטן?
7. וויפֿל לענדער זײַנען דאָ אין צפֿון־אַמעריקע?

געניטונג 6: אָוונט אין לערנטאָן

It's evening at Lernton College, and the students are in their dorm rooms. Their interactions will help prepare you for the following exercise.

אַבֿרהם: דאָס שפּילן שטערט מיר
צום לייענען!

סענדער: הײַנט איז משהס
געבורטסטאָג! ער כאַפּט
אַרײַן אַ וואָדקע.

גיטל: אײדל האָט אַ סך זאָרגן. זי עסט
נישט, זי שלאָפֿט נישט, און זי
אַרבעט מער ווי אַלע: נעכטן
(דינסטיק) — אַן עקזאַמען, הײַנט
(מיטוואָך) — אַן עסיי, מאָרגן
(דאָנערשטיק) — אַ רעפֿעראַט.

חנה: די באָבע איז שוין אויף יענער
וועלט, אָבער דער זיידע איז,
ברוך־השם, בײַם לעבן.

Based on the visual context, figure out the meaning of the blue words and phrases in the captions above. Write each one next to its English equivalent below.

birthday	געבורטסטאָג	worries		tomorrow	
alive		today		*takes a shot of vodka*	
disturbs		yesterday		*in the world to come*	

געניטונג 7: שוין אַוועק דער נעכטן

הער־געניטונג ג־7

טיטל	♫ „שוין אַוועק דער נעכטן“ (פֿראַגמענט) פֿאָלקסליד
זינגער	**מיישקע אַלפּערט (Michael Alpert)** (לאָס־אַנדזשעלעס, פֿאַראייניקטע שטאַטן 1954 –)
רעקאָרדירונג	2006, פֿאַראייניקטע שטאַטן

The exact origins of this popular Yiddish folk song are unknown. Variants of the song, and additional verses, exist in Yiddish and in other languages, including surzhyk, *an intermediate dialect between Russian and Ukrainian. In this latter language, the song (with the title "*Ne zhurite khloptsy,*" or "Don't Worry, Brothers") is popular among Lubavitch Hasidim, who interpret its comment on the ephemeral nature of life on Earth as a philosophy of the attachment of a Hasid to his rebbe. This recording features* **Michael Alpert**, *a multi-instrumentalist, vocalist, songwriter, and a central figure in the klezmer revival of the late twentieth century.*

איידער איר הערט זיך צו צום ליד, לייענט די פֿראַגעס אונטן. זיי וועלן אײַך העלפֿן פֿאַרשטיין דאָס ליד.

- Underline all words and phrases that you recognize from the preceding exercise.

1. מע זינגט דאָ פֿון נעכטן, פֿון מאָרגן, און פֿון הײַנט. פֿון די דרײַ „טעג“, וועלכער איז דער וויכטיקסטער? — which; most important

2. וואָס טאָר מען נישט שטערן מיט זאָרגן? — must one not

3. וואָס דאַרף מען טאָן כּל־זמן מען איז בײַם לעבן? — should; as long as [קאָל־זמאַן]

4. וואָס איז דאָ אויף דער וועלט, וואָס איז נישטאָ אויף יענער וועלט? — this

---

Listen to the audio recording once through, with your book closed. Don't worry if you don't understand every word—just try to get the gist. What sort of a song is this?

Listen to the song once more, this time following along with the text below.

2 מאָל

שוין אַוועק דער נעכטן, — gone
נאָך ניטאָ דער מאָרגן. — still; נישטאָ
ס׳איז נאָר דאָ אַ ביסעלע הײַנט — — only
שטערט אים ניט מיט זאָרגן. — it

2 מאָל

כאַפּט אַרײַן אַ וואָדקע,
כּל־זמן איר זײַט בײַם לעבן.
אם־ירצה־השם אויף יענער וועלט — God willing [מירצעשעם]
וועט מען אײַך ניט געבן. — they won't give you (any)

◀ CONTINUED

CONTINUED

Many of the sentence structures in this song may be somewhat unfamiliar for an English speaker. Group the lines of the song into sentences so that each sentence is understandable on its own.

Once you have done this, label each sentence with **הײַנט**, **מאָרגן**, or **נעכטן**, depending on whether it has to do with the present, future, or past. A sentence may have more than one label.

Now answer the questions above, using words and phrases from the song.

According to the song, what *does* exist—and what doesn't?

- Fill in each of the blanks below using one of the following expressions.

עס איז דאָ	**עס זײַנען דאָ**	**עס איז נישטאָ קיין**	**עס זײַנען נישטאָ קיין**

1. ________ וואָדקע אויף יענער וועלט.
2. ________ נעכטן.
3. ________ אַ ביסעלע הײַנט.
4. ________ אַ סך זאָרגן אין לעבן.
5. ________ מענטשן וואָס שטערן דאָס ביסעלע הײַנט מיט זאָרגן.

Using the template below, compose your own version of **שוין אַוועק דער נעכטן**. Fill in the blanks with academic terminology from **קאַפּיטל 6**, whether names of areas of study (**ליטעראַטור**) or types of schoolwork (**היימאַרבעט**).

- For the fourth line, you may write any imperative phrase (i.e., command) that you like.

שוין אַוועק דער אויספֿרעג,

נאָך ניטאָ דער עקזאַמען.

ס'איז נאָר דאָ אַ ביסעלע היימאַרבעט.

אַרבעט הײַנט נישט צו פֿיל.

כאַפּט אַרײַן אַ(ן) עסיי,

כּל־זמן איר שטודירט ליטעראַטור.

אם־ירצה־השם אויפֿן ביאָלאָגיע־קורס,

וועט מען אײַך ניט געבן.

געניטונג 8: ווו וועלן מיר מאַכן די היימאַרבעט?

Moyshe and Sender are trying to find a place to study. Describe the classrooms pictured below, as in the example.

- Use schoolwork words in your descriptions of the activities going on in each room.

דוגמא:

אין ביאָלאָגיע־צימער איז דאָ אַ פּאָפּוגײַ. ער האַלט אין עקזאַמען.

ביאָלאָגיע

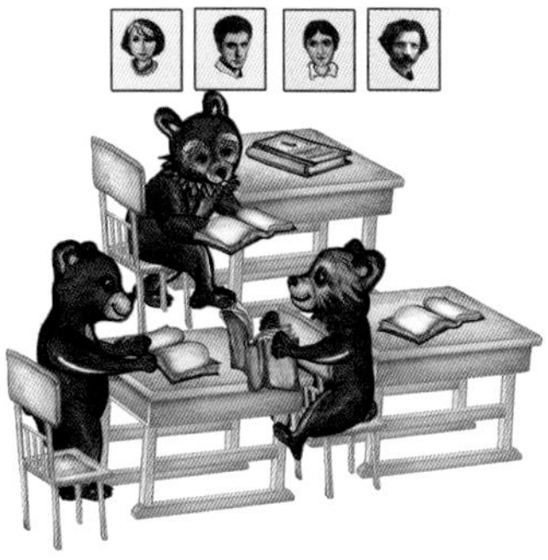

ליטעראַטור

כעמיע

מאַטעמאַטיק

מוזיק

געשיכטע

Now that you've established what the options are, write a dialogue in which Moyshe and Sender decide where to study, based on the model below.

- Use quantifiers, comparatives, probability adverbs, and phrases like **איך בין מסכּים** and **איך מיין אַז יאָ/נישט** to talk about your opinions.
- Be sure to use **עס איז/זײַנען דאָ** in your comparisons of one workspace to the next.

דוגמא:

משה: איך מיין אַז דער ביאָלאָגיע־צימער איז גוט. דאָרטן זײַנען נישטאָ קיין בערן. ביסט מסכּים?

סענדער: ניין, איך בין נישט מסכּים! אין ביאָלאָגיע־צימער האַלט מען אין עקזאַמען! דער מאַטעמאַטיק־צימער איז בעסער. דאָרטן זײַנען דאָ ווייניקער סטודענטן ווי אין ביאָלאָגיע־צימער.

בעסער	better
עמעצער	someone
קיינער (איז נישטאָ)	(there is) no one
דאָרטן	there

NOTE:

In the example, **דאָרטן** is used to specify the location that is being discussed. The word **דאָ** must still appear as part of the phrase **זײַנען דאָ**.

6 וואָקאַבולאַר־איבערבליק

א. לימודים און שולאַרבעט־טערמינען
DISCIPLINES AND SCHOOLWORK TERMS

disciplines	לימודים
history	די געשיכטע
theater arts	די דראַמאַטורגיע
humanities	די הומאַניסטיק
chemistry	די כעמיע
natural science	די נאַטור־וויסנשאַפֿט
social science	די סאָציאַל־וויסנשאַפֿט
art	די קונסט
art history	די קונסט־געשיכטע
Jewish studies	די ייִדישע לימודים

schoolwork	שולאַרבעט
exercise	די געניטונג (ען)
homework	די היימאַרבעט
lesson	די לעקציע (ס)
question	די פֿראַגע (ס)
quiz	דער אויספֿרעג (ן)
(field of) study	דער לימוד (ים) [לימעד (לימודים)]
essay	דער עסיי (ען)
exam	דער עקזאַמען (ס)
presentation	דער רעפֿעראַט (ן)

verbs	ווערבן
to teach	לערנען
to study (a subject)	שטודירן
to take a quiz, exam	האַלטן אַן אויספֿרעג, עקזאַמען איך האַלט, מיר האַלטן
to give a presentation	האַלטן אַ רעפֿעראַט
to hear a lecture	הערן אַ לעקציע
to do homework	מאַכן היימאַרבעט
to do an exercise	מאַכן אַ געניטונג
to write an essay	שרײַבן אַן עסיי

adjectives	אַדיעקטיוון
boring	נודנע
interesting	אינטערעסאַנט

א. לימודים און שולאַרבעט־טערמינען
DISCIPLINES AND SCHOOLWORK TERMS (continued)

useful expressions	נוציקע אויסדרוקן
a little bit (of)	אַ ביסל...
a lot (of)	אַ סך... [סאַך]
less (than)	ווייניקער (ווי)
more (than)	מער (ווי)
of course	אַוודאי [אַוואַדע]
maybe	אפֿשר [עפּשער]
probably	מסתּמא [מיסטאָמע]
I believe that...	איך מיין אַז...
I believe so	איך מיין אַז יאָ
I don't believe so	איך מיין אַז ניין
I agree	איך בין מסכּים [מאַסקעם]
I don't agree	איך בין נישט מסכּים
so	אַזוי
about	וועגן
only	נאָר

די אינזשעניריע; די אַנטראָפּאָלאָגיע; די ביאָלאָגיע;
די געאָגראַפֿיע; די ליטעראַטור; די לינגוויסטיק;
די מאַטעמאַטיק; די מוזיק; די סאָציאָלאָגיע; די עקאָנאָמיק;
די פּאָליטיק; די פּסיכאָלאָגיע; די פֿיזיק; די פֿילאָסאָפֿיע;
די קאָמפּיוטער־וויסנשאַפֿט; די רעליגיע

ג. עס איז דאָ
THERE IS

yesterday is gone	שוין אַוועק דער נעכטן
worry	די זאָרג (ן)
today	הײַנט
tomorrow	מאָרגן
yesterday	נעכטן
to disturb	שטערן
in the world to come	אויף יענער וועלט
alive	בײַם לעבן
take a shot of vodka	כאַפּט אַרײַן אַ וואָדקע
still; after	נאָך

26ב גראַמאַטיק־איבערבליק

NEGATION — פֿאַרניינונג

We know already how to negate intransitive (objectless) verbs, adding **נישט** after the conjugated part of the verb: **זי אַרבעט נישט שבת.**

- An adverb or pronoun may also separate **נישט** and the verb: **זונטיק אַרבעט זי אויך נישט.**

But what about *transitive* verbs? How do we negate an object (or other noun)? If the noun would take the indefinite article in a positive sentence, then we use the **negative** article **קיין**.

- In the negative sentence, **קיין** is placed wherever the indefinite article would have been:

איך בין אַ לערערין. ← איך בין נישט קיין לערערין.

- As seen in the examples below, the negative article **קיין** always precedes the noun to which it refers. (It is *not* bound to the word **נישט**, though the two often co-occur.)

ער איז נישט קיין פּילאָט.

זי עסט נישט קיין באַר.

ער לייגט נישט אַוועק קיין העפֿט.

ער זיצט נישט אויף קיין בענקל.

קיין בער זע איך נישט...

- The plural indefinite article (which is invisible in a positive sentence) is still replaced by **קיין** in a negative sentence.

זי האָט ביכער. ← זי האָט נישט קיין ביכער.

The same goes for uncountable nouns:

ער טרינקט קאַווע. ← ער טרינקט נישט קיין קאַווע.

- Quantitative constructions such as **אַ סך** also take **קיין** in the negative.

איך טרינק נישט קיין סך קאַווע.

- The pronoun **קיינער** (*no one*) also derives from **קיין**.

קיינער אַרבעט נישט פֿרײַטיק אין אָוונט.

If the negated noun is **definite**, then we do **not** use **קיין**, and the article remains:

זי איז נישט די לערערין.

- The same is true of possessives.

ער איז נישט מײַן דאָקטער.

- Proper nouns (used to refer to a specific *real* entity in the world, not to *allude* to a general concept) are also considered definite, and thus do not trigger the use of **קיין** .

דער מאַן איז נישט משה.

גראַמאַטיק־איבערבליק 6ג

THERE IS — עס איז דאָ

- The idiomatic verb phrase **איז / זײַנען דאָ** *(there is / are)* is used to discuss the presence or absence of people and things in a given context.

  There is a pencil. ← עס איז דאָ אַ בלײַער.

- The pronoun **עס** is not the true subject of the verb **זײַן** in this phrase. Rather, the verb conjugates according to the number of the noun that is present or absent.

עס איז דאָ איין בלײַער. ← עס זײַנען דאָ צוויי בלײַערס.

איין סטודענט איז דאָ. ← אַלע סטודענטן זײַנען דאָ.

- Mass nouns behave as singular, as usual.

עס איז דאָ קאַווע.

- Quantitative constructions may also trigger plural verb conjugation, depending on whether the descriptive noun in the construction is plural.

עס זײַנען דאָ אַ סך בלײַערס.

עס איז דאָ אַ סך קאַווע.

Similarly, a question and answer may not match in terms of verb conjugation:

וויפֿל בלײַערס זײַנען דאָ?

עס איז דאָ איין בלײַער.

- As we have seen, **נישט** contracts with **דאָ** (in the case of the verb phrase **איז / זײַנען דאָ**). Hence, this phrase has a particular appearance when it is negated.

עס איז **נישטאָ** קיין קאַווע.

עס זײַנען **נישטאָ** קיין בלײַערס.

- The combination **עס איז** is often contracted to **ס׳איז** (as **מען איז** sometimes becomes **מ׳איז**).

- When something other than the pronoun **עס** occupies the first sentence position, the **עס** disappears, as it is essentially a placeholder, itself devoid of meaning.

זונטיק זײַנען נישטאָ קיין סטודענטן.

מאָנטיק איז דאָ איין סטודענט.

- In order to specify that something is present *here* or *there*, the adverbs **דאָ** and **דאָרטן** must be used. (The **דאָ** included in the verb phrase discussed here is location neutral.)

דאָ זײַנען דאָ אַ סך בלײַערס.

דאָרטן איז דאָ אַ סך קאַווע.

- When saying that *no one* is present, **קיינער** is used, with an obligatory double negative:

קיינער איז דאָרטן נישטאָ.

איבערחזר־געניטונגען 6

געניטונג 1: דער גולם גייט אין קלאַס

Your *goylem* just signed up to take some classes at the local community college. Describe his class schedule Monday–Friday, as in the model.

- Talk about the number of students in each class and the kind (and quantity) of assignments the *goylem* does.

דוגמא:

מאָנטיק גייט דער גולם אויפֿן פּסיכאָלאָגיע־קורס. עס זײַנען דאָ 120 סטודענטן אין קלאַס. ער מאַכט נישט קיין סך היימאַרבעט.

געניטונג 2: מײַן שרײַבטיש

ווידעאָ־געניטונג

איבערחזר־סעקציע־2

Practice classroom vocabulary with these video interviews, which you can find online with the accompanying exercise.

געניטונג 3: וואָס האָבן די סטודענטן?

ענטפֿערט אויף די פֿראַגעס אונטן, לויטן בילד. שרײַבט גאַנצע זאַצן.

- Use the appropriate singular or plural form of **עס איז/זײַנען דאָ**, depending on the noun.

דוגמא: אײדל האָט אַ רוקזאַק?

ניין, אײדל האָט נישט קיין רוקזאַק.

1. גיטל האָט בלײַערס?
2. וויפֿל מענטשן מיט רוקזעק זײַנען דאָ אויפֿן בילד?
3. אײדל האָט די שער?
4. וויפֿל סטודענטקעס מיט ביכער זײַנען דאָ אויפֿן בילד?
5. וויפֿל בענקלעך זײַנען דאָ אויפֿן בילד?
6. משה האָט אַ העפֿט?
7. וויפֿל זייגערס זײַנען דאָ אויפֿן בילד?
8. אַבֿרהם האָט די ביכער?

געניטונג 4: ווּ איז פּערל?

It's the first day of school, and Perl's mother can't find her anywhere. Describe the mother's search for Perl by writing complete negative sentences using the elements provided below.

- All verbs are provided in the infinitive, so be sure to conjugate each one and include the appropriate negation words.

דוגמא: די מאַמע / זען / פּערלען.

די מאַמע זעט נישט פּערלען.

1. פּערל / ליגן / אין / אַ בעט.
2. פּערל / עסן / באַנאַנעס.
3. פּערל / לייענען / אַ בוך.
4. פּערל / זיצן / אויף / דעם בענקל.

פּערל איז אין גאַראַזש! פּערל, ביסט גרייט צו גיין אין שול? (ready: גרייט)

Now that Perl has been found, she's in no rush to get ready for school. What's holding her back from being ready? Make complete negative sentences (as above) out of the elements below and match them to the mother's exasperated responses as she attempts to hurry Perl along.

דוגמא:

7. איך / זײַן / הונגעריק

איך בין נישט הונגעריק.

	פּערל:	מאַמע:
[1]already	5. עס / זײַן / דאָ / אַ רוקזאַק / אין גאַראַזש.	7 פּערל, עס שוין[1]!
	6. איך / האָבן / די העפּטן.	___ די העפּטן זײַנען אויפֿן טיש!
[2]hungry	7. איך / זײַן / הונגעריק[2].	___ דער רוקזאַק איז אויפֿן בענקל!
[3]so	8. עס / זײַן / דאָ / זייגערס / אין הויז.	___ טאָ[3] קום שוין!
[4]time; [5]o'clock	9. מיר / האָבן / אַ סך / צײַט[4].	___ פּערל, עס איז שוין אַכט אַ זייגער[5]!

7

קאַפּיטל זיבן:
אַדיעקטיוון און פּאָסעסיוו

CHAPTER GOALS

- In this chapter, you will learn to use descriptive and possessive adjectives.

וואָקאַבולאַר:	
adjectives	אַדיעקטיוון

גראַמאַטיק:	
possessive adjectives	פּאָסעסיווע אַדיעקטיוון

קולטור — טעקסט:	
"Marzipans" (Kadia Molodowsky)	„מאַרצעפּאַנעס“ (קאַדיע מאָלאָדאָווסקי)

קולטור — אוידיאָ:	
"Vanity of Vanities" (folk song)	„הבֿל איז הבֿלים“ (פֿאָלקסליד)

קולטור — ווידעאָ:	
Mirele Efros (Joseph Berne)	„מירעלע אפֿרת“ (יוסף בערנע)

א וואָקאַבולאַר:
אַדיעקטיוון

הויך ני׳דעריק

ברייט שמאָל

דיק דין

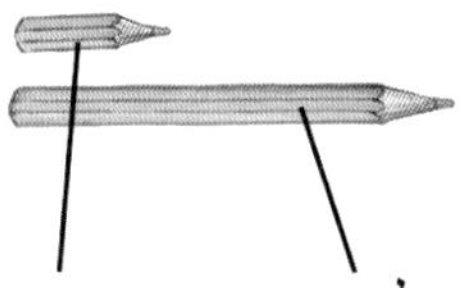

לאַנג קורץ

גלײַך קרום

נײַ אַלט

שווער לײַכט

גרויס קליין

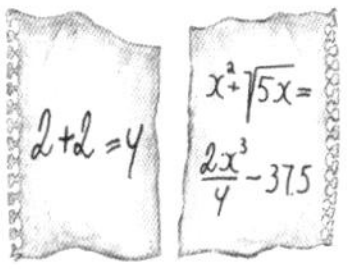

שווער לײַכט

ווייך האַרט

ריין שמוציק

קאַלט הייס

שיין מיאוס [מיִעס]

גיך פּאַמעלעך

קלוג נאַריש

שטאַרק שוואַך

אַלט יונג

טרו׳יעריק פֿריילעך

געניטונג 1: וואָסער אויטאָ איז אַלט?

PDF

אויף רעכטס on the right

אויף לינקס on the left

אויף רעכטס אָדער אויף לינקס? קוקט אויף די בילדער אויבן און שרײַבט אַרײַן די פּעלנדיקע ווערטער אונטן, לויט דער דוגמא.

דוגמא: דער אויטאָ אויף *לינקס* איז אַלט.

1. דער זאַק אויף ______ איז שווער.
2. די פֿרוי (woman) אויף ______ איז טרויעריק.
3. די חיה (animal [כײַע]) אויף ______ איז פּאַמעלעך.
4. די סטודענטקע אויף ______ איז קלוג.
5. דער מאַן אויף ______ איז שוואַך.
6. דער גאָרטן אויף ______ איז מיאוס.
7. די היימאַרבעט אויף ______ איז לײַכט.
8. דאָס וואַסער אויף ______ איז הייס.

גענিטונג 2: דײַן בלײַער איז קלײן?

Write a response to each prompt, as in the model below.

דוגמא:

דער בלײַער (קלײן / גרויס)

מײַן בלײַער איז גרויס.

אָדער

איך האָב נישט קײן בלײַער.

NOTE:

A common synonym for **לײַכט** (in both of its meanings) is **גרינג**.

1. דער רוקזאַק (שווער / לײַכט)
2. דער ברודער (יונג / אַלט)
3. דער צימער (הייס / קאַלט)
4. דער הונט (קלוג / נאַריש)
5. דער ייִדיש־קלאַס (שווער / לײַכט)
6. די טיר (קרום / גלײַך)
7. די העפֿט (נײַ / אַלט)

אין קלאַס

With a partner, take turns asking each other questions based on the prompts above, as in the example.

דוגמא: דער בלײַער (קלײן / גרויס)

א: דײַן בלײַער איז קלײן אָדער גרויס?

ב: מײַן בלײַער איז גרויס.

אָדער

ב: איך האָב נישט קײן בלײַער.

גענײַטונג 3: אײדלס צימער

Eydl has just moved into a new dorm, and her mother has called to ask about the room. Fill in the missing pronoun and verb in each of Eydl's answers below, as in the example.

דוגמא:

מאַמע: ווי איז דער טיש?

אײדל: ער איז לאַנג און רויט.

מאַמע: ווי איז דאָס בענקל?

אײדל: ______ __________ ברוין און שמאָל.

מאַמע: ווי איז דער זייגער?

אײדל: ______ __________ קליין און אָראַנזש.

מאַמע: ווי איז די טיר?

אײדל: ______ __________ בלוי און שווער.

מאַמע: ווי איז דער פֿענצטער?

אײדל: ______ __________ קרום און שמוציק.

מאַמע: ווי זײַנען די ווענט?

אײדל: ______ __________ דין און גרוי.

מאַמע: ווי איז די סטעליע?

אײדל: ______ __________ שוואַרץ און נידעריק.

! געדענקט!

דער ← ער

די ← זי

דאָס ← עס

די (מערצאָל) ← זיי

Draw a quick sketch of Eydl's room, based on the adjectives Eydl uses in her descriptions.

Now answer the following questions about the dialogue. Use complete sentences.

- Note the use of the particle **צו** with the infinitive (following **שווער**).

1. עס איז גוט צו וווינען אין אײדלס צימער?
2. וואָס מיינט אײדלס מאַמע וועגן איר טאָכטערס צימער?
3. וואָס איז די פּראָבלעם?

דוגמא: עס איז שווער צו זען (see) אַ בײַטער וואָס איז קליין.

א) עס איז שווער צו זען דורך (through) אַ ________ וואָס איז ________.

ב) עס איז שווער צו שטיין אונטער (under) אַ ________ וואָס איז ________.

ג) עס איז שווער צו זיצן אויף אַ ________ וואָס איז ________.

ד) עס איז שווער צו שלאָפֿן ווען די ________ זײַנען ________.

ה) עס איז שווער צו עפֿענען אַ ________ וואָס איז ________.

געניטונג 4: פּערל גייט אין שול

הער־געניטונג א־4

פּערל קומט אַהיים פֿון דעם ערשטן טאָג אין שול און זאָגט דער מאַמען וואָס זי מוז האָבן פֿאַר די קלאַסן.

Perl comes home from the first day of school and tells her mother what she must have for her classes. Help Rokhl make her shopping list.

- Listen to the dialogue once, writing down each classroom object Perl mentions.
- Listen again, writing down the adjectives (colors included) that Perl uses.
- Be sure to write each adjective next to the object it refers to.

What objects mentioned in the dialogue does Perl *not* want, and why? Fill in the blanks below.

מוז	must
אָט	here (*with pointing*)
שוין	already
נאַ	here you go!

פּערל וויל נישט דאָס ____________________,

ווײַל עס איז צו ____________________, (because)

און דעם ____________________,

ווײַל ער איז צו ____________________.

NOTE:

Since **ווײַל** is a conjunction (like **און**), it “resets” the sentence unit count to zero. Hence, it is followed by normal subject-verb word order.

געניטונג 5: פֿייגי שרײַבט צו קליין

Shloymele is dissatisfied with the actions of his siblings, and he wants them to behave differently. Based on the prompts and example below, write out the commands he gives.

- Words you’ve seen used as **adjectives**—describing *things* (i.e., nouns)—are used here as **adverbs**, describing *actions* (i.e., verbs). Most Yiddish adjectives can be used as adverbs in this way, without changing their form.
- Pay attention to the placement of **נישט** and the adverb **צו** in the example, and be sure to write your sentences accordingly.

דוגמא: פֿייגי שפּילט פּיאַנע צו גיך. (זינגען; פּאַמעלעך)

פֿייגי, שפּיל נישט אַזוי גיך – ס'איז שווער צו זינגען. שפּיל פּאַמעלעך! (so)

1. מענדל זינגט צו שטיל. (הערן; הויך) (quietly)
2. ליבי רעדט צו גיך. (פֿאַרשטיין; פּאַמעלעך)
3. פֿייגי שרײַבט צו קליין. (לייענען; גרויס)
4. מענדל שפּילט צו קלוג אין קאָרטן. (געווינען; נאַריש)

NOTE:

Adverbs may also modify words and phrases besides verbs, particularly adjectives:

דער לאָמפּ שײַנט העל. ←

דער עפּל איז העל רויט.

ב גראַמאַטיק: פּאָסעסיווע אַדיעקטיוון

עלקע: מײַן פּראָפֿעסאָר איז עטל קלוגער.

אַבֿרהם: דײַן פּראָפֿעסאָר איז עטל קלוגער? זי איז אויך מײַן פּראָפֿעסאָר!

עלקע: זי איז אונדזער פּראָפֿעסאָר!

עלקע: דו קענסט אַריה־לייבן? אָט איז זײַן דירה, נומער 20.

אַבֿרהם: אָבער דאָס איז אויך מײַן דירה!

עלקע: נו, דאָס איז אײַער דירה!

משה: דײַן פּראָפֿעסאָר איז עטל קלוגער? אָט איז איר קלאַסצימער.

אַבֿרהם: ס׳איז אויך הערשל יאָשידאָס קלאַסצימער?

משה: נו יאָ, ס׳איז זייער קלאַסצימער.

גענִיטונג 1: מײַן פּראָפֿעסאָר איז עטל קלוגער

Avrom is going over his class schedule, room assignment, and classroom locations before the new semester starts. Read the short dialogues on the preceding page and answer the following questions.

1. ווער איז אַבֿרהם און עלקעס פּראָפֿעסאָר?
2. ווער וווינט אין דירה נומער 20?
3. ווער לערנט אין איין קלאַסצימער מיט עטל קלוגער?

Now read the dialogues again, paying close attention to the **possessive adjectives** shown in purple. Write these forms next to the corresponding pronouns in the table below.

פּראָנאָם	פּאָסעסיוּוער אַדיעקטיוו	פּראָנאָם	פּאָסעסיוּוער אַדיעקטיוו
איך		מיר	
דו		איר	
ער		זיי	
זי			
עס	מײַן		

גענִיטונג 2: זײַן בלײַער איז בלוי

The students in class are talking about what they have. Fill in the first blank with the appropriate possessive adjective and the second blank with a descriptive adjective from the word box below.

דוגמא: וועלוול האָט אַ בלײַער. מײַן בלײַער איז בלוי.

1. איר שטודירט ייִדיש מיט פּראָפֿעסאָר קלוגער?
 ______ פּראָפֿעסאָר איז ______!
2. דו שרײַבסט אַן עסיי? ______ עסיי איז ______!
3. איך עס אַן עפּל. ______ עפּל איז ______.
4. מיר האָבן אַ טיש. ______ טיש איז ______.
5. דאָס בערעלע האָט אַ רוקזעקל. ______ רוקזעקל איז ______.
6. איידל שפּילט פֿידל. ______ פֿידל איז ______.
7. די סטודענטן וווינען אין אינטערנאַט. ______ אינטערנאַט איז ______.

בלוי	אַלט	רויט
ברוין	קליין	שיין
קלוג	לאַנג	

גענײטונג 3: מײַנע ביכער אָדער דײַנע ביכער?

Etl and Hershl are setting up their shared classroom and discussing which supplies are whose. Read the dialogue below and pay special attention to the purple possessive adjectives.

עטל: מײַנע פֿעדערס זײַנען בלוי. דײַנע פֿעדערס זײַנען שוואַרץ.

הערשל: די ביכער אויפֿן טיש זײַנען מײַנע ביכער, אָדער דײַנע ביכער?

עטל: זיי זײַנען אונדזערע ביכער. מײַנע ביכער זײַנען אויפֿן בענקל.

How are the forms of the possessive adjectives in the dialogue above different from the ones presented at the beginning of this section?

- What causes this change? (Hint: Are the possessed nouns singular or plural?)

Based on the pattern you see here, write out the plural forms for all remaining possessive adjectives you encountered in **גענײטונג 1**.

Describe the items from Etl and Hershl's shared classroom pictured below, as in the model provided. Be sure to use the correct plural form of each possessive adjective.

- Use the dialogue to determine the owner of each set of items.
- Each of your answers should note the owner, quantity, and color of the items in question.
- Your answers should be in the **third person** *only* and so will *not* use any first- or second-person-possessive forms.

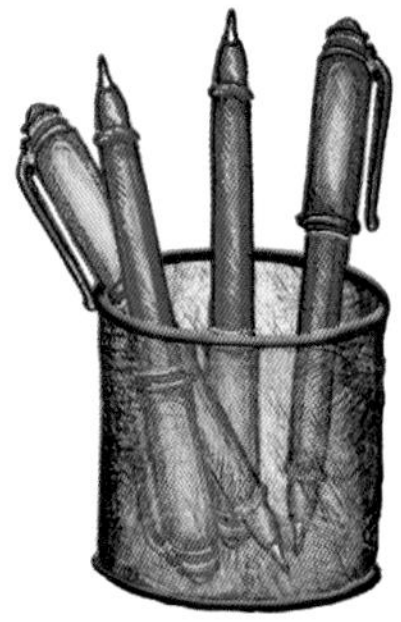

דוגמא:

עטל האָט פֿיר פֿעדערס. אירע פֿעדערס זײַנען בלוי.

.1 ______________________

.2 ______________________

.3 ______________________

גענִיטונג 4: װעמענס פֿעדער?

Elke and Eydl run into a spot of trouble determining the rightful owner of a desired pen. Read the dialogue below.

עלקע: גיב אַ קוק אויף מײַן פֿעדער! *take a look at*

אײדל: דײַן פֿעדער?! דאָס איז מײַן פֿעדער!

עלקע: דאָס איז... אונדזער פֿעדער.

אײדל: ניין, זאָל זײַן דײַן פֿעדער. אָט גייט משה. איך נעם זײַן פֿעדער. *let it be*

עלקע: אָבער זײַן פֿעדער איז צו קליין. אָט גייט שׂרה. נעם איר פֿעדער.

אײדל: איר פֿעדער איז צו דין.

עלקע: אָט גייען סענדער און גיטל. זיי האָבן צװיי פֿעדערס!

אײדל: איך נעם זייערע פֿעדערס!

עלקע: סענדער! גיטל! אײַערע פֿעדערס זײַנען אין סכּנה! *in danger* [סאַקאָנע]

שרײַבט איבער דעם דיאַלאָג מיט אַן אַנדער סובסטאַנטיװ (אַנשטאָט פֿעדער).

- This noun may be singular or plural—if it is plural, adjust the possessive adjectives accordingly.
- You may also replace the descriptive adjectives that appear in the dialogue.

Now identify the owner of each pen described below, according to the dialogue.

- In your answers, attach the possessive suffix ס- to the owner's name, as in the example.

NOTE:

The possessive suffix ס- is attached to a person's name in order to mark them as the **possessor** of another noun: **אײדלס פֿעדער**. This suffix is generally used only when the possessor is a *person,* as opposed to some other entity.

װעמענס whose

דוגמא: װעמענס פֿעדערס זײַנען אין סכּנה?

סענדער און גיטלס פֿעדערס זײַנען אין סכּנה.

1. װעמענס פֿעדער איז צו דין?
2. װעמענס פֿעדער איז צו קליין?

אין קלאַס

מיט אַ חבֿר, חזרט איבער דעם דיאַלאָג אויבן עטלעכע מאָל. רעדט אַזוי גיך און פֿליסיק װי מעגלעך.

Now repeat the dialogue, making the substitutions described above.

7 וואָקאַבולאַר־איבערבליק

א. אַדיעקטיוון ADJECTIVES

broad, wide	ברייט
fast	גיך
even	גלײַך
big	גרויס
easy, light (in weight)	גרינג
thin	דין
thick	דיק
high, tall, loud	הויך
hot	הייס
soft	ווייך
sad	טרויעריק
easy, light (in weight)	לײַכט
ugly	מיאוס [מיִעס]
foolish	נאַריש
low	נידעריק
new	נײַ
slow	פּאַמעלעך
happy	פֿריילעך
short	קורץ
smart	קלוג
small	קליין
crooked	קרום
clean	ריין
weak	שוואַך
heavy, difficult	שווער
strong	שטאַרק
beautiful, nice	שיין
narrow	שמאָל
dirty	שמוציק
	אַלט; האַרט; יונג; לאַנג; קאַלט

א. אַדיעקטיוון ADJECTIVES (continued)

marzipans	מאַרצעפּאַנעס
plum	די פֿלוים (ען)
store	די קראָם (ען)
bean; beans	דער באָב (עס)
tree	דער בוים (ביימער)
mushroom	דער שוואָם (ען)
dumpling	דאָס קניידל (עך)
boiled buckwheat	די הײדעלעך
bent, stooped	אײַנגעבויגן
to buy	קויפֿן
additional vocabulary	**נאָך וואָקאַבולאַר**
like, as	ווי
each, every	יעדער
to; too	צו
(on the) left	(אויף) לינקס
(on the) right	(אויף) רעכטס

ב. פּאָסעסיווע אַדיעקטיוון POSSESSIVE ADJECTIVES

my	מײַנ(ע)
your (*sg informal*)	דײַנ(ע)
his	זײַנ(ע)
her	איר(ע)
its	זײַנ(ע)
our	אונדזער(ע)
your (*pl; sg formal*)	אײַער(ע)
their	זייער(ע)
whose	וועמענס

7ב גראַמאַטיק־איבערבליק

POSSESSIVE ADJECTIVES — פּאָסעסיווע אַדיעקטיוון

In order to express relations of belonging, Yiddish uses **possessive adjectives**.

- Each personal pronoun has its corresponding possessive adjective.

איך האָב אַ העפֿט. ← מײַן העפֿט איז רויט.

דו האָסט אויך אַ העפֿט. ← דײַן העפֿט איז גרין.

- The form of the possessive depends not only on the pronoun to which it corresponds but also on the number (singular or plural) of the noun being possessed.

איך האָב צוויי העפֿטן. ← מײַנע העפֿטן זײַנען רויט.

- To ensure you are using the correct possessive, ask yourself two questions:
  (1) Whose noun is it? Mine? Yours? Hers?... and so on.
  (2) How *many* of this noun are there? Just one, or more than one?

  (As usual, uncountable nouns behave—in *klal-shprakh*—as though they are singular.)

- The full complement of possessive adjectives is to be found in the table below.

Plural Possessive	Singular Possessive	Pronoun
מײַנע	מײַן	איך
דײַנע	דײַן	דו
זײַנע	זײַן	ער
אירע	איר	זי
זײַנע	זײַן	עס
אונדזערע	אונדזער	מיר
אײַערע	אײַער	איר
זייערע	זייער	זיי

- Note that the pronouns **ער** and **עס** share the same possessive forms.

Another common way of marking possession of nouns (typically used only with *human* possessors) is to add the suffix **ס-** to the end of the possessor, whether it is a common or proper noun.

משה האָט אַ בלײַער. ← משהס בלײַער איז שוואַרץ.

דער סטודענט האָט צוויי העפֿטן. ←

דעם סטודענטס העפֿטן זײַנען קליין.

This form of the possessive triggers dative definite articles and adjective endings, which we will learn about in **13 קאַפּיטל**. For now, we will use this possessive ending with names only, where articles and adjectives are generally absent. Note that the ending remains the same *regardless* of the number of the possessed noun.

איבערחזר־געניטונגען 7

געניטונג 1: מײַן גולמס רוקזאַק

Describe the contents of your *goylem's* backpack. Use adjectives, colors, and objects learned in this chapter.

דוגמא:

דער גולם האָט צוויי העפֿטן. בײַדע העפֿטן זײַנען דיק און געל.

געניטונג 2: אַ נײַער צימער

You are redecorating your room and considering the furniture and other items required to pull off the new look. List each type of item you will need (and how many), as well as some characteristics of that item, as in the example below.

דוגמא:

צוויי בענקלעך - ברוין, גרויס

איין פֿענצטער - גלײַך, שמאָל

אין קלאַס

Now find a partner and ask them about the room *they* have planned. Structure your conversation as in the model provided. As your partner talks, sketch the items they describe.

דוגמא:

א: ס׳איז דאָ אַ בוך אין דײַן צימער?

ב: יאָ, עס זײַנען דאָ 12 ביכער וואָס זײַנען רויט, און איין בוך וואָס איז שוואַרץ.

אָדער

א: ס׳איז דאָ אַ זייגער אין דײַן צימער?

ב: ניין, ס׳איז נישטאָ קיין זייגער אין מײַן צימער.

Once your picture of your partner's new room is complete, compare the drawing to your partner's list.

געניטונג 3: גיטלס רוקזאַק

Choose three of the people in the picture on page 189 and describe the things that they are holding.

- Use descriptive adjectives and the possessive suffix **ס-**, as in the example.

דוגמא:

גיטלס רוקזאַק איז שוואַרץ.

געניטונג 4: הבֿל איז הבֿלים

הער־געניטונג
איבערחזר־סעקציע־4

טיטל	♫ **„הבֿל איז הבֿלים“**
	פֿאָלקסליד
זינגער	**לאָרין סקלאַמבערג (Lorin Sklamberg)**
	(לאָס־אַנדזשעלעס, פֿאַראייניקטע שטאַטן 1956 –)
רעקאָרדירונג	2003, פֿאַראייניקטע שטאַטן

The title of this song comes from the Biblical Hebrew phrase **הבֿל הבֿלים** (vanity of vanities [העוול האַוואָלים]), *which opens the extended monologue found in* **קהלת** (Ecclesiastes [קויהעלעס]) *and is traditionally ascribed to King Solomon: "Vanity of vanities, all is vanity!" The phrase made its way into Yiddish—like many citations from Jewish religious texts—and has come to convey a lighthearted sense of absolute futility. In his 1908 Yiddish rendering of* **קהלת** *(never completed), Sholem Aleichem translated the phrase with his usual folksy flair:* **בלאָטע שבבלאָטע** (utter nonsense [שעבעבלאָטע...], *lit.* the muddiest of mud).

Listen to the song once and try to determine the general structure of the four-line stanzas. Do you notice any patterns within the stanzas? Then listen again and fill in the missing words.

NOTE:

Some new vocabulary in the song is not glossed. However, all such words are cognates—that is, they sound like their English counterparts. Try to work out what these unfamiliar words mean based on their sound and the context in which they appear.

◄ CONTINUED

CONTINUED

2 מאָל	אוי הבֿל איז הבֿלים,	[האָוואָלים] ;[העוול]
	און די וועלט איז אַ חלום,	world; dream [כאָלעם]
	און אַ חלום איז די וועלט.	
2 מאָל	אוי הבֿל איז הבֿלים,	
	און אַ חלום איז די וועלט,	
	און די וועלט ______ אויף געלט.	money
	און פֿאַר געלט קויפֿט מען ביר,	buy
	און וואָס דריַ איז ניט ______,	
	און וואָס ______ איז ניט דריַ,	
	און וואָס אַלט איז ניט נײַ.	
	וואָס נײַ איז ניט אַלט,	
	און וואָס וואַרעם איז ניט ______,	
	און וואָס ______ איז ניט וואַרעם,	
	וואָס רײַך איז ניט אָרעם.	rich; poor
2 מאָל	אוי הבֿל איז הבֿלים,	
	און די וועלט איז אַ חלום,	
	אַ חלום איז די וועלט.	
2 מאָל	אוי הבֿל איז הבֿלים,	
	און אַ חלום איז די וועלט,	
	די וועלט שטייט אויף ______.	
	און וואָס אָרעם איז ניט רײַך,	
	און וואָס קרום איז ניט ______,	
	וואָס ______ איז ניט קרום,	
	און וואָס רעדט איז ניט שטום.	mute
	און שטום איז דאָך שלעכט,	of course
	און דער פּויער איז גערעֿכט,	peasant; correct
	און גערעכט איז דער פּויער	
	וואָס זיס איז ניט זויער.	sweet; sour
	און וואָס זויער איז ניט זיס,	
	און וואָס ______ איז ניט מיאוס,	
	און מיאוס איז ניט ______,	
	און וואָס צום זיצן איז ניט צום שטיין.	

◀ CONTINUED

CONTINUED

און וואָס צום שטיין איז ניט צום זיצן,	
און צום לײַב איז גוט צו שוויצן,	body; sweat
און צו שוויצן איז גוט צום לײַב,	
און וואָס אַ ______ איז ניט קיין ווײַב.	wife
און וואָס אַ ווײַב איז ניט קיין ______,	
און וואָס אַ טאָפּ איז ניט קיין פֿאַן,	pot; frying pan
און וואָס אַ פֿאַן איז ניט קיין טאָפּ,	
און וואָס קימל איז ניט קיין קראָפּ.	caraway; dill
און וואָס קראָפּ איז ניט קיין קימל,	
און קיין ערד איז ניט קיין הימל,	earth; sky
און קיין הימל איז ניט קיין ערד,	
און אַ ביקס איז ניט קיין שווערד.	gun; sword
און אַ שווערד איז ניט קיין ביקס,	
און אַ פֿוטער איז פֿון פֿוקס,	fur
און פֿון פֿוקס איז אַ פֿוטער,	
און שמאַלץ איז ניט קיין פוטער.	
און פוטער איז ניט קיין שמאַלץ,	
און מצה באַקט מען אָן זאַלץ,	[מאַצע]; without
און אָן זאַלץ באַקט מען מצה,	
און אַ פֿערד איז ניט קיין קליאַטשע.	horse; nag
4 מאָל: און אַ קליאַטשע איז ניט קיין פֿערד,	
און אַ פויער ליגט אין דר׳ערד,	
און אין דר׳ערד ליגט אַ פויער,	
און עס איז אים זיס און זויער.	for him
2 מאָל: אוי הבֿל איז הבֿלים,	
און די וועלט איז אַ חלום,	
אַ חלום איז די וועלט.	
2 מאָל: אוי הבֿל איז הבֿלים,	
און אַ חלום איז די וועלט,	
די וועלט שטייט אויף ______.	

◀ CONTINUED

CONTINUED

Based on what you discovered about the structure of the song, complete the two new verses below using adjectives you learned in 7 **קאַפּיטל**.

- Make sure that the new verses follow the same rhyming pattern as the rest of the song.

און וואָס שמוציק איז ניט ריין,

____

____

און אַ בער גייט אַרויס.

און אַרויס גייט אַ בער,

____

____

און וואָס טרוקן איז ניט פֿײַכט. — dry; damp

גענִיטונג 5: מאַרצעפּאַנעס

טיטל: „מאַרצעפּאַנעס" (פֿראַגמענט)

פֿון „מאַרצעפּאַנעס: מעשׂהלעך און לידער פֿאַר קינדער און יוגנט" (1970)

מחבר (author) [מעכאַבער]: **קאַדיע מאָלאָדאָווסקי (Kadia Molodowsky)**

(בערעזע, רוסישע אימפּעריע 1894 – פֿילאַדעלפֿיע, פּאַראייניקטע שטאַטן 1975)

In her lifetime, **Kadia Molodowsky** *was a respected editor, educator, and prolific writer across genres and is remembered in particular for her vivid verse and poetry, some of it for children. An advocate for women's artistic expression, her poetry deals with themes such as poverty, working-class life, and the place of women in Jewish religious and artistic traditions. She received the prestigious Itsik Manger Prize in 1971.*

Molodowsky's lighthearted poem "Martsepanes" (appearing in various collections of her works for children) follows the uncompromising Khane in her quest for **מאַרצעפּאַנעס***. At first, it seems her efforts will be in vain, since* **מאַרצעפּאַנעס** *in Yiddish are like ambrosia in English: a mythical delicacy, the proverbial essence of culinary delight—but very hard to find in a restaurant. Nevertheless, Khane remains undaunted and finds a way to cook up the impossible.*

◀ CONTINUED

CONTINUED

באָב

היידעלעך

קניידעלעך

אַ בוים

אַ פֿלוים

שוואָמען

קויפֿן

אַ קראָם

אײַנגעבויגן

The words pictured above will help prepare you for reading the poem. Below is an entry from Reyne's diary. Fill in the blanks with words from the illustration. *Write only the word itself*—articles have already been provided where necessary.

- Use each word once. There may be more than one correct answer for each blank.

אין דער פֿרי גיי איך אין <u>קראָם</u> צו __________ מעקערס.
די מעקערס זײַנען קליין ווי __________! בײַ טאָג עס איך זופּ
מיט __________. די מאַמע עסט __________ מיט __________
און פֿלייש. אין אָוונט גייען מיר אין פּאַרק. די מאַמע זאָגט, „גיב
אַ קוק אויפֿ דעם אַלטן __________. ער איז זייער __________,
אָבער ער האָט נאָך שיינע גרינע בלעטער, און עס הענגט פֿון
אים אַראָפּ אַ __________."

לייענט די פֿראַגעס אונטן אײדער איר לייענט דאָס ליד. זיי וועלן אײַך העלפֿן פֿאַרשטיין דעם טעקסט.

1. וויפֿל מענטשן זײַנען דאָ אין דער <u>משפּחה</u>? — family [מישפּאָכע]
2. וואָס <u>ווילן</u> די קינדער עסן? — want
3. פֿון וואַנען קומען מאַרצעפּאַנעס, לויט יעדער מענטש אין דער משפּחה?

◀ CONTINUED

CONTINUED

Read the text below. Underline the words you learned from the illustration on the preceding page.

געווען אַ טאַטע מיט אַ מאַמע.	(there) was
דער טאַטע איז דין,	
די מאַמע איז גראָב,	דיק
און קינדער ווי באָב.	
וויל איינס עסן הײ́דעלעך,	wants
דאָס צווייטע קניידעלעך,	
און די אויסטראַכטערקע חנה	uncompromising (person)
וויל אַ מאַרצעפּאַנע.	
ווייס ניט קיינער ווו די מאַרצעפּאַנעס קריגן.	*no one knows*; to get
ווייס ניט קיינער ווו האָט עס צו ליגן.	lit. *where they lie*
זאָגט דער טאַטע:	
מאַרצעפּאַנעס וואַקסן אויף אַ בוים,	grow
גלײַך אַן עפּל, גלײַך אַ באַר און גלײַך אַ פֿלוים.	like
זאָגט די מאַמע:	
מאַרצעפּאַנעס קויפֿט מען אין די קראָמען.	
זאָגט די שוועסטער:	sister
מאַרצעפּאַנעס וואַקסן ווי די שוואָמען.	
און די באָבע אַלט און אײַ́נגעבויגן:	
—נישט געהערט פֿון מאַרצעפּאַנעס קיין מאָל.	heard; *never*
נישט געשטויגן,	*preposterous!*
נישט געפֿלויגן.	

נישט געשטויגן, נישט געפֿלויגן

crazy, preposterous
(*lit.* didn't ascend, didn't fly)

This idiom is commonly thought to have originated from an expression of skepticism regarding Jesus's ascension (and possibly that of Moses and Elijah as well)—whatever the speaker is responding to is about as believable, in a traditional Jewish world-view, as that Jesus ascended to heaven. According to some scholars, however, the saying comes from an older idiom about birds (rather than prophets) taking flight. For details, see volumes two and three of YIVO's seminal *Filologishe shriftn*.

Now answer the questions above, using complete sentences. Once you have done so, match each family member below to the adjective that describes them.

___ 1. די מאַמע	א. קליין
___ 2. דער טאַטע	ב. דין
___ 3. די קינדער	ג. אַלט
___ 4. די באָבע	ד. דיק

◀ CONTINUED

CONTINUED

Answer the following questions about the poem in complete sentences.

1. ווער מיינט אַז אַ מאַרצעפּאַנע איז אַ פֿרוכט?
2. וואָס זאָגט די באָבע וועגן מאַרצעפּאַנעס?
3. ווער איז גערעכט? וואָס מיינט איר, ווו נעמט מען מאַרצעפּאַנעס? right
4. איר ווילט עפּעס וואָס איז שווער צו קריגן? וואָס איז עס?

געניטונג 6: מירעלע אפֿרת

וידעאָ־געניטונג
איבערחזר־סעקציע־6

טיטל „מירעלע אפֿרת“ (פֿראַגמענט) (1939)

רעזשיסאָר (director) **יוסף בערנע (Josef Berne)**

(קיִעוו, רוסישע אימפּעריע 1904 – פּאַלם ספּרינגס, פֿאַראייניקטע שטאַטן 1964)

Practice possessives, **עס איז דאָ**, and adjectives with this excerpt from the film *Mirele efros*—based on the play by Jacob Gordin (1853–1909)—which you can find online with its accompanying exercise.

קאַפּיטל אַכט:

8 ראָש־השנה און יום־כּיפּור

CHAPTER GOALS

- In this chapter, you will learn about the *yomim-neroim,* or High Holy Days.

וואָקאַבולאַר:	
Rosh Hashanah and Yom Kippur	ראָש־השנה און יום־כּיפּור

קולטור — טעקסטן:	
"A Word on the Days of Awe" (Hayyim Schauss)	„אַ וואָרט צו ימים־נוראָים" (חיים שויס)
"Holiday Cards" (Zina Rabinowitz)	„לשנה־טובֿהס" (זינאַ ראַבינאָוויטש)
"A Prayer After *Kapores*"	„תּחינה נאָך כּפּרות שלאָגן"

קולטור — אודיאָ:	
"To a Good Year" (Shmuel Tsesler)	„לשנה־טובֿה" (שמואל צעסלער)

איבערחזר־געניטונגען:

קולטור — בילדער:	
A Match (Alexander Vaisman)	„אַ שידוך" (אַלעקסאַנדער ווײַסמאַן)
"Learn English!" (New York Public Library)	„לערנט ענגליש!" (ניו־יאָרקער שטאָט־ביבליאָטעק)

א קולטור:
ימים־נוראָים: ראָש־השנה און יום־כּיפּור

ימים־נוראָים	[יאָמים־נעראָ‌ים]
ראָש־השנה	[ראָשעשאָנע]
יום־כּיפּור	[יאָם־קיפּער]

קולטור
CULTURE

הילכט	echoes
שאַלט	resounds
הײַטערט	cheers
גליק	happiness
פֿרייד	joy

געניטונג 1: דער אָנהייב פֿון יאָר

קולטור
CULTURE

The greeting card for the Jewish New Year on the preceding page was produced in New York in the twentieth century. Below is a description of the scene depicted on the card. Pay special attention to the words and phrases highlighted in purple and use them to label the image.

עס איז ראָש־השנה, דער ערשטער[1] טאָג פֿון נײַעם יאָר. צוויי ייִדן שטייען בײַ אַ טיש, און איינער לייענט פֿון אַ מחזור[2] מיט די תּפֿילות[3] פֿון די ימים־נוראָים (די טעג פֿון ראָש־השנה ביז יום־כּיפּור). ראָש־השנה און יום־כּיפּור דאַוונט מען פֿון דעם ספֿר[4].

דער צווייטער ייִד האַלט אַ האָרן פֿון אַ ווידער[5] — דעם שופֿר[6] — און בלאָזט. דאָס קול[7] פֿון שופֿר מאַכט „טרו־טרו־טרו!“ ס׳איז שוין אַ נײַ יאָר.

דאָס קאַרטל הייסט אַ לשנה־טובֿה[8], ווײַל עס ווינטשט[9] אַ גוט יאָר: לשנה טובֿה תּכּתבֿו[10]!

[1]first
[2][מאַכזער]; [3]prayers [טפֿילעס]
[4]holy book [סײפֿער]
[5]ram; [6][שויפֿער]
[7]voice [קאָל]
[8][לעשאָנע־טויווע]; [9]wishes
[10][טיקאָסייווו]

Perl takes lessons in just about *everything* but has been shirking her studies lately. With the new year, however, has come renewed enthusiasm, and Perl has written cards to all of her various teachers saying so. Match the two halves of each *leshone-toyve* below.

___ **1.** טײַערער הערשל, אַ גוט־יאָר! איך לערן זיך שוין אַ סך מער העברעיִש ווי אין זומער. איר ווייסט פֿאַר וואָס?	**א.** איך מיין אַז עס קומט פֿון דעם וואָס איך הער דאָס שיינע קול פֿון שופֿר אין שול! אַ גרוס, פּערל
___ **2.** טײַערע רבֿקה, לשנה טובֿה תּכּתבֿו! איך זינג שוין אַ סך בעסער איצט, אָבער איך פּראַקטיציר ווייניקער...	**ב.** אַפֿשר איז דאָס אַ דאַנק ראָש־השנה טאַקע: אַ נײַ יאָר הייסט אַ נײַ ביסל געשיכטע, וואָס מיר זשורנאַליסטן מוזן רעקאָרדירן! אַלץ דאָס גוטס, פּערל
___ **3.** טײַערער פּאָל, אַ זיס, געבענטשט יאָר! איך אַרבעט שוין אויף אַ סך אינטערעסאַנטע אַרטיקלען, וואָס איך וויל שרײַבן.	**ג.** ווײַל איך דאַוון אַלע טאָג פֿון מחזור! זײַט געזונט, פּערל

קולטור
CULTURE

טיטל **„אַ וואָרט צו ימים־נוראָים“**
פֿון „דאָס יום־טובֿ־בוך“ (1933)

מחבר **חיים שויס (Hayyim Schauss)**
(גאָרזד, רוסישע אימפּעריע 1884 – לאָס־אַנדזשעלעס, פֿאַראייניקטע שטאַטן 1953)

The historian of Jewish religion **Hayyim Schauss** *immigrated in 1910 to Chicago, where he studied Bible and Semitic history. He used this training as a longtime educator at New York's Jewish Teachers' Seminary, the only Yiddish-language school for advanced Jewish studies and pedagogical training in the United States.*

This essay on the solemnity of the Days of Awe is adapted from a book by Schauss on the histories and meanings behind the Jewish calendar. The Days of Awe are the beginning holidays of the year, when the blast of the shofar, a ram's horn, calls Jews to repent. Here, Schauss describes what sets Rosh Hashanah and Yom Kippur apart, not only from other Jewish holidays but also from non-Jewish celebrations of the New Year. The included verse is from the poet Shimen Frug (1860–1916).

איידער איר לייענט דעם טעקסט, באַטראַכט די ווײַטערדיקע פֿראַגעס.

1. וואָס איז דער קאָלעקטיווער נאָמען פֿון די יום־טובֿים ראָש־השנה און יום־כּיפּור (און אויך פֿון די טעג צווישן זיי)? וואָס מיינט דער נאָמען? [יאָנטויוים]
2. וואָסער געפֿיל האָט מען ראָש־השנה און יום־כּיפּור? צי זײַנען די יום־טובֿים, לויט שויס, מער פֿריילעך אָדער מער ערנסט? פֿאַרגלײַכט דאָס געפֿיל מיט אַנדערע (ייִדישע אָדער נישט־ייִדישע) יום־טובֿים וואָס איר קענט. — feeling; serious; compare; know
3. דער שרײַבער ניצט אַ סך מאָל דעם פּראָנאָם „אונדז“ — וועמען מיינט ער? — whom
4. ווען רייניקן זיך אָפּ רעליגיעזע ייִדן פֿון זינד? — *cleanse*; sin

דער ערשטער טאָג פֿון יאָר

Rosh Hashanah, the first day of the Jewish month Tishrei, is traditionally considered to be the anniversary of Adam and Eve's creation. The counting of Jewish years begins with that date, and thus does not match up with the Gregorian calendar, on two levels: the Jewish year 5778, in terms of Gregorian years, is made up of the last third of 2017 and the first two-thirds of 2018.

The Jewish year is usually expressed in Hebrew letters that carry number values (somewhat like Roman numerals). For example, 5778 is written **תשע״ח** (pronounced [טאַשאַך]).

◀ CONTINUED

קולטור
CULTURE

CONTINUED

לייענט איבער דעם טעקסט. אויב איר דערקענט נישט אַ וואָרט,	recognize
רינגלט עס אַרום.	*circle it*
ראָש־השנה און יום־כּיפּור זײַנען אַנדערש פֿון אַלע אַנדערע ייִדישע יום־טובֿים.	different
זיי טראָגן טאַקע אויך גאָר אַ באַזונדערן נאָמען: „ימים־נוראָים“ פֿאָרכטיקע טעג.	distinct; awe-inspiring
זיי זײַנען נישט פֿריילעך ווי דאָס רובֿ אַנדערע יום־טובֿים: זיי האָבן אַ	*most* [ראָוו]
טיפֿע ערנסטקייט, מיט אַ געפֿיל פֿון דער שווערער אַחריות, וואָס יעדער	responsibility [אַכרײַעס]
מענטש האָט. די ימים־נוראָים האָבן צו טאָן נישט מיטן נאַטור־לעבן	*have to do*
אָדער מיט אונדזער נאַציאָנאַלער געשיכטע (ווי אַנדערע ייִדישע	
יום־טובֿים), נאָר מיטן לעבן פֿון דעם יחיד, מיט זײַן מאָראַלישן געוויסן.	individual [יאָכעד]
ראָש־השנה איז בײַ אונדז דער ערשטער טאָג פֿון יאָר. בײַ אַלע אַנדערע פֿעלקער	first; peoples
איז נײַיאָר אַ הוליאַנקע. בײַ אונדז אָבער, ווען דער שופֿר בלאָזט, פֿאַלט אויף	wild party
אַלעמען אַ שטילער אומעט און אַ פֿרומער ציטער.	gloom; *pious trembling*
אַ מרה־שחורה שוועבט און פֿאַלט	gloom [מאָרע־שכוירע]
אויף אונדזער שטעטל... יונג און אַלט	small town
באַגיסט אַ שווערער, שוואַרצער שאָטן...	shadow
דער קול פֿון שופֿר הילכט און שאַלט,	sounds
דער אַלטער טאָן, די אַלטע נאָטן.	
(ש. פֿרוג)	
אָבער מיט ראָש־השנה אַליין איז מען נאָך נישט יוצא. ראָש־השנה איז נאָר אַ	done [יויצע]
פֿאָרשפּיל צו יום־כּיפּור — דער גרעסטער און הייליקסטער טאָג פֿון יאָר, דער	prelude; holiest
טאָג, ווען ייִדן רייניקן זיך אָפּ פֿון זינד. ערשט נאָך דעם ווי די זינד	*only after*
ווערן פֿאַרגעבן און מ׳פֿילט זיך גײַסטיק ווי אַ נײַער מענטש, פֿײַערט מען	spiritually; celebrate
דעם פֿריילעכן יום־טובֿ פֿון אָנהייב יאָר: סוכּות.	[סוקעס] (see 12 קאַפּיטל)

Answer the questions above using complete sentences.

Now read the text again, finding words you may have circled in the vocabulary list below the text. Use them to fill in your understanding of the text.

לויטן אַרטיקל אויבן, שרײַבט אָן עטלעכע פֿראַגעס וועגן ראָש־השנה און יום־כּיפּור. פֿרעגט אויס די חבֿרים!

דוגמא:

ווי הייסט דער ערשטער טאָג פֿון יאָר?

טראָגן	carry
טאַקע	indeed
גאָר אַ	*an altogether*
טיפֿע	deep
געוויסן	conscience
בײַ אונדז	*for us*
אַלעמען	everyone
שוועבט	hovers
באַגיסט	covers (as liquid), drenches
שאַלט	resounds
נאָך	still
גרעסטער	greatest
ווערן פֿאַרגעבן	*are forgiven*
יום־טובֿ	holiday [יאָנטעו]

קולטור
CULTURE

טיטל — **„לשנה־טובֿהס"** (פֿראַגמענט)
פֿון „דער ליבער יום־טובֿ" (1958)

מחבר — **זינאַ ראַבינאָװיטש (Zina Rabinowitz)**
(בענדער, רוסישע אימפּעריע 1895 – תּל־אָבֿיבֿ, ישׂראל 1965)

Zina Rabinowitz *began publishing stories and poems in her twenties in Russia and continued after her 1921 arrival in New York, where she worked as a Hebrew teacher. In addition to children's literature, she wrote travelogues and historical reportage—her book* Afn veg tsu frayhayt *(On the Road to Freedom) is an account of underground Jewish immigration to Israel during the pre-state years.*

This concluding excerpt of a story from her holiday-themed book Der liber yontef *finds two best friends, Harry and Jerry, encountering each other in a grocery store. They have been quarreling at school and are not on speaking terms. How much longer can they keep up their act, with Rosh Hashanah beginning tonight, and with it the time of most-focused repentance and reconciliation?*

אײדער איר לײענט דעם טעקסט, באַטראַכט די װײַטערדיקע פֿראַגע.

װאָס טוט איר װען איר זײַט ברוגז אויף אַ חבֿר? — *angry with* [ברויגעז]
- איר גײט אַװעק פֿון דעם חבֿר? — away
- איר בלײַבט צעקריגט אַ לאַנגע צײַט? — *stay fighting*; time
- איר בעט זיך איבער? — *make up*

לײענט איבער דעם טעקסט.

As you read, circle any passages where you notice Harry or Jerry taking one of the conflict-resolution approaches described above.

אַז ס׳איז אונטערגעקומען ערבֿ[1]־ראָש־השנה, איז דזשערי
מיטגעגאַנגען[2] מיט זײַן טאַטן העלפֿן דער מאַמען אַהײמשלעפּן די
פּעק פֿון מאַרק[3].

[1] the eve of [ערעװ]
[2] went along
[3] market

אויך הערי איז מיטגעגאַנגען מיט זײַן טאַטן העלפֿן דער מאַמען
אַהײמשלעפּן פֿיש, פֿלײש, און פּרוכט אויף יום־טובֿ. — [יאָנטעװ]

בײדע טאַטעס שטופּן זיך דורך[4] דעם גרויסן עולם[5] אײַנקויפֿער[6],
און בײדע ייִנגלעך כאַפּן[7] בגנבֿה[8] אַ קוק אײנער אויפֿן צװײטן,
אָבער נישט אויף לאַנג, זײ רײַסן[9] אַװעק די טאַטעס,—דעם
אַהין[10] און דעם אַהער[11].

[4] *push through*; [5] crowd [אוילעם]; [6] shoppers
[7] catch; [8] stealthily [ביגניװע]
[9] tear
[10] this way; [11] that way

◀ CONTINUED

CONTINUED

קולטור
CULTURE

— גענוג שוין[12] זײַן ברוגז! ביז וואַנען איז דער שיעור[13] צו זײַן	[12]*enough already;* [13]*what's the limit* **[שיִער]**
ברוגז? — בייזערט זיך[14] העריס טאַטע.	[14]*scolds*
— עס איז דאָך אַ מיצווה[15] ערבֿ־ראָש־השנה זיך איבערצובעטן, —	[15]commandment **[מיצווע]**
טענהט[16] דזשעריס טאַטע, — גיי זאָג אים: „לאָמיר[17] זיך	[16]declares **[טײַנעט]**; [17]let's
איבערבעטן צום[18] נײַעם יאָר“...	[18]for the
— זאָל[19] ער מיר[20] זאָגן! זאָל ער מיך איבערבעטן!	[19]let; [20]to me
און נאָך א מאָל שלעפּט איינער אַהין און אַ צווייטער — אַהער.	
די טאַטעס זײַנען אויסער זיך[21] פֿון פֿאַרדראָס[22].	[21]*beside themselves;* [22]chagrin
צו זייער גליק[23] רופֿט אַ ייִד אויס[24] אויף אַ קול[25]: „לשנה־טובֿה!	[23]*lucky for them;* [24]*calls out;* [25]*loudly* **[קאָל]**
לשנה־טובֿהס צום נײַעם יאָר!“	
דזשעריס טאַטע שטופּט זיך דורך דעם עולם צום ייִדן, וואָס	
פֿאַרקויפֿט[26] לשנה־טובֿהס און רופֿט אויס:	[26]is selling
— גיט מיר צען לשנה־טובֿהס! — דזשערי גיט אַ שלעפּ זײַן	
טאַטן בײַם אַרבל[27]:	[27]sleeve
— ס'איז טאַקע אַ מיצווה זיך איבערצובעטן ערבֿ־ראָש־	
השנה?... — פֿליסטערט[28] ער צו זײַן טאַטן און כאַפּט אַ קוק אויף	[28]whispers
זײַן חבֿר.	
— צי עס איז אַ מיצווה? עס איז די גרעסטע[29] זינד צו בלײַבן	[29]greatest
צעקריגט מיט אַ פֿרײַנד צום נײַעם יאָר!	
— טאָ קויף[30] עלף „שנה־טובֿהס“, איינע פֿון מײַנט וועגן[31]! —	[30]buy; [31]*for me*
זאָגט דזשערי און וואַרפֿט[32] אַ שמייכל[33] צו הערין.	[32]tosses; [33]smile
— קויף אויך איינע פֿון מײַנט וועגן, פּאַ!—רופֿט אויס הערי.	
די טאַטעס זײַנען אַוועק פֿאָרויס[34] און ביידע ייִנגלעך זײַנען	[34]ahead
נאָכגעגאַנגען שוין צוזאַמען[35]...	[35]together

Come up with a new title for the excerpt, based on the events described therein.

Compose your own version of the conciliatory *leshone-toyves* that Harry and Jerry decide to write one another. Use phrases from the text to wish New Year's joy and friendship and to address past foolishness. (See Perl's *leshone-toyves* in **1 געניטונג** for more ideas.)

געניטונג 4: לשנה־טובֿה

הער־געניטונג א־4

קולטור
CULTURE

טיטל	♫ „לשנה־טובֿה“
פּאָעט	**שמואל צעסלער (Shmuel Tsesler)**
	(זאַבלודעווע, רוסישע אימפּעריע 1904 – בוענאָס־אײַרעס, אַרגענטינע 1987)
קאָמפּאָזיטאָר	**חנה מלאָטעק (Chana Mlotek)**
	(ניו־יאָרק, פֿאַראייניקטע שטאַטן 1922 – ניו־יאָרק, פֿאַראייניקטע שטאַטן 2013)
זינגערס	**Children's Chorus of Workmen's Circle Schools**
רעקאָרדירונג	1974, פֿאַראייניקטע שטאַטן

The traditional greetings for the Jewish New Year form the main material of this children's tune, found in 1972's Yontevdike teg *(Festival Days), a compilation of Yiddish songs to sing on Jewish holidays.* **Chana Mlotek***, a dedicated researcher and collector of Jewish music, was dubbed by celebrated writer Isaac Bashevis Singer the "Sherlock Holmes of Yiddish song." The lyricist,* **Shmuel Tsesler***, is known for his children's poetry. This recording features the Children's Chorus of Workmen's Circle Schools, arranged and directed by Zalmen Mlotek. Mlotek is currently the Artistic Director of The National Yiddish Theater-Folksbiene.*

Listen to the song once through without looking at the lyrics. Then listen again and follow along with the text below, filling in any missing words or phrases.

מיר באַגריסן
הויך און קלאָר:
לשנה־טובֿה —
________ !
(2 מאָל)

מיר באַגריסן און מיר ווינטשן, (wish)
אַלע קינדער, הויך און ________ :
לשנה טובֿה תּכּתבֿו!
אַ גוט יאָר! ________ !
(2 מאָל)

טאַטעס, ________ ,
דעם גאַנצן דור: (entire; generation [דאָר])
לשנה־טובֿה —
________ !
(2 מאָל)

טאַטעס, ________ , שוועסטער, ברידער, (sisters)
קרובֿים, פֿרײַנד, ________ : (relatives [קרויוים])
________ כּל־ישׂראל — (all Jews [קאָל־ייִסראָעל])
אַ גוט יאָר! ________ !
(2 מאָל)

אַ גוט יאָר! אַ גוט יאָר!
(2 מאָל)

◀ CONTINUED

CONTINUED

Now it's time to extend your own new year's wishes to *your* family and friends! Examine the list below and decide whom to wish a happy new year.

1. קינד
2. שוועסטער
3. ברודער
4. דאָקטער(שע)
5. פֿרײַנד
6. לערער(ין)

קולטור
CULTURE

לשנה טובֿה תּכּתבֿו

Often, this greeting is expanded to **לשהנה טובֿה תּכּתבֿו ותחתמו** (*may you be inscribed* ***and sealed*** *for a good year* [וועסעכאָסײמו]). This wish refers to the *seyfer-hakhaim*, the Book of Life, in which God is said to record the Jews' deeds and grant another year of living to those deemed worthy. It is said that God opens this ledger on Rosh Hashanah, writes in it in the days following, and seals it on Yom Kippur.

שרײַבט אָן עטלעכע זאַצן, ווו איר באַגריסט די מענטשן פֿון דער ליסטע, לויט דער דוגמא.

- ניצט אַלע באַגריסונגען וואָס איר קענט.

דוגמא:

לשנה טובֿה תּכּתבֿו, מאָלי, מײַן שוועסטער!

אין קלאַס

Ask your classmates whom their new year's wishes are for, as in the model below. Try to find one classmate who is wishing a happy new year to each of the six types of people listed.

- If a classmate answers yes to one of your questions, write their name next to that person on the list.
- You may then ask that classmate whether they'd like to wish a good year to another person on the list.

דוגמא:

א: וועמען ווינטשסטו לשנה־טובֿה? (whom)

ב: איך ווינטש מײַן ברודער לשנה־טובֿה.

א: ווי הייסט דײַן ברודער?

ב: ער הייסט <u>גבֿריאל</u>. [גאַװריִעל]

א: דו ווינטשסט אויך דײַן שוועסטער אַ גוט־יאָר?

ב: ניין, איך האָב נישט קיין שוועסטער.

געניטונג 5: תּחינה נאָך כּפּרות שלאָגן

טיטל ,,תּחינה נאָך כּפּרות שלאָגן" (פֿראַגמענט)
פֿון ,,אַ נײַע ש״ס תּחינה רבֿ פּנינים" (1916)

Tkhines (**תּחינות**) *are personal prayers, generally in Yiddish, and usually recited (and often written) by women. Books containing* tkhines *constituted one of the most popular Yiddish literary genres among women, and they contain prayers meant for all manner of occasions: for a bride to intone before she makes her way to the* khupe; *for mothers who have bad luck with their children; for saying over burning coals, to ward off the evil eye; for plain everyday religious observance; and many to recite on holidays—like this one, intended to be said on the eve of Yom Kippur, after performing the ritual of* shlogn kapores (**כּפּרות**).

קולטור
CULTURE

[טכינע] איידער איר לייענט די תּחינה, קוקט אויף די לשנה־טובֿהס אונטן און ענטפֿערט אויף די פֿראַגעס וועגן זיי.

1. buy — וואָס קויפֿן די פֿרויען?
2. [קאַפּאָרעס] — דער פֿאָטער שלאָגט כּפּרות. וואָס האַלט ער אין דער רעכטער האַנט?
3. wants; may; live; death — דער פֿאָטער וויל, ער און זײַן קינד זאָלן לעבן לאַנגע יאָרן. אָבער דער האָן — ער לעבט לאַנגע יאָרן, אָדער ער גייט צום טויט?

אַצינד — איצט
האָן (הענער) — rooster
הון (הינער) — hen

NOTE:
Traditionally, men perform the ritual with a rooster, while women do so with a hen.

◀ CONTINUED

CONTINUED

Read the *tkhine* once through. Don't worry about words or phrases you don't understand—you will still be able to complete the exercise. As you read, try to gain a sense of the basic purpose and tone of this prayer.

- Consider the connection between the *tkhine* and the ceremony pictured above (as well as the inscribed wish). How does the chicken function to expunge the sins of the people enacting the ritual? Whom does the chicken stand in for in its untimely demise?

קולטור
CULTURE

(די תּחינה זאָגט מען ערבֿ־יום־כּיפּור אין דער פֿרי
איידער מען דאַוונט ווען מען האָט כּפּרות געשלאָגן.)

פֿאַרגיב[1] מיר מײַן פֿאָטער וואָס דו ביסט אַ בעל־הרחמים[2],
אויב איך האָב געטאָן[3] אַזאַ עבֿירה[4] וואָס איך בין דערויף[5]
חייבֿ־כּרת[6], דאָס הייסט, פֿאַרשניטענע[7] יאָרן,
זאָל גערעכנט זײַן[8], דאָס וואָס איך האָב פֿאַרשניטן די יאָרן פֿון
מײַן כּפּרה, גלײַך ווי עס וואָלט פֿאַרשניטן געוואָרן[9] מײַנע
יאָרן, סײַ כּרת בידי־אדם[10] און סײַ כּרת בידי־שמים[11], און
זאָלסט מציל זײַן[12] מיך און מײַן מאַן און מײַנע קינדערלעך
פֿון אַ יונגן טויט און פֿון פֿאַרשניטענע יאָרן. מיר זאָלן
זיך עלטערן[13] אין עושר[14] און אין כּבֿוד[15] ביז הונדערט יאָר.

[1]forgive; [2][באַל־האָראַכאַמים]
[3]*have done*; [4]sin [אַווײרע]; [5]for it
[6]condemned to death [כײַעוו־קאָרעס]; [7]cut short
[8]*let it be taken into account*
[9]*would have been*
[10]brought by man [בידיי־אָדעם]; [11]heaven [שאָמײַם]
[12]*save* [מאַצל]
[13]*grow old*; [14]prosperity [אוישער]; [15]honor [קאָוועד]

Reconstruct the logical structure of the *tkhine* by matching each of the following half sentences to its completion.

____ 1. אפֿשר האָב איך געטאָן אַן עבֿירה,

____ 2. אָבער איך האָב פֿאַרשניטן די יאָרן פֿון מײַן כּפּרה,

____ 3. טאָ, רעכן אַרײַן דעם פֿאַקט אַז איך האָב געשלאָגן כּפּרות,

____ 4. זאָלסט אויך מציל זײַן מײַן פֿאַמיליע,

א. אַזוי אַז זי זאָל שטאַרבן אַנשטאָט מיר.

ב. און פֿאַרגיב מיר פֿאַר דער היפּאָטעטישער עבֿירה.

ג. אַזוי אַז מיר זאָלן אַלע לעבן לאַנגע יאָרן אין געזונט און פֿרייד.

ד. וואָס איבער איר קומט מיר צו האָבן פֿאַרשניטענע יאָרן.

ימים־נוראָים
THE DAYS OF AWE

nouns	סובסטאַנטיוון
Rosh Hashanah greeting card	די **לשנה־טובֿה** (–ות) [לעשאָנע־טויווע (ס)]
commandment; good deed	די **מיצווה** (מיצוות) [מיצווע (ס)]
(women's) personal prayer	די **תּחינה** (–ות) [טכינע (ס)]
death	דער **טויט** (ן)
holiday	דער **יום־טובֿ** (ים) [יאָנטעוו (יאָנטויווים)]
Yom Kippur ("day of atonement")	דער **יום־כּיפּור** [יאָם־קיפּער]
prayer book for the Days of Awe	דער **מחזור** (ים) [מאַכזער (מאַכזוירים)]
person	דער **מענטש** (ן)
Rosh Hashanah ("head of the year")	דער **ראָש־השנה** [ראָשעשאָנע]
ram's horn blown during the Days of Awe	דער **שופֿר** (ות) [שויפֿער (שויפֿרעס)]
feeling	דאָס **געפֿי׳ל** (ן)
voice	דאָס **קול** (ות) [קאָל (קוילעס)]
the Days of Awe (Rosh Hashanah through Yom Kippur)	די **ימים־נוראָים** [יאָמים־נעראָיִם]

adjectives	אַדיעקטיוון
dear	טײַער
serious	ערנסט

verbs	ווערבן
to make up, reconcile	איבערבעטן זיך
to greet	באַגריסן
to blow shofar	בלאָזן שופֿר
to pray	דאַוונען
to perform a ritual in which sins are transferred onto a live chicken by swinging it around one's head	שלאָגן כּפּרות [קאַפּאָרעס]

useful expressions	נוציקע אויסדרוקן
during (in reference to Jewish holidays)	אום
happy holiday!	גוט יום־טובֿ! [יאָנטעוו]
may you be inscribed (and sealed) for a good year!	לשנה טובֿה תּכּתבֿו (ותחתמו)! [לעשאָנע טויווע טיקאָסייווו (וועסעכאָסיימו)]

די **זינד** (—); דאָס **באַגרי׳ס־קאַרטל** (עך); הייליק; ווינטשן; דאָס **יאָר** (ן); דער **נײַיאָר**; קלאָר

איבערחזר־געניטונגען: טעמע צוויי

געניטונג 1: באַשרײַבט אַ בילד

טיטל „אַ שידוך“ (1997)

קינסטלער **אַלעקסאַנדער ווײַסמאַן (Alexander Vaisman)**

(טשערנאָוויץ, ראַטן־פֿאַרבאַנד 1967 –)

The painting here depicts a shidekh*, an arranged match between two people deemed suitable to marry each other. Born in the Soviet Union and now based in Israel,* **Alexander Vaisman** *blends the motifs of traditional Eastern Europe Jewish art together with a modern, playful sensibility and a range of historical and literary references. He and his sister-in-law Shura Vaisman illustrated this textbook.*

Spend two minutes writing as many sentences as you can about the picture above.

- Be sure to write about the room itself, as well as the objects and people within it.

טיטל **לערנט ענגליש!**
(ניו־יאָרק, 1920)

אָרגאַניזאַציע **ניו־יאָרקער שטאָט־ביבליאָטעק**

This poster from the New York Public Library was also printed in Hungarian, Polish, and Italian. As you examine the poster, think about why it was printed in these four languages at that time.

ענטפֿערט אויף די פֿראַגעס אונטן. שרײַבט גאַנצע זאַצן.

1. וואָסער **געשעעניש** אַנאָנסירט די נאָטיץ? event
2. ווען **קומט** עס **פֿאָר**? take place
3. ווער קומט אויף די קלאַסן?
4. וואָס לערנט מען?
5. מיט וואָס **העלפֿט** מען? help
6. ווו קומט דאָס אַלץ פֿאָר?
7. וואָס איז דער אַדרעס?
8. וואָס פֿאַר אַן אינסטיטוציע אָרגאַניזירט דאָס געשעעניש?

לאָמיר שמועסן!

9. וואָס קען מען זאָגן וועגן דעם **אויסלייג** פֿון דער נאָטיץ? וואָס איז אַנדערש אין די ווערטער: „קלאַססען“, „מעננער“, „אידיש“? spelling
10. ווער זײַנען די מענטשן וואָס קומען אויף די קלאַסן? זיי זײַנען קינדער אָדער דערוואַקסענע? פֿון וואַנען קומען זיי? זיי זײַנען סטודענטן אָדער אַרבעטערס?

טעמע III:
עס בלײַבט אין דער משפּחה

UNIT GOALS

- In this unit, you will learn to talk about your family: what family members you have, what professions they practice, what their hobbies are, and what they look like.
- The holidays covered in this unit are Sukkos and Simchas Torah.

אינהאַלט:

9

קאַפּיטל נײַן:
די משפּחה

CHAPTER GOALS

- In this chapter, you will learn how to talk about your family, how to describe your family members, and how to use attributive adjectives.

וואָקאַבולאַר:	
family	משפּחה

גראַמאַטיק:	
nominative adjective endings	אַדיעקטיוו־ענדונגען אין נאָמינאַטיוו

קולטור — טעקסטן:	
"Open the Gate" (Kadia Molodowsky)	„עפֿנט דעם טויער" (קאַדיע מאָלאָדאָווסקי)
Zelmenyaners (Moyshe Kulbak)	„זעלמעניאַנער" (משה קולבאַק)
"Yiddish Is My Mother" (M. M. Shafir)	„ייִדיש איז מײַן מאַמע" (מ. מ. שאַפֿיר)
"A Morning Song" (Mani Leyb)	„אַ מאָרגנליד" (מאַני לייב)

קולטור — אוידיאָ:	
"The In-Laws Are Coming" (Mark Varshavski)	„די מחותּנים גייען" (מאַרק וואַרשאַווסקי)

א וואָקאַבולאַר:
די משפּחה

געניטונג 1: סאַראַ משפּחה!

For a school project, Perl has drawn her family tree and labeled all of her family members in relation to herself. In class, another student, Keyle, interviews Perl about her family. Playing the role of Perl, answer Keyle's questions as in the model below.

דוגמא:

קײלע: װי הײסט דער ברודער?

פּערל: דער ברודער הײסט רפֿאל.

1. װי הײסט דער זײדע?
2. װי הײסט די מומע?
3. װי הײסט דאָס שװעסטערקינד?
4. װי הײסט דער עלטער־פֿעטער?
5. װי הײסט דער טאַטע?
6. װי הײסט די שװעסטער?

NOTE:

The word **שװעסטערקינד** applies to any cousin, regardless of gender, and is grammatically neuter: **דאָס שװעסטערקינד**. The gendered synonyms **דער קוזין** and **די קוזינע** are also used.

געדענקט!

Possessive adjectives are often replaced by the definite article when context makes clear who the possessor is. This is especially common with so-called intimate nouns, like relatives: **די מאַמע** means not only *the mother* but also potentially *my mother, your mother, his mother*, etc. Possessive adjectives *are* sometimes used (**מײַן מאַמע**), but mostly for clarification or emphasis.

געניטונג 2: אַ בילד פֿון דער משפּחה

איציק און דינה זײַנען צו גאַסט בײַ די גרינפֿעלדס. פּערל כאַפּט אַראָפּ אַ בילד.

visiting
snaps

Read the sentences below and determine the meanings of the purple words. Refer to the family tree on page 228 if you need a reminder of the characters' relationships to one another.

NOTE:

The suffix **ס-** is added after a family name to refer to that family collectively: **די גרינפֿעלדס** (*the Grinfelds*).

1. דינה איז רפֿאלס מומע, און ער איז איר פּלימעניק.
2. איציק איז דינהס מאַן, און זי איז זײַן װײַב.
3. איציק איז חיהס פֿעטער, און זי איז זײַן פּלימעניצע.
4. חיה איז אויך באָבע שיינדלס אײניקל און נתנס טאָכטער.
5. רחל איז רפֿאלס מאַמע, און ער איז איר זון.

!געדענקט

In order to form the possessive of a personal name, the suffix **ס-** is added: **רפֿאלס** (*Refoel's*).

!געדענקט

The addition and deletion of suffixes is generally ignored when determining stress placement:
פּלימעניק ← פּלימעניצע

שרײַבט אַרײַן די פֿעלנדיקע װערטער אין דער באַשרײַבונג אונטן.

Write in the missing words in the description below.

- Use the purple words from the sentences above.

while [בעשאַס]

דינה רעדט מיט איר ________, בשעת איר
________, איציק, שפּילט זיך מיט זײַן ________.
נתן קוקט אויף זײַן ________ פּערל (װאָס
פֿאָטאָגראַפֿירט), און זײַן ________, רחל, זיצט אויף
דער סאָפֿע מיט זייער ________. באָבע שיינדל קושט
איר ________.

NOTE:

A common synonym for **װײַב** is **פֿרוי**.

NOTE:

The word **אייניקל** applies to any grandchild, regardless of gender. Along with **װײַב** and **שװעסטערקינד**, it too is grammatically neuter: **דאָס אייניקל**.

געניטונג 3: איציק איז ריינעס טאַטע

שרײַבט אַרײַן די פּעלנדיקע משפּחה־טערמינען לויטן בילד אויף זײַט 228.

דוגמא: איציק איז ריינעס _טאַטע_.

1. בלומע איז זלמנס ________.
2. ריינע איז רחלס ________.
3. דינה איז רחלס ________.
4. רפֿאל איז שיינדלס ________.
5. ריינע איז רפֿאלס ________.
6. דינה איז בלומעס ________.
7. יאַנקל איז רחלס ________.
8. זלמן איז יאַנקלס ________.

געניטונג 4: איידלס משפּחה

הער־געניטונג א־4

[מישפּאָכע] איידל רעדט מיט סענדערן וועגן איר משפּחה. איידער איר הערט זיך צו צום דיאַלאָג, ענטפֿערט אויף די פֿראַגעס וועגן אײַער משפּחה. שרײַבט גאַנצע זאַצן.

1. וויפֿל זײַט איר אין אײַער משפּחה?
2. איר האָט ברידער און שוועסטער?
3. אײַערע ברידער אָדער שוועסטער האָבן קינדער?
4. די עלטערן אײַערע וווינען ווײַט פֿון אײַך, אָדער נאָענט? — parents; *from you*

הערט זיך צו צום דיאַלאָג און שרײַבט אַרײַן די פֿעלנדיקע ווערטער.

Don't worry about words or phrases you don't understand—they will not prevent you from completing the activity.

סענדער: דײַן ________ איז גרויס, איידל?

איידל: יאָ, מיר זײַנען זיבן מענטשן! — people

סענדער: קיין עין־הרע! וויפֿל ברידער און וויפֿל שוועסטער האָסטו?

איידל: איך האָב ________ ברידער און ________ שוועסטער.

סענדער: נישקשה! ווי הייסט די שוועסטער? — not bad [נישקאָשע]

איידל: זי ________ ריווע.

סענדער: ריווע זילבערבערג?

איידל: יאָ, פּונקט אַזוי. דו קענסט זי? — know

סענדער: אַוודאי קען איך זי! זי וווינט אין אינטערנאַט מיט מײַנע צוויי שוועסטערקינדער. אפֿשר קען איך דײַנע ברידער אויך?

איידל: נו, מסתּמא נישט. שײַע וווינט נאָך אין דער היים, מיט די עלטערן הייסט דאָס. לייזער און מיכל ________ ביידע אין ניו־יאָרק. לייזער האָט שוין זײַן אייגן געזינדל: אַ ווײַב מיט צוויי זין — מײַנע פּלימעניקעס... — *at home*; own; משפּחה

סענדער: טאַקע? אוואַ! הייסט דאָס אַז דו און ריווע זײַנען שוין מומעס! און די אַנדערע ברידער גאָר פֿעטערס!

איידל: יאָ, טאַקע אמת. איך גלייב עס קוים! — [עמעס]; *barely believe it*

סענדער: ווו ________ די עלטערן דײַנע? אין ניו־יאָרק מיט די אייניקלעך?

◄ CONTINUED

CONTINUED

איידל:	ניין, טאַטע־מאַמע ווינען נישט ווײַט, אין מאַסאַטשוסעטס, אַזוי אַז זיי קומען אָפֿט צו גאַסט צו אונדז, די **טעכטער**.	us
סענדער:	זייער שיין! און ווי הייסן די עלטערן?	
איידל:	די ________ הייסט מינדל און דער ________ הייסט יחיאל.	[יעכיִעל]
סענדער:	נו, גוט. אַ **גרוס** אין דער היים!	(my) regards

Read through the completed dialogue with the aid of the glosses below.

wow	אוואַ	exactly	פּונקט אַזוי
(so) that means that...	הייסט דאָס אַז...	well	נו
of all things *(expressing surprise)*	גאָר	still	נאָך
truth; true [עמעס]	אמת	*that is (to say)*	הייסט דאָס
very nice	זייער שיין	already	שוין
		really	טאַקע

Find all of the plural family nouns in the dialogue above. Write each one next to its singular counterpart in the table below.

NOTE:

The word קוים (*barely*) is often pronounced [קאָם].

ברודער	בריִדער	שוועסטער	
זון		טאָכטער	
פּלימעניק		פּלימעניצע	
שוועסטערקינד		אייניקל	
טאַטע		מאַמע	
זיידע		באָבע	
פֿעטער		מומע	

The plural forms of the remaining terms follow the patterns you learned in **קאַפּיטל 5**. Figure them out and fill them in above.

Draw and label Eydl's family tree according to the dialogue. Be sure to record the names, ages, and places of residence of all of the relations you know.

Write a few sentences about Eydl's family, using as many of the plural family terms as you can.

דוגמא:

מינדל האָט צוויי אייניקלעך.

טיטל **„עפֿנט דעם טויער“**

פֿון „ייִדישע קינדער (מעשׂהלעך)“ (1945)

מחבר **קאַדיע מאָלאָדאָווסקי (Kadia Molodowsky)**

(בערעזע, רוסישע אימפּעריע 1894 – פֿילאַדעלפֿיע, פּאַראייניקטע שטאַטן 1975)

In this short poem by **Kadia Molodowsky**, a “golden chain” (**גאָלדענע קייט**) of successive generations parades through the gate (**טויער**) of the poem’s title—but in the version below some of the links are missing! Use the context to fill in the missing words and articles.

- When family members are mentioned in the poem, equivalent masculine and feminine terms often come one after the other.

1. עפֿנט דעם טויער, עפֿנט אים[1] ברייט,
ס׳וועט[2] דאָ דורכגיין[3] אַ גאָלדענע קייט:
דער טאַטע, ___ __________,
___ __________, די שוועסטער,
חתן־כּלה[4] אין מיטן[5]
אויף אַ גאָלדענעם שליטן[6].

[1]it
[2]there will; [3]pass through
[4]bride and groom [כאָסן־קאַלע]; [5]middle
[6]sleigh

2. עפֿנט דעם טויער, עפֿנט אים ברייט,
ס׳וועט דאָ דורכגיין אַ גאָלדענע קייט:
___ __________, די באָבע,
דער פֿעטער, ___ __________,
די אייניקלעך אין מיטן
אויף אַ גאָלדענעם שליטן.

3. עפֿנט דעם טויער, עפֿנט אים __________,
ס׳וועט דאָ דורכגיין אַ גאָלדענע קייט:
אַ באַר און ___ __________,
און האָניק אַ טעפּל[7],
און אַ לעקעך[8] אַ געלער
אויף אַ גאָלדענעם טעלער[9].

[7]pot
[8]cake
[9]plate

די גאָלדענע קייט

the golden chain

This phrase refers to the Jewish religious and cultural tradition, particularly the inheritance and continuity of that tradition from generation to generation. The metaphor has long had its place in Jewish folk art and culture, likely predating Yiddish itself.

◀ CONTINUED

CONTINUED

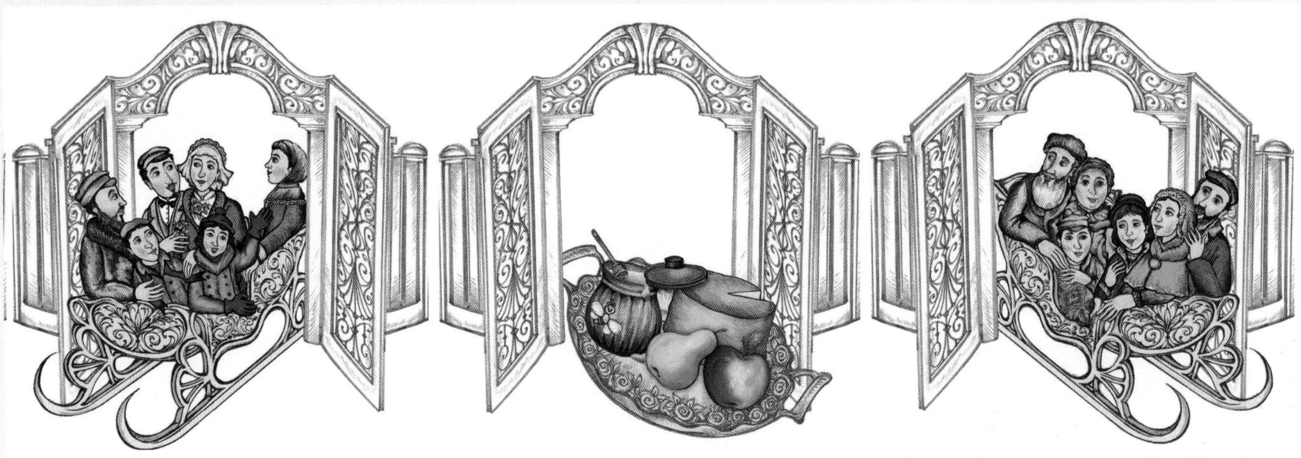

Label each image with the number of the corresponding stanza. Then label the family members and other characters and objects that appear in the images.

איצט, ענטפֿערט אויף די שמועס־פֿראַגעס אונטן.	now; discussion
1. פֿון וואָסער שטאָף איז זי טאַקע, די „גאָלדענע“ קייט?	material
2. ווען עסט מען געוויינטלעך עפּל מיט האָניק?	
3. דאָס ליד באַשרײַבט וואָכעדיקע אָדער יום־טובֿדיקע זאַכן און	describes; festive [...יאָנטעוו]; things
פֿאַסירונגען? וואָסערע ווערטער און אימאַזשן ווײַזן אויף דעם פֿאַקט?	events
4. איר מיינט אַז דאָס איז אַן אמתדיקע באַשרײַבונג פֿונעם טראַדיציאָנעלן ייִדישן לעבן, אָדער אַ מעטאַפֿאָר? פֿאַר וואָס?	true [...עמעס]
5. איר מיינט אַז דאָס ליד איז פֿאַר קינדער אָדער פֿאַר דערוואַקסענע?	adults

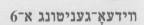

גענימונג 6: איר האָט אַ סך ברידער און שוועסטער?

Practice family vocabulary with these video interviews, which you can find online with the accompanying exercise.

ווידעאָ־גענימונג א־6

טיטל ‫„**זעלמעניאַנער**“ (פֿראַגמענט) (1929-1935)

מחבר **משה קולבאַק (Moyshe Kulbak)**

(סמאַרגאָן, רוסישע אימפּעריע 1896 – לעבן מינסק, ראַטן־פֿאַרבאַנד 1937)

Originally published serially, the novel The Zelmenyaners *is considered a classic satire of the early years of the Soviet Union. With sharply deployed humor and irony, the work depicts a large and idiosyncratic family struggling with modernization, change, and intergenerational conflict. Its author,* **Moyshe Kulbak**, *was a popular poet, prose writer, and teacher who lived in Kovno, Berlin, and Vilna before settling in Minsk. Like many intellectuals in that city, Kulbak was a victim of the Stalinist purges of the late 1930s and was arrested and killed in 1937.*

רפֿאל הערט אַ קורס וועגן דער סאָוועטיש־ייִדישער ליטעראַטור. אויפֿן קורס לייענט מען „זעלמעניאַנער“, משה קולבאַקס קלאַסישע סאַטירע פֿונעם ייִדישן לעבן אין סאָוועטן־פֿאַרבאַנד.

Refoel is taking a course on Soviet Yiddish literature. In the course, the students are reading Zelmenyaner, Moyshe Kulbak's classic satire of Jewish life in the Soviet Union.

In order to keep all of the characters straight as he reads, Refoel has been making a family tree, but he hasn't finished it yet. Use the following excerpts to help Refoel fill in the missing names in the diagram on page 238.

Don't worry about words, phrases, or even entire sentences you don't understand—your goal here is simply to locate the purple names in the text and work out how each person fits into the family tree provided.

- The names with a purple underline are the ones missing from the tree.
- As you read, circle all of the family terms you encounter.
- Use these terms to work out the relationships between the characters named in the text.

געדענקט!

Most of the members of the eldest two generations of Zelmenyaners are referred to as **פֿעטער...**, **מומע...**, or **באָבע...**, followed by the character's actual first name. The prefixed **פֿעטער/מומע** acts basically as a title (like **רב**, *mister*) and does not express a specific familial relation.

◀ CONTINUED

פֿון וואַנען שטאַמט רב זעלמעלע?	[רעב] קומט;
אין דער משפּחה איז אומגעגאַנגען אַ הסבר, אַז ער	[העזבער] מיינט מען
שטאַמט פֿון „טיף ראַסיי“. יעדנפֿאַלס האָט ער שוין דאָ	רוסלאַנד
די חתונה געהאַט מיט דער באָבע באַשען, וואָס איז נאָך	[כאַסענע] married
דעמאָלט, קענטיק, געווען אַ מיידל.	
אַ באַזונדער אָרט פֿאַרנעמט אין דער משפּחה דער	
פֿעטער זישע, וואָס ווערט אין הויף פֿאַררעכנט פֿאַר אַ	
יחסן. צוויי טעכטער האָט אים זײַן ווײַב, די מומע גיטע,	[יאַכסן]
געבראַכט אויף דער וועלט. איינע איז טאָנקע דעם פֿעטער	
זישעס — אַ ריינע זעלמעניאַנערין, די צווייטע האָט שוין	
אין זיך אַ ביסל זיסע מרה־שחורה, וואָס די מומע גיטע,	[מאָרעשכוירע]
זאָל דאָס איר צו קיין גנאַי ניט זײַן, האָט אַרײַנגעשמוגלט	[גנײַ]
אין דער משפּחה.	
פֿעטער יודע איז געווען אַ פֿילאָסאָף און אַן אַלמן.	[אַלמען]
זײַן ווײַב, די מומע העסיע, איז נאָך געשטאָרבן פֿאַר	
די דײַטשן, צוזאַמען מיט אַ שוחט און גאָרניט מיט קיין	[שויכעט]
שיינעם טויט.	
דער פֿעטער יודע האָט זיך געלאָזט האָבן קינדער פֿון	
פֿאַרשיידענעם ווערט. פֿאַר אונדזער געברויך זײַנען פּאַסיק	
בלויז צוויי — חיהלע דעם פֿעטער יודעס און צאַלקע דעם	
פֿעטער יודעס.	
דאָ לוינט נאָך צום סוף אָפּשטעלן זיך גענויער אויף	[סאָף]
איינעם פֿון די ייִנגערע זעלמעניאַנער, אויף דעם	
פֿעטער איטשעס עלטערן זון — בערע כוואַסט.	

◀ CONTINUED

„אָט דאָס איז רב זעלמעלעס הויף.“

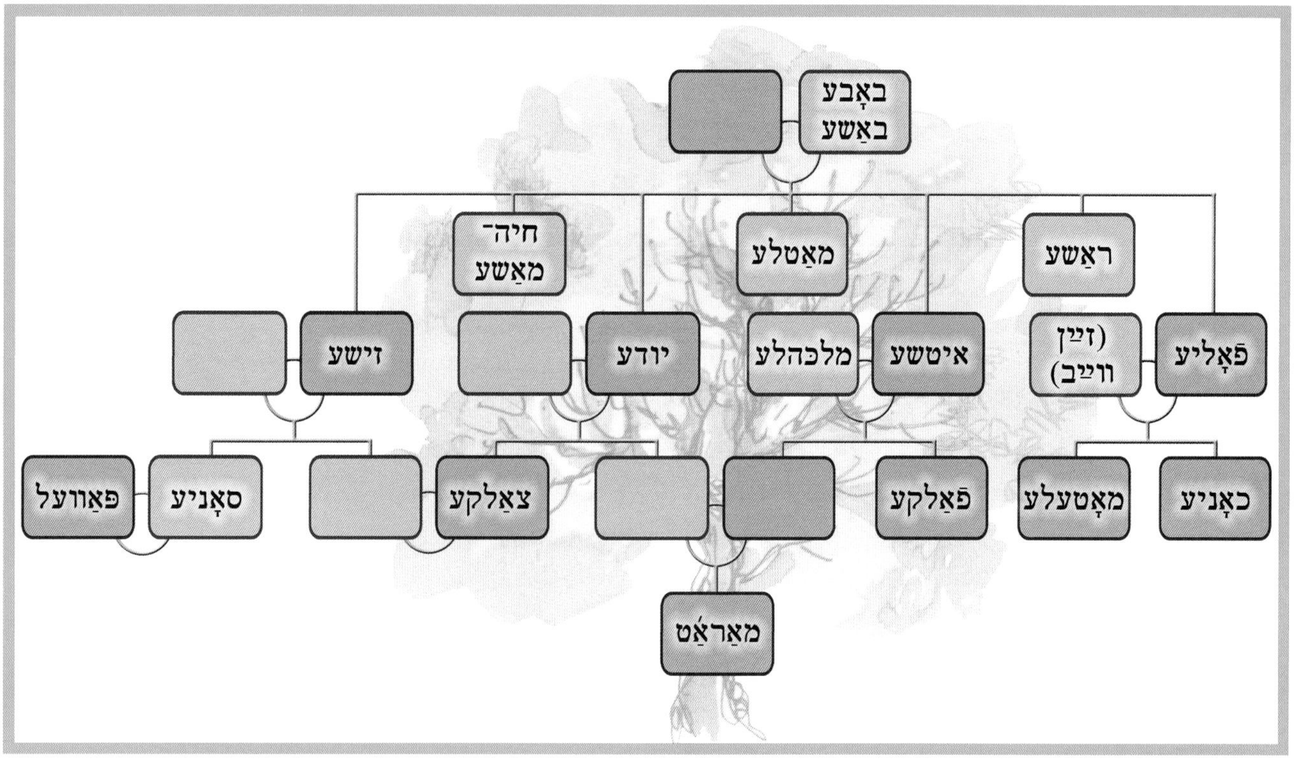

גענិטונג 8: ווער איז פֿעטער פֿאָליעס מאַמע?

With a partner, take turns asking one another questions based on the family tree above. Be sure to use *all* of the family terminology that you know. Follow the model below as a guide.

- Be sure to add necessary endings and suffixes to personal names. After a preposition, the ending ן- is required (**מיט בערען**). In the possessive, the ס- suffix appears (**בערעס מאַמע**).

דוגמא:

א: ווער איז פֿעטער פֿאָליעס מאַמע?

ב: באָבע באַשע איז פֿעטער פֿאָליעס מאַמע. וואָס פֿאַר אַ קרובֿה איז מומע מלכּהלע מיט בערען?

א: מומע מלכּהלע איז בערעס מאַמע!

די קרובֿה	relative (*f*) [קרויווע]
דער קרובֿ	relative (*m*) [קאָרעוו]
קרובֿים	relatives (*m* or mixed) [קרויווים]
קרובֿות	relatives (*f*) [קרויוועס]

היימאַרבעט

Write five to ten sentences describing various Zelmenyaners' relationships to each other. This time, use as many plural relationships as you can.

דוגמא: כאָניע און מאָטעלע זײַנען פֿעטער פֿאָליעס זין.

! גערענקט!

Use the suffix ס- to form the possessive: **פֿעטער פֿאָליעס** *(Uncle Folye's)*.

געניטונג 9: אײַער משפּחה

Draw your own family tree, labeling it with as many names and family relationships as possible. Take note of each family member's age and place of residence as well. Refer to the list below to familiarize yourself with other terms you might need for describing your own family.

half brother	**דער האַלבער ברודער**
half sister	**די האַלבע שוועסטער**
half brothers/sisters	**די האַלבע ברידער / שוועסטער**
great-grandfather	**דער עלטער־זיידע**
great-...	**עלטער־...**
parents	**די עלטערן**
(romantic) partner	**דער פּאַרטנער**
(romantic) partner (*f*)	**די פּאַרטנערין**
stepfather	**דער שטיפֿטאַטע**
stepmother	**די שטיפֿמאַמע**
step...	**שטיפֿ...**

NOTE:

A half brother or half sister is often referred to simply as **ברודער** or **שוועסטער**.

אין קלאַס

Find a partner and tell one another about your families, including all of the information you recorded for homework (but do not look at your family trees). As your partner talks, draw *their* family tree, using the information they provide.

- Be sure to ask for clarification when necessary (**זײַ מיר מוחל, ווי הייסט דײַן טאַטע?**).
- At the end of the conversation, compare the family trees to make sure you noted everything correctly.

דוגמא:

א: איך האָב צוויי פֿעטערס. זיי וווינען אין פֿלאָרידע און טאָראָנטאָ.

ב: ווי הייסן די פֿעטערס?

א: <u>דעם טאַטנס ברודער</u>, וואָס וווינט אין פֿלאָרידע, הייסט מאַרק; <u>דער מאַמעס ברודער</u>, וואָס וווינט אין טאָראָנטאָ, הייסט מאַרטין.

father's brother/sister	**דעם טאַטנס ברודער / שוועסטער**
mother's brother/sister	**דער מאַמעס ברודער / שוועסטער**

NOTE:

Just like personal names, words that describe *people* (like **מאַמע**) have a possessive form created by the **ס**-suffix: **דער מאַמעס** (*the mother's*).

For homework, write up a paragraph about your partner's family, making sure to include as much information as possible.

ב גראַמאַטיק:
אַדיעקטיוו־ענדונגען אין נאָמינאַטיוו

די יונגע מומע טרינקט קאַווע.

דאָס טרויעריקע שוועסטערקינד וויינט.

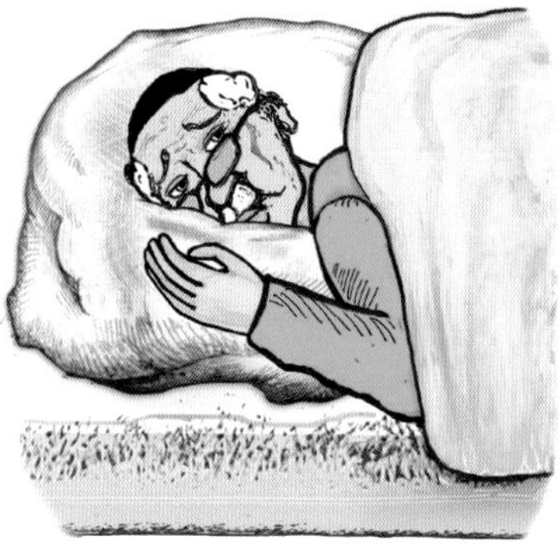

דער שוואַכער זיידע ליגט אין בעט.

די אַלטע באָבעס טרינקען טיי.

די פֿריילעכע אייניקלעך לאַכן.

די שטאַרקע פֿעטערס לויפֿן אין פּאַרק.

געניטונג 1: דער גוטער זיידע

Examine the pictures on the previous page showing what various members of Perl's extended family are up to this afternoon. Read the description below each picture.

- Identify the gender of each of the family nouns used.
- What is the role of these nouns in the sentence? Are they the subject or the object of the verb?
- What is different about the adjectives here? (Compare their introduction in **7 קאַפּיטל**, on page 192.) Where do they appear relative to the noun and definite article?

Look at the pictures where only one person is depicted.

- What is the adjective ending for each gender of noun? Compare the sound of the adjective ending to the sound of the corresponding definite article.

Now look at the pictures with two people. What do you notice about *these* adjective endings?

Pick one of the adjectives from the illustration and make a table showing the forms it would take in connection with each of the types of nouns above—feminine, masculine, neuter, and plural. Write some example sentences on a separate sheet of paper.

> **NOTE:**
> As you examine nouns of various genders in the nominative case, pay attention to the similarities in form between the definite article and adjective endings.

Examine the pictures below and fill in the blank in each sentence with a noun phrase from the word box that best fits each picture.

______ איז אַזוי הויך!

______ האַלט אַ פֿאָטאָ־אַפּאַראַט.

______ שטייט.

______ גייען עסן אין פּאַרק.

די שטאַרקע אייניקלעך	די הויכע טאָכטער
דאָס קלוגע שוועסטערקינד	דער גוטער זיידע

געניטונג 2: דער רויטער בלײַער

Nosn is reorganizing his office and wanted Paul's input on what new supplies he might need, but the text message he sent got a bit garbled. Thankfully, he sent a picture as well. Use what you know about nominative adjective endings to reconstruct Nosn's message from the mixed-up words in the table below.

- Match each nominative adjective to the noun it describes and to that noun's location in Nosn's office. (Two objects are to be found in each location.)
- Fill in the missing definite article that matches each noun phrase.
- Be sure your description matches the object as it is shown in the picture below.

דער	רויטער	דרעטלער איז	
____	דיקע	פֿעדער הענגט	אויפֿן טיש
____	שוואַרצער	בלײַער ליגט	
____	בלויע	בלעטלעך הענגען	אויפֿן טאָוול
____	ווײַסער	זייגער ליגט	אויפֿן דיל
____	ברוינע	בוך שטייט	
____	געלער	בענקל ליגט	אויף דער וואַנט
____	ווײַסע	לאָמפּ שטייט	

! גערדענקט!

The contraction אויפֿן (= אויף + דעם) is pronounced [אַפֿן].

◀ CONTINUED

CONTINUED

Now that you have worked out where everything is, write a paragraph describing the state of Nosn's office, incorporating any objects shown in the illustration. Use the example below as a guide. Remember that you may also use negation to describe the objects that are *not* present.

דוגמא:

דער רויטער בלײַער ליגט אויפֿן דיל.

געניטונג 3: אַ חתונה אין שטעטל ברוקלין

The Eisners' relatives from Antwerp have come to Brooklyn for a wedding. Describe what the various family members are doing by making complete sentences out of the elements below.

- Make sure to add definite articles, decline adjectives, and conjugate verbs (see example).

דוגמא:

קליין / זיידע / טרינקען / אַ גלאָז ווײַן

דער קליינער זיידע טרינקט אַ גלאָז ווײַן.

1. הויך / חתן / זיצן / אויף אַ בענקל
2. קלוג / מומע / שטיין / מיט דעם קינד
3. שוואַך / באָבע / שלאָפֿן / בײַ דעם טיש
4. נאַריש / אייניקל / לויפֿן / צו דער טיר
5. יונג / פֿעטער / נעמען / אַ קיכל — cookie
6. אַלט / זיידע / זאָגן / „שלום־עליכם!“
7. שיין / שוועסטערקינד / זינגען / אַ ליד
8. שטאַרק / מאַמע / טאַנצן / מיט דער טאָכטער
9. פֿריילעך / כּלה / אָנהייבן / לאַכן
10. גרויס / טאַטע / עפֿענען / דעם פֿענצטער

די חתונה	wedding [כאַסענע]
דער חתן	bridegroom [כאָסן]
די כּלה	bride [קאַלע]

! געדענקט

The present-tense forms of a separable-prefix verb differ considerably from the infinitive: **אָנהייבן** but **זי הייבט אָן.**

אין קלאַס

With a partner, take turns miming the actions described above so that your partner is able to guess which of the wedding guests you are imitating. Act out as many of the sentences as you can in the time given.

געניטונג 4: אָראַנזשענע בלומען

Some of the wedding guests have brought colorful arrays of flowers for the newlyweds. Examine the color adjectives used to describe the flowers.

- Identify the grammatical gender of each type of flower.
- Compare all of the instances of *orange* that you see. What, if anything, is different about this adjective when it appears *before* the noun? (Compare to its introduction on page 122.)
- Do the same for *purple* and *pink*.
- Make a table so that you can see how each of the three adjectives changes (or doesn't), depending on gender and number.

After the guests have deposited their floral gifts, the bride and her mother-in-law are appreciating the displays. Well, the mother-in-law *isn't* appreciating them. Write a dialogue in which these two characters describe the positive and negative characteristics of the arrangements pictured above, as in the example.

- Remember, **לילאַ** does not decline.
- All the flowers in this illustration have regular plural forms.
- Be sure to add the masculine ending **ר-** only to the ends of **אָראַנזשענע** and **ראָזעווע.**
- Use adjectives from 7 **קאַפּיטל** to describe the flower displays.

דוגמא:

כּלה: די אָראַנזשענע רויז איז אַזוי שיין!

מאַמע: נו, אפֿשר... אָבער דאָס לילאַ פּאַפּיר איז אַ ביסל שמוציק.

געניטונג 5: אַן אַנדער צימער...

Paul has arrived at Nosn's office to help him reorganize and finds the place still a mess—but no longer in the state Nosn had described in his message! A few new items have appeared and are described below. Note that these nouns are preceded by the *indefinite* article.

אַ רויטע פֿעדער הענגט אויפֿן טאָוול.

אַ בלוי בענקל שטייט בײַם טיש.

אַ גרינער לאָמפּ שטייט אויפֿן דיל.

גרויע ביכער ליגן אויפֿן דיל.

Identify the gender of each of the nouns above and whether it is singular or plural. Now think of the adjective endings you learned in **געניטונג 1** (where the *definite* article was used).

- Now that they are preceded by an *indefinite* article, are the adjective endings here the same or different? Consider each noun separately.

געניטונג 6: אַ באַלאַגאַן

Paul is taking in the new office scenery. Fill in the blanks in the dialogue with appropriate nominative adjectives, according to the image above.

- Pay attention to the gender of each noun and whether it is definite or indefinite.
- Refer to the earlier picture (in **געניטונג 2**) for details about items now *missing* from the office.

! געדענקט!

When an adjective modifies a **singular neuter noun**, the adjective takes one of two forms, depending on whether it is preceded by the definite or indefinite article:

דאָס נײַע בענקל איז אין ווינצימער.

אַ נײַ בענקל איז אין ווינצימער.

This second form exists for singular neuter nouns *only*. Adjectives modifying feminine, masculine, or plural nouns have the same form, whether preceded by definite or indefinite articles.

! געדענקט!

The adjectives **ראָזעווע**, **לילאַ**, and **אָראַנזשן** are irregular: **לילאַ** is always the same, **ראָזעווע** always retains its final **ע-** (which becomes **ער-** for masculine), and **אָראַנזשן** adds a supporting **ע-** along with any case ending (**אַן אָראַנזשן בוך ← דאָס אָראַנזשענע בוך**).

◄ CONTINUED

NOTE:

The neuter indefinite form is generally the same as the base form of the adjective, the same one used in the predicate (**דאָס בענקל איז נײַ**). However, some adjectives have different **predicative** and **attributive** forms: **דאָס בוך איז אָראַנזש** but **אַן אָראַנזשן בוך איז אויפֿן טיש**. The latter gives rise to the attributive definite forms **אָראַנזשענע** and **אָראַנזשענער**. Many adjectives follow this pattern.

NOTE:

The indefinite neuter form is also used when a possessive adjective takes the place of an article: **מײַן נײַ בענקל איז אין ווינצימער.**

פּאָל:	אוי, סאַראַ באַלאַגאַן... אָבער דער צימער איז שוין אַנדערש ווי געווען!	*what a mess*; different
נתן:	ע, זײַ מוחל...	
פּאָל:	נו, מילא. איך זע נישט דאָס ________ בענקל, אָבער ס׳איז שוין דאָ אַ נײַ בענקל — טאַקע זייער אַ שיין, ________ בענקל! און דער ________ זייגער איז שוין מער אָדער ווייניקער אויף דער וואַנט. נישקשה! ווּ איז דער ________ לאָמפּ?	anyway [מײַלע]; see indeed
נתן:	איך ווייס נישט, אָבער ס׳איז שוין דאָ אַ ________ לאָמפּ!	
פּאָל:	טאַקע, און נאָך אַלץ אויפֿן דיל!	*still*
נתן:	נו, אַזוי פֿאַלט ער נישט אַראָפּ!	down
פּאָל:	דאָס ________ בוך איז אָבער אויפֿן טיש.	however
נתן:	אַוודאי איז עס אויפֿן טיש. איך לייען עס!	
פּאָל:	אָבער עס זײַנען דאָ אַ סך ביכער אויך אויפֿן דיל — ________ ביכער, גרינע, גרויע, ווײַ איז מיר, פֿאַר וואָס ליגן זיי אַלע אויפֿן דיל?	
נתן:	גלאַט אַזוי. אַ מאָל זיץ איך בײַם טיש און לייען, און אַ מאָל אויפֿן דיל. דו זעסט אָבער ווי די ________ בלעטלעך הענגען אַזוי שיין אויפֿן טאָוול?	*no particular reason; sometimes*
פּאָל:	טאַקע שיין, ווי אַ שאַגאַל, להבֿדיל! אָבער ווּ איז די ________ פּעדער?	forgive the comparison [לעהאַוודל]
נתן:	כ׳ווייס?	*how shall I put it?*
פּאָל:	אַהאַ! נישט קיין בלויע, אָבער ס׳איז דאָ אַ ________ פּעדער אויפֿן טאָוול! און איך זע שוין אַז דער ________ דרעטלער איז פּונקט ווּ ער דאַרף זײַן — אויפֿן טיש! אָבער ווּ זשע איז דער ________ בלײַער?!	should; then (*emphasis*)
נתן:	השומר אָחי אָנוכי — פֿון וואַנען זאָל איך וויסן?	[האַשוימער אָכי אָנויכי]
פּאָל:	אוי, איך זע שוין דעם בלײַער: ער שטעקט גלײַך אין מיטן דער וואַנט!	right
נתן:	נו, וואָס זאָל איך זאָגן: איך שרײַב מיט ענטוזיאַזם!	*what can I say*
פּאָל:	נו שוין, צו דער אַרבעט!	*all right already*

Now write several sentences describing the current state of Nosn's office, using definite and indefinite articles as appropriate. Make sure the nominative adjective endings match both the gender of the noun and the type of article used, as in the example below.

- Use **עס איז נישטאָ קיין** to talk about things that are *missing* from the room (that were there in **גגעניטונג 2**).

דוגמא:

עס איז דאָ אַ רויטע פּעדער אויפֿן טאָוול. דער גרויער בייגער הענגט אויף דער וואַנט. עס איז נישטאָ קיין ברוין בענקל.

השומר אָחי אָנוכי
[האַשוימער אָכי אָנויכי]

Am I my brother's keeper? (**בראשית ד 9**)

Cain's answer to God, when God asks him if he knows where his brother Abel is to be found. In colloquial speech, this verse is sometimes used to humorously express one's indignance at being asked a supposedly inappropriate question: "How should I know?" (**פֿון וואַנען זאָל איך וויסן?**)

געניטונג 7: די אָפּטימיסטישע באָבע

Many useful descriptive adjectives sound very similar in Yiddish and English. Choose adjectives from the word box below to write sentences describing the people in Perl's family photo (reprinted on the following page).

- Be sure to use the correct form of the nominative adjective ending for each person. Your choice of adjective can be completely subjective.

דוגמא:

די אָפּטימיסטישע באָבע קושט חיהן.

אָפּטימיסטיש	קאָסמאָפּאָליטיש
נאַיִוו	אַריסטאָקראַטיש
ענטוזיאַסטיש	רעליגיעז
אינטעלעקטועל	טעלעפּאַטיש
רײַך	אָריגינעל
אינטערעסאַנט	

! גערענקט!

When a person's name is the object of a verb, the name takes the ending ן- (or ען-, if the name ends on ם-, ן-, or a syllabic ל-).

Examine the form of the adjectives listed above. Write down as many of their English cognates as you can. Find the correspondences between the English and Yiddish suffixes where relevant.

געניטונג 8: אַ שיינע טענצערין

For the same family members you wrote about in the previous exercise, imagine what other nouns might describe each of them: is the grandmother also a dancer? Write another sentence about each family member as in the model, using a noun from the word box below and an adjective from 7 **קאַפּיטל**.

- Remember to decline all adjectives appropriately.

דוגמא:

די ענטוזיאַסטישע באָבע איז אַ שיינע טענצערין.

לייענער	פּראָפֿעסאָר	זינגערין	טענצערין
פּילאָטין	שרײַבער	רעדערין	

NOTE:

Nouns derived from verbs (e.g., **זינגער**, from **זינגען**) are generally formed by adding the suffix **ער-** to the verb stem (usually its first-person present-tense form). To form the feminine versions of these and other similar nouns, the suffix **ין-** is often used, as in **לערערין** (or **פּילאָטין**).

געדענקט!

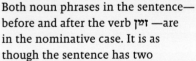

Both noun phrases in the sentence—before and after the verb **זײַן** —are in the nominative case. It is as though the sentence has two subjects; in fact, they are one and the same: the **ענטוזיאַסטישע באָבע** *is* the **שיינע טענצערין**.

9 וואָקאַבולאַר־איבערבליק

א. משפּחה
FAMILY

grandmother	די באָבע (ס)
half sister	די האַלבע שוועסטער (האַלבע שוועסטער)
daughter	די טאָכטער (טעכטער)
aunt	די מומע (ס)
niece	די פּלימעניצע (ס)
woman; wife	די פֿרוי (ען)
sister	די שוועסטער (—)
female relative	די קרובֿה (–ות) [קרויווע(ס)]
grandfather	דער זיידע (ס)
father	דער טאַטע (ס)
husband; man	דער מאַן (מענער)
great-uncle	דער עלטער־פֿעטער (ס)
nephew	דער פּלימעניק (עס)
uncle	דער פֿעטער (ס)
male relative	דער קרובֿ (ים) [קאָרעוו (קרויווים)]
grandchild	דאָס אייניקל (עך)
wife; woman	דאָס ווײַב (ער)
cousin	דאָס שוועסטערקינד (ער)
grandparents	די באָבע־זיידע
parents	די טאַטע־מאַמע
parents	די עלטערן
to know; to be able to	קענען — ער קען
altogether; entirely; quite; unexpectedly	גאָר
indeed, really	טאַקע
that is (to say)	הייסט דאָס
interrogative particle	צי

דער ברודער (ברידער); דער האַלבער ברודער (האַלבע ברידער);
דער זון (זין); די מאַמע (ס); דער פּאַרטנער (ס);
די פּאַרטנערין (ס); דער שטיפֿטאַטע (ס); די שטיפֿמאַמע (ס)

ב. אַדיעקטיוו־ענדונגען אין נאָמינאַטיוו
NOMINATIVE ADJECTIVE ENDINGS

at a wedding	אויף אַ חתונה
wedding	די חתונה (–ות) [כאַסענע(ס)]
bride	די כּלה (–ות) [קאַלע(ס)]
bridegroom	דער חתן (ים) [כאָסן (כאַסאַנים)]

flowers	בלומען
lily	די ליליע (ס)
daisy	די מאַרגעריטקע (ס)
rose	די רויז (ן)
tulip	דער טולפּאַן (ען)
jasmine	דער יאַסמין (ען)
daffodil	דער נאַרציס (ן)
glass	דאָס גלעזל (עך)
pot	דאָס טעפּל (עך)
paper	דאָס פּאַפּיר (ן)

useful expressions	נוציקע אויסדרוקן
sometimes, at one time	אַ מאָל

אינטעלעקטועל; אינטערעסאַנט; אָפּטימיסטיש; אָריגינעל;
אַריסטאָקראַטיש; טעלעפּאַטיש; נאַיִוו; ענטוזיאַסטיש;
קאָסמאָפּאָליטיש; רײַך; רעליגיעז

9 גראַמאַטיק־איבערבליק

ADJECTIVE ENDINGS (NOMINATIVE) — אַדיעקטיוו־ענדונגען (נאָמינאַטיוו)

So far we have seen adjectives used in two different ways.

- In 5 קאַפּיטל we encountered sentences like **דער בלײַער איז בלוי**. Here, **בלוי** is called a **predicative adjective**: connected by a verb (usually **זײַן**) to the noun it describes, its form is always the same, regardless of the gender or number of the corresponding noun.
- In this chapter we have seen sentences like **דער בלויער בלײַער איז אויפֿן טיש**. In this case, **בלויער** is called an **attributive adjective**: linked *directly* to the noun it describes, it acquires an ending that accords to the gender and number of the noun in question.
- The regular declension pattern is demonstrated in the table below. This pattern applies only in the **nominative case** (i.e., to adjectives modifying *subject* nouns). We will learn the patterns that apply to object nouns in **11** **קאַפּיטל**.

❗ **NOTE:** Singular indefinite neuter nouns require a different form of the adjective than their definite counterparts. The same is true when such a noun is preceded by a possessive: **זײַן שטאַרק קינד טאַנצט**.

Some types of adjectives differ slightly from the regular pattern of declension.

- If the adjective's base form ends in **ע**-, that vowel will not be doubled by added endings.

  דאָס בוך איז ראָזעווע ← דאָס ראָזעווע בוך

  (דער ראָזעווער בלײַער, די ראָזעווע פֿעדער,

  אַ ראָזעווע בוך)

- Certain adjectives are invariable, always remaining in their base form.

  דער בלײַער איז לילאַ ← דער לילאַ בלײַער

  (דאָס לילאַ בוך, די לילאַ פֿעדער, אַ לילאַ בוך)

- Adjectives that end on syllabic **ן**- or syllabic **ל**- gain an extra -**ע**- (preceding that *nun* or *lamed*) whenever any ending is added.

  דאָס בוך איז אָפֿן ← דאָס אָפֿענע בוך

  (דער אָפֿענער זשורנאַל, די אָפֿענע טיר, אַן אָפֿן בוך)

- Certain adjectives have different **predicative** and **attributive** base forms. Often the difference is an added **ן**-, which then triggers the same attributive declension pattern described above for the adjective **אָפֿן**.

  דאָס בוך איז אָראַנזש ← אַן אָראַנזשן בוך

  (דאָס אָראַנזשענע בוך...)

❗ **NOTE:** A small number of adjectives appear *only* in the predicate and cannot be made attributive.

	Indefinite	Definite
Masculine	אַ שטאַרקער מאַן טאַנצט.	דער שטאַרקער מאַן טאַנצט.
Neuter	❗ אַ שטאַרק קינד טאַנצט.	דאָס שטאַרקע קינד טאַנצט.
Feminine	אַ שטאַרקע פֿרוי טאַנצט.	די שטאַרקע פֿרוי טאַנצט.
Plural	שטאַרקע מענטשן טאַנצן.	די שטאַרקע מענטשן טאַנצן.

איבערחזר־געניטונגען 9

געניטונג 1: דעם גולמס משפּחה

באַשרײַבט אײַער גולמס משפּחה — וויפֿל ברידער און שוועסטער האָט ער? ווי הייסן זיי? ווי אַלט זײַנען זיי? ניצט אַדיעקטיוון און זײַט **שעפֿעריש**! creative

דוגמא:

דער גולם האָט צוויי שוועסטער - גליקל און טײַבל. גליקל איז אַלט 231 יאָר, און טײַבל איז אַלט 6 יאָר. די אַלטע שוועסטער איז טעלעפּאַטיש.

געניטונג 2: ייִדיש איז מײַן מאַמע

טיטל **„ייִדיש איז מײַן מאַמע“**

פֿון „אַ סטעזשקע“ (1940)

מחבר **מ. מ. שאַפֿיר (M. M. Shafir)**

(שאָץ, עסטרײַך־אונגערן 1909 – מאָנטרעאָל, קאַנאַדע 1988)

M. M. Shafir, *born Moyshe-Mordkhe Shekhter, was a member of Montreal's Yiddish literary circles and an educator in the city's Yiddish schools. As with many immigrants from prewar Europe, Shafir remembered the town of his childhood with great warmth—the pain of separation from that place and time is palpable in his writing. In this poem, living in a bustling city "in di fremdn," he clings to Yiddish not only as his mother tongue but rather as his very* mother, *in whose embrace he can always find home.*

לייענט איבער די פֿראַגעס אונטן איידער איר לייענט דאָס ליד. זיי וועלן אײַך העלפֿן פֿאַרשטיין דעם טעקסט.

1. וואָסערע שפּראַכן רעדט דער נאַראַטאָר?
2. וואָסער שפּראַך איז אים די **טײַערסטע**? dearest
3. וואָסערע אַדיעקטיוון ניצט דער נאַראַטאָר צו באַשרײַבן זײַן **באַליבטסטע** שפּראַך? favorite

◀ CONTINUED

CONTINUED

לייענט איבער דאָס ליד און ענטפֿערט אויף די פֿראַגעס אויבן.

לשון־קודש איז מײַן טאַטע,	
די מאַמע מײַנע — ייִדיש.	
דײַטש איז מיר אַ שוועסטער,	
איז זי שיין — אַ חידוש!	*no surprise there!* [כידעש]
רומעניש איז אַ פֿעטער,	
קיין מומע האָב איך נישט	
פֿון אָט־די אַלע קלאַנגען	*from all of these sounds*
איז מײַן בלוט געמישט.	mixed
נאָר שענער פֿון אַ מאַמען —	מער שיין
אַזוינס איז דען געמאָלט?	*can such a thing even be imagined?*
אויגן — לויטער גוטסקייט,	eyes; pure
אַ האַרץ פֿון גינען־גאָלד.	ריין גאָלד
און אָרעמס פֿול מיט טרייסטונג,	comfort
פֿאַר מיר, איר טײַער קינד,	
וואָס עלנטיקט אין די פֿרעמדן	goes around lonely; foreign lands
און איז הפֿקר ווי דער ווינט.	abandoned [העפֿקער]

איצט, ענטפֿערט אויף די פֿראַגעס אונטן.

1. וואָסערע משפּחה־ווערטער ניצט דער נאַראַטאָר צו באַשרײַבן יעדער שפּראַך וואָס ער קען?
2. וואָס מיינט ער וועגן דײַטש?
3. צי מיינט ער אַז ס׳איז דאָ אַ שפּראַך וואָס איז שענער פֿון ייִדיש?
4. וואָס איז אײַער באַציִונג צו די שפּראַכן וואָס איר קענט? באַשרײַבט זיי לויטן סטיל פֿון ליד.

NOTE:

The word **צי** is an interrogative particle that signals a yes-no question. When **צי** begins a sentence, it functions as a sentence unit and so must be followed directly by the conjugated verb.

relationship

באַטראַכט די פֿראַגעס אונטן, נאָר ענטפֿערט אויף זיי נישט.

1. דער מחבר זאָגט אַז ער „עלנטיקט אין די פֿרעמדן“. ווו איז ער און פֿאַר וואָס פֿילט ער זיך עלנט? ער איז מיט זײַן משפּחה?
2. פֿאַר וואָס, מיינט איר, איז ייִדיש אַ מאַמע, און העברעיִש — אַ טאַטע? וואָס האָבן מאַסקולינקייט און פֿעמינינקייט צו טאָן מיט די שפּראַכן?

NOTE:

In traditional Ashkenazi society, access to texts in *loshn-koydesh* (Hebrew/Aramaic) was generally restricted to men, especially those of means and/or status. Yiddish, by contrast, was considered “feminine,” tied to everyday life and the domestic sphere, despite being the vernacular of all.

געניטונג 3: די מחותּנים גייען

הער־געניטונג
איבערחזר־סעקציע־3

טיטל ♫ „די מחותּנים גייען“

מחבר **מאַרק וואַרשאַווסקי (Mark Varshavski)**

(אַדעס, רוסישע אימפּעריע 1848 – קיִעוו, רוסישע אימפּעריע 1907)

זינגער **דזשודי ברעסלער (Judy Bressler)**

(ניו־יאָרק, פֿאַראייניקטע שטאַטן 1953 –)

רעקאָרדירונג 2000, פֿאַראייניקטע שטאַטן

A lawyer by trade, **Mark Varshavski** *composed some of the most famous Yiddish songs in the entire repertory, tunes that were so widely sung in his lifetime that many assumed them to be folk songs—and still do today. Varshavski was "discovered" by Sholem Aleichem, who published the first written editions of his songs and often invited him to perform these tunes at his readings.*

"Di mekhutonim geyen" *(1901; "The In-Laws Arrive"), originally titled* "A freylekhs (khosns tsad)" *("A Joyous Tune for the Groom's Family") is typical of Varshavski's folk style and evocation of the irreverence inherent in Jewish popular culture. This recording is from The Klezmer Conservatory Band, led by Hankus Netsky (a leading figure in the late 20th century "klezmer revival" movement) and featuring vocalist* **Judy Bressler**, *who descends from a family of Yiddish performers that includes famed actors Menashe Skulnik and Lucy Gehrman.*

דאָס ליד באַשרײַבט אַ חתונה. ענטפֿערט אויף די פֿראַגעס לויט אײַער **דערפֿאַרונג**. (experience)

1. איר גייט אַ מאָל אויף אַ חתונה? איר **פֿרייט זיך** ווען איר זײַט אויף אַ חתונה? (*rejoice*)
2. וואָסערע קרובֿים קומען געוויינטלעך אויף אַ חתונה?
3. וואָס טוט מען אויף אַ חתונה?

לייענט די פֿראַגעס אונטן איידער איר הערט זיך צו צום ליד. זיי וועלן אײַך העלפֿן פֿאַרשטיין דעם טעקסט.

1. אין ליד זײַנען דאָ דרײַ קרובֿים פֿונעם חתן. זיי הייסן פֿריידל, מינדיק, און אליהו. **וואָס פֿאַר אַ** קרובֿים זײַנען זיי אים? ([עליִע]; *what sort of*)
2. וואָס שפּילט מען **דעם** חתנס **צד**? (for the; side (of the family) [צאַד])
3. וואָס טוען די **מחותּנים**? (bride and groom's relatives [מעכוטאָנים])

! געדענקט!

Just like personal names, words that describe *people* (like **חתן** or **כּלה**) have a simple possessive form created by the **ס**- suffix: **דעם חתנס** (*the groom's*).

◀ CONTINUED

CONTINUED

הערט זיך צו צום ליד, נאָר קוקט נישט אויפֿן טעקסט. ענטפֿערט אויף די פֿראַגעס אויבן.

הערט נאָך אַ מאָל, און לייענט דעם טעקסט אונטן. *again*

די מחותּנים גייען, קינדער,
לאָמיר זיך פֿרייען, שאַט נאָר שאַט! *hush!*
דער חתן איז גאָר אַ ווּנדער,
שפּילט אַ לידעלע דעם חתנס צד.

דעם חתנס שוועסטער פֿריידל,
זי דרייט זיך ווי אַ דריידל, שאַט נאָר שאַט! *like*
נעמט זי אַרײַן אין רעדל, *circle*
שפּילט אַ לידעלע דעם חתנס צד.

אָט גייט דער פֿעטער מינדיק,
וואָס האָבן מיר געזינדיקט, שאַט נאָר שאַט! *how did we sin*
ער בלאָזט זיך ווי אַן אינדיק, *puffs himself up; turkey*
שפּילט אַ לידעלע דעם חתנס צד.

דאָרט גייט אליהו דעם חתנס פֿעטער,
דעם בײַכל גלעט ער, שאַט נאָר שאַט! *tummy; strokes*
ער איז פֿעטער פֿון אַלע פֿעטערס, *דיקער*
שפּילט אַ לידעלע דעם חתנס צד.

NOTE:

The word **מחותּנים** is plural—in-laws—and usually refers specifically to the parents of one's son- or daughter-in-law. In the context of a wedding, the term refers to all relatives of the bride and groom who happen to be in attendance.

NOTE:

You may notice that, on paper, some of the rhymes in this song don't quite seem to work (much as in Mani Leyb's *"Morgnlid,"* on page 257). Refer to pages xxxv–xxxvi in the Introduction to read about the dialect differences that lead to this sort of rhyming. Performers sometimes render a text partially or fully in dialect so that the rhymes fit.

ער בלאָזט זיך ווי אַן אינדיק

This idiomatic expression, which literally means "he puffs himself up like a turkey," can express either anger (as it does here) or arrogance.

אין קלאַס

With a partner, take turns acting out the antics of various relatives (as described in the song) and try to guess which relative your partner is imitating. Make sure your guesses are complete sentences, as in the example.

דוגמא:

אַהאַ! דו בלאָזסט זיך ווי אַן אינדיק — דו ביסט דער פֿעטער מינדיק!

טיטל **„אַ מאָרגנליד“**

פֿון „וווּנדער איבער וווּנדער: לידער, באַלאַדן, מעשׂהלעך“ (1930)

מחבר **מאַני לייב (Mani Leyb)**

(ניעזשן, רוסישע אימפּעריע 1883 – ניו־יאָרק, פֿאַראייניקטע שטאַטן 1953)

***Mani Leyb** was born Mani-Leyb Brahinski, the eldest son of a large, poor family. After immigrating to the United States in 1906, he used his training as a bootmaker to find work in New York's shoe factories while publishing his poetry widely. Eventually weakened by tuberculosis, he spent the last several years of his life focused exclusively on writing.*

Mani Leyb was the chief representive of the American Yiddish literary movement that became known as Di yunge *("The Young Ones"). Influenced by larger trends in American poetry in English, this group was interested in freeing Yiddish poetry from overbearing social themes and celebrating sound and image for their own sake. We see this in the fairly unadorned "*A morgnlid,*" which highlights the beauty in the commonplace rituals of everyday life.*

איידער איר לייענט דאָס ליד, קוקט אויפֿן בילד אונטן.

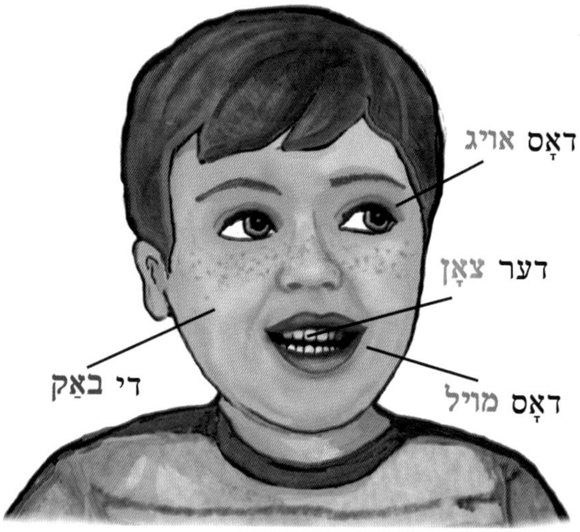

איצט, לייענט דאָס ליד. קאָנצענטרירט זיך אויף די אימאַזשן
וואָס די ווערטער שאַפֿן. words; create

- All four facial features labeled above are mentioned in the poem. Find each one and circle the word. (Hint: Some are diminutivized or pluralized and thus may have suffixes, vowel shifts, or both.)
- The purple words have the same meaning as their English soundalikes.

◀ CONTINUED

CONTINUED

גוט מאָרגן, שיינער טאָג!
גוט מאָרגן און גוט יאָר!
קומט דער נײַער טאָג —
חלום אויפֿן וואָר. — *dream come to life* [כאָלעם]

אייגלעך אָפֿענע —
ווידער אין דער היים. — (once) again
בעקלעך גאָלדיקן — — become golden
עפּל אויפֿן בוים.

וואַסער לויטערע
שווענקט די קליינע הענט, — וואַשט
פֿײַער זוניקער
אויפֿן אויוון ברענט.

אויפֿן גרייטן טיש
שטייט פֿון אַלעם גרייט: — *all things prepared*
מילך, ווי ווײַסער שניי,
האָניק זיס און רויט.

מיט אַ פֿולן מויל
זעץ זיך נאָר און עס. — *just take a seat*
נעמען מאָלן ציין, — *begin to chew*
קלינגען די געפֿעס. — dishes

NOTE:

In the phrase **וואַסער לויטערע** (*pure water*), the adjective follows the noun. Such inversion is particularly common in poetry.

NOTE:

You are not likely to find the word **גאָלדיקן** in a dictionary. In fact, it is possible that Mani Leyb never heard this word before using it here. Such neologisms (in formal as well as informal contexts) are made possible by the prodigious word-creating powers of Yiddish: by adding the right prefix or suffix, you can turn nouns into brand-new verbs (**גאָלדיקן**) or adjectives (**זוניק**), verbs into adjectives, adjectives into nouns, and so on. You saw a similar pattern of word formation using the adjective **עלנט** (*lonely*) in M. M. Shafir's poem *"Yidish iz mayn mame,"* on page 253.

NOTE:

As in the phrase **אייגלעך אָפֿענע** , the adjective **אָפֿן** (*open*) follows a similar pattern of declension as (attributive) **אָראַנזשן** , adding a supporting **-ע-** with all endings. Grammatically speaking, the two adjectives differ only in that the predicative form of **אָפֿן** also has the final **ן-**, which predicative **אָראַנזש** lacks: **דאָס בוך איז אָפֿן.**

Now it's your turn to be the poet! Use the conjunction **ווי** and your knowledge of nominative adjectives to expand the declarative sentences below into scintillating poetic similes. You may use the adjectives and nouns in the word box below or come up with your own.

- Remember to add appropriate nominative adjective endings.
- If a noun is provided *without* an article, it is plural indefinite (where the article vanishes).

סובסטאַנטיוון	אַדיעקטיוון
אַ חלום	שיין
דער שניי	ווײַס
עפּל	רויט
די זון	גרויס
אַ באַנאַנע	געל

דוגמא: דער נײַער טאָג קומט.
דער נײַער טאָג קומט
ווי אַ שיינער חלום.

1. די בעקלעך גאָלדיקן.
2. דער פֿײַער ברענט.
3. די מילך איז ווײַס.
4. דער האָניק איז זיס.

ווי like

! גערעדנקט!

Noun phrases following the conjunction **ווי** are in the nominative case.

10

קאַפּיטל צען:
פּראָפֿעסיעס און פֿאַרוויַילונגען

CHAPTER GOALS

- In this chapter, you will learn how to talk about professions and hobbies.

וואָקאַבולאַר:	
professions	פּראָפֿעסיעס
גראַמאַטיק:	
the pronoun *zikh*	דער פּראָנאָם „זיך“
to like to...	ליב האָבן צו...
קולטור — טעקסטן:	
"Etele" (Y. L. Peretz)	„עטעלע“ (י. ל. פּרץ)
"My Family" (Moyshe Nadir)	„מײַן משפּחה“ (משה נאַדיר)
קולטור — אױדיאָ:	
"What Do You Want?" (folk song)	„װאָס זשע װילסטו“ (פֿאָלקסליד)
"Nothing" (Zvee Scooler)	„גאָרנישט“ (צבֿי סקולער)
קולטור — װידעאָ:	
"A Great Actor" (Fyvush Finkel)	„אַ גרױסער אַקטיאָר“ (פֿײַװיש פֿינקעל)

א וואָקאַבולאַר: פּראָפֿעסיעס

ביבליאָטעקערין
צירל

קרעמער
יואל

קאַסיר
שאָולי

אויפֿראַמערין
בערטע

שנײַדערין
ביילע

אַדוואָקאַטין
רחל

שופֿט [שױפֿעט]
יאַנקל

פֿאָטאָגראַפֿין
מירל

שוסטער
מאיר

קעלנערין
גיטל

בעקער
נתן

קעכין
עלקע

געניטונג 1: די קעלנערין אַרבעט אין אַ רעסטאָראַן

Pictured above are some familiar characters engaging in their professions. Fill in the blanks below to describe where some of them work, using a workplace from the word box, as in the example.

- You may use some workplaces more than once.

דוגמא: גיטל איז אַ קעלנערין. זי אַרבעט אין אַ רעסטאָראַן.

1. נתן איז אַ בעקער. ער אַרבעט אין אַ ___________.
2. יואל איז אַ קרעמער. ער אַרבעט אין אַ ___________.
3. צירל איז אַ ביבליאָטעקערין. זי אַרבעט אין אַ ___________.
4. שאָולי איז אַ קאַסיר. ער אַרבעט אין אַ ___________.
5. עלקע איז אַ קעכין. זי אַרבעט אין אַ ___________.
6. בערטע איז אַן אויפֿראַמערין. זי אַרבעט אין אַ ___________.

רעסטאָראַן	ביבליאָטעק	הויז
בעקערײַ	קראָם	

NOTE:

Just as the verbal prefix -אויפֿ (as in אויפֿהערן) is pronounced [-אופֿ], so is אויפֿראַמערין pronounced with the same [-אופֿ] prefix: [אופֿראַמערן]. This pronunciation generally applies wherever -אויפֿ is prefixed to another word. The suffix ין- is pronounced [ן-], as in לערערין, pronounced [לערערן].

געניטונג 2: אַ בעקער אָדער אַ בעקערקע?

Profession or agent nouns (see page 249) often have two forms: one that serves as both a masculine and general-purpose term, and another that is specifically feminine—usually marked by a suffix. Match the masculine profession words in the right column to their feminine equivalents in the left. Make a list of the various feminine suffixes used.

____ 1. פֿאָטאָגראַ́ף	א. קעלנערין
____ 2. אוי́פֿראַמער	ב. פֿאָטאָגראַפֿין
____ 3. קעלנער	ג. ביבליאָטעקערין
____ 4. שוסטער	ד. אַדוואָקאַטין
____ 5. ביבליאָטעקער	ה. אויפֿראַמערין
____ 6. קרעמער	ו. שנײַדערין
____ 7. שנײַדער	ז. קעכין
____ 8. בעקער	ח. קרע́מערקע
____ 9. קאַסיר	ט. בע́קערקע
____ 10. אַדוואָקאַ́ט	י. שו́סטערקע
____ 11. קוכער	יא. קאַסירשע

NOTE:

Feminine suffixes are sometimes (but not always) interchangeable: **שנײַדערקע** is just as common and has the same meaning as **שנײַדערין**.

NOTE:

The addition or deletion of a suffix generally does not affect word stress, as in all of the masculine-feminine pairs presented here: **בע́קער ← בע́קערקע**.

NOTE:

For all profession terms that end with **ין-**, **קע-** , **שע-**, or **ער-**, the plural may be formed by simply adding the suffix **ס-**: **די קעלנערינס**, **די קעלנערס**, etc. For the remainder of the words presented here, the plural suffix is the usual **ן-** , save for **שופֿט**, which pluralizes to **שופֿטים**, pronounced [**שאָפֿטים**].

געניטונג 3: וווּ אַרבעט אַ שופֿט?

דאָס געלט

דאָס ביוראָ

דאָס געריכט

די צײַטונג

(די) קליידער

די טרעפֿונג

Study the profession-related nouns above. Then fill in the blank in each sentence below with one of these nouns.

- Use each noun only once.
- You will need to use the plural forms of some of the nouns. Remember that nouns ending in **-נג** take a **-ען** plural ending.

1. אַ קאַסיר נעמט ______ פֿון אַ קונה. customer [קוינע]
2. אַן אַדוואָקאַט לייענט אָפֿט אין ______.
3. אַ שופֿט אַרבעט אין ______.
4. אַ שנײַדער אַרבעט מיט ______.
5. אַ ביבליאָטעקערין קאַטאַלאָגירט ______.
6. אַ פֿאָטאָגראַפֿין פּלאַנירט ______ מיט אירע קליענטן.

געניטונג 4: ווער פֿאָטאָגראַפֿירט?

פֿאָטאָגראַפֿירן

פֿאַרקויפֿן

קאָכן

נייען

גיסן

באַקן

שווימען

דערלאַנגען

באַשטעלן

ברענגען

Examine the profession-related verbs above. Then read the statements below, and imagine you see someone engaged in each of these actions. What is their profession likely to be?

1. ער פֿאָטאָגראַפֿירט מענטשן. מסתּמא איז ער אַ ...
   א. קעלנער ב. פּיראַט ג. פֿאָטאָגראַף
2. זי פֿאַרקויפֿט עמעצן אַ מאַנטל. מסתּמא איז זי אַ ...
   א. קאַסירשע ב. פֿאָטאָגראַפֿין ג. אַדוואָקאַטין
3. ער קאָכט זופּ. מסתּמא איז ער אַ ...
   א. שוסטער ב. קוכער ג. שופֿט
4. ער נייט קליידער. מסתּמא איז ער אַ ...
   א. שנײַדער ב. אויפֿראַמער ג. קאַסיר
5. ער גיסט ווײַן. מסתּמא איז ער אַ ...
   א. שוסטער ב. בעקער ג. קעלנער
6. זי באַקט ברויט. מסתּמא איז זי אַ ...
   א. ביבליאָטעקערין ב. בעקערקע ג. קרעמערקע
7. ער שווימט. מסתּמא איז ער אַ ...
   א. פּיראַט ב. זשורנאַליסט ג. קאַסיר
8. ער דערלאַנגט עמעצן אַ בוך. מסתּמא איז ער אַ ...
   א. פֿאָטאָגראַף ב. ביבליאָטעקער ג. שופֿט
9. זי באַשטעלט נײַע קליידער פֿאַר איר קליידערקראָם. מסתּמא איז זי אַ ...
   א. בעקערקע ב. קרעמערקע ג. אויפֿראַמערין
10. ער ברענגט אַ העפֿט אויף אַן אינטערוויו. מסתּמא איז ער אַ ...
   א. שוסטער ב. שנײַדער ג. זשורנאַליסט

עמעצן — (to) someone

גענִיטונג 5: ער איז אַן אַקטיאָר?

Fill in the first blank in each sentence below with the profession word from the word box that best fits the description. (The word box provides more terms than you will need, so don't worry if you don't use them all.)

- Some of the sentences refer to the characters in **גענִיטונג 1** — in those cases, fill in both the profession and the name of the character.
- Both masculine and feminine forms are provided for each profession.
- A number of words appearing in these sentences are cognate with English words that you know. See if you can work out the meanings of such words from context.

דוגמא: דער <u>אַקטיאָר</u> שפּילט אין אַ טעאַטער. זײַן באַליבטסטע ראָלע איז קעניג ליר. ער הייסט דזשאָן. — favorite

1. די ________ אַרבעט אין אַ ביוראָ און רעדט זייער אַ סך אויפֿן טעלעפֿאָן. זי פּלאַנירט אויך טרעפֿונגען צווישן איר <u>בעל־הבית</u> און זײַנע קליענטן. זי הייסט דבֿורה־לאה. — boss [באַלעבאָס]
2. דער ________ פֿאַרקויפֿט ביכער אין אַ ביכערקראָם. ער באַשטעלט נײַע ביכער און קאָנטראָלירט דעם אינווענטאַר. ער הייסט ________.
3. דער ________ שפּילט פֿידל אין אַ קלעזמער־קאַפּעליע. ער שפּילט אויף <u>חתונות</u> און אויף קאָנצערטן. ער הייסט שיקל. — band; [כאַסענעס]
4. די ________ מאַכט קליידער פֿאַר אַנדערע מענטשן. זי נייט קאָסטיומען און בלוזקעס. זי הייסט ________.
5. דער ________ אַרבעט אין אוניווערסיטעט. ער לערנט ייִדישע לימודים און ער האָט אַ סך סטודענטן. ער הייסט הערשל.
6. די ________ אַרבעט אין אַ געריכט. זי לייענט אַ סך ביכער און אַרבעט מיט קליענטן. זי הייסט ________.
7. דער ________ אַרבעט אין אַ שפּיטאָל. ער היילט קראַנקע מענטשן. ער הייסט בער.
8. דער ________ שרײַבט אַרטיקלען פֿאַר אַ צײַטונג. אַ מאָל אינטערוויויִרט ער וויכטיקע מענטשן. ער הייסט פֿאָל. — sometimes; important

זשורנאַליסט זשורנאַליסטקע	קרעמער קרעמערקע	פּראָפֿעסאָר פּראָפֿעסאָרשע	קוכער קעכין
פֿאָטאָגראַף פֿאָטאָגראַפֿין	שרײַבער שרײַבערין	שנײַדער שנײַדערין	סעקרעטאַר סעקרעטאַרשע
מוזיקער מוזיקערין	דאָקטער דאָקטערשע	אַקטיאָר אַקטריסע	אַדוואָקאַט אַדוואָקאַטין

געניטונג 6: דזשאָן איז אַן אינטערעסאַנטער אַקטיאָר

Write a sentence about each of the characters pictured below. Include the person's name, profession (based on the information provided in **5 געניטונג**), and an adjective, as in the model.

- You may use adjectives from page 248 or from **7 קאַפּיטל**.
- Remember to use nominative adjective endings after the verb **זײַן**.

דוגמא:
דזשאָן איז אַן אינטערעסאַנטער אַקטיאָר.

.1

.2

.3

.4

.5

געניטונג 7: ווער פֿאַרדינט אַ סך געלט?

Identify two professions that, in your opinion, match each of the statements below. Try to use as many different professions as possible in your answers, referring to the professions introduced in **1 געניטונג** and **5 געניטונג**.

דוגמא:

מע פֿאָרט אויף קאָנפֿערענצן.

פּראָפֿעסאָר; דאָקטער

1. מע רעדט זייער אָפֿט מיט פֿרעמדע מענטשן. *strangers*
2. מע זעט נישט קיין סך אַנדערע מענטשן. other
3. מען אַרבעט אין אַ ביוראָ.
4. מע מאַכט עפּעס מיט די הענט. something
5. מען אַרבעט פֿון 9 אַ זייגער אין דער פֿרי ביז 5 אַ זייגער נאָך מיטאָג.
6. מען אַרבעט אין אָוונט.
7. מע פֿאַרדי׳נט אַ סך געלט. earns
8. מע פֿאַרדינט ווייניק געלט. little

אין קלאַס

Sender and Khane are reviewing for an upcoming quiz on career vocabulary. They have just completed the above exercise and are comparing their answers. With a partner, read the short dialogue below.

סענדער: איך מיין אַז אַ פּראָפֿעסאָר פֿאָרט אויף קאָנפֿערענצן. ביסט מסכּים?

חנה: יאָ, איך בין מסכּים. און אַ מוזיקער אַרבעט אין אַ ביוראָ.

סענדער: ניין, איך בין נישט מסכּים, ווײַל אַ מוזיקער שפּילט אויף קאָנצערטן! אַן אַדוואָקאַט אַרבעט אין אַ ביוראָ. because

חנה: אָ, דו ביסט גערעכט. *you're right*

Using Sender and Khane's dialogue as a guide, compare and discuss your *own* answers to the above questions. Use vocabulary from **3 געניטונג** and **4 געניטונג** to support your arguments.

גערעדנקט!

The conjunctions **אַז** and **ווײַל** reset the sentence unit count to zero, and so are followed by normal subject-verb word order.

געניטונג 8: וואָס זשע ווילסטו?

הער־געניטונג א־8

טיטל ♫ „וואָס זשע ווילסטו“
פֿאָלקסליד

זינגערס **ראַשע ריפּס (Raasche Rips)**
(שיקאַגע, פֿאַראייניקטע שטאַטן 1916 – לאָס־אַנדזשעלעס, פֿאַראייניקטע שטאַטן 2013)
אַלאַן מילס (Alan Mills)
(מאָנטרעאָל, קאַנאַדע 1913 – מאָנטרעאָל, קאַנאַדע 1977)

רעקאָרדירונג 1962, פֿאַראייניקטע שטאַטן

"Vozhe vilstu" concerns a daughter's expectation of marriage and her ideal choice of bridegroom. Such songs are widespread in the Yiddish folk repertoire. Typically, the learned religious scholar or teacher is held up as the ideal match. In some parodies of "Vozhe vilstu," however, the girl demands a klezmer *(musician) for her groom!*

This 1962 recording is by two participants in the folk revival movement, **Alan Mills** *and* **Raasche Rips***. Alan Mills cowrote the song "I Know an Old Lady Who Swallowed a Fly," while Raasche was renowned for her authentic interpretations of Jewish folk songs—from recitals given at WWII military hospitals to hootenannies in the coffeehouses of Greenwich Village. This track was produced by Moses Asch, founder of Folkways Records and son of prominent Yiddish writer Sholem Asch.*

לייענט איבער דעם קורצן דיאַלאָג, און ענטפֿערט אויף די פֿראַגעס אונטן.

טאַטע: וואָס ווילסטו, טאָכטער? אַ זינגער פֿאַר אַ מאַן?

טאָכטער: אַ זינגער פֿאַר אַ מאַן וויל איך נישט. אַ זינגערס אַ טאָכטער בין איך נישט. לידער זינגען קען איך נישט.

NOTE:
The verb **וויל** can apply either to another verb (**איך וויל לערנען תּורה**) or to a noun (**איך וויל אַ רבין**) Note that its third-person-singular form lacks the usual **ט-** suffix: **איך וויל ← זי וויל**.

1. די טאָכטער וויל אַ מאַן?
2. זי וויל אַ מאַן אַ זינגער?
3. איר טאַטע איז אַ זינגער?
4. זי קען זינגען לידער?

איצט, הערט זיך צו צום ליד. שרײַבט אַרײַן די פֿעלנדיקע ווערטער אינעם טעקסט אונטן.

◄ CONTINUED

CONTINUED

[וואָזשע]	וואָס זשע ווילסטו?	
	אַ ________ פֿאַר אַ ________?	2 מאָל
נישט	אַ ________ פֿאַר אַ ________ וויל איך ניט,	
	אַ ________ אַ טאָכטער בין איך ניט.	
	קליידער נייען קען איך ניט.	
stone	זע איך מיר אַ שטיין,	
	זעץ איך זיך און וויין.	
	אַלע מיידעלעך האָבן חתונה	2 מאָל
remain	נאָר איך בלײַב אַליין.	
	וואָס זשע ווילסטו?	
	אַ ________ פֿאַר אַ ________?	2 מאָל
	אַ ________ פֿאַר אַ ________ וויל איך ניט,	
	אַ ________ אַ טאָכטער בין איך ניט.	
shoemaker's threads; pull	דראַטעווס ציען קען איך ניט.	
	זע איך מיר אַ שטיין,	
	זעץ איך זיך און וויין.	
	אַלע מיידעלעך האָבן חתונה	2 מאָל
	נאָר איך בלײַב אַליין.	
	וואָס זשע ווילסטו טעכטערל?	
traditional religious teacher [רעבן]	אַ רבין פֿאַר אַ ________?	2 מאָל
of course!	אַ רבין פֿאַר אַ ________ וויל איך דאָך,	
after all	אַ רבינס אַ ________ בין איך דאָך.	
[טוירע]	תּורה לערנען קען איך דאָך.	
roof	זיץ איך אויפֿן דאַך,	
down	און קוק אַראָפּ און לאַך.	
	אַלע מיידעלעך האָבן חתונה	2 מאָל
equal	איך מיט זיי בײַ גלײַך.	

NOTE:

The idiom **תּורה לערנען** (*to study Torah*) reveals the blurry line between **לערנען** and **לערנען זיך**. While **לערנען זיך** always means *to learn* or *study*, the bare verb **לערנען** (usually: *to teach*) may *also* refer to study, particularly in the case of *religious* study, or a longer *program* of study.

◄ CONTINUED

CONTINUED

ענטפֿערט אויף די פֿראַגעס אונטן, לויטן ליד.

פֿראַגעס וועגן דעם טעקסט:

1. ווער פֿרעגט, „וואָס זשע ווילסטו“? **וועמען** פֿרעגט מען? — whom
2. פֿאַר וואָס וויל די טאָכטער נישט קיין שוסטער?
3. פֿאַר וואָס וויינט די טאָכטער?
4. **וואָס פֿאַר אַ** מאַן וויל די טאָכטער? פֿאַר וואָס? — *what kind of*
5. פֿאַר וואָס איז די טאָכטער פֿריילעך **בײַם סוף** פֿון ליד? — *at the end of the* [סאָף]

לאָמיר שמועסן!

1. צי איז דאָס אַ ליד וועגן ראָמאַנטישער ליבע?
2. לויטן ליד, וואָס איז **וויכטיק** ווען מע **קלײַבט** אויס אַ חתן אָדער אַ כּלה? — important; *choose*
3. פֿאַר וואָס וויל די טאָכטער חתונה האָבן?
4. איר קלײַבט אויס אַ ליבע־פּאַרטנער **לויט** דער פּראָפֿעסיע? — according to

NOTE:

You may use the conjunction **ווײַל** to answer questions that begin with **פֿאַר וואָס**. Begin by restating the subject and verb from the question, followed by **ווײַל** and your reasoning:

פֿאַר וואָס וויל די טאָכטער נישט קיין שנײַדער?

די טאָכטער וויל נישט קיין שנײַדער ווײַל זי וויל נישט קיין שנײַדערס אַ טאָכטער און זי קען נישט נייען קיין קליידער.

Remember to use correct word order after the conjunction **ווײַל**, as shown.

Compose two additional stanzas in the same format as those above but using different profession words. Decide whether the daughter accepts or rejects each bridegroom.

דוגמא:

וואָס זשע ווילסטו?
אַ *פּשורנאַליסט* פֿאַר אַ מאַן?

אַ *פּשורנאַליסט* פֿאַר אַ מאַן וויל איך ניט,
אַ *פּשורנאַליסטס* אַ טאָכטער בין איך ניט.
אַרטיקלען שרײַבן קען איך ניט.

זע איך מיר אַ שטיין,
זעץ איך זיך און וויין.
אַלע מיידעלעך האָבן חתונה
נאָר איך בלײַב אַליין.

געניטונג 9: בערל באַנדאַזשירט זיך

Our professionals are doing their best to aid their fellow citizens. Match each professional (left column below) to the scenario in which they would be most helpful (right column). Then write a sentence to describe the service rendered, using a verb from the word box, as in the example.

- The person assisted is the direct object of the verb, so their name takes the accusative suffix **(ע)ן**-. If you need help deciding which ending to use, refer to the note in the margin.
- Be sure to conjugate each verb, as in the example.

!געדענקט

The accusative suffix **ן-** takes the form **ען-** when the name it is attached to ends in **ל-** , **ן-**, or **ם-**.

דוגמאַ:

4. חיה פֿאַלט. **א.** בער איז אַ דאָקטער.

בער באַנדאַזשירט חיהן.

____ **1.** צירל שרײַבט אַ בוך.	**א.** בער איז אַ דאָקטער.
____ **2.** ריינע שטייט אויף אַ טישל אין קלאַס.	**ב.** פּאָל איז אַ זשורנאַליסט.
____ **3.** חנה האָט נײַע קליידער.	**ג.** מירל איז אַ פֿאָטאָגראַפֿין.
א **4.** חיה פֿאַלט.	**ד.** דזשאָן איז אַן אַקטיאָר.
____ **5.** מאיר רעדט אַ **זעלטענעם** ייִדישן דיאַלעקט. (rare)	**ה.** הערשל איז אַ לינגוויסט.
____ **6.** נתן האָט אַ סך זאָרגן.	**ו.** שיינדל איז אַ לערערין.

באַנדאַזשירן	פֿאָטאָגראַפֿירן
אינטערוויויִרן	אַמוזירן
רעקאָרדירן	דיסציפּלינירן

NOTE:

The verbs shown here all carry stress on the syllable **-יר-** and have the same meaning as their English cognates. They all conjugate regularly, as with **שטודירן** in **קאַפּיטל 6**.

◀ CONTINUED

CONTINUED

Now the professionals are using their skills to help *themselves* out! Write sentences using the same verbs as above, but replace the direct object with the reflexive pronoun **זיך**, as in the example.

דוגמא: בער פֿאַלט.

בער באַנדאַזשירט זיך.

1. פּאָל גרייט זיך אויף אַ ראַדיאָ־אינטערוויו וועגן זײַן נײַ בוך. — *is preparing*
2. מירל טראָגט שיינע נײַע קליידער.
3. דזשאָן זיצט אין אויטאָבוס און חזרט איבער אַ קאָמישן מאָנאָלאָג.
4. הערשל אימיטירט מאירס ייִדיש און וויל קאָנטראָלירן זײַן אַרויסרעד. — *(to) check; pronunciation*
5. שיינדל קוקט אויף טעלעוויזיע ווען זי דאַרף לייענען אירע סטודענטנס עסייען. — *ought (to)*

These sentences show the **reflexive pronoun** in its most basic role: standing in for the object of the verb when the subject and object are one and the same. For example, Ber is both the one *doing* the bandaging (subject) *and* the one being bandaged (object).

געניטונג 10: אַ יונגע דאָקטערשע לערנט זיך ביאָלאָגיע

In order to become a good doctor, you've got to learn biology first. Write sentences about the seven aspiring professionals listed below, describing the subjects they are studying to prepare for their future careers, as in the example.

דוגמא: ריווע וויל ווערן אַ דאָקטערשע. — *to become*

זי לערנט זיך ביאָלאָגיע.

לערנען זיך	to learn

NOTE:

Here, the pronoun **זיך** has combined with a basic verb (**לערנען**, *to teach*) to create a new two-word verb (**לערנען זיך**, *to learn*). This idiomatic **זיך** is no longer a true pronoun—it does not stand in for any noun—but is simply part of the verb.

1. וועלוול וויל ווערן אַ קאַסיר.
2. ריינע וויל ווערן אַ פּיראַט.
3. חיה וויל ווערן אַ בעקערקע.
4. מענדל וויל ווערן אַ קרעמער.
5. פּערל וויל ווערן אַ שרײַבערין.
6. חווה וויל ווערן אַ מוזיקערין.

געאָגראַפֿיע	כעמיע
מוזיק	מאַטעמאַטיק
עקאָנאָמיק	ליטעראַטור

געניטונג 11: מיר לערנען זיך קאָכן

צוויי סטודענטן רעדן וועגן פּראָפֿעסיעס. לייענט דעם דיאַלאָג.

עלקע: איך וויל ווערן אַ קעכין. איך לערן זיך קאָכן. want to

איידל: דו לערנסט זיך קאָכן?! איך לערן זיך אויך קאָכן!

עלקע: ביידע לערנען מיר זיך קאָכן!

איידל: אָט גייט אַבֿרהם. ער וויל ווערן אַ בעקער.

עלקע: ער לערנט זיך נישט קאָכן, ער לערנט זיך באַקן?

איידל: אין דער פֿרי לערנט ער זיך באַקן און אין אָוונט לערנט ער זיך קאָכן.

עלקע: איר לערנט זיך קאָכן צוזאַמען?

איידל: ניין, אַבֿרהם לערנט זיך קאָכן מיט גיטלען.

Examine the position of the pronoun **זיך** in the following sentences from the dialogue:

איך לערן זיך אויך קאָכן!

ער לערנט זיך נישט קאָכן.

אין דער פֿרי לערנט ער זיך באַקן.

Where does **זיך** appear in the sentence, relative to the verb and adverbs? What sentence element *does* separate **זיך** from the verb?

Rewrite the dialogue, replacing **קעכין**, **קאָכן**, and so on with other career-related nouns and verbs from this section.

NOTE:

The verb that represents the skill being learned (e.g., **קאָכן**) is in the *infinitive*.

NOTE:

The subject comes between the verb and **זיך** only when the subject itself is short or syntactically basic: a pronoun, a name, a noun with an article. Otherwise, the subject will follow **זיך**, as here:

אין דער פֿרי לערנט זיך דער קלוגער סטודענט באַקן.

אין קלאַס

מיט אַ חבֿר, חזרט איבער דעם דיאַלאָג אויבן עטלעכע מאָל. רעדט אַזוי גיך און פֿליסיק ווי מעגלעך.

Now repeat the dialogue, making the substitutions described above.

געניטונג 12: ער לערנט זיך קאַטאַלאָגירן

פּראָפֿעסיעס	ווערבן	
סעקרעטאַרשע	אָרגאַניזירן	אינטערוויויִרן
זשורנאַליסטקע	פֿילמירן	אַנאַליזירן
אַקטריסע	אימיטירן	פּרעזענטירן
אַדוואָקאַט	פּלאַנירן	אימפּראָוויזירן
ביבליאָטעקער	קאַטאַלאָגירן	דיגיטאַליזירן

Pick one of the professions from the word box above and write several sentences describing what a person intending to practice that profession is and is not learning to do at different times of the day.

- Use verbs from among the **ירן**– verbs in the word box, as in the model.
- Pay special attention to the placement of the subject, **זיך**, and **נישט**.

דוגמא:

רפֿאל וויל ווערן אַ זשורנאַליסט. אין דער פֿרי לערנט ער זיך אינטערוויויִרן.

נאָך מיטאָג לערנט ער זיך נישט באַנדאַזשירן - ער לערנט זיך אַנאַליזירן דאָקומענטן.

געניטונג 13: אַ גרויסער אַקטיאָר

וידעאָ־געניטונג א־13

דערציילער פֿײַוויש פֿינקעל **(Fyvush Finkel)** (פֿראַגמענט)

(ניו־יאָרק, פֿאַראייניקטע שטאַטן 1922 – ניו־יאָרק, פֿאַראייניקטע שטאַטן 2016)

אַרכיוו Wexler Oral History Project (2014)

Practice professions with this excerpt from an oral history interview with Fyvush Finkel, which you can find online with its accompanying exercise.

ב גראַמאַטיק:
ליב האָבן

סענדער

ריינע

פּאָל

שלמהלע

שׂרה

חנה און משה

פּערל, חיה, און באָבע שיינדל

געניטונג 1: ווער האָט ליב צו טאַנצן?

Perl is working on a photo album, taking pictures of people doing various activities. Khaye is writing the captions and is adamant that everyone *likes* what they are doing, as in the following two captions.

שׂרה האָט ליב צו טאַנצן.

משה און חנה האָבן ליב צו לויפֿן.

Can you spot the phrase that means to *like*?

- Of how many words does this phrase consist?
- Which of the words *changes* slightly from one sentence to the next?

Consider the verbs that follow the phrase in question.

- Are they conjugated or left in the infinitive?
- What other verbs do you know that trigger a similar construction?

Now write a caption for each snapshot above in the same style as the two provided.

◀ CONTINUED

NOTE:

When ליב האָבן modifies another verb, that verb appears in its infinitive form, preceded by the particle צו (e.g., נתן האָט ליב צו שווימען). This is not the case when לערנען זיך, modifies another verb, in which case that verb's infinitive appears alone (e.g., נתן לערנט זיך שווימען). (After אָנהייבן and אויפֿהערן, the צו is optional.)

אין קלאַס

With a partner, take turns asking who likes to do various activities, as in the example.

- Remember to conjugate **האָבן** appropriately. Note that the question always uses **האָט**, because the interrogative pronoun **ווער** is singular.

דוגמא:

א: ווער האָט ליב צו טאַנצן?

ב: שׂרה האָט ליב צו טאַנצן. ווער האָט ליב צו לויפֿן?

א: משה און חנה האָבן ליב צו לויפֿן.

געניטונג 2: די ביבליאָטעקערין האָט ליב צו לייענען

קוקט אויף די מענטשן דאָ. וואָס זײַנען זייערע פּראָפֿעסיעס, לויט די בילדער?

וואָס, מיינט איר, האָבן די מענטשן ליב צו טאָן (לויט זייערע פּראָפֿעסיעס)? שרײַבט גאַנצע זאַצן, לויט דער דוגמא.

- ניצט סופֿיקסן ווו ס׳איז **נייטיק**. necessary

דוגמא:

די ביבליאָטעקערין האָט ליב צו לייענען.

שווימען	שרײַבן	נייען
לערנען	לויפֿן	שפּילן
קאָכן	רעדן	טאַנצן
לייענען	באַקן	פֿאָטאָגראַפֿירן

גע́ניטונג 3: אַוודאי האָב איך ליב צו טאַנצן

פּאָל אינטערוויויִרט שׂרהן וועגן צײַטפֿאַרטרײַבן. לייענט דעם דיאַלאָג. hobbies

פּאָל: דו האָסט ליב צו ___טאַנצן___?

שׂרה: אַוודאי האָב איך ליב צו ___טאַנצן___. איך ___טאַנץ___ מיט משהן אַלע זונטיק. every

פּאָל: ער האָט אויך ליב צו ___טאַנצן___?

שׂרה: ווייניקער ווי איך, אָבער מיר האָבן ביידע זייער ליב צו ___הערן מוזיק___.

פּאָל: אפֿשר האָט איר אויך ליב צו ___זינגען___?

שׂרה: איך האָב נישט ליב צו ___זינגען___.

פּאָל: אָבער משה האָט יאָ ליב צו ___זינגען___?

שׂרה: יאָ, ער און אַריה־לייב ___זינגען___ צוזאַמען אַלע מיטוואָך. together

---

Consider the purple pronouns and adverbs in the dialogue above.

- Where are they positioned relative to the two parts of the verb **ליב האָבן**?
- What other verbs do you know where a similar arrangement occurs?
- When a pronoun and an adverb appear *together* after **האָבן**, which comes first?
- In Paul's last line, what is the function of the word **יאָ**? (Hint: Can you find a contrasting word in the previous line?)

איצט, שרײַבט איבער דעם דיאַלאָג מיט אַנדערע ווערבן.

- ניצט די פּאַסיקע פֿאָרמע פֿון ווערב: דעם אינפֿיניטיוו אָדער די קאָניוגירטע פֿאָרמע.

געניטונג 4: וואָס האָסטו ליב צו טאָן?

Take turns asking your partner whether they like to do the activities listed in the word box below.

Familiarize yourself with potential responses by first reading the model dialogues below.

- Pay special attention to the placement and ordering of adverbs (in purple).

Take notes on your partner's answers.

א: דו האָסט ליב צו שווימען? **ב:** יאָ, איך האָב זייער ליב צו שווימען! **א:** איך האָב אויך ליב צו שווימען.	**א:** דו האָסט ליב צו שווימען? **ב:** ניין, איך האָב נישט ליב צו שווימען. **א:** איך האָב יאָ ליב צו שווימען.
א: דו האָסט ליב צו שווימען? **ב:** יאָ, איך האָב ליב צו שווימען. **א:** איך האָב נישט ליב צו שווימען.	**א:** דו האָסט ליב צו שווימען? **ב:** ניין, איך האָב נישט ליב צו שווימען. **א:** איך האָב אויך נישט ליב צו שווימען.

שווימען	שרײַבן	נייען
לערנען	לויפֿן	שפּילן
קאָכן	רעדן	טאַנצן
לייענען	באַקן	פֿאָטאָגראַפֿירן

Now present your partner's preferences to the rest of the class. If there are activities that you both like or dislike, mention those too, as in the example below.

- Pay attention to word order, including the juxtaposition **ביידע נישט**.

דוגמא:

סענדער: שׂרה האָט זייער ליב צו טאַנצן, אָבער זי האָט נישט ליב צו לויפֿן. מיר האָבן ביידע ליב צו לייענען.

שׂרה: סענדער האָט ליב צו שווימען. מיר האָבן ביידע נישט ליב צו באַקן.

גענ־טונג 5: האָסט ליב צו לויפֿן אין פּאַרק?

Try to find one classmate who likes to do each of the activities listed below. Ask and answer questions as in the example provided.

- If a classmate answers yes to one of your questions, write their name next to that activity.
- You may ask each classmate up to three questions before changing partners.

דוגמא: לויפֿן אין פּאַרק

א: האָסט ליב צו לויפֿן אין פּאַרק?

ב: יאָ, איך האָב ליב צו לויפֿן אין פּאַרק.

אָדער

ב: ניין, איך האָב נישט ליב צו לויפֿן אין פּאַרק.

1. לויפֿן אין פּאַרק
2. קוקן אויף טעלעוויזיע
3. טרינקען טיי
4. שרײַבן לידער
5. שווימען אין אָזערע
6. שפּילן אין טעניס
7. לייענען פּאָעזיע
8. שפּילן פּיאַנע
9. ליגן אויפֿן דיל
10. עסן בולבעס

היימאַרבעט

yourself

איר האָט אַלײן ליב צו טאָן די אַקטיוויטעטן, אָדער נישט? שרײַבט אָן עטלעכע זאַצן, לויט דער דוגמא.

דוגמא:

איך האָב ליב צו לויפֿן אין פּאַרק, אָבער איך האָב נישט ליב צו קוקן אויף טעלעוויזיע.

געניטונג 6: אויף וואַקאַציע

ענטפֿערט אויף די פֿראַגעס אונטן. שרײַבט גאַנצע זאַצן, און זײַט ספּעציפֿיש.

1. וואָס האָסטו ליב צו טאָן ווען דו ביסט אויף וואַקאַציע?
2. וואָס האָסטו נישט ליב צו טאָן ווען דו ביסט אויף וואַקאַציע?
3. וואָס האָבן דײַנע עלטערן ליב צו טאָן אויף וואַקאַציע?
4. וואָס האָבן דײַנע עלטערן נישט ליב צו טאָן אויף וואַקאַציע?

געניטונג 7: עטעלע

טיטל **„עטעלע“**

פֿון „פּאָר קליינע קינדער (געזאַנג און שפּיל)“ (1925)

מחבר **י. ל. פּרץ (Y. L. Peretz)**

(זאַמיטשט, רוסישע אימפּעריע 1852 – וואַרשע, רוסישע אימפּעריע 1915)

Y. L. (Yitskhok Leybush) Peretz, *together with Mendele Moykher-Sforim and Sholem Aleichem, completes the revered trio of Yiddish literature's "dray klasikers" (three classic writers). Peretz championed Jewish and Yiddish culture throughout his life, producing a formidable corpus of short stories, plays, and poetry while mentoring countless others to follow in his footsteps. Through his literary work and other activities, Peretz fashioned a vision of a culturally autonomous Jewish community, one that would at once be thoroughly secular in nature and yet pull from the vast riches of its ethical and religious traditions. Peretz also wrote for children, particularly after the outbreak of WWI, when he became involved in relief efforts for the displaced and helped found an orphanage for Jewish children.*

דאָס ליד באַשרײַבט וואָס אַ מיידל, עטעלע, האָט ליב און וואָס זי האָט פֿײַנט. וואָס האָט זי ליב און וואָס האָט זי פֿײַנט? לייענט איבער דאָס ליד.

hates

◀ CONTINUED

זאָג מיר, עטעלע, מײַן גאָלד,	*tell me*
וואָס האָסטו פֿײַנט, וואָס האָסטו האָלט?	ליב
בלײַבט זי שטיין, ווי צעמישט,	confused
עטל שווײַגט און ענטפֿערט נישט.	is silent
דאָך ווייסן אַלע, ווי מיר שײַנט,	yet; *it seems to me*
וואָס עטעלע האָט ליב און פֿײַנט!	
ליב האָט אונדזער עטעלע	
צו ליגן לאַנג אין בעטעלע,	
פֿײַנט האָט זי נאָר אויפֿצושטיין,	to get up
אויך בײַ נאַכט דאָס שלאָפֿן גיין...	
ליב האָט עטעלע צו נאַשן,	eat sweets
פֿײַנט — דאָס פּנימל צו וואַשן.	face [פּענעמל]
קנאַקן ניסלעך? גאָרנישט פֿויל;	*cracking nuts; (she's) no slouch*
פֿײַנט צו שווענקען אויס דאָס מויל!	*rinse out*; mouth

ענטפֿערט אויף די פֿראַגעס אונטן, לויטן ליד.

1. עטעלע רעדט, אָדער זי שווײַגט?
2. ווער ווייסט וואָס עטעלע האָט ליב און פֿײַנט?
3. עטעלע האָט פֿײַנט צו ליגן אין בעט?
4. עטעלע האָט ליב צו עסן דעסערט?
5. עטעלע האָט ליב צו וואַשן דאָס פּנימל?
6. עטעלע האָט ליב צו קנאַקן ניסלעך?
7. דער נאַראַטאָר האָט ליב עטעלען אָדער ער האָט זי פֿײַנט?

NOTE:

Both **פֿײַנט האָבן** (*to hate*) and **האָלט האָבן** (*to like*) are grammatically identical to **ליב האָבן**: they have the same patterns of conjugation and word order, and they modify infinitives preceded by **צו**.

NOTE:

The diminutive nouns in this poem are not necessarily *small*. Rather, the diminutive functions mainly to associate these nouns with childlike behavior—the diminutive of cuteness.

Write a few sentences about a child you know, discussing the activities they like and dislike. Start with things mentioned in Peretz's poem, but include other activities as well, using verbs from the previous section, as in the example.

- Practice using the diminutive of cuteness—with classroom nouns, for example. Remember that some nouns have irregular diminutive forms. If you're not sure, check in a dictionary.
- Be sure to use proper conjugation and word order.

דוגמא:

מאָלי האָט פֿײַנט צו ליגן אין בעטעלע, אָבער זי האָט זייער ליב צו באַקן באַרעלעך.

געניטונג 8: וואָס חיה האָט ליב

Khaye has been a bit self-involved lately, spending a lot of time playing on her own. Perl, ever the documentarian, has been taking pictures of Khaye's antics and captioning them in her diary.

חיה האָט ליב זיך צו אַפּלאָדירן.

Compare Perl's caption to the sentences you wrote (with **זיך**) in **געניטונג 9** of the previous section.

- Where does **זיך** appear, relative to the verb of which it is the object?
- What word comes between that verb and **זיך**?

NOTE:

The pronoun **זיך** is the direct object of the verb **אַפּלאָדירן**.

Write captions (like Perl's to the right) about Khaye's other solitary pursuits, based on the following pictures.

- Find three suitable verbs among those provided, and remember to use the reflexive **זיך**.

1. ______________________

2. ______________________

3. ______________________

פֿאָטאָגראַפֿירן	אינטערוויויִרן	קריטיקירן
אַפּלאָדירן	אַנאַליזירן	דיסציפּלינירן
קלאָנירן	רעקאָרדירן	שאָקירן
פּאַרפֿומירן	מאַסאַזשירן	אַמוזירן

◀ CONTINUED

CONTINUED

Khaye is trying to come up with ideas for other self-oriented hobbies she might take up, in light of various future careers she imagines for herself. Write several sentences, combining the adjectives and professions listed below with the verbs provided on the previous page (plus **זיך**).

- Be sure to add appropriate endings to all adjectives used.
- Use **ליב האָבן** to describe both likes and dislikes, as in the examples below.

דוגמא:

אַן אַריסטאָקראַטישע אַקטריסע האָט ליב זיך צו פּאַרפֿומירן.

אָדער

אַן אַריסטאָקראַטישע אַקטריסע האָט נישט ליב זיך צו קריטיקירן.

אַדיעקטיוו	פּראָפֿעסיע
אַריסטאָקראַטיש	אַקטריסע
אָפּטימיסטיש	קרעמערקע
אינטעלעקטועל	שרײַבערין
טעלעפּאַטיש	זינגערין
קאָסמאָפּאָליטיש	דאָקטערשע

א. פּראָפעסיעס
PROFESSIONS

worker	אַרבעטערין	אַרבעטער
lawyer	די אַדוואָקאַטין (ס)	דער אַדוואָקאַ́ט (ן)
cleaner	די אויפֿראַמערין (ס)	דער אוי́פֿראַמער (ס)
librarian	די ביבליאָטעקערין (ס)	דער ביבליאָטעקער (ס)
cashier	די קאַסירשע (ס)	דער קאַסי́ר (ן)
cook	די קעכין (ס)	דער קוכער (ס)
waiter	די קעלנערין (ס)	דער קעלנער (ס)
shopkeeper	די קרעמערקע (ס)	דער קרעמער (ס)
shoemaker	די שוסטערקע (ס)	דער שוסטער (ס)
judge	[same as masculine]	דער שופֿט (ים) [שויפֿעט (שאָפֿטים)]
tailor	די שנײַדערין (ס)	דער שנײַדער (ס)
writer	די שרײַבערין (ס)	דער שרײַבער (ס)

verbs	ווערבן
to order	באַשטעלן
to pour	גיסן
to pass	דערלאַנגען
to heal	היילן
to learn	לערנען זיך
to sew	נייען
to earn	פֿאַרדינען
to sell	פֿאַרקויפֿן
to cook	קאָכן

א. פּראָפעסיעס
PROFESSIONS

work	אַרבעט
meeting	די טרעפֿונג (ען)
newspaper	די צײַטונג (ען)
office	דאָס ביוראָ (ען)
money	דאָס געלט (ן)
court	דאָס געריכט (ן)
clothes	די קליידער

useful expressions	נוציקע אויסדרוקן
I don't agree, because...	איך בין נישט מסכּים, ווײַל...
after all; obviously; yet	דאָך
you're right	דו ביסט גערעכט
because	ווײַל
important	וויכטיק
someone	עמעצער

דער אַקטיאָ́ר (ן); **די אַקטריסע** (ס); **דער בעקער** (ס);
די בעקערקע (ס); **דער דאָקטער** (דאָקטוירים);
די דאָקטערשע (ס); **דער זינגער** (ס); **די זינגערין** (ס);
דער זשורנאַלי́סט (ן); **די זשורנאַליסטקע** (ס);
דער מוזיקער (ס); **די מוזיקערין** (ס); **דער סעקרעטאַ́ר** (ן);
די סעקרעטאַרשע (ס); **די פּראָפֿעסאָרשע** (ס);
דער פֿאָטאָגראַ́ף (ן); **די פֿאָטאָגראַפֿין** (ס)

באַקן; ברענגען; פֿאָטאָגראַפֿירן; שווימען

אימיטירן; אימפּראָוויזירן; אינטערוויויִרן; אַמוזירן;
אַנאַליזירן; אָרגאַניזירן; באַנדאַזשירן; דיגיטאַליזירן;
דיסציפּלינירן; פּלאַנירן; פּרעזענטירן; קאַטאַלאָגירן;
רעקאָרדירן

ב. ליב האָבן
TO LIKE

to like, to love	איך האָב ליב	ליב האָבן
to hate	איך האָב פֿײַנט	פֿײַנט האָבן

אַטאַקירן; איגנאָרירן; אינספּירירן; אַפּלאָדירן; מאָטיווירן;
מאַסאַזשירן; פּאַרפֿומירן; קריטיקירן; קלאָנירן; שאָקירן

די וואַקאַציע (ס); **די טעלעוויזיע**

10 גראַמאַטיק־איבערבליק

PROFESSIONS AND FEMININE SUFFIXES — פּראָפֿעסיעס און פֿעמינין־סופֿיקסן

Profession nouns usually have two forms: a general (or masculine) one and a feminine one.

- The masculine form often ends with ער- (דער שנײַדער, קרעמער) or with אַר- יסט- ,-אָר, or -אָר (דער דענטיסט, סעקרעטאַר, פּראָפֿעסאָר). Some have no special ending (דער פֿאָטאָגראַף).
- These terms are used both to designate a particular *man* who holds a given profession and to refer *generally* to that profession, irrespective of individual practitioners. In this way, a male tailor is simply a *tailor* (שנײַדער) like any other, but a female tailor (see below) is generally marked as a *tailoress* (שנײַדערין).

NOTE: When referring to a specific person, the gendered form is used. However, the masculine form appears in personal *titles*, regardless of gender:

פּראָפֿעסאָר קלוגער איז זייער אַ טאַלאַנטירטע פּראָפֿעסאָרשע.

The feminine form of the noun is typically created by adding a suffix to the masculine form.

- The most widely applicable suffixes are ין- and קע- (די שנײַדערין, קרעמערקע). Often, these suffixes may be used interchangeably: די שנײַדערקע is also perfectly correct.
- The suffix ין- is pronounced simply as a syllabic *nun*: [שנײַדערן].
- For masculine forms ending in אַר- or אָר-, the suffix שע- is used (די סעקרעטאַרשע, פּראָפֿעסאָרשע). A variety of other suffixes exist and will be pointed out when they occur.
- Added suffixes are generally ignored when determining the placement of word stress. For example, שנײַדערין is stressed as it is because it derives from שנײַדער. There are of course exceptions to this rule, as in פּראָפֿעסאָרשע (versus פּראָפֿעסאָר).
- Some profession words lack a special feminine form (e.g., דער שופֿט), and the masculine form (*including* the masculine definite article) is also used for women in the profession: דער שופֿט איז טײַבלס מאַמע.

NOTE: The feminine form of a profession word may also be used to refer to the wife of a man who holds that profession. This usage is more common in traditional contexts.

TO LIKE — ליב האָבן

- The verb ליב האָבן is **periphrastic**—composed of two or more elements—in this case ליב (which does not vary) and האָבן (which is conjugated as usual).
- The verb means *to like* or *to love* and may be paired with a noun object (איך האָב ליב מײַן משפּחה) or with a verb (איך האָב ליב צו זינגען). When paired with a verb, that verb must be in the **infinitive** and preceded by the particle צו.
- When we say that the verb must be the second unit in a sentence, what we really mean is that the **conjugated verb** must come second. Since האָבן is the only part of ליב האָבן that is conjugated, then *this* is the bit that has to occupy second position:

איך האָב ליב צו טאַנצן.

- When we negate this kind of verb, we place נישט after the conjugated bit (האָבן) but *before* the invariable (ליב):

ער האָט נישט ליב צו טאַנצן.

- Adverbs such as אויך (*also*) and זייער (*very much*) can also go in this position:

איר האָט אויך ליב צו טאַנצן?

מיר האָבן זייער ליב צו טאַנצן.

- If the subject does not occupy the first position in the sentence, it generally follows the conjugated portion of the verb. In negative sentences, נישט comes after the subject:

אַ טאַנגאָ האָב איך ליב צו טאַנצן.

קיין וואַלס האָב איך נישט ליב צו טאַנצן.

איבערחזר־געניטונגען 10

געניטונג 1: וואָס האָט דער גולם ליב צו טאָן?

Having completed his course of studies at the community college, your *goylem* is considering what profession to pursue. Describe what the *goylem* enjoys doing and speculate about which professions would suit such interests, as in the model.

- Use professions vocabulary, as well as **־ירן** verbs from this chapter.
- Offer the *goylem* a few different options to choose from, based on their varied interests.

דוגמא:

דער גולם האָט זייער ליב צו שרײַבן און צו אינטערוויויִרן מענטשן.
אפֿשר וועט ער ווערן אַ זשורנאַליסט.

וועט ווערן *will become*

געניטונג 2: מײַן משפּחה

טיטל **„מײַן משפּחה“** (פֿראַגמענט)
פֿון „קינד אָן קייט“ (1936)

מחבר **משה נאַדיר (Moyshe Nadir)**
(נרײַעוו, עסטרײַך־אונגערן 1885 – וווּדסטאָק, פֿאַראייניקטע שטאַטן 1943)

Moyshe Nadir *was the pen name of Yitskhok Rayz, a Galician Jew who, in 1898, arrived with his family in New York, where he became known for his satirical prose and poetry. Often, as in "Mayn mishpokhe," Nadir aims his satire at the living and working conditions of the new Americans residing in New York's Lower East Side, always writing with irony, linguistic playfulness, and political pointedness.*

This poem appeared in Nadir's 1936 collection of children's verse, Kind on keyt *(Child Unchained, New York: 1936)—the title is a play on the expression* kind un keyt*, meaning "young and old" or "the whole family." It was published by the* Internatsyonaler arbeter ordn *(International Workers Order, or IWO), a largely Jewish Communist fraternal organization. As in the publications of many other leftist Yiddish organizations, the poem was printed with the new, de-Hebraicized orthography developed by the Soviet Union. Some changes have been made here to reflect the conventions of* klal-shprakh.

◀ CONTINUED

CONTINUED

לייענט איבער די פֿראַגעס אונטן איידער איר לייענט דאָס ליד. זיי וועלן אײַך העלפֿן פֿאַרשטיין דעם טעקסט.

1. וואָס איז דעם טאַטנס פּראָפֿעסיע? וואָס מאַכט ער נישט פֿאַר זײַן זון? פֿאַר וואָס?
2. וואָס איז דעם פֿעטערס פּראָפֿעסיע? ווו אַרבעט ער? וואָס וויל ער געבן דער משפּחה? פֿאַר וואָס קען ער זיי נישט געבן די זאַכן?
3. וואָסער שפּראַך רעדט די מומע?

אין ליד זײַנען דאָ אַ סך ענגלישע ווערטער. לייענט דאָס ליד אויף אַ קול און פּרוווט זיי צו געפֿינען. שטרײַכט זיי אונטער. — *out loud*; try; *underline them*

לייענט דאָס ליד נאָך אַ מאָל און ענטפֿערט אויף די פֿראַגעס אויבן.

1. איך שטאַם פֿון אַ משפּחה	קום
אַן אָרנטלעכע זייער	honest
ניטאָ בײַ אונדז קיין באָסעס	
ניטאָ קיין לײדיק־גייער.	unemployed
מײַן טאַטע איז אַ שנײַדער	
אַ גוטער אָנצוג־נייער.	suit maker
2. ער וואָלט מאַכן אַ גאַרניטער	would; suit
פֿאַר מיר — אָלרײַט, אָלרײַט,	
נאָר ער אַרבעט שווער און ביטער,	
האָט ער נישט קיין צײַט.	time
3. איך שטאַם פֿון אַ משפּחה,	
אָרנטלעך ביז גאָר,	as can be
די פֿרויען — אַרבעטאָרינס,	
די מענער — אַרבעטורער.	
4. מײַן פֿעטער איז אַ בעקער	
אין ליפֿשיצס בעקער־סטאָר,	
ער באַקט די בעסטע ברויטן,	
די שענסטע פּאַיס און קייקס.	
ער פֿלעכט און ווינזעלט קנויטן	braids; *winds knots (of dough)*
ער ציט און ציט דאָס טייג.	knead; dough

◄ CONTINUED

5. ער וואָלט אונדז געבן קוכן — would; cakes
און שוואַרצן פּאָמפּעניק, — pumpernickel
די באָסעס אָבער קוקן
און געבן טאָר מען ניט. — *is not permitted*

6. מײַן מומע רעדט באַלעזנט — expertly
און ווײַזט אויף אָנקל דזשאָ:
„הי מעיקס דהי דאָו, באָט העזנט, — "the"
הי העזנט גאָט דהי דאָו.“

7. איך שטאַם פֿון העכסטן ייִחוס — highest; pedigree [ייִכעס]
קיין העכערס איז ניטאָ,
און יעדער אַרבעט ריכטיק
ווען אַרבעט איז נאָר דאָ.

איצט, ענטפֿערט אויף די פֿראַגעס אונטן.

1. ווי הייסט דער פֿעטער? וואָס באַקט ער?
2. ווי אַזוי שפּילט זיך נאַדיר מיט דעם וואָרט „דאָו“? וויפֿל טײַטשן האָט דאָס וואָרט אויף ענגליש? ווי זאָגט מען „דאָו“ אויף ייִדיש? — meanings
3. וואָס מיינט איר, צי האָט די משפּחה אַ סך געלט אָדער ווייניק געלט? אַלע זײַנען צופֿרידן וואָס זיי וווינען און אַרבעטן אין די פֿאַראייניקטע שטאַטן? פֿאַר וואָס אָדער פֿאַר וואָס נישט? — happy
4. דער נאַראַטאָר איז שטאָלץ מיט זײַן משפּחה, אָדער ער שעמט זיך? ווי אַזוי ווייסט איר? ניצט ווערטער פֿון דעם ליד אין אײַער ענטפֿער. — proud

געניטונג 3: גאָרנישט

הער־געניטונג
איבערחזר־סעקציע־3

טיטל	**„גאָרנישט“** (פֿראַגמענט)
דיקטאָר	**צבֿי סקולער (Zvee Scooler)** (קאָמעניץ־פּאָדאָלסק, רוסישע אימפּעריע 1899 – ניו־יאָרק, פֿאַראייניקטע שטאַטן 1985)
רעקאָרדירונג	1947, פֿאַראייניקטע שטאַטן

Practice family vocabulary and professions with this segment from the radio show *Di forverts sho* (*The Forward Hour*), which you can find online with the accompanying exercise.

11

קאַפּיטל עלף:
אַקוזאַטיוו און אויסזען

CHAPTER GOALS

- In this chapter, you will learn how to talk about a person's physical appearance and how to use the accusative case.

וואָקאַבולאַר:	
physical appearances	אויסזען

גראַמאַטיק:	
accusative articles and adjective endings	אַרטיקלען און אַדיעקטיוו־ענדונגען אין אַקוזאַטיוו
accusative pronouns	פּראָנאָמען אין אַקוזאַטיוו
grammatical gender	גראַמאַטישער מין

קולטור — טעקסטן:	
"A Dream About a Shop" (J. I. Sigal)	„אַ חלום וועגן אַ קרעמל“ (י. י. סיגאַל)
"Relatives" (anecdote)	„קרובֿישאַפֿט“ (אַנעקדאָט)

קולטור — אודיאָ:	
"The Lord Sends..." (folk song)	„שיקט דער האַר“ (פֿאָלקסליד)

א גראַמאַטיק:
אַקוזאַטיוו און גראַמאַטישער מין

משה פֿאַרמאַכט
די שווערע טיר.

אַריה־לייב עפֿנט
דעם גרויסן פֿענצטער.

איידל נעמט אַרויס
דאָס אַלטע ווערטערבוך.

חנה פֿאָטאָגראַפֿירט
די קלוגע סטודענטן.

געניטונג 1: עפֿענען אַ פֿענצטער

Professor Kluger's students are keeping busy as they wait for class to begin. Read the descriptions of what they are doing. In each of these sentences, the verb describes an action that involves two nouns: a **subject** (*performing* the action) and a **direct object** (*immediately affected* by that action).

- Identify the direct object of each verb. (You may notice certain changes in articles and adjectives; we will return to these later.)

Many verbs we have seen so far have had *only* a subject. Consider the short sentences below; all are correct as is, but some *could* be extended further by adding an object noun while others cannot. Match each noun provided below with one extendable sentence, as in the example.

דוגמאַ:

שׂרה טאַנצט *אַ טאַנגאָ.*

1. שׂרה טאַנצט
2. גיטל הערט
3. משה שפּרינגט
4. חנה לויפֿט
5. איידל שפּילט
6. אַריה־לייב זיצט
7. חווה זינגט
8. סענדער שטייט
9. וועלוול עסט

אַ טאַנגאָ	אַ ליד
אַ סאָנאַטע	אַ בולבע
אַ לעקציע	

◀ CONTINUED

NOTE:

To illustrate the concepts discussed here, consider the sentence **אַריה־לייב עפֿנט דעם גרויסן פֿענצטער.** The verb **עפֿענען** describes the action of *opening*, which involves two nouns: a **subject** (**אַריה־לייב**) that *opens* something and a **direct** *object* (**דעם גרויסן פֿענצטער**) that is *being opened.*

NOTE:

A verb that has an object is said to be **transitive**, while a verb *without* an object is **intransitive**. Many verbs (like **זינגען**) may be used both transitively and intransitively, as demonstrated in this exercise. However, certain verbs (like **עפֿענען**) *require* an object (at least an implicit one) and are thus *always* transitive. Others (like **שפּרינגען**) can *never* have an object, and are always intransitive.

CONTINUED

Now let's return to the direct-object nouns themselves. We saw in **קאַפּיטל 9** that, when a noun is modified directly by an adjective, that adjective takes endings according to the gender of the noun. In fact, these endings depend not only on the noun's gender but also its role in the sentence: when it is the subject of a verb, it (and its associated articles and adjectives) are said to be in the **nominative case**. By contrast, a direct-object noun is said to be in the **accusative case**.

Identify the gender and number of each direct-object noun in the four sentences illustrated on the preceding page. Now examine the definite articles and adjectives modifying these nouns.

- Are they the same as the *nominative* articles and adjectives of the corresponding gender?
- If not, which of the accusative articles and adjectives differ, and in what way?

Make a table showing the forms a definite article and the adjective **גרויס** would take in the accusative case in connection with each of the types of nouns above—feminine, masculine, neuter, and plural. The resultant noun phrase in each table cell should complete the sentence **...איך זע**.

געניטונג 2: וועמען היפּנאָטיזירט דער פּעטער?

Fill in the missing definite articles and adjectives in the sentences below. Be sure to use the appropriate accusative forms of all articles and matching adjectives (as provided below).

1. דער קאָסמאָפּאָליטישער פּעטער היפּנאָטיזירט ______ ______ פלימעניק.
2. די אָפּטימיסטישע זשורנאַליסטקע אינטערוויוִירט ______ ______ שרײַבערין.
3. די יונגע סטודענטקע אימיטירט ______ ______ שוועסטערקינד.
4. דער קלוגער שרײַבער אינספּירירט ______ ______ לייענערס.

אינטעלעקטועלע	נאַיִוון
אינטערעסאַנטע	ענטוזיאַסטישע

Write four more sentences using verbs of your choice, with the direct objects below.

- The adjectives have already been declined, but you will need to add appropriately declined definite articles.

טעלעפּאַטישן אַדוואָקאַט	מידע קעלנערין
שטאַרקע אייניקל	אַריסטאָקראַטישע פּראָפֿעסאָרן

געניטונג 3: וועלוול נעמט אַ רויטע פֿעדער

וועלוול נעמט
אַ רויטע פֿעדער.

עלקע לייענט
אַ שווער בוך.

אַבֿרהם שרײַבט
אַ לאַנגן עסיי.

גיטל עסט
געלע בולבעס.

Compare the adjectives in the sentences above to the ones at the beginning of this section. Do you notice any endings that are different?

- This is the same phenomenon as that described on page 245 with regard to neuter nouns in the *nominative* case. The formal properties of nominative and accusative neuter nouns are the same in this respect.

גענִיטונג 4: חנה האָט אַ רויטע שער

Write a sentence about each character, using the accusative adjectives provided. Use indefinite articles only.

- Make sure each adjective you use matches the gender of the noun it modifies, just as **רויטע** matches the feminine noun **שער** in the example.
- Remember to use the appropriate adjective form with singular neuter nouns.

דוגמא:

חנה האָט אַ רויטע שער.

לײַכטן	רויטע	געל	שיינע
גרויסע	ברוין	שוואַרצן	

! געדענקט!

Singular *indefinite* neuter nouns require a different form of the adjective than their definite counterparts:

עלקע לייענט דאָס שווערע בוך.
עלקע לייענט אַ שווער בוך.

געניטונג 5: טאַטע־מאַמע אױף װאַקאַציע

טאַטע־מאַמע גרינפֿעלד פֿאָרן אַװעק אױף װאַקאַציע, און די קינדער בלײַבן אין דער הײם מיט באָבע שײנדל. פּערל שרײַבט די עלטערן אַ בריוו.

דער בריוו	letter

טײַערע טאַטע־מאַמע,

באָבע שײנדל עסט בולבעס אין קיך און זי זעט נישט װאָס חיה טוט. חיה נעמט אַ בלױען בלײַער און זי שרײַבט גרױסע װערטער אױף די װענט. דערנאָך נעמט זי אַ רײן, װײַס בלעטל פּאַפּיר און זי מאַכט אַ קרומען עראָפּלאַן. זי װאַרפֿט אַרױס דעם װײַסן עראָפּלאַן דורכן פֿענצטער.

איך ברענג דעם באַקװעמען האַמאַק אין גאָרטן אַרײַן און איך עס אַ רױטע טרוסקאַפֿקע. דאָס קעצל טרינקט דאָס קאַלטע װאַסער פֿון דעם אַלטן עמער.

הײַנט האָט רפֿאל אַ פֿרײַען טאָג. ער עפֿנט אַ שײנעם, ברױנעם רוקזאַק און ער נעמט אַרױס אַ דיק בוך מיט אַלען גינזבורגס פּאָעזיע.

זײַט געזונט,

פּערעלע

kitchen

words

then

throws out

through the

comfortable

strawberry

bucket

Read through the letter again, drawing a box around every verb. Underline the subject of each verb and circle the direct object.

- There will be some nouns left over. These are contained in **prepositional phrases** and are neither subjects nor direct objects. We will learn more about prepositions in **13 קאַפּיטל**.

List all the direct-object noun phrases, including any articles and adjectives, as in the example. Label each noun with its gender and whether it is singular or plural.

- If you are unsure of a given noun's gender, determine it using the form of the definite article. Remember, direct-object nouns take the accusative case.

אײנצאָל	singular
מערצאָל	plural
מאַסקולין	masculine
פֿעמינין	feminine
נײטראַל	neuter

דוגמא:

אַ בלױען בלײַער (מאַסקולין)

◀ CONTINUED

CONTINUED

Now look specifically at the masculine nouns.

- What do you notice about the adjectives attached to them?
- Circle the stem of each adjective.

Group these adjectives according to the ending following the stem.

- Which of these endings have you seen before?
- What seems to cause the other two endings?
- Write down the final letters corresponding to each variant ending.

NOTE:

The adjective **נײַ** is an exception to the patterns demonstrated here, forming its masculine accusative form with **-עם** (despite ending in a vowel):

רפֿאל עפֿנט דעם נײַעם רוקזאַק.

גענישונג 6: חיהס בריוו

Khaye, not one to be upstaged, has *also* written a letter to her parents in their absence—but her spelling is still a little shaky when it comes to representing adjective endings. Use your knowledge of masculine accusative adjective forms to help Khaye fill in the missing endings.

טײַערע טאַטע־מאַמע,

די זון שײַנט און עס איז וואַרעם. איך האָב ליב דעם
וואַרעמ___ טאָג. איך שרײַב אַ קלײנ___ בריוו אויף די ווענט.
דאָס קעצל איז אין גאָרטן און עס לעקט דעם גרוי___ עמער.
פֿערל איז אויך אין גאָרטן, און זי צעקנייטשט מײַן גרויס___
פּאַפּירענעם עראָפּלאַן. רפֿאל האָט אַ נײַ___ רוקזאַק, און
ער מיינט אַז ער איז זייער אינטעלעקטועל.

קומט שוין אַהיים,

חיהלע

crumples

גערעדעט! ⓘ

The adjective **נײַ** is irregular in the accusative (see **גענישונג 5**).

געניטונג 7: איר זעט דעם שיינעם גאָרטן?

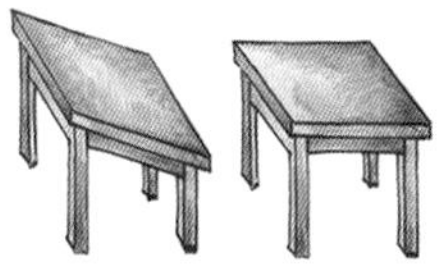

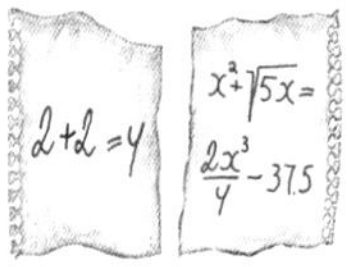

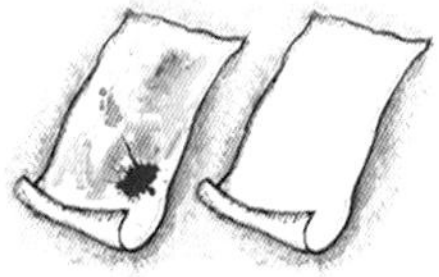

די פֿראַגעס אונטן דערמאָנען עטלעכע אָביעקטן. איר קענט זיי געפֿינען אויפֿן בילד?

- ווען איר זעט אַ ספּעציפֿישן אָביעקט אויפֿן בילד, באַשרײַבט ווו ער געפֿינט זיך, לויט דער דוגמא.
- עטלעכע אָביעקטן זײַנען נישטאָ אויפֿן בילד. אויב איר געפֿינט עפּעס נישט, שרײַבט „ניין, ער איז נישטאָ.“

אויב if

דוגמא: איר זעט דעם שיינעם גאָרטן?
יאָ, ער איז אויף רעכטס.

1. איר זעט דעם נײַעם אויטאָ?
2. איר זעט דעם דינעם מאַנטל?
3. איר זעט דעם קליינעם פֿענצטער?
4. איר זעט דעם גרויען זייגער?
5. איר זעט דעם בלויען בלײַער?
6. איר זעט דעם קרומען טיש?
7. איר זעט דעם גרינעם זאַק?

געניטונג 8: ווער האָט אַ גרינעם לאָמפּ?

Try to find one classmate who owns each of the items listed below. Ask and answer questions as in the example provided.

- Adjectives are provided in their base form. Be sure to add appropriate accusative endings.
- If a classmate answers yes to one of your questions, write their name next to that object.
- You may ask each classmate up to three questions before changing partners.

דוגמא: לאָמפּ (גרין)

א: דו האָסט אַ גרינעם לאָמפּ?

ב: יאָ, איך האָב אַ גרינעם לאָמפּ.

אָדער

ב: ניין, איך האָב נישט קיין גרינעם לאָמפּ.

1. לאָמפּ (גרין)
2. זייגער (גרוי)
3. מעקער (נײַ)
4. פֿענצטער (ריין)
5. דרעטלער (שוואַרץ)
6. דיל (בלוי)
7. טיש (קרום)
8. מאַנטל (דין)

היימאַרבעט

איר האָט אַליין די זאַכן, אָדער נישט? שרײַבט אָן עטלעכע זאַצן, לויט דער דוגמא.

דוגמא:

איך האָב אַ גרינעם לאָמפּ, אָבער איך האָב נישט קיין גרויען זייגער.

געניטונג 9: שיקט דער האַר

הער־געניטונג א־9

טיטל ♫ „שיקט דער האַר“

פֿאָלקסליד

זינגער **סידאָר בעלאַרסקי (Sidor Belarsky)**

(קריזשאָפּאָל, רוסישע אימפּעריע 1898 – ניו־יאָרק, פֿאַראייניקטע שטאַטן 1975)

רעקאָרדירונג פֿאַראייניקטע שטאַטן

"Shikt der har" is an example of a cumulative song, a type of folk song common to many European cultures in which each stanza builds on the last. This song bears a striking resemblance to another cumulative song in the Jewish tradition—"Khad gadyo," which is traditionally sung at Passover. Although written in Aramaic (a language associated with ancient Middle Eastern texts), the musical form of "Khad gadyo" indicates that it was likely composed in Europe at about the same time as "Shikt der har," approximately the 16th century.

Sidor Belarsky *(born Isidor Livshitz) was an internationally renowned opera singer who performed with opera companies across the globe. In the 1930s he became an important collector and interpreter of cantorial music, Hasidic nigunim, and Yiddish and Hebrew songs.*

Having tired of letter-writing, Khaye and Perl have taken to drawing pictures. Examine their illustration of the song *Shikt der har* below.

- Write five sentences using the nouns and verbs in Khaye's and Perl's drawings.
- Remember that nouns functioning as direct objects need to be in the accusative case.

דוגמא: דער פֿײַער ברענט דעם שטעקן.

דער פּויער* | דער האַר* | דער שוחט* [שויכעט] | די בהמה* [בעהיימע] | דער וואַלד | דער שטעקן* | דער פֿײַער* | דאָס וואַסער

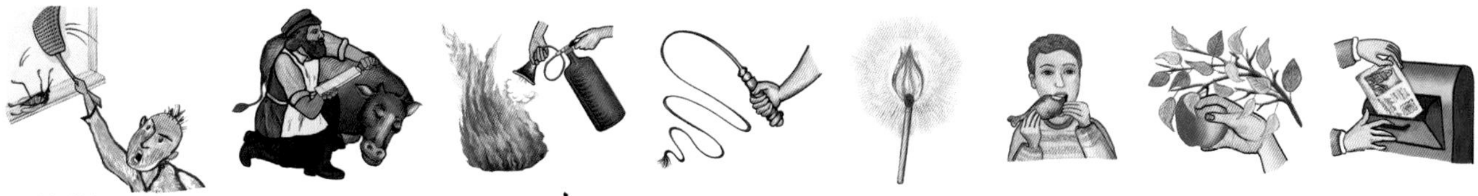

שיקן | רײַסן | בײַסן | ברענען | שמײַסן | לעשן | שעכטן | טייטן

◄ CONTINUED

CONTINUED

Although there is no surefire way of ascertaining a noun's grammatical gender from its form alone, there are common trends among certain groups of words. Each of the nouns marked with an asterisk on the preceding page belongs to one of the six groups shown in the table below. Place each word in the appropriate group.

- Note that we have provided two categories *not* represented in the song, so some groups may receive more than one word and others none at all.

לערערין, פּראָפֿעסאָרשע, סטודענטקע, חבֿרטע	לערער, פּראָפֿעסאָר, סטודענט, חבֿר
קאַווע, סטעליע, דירה, דוגמא	צימער, פֿענצטער, בלײַער
	האָרן, רעגן־בויגן
	טאָוול, עפּל

Now that your table is complete, label each column with the corresponding grammatical gender and identify the feature that unites the words in each cell.

- Note that this feature may have to do with the form of the word itself (e.g., a suffix or final sound) or with some aspect of the word's meaning.

Read the song (on the following page) once through for comprehension.

- Refer to the illustration in the margin to help you make sense of the first stanza.

◄ CONTINUED

CONTINUED

NOTE:

This song is structured around the two verbs **זאָל** and **וויל**. Rather than describing actions or circumstances, these **modal verbs** express a *feeling or intention* regarding some other event: the lord *intends* for the peasant to pick the pears; the peasant doesn't *want* to. The verb **זאָלן** signals the **subjunctive mood** and might be translated in slightly archaic English: "The lord sends the peasant into the forest, that he *might* pick the pears."

NOTE:

Modal verbs like **זאָלן** and **וועלן** (the irregular infinitive of **וויל**) are followed by the infinitive of the verb they modify, *without* the particle **צו**. Such verbs also have a special conjugation in the third-person singular, which lacks the regular ending **ט**- and thus matches the **איך** form.

1. שיקט דער האַר
אַ פּויער אין וואַלד [2 מאָל]
ער זאָל די באַרעלעך רײַסן. [2 מאָל]
דער פּויער וויל נישט די באַרעלעך רײַסן,
די באַרעלעך ווילן נישט פֿאַלן. [2 מאָל]

2. שיקט דער האַר
אַ הונט אין וואַלד [2 מאָל]
ער זאָל דעם פּויער בײַסן. [2 מאָל]
דער הונט וויל נישט דעם פּויער בײַסן,
דער פּויער וויל נישט די באַרעלעך רײַסן,
די באַרעלעך ווילן נישט פֿאַלן. [2 מאָל]

3. שיקט דער האַר
אַ שטעקן אין וואַלד [2 מאָל]
ער זאָל דעם הונט שמײַסן. [2 מאָל]
דער שטעקן וויל נישט דעם הונט שמײַסן,
דער הונט וויל נישט דעם פּויער בײַסן...

4. שיקט דער האַר
אַ פֿײַער אין וואַלד [2 מאָל]
ער זאָל דעם שטעקן ברענען. [2 מאָל]
דער פֿײַער וויל נישט דעם שטעקן ברענען,
דער שטעקן וויל נישט דעם הונט שמײַסן...

5. שיקט דער האַר
אַ וואַסער אין וואַלד [2 מאָל]
עס זאָל דעם פֿײַער לעשן. [2 מאָל]
דאָס וואַסער וויל נישט דעם פֿײַער לעשן,
דער פֿײַער וויל נישט דעם שטעקן ברענען...

6. שיקט דער האַר
אַ בהמה אין וואַלד [2 מאָל]
זי זאָל דאָס וואַסער טרינקען. [2 מאָל]
די בהמה וויל נישט דאָס וואַסער טרינקען,
דאָס וואַסער וויל נישט דעם פֿײַער לעשן...

◄ CONTINUED

CONTINUED

7. שיקט דער האַר
אַ שוחט אין וואַלד — 2 מאָל
ער זאָל די בהמה שעכטן — 2 מאָל
דער שוחט וויל נישט די בהמה שעכטן,
די בהמה וויל נישט דאָס וואַסער טרינקען...

8. שיקט דער האַר
דעם מלאך־המוות אין וואַלד — 2 מאָל
ער זאָל דעם שוחט טייטן. — 2 מאָל
דער מלאך־המוות וויל נישט דעם שוחט טייטן,
דער שוחט וויל נישט די בהמה שעכטן...

angel of death [מאַלעכאַמאָוועס]

9. קומט דער האַר
אַליין אין וואַלד אַרײַן — 2 מאָל
...
דער מלאך־המוות וויל שוין דעם שוחט טייטן,
דער שוחט וויל שוין די בהמה שעכטן,
די בהמה וויל שוין דאָס וואַסער טרינקען,
דאָס וואַסער וויל שוין דעם פֿײַער לעשן,
דער פֿײַער וויל שוין דעם שטעקן ברענען,
דער שטעקן וויל שוין דעם הונט שמײַסן,
דער הונט וויל שוין דעם פּויער בײַסן,
דער פּויער וויל שוין די באַרעלעך רײַסן,
די באַרעלעך ווילן שוין פֿאַלן,
די באַרעלעך ווילן שוין פֿאַלן.

Write a narrative summary of what each character refuses to do, as in the model below. Be sure to use the accusative case when appropriate.

דוגמא:

דער פּויער רײַסט נישט די באַרעלעך.

Now listen to the recording and compare the singer's words to the lyrics printed above. How do the two versions differ?

! גערעדנקט!

Unlike the indefinite article, the **definite article** *is* often used in negative sentences, as in the example here. In such cases, the negative article **קיין** does not appear.

ב וואָקאַבולאַר: אויסזען

דער פּיראַט
די **רויטע** באָרד

דבֿורה־לאה
דאָס טיכל

רחל
(די) **ברוינע**
אויגן

אַריה־לייב
(די) וואָנצעס

רפֿאל
דאָס היטל

דזשאָן
דער הוט

פּראָפֿעסאָר קלוגער
(די) ברילן

ד״ר הערשקאָוויטש
(די) **קורצע,**
ווײַסע האָר

שלמהלע
(די) זומער־
שפּרענקלעך

מענדל
(די) פּאות
[פּייעס]

יואל
די **שוואַרצע**
יאַרמלקע

שאָולי
דאָס לאָשיק־
עקל

נתן
(די) **בלויע** אויגן

רבֿקה
(די) **לאַנגע,**
געקרײַזלטע
האָר

חנה
(די) **גלאַטע, העל**
ברוינע האָר

וועלוול
דאָס בערדל

שׂרה
(די) **קורצע,**
געקרײַזלטע
האָר

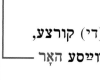

גיטל
(די) **לאַנגע,**
בלאָנדע האָר

געניטונג 1: ווער טראָגט אַ היטל?

Pictured above are some of the characters you have encountered thus far. Which of them matches each of the descriptions below? Write the name of the character corresponding to each description.

- Some of the descriptions match more than one character; write the names of all characters that match those descriptions.

דוגמא: ווער טראָגט אַ היטל?

פיראט

1. ווער טראָגט אַ רויטן הוט און רויטעברילן?
2. ווער האָט אַ ווײַסע באָרד און ווײַסע וואָנצעס?
3. ווער טראָגט אַ ברוינע יאַרמלקע?
4. ווער טראָגט אַ בלוי טיכל?
5. ווער האָט שוואַרצע האָר און בלויע אויגן?
6. ווער האָט געקרײַזלטע האָר?

NOTE:

Plural nouns are shown with the plural definite article **די** in parentheses: **אויגן (די)**. All nouns are color-coded according to grammatical gender.

טראָגן	to wear

! געדענקט!

When referring to someone's (head of) hair in Yiddish, the noun is grammatically plural:

אירע האָר זײַנען שוואַרץ.

What two verbs are used in the above questions? Can you determine the pattern governing which verb is used when?

אין קלאַס

With a partner, take turns asking and answering questions about the pictures, as in the model provided.

- Use only the indefinite article, as in the example.
- Remember to use appropriate accusative adjective endings.

דוגמא:

א: ווער טראָגט אַ בלויע יאַרמלקע?

ב: ד״ר הערשקאָוויטש טראָגט אַ בלויע יאַרמלקע. ווער האָט לאַנגע, בלאָנדע האָר?

א: גיטל האָט לאַנגע, בלאָנדע האָר. ווער טראָגט אַ הוט?

ב: דער פּיראַט טראָגט אַ הוט.

געניטונג 2: ווער איז דער שרײַבער?

1

2

3

4

5

6

לייענט איבער די זעקס ביאָגראַפֿישע סקיצעס פֿון באַקאַנטע ייִדישע שרײַבערס. **פּאַסט צו** די ביאָגראַפֿיעס צו די פֿאָטאָגראַפֿיעס אויבן.

match

____ ער הייסט ש. אַנ־סקי (1863–1920). זײַנע האָר זײַנען ברוין און ווײַס. ער האָט וואָנצעס און אַ קליינע באָרד. ער קומט פֿון רוסלאַנד. ער רעדט מיט אַ סך ייִדן וועגן זייער לעבן אין שטעטל. איינע פֿון זײַנע פּיעסעס הייסט „דער דיבוק“.

spirit that possesses a living person [דיבעק]

____ ער הייסט שלום־עליכם (1859–1916). אויפֿן בילד איז ער נישט אַזוי אַלט. ער האָט ברוינע האָר, גרויסע וואָנצעס, און ער טראָגט ברילן. זײַן פֿאַמיליע־נאָמען איז ראַבינאָוויטש. ער קומט פֿון אוקראַיִנע. ער שרײַבט הומאָריסטישע דיאַלאָגן, און עטלעכע מאָנאָלאָגן פֿון אַ מענטש וואָס הייסט טבֿיה.

[טעוויע]

____ זי הייסט אסתּר קרייטמאַן (1891–1954). זי האָט געקרײַזלטע האָר. זי קומט פֿון פּוילן און וווינט לאַנגע יאָרן אין ענגלאַנד. קרייטמאַן שרײַבט אָפֿט וועגן די פּראָבלעמען פֿון מיידלעך און פֿרויען אין אירע צײַטן. אירע צוויי ייִנגערע ברידער, י. י. זינגער און יצחק באַשעוויס זינגער זײַנען אויך גרויסע ייִדישע שרײַבערס.

[עסטער]

times

____ זי הייסט קאַדיע מאָלאָדאָווסקי (1894–1975). זי האָט גלאַטע האָר. זי קומט פֿון פּוילן און וווינט לאַנגע יאָרן אין די פֿאַראייניקטע שטאַטן. זי שרײַבט פּאָעזיע, פּראָזע, און אויך מעשׂהלעך פֿאַר קינדער. זי איז אַ לערערין פֿון ייִדיש און העברעיִש.

[מײַסעלעך]

____ ער הייסט מענדעלע מוכר־ספֿרים (1835–1917). אויפֿן בילד איז ער שוין אַלט. ער האָט קורצע ווײַסע האָר, אַ קליינע ווײַסע באָרד, און ער טראָגט ברילן. ער קומט פֿון ווײַסרוסלאַנד און וווינט אַ לאַנגע צײַט אין אוקראַיִנע. ער איז „דער זיידע“ פֿון דער ייִדישער ליטעראַטור. איינס פֿון זײַנע ביכער הייסט „מסעות בנימין השלישי“.

[מאַסאָעס בעניאָמען האַשלישי]

____ זי הייסט רחל קאָרן (1898–1982). אויפֿן בילד איז זי אַ יונגע פֿרוי. זי האָט קורצע ברוינע האָר. זי קומט פֿון פּוילן און וווינט לאַנגע יאָרן אין קאַנאַדע. זי שרײַבט פּאָעזיע און דערציילונגען וועגן דעם ייִדישן לעבן אין מיזרח־אייראָפּע. די נאַטור שפּילט אַ גרויסע ראָלע אין איר שרײַבן.

געניטונג 3: אַריה־לייב האָט אַ שוואַרצע באָרד

דזשאָן / **הוט**

רפֿאל / **היטל**

גיטל / **האָר**

אַריה־לייב / **באָרד**

ד״ר הערשקאָוויטש / **באָרד**

וועלוול / **האָר**

דער פּיראַט / **הוט**

דבֿורה־לאה / **טיכל**

Write a sentence about each character using accusative adjectives, as in the model.

- Use indefinite articles only.
- Use the verb **טראָגן** when talking about articles of clothing.

דוגמא:

אַריה־לייב האָט אַ שוואַרצע באָרד.

! גערענקט!

- Some adjectives (e.g., **ראָזעווע**, **אָראַנזש**, **לילאַ**) have special patterns of case marking. If you need a refresher, see page 251.
- When an adjective modifies a singular *indefinite* neuter noun, that adjective will appear in its attributive base form.

געניטונג 4: וויפֿל מענטשן טראָגן היט?

Answer the questions below based on the image in **געניטונג 1**.
Be sure to use the appropriate form of **עס איז דאָ** and negation where necessary.

דוגמא:

רפֿאל האָט אַ באָרד?

ניין, רפֿאל האָט נישט קיין באָרד.

1. וויפֿל פֿרויען זײַנען דאָ אויפֿן בילד?
2. וויפֿל פֿרויען מיט ווײַסע האָר זײַנען דאָ אויפֿן בילד?
3. רחל האָט וואָנצעס?
4. וויפֿל מענטשן מיט בלאָנדע האָר זײַנען דאָ אויפֿן בילד?
5. מענדל האָט אַ באָרד?
6. ווער טראָגט אַ היטל?
7. ווער איז אַלט?
8. ווער טראָגט ברילן?

Now respond to the questions below about where the following articles of clothing or facial features can be found in the picture. Practice negating with the definite article, as in the example.

דוגמא:

אַריה־לייב האָט די ווײַסע וואָנצעס?

ניין, אַריה־לייב האָט נישט די ווײַסע וואָנצעס, ד״ר הערשקאָוויטש האָט די ווײַסע וואָנצעס.

9. יואל האָט די רויטע באָרד?
10. נתן טראָגט די ברוינע יאַרמלקע?
11. שאָולי טראָגט די רויטע ברילן?

Describe three of the people in the picture using three features of each and at least one possessive adjective.

דוגמא:

ד״ר הערשקאָוויטש איז אַלט. ער האָט אַ באָרד און ווײַסע האָר. זײַן באָרד איז ווײַס.

געניטונג 5: ווער ביסטו?

Using the illustration that begins this section as a game board, play several rounds of "**ווער ביסטו**" with your partner. First, secretly choose one of the characters pictured. The object of the game is to determine your opponent's chosen character before they guess *yours*. Take turns asking yes-or-no questions to eliminate candidates until only one remains. Be specific, as in the model.

- Remember to add adjective endings according to case, gender, and number.

דוגמא:

א: דער מענטש טראָגט רויטע ברילן?

ב: ניין, דער מענטש טראָגט נישט קיין רויטע ברילן. דער מענטש האָט שוואַרצע וואָנצעס?

א: יאָ, דער מענטש האָט שוואַרצע וואָנצעס.

NOTE:
The word **מענטש**, though grammatically masculine, just means *person* and is used to talk about both men and women.

When you think you've figured out who your partner's character is, you may make your guess, as in the example below.

דוגמא:

א: דער מענטש הייסט אַריה־לייב?

ב: יאָ, דער מענטש הייסט אַריה־לייב.

א: הוראַ!

אָדער

ב: ניין, דער מענטש הייסט נישט אַריה־לייב.

א: אַ שאָד. *too bad*

טיטל „אַ חלום וועגן אַ קרעמל“

פֿון „לידער פֿאַר ייִדישע קינדער: זיבן בינטלעך“ (1961)

מחבר **י. י. סיגאַל (J.I. Sigal)**

(קאָריץ, רוסישע אימפּעריע 1896 – מאָנטרעאָל, קאַנאַדע 1954)

J. I. Sigal *was a leading figure in Montreal's Yiddish culture. A prolific poet and admired teacher in the city's Yiddish schools, Sigal was also a columnist, essayist, and eventually an editor for the newspaper* Keneder adler *(The Canadian Eagle). His poetry has influenced several generations of Canadian Jewish poets, including those writing in English.*

Having spent most of his adult life as a teacher of Jewish children, it is not surprising that he wrote countless poems for this very audience. "A kholem vegn a kreml" is just such a poem, proclaiming the innocent joys of being young, a world in which even a dolly has a zeyde*, a* bobe*, and a devoted extended family.*

מיר לייענען אַ מעשה וועגן אַ ייִנגל וואָס הייסט יאָסקעלע. ער וויל ווערן אַ קרעמער. איידער איר לייענט דאָס ליד, ענטפֿערט אויף די פֿראַגעס אונטן. (story [מײַסע])

1. **שטעלט זיך פֿאָר** אַז איר האָט אַ **קראָם**. וואָס פֿאַרקויפֿט איר? עסן? קליידער? **שפּילצײַגן**? ביכער? (imagine; store; toys)
2. דאָס ליד **באַשרײַבט** אַ סך ליאַלקעס. איר **האָט זיך געשפּילט** מיט ליאַלקעס, ווען איר **זײַט געווען** אַ קינד? (describes; played; were)
   - **א.** אויב יאָ, באַשרײַבט אײַערע **באַליבטסטע** צוויי ליאַלקעס. (favorite)
   - **ב.** אויב ניט, באַשרײַבט צוויי אַנדערע שפּילצײַגן.

דוגמאַ:

א. *מײַן ליאַלקע האָט געלע האָר און ברוינע אויגן. זי איז כּמעט פֿיר פֿוס הויך.*

ב. *מײַן בערעלע איז ברוין און ווייך. עס טראָגט אַ הוט.*

◀ CONTINUED

CONTINUED

Read the text below. Don't worry about words you don't understand—simply read to get the gist. See if you can tell what kind of text this is, what genre it belongs to, and who the intended audience might be.

> **NOTE:**
>
> The modal verbs **וויל** and **זאָל** are used in this poem in much the same way they are used in "Shikt der har" (see page 300). We will learn more about modal verbs in **19 קאַפּיטל**.

1. ס׳מעשׂהלע פֿון הײַנטיקן זמר	[מײַסעלע]; [זעמער]
איז פֿון אַ יאָסקעלע, אַ ייִנגל,	
וואָס חלומט: אויסוואַקסן אַ קרעמער,	[כאָלעמט]
אַז די גאַס זאָל פֿון אים זינגען,	
2. און אַ קראָם זאָל ער פֿאַרמאָגן	
שפּילצײַגן מכּל־המינים:	[מיקאָל־האַמי׳נים]
פֿון אַ פֿערדל מיט אַ וואָגן	*a horse and buggy*
ביז אַ בינשטאָקל פֿאַר בינען,	*a beehive for bees*
און אַלצדינג – בחצי־חינם.	[בעכאָצע־כינעם]
3. און דער עיקר: ליאַלקעס, ליאַלקעס	[איקער]
און מיט שיינע ייִדישע נעמען:	
חיה־רחל׳ס, שׂרה־מלכּה׳ס,	
פֿייגע־לאה׳ס, גיטע־טעמע׳ס.	
4. בלאָנדע, שוואַרצע און שאַטינע,	
פֿעטינקע און שלאַנקע, דינע,	
בלויע אויגן, שוואַרצע אויגן	
ברוינע און אַפֿילו גרינע.	[אַפֿילע]
5. קומט אַרײַן אַ גוטער קונה	customer [קוינע]
איז פֿאַראַן אויף אויסצוקלויבן:	
מיט אַ טשופּיקל אַ ברוינעם,	
אויגן בלויע, מילדע טויבן,	
6. ליאַלקעס מומעס,	
ליאַלקעס פֿעטערס,	
ליאַלקעס זיידעס,	
ליאַלקעס באָבעס,	
ליאַלקעס שטיפֿמאַמעס אַפֿילו,	
אַלץ קומט דאָך צו נוץ צום שפּילן.	

◀ CONTINUED

CONTINUED

Now look at the illustrations of the six numbered sections of the poem and try to match each picture to a section. Then label the characters and objects that appear in the images with words or phrases from the poem.

◀ CONTINUED

CONTINUED

לייענט די ווערטער אין גלאָסאַר אונטן. זוכט זיי אָפּ אין ליד און שטרײַכט זיי אונטער.

Read the words in the glossary below. Look for them in the poem and underline them.

today's	הײַנטיקן
ליד	זמר
dreams	חלומט
grow up to be	אויסוואַקסן
should	זאָל
own	פֿאַרמאָגן
of all kinds	מכּל־המינים
to	ביז
very cheap	בחצי־חינם
in particular	דער עיקר
chestnut-colored	שאַטינע
דינע	שלאַנקע
even	אַפֿילו
there is plenty to choose from	איז פֿאַראַן אויף אויסצוקלויבן
tuft of hair	טשופּיקל
doves	טויבן
is of use	קומט צו נוץ

Describe Yosl's future as a storekeeper in your own words, retelling the story stanza by stanza, using the pictures (correctly ordered) as a guide.

דוגמא:

יאָסקעלע איז אַ קרעמער. ער האָט אַ סך שפּילצײַגן אין זײַן קראָם: אַ פֿערדל מיט אַ וואָגן און אַ בינשטאָקל פֿאַר בינען.

ג גראַמאַטיק:
פּראָנאָמען אין אַקוזאַטיוו

געניטונג 1: יאָ, איך טרינק עס

In each of the sentences above, the direct object is printed in purple. In the first sentence of each miniature dialogue, the direct object is a noun (with its accusative definite article); in the second, it's a pronoun.

Make a table of accusative articles and corresponding third-person pronouns. Label the pronouns according to gender and number.

! געדענקט!

A pronoun generally matches the grammatical gender of the noun it replaces, even if that noun refers to a nonhuman animal or an object.

געניטונג 2: איך האָב אים!

Compare the contents of your backpack (as shown below right) with the accompanying snapshot of your desk (below left). Identify the items missing from your backpack and ask if your partner has them.

- Be sure to use appropriate accusative articles, adjective endings, and third-person pronouns, as in the model.
- Your partner will work from the corresponding exercise on page A7.

דוגמא:

א: דו האָסט דעם שוואַרצן דרעטלער?

ב: יאָ, איך האָב אים.

אָדער

ב: ניין, איך האָב **אים** נישט.

סטודענט א

NOTE:

When negating a sentence with a direct object, the order of elements depends on whether the object is a noun or a pronoun:

איך האָב נישט דעם דרעטלער.

איך האָב אים נישט.

געדענקט!

The adjectives **לילאַ** and **אָראַנזש** are irregular: **לילאַ** never takes any ending; **אָראַנזש** has a different set of forms (based on the stem **אָראַנזשן**) when used as an **attributive** adjective:

ער האָט די לילאַ העפֿט.

זי האָט די אָראַנזשענע העפֿט.

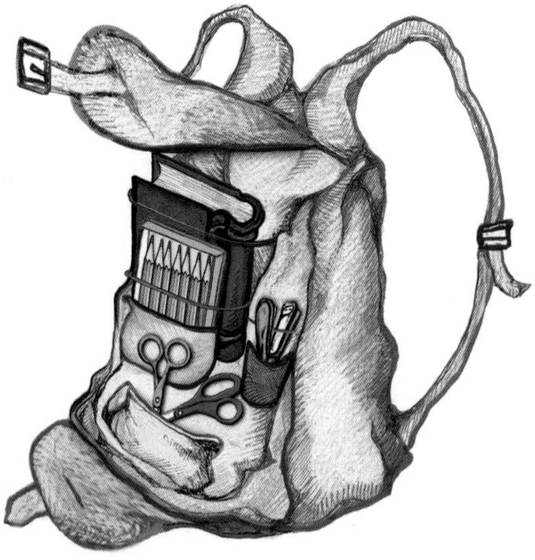

הײמאַרבעט

שרײַבט אָן אַ פּאָר זאַצן וועגן די זאַכן וואָס נישט איר און נישט אײַער חבֿר האָבן זיי.

דוגמא:

מיר האָבן נישט די גרינע העפֿט.

גענײטונג 3: לאָמיר זיך צעקושן

חיה שפּילט זיך מיט אירע פּליושענע חיהלעך, און מאַכט זיי חתונה! ווי דער שטייגער איז אויף חתונות, מוז מען זיך קושן מיט אַלע קרובֿים און גוטע־פֿרײַנד.

Khaye is playing with her stuffed animals, and marrying them! As is the custom at weddings, they must embrace all their relatives and good friends.

Read the questions below before you read the comic; they will help you understand the text.

- Don't worry about unfamiliar words or phrases—focus on getting the gist.

1. ווער האָט חתונה?
2. וועמען קושן חתן־כּלה? זיי קושן חיהן? — whom
3. וואָסערע קרובֿים זײַנען דאָ אויף דער חתונה?
4. ווער זײַנען די לעצטע צוויי מענטשן וואָס קומען אויף דער חתונה?

לייענט איצט איבער דעם טעקסט, און ענטפֿערט אויף די פֿראַגעס אויבן.

Now read the comic again, paying special attention to the purple words. These are the accusative forms of the personal pronouns. Make a table of all of the personal pronouns you know in both their nominative and accusative forms.

Fill in the blanks below with appropriate pronouns, describing the action in each panel of the comic (from Ketsl's perspective).

1. **קעצל:** קראָליקל קושט _מיך_.
2. **קעצל:** חיה, מיר קושן ______.
3. **קעצל:** חיה און פּערל, מיר קושן ______.
4. **קעצל:** אָט איז אונדזער עלטער־באָבע! איצט קושן מיר ______.
5. **קעצל:** קראָליקל, מיר קושן אַלעמען, אָבער קיינער קושט ______ נישט... — everyone (*accusative*)
6. **קעצל:** נתן און רחל זײַנען שוין דאָ. מיר קושן ______ אויך.

◀ CONTINUED

חיה: קום באָבע! קעצל און קראָליקל האָבן חתונה!

באָבע: טאַקע אַ שיינע כּלה! אוי, דער חתן קושט זי שוין?

פּערל: דאָס איז נישט אַלץ!

חיה: איצט קושן זיי מיך...

פּערל: און איצט קושן זיי אונדז ביידע...

חיה: כאַ־כאַ! קעצל, דאָס קיצלט!

tickles

חיה: און זיי קושן אַוודאי אויך דיך. דו ביסט זייער עלטער־באָבע!

באָבע: אַ! נו, וועמען דען קושט מען, ווען נישט אַן עלטער־באָבע?

פּערל: חיה, גיב אַ קוק! טאַטע־מאַמע זײַנען שוין דאָ!

באָבע: חתן־כּלה קושן זיי נישט? זיי זײַנען דאָך זייערע באָבע־זיידע!

חיה: אַוודאי יאָ! טאַטע־מאַמע, חתן־כּלה קושן אײַך!

מאַמע: און מיר ווינטשן זיי מזל־טובֿ!

wish; congratulations (*lit.* good luck) [מאַ́זל־טאָוו]

after all

געניטונג 4: זי האָט מיך ליב

צוויי סטודענטן רעדן וועגן זייער פּראָפֿעסאָרשע. לייענט דעם דיאַלאָג.

אַבֿרהם: סענדער, איך מיין אַז פּראָפֿעסאָר קלוגער האָט מיך ליב.

סענדער: אַוודאי! פּראָפֿעסאָר קלוגער האָט אונדז אַלעמען ליב.

אַבֿרהם: פּראָפֿעסאָר קלוגער האָט דיך ליב?

סענדער: פֿאַרשטייט זיך! אָט גייט וועלוול. פּראָפֿעסאָר קלוגער האָט אויך אים ליב. *of course*

אַבֿרהם: איך אָבער האָב וועלוולען פֿײַנט. אָט גייט גיטל. פּראָפֿעסאָר קלוגער האָט זי זיכער ליב. *אַוודאי*

סענדער: פּראָפֿעסאָר קלוגער האָט זיי ביידע ליב.

אַבֿרהם: וועלוול, גיטל! פּראָפֿעסאָר קלוגער האָט אײַך ליב!

NOTE:

The verb **ליב האָבן** can be used (*without* the particle **צו**) to express fondness for a person or thing. That person or thing is then the direct object of the verb and takes the accusative case. As we saw on page 313, word order depends on whether the direct object is a noun or a pronoun:

פּראָפֿעסאָר קלוגער האָט ליב **דעם סטודענט**.
פּראָפֿעסאָר קלוגער האָט **אים** ליב.

Now rewrite the dialogue, replacing **פּראָפֿעסאָר קלוגער** with a different noun, such as **די באָבע** or **מײַן קעצעלע**. You may also choose to replace **ליב האָבן** with **פֿײַנט האָבן**.

Write several sentences describing in detail whom Professor Kluger likes, as in the model.

- Remember to add the suffix **ן-** (or **ען-**) to any name that is the object of a verb (see page 248).

דוגמא:

פּראָפֿעסאָר קלוגער האָט ליב אַבֿרהאמען.

אין קלאַס

מיט אַ חבֿר, חזרט איבער דעם דיאַלאָג אויבן עטלעכע מאָל. רעדט אַזוי גיך און פֿליסיק ווי מעגלעך.

Now repeat the dialogue, making the substitutions described above.

גענִיטונג 5: דער בעל־הבית שיקט דיך אין פּאַרק?

סטודענט א

You are the personal assistant to a very busy boss, who sends you to a different location every day on an important errand. Compare notes with your partner, who also works for such a boss, on where your respective bosses send you, as in the model.

- Pay attention to the relative position of the subject and direct object in the sentence. How does it change when the subject is a full noun, as opposed to a pronoun?
- Make sure to place **נישט** in the correct position in the sentence.
- Your partner will work from the table on page A8.

דוגמא:

דער בעל־הבית [באַלעבאָס] boss

א: זונטיק שיקט דיך דער בעל־הבית אין ביוראָ?

ב: ניין, זונטיק שיקט ער מיך נישט אין ביוראָ. זונטיק שיקט ער מיך אין פּאַרק. זונטיק שיקט דיך דײַן בעל־הבית אין פּאַרק?

א: ניין, זונטיק שיקט מיך מײַן בעל־הבית נישט אין פּאַרק. זונטיק, שיקט ער מיך אין קראָם.

טאָג	איך	דער חבֿר
זונטיק	אין קראָם	
מאָנטיק	אין ביוראָ	
דינסטיק	אין אוניווערסיטעט	
מיטוואָך	אין רעסטאָראַן	
דאָנערשטיק	אין געריכט	
פֿרײַטיק	אין פּאַרק	

היימאַרבעט

Write several sentences describing where your boss sends you on various days of the week and explain what he intends for you to do in each of those locations, as in the model.

דוגמא:

זונטיק שיקט מיך דער בעל־הבית אין קראָם קויפֿן בלײַערס.

מאָנטיק שיקט ער מיך אין ביוראָ רעקאָרדירן אַ טעלעפֿאָן.

גענִיטונג 6: שלמהלע לערנט זיך כּיבוד־אָבֿ־ואם

Shloymele is learning about respectful behavior. Read the sentences below and circle the one in each pair that reflects good behavior.

שלמהלע פֿאָטאָגראַפֿירט די מאַמע.	שלמהלע בײַסט די מאַמע.
שלמהלע שמײַסט דעם טאַטן.	שלמהלע פֿילמירט דעם טאַטן.
שלמהלע קריטיקירט דעם זיידן.	שלמהלע אַמוזירט דעם זיידן.
שלמהלע אינטערוויוּירט די באָבע.	שלמהלע איגנאָרירט די באָבע.

Now read the sentences again, paying special attention to words that refer to family members.

- Which words have a different form now that they are direct objects?
- What part of these words changes? What is the substitution that occurs?

Help guide Shloymele in making the right behavioral choices. Tell him how to treat each of his family members by giving one positive and one negative command, as in the example.

- Remember to decline family terms when necessary.
- Use the appropriate accusative *pronoun* in the second command of each pair.

דוגמא:

שלמהלע, בײַס נישט די מאַמע! פֿאָטאָגראַפֿיר זי!

כּיבוד־אָבֿ־ואם [קיבעד־אָוו־וואָיים]

honoring one's father and mother

This phrase, echoing the language of the Fifth Commandment, is used in both religious and secular circles to call forth an appropriate sense of filial duty.

NOTE:

A small number of other nouns decline in the accusative like **טאַטע** and **זיידע**, though sometimes this declension is optional:

דער רבי [רעבע] ← **דעם רבין** [רעבן]

דער מענטש ← **דעם מענטשן** (optional)

דער ייִד ← **דעם ייִדן** (optional)

Note that the accusative declension ן- actually *replaces* the nominative [ע-] in **טאַטע**, **זיידע**, and **רבי** . This stands in contrast to the ending on a personal name in the accusative case, which only *adds* its sound to the end of the name.

11 וואָקאַבולאַר־איבערבליק

א. אַקוזאַטיוו און גראַמאַטישער מין
THE ACCUSATIVE AND GRAMMATICAL GENDER

the lord sends	שיקט דער האַר
pear	די באַר (ן)
cow	די בהמה (–ות) [בעהיימע (ס)]
letter	דער בריוו (—)
lord	דער האַר (ן)
dog	דער הונט (הינט)
forest	דער וואַלד (וועלדער)
peasant	דער פּויער (ים)
ritual slaughterer	דער שוחט (ים) [שויכעט (שאָכטים)]
stick	דער שטעקן (ס)
water	דאָס וואַסער (ן)

verbs	ווערבן
to bite	בײַסן
to burn	ברענען
to kill	טייטן
to extinguish	לעשן
to pick (fruit), to tear	רײַסן
to send	שיקן
to hit, to whip	שמײַסן
to slaughter	שעכטן

דער פּײַער (ן)

ב. אויסזען
PHYSICAL APPEARANCE

to wear	טראָגן
curly	געקרײַזלט
straight	גלאַט

ב. אויסזען
PHYSICAL APPEARANCE (continued)

side lock	די פּאה (–ות) [פּייע (ס)]
person	דער מענטש (ן)
eye	דאָס אויג (ן)
cap	דאָס היטל (עך)
freckle	דאָס זומער־שפּרענקל (עך)
kerchief	דאָס טיכל (עך)
ponytail	דאָס לאָשיק־עקל (עך)
hair	די האָר
moustache	די וואָנצעס
eyeglasses	די ברילן

בלאָנד; די באָרד (בערד); דער הוט (היט); די יאַרמלקע (ס)

ג. פּראָנאָמען אין אַקוזאַטיוו
ACCUSATIVE PRONOUNS

accusative pronouns	פּראָנאָמען אין אַקוזאַטיוו
me	מיך
you (*sg informal*)	דיך
him	אים
her	זי
it	עס
us	אונדז
you (*pl; sg formal*)	אײַך
them	זיי
whom	וועמען

useful words	נוציקע ווערטער
to kiss	קושן
to wish	ווינטשן
if	אויב
certainly	זיכער
congratulations!	מזל־טובֿ! [מאַ́זל־טאָוו]
store	די קראָם (ען)
boss	דער בעל־הבית (בעלי־בתּים) [באַלעבאָס (באַלעבאַטים)]

11 גראַמאַטיק־איבערבליק

THE ACCUSATIVE — אַקוזאַטיוו

- Just as attributive adjectives may apply to subject nouns (taking appropriate nominative case endings as they do), so may they apply to *object* nouns—in the **accusative case**.
- As we saw in the nominative, definite articles and attributive adjectives are most commonly marked according to case. Accusative case markings are exactly like the nominative except for **singular masculine nouns**, which require new articles and adjective endings, as in the table below.
- Plural nouns, regardless of gender or case, always take the same adjective and article forms.

❗ **NOTE:** Singular indefinite neuter nouns require a different form of the adjective than their definite counterparts.

	Nominative	Accusative
Masculine	דער שטאַרקער מאַן טאַנצט.	איך זע דעם שטאַרקן מאַן.
	אַ שטאַרקער מאַן טאַנצט.	איך זע אַ שטאַרקן מאַן.
Neuter	דאָס שטאַרקע קינד טאַנצט.	איך זע דאָס שטאַרקע קינד.
	אַ שטאַרק קינד טאַנצט.	איך זע אַ שטאַרק קינד. ❗
Feminine	די שטאַרקע פֿרוי טאַנצט.	איך זע די שטאַרקע פֿרוי.
	אַ שטאַרקע פֿרוי טאַנצט.	איך זע אַ שטאַרקע פֿרוי.
Plural	די שטאַרקע מענטשן טאַנצן.	איך זע די שטאַרקע מענטשן.
	שטאַרקע מענטשן טאַנצן.	איך זע שטאַרקע מענטשן.

Not all adjectives follow exactly the declension pattern outlined above.

- If the base form of an adjective ends on ן-, the masculine ending becomes **עם**-.

דער מאַן איז שיין. ← איך זע דעם שיינעם מאַן.

- If the base form of an adjective ends on ם-, a vowel, or a diphthong, the masculine ending becomes **ען**-.

דער טיש איז קרום. ← איך זע דעם קרומען טיש.

דער בלײַער איז בלוי. ← איך זע דעם בלויען בלײַער.

- The adjective **נײַ** is an exception to the above: its masculine accusative ending is **עם**-.

דער רוקזאַק איז נײַ. ← איך זע דעם נײַעם רוקזאַק.

A small number of *nouns* are also affected by case.

- For example, **טאַטע** and **זיידע** become **טאַטן** and **זיידן** in the accusative.
- As you have already seen, personal names acquire a ן- (or ען-) ending in the accusative.

11 גראַמאַטיק־איבערבליק

GRAMMATICAL GENDER OF NOUNS — גראַמאַטישער מין פֿון סובסטאַנטיוון

Every Yiddish noun has a **grammatical gender**: feminine, masculine, or neuter.

- These genders are essentially formal properties of the noun, which determine the way other words (mostly adjectives and articles) interact with it.
- Noun genders are rarely self-evident and often must be memorized. Nevertheless, there are certain guidelines that can help us work out the gender of an unfamiliar word when surrounding articles and adjectives don't help.
- These guidelines typically relate the word's gender to one of three things: the meaning of the word, its sound, or its grammatical form.

NOTE: The noun-gender system in present-day Yiddish is in flux, and usage varies considerably from one community to another. This synthesis will attempt to present the approach of the standard language. (Sometimes more than one grammatical gender is admissible for a given word. We have tried to use the more common form in such cases.)

Meaning-Based Rules

- Nouns that refer to males are generally grammatically masculine in gender (**דער זיידע**), and nouns that refer to females, grammatically feminine (**די באָבע**).
- As we saw in **10 קאַפּיטל**, the base forms of nouns referring to professions or social roles are generally masculine in gender. Corresponding feminine forms are typically formed by the suffixes **-ין**, **-קע**, **-שע**, **-טע**, or **-ניצע** (see below) and are feminine in gender.
- Nouns referring to professions and social roles traditionally held by women are grammatically feminine: **די רביצין** (*rabbi's wife* [רעבעצן]) or **די הייבאַם** (*midwife*).

מאַסקולין	פֿעמינין
זיידע	באָבע
רבֿ [ראָוו] (*rabbi*)	הייבאַם
לערער	לערערין
סטודענט	סטודענטקע
סעקרעטאַר	סעקרעטאַרשע
חבֿר	חבֿרטע
פּלימעניק	פּלימעניצע

- Nouns describing people may also be neutral in gender (**דאָס קינד**), sometimes even contradicting the meaning-based rule above (**דאָס ווײַב / ייִנגל / מיידל**). For some speakers, however, the latter three words *are* gendered masculine or feminine.

NOTE: The noun **דער מענטש** (*person*) may refer to a man or a woman and retains its masculine definite article either way.

Sound-Based Rules

- Multisyllabic nouns ending in **-ער**, syllabic **-ן**, or syllabic **-ל** (nondiminutive) are typically masculine.
- Nouns ending in an unstressed [**ע**-]-sound (which can be spelled **-ע**, **-ה**, **-א**, or **-י**) are typically feminine.

מאַסקולין	פֿעמינין
צימער	קאָווע
שטערן (*star*)	דירה [דירע]
טאָוול	דוגמא [דוגמע]
	כּלי [קיילע] (*dish*)

11 גראַמאַטיק־איבערבליק

GRAMMATICAL GENDER OF NOUNS (continued) — גראַמאַטישער מין פֿון סובסטאַנטיוון

- There are many exceptions to both of these tendencies. For example, **שוועסטער** (*sister*) is feminine in gender, while **זיידע** (*grandfather*) is masculine, simply due to meaning. Many *loshn-koydesh* terms for traditionally male professions and social roles end in [**ע**] and yet are masculine:

דער קונה [קוינע] (*customer*)

דער רופֿא [רויפֿע] (*traditional healer*)

דער רבי [רעבע] (*Hasidic spiritual leader; teacher*)

- Some of the exceptions to the preceding rules, however, are entirely unpredictable:

די פֿעדער; דאָס וואַסער

דאָס לעבן (*life*)

די שיסל (*bowl*)

Form-Based Rules

- Many Yiddish nouns are derived from other words (or forms of words) by the attachment of a prefix or suffix. Some of these prefixes and suffixes, in addition to changing the meaning of the word in a specific way, also change the word's grammatical gender.
- For example, when the suffix **ל**- or **לע**(**ע**)- is used to derive the diminutive form of a word, that word loses its initial grammatical gender and adopts the neuter gender:

דער טיש (*masculine*) ← דאָס טישל (*neuter*)

די דירה (*feminine*) ← דאָס דירהלע (*neuter*)

דער עפּל (*masculine*) ← דאָס עפּעלע (*neuter*)

- Another common suffix that affects noun gender is **ונג**- , which forms feminine nouns, often from verb stems: **די זיצונג** (*meeting*), from the verb **זיצן**.

NOTE: Compound nouns usually have the same gender as their second component:

<u>דאָס</u> בוך ← <u>דאָס</u> ווערטערבוך

ACCUSATIVE PRONOUNS — פּראָנאָמען אין אַקוזאַטיוו

Though nouns *themselves* generally do not change form depending on their role as a subject or object, **pronouns** do.

	Pronoun	Noun
Nominative	ער איז דאָ.	דער מאַן איז דאָ.
Accusative	איך זע אים.	איך זע דעם מאַן.

As with adjective endings and definite articles, some pronouns are the same in both nominative and accusative, but most do change (see below).

- Note the similarity between the third-person accusative pronouns and corresponding definite articles: **דעם**, **די**, and **דאָס**.

Accusative	Nominative
ער זעט מיך.	איך בין דאָ.
ער זעט דיך.	דו ביסט דאָ.
ער זעט אים.	ער איז דאָ.
ער זעט זי.	זי איז דאָ.
ער זעט עס.	עס איז דאָ.
ער זעט אונדז.	מיר זײַנען דאָ.
ער זעט אײַך.	איר זײַט דאָ.
ער זעט זיי.	זיי זײַנען דאָ.

Pronouns and Word Order

- In a negative sentence, the direct object pronoun comes before **נישט**. Note that this is not the case when the direct object is a full noun:

איך זע <u>נישט</u> דעם מאַן.

איך זע אים <u>נישט</u>.

- When an accusative pronoun is used with a periphrastic or separable-prefix verb, the pronoun comes after the conjugated part of the verb and before the invariable. Again, this is not the case with full nouns:

איך <u>האָב</u> <u>ליב</u> דעם מאַן.

איך <u>האָב</u> אים <u>ליב</u>.

איבערחזר־געניטונגען 11

געניטונג 1: דער גולם קוקט אין שפיגל

Describe your *goylem's* appearance in as much detail as possible.

דוגמא:

דער גולם האָט לאַנגע, בלאָנדע, געקרײַזלטע האָר. ער טראָגט גרינע ברילן און אַ ווײַס היטל. ער האָט אַ סך זומער־שפּרענקלעך.

געניטונג 2: וואָס טוען די מענטשן?

Yosl is looking through photos of various people engaged in their professions, but he's a bit mixed up about what they're actually doing. Help him sort things out by answering each of the following questions with a verb characteristic of the profession in question.

- Use appropriate pronouns.

NOTE:

In basic sentence order, the accusative pronoun follows the verb and precedes **נישט**. Be sure to use this word order in your answers here.

דוגמא:

די קעכין באַקט די זופּ?

ניין, זי באַקט זי נישט. זי קאָכט זי.

1. דער שרײַבער נייט דאָס בוך?
2. דער פּראָפֿעסאָר פֿאָטאָגראַפֿירט די סטודענטן?
3. די שנײַדערין קאָכט דעם מאַנטל?
4. דער בעקער לערנט דאָס ברויט?
5. די פֿאָטאָגראַפֿין פֿאַרקויפֿט דעם אַקטיאָר?
6. דער קרעמער שרײַבט די ביכער?

געניטונג 3: קרובֿישאַפֿט

טיטל **,,קרובֿישאַפֿט“** (פֿראַגמענט)

פֿון ,,לחיים!“ [לעכאַיִם] (1949)

רעדאַקטאָר **עמנואל אָלשוואַנגער** [אימאַנועל] **(Immanuel Olsvanger)**

(גרייִוווע, רוסישע אימפּעריע 1888 – ירושלים, ישׂראל 1961)

This parody of the extended Jewish family appears in L'chayim! Jewish Wit and Humor*, edited by* **Immanuel Olsvanger***. Olsvanger's compilations of anecdotes and aphorisms, published "just as they were told to [him] by the Jews of Eastern Europe themselves," are unusual among Yiddish books for their having been printed in transliteration. Olsvanger's work with Jewish folklore began during his involvement in an official ethnographic project in Switzerland (where he had studied medicine). After settling in Palestine in 1933, he continued his work as a folklorist and a translator into Hebrew from such languages as Sanskrit, Japanese, and Italian. He also wrote on Jewish themes in Esperanto and served as the honorary president of the Hebrew Esperanto Association.*

Read the text on the following page. For now, don't worry about words you don't understand—just read to get the gist. See if you can tell what kind of text this is, what genre it belongs to, who might be writing or recounting it, and to whom it is being recounted. The first two sentences set the backdrop.

◀ CONTINUED

CONTINUED

אין שטעטל איז אַ חתונה. צוויי יאַטן שטייען בײַ דער טיר, און לאָזן אַרײַן נאָר קרובֿים פֿון חתן־כּלה.
קומען אָן ייִדן נאָך ייִדן, און די יאַטן פֿרעגן זיך נאָך, ווער זיי זײַנען. זאָגט איינער:

— איך בין דער כּלהס פֿעטערס באָבעס אַ שוואָגער!
— אַרײַן!
— איך בין דעם חתנס אַ שוועסטערקינד!
— אָך! אַוודאי אַרײַן!
— איך בין דער מאָן־שטויסער!
— דער מאָן־שטויסער? אַרײַן!
— איך בין דער פֿעפֿער־שטויסער!
— לאָזט אַרײַן דעם פֿעפֿער־שטויסער!

דאַן האָט זיך גענומען שטויסן עפּעס קענטיק גאָר אַ פֿרעמדער ייִד. פֿרעגט מען אים:

— ווער זײַט איר?

ענטפֿערט ער:

— לאָזט מיך אַרײַן! איך בין דעם פֿעפֿער־שטויסערס אַן איידעם!
— אויך אַרײַן!

יונגע שטאַרקע מענער; *let in*	
and more	
brother-in-law	
poppyseed-crusher	
pepper	
started pushing; unfamiliar	
son-in-law	

Based on the wedding guests described in the text above, create two or three more hopeful attendees. Using the vocabulary you learned in **11–9 קאַפּיטלען**, jot down a few notes about each character's appearance and their relationship to the bride or groom.

דוגמא:

ווײַסע האָר, גרויסע וואָנצעס; חתנס קעצלס עלטער־זיידע

Your new characters are now trying to get into the wedding, but the bouncers have started turning people away, usually citing some spurious element of the characters' appearance. Based on the example below, write a few lines of dialogue between your characters and the bouncers.

- Be sure to practice your accusative personal pronouns (and associated word-order rules) by using the separable-prefix verb **אַרײַנלאָזן**.

דוגמא:

— לאָזט מיך אַרײַן! איך בין דעם חתנס קעצלס עלטער־זיידע!
— אוי! ניין, מיר לאָזן אײַך נישט אַרײַן. אײַערע וואָנצעס זײַנען צו גרויס!

NOTE:

Can you spot the wordplay happening here with the verb **שטויסן** (*to push, to crush*) and the "doer"-construction **שטויסער**?

! גערעדנקט!

When a separable-prefix verb has a *pronoun* object, that pronoun must precede the invariable portion of the verb. (When **נישט** is used to negate the verb, it too follows the pronoun object.)

איך לאָז אים אַרײַן. ←
איך לאָז אים נישט אַרײַן.

too	צו

אין קלאַס

With a partner, perform your skit for the class. Make sure to act out your characters' personalities—with feeling!

12

קאַפּיטל צוועלף:
סוכּות און שׂימחת־תּורה

CHAPTER GOALS

- In this chapter, you will learn how to talk about Sukkos and Simchas Torah.

וואָקאַבולאַר:	
Sukkos and Simchas Torah	סוכּות און שׂימחת־תּורה

קולטור — טעקסטן:	
"Sukkos" and "Simchas Torah" (Symcha Petrushka)	„סוכּות" און „שׂימחת־תּורה" (שׂמחה פּיעטרושקאָ)
Burning Lights (Bella Chagall)	„ברענענדיקע ליכט" (בעלאַ שאַגאַל)

קולטור — אױדיאָ:	
"In the Sukkah" (Avrom Reyzen)	„אין סוכּה" (אַבֿרהם רייזען)
"Children, It's Simchas Torah" (Mark Varshavski)	„קינדער, מיר האָבן שׂימחת־תּורה" (מאַרק וואַרשאַווסקי)

קולטור — װידעאָ:	
Mamele (Joseph Green)	„מאַמעלע" (יוסף גרין)

איבערחזר־געניטונגען:

קולטור — בילדער:	
Dancing Lesson (Raphael Soyer)	„טאַנץ־לעקציע" (רפֿאל סויער)
"10 Questions. 10 Minutes." (United States Census Bureau)	„10 פֿראַגעס. 10 מינוטן." (פֿאַראייניקטע שטאַטן־צענזוס־ביוראָ)

א קולטור:
זמן־שׂמחתנו: סוכּות און שׂימחת־תּורה

קולטור
CULTURE

סוכּות
[סוקעס]

שׂימחת־תּורה
[סימכעס־טוירע]

גענիטונג 1: שיין ווי אַן אתרוג

Depicted here are scenes characteristic of the holidays Sukkos and Simchas Torah. List the items labeled in each picture and describe each object with an adjective from the word box below.

- Use **עס איז / זײַנען דאָ** and appropriate nominative adjective endings.
- A variety of noun-adjective pairings are possible. There is no one right answer.

קולטור
CULTURE

דוגמא:

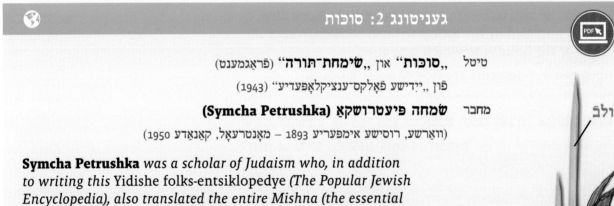

אויפֿן בילד פֿון סוכּות איז דאָ אַ געלער אתרוג.
דאָרטן איז אויך דאָ בײער אַ שיינער, לײַכטער לולבֿ.

גרין	ברוין	ליכטיק
רויט	הויך	מיאוס
ריין	אַלט	נײַ
ווייך	האַרט	הייליק
קורץ	לאַנג	שווער
גרויס	קליין	גלאַט

גענիטונג 2: סוכּות

טיטל „**סוכּות**“ און „**שׂימחת־תּורה**“ (פֿראַגמענט)
פֿון „ייִדישע פֿאָלקס־ענציקלאָפּעדיע“ (1943)

מחבר **שׂמחה פּיעטרושקאַ (Symcha Petrushka)**
(וואַרשע, רוסישע אימפּעריע 1893 – מאָנטרעאָל, קאַנאַדע 1950)

Symcha Petrushka *was a scholar of Judaism who, in addition to writing this* Yidishe folks-entsiklopedye *(The Popular Jewish Encyclopedia), also translated the entire Mishna (the essential compilation of early postbiblical Jewish law) into Yiddish. These summaries of the autumnal holidays Sukkos and Simchas Torah have been adapted from his encyclopedia.*

Examine the close-up of a *lulev* pictured here. Although *lulev* literally means “palm,” the term also refers to this ritual object, which is made up of palm, willow and myrtle branches bound together.

◄ CONTINUED

CONTINUED

Below is a list of statements about Sukkos and Simchas Torah. Some apply to both holidays, and some apply only to one holiday or the other. Read the statements.

- Glossed words will appear in the articles. Take a moment to integrate their meaning.

קולטור
CULTURE

1. מע פּראַוועט דעם סוף פֿונעם יערלעכן ציקל פֿון לייענען די תּורה. — celebrates; end [סאָף]; Torah (Pentateuch) [טוירע]
2. מע טאָר נישט אַרבעטן. — *must not*; work
3. מע טאַנצט אַרום מיט די ספֿרי־תּורות. — around; Torah scrolls [סיפֿרײ־טוירעס]
4. מען עסט אין אַ סוכּה — אַ בײַדל. — hut
5. דאָס איז אַ פֿריילעכער יום־טובֿ — אַ יום־טובֿ פֿון פֿרייד. — joy
6. דער יום־טובֿ איז אין תּשרי. — an autumn month [טישרע]
7. מע מאַכט אַ ברכה איבער אַן אתרוג און אַ לולבֿ. — blessing [בראָכע]

לייענט דעם אַרטיקל אונטן.

- When you come across one of the glossed words from the activity above, circle it.

After you've read the article, return to the statements above. Use the information provided by the article to label each statement with the name of the holiday to which it applies.

- Remember, some statements are true of both holidays.

איצט, שרײַבט אָן עטלעכע פֿראַגעס וועגן סוכּות און שׂימחת־תּורה, לויטן אַרטיקל. פֿרעגט אויס די חבֿרים!

דוגמא:

ווו שטייט אַ סוכּה?

לאָמיר שמועסן!

סוכּות און שׂימחת־תּורה הייסן „זמן־שׂמחתנו“ — די צײַט פֿון אונדזער פֿרייד.

1. וואָס טוט מען אין דער צײַט, וואָס ווײַזט אַז מען איז פֿריילעך? — *shows that*
2. שרײַבט וועגן נאָך אַ צײַט ווען איר פֿילט גרויס פֿרייד. וואָס האָט איר ליב צו טאָן אין דער צײַט? — *another*

◀ CONTINUED

קולטור
CULTURE

סוכּות

סוכּות איז דער נאָמען פֿון יום־טובֿ, וועלכער דויערט נײַן טעג, הייבט זיך אָן דעם 15טן תּישרי און ענדיקט זיך דעם 23סטן תּישרי. די ערשטע[1] צוויי טעג און די לעצטע[2] צוויי טעג זײַנען פֿולער יום־טובֿ, מען טאָר נישט אַרבעטן.

[1]first; [2]last

אין די ערשטע זיבן טעג פֿון סוכּות עסט מען (טייל פֿרומע[3] ייִדן שלאָפֿן אויך) אין סוכּה, דאָס הייסט אין אַ בײַדל, אויפֿגעשטעלט אונטערן פֿרײַען הימל, אָן אַ דאַך[4]. אַנשטאָט[5] דעם דאַך לייגט מען אַרויף „סכך“, בלעטער[6] און שטעקעלעך פֿון ביימער[7]. דער חומש[8] זאָגט אַז דאָס איז אַן אָנדענק[9] פֿון דער צײַט[10] ווען ייִדן זײַנען אַרויס[11] פֿון מצרים[12] און געווען אין מדבר[13] און געוווינט נישט אין פֿעסטע[14] הײַזער נאָר אין „סוכּות“, בײַדלעך.

[3]devout; [4]roof; [5]instead; [6]leaves; [7]trees; [8]Pentateuch [כומעש]; [9]memorial; [10]time; [11]*went out*; [12]Egypt [מיצראַיִם]; [13]desert [מידבער]; [14]שטאַרקע

יעדן[15] טאָג פֿון די ערשטע זיבן טעג סוכּות בענטשט מען אתרוג, דאָס הייסט מען נעמט אַן אתרוג און אַ לולבֿ און הדסים און ערבֿות און מע מאַכט אויף זיי אַ ברכה. עס איז פֿאַראַן אַ מיינונג[16], אַז דאָס זיצן אין סוכּות און בענטשן איבער אתרוג און לולבֿ האָט אַ שײַכות[17] מיט דעם פֿעלד־כאַראַקטער פֿון יום־טובֿ, ווײַל ביז[18] מע נעמט אַראָפּ און מע זאַמלט אײַן[19] אין ארץ־ישׂראל[20] די תּבֿואות[21] און פֿרוכטן נעכטיקט[22] מען געוויינטלעך אין בײַדלעך אויפֿן פֿעלד. דער יום־טובֿ הייסט אויך „זמן־שׂמחתנו“[23] — די צײַט פֿון אונדזער פֿרייד.

[15]every; [16]opinion; [17]connection [שײַכעס]; [18]until; [19]*gather*; [20]the Land of Israel [ערעץ]; [21]grains [טוווּעס]; [22]שלאָפֿט; [23][זמאַן־סימכאָסיינו]

***

שׂימחת־תּורה

שׂימחת־תּורה (די פֿרייד פֿון דער תּורה) איז דער 9טער טאָג פֿון סוכּות, ווען מען ענדיקט לייענען די תּורה און מע הייבט אָן די ערשטע פּרשה[24] פֿון בראשית[25]. בײַ נאַכט און צו מאָרגנס אין דער פֿרי בײַם דאַווענען מאַכט מען אין שול „הקפֿות[26]“. מע גייט אַרום מיט די ספֿרי־תּורות אַרום דער בימה אין שול מיט געזאַנג און טענץ. צו די הקפֿות קומען אויך פֿרויען אין דער מענער שול[27] און קושן די ספֿרי־תּורות. די קינדער טראָגן פֿאָנען מיט אָנגעצונדענע ליכטלעך. אין שׂימחת־תּורה איז מען זיך משׂמח[28], מע גייט אַרום איבער די הײַזער און מע פּראַוועט בשותּפֿותדיקע[29] סעודות.

[24]weekly Torah portion [פּאַרשע]; [25][ברייִשעס]; [26]processions [האַקאָפֿעס]; [27]*men's section of synagogue sanctuary*; [28]*makes merry* [מעסאַמייעך]; [29]joint [בעשוטפֿעסדיקע]

גענײטונג 3: מאַמעלע

וידעאָ־גענײטונג א־3

קולטור
CULTURE

טיטל „**מאַמעלע**“ (1938) (פֿראַגמענט)

רעזשיסאָרן **יוסף גרין (Joseph Green)**

(לאָדזש, רוסישע אימפּעריע 1900 – לאָנג־אײַלענד, פֿאַראייניקטע שטאַטן 1996)

קאָנראַד טאָם (Konrad Tom)

(וואַרשע, רוסישע אימפּעריע 1887 – לאָס־אַנדזשעלעס, פֿאַראייניקטע שטאַטן 1957)

Practice Sukkos vocabulary with this excerpt from the film *Mamele,* which you can find online with its accompanying exercise.

געניטונג 4: ברענענדיקע ליכט

טיטל: „**סוכּות**“ (פֿראַגמענט)

פֿון „ברענענדיקע ליכט“ (1939)

מחבר: **בעלאַ שאַגאַל (Bella Chagall)**

(וויטעבסק, רוסישע אימפּעריע 1895 – ניו־יאָרק, פֿאַראייניקטע שטאַטן 1944)

קינסטלער: **מאַרק שאַגאַל (Marc Chagall)**

(וויטעבסק, רוסישע אימפּעריע 1887 – סען-פּאָל-דע-וואַנס, פֿראַנקרײַך 1985)

קולטור
CULTURE

***Bella Chagall** was born Berta Rosenfeld to a family in the jewelry business who belonged to the Lubavitcher Hasidic sect. By the time she wrote this memoir, she was living in France with her husband, famed painter **Marc Chagall**. Both of them from Vitebsk, they chose to collaborate on the book* Brenendike likht *(Burning Lights), a tribute to the town of their youth. Bella Chagall deliberately chose Yiddish as the language most appropriate for these memories, explaining, "It is an odd thing: a desire comes to me to write, and to write in my faltering mother tongue, which, as it happens, I have not spoken since I left the home of my parents."*

In this passage, Bella Chagall narrates a Sukkos observance. Examine Marc Chagall's illustration on this page, which will help you to visualize the scene as Bella describes it.

סוכות

אויף מאָרגן נאָך יום־כּיפּור וואַרטן מיר אויף אַ שליח פֿון גאָט. ער מוז דאָך קומען נאָך אונדזערע נעכטיקע תּפֿילות און טרערן.

פֿאָרט אַרײַן אין הויף אַ פּויער מיט אַ וואָגן סכך. ער קערט איבער דעם וואָגן. שטעכנדיקע צווײַגן פֿאַלן אַנידער, לייגן זיך אָן איינע אויף די אַנדערע.

דער הויף ווערט ווי אַ וואַלד. ס׳שמעקט מיט סמאָלע, מיט סאָסנע. דער סכך איז פֿריש, ווי ערשט נאָך אַ רעגן. ווי גרויסע

89

איצט, ענטפֿערט אויף די פֿראַגעס וועגן דעם בילד.

- Purple words will appear in the story. Take a moment to integrate their meaning.

1. ווער דערלאַנגט דאָס עסן — אַ מאַן אָדער אַ פֿרוי?
2. ווו איז דער מענטש וואָס דערלאַנגט — אין שטוב[1] אָדער אין דער סוכּה? — [1] הויז
3. ווער עסט דאָס עסן — פֿרויען אָדער מאַנצבילן[2]? — [2] מענער
4. וויפֿל טעלערס[3] זעט מען אויפֿן טיש? — [3] plates
5. מיט וואָס איז די סוכּה פֿאַרדעקט[4]? — [4] covered

◄ CONTINUED

CONTINUED

Prepare a Venn diagram. Label one circle **אין שטוב** and the other **אין דער סוכּה**. As you read the text, take note of which characters and things appear in only one of these locations and which appear in both.

- When you come across one of the purple words from the questions on the preceding page, circle it.

When you have finished reading, fill in the Venn diagram accordingly.

- Write at least two elements in each of the three sections.

Go back to Marc Chagall's picture and label it with words and information you have obtained from the story: who is who, what might be in the dishes, and so on.

ענטפֿערט אויף די פֿראַגעס וועגן דער קליינער בערטעס סוכּות.

1. פֿאַר וואָס איז בערטען אומעטיק?
2. בערטעס משפּחה עסט געוויינטלעך צוזאַמען, אָדער באַזונדער?
3. זיי עסן צוזאַמען אום סוכּות? פֿאַר וואָס (אָדער פֿאַר וואָס נישט)?
4. באַטראַכט דעם ציטאַט:

„די ברידער קאָנען מיינען, אַז די טעלערלעך מיט דעם עסן קומען
זיי גלײַך פֿון הימל אַראָפּ. גיבן זיי גאָר נישט אַ טראַכט וועגן אונדז,
וואָס זײַנען איבערגעבליבן אַליין אין שטוב?“
איר מיינט אַז די מענטשן אין סוכּה טראַכטן וועגן די וואָס אין
שטוב? און די מענטשן אין שטוב, זיי טראַכטן וועגן די וואָס
אין סוכּה? ווי אַזוי ווייסט איר? ווײַזט אויף ספּעציפֿישע ציטאַטן *how*
פֿון טעקסט.

5. וואָס מיינט דער מאַמעס ענטפֿער: „זיי זײַנען דאָך מאַנצבילן“?
6. מיר ווייסן וואָס בערטע טראַכט וועגן די געשעענישן, אָבער וואָס *events*
טראַכט די מאַמע? באַשרײַבט אירע געדאַנקען — אַן „אינערלעכער *thoughts*
מאָנאָלאָג“ אַזאַ. *of sorts*
7. איר האָט אַ מאָל געמוזט ענטפֿערן אויף אַ שווערער פֿראַגע — אַ *once had to*
„פֿאַר וואָס“ — פֿון אַ יונג קינד? פֿאַרגלײַכט די צוויי סיטואַציעס:
די פֿראַגע (און אײַער ענטפֿער) מיט בערטעס פֿראַגעס, און איר
מאַמעס ענטפֿער.

◀ CONTINUED

CONTINUED

צום אָוונט טוען אָן[1] דער טאַטע מיט די ברידער זייערע מאַנטלען,
ווי זיי וואָלטן זיך געקליבן[2] אַוועקגיין פֿון דער היים. זיי גייען עסן
וועטשערע[3] אין דער סוכּה.

[1]*put on*
[2]*as though they were about to*
[3]dinner

נישט די מאַמע, נישט איך, נישט די קעכין גייען אַהין אַרײַן[4]. אַפֿילו[5]
דעם טאַטנס קידוש האָבן מיר, זאַלבעדריט, אויסגעהערט בײַ דער טיר
פֿון דער סוכּה.

[4]*in there;* [5]even [אַפֿילע]

און דאָס עסן דערלאַנגט מען אין סוכּה דורך[6] אַ פֿענצטערל, ווי דורך
אַ לאָך אַרײַן, איין טעלער נאָך[7] אַן אַנדערן. די ברידער קאָנען[8] מיינען,
אַז די טעלערלעך מיט דעם עסן קומען זיי גלײַך פֿון הימל אַראָפּ[9].

[6]through
[7]after; [8]קענען
[9]*straight down from heaven*

גיבן זיי גאָר נישט אַ טראַכט[10] וועגן אונדז, וואָס זײַנען
איבערגעבליבן[11] אַליין אין שטוב?

[10]thought
[11]left

אין דער שטוב איז קאַלט. זי איז, ווי אַ פּוסטע[12], ווי אָן[13] טיר און
פֿענצטער. מיר זיצן זאַלבענאַנד[14] מיט דער מאַמען און עסן אָן הנאה[15].

[12]empty; [13]without
[14]צוזאַמען; [15]pleasure [האַנאָע]

— מאַמע, פֿאַר וואָס זײַנען נאָר מיר אַליין איבערגעבליבן דאָ מיט די
דינסטן[16], ווי מיר וואָלטן אַליין געווען[17] דינסטן?
וואָס איז דאָס פֿאַר[18] אַ יום־טובֿ, מאַמע?

[16]maids; [17]*as if we ourselves were*
[18]*what kind of … is that?!*

איך שטיי נישט אָפּ פֿון[19] איר.

[19]*leave … alone*

— פֿאַר וואָס עסן זיי באַזונדער[20]?

[20]separately

— אַך, קינדיטשקע, זיי זײַנען דאָך מאַנצבילן, —
שלינגט[21] די מאַמע אַליין אומעטיק[22] אַראָפּ איר קאַלטן ביסן פֿלייש[23].

[21]swallows; [22]gloomily; [23]*bit (of) meat*

פּלוצעם[24] ווערט אַ טומל[25] אין קיך[26]. די דינסטן לויפֿן הין און קריק[27]
פֿון הויף[28] אין שטוב אַרײַן.

[24]suddenly; [25]ruckus; [26]kitchen; [27]*to and fro*
[28]courtyard

— באַלעבאָסטע[29], ס׳האָט זיך אָנגעהויבן אַ רעגן[30]!

[29]madam; [30]rain

— טראָג זיי גלײַך אַרײַן[31] דאָס גאַנצע עסן,
זיי זאָלן קענען[32] גיכער אָפּבענטשן[33]! — פֿאַרטומלט זיך אויך די מאַמע.

[31]*bring them in right away*
[32]*so they can;* [33]say the after-meal blessing

איך בין צופֿרידן[34], וואָס ס׳רעגנט אין מיטן דער וועטשערע. פֿאַר
אונדז מיט דער מאַמען איז דער יום־טובֿ אַזוי אומעטיק!

[34]glad

זיי זאָלן קענען גיכער אָפּבענטשן

It is a mitzvah to eat in the sukkah. Such a mitzvah can only be successfully completed with the saying of the traditional post-meal blessings, which must also be recited within the sukkah walls.

געניטונג 5: אין סוכּה

הער־געניטונג א־5

קולטור
CULTURE

טיטל	♫ „אין סוכּה“ (פֿראַגמענט) פֿון „נײַע ווערק“ (1911)
מחבר	**אַבֿרהם רייזען (Avrom Reyzen)** (קיידענעווו, רוסישע אימפּעריע 1876 – ניו־יאָרק, פֿאַראייניקטע שטאַטן 1953)
זינגער	**לאָרין סקלאַמבערג (Lorin Sklamberg)** (לאָס־אַנדזשעלעס, פֿאַראייניקטע שטאַטן 1956 –)
רעקאָרדירונג	2009, פֿאַראייניקטע שטאַטן

Avrom Reyzen *was a prolific poet, short story writer, and literary activist whose verse was much beloved by Yiddish readers and often set to music. In Warsaw and later in New York, Reyzen was also a central figure in the publishing, editing, and dissemination of Yiddish literature. His work often portrayed the lives of ordinary people, bringing the margins of society into the pages of Yiddish literature.*

In his poem "In suke," Reyzen contrasts the temporary dwelling's impermanence and fragility with its longevity as a symbol of the Jewish people's resilience through the ages. The accompanying recording comes from the album Tsuker Zis, *featuring singer* **Lorin Sklamberg** *and multi-instrumentalist* **Frank London**.

לייענט די פֿראַגעס אונטן איידער איר הערט זיך צו צום ליד. זיי וועלן אײַך העלפֿן פֿאַרשטיין דעם טעקסט.

1. די סוכּה איז פֿון מעטאַל, אָדער פֿון ברעטער? — boards
2. עס זײַנען דאָ שפּאַלטן אין די ווענט פֿון דער סוכּה? — cracks
3. דער דאַך פֿון דער סוכּה איז געדעקט מיט אַ לולבֿ, אָדער מיט סכך? — roof; covered
4. דאָס ליכטל לעשט זיך, אָדער עס ברענט רויִק? — *goes out*; peacefully

◄ CONTINUED

CONTINUED

הערט זיך צו צום ליד, נאָר קוקט נאָך נישט אויפֿן טעקסט אונטן.
ענטפֿערט אויף די פֿראַגעס אויבן.

הערט דאָס ליד נאָך אַ מאָל, און לייענט די ווערטער אונטן.

- When you come across one of the glossed words from the questions on the preceding page, circle it.

קולטור
CULTURE

2 מאָל	אַ סוכּה אַ קליינע	
	פֿון ברעטער געמיינע	commonplace
	האָב איך קוים מיט צרות געמאַכט!	*barely (and) with hardship* [צאָרעס]
	געדעקט דעם דאַך	
	מיט אַ ביסעלע סכך	
	און איך זיץ אין איר סוכּות בײַ נאַכט.	
2 מאָל	פֿון ווינט דעם קאַלטן,	
	וואָס בלאָזט דורך די שפּאַלטן,	through
	מײַן ליכטעלע לעשן זיך וויל:	wants to
	דאָך מאַך איך מיר קידוש,	yet
	און זעט נאָר אַ חידוש,	*just look at this surprise* [כידעש]
	דאָס ליכטל ברענט רויִק און שטיל!	unwaveringly

Sukkos is tomorrow, and you are going to help build a shared sukkah. Write a list of items that you have at home (not necessarily in reality), as in the example.

- Be sure to use appropriate accusative adjective endings.
- Use nouns learned in this song, as well as earlier in the section.

דוגמא:

איך האָב אַ געלן אתרוג.

געניטונג 6: קינדער, מיר האָבן שׂימחת־תּורה

קולטור
CULTURE

טיטל	♫ „קינדער, מיר האָבן שׂימחת־תּורה“
מחבר	**מאַרק וואַרשאַווסקי (Mark Varshavski)** (אָדעס, רוסישע אימפּעריע 1848 – קיִעוו, רוסישע אימפּעריע 1907)
זינגערס	**מאָריס פֿרידמאַן (Maurice Friedman)** (ווילנע, רוסישע אימפּעריע 1893 – סיִעטל, פֿאַראייניקטע שטאַטן 1962) **סוזי מײַקל (Susie Michael)** (פּאָרטלענד, פֿאַראייניקטע שטאַטן 1898 – סיִעטל, פֿאַראייניקטע שטאַטן 1990)
רעקאָרדירונג	1965, פֿאַראייניקטע שטאַטן

Maurice Friedman *(vocals) and* **Susie Michael** *(narrator, piano) toured the United States in what they called a "Cavalcade of Jewish Music." In Michael's spoken introduction to the song, she stresses its familial motif: "And even when celebrating a religious festival, such as Simchas Torah, our people, like the gentleman in this song, call upon their nearest and dearest to join together in celebrating this day of joy."*

The narrator seems to hold the following concepts particularly dear. Read the list, then look at the illustration in **געניטונג 1** and label its various elements with each of the four terms below.

משפּחה	פֿריילעכקייט
ייִדישקייט	געזונט

הערט זיך צו צום ליד, נאָר קוקט נאָך נישט אויף די ווערטער אונטן.
זאָרגט זיך נישט ווען איר פֿאַרשטייט נישט אַלץ.

- Listen for moments in the song when the lyric seems to refer to any of the concepts in the list above. Make note of these as you listen.

◀ CONTINUED

CONTINUED

הערט דאָס ליד נאָך אַ מאָל, און לייענט די ווערטער אונטן.

When you have finished listening and reading, underline the phrases in the text that relate to the concepts listed on the previous page. Beside those phrases, write the concept to which they relate.

קולטור
CULTURE

דוגמא:

קינדער, מיר האָבן שׂימחת־תּורה...

משפּחה; ייִדישקייט

קינדער, מיר האָבן שׂימחת־תּורה,	
שׂימחת־תּורה אויף דער גאַנצער וועלט[1]!	[1]world
— תּורה איז די בעסטע סחורה[2] —	[2]merchandise [סכוירע]
אַזוי האָט דער רבי[3] מיט אונדז געקנעלט[4].	[3][רעבע]; [4]געלערנט
אוי־ווײ, אײַ־אײַ־אײַ!	
פֿריילעך, קינדער, אָט אַזוי!	
רענדלעך[5] שיטן זיך[6] פֿון די זעק,	[5]gold coins; [6]*pour out*
פֿריילעך אָן אַן עק[7]!	[7]*endlessly*
כאָטש איך בין מיר אַן אָרעם[8] ייִדל	[8]poor
און עס דאַרט מיר גוט דער מוח[9],	[9]*I'm plagued with worry* [מויעך]
שׂימחת־תּורה זינג איך אַ לידל,	
און מאַך אַ גוטע כּוסה[10] אויך!	[10]*have a nice drink* [קויסע]
אוי־ווײ...	
דבֿורה, גיב מיר די נײַע קאַפּאָטע[11],	[11]long coat
איך וועל[12] זי אָנטאָן[13] טאַקע אַצינד[14].	[12]will; [13]put on; [14]איצט
איך וועל דיר זאָגן, — אַלצדינג איז בלאָטע,	
אַבי[15] מ'איז, ברוך־השם, געזונט!	[15]as long as
אוי־ווײ...	
ווו איז בערל? ווו איז דוואָשע?	
רוף[16] זיי אַלע אין שטוב אַרײַן!	[16]call
די מומע שאָשע, דעם פֿעטער יאָשע,	
זאָלן[17] זיי אַלע פֿריילעך זײַן!	[17]may
אוי־ווײ...	
קינדער, מיר האָבן שׂימחת־תּורה...	
אוי־ווײ...	

◀ CONTINUED

CONTINUED

In this song, Varshavski gives us the dialogue of the narrator. But he does not give us the physical context for his pronouncements—where he is, who exactly is with him, what they are doing, what they look like. Answer all of these questions by imagining the song as taking place within a stage musical, and write the stage directions for the scene.

- Use vocabulary from this section and the locational adverbs **רעכטס**, **לינקס**, and **אין מיטן**.
- Be sure to use appropriate nominative and accusative adjective endings.

דוגמא:

(קליינער צימער אין אַ הויז אין ספּרינגפֿילד, מאַסאַטשוסעטס. עס שטייט אַ טיש אין מיטן צימער, און אַ ספֿר־תּורה לינקס. דער טאַטע שטייט רעכטס און זינגט. ער איז הויך, און ער טראָגט רויטע ברילן...)

קולטור
CULTURE

12 וואָקאַבולאַר־איבערבליק

זמן־שׂמחתנו: סוכּות און שׂימחת־תּורה THE SEASON OF OUR HAPPINESS: SUKKOS AND SIMCHAS TORAH		
bimah		די **בימה** (–ות) [בימע (ס)]
sukkah		די **סוכּה** (–ות) [סוקע (ס)]
flag		די **פֿאָן** (ען)
house		די **שטוב** (שטיבער)
citron		דער **אתרוג** (ים) [עסרעג (עסרויגים)]
roof		דער **דאַך** (דעכער)
month		דער **חודש** (חדשים) [כוידעש (כאַדאָשים)]
lulov		דער **לולבֿ** (ים) [לולעוו (לולאָווים)]
Sukkos		דער **סוכּות** [סוקעס]
end		דער **סוף** (ן) [סאָף]
sukkah covering		דער **סכך** [סכאַך]
Torah scroll		דער **ספֿר־תּורה** (ספֿרי־...) [סײפֿער־טוירע (סיפֿרע־...)]
Shemini Atzereth		דער **שמיני־עצרת** [שמינאַצערעס]
Simchas Torah		דער **שׂימחת־תּורה** [סימכעס־טוירע]
to build	איך בוי	בויען
to cover		דעקן
to shake	איך שאָקל	שאָקלען

איבערחזר־געניטונגען: טעמע דרײַ

געניטונג 1: באַשרײַבט אַ בילד

טיטל „טאַנץ־לעקציע“ (1926)

קינסטלער **רפֿאל סויער (Raphael Soyer)**

(באָריסאָגלעבסק, רוסישע אימפּעריע 1899 – ניו־יאָרק, פֿאַראייניקטע שטאַטן 1987)

Fleeing political upheaval in Czarist Russia, **Raphael Soyer**'*s family immigrated to the Bronx in 1910. He considered his new city his true homeland, and his canvases are filled with depictions of life there; he once said in an interview, "I painted only what I saw in my neighborhood in New York City, which I call my country rather than my city." This painting,* Dancing Lesson, *was completed in the mid-1920s.*

◀ CONTINUED

CONTINUED

קוקט אויפֿן בילד און באַטראַכט די פֿראַגעס אונטן, נאָר ענטפֿערט אויף זיי נישט.

1. ווי הייסט די צײַטונג וואָס די פֿרוי האַלט?
2. ווער זײַנען די מענטשן אין צימער? זיי זײַנען קרובֿים?
3. ווער זײַנען די מענטשן אויפֿן פּאָרטרעֶט אויף דער וואַנט? זיי זײַנען קרובֿים מיט די מענטשן אין צימער?

איצט, שרײַבט וועגן דעם בילד, אַזוי פֿיל ווי איר קענט אין צוויי מינוׂט. *as much as*

- שרײַבט גאַנצע זאַצן. ניצט ווערטער און פֿראַזעס פֿון קאַפּיטלען 9 - 11.

גענִיטונג 2: דעם קינסטלערס קרעדאָ

A painting of Soyer's, and also works by his identical twin Moses and younger brother Isaac, are presented in the 1947 book *Hundert haynttsaytike amerikaner yidishe moler un skulptorn (One Hundred Contemporary American Jewish Painters and Sculptors)*, published by YKUF, the *Yidisher kultur farband*. This association, founded in Paris in 1937, promoted Jewish literary and visual artists, particularly those tied to Yiddish culture. To that end, all of the paintings in the book appear beside the artist's credo printed in both Yiddish and English.

איידער איר לייענט איבער דעם פֿראַגמענט פֿונעם קינסטלערס קרעדאָ, באַטראַכט די ווײַטערדיקע פֿראַגעס.

1. וואָס איז סויערס ציל וואָס ער פּאָלגט שטענדיק נאָך: וואָסער סאָרט בילדער מאַכט ער — נאַטוראַליׂסטישע אָדער אַבסטראַקטע? *goal; pursues*
2. אין „טאַנץ־לעקציע“, צי זעט מען די פֿיגורן אין אַ נאַטיׂרלעכער סבֿיבֿה? ווו זײַנען זיי? *environment [סוויווע]*
3. סויערס קרעדאָ פּאַסט דעם בילד אין גענִיטונג 1? ווי אַזוי? וואָס איז „טאָג־טעגלעך“ אינעם בילד? *matches; commonplace*

איצט, לייענט דעם קרעדאָ.

- When you see a word in the text that was glossed in the questions above, circle it.

ווען איך כאַפּ אַ בליק צוריק אויף מײַן אַרבעט אַזוי אָביעקטיׂוו ווי מעגלעך, זע איך, אַז איך האָב נאָכגעפּאָלגט אַ באַשטימטן ציל — און דאָס איז אַ בילד פֿונעם לעבן וואָס איז מיר באַקאַנט; אַ פּרוּוו אָפּצושפּיגלען די מענטשן אין זייער סבֿיבֿה; נישט קיין איזאָלירטע פּאָרטרעטוׂר, נאָר דעם סוביעֶקט אין זײַן נאַטירלעכער אומגעבונג, אין זײַן טאָג־טעגלעכן ראַם.

look back; possible; ספּעציפֿיש; familiar; *attempt to reflect*; סבֿיבֿה*; frame*

ענטפֿערט אויף די פֿראַגעס אויבן.

טיטל „10. פֿראַגעס. 10 מינוטן.“

פֿון פֿאַראייניקטע שטאַטן־צענזוס, 2010

אָרגאַניזאַציע פֿאַראייניקטע שטאַטן־צענזוס־ביוראָ

This form comes from the United States Census Bureau, which translated the 2010 census into many languages, including Yiddish. In 2011, the American Community Survey, a more detailed fact-finding mission also organized by the Census Bureau, found the number of Americans above the age of five who speak Yiddish at home to be 160,968.

לייענט דעם אָפֿיציעלן פּלאַקאַט, וואָס רעקלאַמירט דעם צענזוס. — poster; publicizes

are confident that	פֿאַרלאָזן זיך אַז
education	דערציִונג
will	וועט
villages	דערפֿער
have an influence	זײַט משפּיע [מאַשפּיִע]

NOTE:

A higher-resolution copy of this image may be found on the textbook website. If you find the font here to be too small, please refer to the online version.

◀ CONTINUED

CONTINUED

Using the text of the poster as a model, write four or five sentences on likes and dislikes among people in your Yiddish class, family, or hometown. Follow with an imperative that presents a call to action related to the preceding sentences, as the poster does.

- Write out numbers in full.
- You need not poll people as to their likes and dislikes—you may make up the numbers.

דוגמא:

צוויי הונדערט פֿינף און פֿופֿציק מענטשן וווינען אין מײַן דערפֿל אין קליינסוויל, אַלאַבאַמע. פֿון זיי האָבן הונדערט צוויי און זיבעציק ליב צו טאַנצן קוואַדראַ́טטענץ, זעקס און אַכציק האָבן ליב צו טאַנצן דזשעז, פֿינף און צוואַנציק האָבן ליב צו טאַנצן טאַנגאָ, און צוויי האָבן ליב צו טאַנצן אַ שער, אַ ייִדישער טאַנץ. אָבער אַ שער איז פֿאַר אַכט מענטשן אָדער מער. לערנט זיך טאַנצן דעם שער, מענטשן פֿון קליינסוויל!

REFERENCE

TABLE OF CONTENTS (VOL. 1)

APPENDIX A: INFORMATION GAP EXERCISES

טעמע I, קאַפּיטל 3, סעקציע ב

געניטונג 3: וואָס איז דאָס?

סטודענט ב

Help your partner connect the dots in the image provided (in the corresponding exercise in קאַפּיטל 3, page 94) by reciting the text below.

begin with הייב אָן מיט 1. גיי צו 35, צו 76, צו 13, צו 52, צו 24,
צו 4, צו 58, צו 84, צו 30, צו 11, צו 92, צו 70, צו 36,
צו 3, צו 97, צו 59, צו 2, צו 60, צו 48, צו 29, צו 9, צו
42, צו 83, צו 67, צו 74, צו 64, צו 17, צו 21, צו 7, צו
15, צו 79, צו 34, צו 96, צו 26, צו 43, צו 38, צו 56,
צו 27, צו 71, צו 88, צו 91, צו 86, צו 40, צו 94, און
finally [סאָף] צום סוף צו 46. דאָס איז אַ ציגעלע!

Now follow your partner's instructions to connect the dots in the image below.

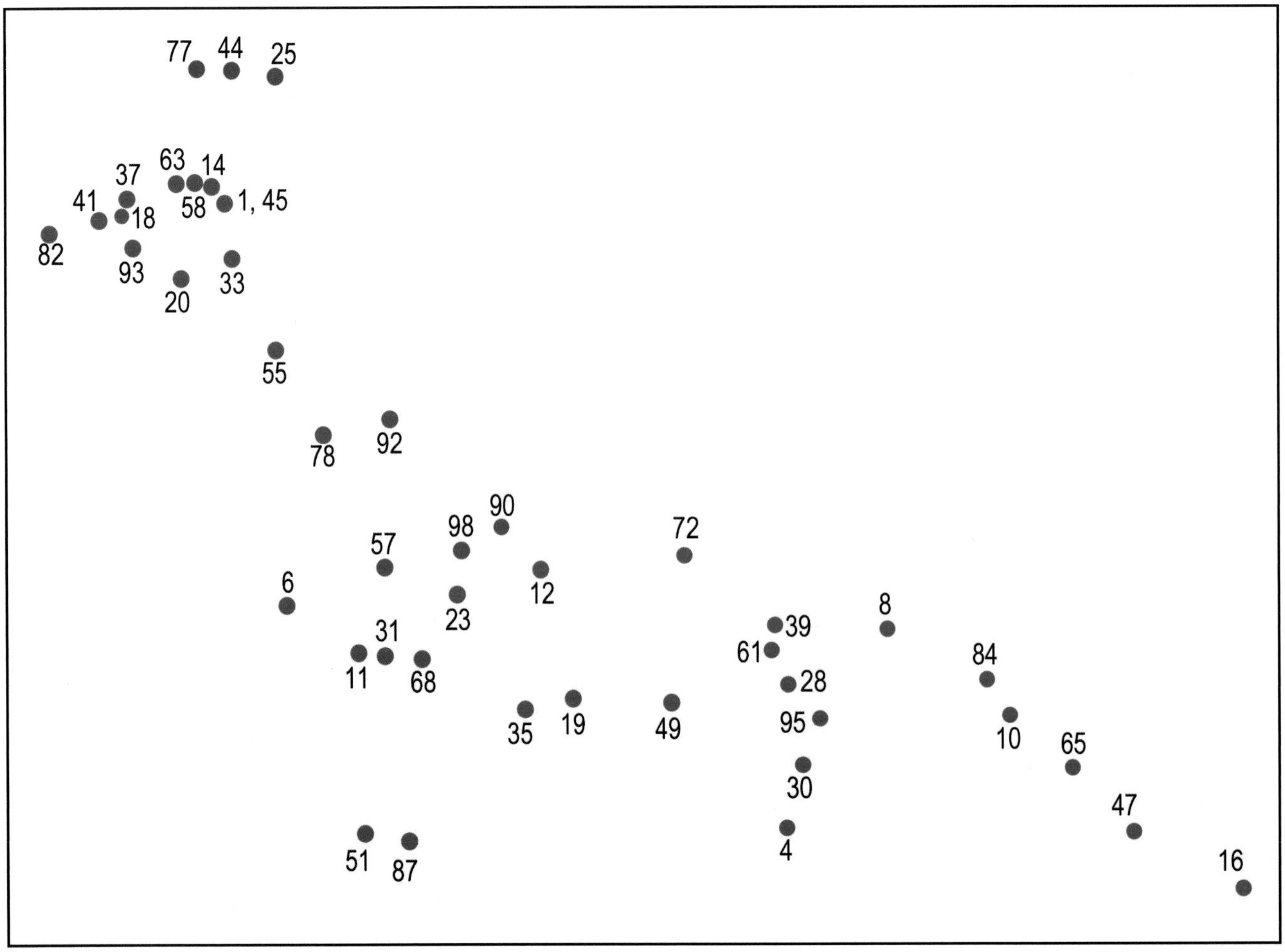

געניטונג 3: ווער בין איך?

סטודענט ב

With a partner, take turns role-playing some of the characters we've met so far. Your partner will work from the corresponding exercise in 3 **קאַפּיטל** (see page 104).

Each column in the table below pertains to a separate character. Using the model provided, ask your partner questions to fill in the missing information in columns 3 and 4.

- You will need to ask both open-ended (**?פֿון וואַנען קומסטו**) and yes-or-no questions (**?דו ביסט אַ סטודענט**).
- Once your table is complete, answer your partner's questions according to the information in columns 1 and 2.
- Be sure to use the pronoun provided at the top of each column when asking or answering the corresponding questions.

דוגמא:

א: דו ביסט אַ סטודענטקע?

ב: ניין, איך בין אַ סטודענט.

א: פֿון וואַנען קומסטו?

ב: איך קום פֿון ישׂראל.

[...]

א: דו הייסט ________!

ב: אַ יישר־כּוח[1]!

אָדער

ב: ניין, פּרוּװ[2] נאָך אַ מאָל[3].

[1] *well done!* [יאַשער־קויעך]

[2] try; [3] *again*

	1. (איך)	2. (איך)	3. (איר)	4. (דו)
זײַן	אַ סטודענט	אַ פּראָפֿעסאָרשע		
קומען	פֿון ישׂראל	פֿון ניו־יאָרק		
רעדן	העברעיִש, אַראַביש, און ענגליש	ייִדיש, רוסיש, און ענגליש		
וווינען	אין לערנטאָן	אין לערנטאָן		
זײַן	24 יאָר אַלט	40 יאָר אַלט		
הייסן	אַבֿרהם	פּראָפֿעסאָר קלוגער		

טעמע II, קאַפּיטל 5, סעקציע ג

גענײטונג 2: איך לײג אַרײַן אַ פּאָפּוגײַ

סטודענט ב (חיה)

Rokhl is getting Khaye ready for school, packing her backpack. Khaye wants to help but has her own ideas about what she needs to bring. With a partner, act out their interaction.

- Take turns putting things into Khaye's backpack (or taking them out) until the items in the backpack are *all* things that both Rokhl and Khaye intended.
- Khaye should work from the list below; Rokhl's list is to be found in **קאַפּיטל** 5 (see page 142).
- When referring to something your partner has already mentioned, replace the article with the possessive adjective **דײַן** (*your*), as in the example.
- When you choose *not* to take something out, use **נישט** as Rokhl does below.

דוגמא:

חיה: איך לײג אַרײַן אַ פּאָפּוגײַ.

רחל: איך נעם אַרויס דײַן פּאָפּוגײַ.

חיה: איך לײג אַרײַן אַ בלײַער.

רחל: איך נעם **נישט** אַרויס דײַן בלײַער. איך לײג אַרײַן אַ באַר.

חיה: איך נעם אַרויס דײַן באַר.

אַרײַנלײגן — to put in

Keep track of what remains in the backpack and what doesn't, as shown below.

[רעשימע]

חיהס רשימה	אין רוקזאַק
פּאָפּוגײַ	נײן
בלײַער	יאָ
שאָקאָלאַדקע	
מעקער	
גיטאַרע	
העפֿט	
שער	
פֿעדער	

געניטונג 6: וואָס לערנט פּראָפֿעסאָר קלוגער?

סטודענט ב

Among the characters we've met so far, there are many part-time and full-time teachers. With a partner, take turns asking questions to find out who teaches what and then fill in the table below.

- Your partner will work from the table in **6 קאַפּיטל** (see page 165).
- Model your dialogue on the example below.

NOTE:

The verb **לערנען** means *to teach* (though it does also have other meanings, depending on context).

דוגמא:

ב: וואָס לערנט פּראָפֿעסאָר קלוגער?

א: פּראָפֿעסאָער קלוגער לערנט ייִדיש.

נאָמען:	פּראָפֿעסאָר קלוגער	הערשל	נתן	רחל	צירל	פּאָל
לימוד:	ייִדיש		געשיכטע	סאָציאָלאָגיע		זשורנאַליסטיק

געניטונג 7: ווען איז דער אויספֿרעג?

סטודענט ב

With a partner, fill in the missing information about Elke's schoolwork in the schedule below. Structure your conversation as in the model provided.

- Your partner will work from the corresponding exercise in **6 קאַפּיטל** (see page 165).
- Be sure to use the appropriate verb for each schoolwork noun. Refer to the list you made in **3 געניטונג** for a reminder.

דוגמא:

א: עלקע האַלט פֿרײַטיק אַן עקזאַמען?

ב: יאָ, פֿרײַטיק האַלט זי אַן עקזאַמען אויף קאַפּיטל 2. זי האָט זונטיק אַן אויספֿרעג?

א: ניין, זונטיק מאַכט זי געניטונג 3 אין קאַפּיטל 2.

זונטיק	מאָנטיק	דינסטיק	מיטוואָך	דאָנערשטיק	פֿרײַטיק
	רעפֿעראַט וועגן פּוילן			געניטונג 5 אין קאַפּיטל 2	עקזאַמען אויף קאַפּיטל 2

טעמע II, קאַפּיטל 6, סעקציע ב

געניטונג 5: קאַווע און אײַזקרעם

סטודענט ב (חנה)

Khane and Sender are hoping to go out for both coffee *and* ice cream this week. With a partner, compare their schedules to figure out which days they are both relatively free, as in the model below.

- Sender's schedule appears in **קאַפּיטל 6** (see page 172). Khane's is below.

דוגמא:

חנה: זונטיק האָב איך נישט קיין סך היימאַרבעט. וויפֿל היימאַרבעט האָסט דו זונטיק?

סענדער: איך האָב אַ סך היימאַרבעט זונטיק, אָבער מאָנטיק האָב איך נישט קיין סך היימאַרבעט.

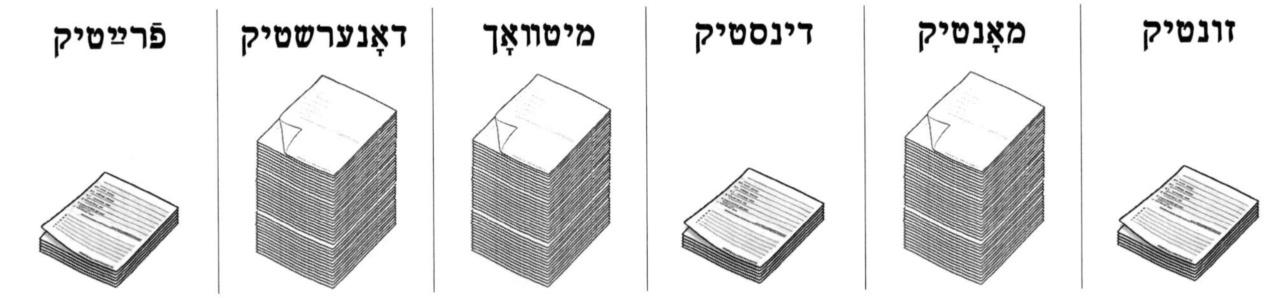

געניטונג 4: אין קלאַס און אין הויז

סטודענט ב (אין הויז)

Professor Kluger is at the stationery store shopping for school supplies, but she has forgotten to check which items she already owns.

- Help Professor Kluger check what's already in her house (see below) while your partner checks her classroom (see **קאַפּיטל 6**, page 179).
- Ask your partner about each item listed below, as in the model provided, and write down (in the corresponding blank) how many of that item Professor Kluger owns.

דרעטלערס ____	שערן ____	בלעטלעך ____	מעקערס __1__	זייגערס ____
לאָמפּן ____	ביכער ____	העפֿטן ____	בלײַערס ____	פֿעדערס ____

אין הויז

NOTE:

The question **וויפֿל מעקערס זײַנען דאָ** (and others like it) are asked in the plural (**מעקערס זײַנען**). However, the answer may be either in the plural or in the singular, depending on the number of items actually present: **עס איז דאָ איין מעקער** or **עס זײַנען דאָ פֿינף מעקערס**.
If there are *no* items present at all, the answer may be either plural or singular: **עס זײַנען נישטאָ קיין מעקערס** or **עס איז נישטאָ קיין מעקער**.

דוגמא:

א: וויפֿל מעקערס זײַנען דאָ אין הויז?

ב: עס איז דאָ איין מעקער אין הויז. וויפֿל מעקערס זײַנען דאָ אין קלאַס?

א: עס זײַנען נישטאָ קיין מעקערס אין קלאַס. אין גאַנצן איז דאָ איין מעקער.

אין גאַנצן — in total

טעמע III, קאַפּיטל 11, סעקציע ג

געניטונג 2: איך האָב אים!

סטודענט ב

NOTE:

When negating a sentence with a direct object, the order of elements depends on whether the object is a noun or a pronoun:

איך האָב נישט דעם דרעטלער.

איך האָב אים נישט.

געדענקט!

The adjectives **לילאַ** and **אָראַנזש** are irregular: **לילאַ** never takes any ending; **אָראַנזש** has a different set of forms (based on the stem **אָראַנזשן**) when used as an **attributive** adjective:

ער האָט די לילאַ העפֿט.

זי האָט די אָראַנזשענע העפֿט.

Compare the contents of your backpack (as shown below right) with the accompanying snapshot of your desk (below left). Identify the items missing from your backpack and ask if your partner has them.

- Be sure to use appropriate accusative articles, adjective endings, and third-person pronouns, as in the model.
- Your partner will work from the corresponding exercise in **11 קאַפּיטל** (see page 313).

דוגמא:

א: דו האָסט דעם שוואַרצן דרעטלער?

ב: יאָ, איך האָב אים.

אָדער

ב: ניין, איך האָב אים נישט.

טעמע III, קאַפּיטל 11, סעקציע ג

געניטונג 5: דער בעל־הבית שיקט דיך אין פּאַרק?

סטודענט ב

You are the personal assistant to a very busy boss, who sends you to a different location every day on an important errand. Compare notes with your partner, who also works for such a boss, on where your respective bosses send you, as in the model.

- Pay attention to the relative position of the subject and direct object in the sentence. How does it change when the subject is a full noun, as opposed to a pronoun?
- Make sure to place **נישט** in the correct position in the sentence.
- Your partner will work from the table in **קאַפּיטל 11** (see page 317).

דוגמא:

א: זונטיק שיקט דיך דער בעל־הבית אין ביוראָ?

ב: ניין, זונטיק שיקט ער מיך נישט אין ביוראָ. זונטיק שיקט ער מיך אין פּאַרק. זונטיק שיקט דיך דײַן בעל־הבית אין פּאַרק?

א: ניין, זונטיק שיקט מיך מײַן בעל־הבית נישט אין פּאַרק. זונטיק, שיקט ער מיך אין קראָם.

דער בעל־הבית [באַלעבאָס] boss

טאָג	איך	דער חבֿר
זונטיק	אין פּאַרק	
מאָנטיק	אין געריכט	
דינסטיק	אין קראָם	
מיטוואָך	אין אוניווערסיטעט	
דאָנערשטיק	אין ביוראָ	
פֿרײַטיק	אין רעסטאָראַן	

APPENDIX B: GRAMMAR SUMMARY TABLES

VERB CONJUGATIONS

REGULAR VERBS (P. 80)

Infinitive	קומען (!)	אַרבעטן	עסן	שלאָפֿן	
First-person singular	קום	אַרבעט	עס	שלאָף	איך
Second person singular (*informal*)	קומסט	אַרבעטסט	עסט (!)	שלאָפֿסט	דו
Third-person singular	קומט	אַרבעט (!)	עסט	שלאָפֿט	ער/זי/עס
First-person plural	קומען (!)	אַרבעטן	עסן	שלאָפֿן	מיר
Second person plural (and *singular formal*)	קומט	אַרבעט (!)	עסט	שלאָפֿט	איר
Third-person plural	קומען (!)	אַרבעטן	עסן	שלאָפֿן	זיי

NOTES:

- Verbs like **שלאָפֿן** constitute the most common class of regular verbs. To form the present tense, the stem of the verb (-**שלאָפֿ**) combines with the endings shown in **bold** above.
- Verbs with stems ending in **ס**- (e.g., **עסן**) have a special conjugation for **דו**, adding only **ט**- (rather than **סט**-) in order to avoid doubling the **ס**.
- Similarly, verbs with stems ending in **ט**- (e.g., **אַרבעטן**) omit the usual third-person singular and second-person-plural/formal endings in order to avoid doubling the final **ט**.
- Verbs with stems ending in **מ**-, **נ**-, **נג**-, **נק**-, an accented vowel, or a syllabic **ל**- have a special ending in the first- and third-person plural: **ען**- (instead of **ן**- alone). For example:

מיר קומען, ווינען, זינגען, טרינקען, פֿליִען *(fly)*, שמייכלען *(smile)*

These usually form the infinitive too (with some exceptions, such as (**גיין ← מיר גייען**).

THE VERBS **האָבן** AND **זײַן** (P. 101)

	האָבן	זײַן
איך	האָב	בין
דו	האָסט (!)	ביסט
ער/זי/עס	האָט (!)	איז
מיר	האָבן	זײַנען
איר	האָט (!)	זײַט
זיי	האָבן	זײַנען

THE VERB **עפֿענען** (P. 155)

עפֿענען (!)	Plural	Singular
First Person	מיר עפֿענען (!)	איך עפֿן
Second Person	איר עפֿנט	דו עפֿנסט
Third Person	זיי עפֿענען (!)	ער/זי/עס עפֿנט

NOTES:

- The stem of this verb (**עפֿן**) ends with a **syllabic** *nun*, requiring a supporting *ayin* to be inserted before this *nun* in the infinitive and first- and third-person plural conjugations. This rule applies widely to verbs with stems ending in a syllabic *nun*.

VERB CONJUGATIONS (continued)

THE VERB געבן (P. 155)

געבן (!)	Plural	Singular
First Person	מיר גיבן	איך גיב
Second Person	איר גיט (!)	דו גיסט (!)
Third Person	זיי גיבן	ער/זי/עס גיט (!)

VERBS WITH ע- STEM (P. 467)

מיר פראַוועו	איך פראַוועו
איר פראַוועט	דו פראַוועסט
זיי פראַוועו	ער/זי/עס פראַוועט

MODAL VERBS (P. 565)

מיר דאַרפֿן	איך דאַרף
איר דאַרפֿט	דו דאַרפֿסט
זיי דאַרפֿן	ער/זי/עס דאַרף (!)

NOTES:

- All seven modal verbs (**דאַרפֿן**, **קענען**, **מוזן**, **מעגן**, **נישט טאָרן**, **וועלן**, and **זאָלן**) conjugate without the **ט-** ending in the third-person-singular conjugation.
- The verb **וועלן** has an irregular infinitive; the stem of the verb (and thus the basis of its present-tense conjugations) is **-וויל**.

THE FUTURE AUXILIARY VERB וועלן (P. 625)

מיר וועלן	איך וועל
איר וועט (!)	דו וועסט (!)
זיי וועלן	ער/זי/עס וועט (!)

IRREGULAR INFINITIVES (P. 156)

First- and Third-Person Plural	Infinitive
מיר/זיי גייען	גיין
מיר/זיי שטייען	שטיין
מיר/זיי זעען	זען
מיר/זיי זײַנען	זײַן
מיר/זיי גיבן	געבן
מיר/זיי טוען	טאָן

POSITION VERBS (P. 381)

	Intransitive	Transitive
Upright	שטיין	שטעלן
Horizontal	ליגן	לייגן
Seated	זיצן	זעצן
Suspended	הענגען	הענגען

VERB PARTICIPLES

COMMON VERBS THAT TAKE זײַן AS AUXILIARY (P. 497)

בלײַבן	געבליבן	זיצן	געזעסן	רײַטן	געריטן
גיין	געגאַנגען	לויפֿן	געלאָפֿן	רינען	גערונען
געפֿעלן	געפֿעלן	ליגן	געלעגן	שווימען	געשוווּמען
געשען	געשען	פֿאַלן	געפֿאַלן	שטאַרבן	געשטאָרבן
הענגען	געהאָנגען	פֿאָרן	געפֿאָרן	שטיין	געשטאַנען
וואַקסן	געוואַקסן	פֿליִען	געפֿלויגן	שלאָפֿן	געשלאָפֿן
ווערן	געוואָרן	קומען	געקומען	שפרינגען	געשפרונגען
זײַן	געווען	קריכן	געקראָכן		

COMMON VERBS WITH IRREGULAR PARTICIPLES (P. 505)

בײַסן	געביסן	ווינטשן	געווונטשן	גיסן	געגאָסן
ווײַזן	געוויזן	זינגען	געזונגען		
רײַסן	געריסן	טרינקען	געטרונקען		
שמײַסן	געשמיסן				
שרײַבן	געשריבן				

בלאָזן	געבלאָזן	טרעפֿן	געטראָפֿן	אָנהייבן	אָנגעהויבן (!)
געבן	געגעבן	לעשן	געלאָשן	האָבן	געהאַט (!)
האַלטן	געהאַלטן	שעכטן	געשאָכטן	וועלן	געוואָלט (!)
הייסן	געהייסן			נעמען	גענומען (!)
זען	געזען			עסן	געגעסן (!)
טאָן	געטאָן				
טראָגן	געטראָגן				

SOME COMMON VERBS WITH INSEPARABLE PREFIXES AND THEIR PARTICIPLES (P. 509)

אַנט־		גע־		פֿאַר־	
אַנטלויפֿן	אַנטלאָפֿן	געדענקען	געדענקט	פֿאַרגעסן	פֿאַרגעסן
		געפֿינען	געפֿונען	פֿאַרמאַכן	פֿאַרמאַכט
				פֿאַרקויפֿן	פֿאַרקויפֿט
				פֿאַרשטיין	פֿאַרשטאַנען

באַ־		דער־		צע־	
באַקומען	באַקומען	דערלאַנגען	דערלאַנגט	צעטאַנצן	צעטאַנצט
באַשטעלן	באַשטעלט	דערציילן	דערציילט	צעלאַכן	צעלאַכט

NOUN GENDERS

GENDER PATTERNS OF NOUNS (PP. 299, 321)

Every Yiddish noun has a **grammatical gender**: feminine, masculine, or neuter.

- Noun genders are rarely self-evident and often must be memorized. Nevertheless, there are certain guidelines that can help us work out the gender of an unfamiliar word.
- Note that there are exceptions to each of the patterns provided below.

MEANING-BASED PATTERNS:

Nouns that refer to males are generally grammatically masculine	דער זיידע; דער מאַן
Nouns that refer to females are generally grammatically feminine	די באָבע; די פֿרוי
The base forms of nouns referring to professions or social roles are generally grammatically masculine	דער לערער; דער סטודענט; דער סעקרעטאַר; דער חבֿר; דער ליובאָווניק (lover)
Corresponding feminine forms are typically formed by adding the suffixes ין-, קע-, שע-, טע-, or **ניצע-** and are grammatically feminine	די לערערין; די סטודענטקע; די סעקרעטאַרשע; די חבֿרטע; די ליובאָווניצע

SOUND-BASED PATTERNS:

Multisyllabic nouns with the following endings are typically masculine:

ער-	דער בלײַער; דער צימער; דער פֿענצטער
syllabic ן-	דער שטעקן; דער האָרן; דער רעגן־בויגן
syllabic ל- (nondiminutive)	דער טאָוול; דער עפּל

Nouns ending in an unstressed [ע] sound (with the following spellings) are typically feminine:

ע-	די קאַווע; די סטעליע
ה-	די דירה; די סוכּה
א-	די דוגמא; די גמרא [געמאָרע]
י-	די כּלי [קיילע] (dish)

FORM-BASED PATTERNS:

When the suffix ל- or **(ע)לע-** is used to derive the diminutive form of a word, that word adopts the neuter gender	דער טיש ← דאָס טישל די דירה ← דאָס דירהלע דאָס בוך ← דאָס ביכעלע
Words with the suffix **ונג-** are generally feminine, often formed from verb stems	טרעפֿן ← די טרעפֿונג זיצן ← די זיצונג
Compound nouns usually have the same gender as their second component	דאָס בוך ← דאָס ווערטערבוך

NOUN PLURALS

SOME PLURAL PATTERNS OF NOUNS (P. 153)

There are several types of plural forms in Yiddish. These forms are rarely self-evident and often must be memorized. Nevertheless, there are certain guidelines that can help us work out the plural form of some unfamiliar words.

- The table below presents four common plural suffixes and the types of nouns that often form their plural with each suffix.
- Note that there are exceptions to each of the patterns provided below.

ן(ע)-	**Most nouns form their plural with the suffix ן-.**	העפּט ← העפּטן
	The -ע- is added when the base noun ends in	
	-נג	געניטונג ← געניטונגען
	-נק	פֿונק ← פֿונקען (*spark*)
	a syllabic ל- and is not a diminutive	טאָוול ← טאָוולען
	a stressed syllable terminating with ן-	באַן ← באַנען
	a stressed syllable terminating with ם-	בלום ← בלומען
	a vowel or diphthong	פּאָפּוגײַ ← פּאָפּוגײַען
ס-	**• If a word ends in ם- or ן- but the last syllable is not emphasized, the plural ending is ס-.**	
	ן-	עקזאַמען ← עקזאַמענס
	ם-	אָרעם ← אָרעמס (*arm*)
	• Nouns ending in an unstressed ע- form their plural with the suffix ס-.	מאָבילקע ← מאָבילקעס
	• Nouns ending in unstressed ער- also commonly form their plurals with ס-.	בלײַער ← בלײַערס
ות-	**Nouns from *loshn-koydesh* that end in an unstressed [ע] sound form their plural with the suffix ות-, which takes the place of the final letter of the noun.**	
	ה-	דירה ← דירות
	א-	דוגמא ← דוגמות
ך(ע)-	**Diminutive nouns form plurals with עך-.**	בענקל ← בענקלעך
	Iminutive nouns form plurals with ך- alone.	בענקעלע ← בענקעלעך

NOUN PHRASE CASES

NOMINATIVE ARTICLES AND ADJECTIVE ENDINGS (P. 251)

	Indefinite	Definite
Masculine	אַ שטאַרקער מאַן טאַנצט.	דער שטאַרקער מאַן טאַנצט.
Neuter	אַ שטאַרק קינד טאַנצט. (!)	דאָס שטאַרקע קינד טאַנצט.
Feminine	אַ שטאַרקע פֿרוי טאַנצט.	די שטאַרקע פֿרוי טאַנצט.
Plural	שטאַרקע מענטשן טאַנצן.	די שטאַרקע מענטשן טאַנצן.

ACCUSATIVE AND DATIVE ARTICLES AND ADJECTIVE ENDINGS (PP. 320, 381)

	Nominative	Accusative	Dative
Masculine	דער שטאַרקער מאַן טאַנצט. אַ שטאַרקער מאַן טאַנצט.	איך זע דעם שטאַרקן מאַן. איך זע אַ שטאַרקן מאַן.	איך שטיי לעבן דעם שטאַרקן מאַן. איך שטיי לעבן אַ שטאַרקן מאַן.
Neuter	דאָס שטאַרקע קינד טאַנצט. אַ שטאַרק קינד טאַנצט. (!)	איך זע דאָס שטאַרקע קינד. איך זע אַ שטאַרק קינד. (!)	איך שטיי לעבן דעם שטאַרקן קינד. איך שטיי לעבן אַ שטאַרק קינד. (!)
Feminine	די שטאַרקע פֿרוי טאַנצט. אַ שטאַרקע פֿרוי טאַנצט.	איך זע די שטאַרקע פֿרוי. איך זע אַ שטאַרקע פֿרוי.	איך שטיי לעבן דער שטאַרקער פֿרוי. איך שטיי לעבן אַ שטאַרקער פֿרוי.
Plural	די שטאַרקע מענטשן טאַנצן. שטאַרקע מענטשן טאַנצן.	איך זע די שטאַרקע מענטשן. איך זע שטאַרקע מענטשן.	איך שטיי לעבן די שטאַרקע מענטשן. איך שטיי לעבן שטאַרקע מענטשן.

NOTES:

When declining masculine adjectives in the accusative and masculine and neuter adjectives in the dative, not all adjectives follow exactly the declension pattern outlined above.

- If the base form of an adjective ends on ן-, the ן- declension ending becomes **עם-**.

  דער מאַן איז שיין. ← איך זע דעם שיינעם מאַן; איך שטיי צווישן דעם שיינעם מאַן און דעם שיינעם קינד.

- If the base form of an adjective ends on **ם-**, a vowel, or a diphthong, the ן- declension ending becomes **ען-**.

  דער טיש איז קרום. ←
  איך זע דעם קרומען טיש; איך שטיי צווישן דעם קרומען טיש און דעם קרומען בענקל.
  דער טאָוול איז בלוי. ←
  איך זע דעם בלויען טאָוול; איך שטיי צווישן דעם בלויען טאָוול און דעם בלויען בענקל.

- The adjective **ניי** is an exception to the above: its masculine accusative and masculine or neuter dative ending is **עם-**.

  דער רוקזאַק איז ניי. ←
  איך זע דעם נייעם רוקזאַק; איך שטיי צווישן דעם נייעם רוקזאַק און דעם נייעם בענקל.

NOUN PHRASE CASES (continued)

DECLINABLE NOUNS (P. 413)

Nominative	Accusative	Dative
די מאַמע	די מאַמע	דער מאַמען
די באָבע	די באָבע	דער באָבען
דער טאַטע	דעם טאַטן	דעם טאַטן
דער זיידע	דעם זיידן	דעם זיידן
דער רבי [רעבע]	דעם רבין [רעבן]	דעם רבין [רעבן]

NOTES:

- Personal names inflect identically in the accusative and dative cases, with the addition of ן(ע)-.
- There are a few nouns for which declension is optional:

Nominative	Accusative	Dative
די מומע	די מומע	דער מומען
דער ייִד	דעם ייִדן	דעם ייִדן
דער מענטש	דעם מענטשן	דעם מענטשן

PRONOUNS

POSSESSIVE ADJECTIVES (P. 201)

Plural Possessive	Singular Possessive	Pronoun
מײַנע	מײַן	איך
דײַנע	דײַן	דו
זײַנע	זײַן	ער
אירע	איר	זי
זײַנע	זײַן	עס
אונדזערע	אונדזער	מיר
אײַערע	אײַער	איר
זייערע	זייער	זיי

NOMINATIVE, ACCUSATIVE, AND DATIVE PRONOUNS (PP. 322, 413)

Dative	Accusative	Nominative
ער שטייט לעבן מיר.	ער זעט מיך.	איך בין דאָ.
ער שטייט לעבן דיר.	ער זעט דיך.	דו ביסט דאָ.
ער שטייט לעבן אים.	ער זעט אים.	ער איז דאָ.
ער שטייט לעבן איר.	ער זעט זי.	זי איז דאָ.
ער שטייט לעבן אים.	ער זעט עס.	עס איז דאָ.
ער שטייט לעבן אונדז.	ער זעט אונדז.	מיר זײַנען דאָ.
ער שטייט לעבן אײַך.	ער זעט אײַך.	איר זײַט דאָ.
ער שטייט לעבן זיי.	ער זעט זיי.	זיי זײַנען דאָ.

PREPOSITIONS

PREPOSITIONS THAT DO AND DO NOT FORM CONTRACTIONS WITH דעם (P. 412)

FORM OF ARTICLE	דעם	ם(ע)-	ן-
Prepositions with Article	לעבן דעם	בײַם	איבערן
	צווישן דעם	צום	אונטערן
	וועגן דעם	אינעם	פֿאַרן
	אַרום דעם	פֿונעם	הינטערן
			אויפֿן
			מיטן
			דורכן

NOTES:

- Most prepositions that contract take the ן- ending by default. A final vowel, diphthong, or nonsyllabic *nun* triggers the ם(ע)- ending. A final syllabic *nun* ensures that there will be no contraction.

PREPOSITIONS WITH LOCATIONS AND DESTINATIONS (P. 466)

	Destination	Location
Place	איך גיי אין טעאַטער.	איך בין אין טעאַטער.
Event	איך גיי אויף אַ קאָנצערט.	איך בין אויף אַ קאָנצערט.
Person	איך גיי צו סענדערן.	איך בין בײַ סענדערן.
Home	איך גיי אַהיים.	איך בין אין דער היים.
Work	איך גיי צו דער אַרבעט.	איך בין בײַ דער אַרבעט.

APPENDIX C: GEOGRAPHY SUPPLEMENT

The Yiddish names of some countries and languages were introduced in **קאַפּיטל 1** (see page 50 for a summary). This supplement provides the names of United States states and territories, Canadian provinces and territories, and the languages most commonly studied in the United States (with the exception of those that appear on page 50). The list is alphabetical by Yiddish name. Additional country names can be found on the website.

Yiddish place-names are spelled, where possible, according to Hanan-Michael Bordin's *English-Yiddish Dictionary of Place-Names* (2015).

ערטער PLACES	
United States	**די פֿאַראייניקטע שטאַטן**
Ohio	אָהײַאָ
Iowa	אײַאָווע
Idaho	אײַדאַהאָ
Illinois	אילינוי
Indiana	אינדיאַנע
Alabama	אַלאַבאַמע
Alaska	אַלאַסקע
Oklahoma	אָקלאַהאָמע
Arizona	אַריזאָנע
Oregon	אָרעגאָן
Arkansas	אַרקענסאָ
Georgia	דזשאָרדזשיע
Delaware	דעלאַווער
South Dakota	דרום־דאַקאָטע
South Carolina	דרום־קאַראָלײַנע
Hawaii	האַווײַי
Washington	וואַשינגטאָן
Wyoming	ווײַאָמינג
Wisconsin	וויסקאָנסין
Virginia	ווירדזשיניע
Vermont	ווערמאָנט
Tennessee	טענעסי
Texas	טעקסאַס
Utah	יוטע

ערטער PLACES (continued)	
Louisiana	לויִזיאַנע
Montana	מאָנטאַנע
Massachusetts	מאַסאַטשוסעטס
Maine	מײן
Minnesota	מינעסאָטע
Missouri	מיסורי
Mississippi	מיסיסיפּי
Michigan	מישיגען
West Virginia	מערבֿ־ווירדזשיניע
Maryland	מערילענד
New Jersey	ניו־דזשערסי
New Hampshire	ניו־האַמפּשיר
New York	ניו־יאָרק
New Mexico	ניו־מעקסיקע
Nebraska	נעבראַסקע
Nevada	נעוואַדע
Pennsylvania	פּענסילוואַניע
Florida	פֿלאָרידע
North Dakota	צפֿון־דאַקאָטע
North Carolina	צפֿון־קאַראָלײַנע
Colorado	קאָלאָראַדאָ
California	קאַליפֿאָרניע
Kansas	קאַנזאַס
Connecticut	קאָנעטיקעט
Kentucky	קענטאַקי
Rhode Island	ראָד־אײַלענד

שפּראַכן
LANGUAGES (continued)

Danish	דעניש
Hausa	האַוסע
Dutch	האָלענדיש
Hindi	הינדי
Vietnamese	וויעטנאַמיש
Zulu	זולוסיש
Tamil	טאַמיליש
Thai	טײַלענדיש
Turkish	טערקיש
Czech	טשעכיש
Judeo-Arabic	יאַהודיש
Ladino	לאַדינאָ
Latin	לאַטײַן
Mandarin	מאַנדאַריניש
Egyptian	מיצריש
Navajo	נאַוואַהאָ
Norwegian	נאָרוועגיש
Sanskrit	סאַנסקריטיש
Swahili/Kiswahili	סוואַהיליש
Serbo-Croatian	סערבאָקראָאַטיש
Portuguese	פּאָרטוגעזיש
Farsi	פּערסיש
Finnish	פֿיניש
Catalan	קאַטאַלאַניש
Korean	קאָרעיִש
Swedish	שוועדיש

ערטער
PLACES (continued)

North American U.S. Territories	טעריטאָריעס פֿון די פֿאַראייניקטע שטאַטן
United States Virgin Islands	אַמעריקאַנער בתולה־אינדזלען [פּסולע]
Puerto Rico	פּוערטאָ־ריקאָ

Canadian Provinces	קאַנאַדישע פּראָווינצן
Alberta	אַלבערטע
Ontario	אָנטאַריאָ
British Columbia	בריטיש־קאָלומביע
Manitoba	מאַניטאָבע
New Brunswick	ניו־בראַנזוויק
Newfoundland and Labrador	ניופֿאַונדלענד און לאַבראַדאָר
Nova Scotia	נײַ־שאָטלאַנד
Saskatchewan	סאַסקאַטשעוואַן
Prince Edward Island	פּרינץ עדוואַרד־אינדזל
Quebec	קוועבעק

Canadian Territories	קאַנאַדישע טעריטאָריעס
Yukon	יוקאָן
Nunavut	נונאַוווּט
Northwest Territories	צפֿון־מערבֿ־טעריטאָריעס

שפּראַכן
LANGUAGES

Ojibwa	אָדזשיבוויי
Urdu	אורדו
Indonesian	אינדאָנעזיש
Irish Gaelic	אירישע געליש
Amharic	אַמהאַריש
American Sign Language (ASL)	אַמעריקאַנער שטום־לשון [לאָשן]
Aramaic	אַרמיש [אַראַמיש]
Armenian	אַרמעניש
Bengali/Bangla	בענגאַליש
Greek	גריכיש

VOCABULARY

The vocabulary list provided here contains all of the words that appear in vocabulary overviews at the end of every chapter, as well as other useful words that are used multiple times throughout the book. Only those meanings that are used in this book appear in the vocabulary list. For additional meanings, please refer to a dictionary. (You can find some dictionaries listed in the Bibliography.)

The words from vocabulary overviews are accompanied in the English column by a number or letters indicating the chapter in which they are taught (*AB* = **Alef-beys chapter**; *SC* = **Supplementary chapter**; *CE* = **Classroom expressions list**).

Words that do not use phonetic spelling (such as words of *loshn-koydesh* origin) are followed by their pronunciation, spelled in Yiddish characters and set off in brackets. Words that are not stressed on the penultimate syllable are marked with an accent over the stressed vowel.

Nouns are listed with their gender and plural form. Gender immediately follows the noun, indicated by the appropriate definite article (**דאָס, דער, די**). Plural endings are listed in parentheses after the gender. A long dash (—) indicates that the plural form of a noun is the same as its singular form. A shorter dash preceding a plural ending means that the last letter of the stem is dropped before adding the plural ending; thus, **דירה** (–ות) indicates that the plural of **דירה** is **דירות**. If the stem of the word changes in the plural, the entire plural form is provided. Some nouns appear with a symbol (^) indicating that the noun declines in the accusative and/or dative cases.

Verbs are listed in the infinitive, with any irregular conjugations and irregular participles supplied in parentheses after the verb. When the past tense of a verb is formed with **זײַן**, its participle is preceded by **איז**. Separable prefix verbs appear with an interpoint (·) separating the prefix from the main verb for clarity.

Some adjectives have irregular forms when declined. When applicable, these forms are provided in parentheses after the base form of the adjective.

ABBREVIATIONS	
acc	accusative
adj	adjective
alt.	alternatively
aux	auxiliary
dat	dative
f	feminine
gramm	grammatical
lit.	literally
m	masculine
n	neuter
pl	plural
poss	possessive
pron	pronoun
sg	singular

VOCABULARY: YIDDISH-ENGLISH

א

אַ — a
אַ ביסל — a few; some, a little bit (of)
אָבער — but (2)
אָבֿ [אָוו] — Av (20)
אַדוואָקאַט דער (ן) / אַדוואָקאַטין די (ס) — lawyer (10)
אַדיעקטיוו דער (ן) — adjective (1)
אָדלער דער (ס) — eagle (17)
אָדער — or (1)
אָדר [אָדער] — Adar (20)
אַדרעס דער (ן) — address (3)
אַהיים — homeward (16)
אוגערקע די (ס) — cucumber (13)
אַוואָקאַדאָ דער (ס) — avocado (13)
אַוודאי [אַוואַדע] — of course (6)
אוואַ! — wow!
אָוונט דער (ן) — evening (2)
  אין אָוונט — in the evening (2, 16)
אָוונטברויט דאָס (ן) — supper (13)
אַוועק — gone (6)
אַוועק·זעצן זיך (אַוועקגעזעצט) — to sit down (CE)
אַוועק·לייגן (אַוועקגעלייגט) — to put away, to put down (5)
אויב — if
אויבן [אויבם] — above (13)
אויג דאָס (ן) — eye (11, SC)
אויגוסט — August (20)
אוי־ווײ — oh dear! alas! (2)
אויטאָ דער (ס) — car (21)
אויטאָבוס דער (ן) — bus (21)
אויך — also (2)
אויסגעצייכנט — excellent (CE)
אויסדרוק דער (ן) — expression (1)
אויס·דריקן (אויסגעדריקט) — to express
אויסזען דאָס — looks, appearance (11)
אויס·טאָן (אויסגעטאָן) — to take off (clothing) (SC)
  אויס·טאָן זיך — to get undressed (SC)
אויסטראַליע די — Australia (1)
אויסערגעוויינטלעך — extraordinary (CE)
אויספֿרעג דער (ן) — quiz (6)
  האַלטן אַן אויספֿרעג — to take a quiz (6)
אויס·צירן (אויסגעצירט) — to decorate (SC)
אויס·קלײַבן (אויסגעקליבן) — to choose
אויס·קעמען (אויסגעקעמט) — to comb out (SC)
אויסשטעלונג די (ען) — exhibit (16)

אויס·שפּילן (אויסגעשפּילט) — to win (15)
אויער דער (ן) — ear (SC)
אויף [אַף] — on; at (1, 14)
  אויף אַ קול [קאָל] — aloud, out loud (CE)
  אויף ייִדיש — in Yiddish (CE)
אויפֿ·הערן [אוף] (אויפֿגעהערט) — to stop (doing) (5)
אויפֿ·וואַכן [אוף] (אויפֿגעוואַכט) — to wake up
אויפֿ·כאַפּן זיך [אוף] (אויפֿגעכאַפּט) — to wake up (SC)
אויפֿראַמער דער (ס) / אויפֿראַמערין די (ס) — cleaner (10)
אויפֿ·שטיין [אוף] (איז אויפֿגעשטאַנען) — to get up (SC)
אום — during (in reference to Jewish holidays) (8)
אומגעלומפּערט — clumsy
אומגליק דאָס (ן) — calamity; misfortune
און — and (2)
אונגעריש דאָס — Hungarian (1)
אונגערן דאָס — Hungary (1)
אונדז — us (acc/dat) (11, 14)
אונדזער (אונדזערע) — our (7)
אונטן — below (13)
אונטער — under (14)
אונטערבאַן די (ען) — subway (21)
אונטער·שטרײַכן (אונטערגעשטראָכן / אונטערגעשטרײַכט) — to underline
אוניווערסיטעט די (ן) — university (1)
אות דער (יות) [אָס (אויסיעס)] — letter (of the alphabet)
אוקראַיִניש דאָס — Ukrainian (1)
אוקראַיִנע די — Ukraine (1)
אַז — that; if, when (19)
אַזאַ (אַזעלכע) — a sort of; such a ...
אַזוי — so (6)
  אַזוי ווי — like
  אַזוי פֿיל ... ווי — as much/many ... as
  אָט אַזוי — that's the way
  ווי אַזוי — in what way, how
  פּונקט אַזוי — exactly (CE)
אַזיע די — Asia (1)
אָזערע די (ס) — lake (AB)
אָט — here (with pointing)
  אָט (גייט) — there (goes) (2)
  אָט אַזוי — that's the way
  אָט דער/די/דאָס/דעם — this, these; that, those
אַטאַקירן (אַטאַקירט) — to attack (10)
איבער — over (14)
איבער·בעטן זיך (איבערגעבעטן) — to make up, reconcile (8)

to address someone with **איר** (2) — **אירצן**
eight (3) — **אַכט**
eighty (3) — **אַכציק**
eighteen (3) — **אַכצן**
Elul (20) — **אלול** [עלעל]
Algeria (1) — **אַלזשיריע** די
old (7) — **אַלט**
  I am ... years old (3) — איך בין אַלט ... יאָר
  how old are you? (*informal*) (3) — ווי אַלט ביסטו?
Elijah the Prophet (22) — **אליהו־הנבֿיא** [עליִאָהו־האַנאָווי]
alone; (one)self — **אַליין**
wardrobe (14) — **אַלמער** דער (ס)
all; everyone (*AB*) — **אַלע**
  every day — אַלע טאָג
  every year — אַלע יאָר
  always — אַלע מאָל
everyone (*acc/dat*) — **אַלע(מען)**
everything (*CE*) — **אַלץ**
  still — נאָך אַלץ
to amuse (10) — **אַמוזירן** (אַמוזירט)
God willing — **אם־ירצה־השם** [מירצעשעם]
true (*CE*) — **אמת** [עמעס]
an — **אַן**
without — **אָן**
to analyze (10) — **אַנאַליזירן** (אַנאַליזירט)
pineapple (13) — **אַנאַנאַס** דער (ן)
other (13) — **אַנדער**
  one another — איינער דעם אַנדערן
different (22) — **אַנדערש**
to start (doing) (5) — **אָנ·הייבן** (אָנגעהויבן)
instructions (*CE*) — **אָנווײַזונג** די (ען)
to put on (clothing) (*SC*) — **אָנ·טאָן** (אָנגעטאָן)
  to get dressed (*SC*) — **אָנ·טאָן זיך**
Antarctica (1) — **אַנטאַרקטיק** דער
to flee, to run away — **אַנטלויפֿן** (איז אַנטלאָפֿן)
in front of, across from — **אַנטקעגן**
anthropology (6) — **אַנטראָפּאָלאָגיע** די
to light (15) — **אָנ·צינדן** (אָנגעצונדן)
astronaut (3) — **אַסטראָנויט** דער (ן) / **אַסטראָנויטין** די (ס)
a lot (of) (6) — **אַ סך** [סאַך]
to wipe (*SC*) — **אָפּ·ווישן** (אָפּגעווישט)
  to dry oneself (*SC*) — **אָפּ·ווישן זיך**
optimism — **אָפּטימיזם** דער
optimistic (9) — **אָפּטימיסטיש**
to applaud (10) — **אַפּלאָדירן** (אַפּלאָדירט)
to count off (*SC*) — **אָפּ·ציילן** (אָפּגעציילט)
feedback (*CE*) — **אָפּרוף** דער (ן)

translation — **איבערזעצונג** די (ען)
to repeat (*CE*) — **איבער·חזרן** [איבערכאַזערן] (איבערגעחזרט)
to rewrite — **איבער·שרײַבן** (איבערגעשריבן)
to ignore (10) — **איגנאָרירן** (איגנאָרירט)
idea (*AB*) — **אידעע** די (ס)
so... (*CE*) — **איז...**
Italy (1) — **איטאַליע** די
Italian (1) — **איטאַליעניש** דאָס
egg (13) — **איי** דאָס (ער)
wonderful! — **אײַ־אײַ־אײַ**
  not so great (2) — נישט אַזוי אײַ־אײַ־אײַ
(one's) own — **אייגן** (אייגענע)
before (*SC*) — **איידער**
donkey (17) — **אייזל** דער (ען)
ice cream (2) — **אײַזקרעם** דער
you (*pl; sg formal acc/dat*) (11, 14) — **אײַך**
bent, stooped (7) — **אײַנגעבויגן**
jam, preserves (13) — **אײַנגעמאַכטס** דאָס (ן)
pleasant — **אײַנגענעם**
  very pleased (to meet you) (1) — זייער אײַנגענעם
to divide — **אײַנ·טיילן** (אײַנגעטיילט)
grandchild (9) — **אייניקל** דאָס (עך)
one (3) — **איינס** (איין)
singular (*gramm*) — **איינצאָל** די (ן)
to fall asleep (*SC*) — **אײַנ·שלאָפֿן** (איז אײַנגעשלאָפֿן)
your (*pl; sg formal*) (7) — **אײַער** (אײַערע)
Iyar (20) — **אייר** [איִער]
Europe (1) — **אייראָפּע** די
I (1) — **איך**
him; it (*m acc; m/n dat*) (11, 14) — **אים**
to imitate (10) — **אימיטירן** (אימיטירט)
to improvise (10) — **אימפּראָוויזירן** (אימפּראָוויזירט)
in; at (1, 14) — **אין**
  in the evening (2, 16) — אין אָוונט
  in the morning (2, 16) — אין דער פֿרי
  outside, outdoors (*AB*, 20) — אין דרויסן
  in the middle (13) — אין מיטן
engineering (6) — **אינזשעניריע** די
intellectual (9) — **אינטעלעקטועל**
to interview (10) — **אינטערוויויִרן** (אינטערוויויִרט)
dormitory (1) — **אינטערנאַט** דער (ן)
interesting (6) — **אינטערעסאַנט**
to inspire (10) — **אינספּירירן** (אינספּירירט)
instrument — **אינסטרומענט** דער (ן)
now (2) — **איצט**
you (*pl; sg formal*) (2) — **איר**
her, it (*f dat*) (14) — **איר**
her, its (*f poss adj*) (7) — **איר** (אירע)

אַפּריל	April (20)
אַפֿילו [אַפֿילע]	even (21)
אַפֿיקומן דער (ס) [אַפֿיקוימען]	afikomen (ceremonially hidden piece of matzoh) (22)
אַפֿריקע די	Africa (1)
אפֿשר [עפֿשער]	maybe (6)
אַקוזאַטיוו דער (ן)	accusative (*gramm*) (11)
אָקטאָבער	October (20)
אַקטיאָר דער (ן) / **אַקטריסע** די (ס)	actor (10)
אַקטיוויטעט די (ן)	activity (16)
אַקטריסע די (ס)	actress (10)
אַקסל דער (ען)	shoulder (*SC*)
אַראַביש דאָס	Arabic (1)
אָראַנזש (אָראַנזשן, אָראַנזשענע)	orange (color) (5)
אַראָפּ·פֿאַלן (איז אַראָפּגעפֿאַלן)	to fall (down)
אַרבוז דער (ן)	watermelon (13)
אַרבעט די (ן)	work (10)
אַרבעטן (איך אַרבעט, ער אַרבעט; געאַרבעט)	to work (*AB*, 4)
אַרבעטער דער (ס) / **אַרבעטערין** די (ס)	worker (10)
אָרגאַניזירן (אָרגאַניזירט)	to organize (10)
אַרויס·גיין (פֿון) (איך גיי אַרויס, מיר גייען אַרויס; איז אַרויסגעגאַנגען)	to go out (from) (5)
אַרויס·וואַרפֿן (אַרויסגעוואָרפֿן)	to throw out
אַרויס·נעמען (פֿון) (אַרויסגענומען)	to take out (from) (5)
אַרום	around (14)
אַרומ·רינגלען (אַרומגערינגלט)	to circle
אָרט דער (ערטער)	place, location (16)
אַרטיקל דער (ען)	article
אָריגינעל	original (9)
אַרײַנ·כאַפּן (אַרײַנגעכאַפּט)	to consume hastily
אַרײַנכאַפּן אַ וואָדקע	to take a shot of vodka (6)
אַרײַנ·לייגן (אין) (אַרײַנגעלייגט)	to put in (into) (5)
אַריסטאָקראַטיש	aristocratic (9)
אתרוג דער (ים) [עסרעג (עסרויגים)]	citron (12)

ב

באָב דער (עס)	bean; beans (7)
באָבע^ די (ס)	grandmother (9)
באַגריס־קאַרטל דאָס (עך)	greeting card (8)
באַגריסונג די (ען)	greeting (2)
באַגריסן (באַגריסט)	to greet (8)
באַגריסן זיך	to exchange greetings (2)
באָדן (געבאָדן)	to bathe (*SC*)
באָדקאָסטיום דער (ען)	bathing suit (19)
באַהאַלטן זיך (באַהאַלטן)	to hide
באַטײַט דער (ן)	meaning; significance
באַטראַכטן (באַטראַכט)	to consider
באַל דער (ן)	ball (*AB*)
באַלאַגאַן דער (ען)	mess
באַלד	soon (16)
באַליבטסט	favorite
באַן די (ען)	train (21)
באַנאַנע די (ס)	banana (*AB*, 13)
באַנדאַזשירן (באַנדאַזשירט)	to bandage (10)
באַנק די (בענק)	bench; bank
באַס דער (ן)	bass (instrument)
באַציִונג די (ען)	relationship
באַק די (ן)	cheek (*SC*)
באַקאַנט	famous, known
באַקוועם	comfortable
באַקומען (באַקומען)	to receive (15)
באַקן (געבאַקן / געבאַקט)	to bake (10)
באַקענען זיך (באַקענט)	to get acquainted (1)
באַר די (ן)	pear (*AB*, 11, 13)
באַרג סיני דער [סינײַ]	Mount Sinai (*SC*)
באָרד די (בערד)	beard (11)
באָרשט דער (ן)	borscht, beet soup (13)
באַשטעלן (באַשטעלט)	to order (10)
באַשערן (באַשערט)	to predestine, to foreordain
באַשרײַבן (באַשריבן)	to describe (14)
בהמה די (–ות) [בעהיימע (ס)]	cow (11)
בויך דער (בײַכער)	stomach (*SC*)
בוים דער (ביימער)	tree (*AB*, 7, 17)
בוימל דער (ען)	oil (13)
בויען (איך בוי)	to build (12)
בוך דאָס (ביכער)	book (*AB*, 5)
בולבע די (ס)	potato (2)
בוריק דער (עס)	beet (13)
ביאָלאָגיע די	biology (6)
ביבליאָטעק די (ן)	library (16)
ביבליאָטעקער דער (ס) / **ביבליאָטעקערין** די (ס)	librarian (10)
ביוראָ דאָס (ען)	office (10)
ביז	until (16)
ביטער	bitter (13)
בײַ	by; at; while (14)
בײַ טאָג	during the day (2)
בײַם לעבן	alive (6)
בײַ נאַכט	at night (2, 16)
בייגל דער (—)	bagel (2, 13)
בײַדל דאָס (עך)	hut, cabin; booth
ביידע	both (5)
בייז	angry
בײַטל דאָס (ען)	handbag (19)
בײַסן (געביסן)	to bite (11)
ביכערשאַנק די (...שענק)	bookcase (14)

picture	**בילד** דאָס (ער)
comic strip	**בילדערשטרײַף** דער (ן)
ticket (16)	**בילעט** דער (ן)
bimah (12)	**בימה** די (–ות) [בימע (ס)]
bit (13)	**ביסל** דאָס (עך)
a few; some, a little bit (of) (6)	אַ ביסל
beer (13)	**ביר** דאָס
to blow	**בלאָזן** (געבלאָזן)
to blow shofar (8)	בלאָזן שופֿר
it's windy (*lit.* a wind is blowing) (20)	עס בלאָזט אַ ווינט
leaf, sheet (of paper)	**בלאַט** דער (בלעטער)
blond (11)	**בלאָנד**
blouse (19)	**בלוזקע** די (ס)
blue (5)	**בלוי**
only (17)	**בלויז**
flower (*AB*, 9)	**בלום** די (ען)
to stay (17)	**בלײַבן** [בלײַבם] (איז געבליבן)
pencil (*AB*, 5)	**בלײַער** דער (ס)
cheese-filled crepe (13)	**בלינצע** די (ס)
lightning (20)	**בליץ** דער (ן)
e-mail	**בליצבריוו** דער (—)
to flash	**בליצן**
there are flashes of lightning (20)	עס בליצט
leaf, sheet (of paper) (5)	**בלעטל** דאָס (עך)
building	**בנין** דער (ים) [ביניען (ביניאָנים)]
bed (*AB*)	**בעט** דאָס (ן)
to ask for, to beg	**בעטן** (געבעטן)
boss (11)	**בעל־הבית** דער (בעלי־בתּים) [באַלעבאָס (באַלעבאַטים)]
to bless (4, 15)	**בענטשן**
chair (5)	**בענקל** דאָס (עך)
to yearn (for)	**בענקען** (נאָך)
better; rather (2)	**בעסער**
baker (10)	**בעקער** דער (ס) / **בעקערקע** די (ס)
bear (*AB*, 17)	**בער** דער (ן)
brush (*SC*)	**בערשטל** דאָס (עך)
to brush (*SC*)	**בערשטן** (געבערשט)
blessing	**ברכה** די (–ות) [בראָכע (ס)]
broccoli (13)	**בראָקאָלי** דער
brother (9)	**ברודער** דער (ברידער)
bread (13)	**ברויט** דאָס (ן)
brown (5)	**ברוין**
thank God (2)	**ברוך־השם** [באָרעכאַשעם]
chest; breast (*SC*)	**ברוסט** די (בריסט)
letter (11)	**בריוו** דער (—)
broad, wide (7)	**ברייט**
eyeglasses (11)	**ברילן** די
border; bank, shore	**ברעג** דער (ן)
to vomit (*SC*)	**ברעכן** (געבראָכן)
eyebrow (*SC*)	**ברעם** די (ען)
to bring (10)	**ברענגען** (געברענגט / געבראַכט)
to burn (11)	**ברענען**
during; while (*SC*)	**בשעת** [בעשאַס]

ג

whole; complete (5)	**גאַנץ**
in total; completely	אין גאַנצן
street (1)	**גאַס** די (ן)
guest	**גאַסט** דער (געסט)
to visit	קומען/זײַן צו גאַסט
fork (13)	**גאָפּל** דער (ען)
altogether; entirely; quite; unexpectedly (9)	**גאָר**
nothing (15)	**גאָרניסט**
good; well (2)	**גוט**
(have a) good day (*reply*) (2)	אַ גוטן טאָג (אַ גוט יאָר)
(have a) good Shabbos (*reply*) (4)	אַ גוטן שבת (אַ גוט יאָר)
(have a) good week (*reply*) (4)	אַ גוטע וואָך (אַ גוט יאָר)
good night (2)	אַ גוטע נאַכט
good evening (*after Havdalah*) (4)	גוט־וואָך
happy holiday (8)	גוט־יום־טובֿ [יאָנטעוו]
good morning/afternoon (*reply*) (2)	גוט־מאָרגן (גוט־יאָר)
good evening (*reply*) (2)	גוטן־אָוונט (גוט־יאָר)
good Shabbos (*reply*) (4)	גוט־שבת (גוט־יאָר)
please (*formal/informal*) (*lit.* be so good) (2)	זײַ(ט) אַזוי גוט
golem	**גולם** דער (ס) [גוילעם (ס)]
body (*SC*)	**גוף** דער (ים)
fate, destiny	**גורל** דער (ות) [גוירל (גויראָלעס)]
guitar (*AB*)	**גיטאַרע** די (ס)
to go (by foot) (2)	**גיין** (איך גיי, מיר גייען; איז געגאַנגען)
to go on foot (21)	גיין צו פֿוס
it's raining (20)	עס גייט אַ רעגן
fast (7)	**גיך**
to pour (10)	**גיסן** (געגאָסן)
glass (13)	**גלאָז** די (גלעזער)
smooth; straight (hair) (11)	**גלאַט**
for no particular reason	גלאַט אַזוי
even; straight (7)	**גלײַך**
glass (9)	**גלעזל** דאָס (עך)
geography (1, 6)	**געאָגראַפֿיע** די
commandment	**געבאָט** דאָס (—)
the Ten Commandments (*SC*)	די צען געבאָט
to be born	**געבוירן ווערן** (איז געבוירן געוואָרן)

grapefruit (13)	**גרייפּפֿרוכט** דער (ן)
green (5)	**גרין**
easy, light (in weight) (7)	**גרינג**
vegetable; greenery (13, supplement)	**גרינס** דאָס (ן)

ד

here (5)	**דאָ**
there is/are (6)	עס איז/זײַנען דאָ
to pray (8, 16)	**דאַוונען**
dative (*gramm*) (14)	**דאַטי׳וו** דער (ן)
roof	**דאַך** דער (דעכער)
after all; obviously; yet	**דאָך**
(on) Thursday (2)	**דאָ׳נערשטיק**
gratitude, thanks	**דאַנק** דער (ען)
thank you very much	אַ גרויסן/שיינעם דאַנק
thank you, thanks (2)	אַ דאַנק
the, this (*n nom/acc*) (1, 11)	**דאָס**
doctor (10)	**דאָקטער** דער (דאָקטוירים) / **דאָקטערשע** די (ס)
there, over there	**דאָרטן**
to need; to have to (19)	**דאַרפֿן** (ער דאַרף)
you (*sg informal*) (1)	**דו**
example, model (1)	**דוגמא** די (–ות) [דוגמע (ס)]
thunder (20)	**דונער** דער (ן)
to thunder	**דונערן**
it's thundering (20)	עס דונערט
to address someone with **דו** (2)	**דוצן**
through (14)	**דורך**
the, this (*f nom/acc*) (1, 11); the, these (*pl nom/acc/dat*) (1, 11, 13)	**די**
spirit that possesses a living person	**דיבוק** דער (ים) [דיבעק (דיבו׳קים)]
to digitalize (10)	**דיגיטאַליזירן** (דיגיטאַליזי׳רט)
German (1)	**דײַטש** דאָס
Germany (1)	**דײַטשלאַנד** דאָס
your (*sg informal*) (7)	**דײַן** (דײַנע)
you (*sg informal acc*) (11)	**דיך**
floor (5)	**דיל** דער (ן)
thin (7)	**דין**
(on) Tuesday (2)	**דינסטיק**
to discipline (10)	**דיסציפּלינירן** (דיסציפּליני׳רט)
thick (7)	**דיק**
you (*sg informal dat*) (14)	**דיר**
apartment (1)	**דירה** די (–ות) [דירע (ס)]
the, this (*m acc/dat; n dat*) (11, 13)	**דעם**
then (19)	**דעמאָלט**
December (20)	**דעצעמבער**
to cover (12)	**דעקן**
the, this (*m nom; f dat*) (1, 13)	**דער**

birthday	**געבורטסטאָג** דער (...טעג)
to give (5)	**געבן** [געבם] (איך גיב, דו גיסט; געגעבן)
he takes a look (*CE*)	ער גיט אַ קוק
thought, idea	**געדאַ׳נק** דער (ען)
patience	**געדו׳לד** די
to remember (1)	**געדענקען** (געדע׳נקט)
chopped liver (13)	**געהאַקטע לעבער** די
cloth (13)	**געוואַ׳נט** דאָס (ן)
usually (2)	**געוויינטלעך**
to win	**געווינען** (געוווּנען)
certain, given	**געווי׳ס**
healthy (2)	**געזו׳נט**
good-bye (*formal/informal*) (*lit.* be well) (2)	זײַ(ט) געזו׳נט
bless you! (after sneeze) (*lit.* to health) (*CE*)	צו געזו׳נט!
farewell (2)	**געזע׳גענונג** די (ען)
divided by (3)	**געטיי׳לט אויף**
beverage	**געטראַ׳נק** דאָס (ען)
faithful, loyal	**געטרײַ׳**
yellow (5)	**געל**
money (10)	**געלט** דאָס (ן)
enough	**גענו׳ג**
exercise (6)	**געניטונג** די (ען)
to do an exercise (6)	מאַכן אַ געניטונג
feeling (8)	**געפֿי׳ל** דאָס (ן)
gefilte fish (2)	**געפֿילטע פֿיש** די
to find (13)	**געפֿינען** (געפֿונען)
curly (11)	**געקרײַזלט**
court (10)	**גערי׳כט** דאָס (ן)
right, fair (10)	**גערע׳כט**
history (6)	**געשיכטע** די
tasty (13)	**געשמאַ׳ק**
to happen	**געשע׳ן** (זיי געשעען; איז געשע׳ן)
event	**געשע׳עניש** דאָס (ן)
noisemaker (18)	**גראַגער** דער (ס)
degree	**גראַד** דער (ן)
degree(s) Fahrenheit (20)	גראַד פֿאַ׳רנהײַט
grammatical (11)	**גראַמאַטיש**
gray (5)	**גרוי**
big (7)	**גרויס**
basic (2)	**גרונטיק**
greeting	**גרוס** דער (ן)
my regards (to)... (19)	אַ גרוס...
fried goose/chicken skin (*pl*) (13)	**גרי׳בענעס** די
ready (*CE*)	**גרייט**
to prepare	**גרייטן** (געגרייט)
to set the table (13)	גרייטן צום טיש

hat (11)	**הוט** דער (היט)
house (1)	**הויז** דאָס (הײַזער)
pants (19)	**הויזן** די
shorts (19)	קורצע הייזלעך
high, tall, loud (7)	**הויך**
capital city (1)	**הויפּטשטאָט** די (...שטעט)
humanities (6)	**הומאַניסטיק** די
hungry	**הונגעריק**
(a) hundred (*alt.* one hundred) (3)	**הונדערט**
(may you so live) until 120! (2)	ביז הונדערט און צוואַנציק!
dog (*AB*, 11)	**הונט** דער (הינט)
to cough (*SC*)	**הוסטן** (געהוסט)
appendix (*CE*)	**הוספה** די (–ות) [העסאָפֿע (ס)]
hooray! (*CE*)	**הוראַ!**
cap (11)	**היטל** דאָס (עך)
boiled buckwheat (*pl*) (7)	**הײַדעלעך** די
holy (8)	**הייליק**
to heal, to cure (10)	**היילן**
home (16)	**היים** די (ען)
at home	אין דער היים
homework (6)	**היימאַרבעט** די
to do homework (6)	מאַכן היימאַרבעט
today (4, 6)	**הײַנט**
hot (7)	**הייס**
to be called, named (1)	**הייסן** (געהייסן)
that is (to say) (9)	הייסט דאָס
(so) that means that...	הייסט דאָס אַז...
what's your name? (*informal*) (1)	ווי הייסטו?
sky (20)	**הימל** דער (ען)
behind (14)	**הינטער**
opposite, contrary	**היפּוך** דער (ים) [הייפּעך (היפּוכים)]
fever	**היץ** די (ן)
to have a fever (*SC*)	האָבן היץ
deer (17)	**הירש** דער (ן)
income	**הכנסה** די (–ות) [האַכנאָסע (ס)]
three-cornered filled pastry (18)	**המן־טאַש** דער (ן) [האָמען]
Hebrew (1)	**העברעיִש** דאָס
light (in color) (5)	**העל**
light blue (5)	העל בלוי
stuffed neck of fowl (13)	**העלדזל** דאָס (עך)
elephant (17)	**העלפֿאַנד** דער (ן)
half	**העלפֿט** די (ן)
to help	**העלפֿן** (געהאָלפֿן)
shirt (19)	**העמד** דאָס (ער)
chandelier (14)	**הענגלײַכטער** דער (ס)
to hang (13)	**הענגען** (איז געהאָנגען)
glove (19)	**הענטשקע** די (ס)
adult	**דערוואַקסן** (דערוואַקסענע)
to pass (10)	**דערלאַנגען** (דערלאַנגט)
to mention	**דערמאָנען** (דערמאָנט)
to remember	**דערמאָנען זיך**
then; afterward (16)	**דערנאָך**
experience	**דערפֿאַרונג** די (ען)
(short) story	**דערציילונג** די (ען)
to tell (a story)	**דערציילן** (דערציילט)
to recognize	**דערקענען** (דערקענט)
theater arts (6)	**דראַמאַטורגיע** די
outside, outdoors	**דרויסן**
outside, outdoors (*AB*, 20)	אין דרויסן
south (1)	**דרום** [דאָרעם]
South America (1)	**דרום־אַמעריקע** די
three (3)	**דרײַ**
spinning top (15)	**דריידל** דאָס (עך)
thirty (3)	**דרײַסיק**
to spin, to turn (15)	**דרייען**
thirteen (3)	**דרײַצן**
stapler (5)	**דרעטלער** דער (ס)
	ה
habitat (17)	**האַביטאַט** דער (ן)
to have (3)	**האָבן** [האָבם] (איך האָב, דו האָסט; געהאַט)
hare	**האָז** דער (ן)
half	**האַלב**
thirty minutes to (nine) (16)	האַלב (נײַן)
midnight (16)	האַלבע נאַכט
noon (16)	האַלבער טאָג
half-brother (9)	**האַלבער ברודער** דער (האַלבע ברידער)
half-sister (9)	**האַלבע שוועסטער** די (האַלבע שוועסטער)
to hold	**האַלטן** (איך האַלט, מיר האַלטן; געהאַלטן)
to take a quiz, exam (6)	האַלטן אַן אויספֿרעג, עקזאַמען
to give a presentation (6)	האַלטן אַ רעפֿעראַט
what time is it? (16)	וויפֿל האַלט דער זייגער?
hand; arm (*SC*)	**האַנט** די (הענט)
towel (19, *SC*)	**האַנטעך** דער (ער)
honey (13)	**האָניק** דער
hope	**האָפֿענונג** די (ען)
hair (*pl*) (11)	**האָר** די
lord (11)	**האַר** דער (ן)
fall (20)	**האַרבסט** דער (ן)
hard, stiff (7)	**האַרט**
hora (dance)	**האָרע** די (ס)
Havdalah (4)	**הבֿדלה** די (–ות) [האַוודאָלע (ס)]
Haggadah (22)	**הגדה** די (–ות) [האַגאָדע (ס)]
to read from the Haggadah (22)	זאָגן די הגדה

notebook (5)	**העפֿט** די (ן)
Mr.	**הער**
herring (2, 13)	**הערינג** דער (—)
to hear (2)	**הערן**

וו

vodka	**וואָדקע** די (ס)
to take a shot of vodka (6)	אַרײַנכאַפּן אַ וואָדקע
vase (14)	**וואַזע** די (ס)
week (2, 4)	**וואָך** די (ן)
last week (17)	פֿאַרגאַנגענע וואָך
forest (11, 17)	**וואַלד** דער (וועלדער)
wolf (17)	**וואָלף** דער (וועלף)
cloud (20)	**וואָלקן** דער (ס)
cloudy (20)	**וואָלקנדיק**
wall (5)	**וואַנט** די (ווענט)
bath (*SC*)	**וואַנע** די (ס)
moustache (*pl*) (11)	**וואָנצעס** די
what (1); that	**וואָס**
how are you? (*informal*) (2)	וואָס מאַכסטו?
what kind of	וואָס פֿאַר אַ
why (5)	פֿאַר וואָס
which (1)	**וואָסער** (וואָסערע)
water (*AB*, 11)	**וואַסער** דאָס (ן)
stream (17)	**וואַסערל** דאָס (עך)
vocabulary (2)	**וואָקאַבולאַר** דער (ן)
vacation (10)	**וואַקאַציע** די (ס)
to grow (17)	**וואַקסן** (איז געוואַקסן)
word (1)	**וואָרט** דאָס (ווערטער)
to wait (15)	**וואַרטן** (געוואַרט)
warm (20)	**וואַרעם**
sink (*SC*)	**וואַשטיש** דער (ן)
to wash (*SC*)	**וואַשן** (געוואַשן)
bathroom (*SC*)	**וואַשצימער** דער (ן)
where (1)	**וווּ**
place of residence (1)	**וווינאָרט** דער (וווינערטער)
to live, reside (1)	**וווינען**
how (1)	**ווי**
in what way, how	ווי אַזוי׳
what's your name? (*informal*) (1)	ווי הייסטו?
how does one say ... in Yiddish? (1)	ווי זאָגט מען ... אויף ייִדיש?
like, as; than (7)	**ווי**
like	אַזוי׳ ווי
lullaby	**וויגליד** דאָס (ער)
rocking chair (14)	**וויגשטול** דער (ן)
again, anew	**ווידער**
once again	ווידער אַ מאָל
wife; woman (9)	**ווײַב** דאָס (ער)
to show	**ווײַזן** (געוויזן)
to point to (5)	ווײַזן אויף
far (from) (1)	**ווײַט** (פֿון)
to hurt, ache (*SC*)	**וויי טאָן** (עס טוט וויי; עס האָט וויי געטאָן)
further; again (15)	**ווײַטער**
subsequent; additional (3)	**ווײַטערדיק**
soft (7)	**ווייך**
because (10)	**ווײַל**
wine (4, 13)	**ווײַן** דער (ען)
grape (13)	**ווײַנטרויב** די (ן)
few; little (*SC*)	**ווייניק**
less (than) (6)	**ווייניקער** (ווי)
to cry (2)	**וויינען**
white (5)	**ווײַס**
Belarussian (1)	**ווײַסרוסיש** דאָס
Belarus (1)	**ווײַסרוסלאַנד** דאָס
important (10)	**וויכטיק**
wind (20)	**ווינט** דער (ן)
it's windy (*lit.* a wind is blowing) (20)	עס בלאָזט אַ ווינט
winter (20)	**ווינטער** דער (ן)
to wish (8, 11)	**ווינטשן** (געווונטשן)
corner	**ווינקל** דער (ען)
to know (1)	**וויסן** (איך ווייס, מיר ווייסן; געוווּסט)
how shall I put it?	כ׳ווייס?
how many; how much (3)	**וויפֿל**
(at) what time . . . (16)	וויפֿל אַ זייגער...
what time is it? (16)	וויפֿל האַלט דער זייגער?
road; way	**וועג** דער (ן)
about (6)	**וועגן**
weather (20)	**וועטער** דער (ן)
meteorologist, weather forecaster	**וועטער־נבֿיא** דער (ים) [...־נאָווי (...־נעוויִים)]
will (*future tense aux*) (21)	**וועל** (איך וועל, דו וועסט)
bicycle (21)	**וועלאָסיפּעד** דער (ן)
world (6)	**וועלט** די (ן)
in the world	אויף דער וועלט
in the world to come (6)	אויף יענער וועלט
which	**וועלכער** (וועלכע, וועלכעס)
to want (19)	**וועלן** (ער וויל; געוואָלט)
whom (11)	**וועמען**
whose (7)	**וועמענס**
when	**ווען**
vest (19)	**וועסט** דער (ן)
alarm clock (*SC*)	**וועקער** דער (ס)
who (1)	**ווער**

very (1)	**זייער**
very pleased (to meet you) (1)	זייער אײַנגענעם
their (7)	**זייער** (זייערע)
soap (*SC*)	**זייף** די (ן)
oneself (*reflexive pron*) (10)	**זיך**
certainly	**זיכער**
to sing (2)	**זינגען** (געזונגען)
singer (3, 10)	**זינגער** דער (ס) / **זינגערין** די (ס)
sin (8)	**זינד** די (—)
sweet (13)	**זיס**
to sit (2, 13)	**זיצן** (איז געזעסן)
sixty (3)	**זעכציק**
sixteen (3)	**זעכצן**
same	**זעלבער**
rare	**זעלטן** (זעלטענע)
to see (3)	**זען** (איך זע, מיר זעען; געזען)
to set (13)	**זעצן**
six (3)	**זעקס**
frog (17)	**זשאַבע** די (ס)
journalist (10)	**זשורנאַליסט** דער (ן) / **זשורנאַליסטקע** די (ס)
so; then (*emphasis*) (16)	**זשע**

ח

friend (2)	**חבֿר** דער (ים) [כאַווער (כאַווײרים)]
friend (*f*) (2)	**חבֿרטע** די (ס) [כאַווערטע (ס)]
month (12, 20)	**חודש** דער (חדשים) [כוידעש (כאַדאָשים)]
wedding canopy; wedding	**חופּה** די (–ות) [כופּע (ס)]
except, besides	**חוץ**
catastrophe; the Holocaust (18)	**חורבן** דער [כורבם]
cantor	**חזן** דער (ים) [כאַזן (כאַזאָנים)]
animal (17)	**חיה** די (–ות) [כײַע (ס)]
challah (4)	**חלה** די (–ות) [כאַלע (ס)]
dream	**חלום** דער (ות) [כאָלעם (כאַלוימעס)]
to dream	**חלומען** [כאָלעמען]
God forbid (21)	**חלילה** [כאָלילע]
to faint (*SC*)	**חלשן** [כאַלעשן]
leavening; leavened food (22)	**חמץ** דער [כאָמעץ]
Hanukkah (15)	**חנוכּה** דער [כאַניקע]
money (or chocolate coins) given to children on Hanukkah (15)	**חנוכּה־געלט** דאָס [כאַניקע־...]
nine-branched candelabrum lit on Hanukkah (15)	**חנוכּה־לאָמפּ** דער (ן) [כאַניקע־...]
charoseth (sweet paste of fruit and nuts) (22)	**חרוסת** דאָס [כרויסעס]
Heshvan (20)	**חשוון** [כעזשוון]
wedding (9)	**חתונה** די (–ות) [כאַסענע (ס)]
to get married	חתונה האָבן (געהאַט)
bridegroom (9)	**חתן** דער (ים) [כאָסן (כאַסאַנים)]

verb (1)	**ווערב** דער (ן)
dictionary (5)	**ווערטערבוך** דאָס (ווערטערביכער)
to become (17)	**ווערן** (איז געוואָרן)

ז

to say; to tell (1)	**זאָגן**
I should be so lucky	אויף מיר געזאָגט
how does one say ... in Yiddish? (1)	ווי זאָגט מען ... אויף ייִדיש?
to read from the Haggadah (22)	זאָגן די הגדה
thing (17)	**זאַך** די (ן)
should (19)	**זאָלן** (ער זאָל)
let it be...	זאָל זײַן...
salt (13)	**זאַלץ** די (ן)
salty (13)	**זאַלציק**
juice (13)	**זאַפֿט** דער (ן)
juicy (13)	**זאַפֿטיק**
sentence (5)	**זאַץ** דער (ן)
sock (19)	**זאָק** דער (ן)
worry (6)	**זאָרג** די (ן)
to worry	**זאָרגן**
sour (13)	**זויער**
pickle (13)	**זויערע אוגערקע** די (ס)
to search (for)	**זוכן**
summer (20)	**זומער** דער (ן)
freckle (11)	**זומער־שפּרענקל** דאָס (עך)
sun (20)	**זון** די (ען)
the sun is shining (20)	עס שײַנט די זון
son (9)	**זון** דער (זין)
sunglasses (19)	**זונברילן** די
(on) Sunday (2)	**זונטיק**
she, it; her, it (*f nom/acc*) (1, 11)	**זי**
seven (3)	**זיבן** [זיבם]
seventy (3)	**זיבעציק**
seventeen (3)	**זיבעצן**
they; them (*nom/acc/dat*) (2, 11, 14)	**זיי**
clock (5)	**זייגער** דער (ס)
o'clock (16)	אַ זייגער
(at) what time . . . (16)	וויפֿל אַ זייגער...
what time is it? (16)	וויפֿל האַלט דער זייגער?
grandfather (9)	**זיידע^** דער (ס)
page (*CE*); side	**זײַט** די (ן)
to be (3)	**זײַן** (איך בין, דו ביסט, ער איז, מיר זײַנען, איר זײַט, זיי זײַנען; איז געווען; זײַ, זײַט)
please (*formal/informal*) (*lit.* be so good) (2)	זײַ(ט) אַזוי גוט
good-bye (*formal/informal*) (*lit.* be well) (2)	זײַ(ט) געזונט
his; its (*m/n poss adj*) (7)	**זײַן** (זײַנע)

ט

so (16)	טאָ
day (2)	טאָג דער (טעג)
during the day (2)	בײַ טאָג
noon (16)	האַלבער טאָג
daily, everyday	טאָג־טעגלעך
board (5)	טאָוול דער (ען)
father (9)	טאַטע^ דער (ס)
daughter (9)	טאָכטער די (טעכטער)
to do (2)	טאָן (איך טו, מיר טוען; געטאָן)
tango	טאַנגאָ דער (ס)
to dance (2)	טאַנצן
taxi (21)	טאַקסי דער (ס)
indeed, really (*CE*, 9)	טאַקע
to not be allowed to (19)	טאָרן: נישט טאָרן (ער טאָר נישט)
Tevet (20)	טבֿת [טייוועס]
(a) thousand (*alt.* one thousand) (3)	טויזנט
death (8)	טויט דער (ן)
tulip (9)	טולפּאַן דער (ען)
dark (in color) (5)	טונקל (טונקעלע)
dark blue (5)	טונקל בלוי
tea (*AB*, 13)	טיי די (ען)
to kill (11)	טייטן (געטייט)
meaning	טײַטש דער (ן)
river (17)	טײַך דער (ן)
part, portion	טייל דער (ן)
dear (8)	טײַער
kerchief (11)	טיכל דאָס (עך)
deep	טיף
door (5)	טיר די (ן)
table (5)	טיש דער (ן)
to set the table (13)	גרייטן צום טיש
tablecloth (13)	טישטעך דער (ער)
theater (16)	טעאַטער דער (ס)
television set (14)	טעלעוויזאָר דער (טעלעוויזאָרן)
television (programming) (10)	טעלעוויזיע די
telepathic (9)	טעלעפּאַטיש
telephone number (3)	טעלעפֿאָן־נומער דער (ן)
plate (13)	טעלער דער (—)
saucer (13)	טעלערל דאָס (עך)
dancer (3)	טענצער דער (ס) / טענצערין די (ס)
pot (9); cup (13)	טעפּל דאָס (עך)
carpet, rug (14)	טעפּעך דער (ער)
deadline	טערמין דער (ען)
Turkey (1)	טערקײַ די
to wear; to carry (11)	טראָגן (געטראָגן)
to think, reflect	טראַכטן (געטראַכט)
streetcar, trolley (21)	טראַמווײַ דער (ען)
sadness	טרויער דער
sad (7)	טרויעריק
strawberry (13)	טרוסקאַפֿקע די (ס)
dry (20)	טרוקן (טרוקענע)
to drink (2)	טרינקען (געטרונקען)
meeting (10)	טרעפֿונג די (ען)
to guess	טרעפֿן (געטראָפֿן)
to meet up (3, 16)	טרעפֿן זיך (געטראָפֿן)
tear	טרער די (ן)
Shabbos stew (often with meat, potato, beans) (13)	טשאָלנט דער (ן)
suitcase (19)	טשעמאָדאַן דער (ען)
turtle (17)	טשערעפּאַכע די (ס)

י

yes (1)	יאָ
January (20)	יאַנואַר
jasmine (9)	יאַסמין דער (ען)
Japan (1)	יאַפּאַן דאָס
Japanese (1)	יאַפּאַניש דאָס
year (8)	יאָר דאָס (ן)
I am ... years old (3)	איך בין אַלט ... יאָר
bless you! (after third sneeze) (*lit.* to long years) (*CE*)	צו לאַנגע יאָר!
yarmulke, kippah (11)	יאַרמלקע די (ס)
lizard (17)	יאַשטשערקע די (ס)
(chicken) soup, broth (13)	יויך די (ן)
July (20)	יולי
holiday (8)	יום־טובֿ דער (ים) [יאָנטעוו (יאָנטויווים)]
happy holiday (8)	גוט־יום־טובֿ
Yom Kippur ("day of atonement") (8)	יום־כּיפּור דער [יאָם־קיפּער]
young (7)	יונג
June (20)	יוני
memorial book for a destroyed Jewish community (18)	יזכּור־בוך דאָס (...־ביכער) [ייִסקער]
Jew	ייִד דער (ן)
Jewish (13); Yiddish	ייִדיש
Yiddish (1)	ייִדיש דאָס
in Yiddish (*CE*)	אויף ייִדיש
Jewish studies (6)	ייִדישע לימודים די
boy (4)	ייִנגל דאָס (עך)
younger (than) (3)	ייִנגער (פֿון)
well done!, congratulations!	יישר־כּוח [יאַשער־קויעך]
sea, ocean	ים דער (ען) [יאַם (ען)]
the Days of Awe (Rosh Hashanah through Yom Kippur) (8)	ימים־נוראָים די [יאָמים־נעראָיִם]
each, every (7)	יעדער

purple (*invariable*) (5)	**לילאַ**
lily (9)	**ליליע** די (ס)
(field of) study (6)	**לימוד** דער (ים) [לימעד (לימודים)]
lemon (13)	**לימענע** די (ס)
linguistics (6)	**לינגוויסטיק** די
(to the) left	**לינקס**
(on the) left (7, 13)	(אויף) לינקס
lip (*SC*)	**ליפּ** די (ן)
in honor of	**לכּבֿוד** [לעקאָוועד]
for example (*CE*)	**למשל** [לעמאָשל]
near (14)	**לעבן** [לעבם]
to live	**לעבן** [לעבם]
life (6)	**לעבן** דאָס (ס) [לעבם]
alive (6)	בײַם לעבן
bless you! (after second sneeze) (*lit.* to life) (*CE*)	צום לעבן!
spoon (13)	**לעפֿל** דער (—)
teaspoon (13)	**לעפֿעלע** דאָס (ך)
recently (17)	**לעצטנס**
to lick (*SC*)	**לעקן**
lesson (6); lecture (16)	**לעקציע** די (ס)
to teach (6)	**לערנען**
to learn (10)	**לערנען זיך**
teacher (2, 5)	**לערער** דער (ס) / **לערערין** די (ס)
to extinguish (11)	**לעשן** (געלאָשן)
Rosh Hashanah greeting card (8)	**לשנה־טובֿה** די (–ות) [לעשאָנע־טויווע (ס)]
may you be inscribed (and sealed) for a good year! (8)	**לשנה טובֿה תּכּתבֿו (ותּחתמו)!** [לעשאָנע טויווע טיקאָסייווו (וועסעכאָסיימו)]

מ

cell phone (3)	**מאָבילקע** די (ס)
modal (*gramm*) (19)	**מאָדאַל**
strange	**מאָדנע**
style, fashion	**מאָדע** די (ס)
fashionable, in style	אין דער מאָדע
motorcycle (21)	**מאָטאָציקל** דער (ען)
to motivate (10)	**מאָטיווירן** (מאָטיווירט)
mathematics (3, 6)	**מאַטעמאַטיק** די
material (13)	**מאַטעריאַל** דער (ן)
food, dish (13)	**מאכל** דאָס (ים) [מײַכל (מײַכאָלים)]
to make, to do	**מאַכן**
how are you? (*informal*) (*lit.* what are you doing?) (2)	וואָס מאַכסטו?
to do an exercise (6)	מאַכן אַ געניטונג
to do homework (6)	מאַכן היימאַרבעט

that; the other	**יענער**
in the world to come (6)	אויף יענער וועלט
Israel (1)	**ישׂראל** דאָס [ייִסראָעל]

כּ

Kislev (20)	**כּיסלו** [קיסלעוו]
bride (9)	**כּלה** די (–ות) [קאַלע (ס)]
as long as	**כּל־זמן** [קאָל־זמאַן]
utensil, dish	**כּלי** די (ם) [קיילע (קיילים)]
almost (*CE*)	**כּמעט** [קימאַט]
atonement ceremony performed the day before Yom Kippur (*pl*)	**כּפּרות** די [קאַפּאָרעס]
to perform a ritual in which sins are transferred onto a live chicken by swinging it around one's head (8)	שלאָגן כּפּרות

כ

sly	**כיטרע**
China (1)	**כינע** די
Chinese (1)	**כינעזיש** דאָס
chemistry (6)	**כעמיע** די
horseradish (22)	**כריין** דער

ל

latke, (potato) pancake (13)	**לאַטקע** די (ס)
to laugh (2)	**לאַכן**
let's (3)	**לאָמיר**
lamp (5)	**לאָמפּ** דער (ן)
long (7)	**לאַנג**
country (1)	**לאַנד** דאָס (לענדער)
salmon, lox (13)	**לאַקס** דער (ן)
noodle (13)	**לאָקש** דער (ן)
ponytail (11)	**לאָשיק־עקל** דאָס (עך)
forgive the comparison	**להבֿדיל** [לעהאַוודל]
according to (5)	**לויט**
to run (2)	**לויפֿן** (איז געלאָפֿן)
lulov (12)	**לולבֿ** דער (ים) [לולעוו (לולאָווים)]
to like, to love (10)	**ליב האָבן** (איך האָב ליב; ליב געהאַט)
to lie (13)	**ליגן** (איז געלעגן)
song; poem (*AB*, 2)	**ליד** דאָס (ער)
Lithuanian (1)	**ליטוויש** דאָס
Lithuania (1)	**ליטע** די
literature (6)	**ליטעראַטור** די
lion (17)	**לייב** דער (ן)
to place, to lay (down) (5, 13)	**לייגן**
to go to bed (*SC*)	לייגן זיך שלאָפֿן
easy, light (in weight) (7)	**לײַכט**
to read (2)	**לייענען**
bright (20)	**ליכטיק**
candle (15)	**ליכט** דאָס (עך)

with (2, 14) — **מיט**
- with the greatest pleasure (2) — מיטן גרעסטן פֿאַרגעניגן

lunch (13) — **מיטאָג** דער (ן)
- in the afternoon (16) — נאָך מיטאָג
- p.m. (16) — נ״מ (נאָך מיטאָג)
- a.m. (16) — פֿ״מ (פֿאַר מיטאָג)

to bring along — **מיט·ברענגען** (מיטגעברענגט / מיטגעבראַכט)

(on) Wednesday (2) — **מיטוואָך**

roommate — **מיטוווינער** דער (ס) / **מיטוווינערין** די (ס)

middle, center — **מיטן** דער (ס)
- in the middle (13) — אין מיטן

May (20) — **מײַ**

girl (*AB*, 4) — **מיידל** דאָס (עך)

my (7) — **מײַן** (מײַנע)

to mean (1) — **מיינען**
- I believe so (6) — איך מיין אַז יאָ
- I don't believe so (6) — איך מיין אַז ניין
- what does ... mean? (1) — וואָס מיינט ... ?
- to think that (6) — מיינען אַז

me (*acc*) (11) — **מיך**

anyway; so be it — **מילא** [מיילע]

milk (13) — **מילך** די

of (or including) dairy (13) — **מילכיק**

gender (*gramm*) (11); kind, sort — **מין** דער (ים)

custom (18) — **מינהג** דער (ים) [מינעג (מינהאָגים)]

minute — **מינוט** די (ן)
- (twenty) minutes past (nine) (16) — (צוואַנציק) מינוט נאָך (נײַן)
- (five) minutes to (nine) (16) — (פֿינף) מינוט צו (נײַן)

minus (3) — **מינוס**

commandment; good deed (8) — **מיצווה** די (מיצוות) [מיצווע (ס)]

we (2) — **מיר**

me (*dat*) (14) — **מיר**

angel — **מלאך** דער (מלאָכים) [מאַלעך (מאַלאָכים)]

angel of death — **מלאך־המוות** דער [מאַלעכאַמאָוועס]

queen — **מלכּה** די (–ות) [מאַלקע (ס)]

to agree (6) — **מסכּים זײַן** [מאַסקעם] (איך בין מסכּים; מסכּים געווען)

probably (6) — **מסתּמא** [מיסטאָמע]

furniture (14) — **מעבל** דאָס

possible — **מעגלעך**

possibility — **מעגלעכקייט** די (ן)

may (19) — **מעגן** (ער מעג)

medicine — **מעדיצין** די (ען)

metal (13) — **מעטאַל** דער (ן)

flour (13) — **מעל** די

time — **מאָל** דאָס (—)
- always — אַלע מאָל
- sometimes, at one time (9) — אַ מאָל
- three times four (3) — דרײַ מאָל פֿיר
- once again — ווידער אַ מאָל
- at once; suddenly — מיט אַ מאָל
- again (*CE*) — נאָך אַ מאָל
- never (17) — קיין מאָל נישט

raspberry (13) — **מאַלינע** די (ס)

monkey (17) — **מאַלפּע** די (ס)

meal (13) — **מאָלצײַט** דער (ן)

mother, mom (9) — **מאַמע^** די (ס)

polenta, corn mush (13) — **מאַמעליגע** די

husband; man (9) — **מאַן** דער (מענער)

(on) Monday (2) — **מאָנטיק**

coat (*AB*, 19) — **מאַנטל** דער (ען)

to massage (10) — **מאַסאַזשירן** (מאַסאַזשירט)

masculine (*gramm*) — **מאַסקולין**

orange (fruit) (13) — **מאַראַנץ** דער (ן)

Morocco (1) — **מאַראָקאָ** דאָס

tomorrow (6) — **מאָרגן**

daisy (9) — **מאַרגעריטקע** די (ס)

March (20) — **מאַרץ**

marzipan (7) — **מאַרצעפּאַן** דער (עס)

market — **מאַרק** דער (מערק)

scroll; any of the five Biblical books designated as such (18) — **מגילה** די (–ות) [מעגילע (ס)]

museum (16) — **מוזיי** דער (ען)

music (6) — **מוזיק** די

musician (10) — **מוזיקער** דער (ס) / **מוזיקערין** די (ס)

must (19) — **מוזן** (ער מוז)

to forgive — **מוחל זײַן** [מויכל] (מוחל געווען)
- (I'm) sorry; excuse me (*formal/informal*) (2) — זײַ(ט) (מיר) מוחל

mouth (*SC*) — **מויל** דאָס (מײַלער)

aunt (9) — **מומע** די (ס)

to be afraid (of) — **מורא האָבן** (פֿאַר) [מוירע] (איך האָב מורא; מורא געהאַט)

luck — **מזל** דאָס [מאַזל]
- good luck! — זאָל זײַן מיט מזל

congratulations! (11) — **מזל־טובֿ!** [מאַזל־טאָוו]

prayer book for the Days of Awe (8) — **מחזור** דער (ים) [מאַכזער (מאַכזוירים)]

coin (15) — **מטבע** די (ות) [מאַטבייע (ס)]

ugly (7) — **מיאוס** [מיִעס]

tired (2) — **מיד**

east (1) — **מיזרח** [מיזרעך]

melon (13)	מעלאָן דער (ען)
one; they (*impersonal pron*) (1)	מען (מע)
person (8, 11)	מענטש דער (ן)
knife (13)	מעסער דער (ס)
eraser (5)	מעקער דער (ס)
more (than) (6)	מער (ווי)
carrot (13)	מער די (ן)
west (1)	מערבֿ [מײַרעוו]
to multiply, to increase	מערן
plural (*gramm*)	מערצאָל די (ן)
story (15)	מעשה די (–ות) [מײַסע (ס)]
matzoh (2, 22)	מצה די (–ות) [מאַצע (ס)]
Egypt	מצרים דאָס [מיצראַיִם]
the Messiah (22)	משיח דער (ים) [מעשיִעך (מעשיכים)]
family (4, 9)	משפּחה די (–ות) [מישפּאָכע (ס)]

נ

here!, here you go	נאַ
nail (*SC*)	נאָגל דער (נעגל)
November (20)	נאָוועמבער
nose (*SC*)	נאָז די (נעזער)
natural science (6)	נאַטור־וויסנשאַפֿט די
naïve (9)	נאַיִוו
still, yet; more; another, additional (6)	נאָך
still	נאָך אַלץ
again (*CE*)	נאָך אַ מאָל
not yet	נאָך נישט
after (6)	נאָך
afterwards	נאָך דעם
in the afternoon (16)	נאָך מיטאָג
after (*SC*)	נאָך דעם ווי
to repeat (another's words) (*CE*)	נאָכ·זאָגן (נאָכגעזאָגט)
night (2)	נאַכט די (נעכט)
at night (2, 16)	בײַ נאַכט
midnight (16)	האַלבע נאַכט
to copy (written text)	נאָכ·שרײַבן (נאָכגעשריבן)
nominative (*gramm*) (9)	נאָמינאַטיוו דער (ן)
name (3)	נאָמען דער (נעמען)
wet (20)	נאַס
near (to) (1)	נאָענט (צו)
neck (*SC*)	נאַקן דער (ס)
only; but (6)	נאָר
fool	נאַר דער (נאַראָנים)
foolish (7)	נאַריש
hole, den	נאָרע די (ס)
daffodil (9)	נאַרציס דער (ן)
prophet	נבֿיא דער (ים) [נאָווי (נעוויִים)]
prophet (*f*)	נבֿיאה די (–ות) [נעוויִע (ס)]
well (*interjection*) (2)	נו
well, all right (2)	נו, גוט
boring (6)	נודנע
zero (3)	נול
number; issue (of a periodical)	נומער דער (ן)
nut (13)	נוס (ניס)
useful (1)	נוציק
low (7)	נידעריק
new (7)	נײַ
necessary	נייטיק
neuter (*gramm*)	נייטראַל
New Year (8)	נײַיאָר דער
no (1)	ניין
nine (3)	נײַן
ninety (3)	נײַנציק
nineteen (3)	נײַנצן
to sew (10)	נייען
to sneeze (*SC*)	ניסן (געניאָסן)
Nisan (20)	ניסן [ניסן]
to use (5)	ניצן
not (2)	נישט
absent (5)	נישטאָ
she is not here (5)	זי איז נישטאָ
there isn't/aren't any ... (6)	עס איז/זײַנען נישטאָ קיין ...
you're welcome; no problem (2)	נישטאָ פֿאַר וואָס
not bad (2); no problem	נישקשה [נישקאָשע]
miracle (15)	נס דער (ים) [נעס (ניסים)]
trip, voyage	נסיעה די (–ות) [נעסיִע (ס)]
poor thing! alas! (2)	נעבעך
yesterday (6)	נעכטן
to take (5)	נעמען (גענומען)
fog (20)	נעפּל דער (ען)
foggy (20)	נעפּלדיק

ס

Saudi Arabia (1)	סאַוד־אַראַביע די
sonata	סאָנאַטע די (ס)
sandal (19)	סאַנדאַל דער (ן)
sofa (14)	סאָפֿע די (ס)
social science (6)	סאָציאַל־וויסנשאַפֿט די
sociology (6)	סאָציאָלאָגיע די
what a...	סאַראַ...
seder; order (22)	סדר דער (ים) [סיידער (סדאָרים)]
to hold or take part in a seder (22)	פּראַווען אַ סדר
noun (8)	סובסטאַנטיוו דער (ן)
secret; mystery	סוד דער (ות) [סאָד (סוידעס)]
sweater (19)	סוועטער דער (ס)
sukkah (12)	סוכּה די (–ות) [סוקע (ס)]

to finish (*CE*)	**ענדיקן**
enthusiastic (9)	**ענטוזיאַסטיש**
answer, reply (2)	**ענטפֿער** דער (ס)
to answer, to respond (to) (2)	**ענטפֿערן**
similar	**ענלעך**
it (*n nom/acc*) (1, 11)	**עס**
essay (6)	**עסיי** דער (ען)
vinegar (13)	**עסיק** דער
to eat (2)	**עסן** (געגעסן)
food (13)	**עסן** דאָס (ס)
food	**עסנוואַרג** דאָס
apple (*AB*, 13)	**עפּל** דער (—)
something (19)	**עפּעס**
I have a question (*lit.* I want to ask something) (1)	איך וויל עפּעס פֿרעגן
to open (5)	**עפֿענען** (איך עפֿן, מיר עפֿענען)
(piece of) advice	**עצה** די (–ות) [אייצע (ס)]
economics (6)	**עקאָנאָמיק** די
exam (6)	**עקזאַמען** דער (ס)
to take an exam (6)	האַלטן אַן עקזאַמען
he, it (*m*) (1)	**ער**
airplane (21)	**עראָפּלאַן** דער (ען)
worse	**ערגער**
serious (8)	**ערנסט**
first (15)	**ערשט**
for the first time	צום ערשטן מאָל
at first	צו ערשט

פּ

side lock (11)	**פּאה** די (–ות) [פּייע (ס)]
peacock (17)	**פּאַווע** די (ס)
position (13)	**פּאָזיציע** די (ס)
political science; politics (6)	**פּאָליטיק** די
shelf (14)	**פּאָליצע** די (ס)
tomato (13)	**פּאָמידאָר** דער (ן)
slow (7)	**פּאַמעלעך**
passenger (2)	**פּאַסאַזשיר** דער (ן)
appropriate	**פּאַסיק**
belt (19)	**פּאַסיק** דער (עס)
event	**פּאַסירונג** די (ען)
to fit, to suit; to match	**פּאַסן**
poet (*AB*)	**פּאָעט** דער (ן)
parrot (*AB*)	**פּאַפּוגײַ** דער (ען)
paper (9, 13)	**פּאַפּיר** דאָס (ן)
partner (9)	**פּאַרטנער** דער (ס) / **פּאַרטנערין** די (ס)
neutral (neither dairy nor meat) (13)	**פּאַרעווע**
to perfume (10)	**פּאַרפֿומירן** (פּאַרפֿומירט)
porcelain (13)	**פּאָרצעלײַ** דאָס
park (2, 16, *AB*)	**פּאַרק** דער (ן)

Sukkos (12)	**סוכּות** דער [סוקעס]
end (12)	**סוף** דער (ן) [סאָף]
at the end (of)	בײַם סוף (פֿון)
finally	צום סוף
weekend (19)	**סוף־וואָך** דער (ן) [סאָף־...]
station	**סטאַנציע** די (ס)
student (1)	**סטודענט** דער (ן) / **סטודענטקע** די (ס)
ceiling (5)	**סטעליע** די (ס)
stanza (15)	**סטראָפֿע** די (ס)
reason	**סיבה** די (–ות) [סיבע (ס)]
prayer book	**סידור** דער (ים) [סידער (סידורים)]
Sivan (20)	**סיון** [סיוון]
both ... and ... (22)	**סײַ** ... **סײַ** ...
a lot (of) (6)	**סך: אַ סך** [סאַך]
sukkah covering (12)	**סכך** דער [סכאַך]
danger	**סכּנה** די (–ות) [סאַקאָנע (ס)]
sour cream (13)	**סמעטענע** די
festive meal; feast (4, 16)	**סעודה** די (–ות) [סודע (ס)]
September (20)	**סעפּטעמבער**
secretary (10)	**סעקרעטאַר** דער (ן) / **סעקרעטאַרשע** די (ס)
napkin (13)	**סערוועטקע** די (ס)
holy book	**ספֿר** דער (ים) [סייפֿער (ספֿאָרים)]
Torah scroll (12)	**ספֿר־תּורה** דער (ספֿרי־...) [סייפֿער־טוירע (סיפֿרע־...)]
simply; for no special reason	**סתּם** [סטאַם]

ע

audience, crowd	**עולם** דער (ס) [אוילעם (ס)]
Omer, the 49-day period between Pesach and Shavuos (*SC*)	**עומר** דער [אוימער]
chicken (13)	**עוף** דאָס (ות) [אָף (אויפֿעס)]
some, several	**עטלעכע**
the evil eye	**עין־הרע** די (ס) [אײַנהאָרע]
no evil eye! (2)	קיין עין־הרע! [קייניינאָרע]
older (than) (3)	**עלטער** (פֿון)
great-... (relative) (9)	**עלטער־**...
age (3)	**עלטער** דער (ס)
great-uncle (9)	**עלטער־פֿעטער** דער (ס)
parents (9)	**עלטערן** די
nice to meet/see you (*response to* **שלום־עליכם**) (1)	**עליכם־שלום** [אַלייכעם־שאָלעם]
elbow (*SC*)	**עלנבויגן** דער (ס)
eleven (3)	**עלף**
someone (10)	**עמעצער**
someone (*acc/dat*)	עמעצן
bucket	**עמער** דער (ס)
England (1)	**ענגלאַנד** דאָס
English (1)	**ענגליש** דאָס
ending (*gramm*) (9)	**ענדונג** די (ען)

surname (*lit.* family) (3)	**פֿאַמיליע** די (ס)
flag (12)	**פֿאָן** די (ען)
in front of (14); before; for	**פֿאַר**
what kind of	וואָס פֿאַר אַ
why (5)	פֿאַר וואָס
The United States (1)	**פֿאַראײ́ניקטע שטאַטן** די
to go past (16)	**פֿאַרבײַ́·גיין** (איך גיי פֿאַרבײַ́, מיר גייען פֿאַרבײַ́; איז פֿאַרבײַ́געגאַנגען)
to spend time	**פֿאַרברענגען** (פֿאַרברענגט / פֿאַרבראַ́כט)
past, last	**פֿאַרגאַנגען**
last week (17)	פֿאַרגאַנגענע וואָך
past tense (17)	פֿאַרגאַנגענע צײַט
to compare (14)	**פֿאַרגלײַכן** (פֿאַרגלײַכט / פֿאַרגליכן)
pleasure	**פֿאַרגעניגן** דאָס (ס)
with the greatest pleasure (2)	מיטן גרעסטן פֿאַרגעניגן
to forget (1)	**פֿאַרגעסן** (פֿאַרגעסן)
to earn (10)	**פֿאַרדינען** (פֿאַרדינט)
to lose (15)	**פֿאַרלירן** (פֿאַרלוירן)
to close (5)	**פֿאַרמאַכן** (פֿאַרמאַכט)
mode of transportation, vehicle	**פֿאָ́רמיטל** דאָס (ען)
Fahrenheit	**פֿאַ́רנהײַט**
degree(s) Fahrenheit (20)	גראַד פֿאַ́רנהײַט
to sell (10)	**פֿאַרקויפֿן** (פֿאַרקויפֿט)
to take place (16)	**פֿאָ́ר·קומען** (זי קומט פֿאָר, זיי קומען פֿאָר; איז פֿאָ́רגעקומען)
to turn (16)	**פֿאַרקע́רעווען זיך** (איך פֿאַרקע́רעווע זיך, מיר פֿאַרקע́רעווען זיך; פֿאַרקע́רעוועט)
to fix, to repair	**פֿאַרריכטן** (פֿאַרריכט / פֿאַרראָכטן)
to understand (1)	**פֿאַרשטיי́ן** (איך פֿאַרשטיי́, מיר פֿאַרשטייען; פֿאַרשטאַנען)
of course (*CE*)	פֿאַרשטיי́ט זיך
performance	**פֿאָ́רשטעלונג** די (ען)
dressed, disguised (as) (18)	**פֿאַרשטע́לט** (פֿאַר)
assorted; different (13)	**פֿאַרשיידן** (פֿאַרשיידענע)
bird	**פֿויגל** דער (פֿייגל)
from; of; than (*after a comparative*) (1, 14)	**פֿון**
from where (1)	**פֿון וואַנען**
foot; leg (*SC*)	**פֿוס** דער (פֿיס)
to go on foot (21)	גיין צו פֿוס
fifty (3)	**פֿופֿציק**
fifteen (3)	**פֿופֿצן**
fox (17)	**פֿוקס** דער (ן)
violin, fiddle	**פֿידל** דער (ען)
physics (6)	**פֿיזי́ק** די
humid, damp (20)	**פֿײַכט**
to hate (10)	**פֿײַנט האָבן** (איך האָב פֿײַנט; פֿײַנט געהאַט)
fire (11)	**פֿײַער** דער (ן)
character; person	**פּאַרשוי́ן** דער (ען)
butter (13)	**פּוטער** די
Polish (1)	**פּויליש** דאָס
Poland (1)	**פּוילן** דאָס
peasant (11)	**פּויער** דער (ים)
exactly (3)	**פּונקט**
exactly (*CE*)	פּונקט אַזוי́
to brush (one's teeth) (*SC*)	**פּוצן** (די ציין)
Purim (18)	**פּורים** דער
a play performed on Purim (18)	**פּו́רים־שפּיל** די (ן)
piano (14)	**פּיאַנע** די (ס)
pilot (2)	**פּילאָ́ט** דער (ן) / **פּילאָטין** די (ס)
play (16)	**פּיעסע** די (ס)
pizza (13)	**פּיצע** די (ס)
spicy (13)	**פּיקאַ́נט**
to plan (10)	**פּלאַנירן** (פּלאַני́רט)
poster	**פּלאַקאַ́ט** דער (ן)
plus (3)	**פּלוס**
suddenly (20)	**פּלוצלינג**
niece (9)	**פּלימעניצע** די (ס)
nephew (9)	**פּלימעניק** דער (עס)
face (*SC*)	**פּנים** דאָס (ער) [פּאָנעם (פּע́נעמער)]
Pesach (Passover) (22)	**פּסח** דער [פּייסעך]
psychology (6)	**פּסיכאָלאָגיע** די
pen (5)	**פּען** די (ען)
pension	**פּענסיע** די (ס)
retired	אויף פּענסיע
forecast, prediction	**פּראָגנאָ́ז** דער (ן)
to celebrate; to conduct, carry out (16)	**פּראַווען**
to hold or take part in a seder (22)	פּראַווען אַ סדר
pronoun (1)	**פּראָנאָ́ם** דער (ען)
professor (1)	**פּראָפֿע́סאָר** דער (ן) / **פּראָפֿעסאָ́רשע** די (ס)
profession (10)	**פּראָפֿעסיע** די (ס)
to try (*CE*)	**פּרוּוון**
detail	**פּרט** דער (ים) [פּראַט (פּראָטים)]
seasoning, condiment (13)	**פּריפּראַווע** די (ס)
pharaoh (22)	**פּרעה** דער (ס) [פּאַרע]
to present (10)	**פּרעזענטירן** (פּרעזענטי́רט)
preposition (1)	**פּרעפּאָזיציע** די (ס)
section of the Torah (*SC*)	**פּרשה** די (–יות) [פּאַרשע (ס)]

פֿ

photographer (10)	**פֿאָטאָגראַ́ף** דער (ן) / **פֿאָטאָגראַפֿין** די (ס)
to photograph (10)	**פֿאָטאָגראַפֿירן** (פֿאָטאָגראַפֿי́רט)
armchair (14)	**פֿאָטע́ל** דער (ן)
to fall (17)	**פֿאַלן** (איז געפֿאַלן)
it is snowing (20)	עס פֿאַלט אַ שניי
nation, people	**פֿאָלק** דאָס (פֿעלקער)

much, many	**פֿיל**
as much/many ... as	אַזוי׳ פֿיל ... ווי
too much/many (*SC*)	צו פֿיל
philosophy (6)	**פֿילאָסאָפֿיע** די
film (16)	**פֿילם** דער (ען)
finger (*SC*)	**פֿינגער** דער (—)
five (3)	**פֿינף**
dark (20)	**פֿינצטער**
four (3)	**פֿיר**
curtain (14)	**פֿירהאַנג** דער (ען)
to suggest, to propose	**פֿי׳ר־לייגן** (פֿי׳רגעלייגט)
to lead; to drive (a vehicle)	**פֿירן**
fish (13, 17)	**פֿיש** דער (—)
butterfly (17)	**פֿלאַטערל** דאָס (עך)
bottle	**פֿלאַש** די (פֿלעשער)
plum (7, 13)	**פֿלוים** די (ען)
meat (2, 13)	**פֿלייש** דאָס (ן)
of (or including) meat (13)	**פֿליישיק**
to fly (17)	**פֿליִען** (איז געפֿלויגן)
bat (17)	**פֿלע׳דערמויז** די (...מײַז)
February (20)	**פֿעברואַר**
pen (5)	**פֿעדער** די (ס)
uncle (9)	**פֿעטער** דער (ס)
field (17)	**פֿעלד** דאָס (ער)
feminine (*gramm*)	**פֿעמינין**
window (5)	**פֿענצטער** דער (—)
pepper (13)	**פֿעפֿער** דער
horse (17)	**פֿערד** דאָס (—)
quarter	**פֿערטל** דאָס (עך)
a quarter past (nine) (16)	אַ פֿערטל נאָך (נײַן)
a quarter to (nine) (16)	אַ פֿערטל צו (נײַן)
forty (3)	**פֿערציק**
fourteen (3)	**פֿערצן**
peach (13)	**פֿערשקע** די (ס)
question (6)	**פֿראַגע** די (ס)
French (1)	**פֿראַנצייזיש** דאָס
France (1)	**פֿראַנקרײַך** דאָס
Ms.	**פֿרוי**
woman; wife (9)	**פֿרוי** די (ען)
fruit (13)	**פֿרוכט** די (ן)
pious; (religiously) observant	**פֿרום**
early	**פֿרי**
in the morning (2, 16)	אין דער פֿרי
joy	**פֿרייד** די (ן)
(on) Friday (2)	**פֿרײַטיק**
happy (7)	**פֿריילעך**
to rejoice; to be delighted (by)	**פֿרייען זיך**
spring (20)	**פֿרילינג** דער (ען)
breakfast (13)	**פֿרישטיק** דער (ן)
question word (1)	**פֿרעגוואָרט** דאָס (...ווערטער)
to ask (5)	**פֿרעגן**
I have a question (*lit.* I want to ask something) (1)	איך וויל עפּעס פֿרעגן
unfamiliar; foreign; someone else's	**פֿרעמד**
strangers	פֿרעמדע מענטשן

צ

numeral (3)	**צאָלוואָרט** דאָס (...ווערטער)
tooth (*SC*)	**צאָן** דער (ציין)
side (of a family)	**צד** דער (צדדים) [צאַד (צדאָדים)]
charity (18)	**צדקה** די [צדאָקע]
to; too (7, 14)	**צו**
bless you! (after sneeze) (*lit.* to health) (*CE*)	צו געזונט!
bless you! (after third sneeze) (*lit.* to long years) (*CE*)	צו לאַנגע יאָר!
bless you! (after second sneeze) (*lit.* to life) (*CE*)	צום לעבן!
to add	**צו׳־געבן** (איך גיב צו, דו גיסט צו; צו׳געגעבן)
to listen (*CE*)	**צו׳־הערן זיך** (צו׳געהערט)
twenty (3)	**צוואַנציק**
farmers cheese (13)	**צוואָרעך** דער
two (3)	**צוויי**
second; another; next	**צווייט**
between, among (13)	**צווישן**
twelve (3)	**צוועלף**
together (3)	**צוזאַמען**
because of; for the sake of	**צולי׳ב**
tongue (*SC*)	**צונג** די (ען)
happy, pleased	**צופֿרידן** (צופֿרידענע)
sugar (13)	**צוקער** דער
to come back (to) (5)	**צורי׳ק־קומען** (אין) (איז צורי׳קגעקומען)
interrogative particle (9)	**צי**
onion (13)	**צי׳בעלע** די (ס)
time; tense (*gramm*) (2, 16)	**צײַט** די (ן)
past tense (17)	פֿאַרגאַנגענע צײַט
season (20)	צײַט פֿון יאָר
newspaper (10)	**צײַטונג** די (ען)
grade, mark; sign	**צייכן** דער (ס)
toothbrush (*SC*)	**ציי׳נבערשטל** דאָס (עך)
sweet fruit or vegetable (often carrot) stew (13)	**צימעס** דער (ן)
room (1)	**צימער** דער (ן)
ten (3)	**צען**
to crumple	**צעקנייטשן** (צעקנייטשט)
north (1)	**צפֿון** [צאָפֿן]
North America (1)	**צפֿון־אַמעריקע** די

ק

קאַווע די — coffee (*AB*)
קאַטאַלאָגירן (קאַטאַלאָגירט) — to catalog (10)
קאַטשקע די (ס) — duck (17)
קאָכן — to cook (10)
קאַלוזשע די (ס) — puddle
קאַלט — cold (7)
קאַליפֿיאָר דער (ן) — cauliflower (13)
קאָליר דער (ן) — color (5)
קאָלעדזש דער (ן) — college (1)
קאָמיש — funny
קאָמפּאַס דער (ן) — compass (1)
קאָמפּיוטער־וויסנשאַפֿט די — computer science (6)
קאָנוועׂרב דער (ן) — separable verbal prefix (5)
קאָנטינעׂנט דער (ן) — continent (1)
קאָנטראָלירן (קאָנטראָלירט) — to check; to control
קאָניונקציע די (ס) — conjunction (*SC*)
קאָנצעׂרט דער (ן) — concert (2, 16, *AB*)
קאָנצערטזאַל דער (ן) — concert hall (16)
קאָסטיום דער (ען) — suit (19)
קאַסיׂר דער (ן) / **קאַסירשע** די (ס) — cashier (10)
קאָסמאָפּאָליטיש — cosmopolitan (9)
קאָפּ דער (קעפּ) — head (*SC*)
קאַפּעליע די (ס) — band (of musicians)
קאַפֿעׂ די (ען) — café (16)
קאַץ די (קעץ) — cat (*AB*)
קאָקאָשעס די — popcorn (*pl*) (16)
קאָרט די (ן) — playing card
קאַרש די (ן) — cherry (13)
קאַשע די (ס) — porridge (esp. of buckwheat) (13)
קוגל דער (ען) — kugel, noodle or potato casserole, usually eaten on Shabbos (2, 13)
קויפֿן — to buy (7, 13)
קוכן דער (ס) — cake (13)
קוכער דער (ס) / **קעכין** די (ס) — cook (10)
קול דאָס (ער) [קאָל (קעלער)] — voice (8)
  אויף אַ קול — aloud, out loud (*CE*)
קומעדיק — future; next, coming
קומען (איז געקומען) — to come (1)
קונה דער (ים) [קוינע (קוינים)] — customer
קונסט־געשיכטע די — art history (6)
קונסט די — art (6)
קוקורוזע די — corn (13)
קוקן (אויף) — to look (at) (5)
קורץ — short (7)
  קורצע הייזלעך — shorts (19)
קושן — to kiss (11)
קידוש דער — kiddush (4)

קיין — no, (not) any; to (*with place name*)
  נישט קיין — not a, not any (6)
  קיין מאָל נישט — never (17)
  קיין עין־הרע! [קייניינאָרע] — no evil eye! (2)
קיינער (...) **נישט** — no one (19)
קיך די (ן) — kitchen
קיכל דאָס (עך) — cookie (13)
קיל — cool (20)
קין דער (ען) — chin (*SC*)
קינאָ דער (ס) — movie theater (16)
קינד דאָס (ער) — child (2)
קיצלען — to tickle
קישן דער (ס) — cushion (14)
קלאָנירן (קלאָנירט) — to clone (10)
קלאַס דער (ן) — class (2, 5)
קלאַסצימער דאָס (ן) — classroom (*CE*)
קלאָר — clear (8, 20)
קלאַרנעׂט דער (ן) — clarinet
קלוג — smart (7)
קלייד דאָס (ער) — dress; item of clothing (19)
קליידל דאָס (עך) — skirt (19)
קליידער די — clothes (*pl*) (10, 19)
קליין — small (7)
קלערן — to ponder, to think about
קנאָבל דער — garlic (13)
קני דער (—) — knee (*SC*)
קניידל דאָס (עך) — dumpling (7)
קעז דער (ן) — cheese (13)
קעכין די (ס) — cook (*f*) (10)
קעלנער דער (ס) / **קעלנערין** די (ס) — waiter (10)
קעמל דאָס (עך) — comb (*SC*)
קענען (ער קען) — to know (how to); to be able to (9, 19)
קערה די (–ות) [קײַרע (ס)] — seder plate (for ritual food items) (22)
קערפּער דער (ס) — body (*SC*)
קראַוואַט דער (ן) — tie (19)
קראָם די (ען) — store (7, 16)
קראַנק — sick (2)
קרובֿ דער (ים) [קאָרעוו (קרויווים)] — male relative (9)
קרובֿה די (–ות) [קרויווע (ס)] — female relative (9)
קרויט דאָס (ן) — cabbage (13)
קרום — crooked (7)
קריטיקירן (קריטיקירט) — to criticize (10)
קרײַז דער (ן) — circle
קריכן (איז געקראָכן) — to crawl (17)
קרעמער דער (ס) / **קרעמערקע** די (ס) — shopkeeper (10)
קרעפּל דאָס (עך) — meat-filled dumpling (13)
קשיא די (–ות) [קאַשע (ס)] — question, problem (22)

ר

wheel	ראָד די (רעדער)
pink (5)	ראָזעווע
raisin (13)	ראָזשינקע די (ס)
date (16)	ראַנדקע די (ס)
to date (16)	ראַנדקעווען זיך
Rosh Hashanah ("head of the year") (8)	ראָש־השנה דער [ראָשעשאָנע]
God Almighty	רבונו־של־עולם דער [רעבוינע־שעלוילעם]
Hasidic leader; teacher in a religious school	רבי^ דער (ס) [רעבע (ס)]
rest (4)	רו די
rose (9)	רויז די (ן)
red (5)	רויט
peaceful	רויִק
Romania (1)	רומעניע די
Romanian (1)	רומעניש דאָס
Russian (1)	רוסיש דאָס
Russia (1)	רוסלאַנד דאָס
backpack (5)	רוקזאַק דער (רוקזעק)
back (SC)	רוקן דער (ס)
row; turn	ריי די (ען)
rice (13)	רײַז דער
to ride (17)	רײַטן (איז געריטן)
rich (9)	רײַך
clean (7)	ריין
to pick (fruit), to tear (11)	רײַסן (געריסן)
correct (CE)	ריכטיק
to trickle (17)	רינען (איז גערונען)
rain (20)	רעגן דער (ס)
it's raining (20)	עס גייט אַ רעגן
editorial office (2)	רעדאַקציע די (ס)
to speak (1)	רעדן
radish (13)	רעטעכל דאָס (עך)
buckwheat (13)	רעטשקע די
(to the) right	רעכטס
(on the) right (7, 13)	(אויף) רעכטס
religion (6)	רעליגיע די
religious (9)	רעליגיעז
rail	רעלס דער (ן)
restaurant (16)	רעסטאָראַן דער (ען)
presentation (6)	רעפּעראַט דער (ן)
to give a presentation (6)	האַלטן אַ רעפּעראַט
to record (10)	רעקאָרדירן (רעקאָרדירט)
jacket (19)	רעקל דאָס (עך)
to advertise	רעקלאַמירן (רעקלאַמירט)
advertisement	רעקלאַמע די (ס)
noise, tumult (18)	רעש דער [ראַש]
complete recovery	רפֿואה־שלמה די [רעפֿועס־שליימע]
get well soon! (lit. a complete recovery!) (2)	אַ רפֿואה־שלמה!
list (5)	רשימה די (–ות) [רעשימע (ס)]

ש

regrettable thing	שאָד דער
too bad, a pity (CE)	אַ שאָד
shawl, scarf (19)	שאַל די (ן)
lettuce (pl) (13)	שאַלאַטן די
cabinet (14)	שאַפֿקע די (ס)
chocolate (2)	שאָקאָלאַד דער (ן)
to shock (10)	שאָקירן (שאָקירט)
to shake (12)	שאָקלען (איך שאָקל)
(on) Saturday, (on) Shabbos (2, 4)	שבת [שאַבעס]
Shabbos (2, 4)	שבת דער (ים) [שאַבעס (שאַבאָסים)]
Shabbos candle (4)	שבת־ליכט דאָס (—)
Shavuos (SC)	שבֿועות דער [שוועס]
Shevat (20)	שבֿט [שוואַט]
matchmaker	שדכן דער (ים) [שאַטכן (שאַטכאָנים)]
matchmaker (f)	שדכנטע די (ס) [שאַטכנטע (ס)]
weak (7)	שוואַך
mushroom (7, 13)	שוואָם דער (ען)
black (5)	שוואַרץ
to swim (10)	שווימען (איז געשווומען)
swimming trunks (19)	שווימקעס די
sister (9)	שוועסטער די (—)
cousin (9)	שוועסטערקינד דאָס (ער)
heavy, difficult (7)	שווער
ritual slaughterer (11)	שוחט דער (ים) [שויכעט (שאָכטים)]
already (5)	שוין
that's all! (CE)	שוין!
shoe (19)	שוך דער (שיך)
synagogue; school (16)	שול די (ן)
schoolwork (6)	שולאַרבעט די
shoemaker (10)	שוסטער דער (ס) / שוסטערקע די (ס)
judge (10)	שופֿט דער (ים) [שויפֿעט (שאָפֿטים)]
shofar, ram's horn blown during the Days of Awe (8)	שופֿר דער (ות) [שויפֿער (שויפֿרעס)]
to blow shofar (8)	בלאָזן שופֿר
line (of writing) (CE)	שורה די (–ות) [שורע (ס)]
city (1)	שטאָט די (שטעט)
state (1)	שטאַט דער (ן)
proud	שטאָלץ
to die (17)	שטאַרבן [שטאַרבם] (איז געשטאָרבן)
strong (7)	שטאַרק
house (12, 16)	שטוב די (שטיבער)
to study (a subject) (6)	שטודירן (שטודירט)

שטורעם דער (ס)	storm (20)
עס איז אַ שטורעם	it's stormy (*lit.* it's a storm) (20)
שטיוול דער (—)	boot (19)
שטיין (איך שטיי, מיר שטייען; איז געשטאַנען)	to stand (2, 13)
שטיל	quiet
שטיפּ...	step... (relative) (9)
שטיפֿפּאַטע^ דער (ס)	stepfather (9)
שטיפֿמאַמע^ די (ס)	stepmother (9)
שטיק דאָס (ער)	piece
שטעלן	to put (13)
שטענדיק	always
שטעקן דער (ס)	stick (11)
שטערן	to disturb (6)
שטערן דער (ס)	forehead (*SC*)
שידוך דער (ים) [שידעך (שידוכים)]	(marriage) match
שיין	beautiful, nice (7, *CE*)
שײַנען	to shine
עס שײַנט די זון	the sun is shining (20)
שיסל די (ען)	bowl (13)
שיף די (ן)	ship (21)
שיקן	to send (11)
שירעם דער (ס)	umbrella (20)
שלאָגן (געשלאָגן)	to beat
שלאָגן כּפּרות [קאַפּאָרעס]	to perform a ritual in which sins are transferred onto a live chicken by swinging it around one's head (8)
שלאַנג די (ען)	snake (17)
שלאָפֿן (איז געשלאָפֿן)	to sleep (2)
לייגן זיך שלאָפֿן	to go to bed (*SC*)
שלום־עליכם [שאָלעם־אַלייכעם]	nice to meet/see you (1)
שלח־מנות דער [שאַלאַכמאָנעס]	parcel of treats given to friends and neighbors on Purim (18)
שלייערל דאָס (עך)	caterpillar (17)
שלעכט	bad; badly (2)
שמאָל	narrow (7)
שמאַלץ דאָס	rendered animal fat (13)
שמועס דער (ן)	conversation, discussion
שמו́עסן	to converse, to discuss
שמוציק	dirty (7)
שמײַסן (געשמיסן)	to hit, to whip (11)
שמיני־עצרת דער [שמינאַצערעס]	Shemini Atzereth (12)
שמעקן	to smell (*SC*)
שמש דער (ים) [שאַמעס (שאַמאָסים)]	"helper" candle used to light other candles (*lit.* beadle in synagogue) (15)
שניי דער (ען)	snow (20)
עס פֿאַלט אַ שניי	it is snowing (20)
שנײַדער דער (ס) / **שנײַדערין** די (ס)	tailor (10)
שנייעלע דאָס (ך)	snowflake (20)
שעכטן (געשאָכטן)	to slaughter (11)
שענק די (ען)	bar, tavern (16)
שעפֿעריש	creative
שער די (ן)	(pair of) scissors (5)
שפּאַניע די	Spain (1)
שפּאַניש דאָס	Spanish (1)
שפּאַציר דער (ן)	stroll, walk (16)
שפּאַצירן (שפּאַצי́רט)	to stroll, walk (16)
שפּיגל דער (ען)	mirror (14)
שפּײַז די (ן)	food (13)
שפּילן	to play (2)
שפּעט	late
שפּראַך די (ן)	language (1)
שפּרינגען (איז געשפּרונגען)	to jump (2)
שפּריץ דער (ן)	shower (*SC*)
שקלאַף דער (ן)	slave (22)
שרײַבן [שרײַבם] (געשריבן)	to write (1, 2)
שרײַבער דער (ס) / **שרײַבערין** די (ס)	writer (3, 10)

שׂ

שׂמחה די (–ות) [סימכע (ס)]	party, celebration (16)
שׂמחת־תּורה דער [סימכעס־טוירע]	Simchas Torah (12)

ת

תּבֿואה די (–ות) [טווּוע (ס)]	grain (*SC*)
תּורה די [טוירע]	Torah, Pentateuch
תּחינה די (–ות) [טכינע (ס)]	(women's) personal prayer (8)
תּירוץ דער (ים) [טערעץ (טערוצים)]	excuse, justification
תּמוז [טאַמעז]	Tammuz (20)
תּפֿילה די (–ות) [טפֿילע (ס)]	prayer
תּשרי [טישרע]	Tishri (20)

VOCABULARY: ENGLISH-YIDDISH

ABBREVIATIONS			
acc	accusative	*lit.*	literally
adj	adjective	*m*	masculine
alt.	alternatively	*n*	neuter
aux	auxiliary	*pl*	plural
conj	conjunction	*poss*	possessive
dat	dative	*pron*	pronoun
f	feminine	*sg*	singular
gramm	grammatical	*v*	verb

A

a	**אַ**
a.m. (16)	**פֿ״מ** (פֿאַר מיטאָג)
able: be able to (*v*) (9, 19)	**קענען** (ער קען)
about (6)	**וועגן**
above (13)	**אויבן** [אויבם]
absent (5)	**נישטאָ**
she is not here (5)	זי איז נישטאָ
according to (5)	**לויט**
accusative (*gramm*) (11)	**אַקוזאַטיוו** דער (ן)
ache (*v*) (*SC*)	**וויי טאָן** (עס טוט וויי; עס האָט וויי געטאָן)
across from	**אַנטקעגן**
activity (16)	**אַקטיוויטעט** די (ן)
actor (10)	**אַקטיאָר** דער (ן) / **אַקטריסע** די (ס)
actress (10)	**אַקטריסע** די (ס)
Adar (20)	**אָדר** [אָדער]
add (*v*)	**צו·געבן** (איך גיב צו, דו גיסט צו; צוגעגעבן)
additional (3)	**ווײַטערדיק**
address (3)	**אַדרעס** דער (ן)
address someone with **איר** (*v*) (2)	**אירצן**
address someone with **דו** (*v*) (2)	**דוצן**
adjective (1)	**אַדיעקטיוו** דער (ן)
adult	**דערוואַקסן** (דערוואַקסענע)
advertise (*v*)	**רעקלאַמירן** (רעקלאַמירט)
advertisement	**רעקלאַמע** די (ס)
advice	**עצה** די (–ות) [אייצע (ס)]
afikomen (ceremonially hidden piece of matzoh) (22)	**אַפּיקומן** דער (ס) [אַפּיקוימען]
afraid: be afraid (of) (*v*)	**מורא האָבן** (פֿאַר) [מוירע] (איך האָב מורא; מורא געהאַט)
Africa (1)	**אַפֿריקע** די
after (6)	**נאָך**
afternoon (16)	**נאָך מיטאָג**
in the afternoon (16)	נאָך מיטאָג
afterward (16)	**דערנאָך; נאָך דעם**
again (*CE*)	**נאָך אַ מאָל**
age (3)	**עלטער** דער (ס)
agree (*v*) (6)	**מסכּים זײַן** [מאַסקעם] (איך בין מסכּים; מסכּים געווען)
airplane (21)	**עראָפּלאַן** דער (ען)
alarm clock (*SC*)	**וועקער** דער (ס)
alas! (2)	**אוי־וויי; נעבעך**
Algeria (1)	**אַלזשיריע** די
alive (6)	**בײַם לעבן**
all (*AB*)	**אַלע**
allowed: not be allowed to (*v*) (19)	**נישט טאָרן** (ער טאָר נישט)
almost (*CE*)	**כּמעט** [קימאַט]
alone	**אַליין**
aloud (*CE*)	**אויף אַ קול** [אַף אַ קאָל]
already (5)	**שוין**
also (2)	**אויך**
altogether	**אין גאַנצן**
always	**אַלע מאָל; שטענדיק**
among (13)	**צווישן**
amuse (*v*) (10)	**אַמוזירן** (אַמוזירט)
an	**אַן**
analyze (*v*) (10)	**אַנאַליזירן** (אַנאַליזירט)
and (2)	**און**
angel	**מלאך** דער (מלאָכים) [מאַלעך (מאַלאָכים)]
angel of death	**מלאך־המוות** דער [מאַלעכאַמאָוועס]
angry	**בייז**
animal (17)	**חיה** די (–ות) [כײַע (ס)]
another	**נאָך אַ**
answer (2)	**ענטפֿער** דער (ס)
answer (*v*) (2)	**ענטפֿערן**
Antarctica (1)	**אַנטאַרקטיק** דער
anthropology (6)	**אַנטראָפּאָלאָגיע** די
anyway	**מילא** [מיילע]
apartment (1)	**דירה** די (–ות) [דירע (ס)]
appearance (11)	**אויסזען** דאָס

appendix (*CE*)	**הוספֿה** די (–ות) [העסאָפֿע (ס)]
applaud (*v*) (10)	**אַפּלאָדירן** (אַפּלאָדי׳רט)
apple (*AB*, 13)	**עפּל** דער (—)
appropriate	**פּאַסיק**
April (20)	**אַפּרי׳ל**
Arabic (1)	**אַראַביש** דאָס
aristocratic (9)	**אַריסטאָקראַטיש**
arm (*SC*)	**האַנט** די (הענט)
armchair (14)	**פֿאָטעל** דער (ן)
around (14)	**אַרום**
art (6)	**קונסט** די
art history (6)	**קונסט־געשיכטע** די
article	**אַרטיקל** דער (ען)
as	**ווי**
Asia (1)	**אַזיע** די
ask (*v*) (5)	**פֿרעגן**
ask for (*v*)	**בעטן** (געבעטן)
astronaut (3)	**אַסטראָנוי׳ט** דער (ן) / **אַסטראָנויטין** די (ס)
at (14)	**אין; אויף** [אַף]
at the theater	אין טעאַטער
at a concert	אויף אַ קאָנצערט
at (someone's house) (14)	**בײַ**
attack (*v*) (10)	**אַטאַקירן** (אַטאַקי׳רט)
audience	**עולם** דער (ס) [אוילעם (ס)]
August (20)	**אויגוסט**
aunt (9)	**מומע** די (ס)
Australia (1)	**אויסטראַליע** די
Av (20)	**אָבֿ** [אָוו]
avocado (13)	**אַוואָקאַדאָ** דער (ס)

B

back (*SC*)	**רוקן** דער (ס)
backpack (5)	**רוקזאַק** דער (רוקזעק)
bad (2)	**שלעכט**
too bad (*CE*)	**אַ שאָד**
bagel (2, 13)	**בייגל** דער (—)
bake (*v*) (10)	**באַקן** (געבאַקן / געבאַקט)
baker (10)	**בעקער** דער (ס) / **בעקערקע** די (ס)
ball (*AB*)	**באַל** דער (ן)
banana (*AB*, 13)	**באַנאַנע** די (ס)
band (of musicians)	**קאַפּעליע** די (ס)
bandage (*v*) (10)	**באַנדאַזשירן** (באַנדאַזשי׳רט)
bar (tavern) (16)	**שענק** די (ען)
basic (2)	**גרונטיק**
bass (instrument)	**באַס** דער (ן)
bat (17)	**פֿלעדערמויז** די (...מײַז)
bath (*SC*)	**וואַנע** די (ס)
bathe (*v*) (*SC*)	**באָדן** (געבאָדן)
bathing suit (19)	**באָדקאָסטיום** דער (ען)
bathroom (*SC*)	**וואַשצימער** דער (ן)
be (*v*) (3)	**זײַן** (איך בין, דו ביסט, ער איז, מיר זײַנען, איר זײַט, זיי זײַנען; איז געווען; זײַ, זײַט)
bean (7)	**באָב** דער (עס)
bear (*AB*, 17)	**בער** דער (ן)
beard (11)	**באָרד** די (בערד)
beat (*v*)	**שלאָגן** (געשלאָגן)
beautiful (7, *CE*)	**שיין**
because (10)	**ווײַל**
because of	**צולי׳ב**
become (*v*) (17)	**ווערן** (איז געוואָרן)
bed (*AB*)	**בעט** דאָס (ן)
go to bed (*v*) (*SC*)	לייגן זיך שלאָפֿן
beer (13)	**ביר** דאָס
beet (13)	**בוריק** דער (עס)
before	**פֿאַר**
before (*conj*) (*SC*)	**איידער**
behind (14)	**הינטער**
Belarus (1)	**ווײַסרוסלאַנד** דאָס
Belarussian (1)	**ווײַסרוסיש** דאָס
below (13)	**אונטן**
belt (19)	**פּאַסיק** דער (עס)
bench	**באַנק** די (בענק)
bent (7)	**אײַנגעבויגן**
better (2)	**בעסער**
between (13)	**צווישן**
beverage	**געטראַנק** דאָס (ען)
bicycle (21)	**וועלאָסיפּעד** דער (ן)
big (7)	**גרויס**
bimah (12)	**בימה** די (–ות) [בימע (ס)]
biology (6)	**ביאָלאָגיע** די
bird	**פֿויגל** דער (פֿייגל)
birthday	**געבורטסטאָג** דער (...טעג)
happy birthday! (*lit.* until 120) (2)	ביז הונדערט און צוואַנציק!
bit (13)	**ביסל** דאָס (עך)
a little bit (of) (6)	אַ ביסל
bite (*v*) (11)	**בײַסן** (געביסן)
bitter (13)	**ביטער**
black (5)	**שוואַרץ**
bless (*v*) (4, 15)	**בענטשן**
bless you! (after sneeze) (*lit.* to health) (*CE*)	צו געזו׳נט!
bless you! (after second sneeze) (*lit.* to life) (*CE*)	צום לעבן!
bless you! (after third sneeze) (*lit.* to long years) (*CE*)	צו לאַנגע יאָר!

blond (11)	בלאָנד
blouse (19)	בלוזקע די (ס)
blow (*v*)	בלאָזן (געבלאָזן)
blow shofar (*v*) (8)	בלאָזן שופֿר [שויפֿער]
blue (5)	בלוי
board (5)	טאָוול דער (ען)
body (*SC*)	גוף דער (ים); קערפּער דער (ס)
book (*AB*, 5)	בוך דאָס (ביכער)
bookcase (14)	ביכערשאַנק די (...שענק)
boot (19)	שטיוול דער (—)
booth	בײַדל דאָס (עך)
boring (6)	נודנע
born: be born (*v*)	געבוירן ווערן (איז געבוירן געוואָרן)
borscht (beet soup) (13)	באָרשט דער (ן)
boss (11)	בעל־הבית דער (בעלי־בתּים) [באַלעבאָס (באַלעבאַטים)]
both (5)	ביידע
both ... and ... (22)	סײַ ... סײַ ...
bottle	פֿלאַש די (פֿלעשער)
bowl (13)	שיסל די (ען)
boy (4)	ייִנגל דאָס (עך)
bread (13)	ברויט דאָס (ן)
breakfast (13)	פֿרישטיק דער (ן)
breast (*SC*)	ברוסט די (בריסט)
bride (9)	כּלה די (–ות) [קאַלע (ס)]
bridegroom (9)	חתן דער (ים) [כאָסן (כאַסאַנים)]
bright (20)	ליכטיק
bring (*v*) (10)	ברענגען (געברענגט / געבראַכט)
bring along (*v*)	מיט·ברענגען (מיטגעברענגט / מיטגעבראַכט)
broad (7)	ברייט
broccoli (13)	בראָקאָלי דער
brother (9)	ברודער דער (ברידער)
brown (5)	ברוין
brush (*SC*)	בערשטל דאָס (עך)
brush (*v*) (*SC*)	בערשטן (געבערשט)
brush (one's teeth) (*v*) (*SC*)	פּוצן (די ציין)
bucket	עמער דער (ס)
buckwheat (13)	רעטשקע די
build (*v*) (12)	בויען (איך בוי)
building	בנין דער (ים) [ביניען (ביניאָנים)]
burn (*v*) (11)	ברענען
bus (21)	אויטאָבוס דער (ן)
but (2; 6)	אָבער; נאָר
butter (13)	פּוטער די
butterfly (17)	פֿלאַטערל דאָס (עך)
buy (*v*) (7, 13)	קויפֿן
by (14)	בײַ

C

cabbage (13)	קרויט דאָס (ן)
cabin	בײַדל דאָס (עך)
cabinet (14)	שאַפֿקע די (ס)
café (16)	קאַפֿע די (ען)
cake (13)	קוכן דער (ס)
call: be called (*v*) (1)	הייסן (געהייסן)
candle (15)	ליכטל דאָס (עך)
cantor	חזן דער (ים) [כאַזן (כאַזאָנים)]
cap (hat) (11)	היטל דאָס (עך)
capital city (1)	הויפּטשטאָט די (...שטעט)
car (21)	אויטאָ דער (ס)
carrot (13)	מער די (ן)
carry (*v*) (11)	טראָגן (געטראָגן)
cashier (10)	קאַסיר דער (ן) / קאַסירשע די (ס)
cat (*AB*)	קאַץ די (קעץ)
catalog (*v*) (10)	קאַטאַלאָגירן (קאַטאַלאָגירט)
catastrophe (18)	חורבן דער [כורבם]
caterpillar (17)	שלייערל דאָס (עך)
cauliflower (13)	קאַליפֿיאָר דער (ן)
ceiling (5)	סטעליע די (ס)
celebrate (*v*) (16)	פּראַווען
celebration (16)	שׂימחה די (–ות) [סימכע (ס)]
cell phone (3)	מאָבילקע די (ס)
certain	געוויס
certainly	זיכער
chair (5)	בענקל דאָס (עך)
challah (4)	חלה די (–ות) [כאַלע (ס)]
chandelier (14)	הענגלײַכטער דער (ס)
character	פּאַרשוין דער (ען)
charity (18)	צדקה די [צדאָקע]
charoseth (sweet paste of fruit and nuts) (22)	חרוסת דאָס [כרויסעס]
check (*v*)	קאָנטראָלירן (קאָנטראָלירט)
cheek (*SC*)	באַק די (ן)
cheese (13)	קעז דער (ן)
chemistry (6)	כעמיע די
cherry (13)	קאַרש די (ן)
chest (*SC*)	ברוסט די (בריסט)
chicken (13)	עוף דאָס (ות) [אָף (אויפֿעס)]
chicken soup (13)	יויך די (ן)
child (2)	קינד דאָס (ער)
chin (*SC*)	קין דער (ען)
China (1)	כינע די
Chinese (1)	כינעזיש דאָס
chocolate (2)	שאָקאָלאַד דער (ן)

cholent (stew with meat, potato, beans) (13)	טשאָלנט דער (ן)
choose (*v*)	אוי֜ס·קלײַבן (אוי֜סגעקליבן)
chopped liver (13)	געהאַקטע לעבער די
circle	קרײַז דער (ן)
circle (*v*)	אַרו֜ם·רינגלען (אַרו֜מגערינגלט)
city (1)	שטאָט די (שטעט)
clarinet	קלאַרנע֜ט דער (ן)
class (2, 5)	קלאַס דער (ן)
classroom (*CE*)	קלאַ֜סצימער דאָס (ן)
clean (7)	ריין
clear (8, 20)	קלאָר
clock (5)	זייגער דער (ס)
o'clock (16)	אַ זייגער
clone (*v*) (10)	קלאָנירן (קלאָני֜רט)
close (*v*) (5)	פֿאַרמאַכן (פֿאַרמאַכט)
cloth (13)	געוואַ֜נט דאָס (ן)
clothes (*pl*) (10, 19)	קליידער די
cloud (20)	וואָלקן דער (ס)
cloudy (20)	וואָלקנדיק
clumsy	אומגעלומפּערט
coat (*AB*, 19)	מאַנטל דער (ען)
coffee (*AB*)	קאַווע די
coin (15)	מטבע די (ות) [מאַטבייע (ס)]
cold (7)	קאַלט
college (1)	קאַלעדזש דער (ן)
color (5)	קאָליר דער (ן)
comb (*SC*)	קעמל דאָס (עך)
comb out (*v*) (*SC*)	אוי֜ס·קעמען (אוי֜סגעקעמט)
come (*v*) (1)	קומען (איז געקומען)
come back (to) (*v*) (5)	צורי֜ק·קומען (אין) (איז צורי֜קגעקומען)
comfortable	באַקווע֜ם
comic strip	בי֜לדערשטרײַף דער (ן)
commandment (8)	געבאָ֜ט דאָס (—); מיצווה די (מיצוות) [מיצווע (ס)]
the Ten Commandments (*SC*)	די צען געבאָט
compare (*v*) (14)	פֿאַרגלײַכן (פֿאַרגלײַכט / פֿאַרגליכן)
compass (1)	קאָמפּאַס דער (ן)
computer science (6)	קאָמפּיו֜טער־וויסנשאַפֿט די
concert (2, 16, *AB*)	קאָנצע֜רט דער (ן)
concert hall (16)	קאָנצערטזאַל דער (ן)
congratulations! (11)	יישר־כּוח [יאַשער־קויעך]; מזל־טובֿ! [מאַ֜זל־טאָוו]
conjunction (*SC*)	קאָניונקציע די (ס)
consider (*v*)	באַטראַכטן (באַטראַ֜כט)
consume hastily (*v*)	אַרײַ֜נ·כאַפּן (אַרײַ֜נגעכאַפּט)
continent (1)	קאָנטינע֜נט דער (ן)
control (*v*)	קאָנטראָלירן (קאָנטראָלי֜רט)
conversation	שמועס דער (ן)
converse (*v*)	שמו֜עסן
cook (10)	קוכער דער (ס) / קעכין די (ס)
cook (*v*) (10)	קאָכן
cookie (13)	קיכל דאָס (עך)
cool (20)	קיל
copy (written text) (*v*)	נאָ֜כ·שרײַבן (נאָכגעשריבן)
corn (13)	קוקורוזע די
corner	ווינקל דער (ען)
correct (*CE*)	ריכטיק
cosmopolitan (9)	קאָסמאָפּאָליטיש
cough (*v*) (*SC*)	הוסטן (געהוסט)
count off (*v*) (*SC*)	אָ֜פּ·ציילן (אָ֜פּגעציילט)
country (1)	לאַנד דאָס (לענדער)
course: of course (6; *CE*)	אַוודאי [אַוואַדע]; פֿאַרשטיי֜ט זיך
court (10)	געri֜כט דאָס (ן)
cousin (9)	שוועסטערקי֜נד דאָס (ער)
cover (*v*) (12)	דעקן
cow (11)	בהמה די (–ות) [בעהיימע (ס)]
crawl (*v*) (17)	קריכן (איז געקראָכן)
creative	שע֜פֿעריש
criticize (*v*) (10)	קריטיקירן (קריטיקי֜רט)
crooked (7)	קרום
crumple (*v*)	צעקנייטשן (צעקנייטשט)
cry (*v*) (2)	וויינען
cucumber (13)	או֜גערקע די (ס)
cup (13)	טעפּל דאָס (עך)
curly (11)	געקרײַזלט
curtain (14)	פֿירהאַנג דער (ען)
cushion (14)	קישן דער (ס)
custom (18)	מינהג דער (ים) [מינעג (מינהאָגים)]
customer	קונה דער (ים) [קוינע (קוינים)]

D

daffodil (9)	נאַרצי֜ס דער (ן)
dairy (13)	מילכיק
daisy (9)	מאַרגעריטקע די (ס)
dance (*v*) (2)	טאַנצן
dancer (3)	טענצער דער (ס) / טענצערין די (ס)
danger	סכּנה די (–ות) [סאַקאָנע (ס)]
dark (20)	פֿינצטער
dark (in color) (5)	טונקל (טונקעלע)
dark blue (5)	טונקל בלוי
date (16)	ראַנדקע די (ס)
date (*v*) (16)	ראַ֜נדקעווען זיך
dative (*gramm*) (14)	דאַטי֜וו דער (ן)
daughter (9)	טאָכטער די (טעכטער)

day (2)	**טאָג** דער (טעג)
during the day (2)	בײַ טאָג
Days of Awe (Rosh Hashanah through Yom Kippur) (8)	**ימים־נוראָים** די [יאָמים־נעראָים]
deadline	**טערמין** דער (ען)
dear (8)	**טײַער**
oh dear! (2)	**אוי־וויי**
death (8)	**טויט** דער (ן)
December (20)	**דעצעמבער**
decorate (*v*) (*SC*)	**אויס·צירן** (אויסגעצירט)
deep	**טיף**
deer (17)	**הירש** דער (ן)
degree	**גראַד** דער (ן)
degree(s) Fahrenheit (20)	גראַד פֿאַרנהײַט
den (for animals)	**נאָרע** די (ס)
describe (*v*) (14)	**באַשרײַבן** (באַשריבן)
detail	**פּרט** דער (ים) [פּראַט (פּראָטים)]
dictionary (5)	**ווערטערבוך** דאָס (ווערטערביכער)
die (*v*) (17)	**שטאַרבן** [שטאַרבם] (איז געשטאָרבן)
different (13; 22)	**פֿאַרשיידן** (פֿאַרשיידענע); **אַנדערש**
difficult (7)	**שווער**
digitalize (*v*) (10)	**דיגיטאַליזירן** (דיגיטאַליזירט)
dirty (7)	**שמוציק**
discipline (*v*) (10)	**דיסציפּלינירן** (דיסציפּלינירט)
disguised (as) (18)	**פֿאַרשטעלט** (פֿאַר)
disturb (*v*) (6)	**שטערן**
divide (*v*)	**אײַנ·טיילן** (אײַנגעטיילט)
divided by (3)	**געטיילט אויף** [אַף]
do (*v*) (2)	**טאָן** (איך טו, מיר טוען; געטאָן); **מאַכן**
do an exercise, homework (*v*)	מאַכן אַ געניטונג, היימאַרבעט
how are you doing? (*informal*) (2)	וואָס מאַכסטו?
doctor (10)	**דאָקטער** דער (דאָקטוירים) / **דאָקטערשע** די (ס)
dog (*AB*, 11)	**הונט** דער (הינט)
donkey (17)	**אייזל** דער (ען)
door (5)	**טיר** די (ן)
dormitory (1)	**אינטערנאַט** דער (ן)
dream	**חלום** דער (ות) [כאַלעם (כאַלוימעס)]
dream (*v*)	**חלומען** [כאַלעמען]
dreidel (spinning top) (15)	**דריידל** דאָס (עך)
dress (19)	**קלייד** דאָס (ער)
dressed: get dressed (*v*) (*SC*)	**אָנ·טאָן זיך** (איך טו זיך אָן, מיר טוען זיך אָן; אָנגעטאָן)
drink (*v*) (2)	**טרינקען** (געטרונקען)
drive (a vehicle) (*v*)	**פֿירן**
dry (20)	**טרוקן** (טרוקענע)
dry oneself (*v*) (*SC*)	**אָפּ·ווישן זיך**
duck (17)	**קאַטשקע** די (ס)
dumpling (7; 13)	**קניידל** דאָס (עך); **קרעפּל** דאָס (עך)
during (*SC*)	**בשעת** [בעשאַס]
during (in reference to Jewish holidays) (8)	**אום**
dybbuk (spirit that possesses a living person)	**דיבוק** דער (ים) [דיבעק (דיבוקים)]

E

each (7)	**יעדער**
eagle (17)	**אָדלער** דער (ס)
ear (*SC*)	**אויער** דער (ן)
early	**פֿרי**
earn (*v*) (10)	**פֿאַרדינען** (פֿאַרדינט)
east (1)	**מיזרח** [מיזרעך]
easy (7)	**גרינג**; **לײַכט**
eat (*v*) (2)	**עסן** (געגעסן)
economics (6)	**עקאָנאָמיק** די
editorial office (2)	**רעדאַקציע** די (ס)
egg (13)	**איי** דאָס (ער)
Egypt	**מצרים** דאָס [מיצראַיִם]
eight (3)	**אַכט**
eighteen (3)	**אַכצן**
eighty (3)	**אַכציק**
elbow (*SC*)	**עלנבויגן** דער (ס)
elephant (17)	**העלפֿאַנד** דער (ן)
eleven (3)	**עלף**
Elijah the Prophet (22)	**אליהו־הנבֿיא** [עליאָהו־האַנאָווי]
Elul (20)	**אלול** [עלעל]
e-mail	**בליצבריוו** דער (—)
end (12)	**סוף** דער (ן) [סאָף]
at the end (of)	בײַם סוף (פֿון)
ending (*gramm*) (9)	**ענדונג** די (ען)
engineering (6)	**אינזשעניריע** די
England (1)	**ענגלאַנד** דאָס
English (1)	**ענגליש** דאָס
enough	**גענוג**
enthusiastic (9)	**ענטוזיאַסטיש**
eraser (5)	**מעקער** דער (ס)
esrog (citron) (12)	**אתרוג** דער (ים) [עסרעג (עסרויגים)]
essay (6)	**עסיי** דער (ען)
Europe (1)	**אייראָפּע** די
even (21)	**אפֿילו** [אַפֿילע]
evening (2)	**אָוונט** דער (ן)
in the evening (2, 16)	אין אָוונט
event	**געשעעניש** דאָס (ן); **פּאַסירונג** די (ען)

every (7)	**יעדער**
every day	אַלע טאָג
every year	אַלע יאָר
everyone (*acc/dat*) (*AB*)	**אַלע(מען)**
everything (*CE*)	**אַלץ**
evil eye	**עין־הרע** די (ס) [אײנהאָרע]
no evil eye! (2)	קיין עין־הרע! [קײנײנאָרע]
exactly (3; *CE*)	**פּונקט; פּונקט אַזוי**
exam (6)	**עקזאַמען** דער (ס)
take an exam (*v*) (6)	האַלטן אַן עקזאַמען
example (1)	**דוגמא** די (–ות) [דוגמע (ס)]
for example (*CE*)	**למשל** [לעמאָשל]
excellent (*CE*)	**אױסגעצײכנט**
except	**חוץ**
excuse	**תּירוץ** דער (ים) [טערעץ (טערוצים)]
excuse me (*formal/informal*) (2)	**זײַ(ט) (מיר) מוחל**
exercise (6)	**געניטונג** די (ען)
do an exercise (*v*) (6)	מאַכן אַ געניטונג
exhibit (16)	**אױסשטעלונג** די (ען)
experience	**דערפֿאַרונג** די (ען)
express (*v*)	**אױס·דריקן** (אױסגעדריקט)
expression (1)	**אױסדרוק** דער (ן)
extinguish (*v*) (11)	**לעשן** (געלאָשן)
extraordinary (*CE*)	**אױסערגעװײנטלעך**
eye (11, *SC*)	**אױג** דאָס (ן)
eyebrow (*SC*)	**ברעם** די (ען)
eyeglasses (11)	**ברילן** די

F

face (*SC*)	**פּנים** דאָס (ער) [פּאָנעם (פּענעמער)]
Fahrenheit	**פֿאַרנהײַט**
degree(s) Fahrenheit (20)	גראַד פֿאַרנהײַט
faint (*v*) (*SC*)	**חלשן** [כאַלעשן]
faithful	**געטרײַ**
fall (20)	**האַרבסט** דער (ן)
fall (*v*) (17)	**פֿאַלן** (איז געפֿאַלן)
fall (down) (*v*)	**אַראָפּ·פֿאַלן** (איז אַראָפּגעפֿאַלן)
fall asleep (*v*) (*SC*)	**אײַנ·שלאָפֿן** (איז אײַנגעשלאָפֿן)
family (4, 9)	**משפּחה** די (–ות) [מישפּאָכע (ס)]
famous	**באַקאַנט**
far (from) (1)	**װײַט** (פֿון)
farewell (2)	**געזעגענונג** די (ען)
fashion	**מאָדע** די (ס)
fashionable	אין דער מאָדע
fast (7)	**גיך**
fat (animal) (13)	**שמאַלץ** דאָס
fate	**גורל** דער (ות) [גױרל (גױראָלעס)]
father (9)	**טאַטע^** דער (ס)
favorite	**באַליבטסט**
feast (4, 16)	**סעודה** די (–ות) [סודע (ס)]
February (20)	**פֿעברואַר**
feedback (*CE*)	**אָפּרוף** דער (ן)
feeling (8)	**געפֿיל** דאָס (ן)
feminine (*gramm*)	**פֿעמינין**
fever	**היץ** די (ן)
have a fever (*v*) (*SC*)	האָבן היץ
few (*SC*)	**װײניק**
a few	**אַ ביסל**
fiddle	**פֿידל** דער (ען)
field (17)	**פֿעלד** דאָס (ער)
fifteen (3)	**פֿופֿצן**
fifty (3)	**פֿופֿציק**
film (16)	**פֿילם** דער (ען)
finally	**צום סוף**
find (*v*) (13)	**געפֿינען** (געפֿונען)
finger (*SC*)	**פֿינגער** דער (—)
finish (*v*) (*CE*)	**ענדיקן**
fire (11)	**פֿײַער** דער (ן)
first (15)	**ערשט**
for the first time	צום ערשטן מאָל
at first	צו ערשט
fish (13, 17)	**פֿיש** דער (—)
fit (*v*)	**פּאַסן**
five (3)	**פֿינף**
fix (*v*)	**פֿאַרריכטן** (פֿאַרריכט / פֿאַרראַכטן)
flag (12)	**פֿאָן** די (ען)
flash (*v*)	**בליצן**
there are flashes of lightning (20)	עס בליצט
flee (*v*)	**אַנטלױפֿן** (איז אַנטלאָפֿן)
floor (5)	**דיל** דער (ן)
flour (13)	**מעל** די
flower (*AB*, 9)	**בלום** די (ען)
fly (*v*) (17)	**פֿליִען** (איז געפֿלױגן)
fog (20)	**נעפּל** דער (ען)
foggy (20)	**נעפּלדיק**
food (13)	**עסנװאַרג** דאָס; **עסן** דאָס (ס); **שפּײַז** די (ן); **מאכל** דאָס (ים) [מײַכל (מײַכאָלים)]
fool	**נאַר** דער (נאַראָנים)
foolish (7)	**נאַריש**
foot (*SC*)	**פֿוס** דער (פֿיס)
go on foot (*v*) (21)	גײן צו פֿוס
for	**פֿאַר**
forecast	**פּראָגנאָז** דער (ן)
forecaster	**װעטער־נבֿיא** דער (ים) [...־נאָװי (...־נעװיִים)]
forehead (*SC*)	**שטערן** דער (ס)
foreign	**פֿרעמד**

forest (11, 17)	**וואַלד** דער (וועלדער)
forget (*v*) (1)	**פֿאַרגעסן** (פֿאַרגעסן)
forgive (*v*)	**מוחל זײַן** [מויכל] (מוחל געווען)
fork (13)	**גאָפּל** דער (ען)
forty (3)	**פֿערציק**
four (3)	**פֿיר**
fourteen (3)	**פֿערצן**
fox (17)	**פֿוקס** דער (ן)
France (1)	**פֿראַנקרײַך** דאָס
freckle (11)	**זומער־שפּרענקל** דאָס (עך)
French (1)	**פֿראַנצייזיש** דאָס
Friday (2)	**פֿרײַטיק**
friend (2)	**חבֿר** דער (ים) [כאַווער (כאַווײרים)] / **חבֿרטע** די (ס) [כאַווערטע (ס)]
frog (17)	**זשאַבע** די (ס)
from (1, 14)	**פֿון**
from where (1)	**פֿון וואַנען**
front: in front of (14)	**פֿאַר**
fruit (13)	**פֿרוכט** די (ן)
funny	**קאָמיש**
furniture (14)	**מעבל** דאָס
further (15)	**ווײַטער**
future	**קומעדיק**

G

garlic (13)	**קנאָבל** דער
gefilte fish (2)	**געפֿילטע פֿיש** די
gender (*gramm*) (11)	**מין** דער (ים)
geography (1, 6)	**געאָגראַפֿיע** די
German (1)	**דײַטש** דאָס
Germany (1)	**דײַטשלאַנד** דאָס
get acquainted (*v*) (1)	**באַקענען זיך** (באַקענט)
get up (*v*) (*SC*)	**אויפֿ·שטיין** [אוף] (איז אויפֿגעשטאַנען)
girl (*AB*, 4)	**מיידל** דאָס (עך)
give (*v*) (5)	**געבן** [געבם] (איך גיב, דו גיסט; געגעבן)
glass (9, 13)	**גלאָז** די (גלעזער); **גלעזל** דאָס (עך)
glove (19)	**הענטשקע** די (ס)
go (by foot) (*v*) (2)	**גיין** (איך גיי, מיר גייען; איז געגאַנגען)
go on foot (*v*) (21)	גיין צו פֿוס
go out (from) (*v*) (5)	**אַרויס·גיין** (פֿון) (איך גיי אַרויס, מיר גייען אַרויס; איז אַרויסגעגאַנגען)
go past (*v*) (16)	**פֿאַרבײַ·גיין** (איך גיי פֿאַרבײַ, מיר גייען פֿאַרבײַ; איז פֿאַרבײַגעגאַנגען)
God	**גאָט** דער
God forbid (21)	**חלילה** [כאָלילע]
God willing	**אם־ירצה־השם** [מירצעשעם]
golem	**גולם** דער (ס) [גוילעם (ס)]
good (2)	**גוט**
(have a) good day (*reply*) (2)	אַ גוטן טאָג (אַ גוט יאָר)
(have a) good Shabbos (*reply*) (4)	אַ גוטן שבת (אַ גוט יאָר)
(have a) good week (*reply*) (4)	אַ גוטע וואָך (אַ גוט יאָר)
good evening (*reply*) (2)	גוטן־אָוונט (גוט־יאָר)
good evening (*after Havdalah*) (4)	גוט־וואָך
good morning/afternoon (*reply*) (2)	גוט־מאָרגן (גוט־יאָר)
good night (2)	אַ גוטע נאַכט
good Shabbos (*reply*) (4)	גוט־שבת (גוט־יאָר)
not too good (2)	נישט אַזוי אײַ־אײַ־אײַ
good-bye (*formal/informal*) (*lit.* be well) (2)	**זײַ(ט) געזונט**
grade	**צייכן** דער (ס)
grain (*SC*)	**תּבֿואה** די (–ות) [טוווּע (ס)]
grammatical (11)	**גראַמאַטיש**
grandchild (9)	**אייניקל** דאָס (עך)
grandfather (9)	**זיידע^** דער (ס)
grandmother (9)	**באָבע^** די (ס)
grape (13)	**ווײַנטרויב** די (ן)
grapefruit (13)	**גרייפּפֿרוכט** דער (ן)
gray (5)	**גרוי**
great-... (relative) (9)	**עלטער־...**
great-uncle (9)	**עלטער־פֿעטער** דער (ס)
green (5)	**גרין**
greenery (13, supplement)	**גרינס** דאָס (ן)
greet (*v*) (8)	**באַגריסן** (באַגריסט)
exchange greetings (*v*) (2)	**באַגריסן זיך**
greeting (2)	**גרוס** דער (ן); **באַגריסונג** די (ען)
greeting card (8)	**באַגריס־קאַרטל** דאָס (עך)
grow (*v*) (17)	**וואַקסן** (איז געוואַקסן)
guess (*v*)	**טרעפֿן** (געטראָפֿן)
guest	**גאַסט** דער (געסט)
guitar (*AB*)	**גיטאַרע** די (ס)

H

habitat (17)	**האַביטאַט** דער (ן)
Haggadah (22)	**הגדה** די (–ות) [האַגאָדע (ס)]
read from the Haggadah (*v*) (22)	זאָגן די הגדה
hair (*pl*) (11)	**האָר** די
half	**האַלב; העלפֿט** די (ן)
half-brother (9)	**האַלבער ברודער** דער (האַלבע ברידער)
half-sister (9)	**האַלבע שוועסטער** די (האַלבע שוועסטער)
hamantasch (three-cornered filled pastry) (18)	**המן־טאַש** דער (ן) [האָמען]
hand (*SC*)	**האַנט** די (הענט)
handbag (19)	**בײַטל** דאָס (עך)
hang (*v*) (13)	**הענגען** (איז געהאָנגען)

Hanukkah (15)	**חנוכּה** דער [כאַ́ניקע]
happen (*v*)	**געשע́ן** (זיי געשעען; איז געשע́ן)
happy (7)	**פֿריילעך**; **צופֿרידן** (צופֿרידענע)
happy holiday (8)	גוט־יום־טובֿ [יאָנטעוו]
hard (7)	**האַרט**
hare	**האָז** דער (ן)
Hasidic leader	**רבי^** דער (ס) [רעבע (ס)]
hat (11)	**הוט** דער (היט)
hate (*v*) (10)	**פֿײַנט האָבן** (איך האָב פֿײַנט; פֿײַנט געהאַט)
Havdalah (4)	**הבֿדלה** די (–ות) [האַוודאָלע (ס)]
have (*v*) (3)	**האָבן** [האָבם] (איך האָב, דו האָסט; געהאַט)
have to (*v*) (19)	**דאַרפֿן** (ער דאַרף)
he (1)	**ער**
head (*SC*)	**קאָפּ** דער (קעפּ)
heal (someone) (*v*) (10)	**היילן**
healthy (2)	**געזו́נט**
hear (*v*) (2)	**הערן**
heavy (7)	**שווער**
Hebrew (1)	**העברעיִש** דאָס
hello, nice to meet/ see you (*reply*) (1)	**שלום־עליכם** [שאָלעם־אַלייכעם] (**עליכם־שלום** [אַלייכעם־שאָלעם])
help (*v*)	**העלפֿן** (געהאָלפֿן)
her (*acc*) (11)	**זי**
her (*dat*) (14)	**איר**
her (*poss adj*) (7)	**איר** (אירע)
here (5)	**דאָ**
here you go	**נאַ**
here (*with pointing*)	**אָט**
herring (2, 13)	**הערינג** דער (—)
Heshvan (20)	**חשוון** [כעזשוון]
hide (*v*)	**באַהאַלטן זיך** (באַהאַלטן)
high (7)	**הויך**
him (*acc/dat*) (11, 14)	**אים**
his (*poss adj*) (7)	**זײַן** (זײַנע)
history (6)	**געשיכטע** די
hold (*v*)	**האַלטן** (איך האַלט, מיר האַלטן; געהאַלטן)
holiday (8)	**יום־טובֿ** דער (ים) [יאָנטעוו (יאָנטויווים)]
happy holiday (8)	גוט־יום־טובֿ
Holocaust (18)	**חורבן** דער [כורבם]
holy (8)	**הייליק**
holy book	**ספֿר** דער (ים) [סייפֿער (ספֿאָרים)]
home (16)	**היים** די (ען)
at home	אין דער היים
homeward (16)	**אַהיי́ם**
homework (6)	**היי́מאַרבעט** די
do homework (*v*) (6)	מאַכן היימאַרבעט
honey (13)	**האָניק** דער
hooray! (*CE*)	**הוראַ́!**

hope	**האָ́פֿענונג** די (ען)
hora (dance)	**האָרע** די (ס)
horse (17)	**פֿערד** דאָס (—)
horseradish (22)	**כריין** דער
hot (7)	**הייס**
house (1; 12, 16)	**הויז** דאָס (הײַזער); **שטוב** די (שטיבער)
housecleaner (10)	**אוי́פֿראַמער** דער (ס) / **אויפֿראַמערין** די (ס)
how (1)	**ווי**; **ווי אַזוי́**
how does one say ... in Yiddish? (1)	ווי זאָגט מען ... אויף ייִדיש?
how are you? (*informal*) (2)	וואָס מאַכסטו?
how many (3)	**וויפֿל**
how much (3)	**וויפֿל**
humanities (6)	**הומאַניסטיק** די
humid (20)	**פֿײַכט**
hundred (*alt.* one hundred) (3)	**הונדערט**
Hungarian (1)	**או́נגעריש** דאָס
Hungary (1)	**או́נגערן** דאָס
hungry	**הו́נגעריק**
hurt (*v*) (*SC*)	**וויי טאָן** (עס טוט וויי; עס האָט וויי געטאָן)
husband (9)	**מאַן** דער (מענער)

I

I (1)	**איך**
ice cream (2)	**אײַזקרעם** דער
idea (*AB*)	**אידעע** די (ס)
if	**אויב**; **אַז**
ignore (*v*) (10)	**איגנאָרירן** (איגנאָרי́רט)
imitate (*v*) (10)	**אימיטירן** (אימיטי́רט)
important (10)	**וויכטיק**
improvise (*v*) (10)	**אימפּראָוויזירן** (אימפּראָוויזי́רט)
in (1)	**אין**
in Yiddish (*CE*)	אויף ייִדיש [אַף]
income	**הכנסה** די (–ות) [האַכנאָסע (ס)]
increase (*v*)	**מערן**
indeed (*CE*, 9)	**טאַקע**
inspire (*v*) (10)	**אינספּירירן** (אינספּירי́רט)
instructions (*CE*)	**אָנווײַזונג** די (ען)
instrument	**אינסטרומע́נט** דער (ן)
intellectual (9)	**אינטעלעקטוע́ל**
interesting (6)	**אינטערעסאַ́נט**
interview (*v*) (10)	**אינטערוויוּירן** (אינטערוויוּי́רט)
Israel (1)	**ישׂראל** דאָס [ייִסראָעל]
it (*nom/acc*) (1, 11)	**עס**
it (*dat*) (14)	**אים**
Italian (1)	**איטאַליעניש** דאָס
Italy (1)	**איטאַליע** די
its (*poss adj*) (7)	**זײַן** (זײַנע)
Iyar (20)	**אייר** [איִער]

J

jacket (19)	רעקל דאָס (עך)
jam (13)	אײַנגעמאַכטס דאָס (ן)
January (20)	יאַנואַר
Japan (1)	יאַפּאַן דאָס
Japanese (1)	יאַפּאַניש דאָס
jasmine (9)	יאַסמין דער (ען)
Jew	ייִד דער (ן)
Jewish (13)	ייִדיש
Jewish studies (6)	ייִדישע לימודים די
journalist (10)	זשורנאַליסט דער (ן) / זשורנאַליסטקע די (ס)
joy	פֿרייד די (ן)
judge (10)	שופֿט דער (ים) [שויפֿעט (שאָפֿטים)]
juice (13)	זאַפֿט דער (ן)
juicy (13)	זאַפֿטיק
July (20)	יולי
jump (*v*) (2)	שפּרינגען (איז געשפּרונגען)
June (20)	יוני

K

kerchief (11)	טיכל דאָס (עך)
kiddush (4)	קידוש דער
kill (*v*) (11)	טייטן (געטייט)
kind: what kind of	וואָס פֿאַר אַ
kippah (11)	יאַרמלקע די (ס)
Kislev (20)	כּיסלו [קיסלעוו]
kiss (*v*) (11)	קושן
kitchen	קיך די (ן)
knee (*SC*)	קני דער (—)
knife (13)	מעסער דער (ס)
know (*v*) (1)	וויסן (איך ווייס, מיר ווייסן; געוווּסט)
know (how to) (*v*) (9, 19)	קענען (ער קען)
kugel (noodle or potato casserole, usually eaten on Shabbos) (2, 13)	קוגל דער (ען)

L

lake (*AB*)	אָזערע די (ס)
lamp (5)	לאָמפּ דער (ן)
language (1)	שפּראַך די (ן)
last	פֿאַרגאַנגען
last week (17)	פֿאַרגאַנגענע וואָך
late	שפּעט
latke, (potato) pancake (13)	לאַטקע די (ס)
laugh (*v*) (2)	לאַכן
lawyer (10)	אַדוואָקאַט דער (ן) / אַדוואָקאַטין די (ס)
lay (down) (*v*) (5, 13)	לייגן
lead (*v*)	פֿירן
leaf, sheet (of paper) (5)	בלאַט דער (בלעטער); בלעטל דאָס (עך)
learn (*v*) (10)	לערנען זיך
leavened food (22)	חמץ דער [כאָמעץ]
lecture (16)	לעקציע די (ס)
left	לינקס
(on the) left (7, 13)	(אויף) לינקס
leg (*SC*)	פֿוס דער (פֿיס)
lemon (13)	לימענע די (ס)
less (than) (6)	ווייניקער (ווי)
lesson (6)	לעקציע די (ס)
let's (3)	לאָמיר
letter (11)	בריוו דער (—)
letter (of the alphabet)	אות דער (יות) [אָס (אויסיעס)]
lettuce (*pl*) (13)	שאַלאַטן די
librarian (10)	ביבליאָטעקער דער (ס) / ביבליאָטעקערין די (ס)
library (16)	ביבליאָטעק די (ן)
lick (*v*) (*SC*)	לעקן
lie (*v*) (13)	ליגן (איז געלעגן)
life (6)	לעבן דאָס (ס) [לעבם]
light (in color) (5)	העל
light blue (5)	העל בלוי
light (in weight) (7)	גרינג; לײַכט
light (*v*) (15)	אָנ·צינדן (אָנגעצונדן)
lightning (20)	בליץ דער (ן)
like (7)	ווי; אַזוי ווי
like (*v*) (10)	ליב האָבן (איך האָב ליב; ליב געהאַט)
lily (9)	ליליע די (ס)
line (of writing) (*CE*)	שורה די (–ות) [שורע (ס)]
linguistics (6)	לינגוויסטיק די
lion (17)	לייב דער (ן)
lip (*SC*)	ליפּ די (ן)
list (5)	רשימה די (–ות) [רעשימע (ס)]
listen (*v*) (*CE*)	צו·הערן זיך (צוגעהערט)
literature (6)	ליטעראַטור די
Lithuania (1)	ליטע די
Lithuanian (1)	ליטוויש דאָס
little (*SC*)	ווייניק
a little bit (of)	אַ ביסל
live (*v*)	לעבן [לעבם]; וווינען
lizard (17)	יאַשטשערקע די (ס)
location (16)	אָרט דער (ערטער)
long (7)	לאַנג
as long as	כּל־זמן [קאָל־זמאַן]
look (at) (*v*) (5)	קוקן (אויף)
lord (11)	האַר דער (ן)
lose (*v*) (15)	פֿאַרלירן (פֿאַרלוירן)

lot: a lot (of) (6)	אַ סך [סאַך]
loud (7)	הויך
love (*v*) (10)	ליב האָבן (איך האָב ליב; ליב געהאַט)
low (7)	נידעריק
lox (13)	לאַקס דער (ן)
luck	מזל דאָס [מאַזל]
good luck!	זאָל זײַן מיט מזל
lullaby	וויגליד דאָס (ער)
lulov (12)	לולבֿ דער (ים) [לולעוו (לולאָווים)]
lunch (13)	מיטאָג דער (ן)

M

make (*v*)	מאַכן
make up (*v*) (8)	איבער·בעטן זיך (איבערגעבעטן)
man (9)	מאַן דער (מענער)
many (6)	אַ סך [סאַך]; פֿיל
how many (3)	וויפֿל
March (20)	מאַרץ
market	מאַרק דער (מערק)
married: get married (*v*)	חתונה האָבן [כאַסענע (ס)] (געהאַט)
marzipan (7)	מאַרצעפּאַן דער (עס)
masculine (*gramm*)	מאַסקולין
massage (*v*) (10)	מאַסאַזשירן (מאַסאַזשירט)
matchmaker	שדכן דער (ים) [שאַטכן (שאַטכאָנים)] / שדכנטע די (ס) [שאַטכנטע (ס)]
material (13)	מאַטעריאַל דער (ן)
mathematics (3, 6)	מאַטעמאַטיק די
matzoh (2, 22)	מצה די (–ות) [מאַצע (ס)]
may (19)	מעגן (ער מעג)
May (20)	מײַ
maybe (6)	אפֿשר [עפֿשער]
me (*acc*) (11)	מיך
me (*dat*) (14)	מיר
meal (13)	מאָלצײַט דער (ן)
mean (*v*) (1)	מיינען
what does ... mean? (1)	וואָס מיינט ... ?
meaning	טײַטש דער (ן); באַטײַט דער (ן)
meat (2, 13)	פֿלייש דאָס (ן)
of (or including) meat (13)	פֿליישיק
medicine	מעדיצין די (ען)
meet up (*v*) (3, 16)	טרעפֿן זיך (געטראָפֿן)
pleased to meet you (1)	זייער אײַנגענעם
meeting (10)	טרעפֿונג די (ען)
melon (13)	מעלאָן דער (ען)
menorah (nine-branched candelabrum lit on Hanukkah) (15)	חנוכּה־לאָמפּ דער (ן) [כאַניקע־...]
mention (*v*)	דערמאָנען (דערמאָנט)
mess	באַלאַגאַן דער (ען)
Messiah (22)	משיח דער (ים) [מעשיִעך (מעשיכים)]
metal (13)	מעטאַל דער (ן)
meteorologist	וועטער־נבֿיא דער (ים) [...־נאָווי (...־נעוויִים)]
middle	מיטן דער (ס)
in the middle (13)	אין מיטן
midnight (16)	האַלבע נאַכט
milk (13)	מילך די
minus (3)	מינוס
minute	מינוט די (ן)
(twenty) minutes past (nine) (16)	(צוואַנציק) מינוט נאָך (נײַן)
(five) minutes to (nine) (16)	(פֿינף) מינוט צו (נײַן)
thirty minutes to (nine) (16)	האַלב (נײַן)
miracle (15)	נס דער (ים) [נעס (ניסים)]
mirror (14)	שפּיגל דער (ען)
misfortune	אומגליק דאָס (ן)
modal (*gramm*) (19)	מאָדאַל
model (1)	דוגמא די (–ות) [דוגמע (ס)]
Monday (2)	מאָנטיק
money (10)	געלט דאָס (ן)
monkey (17)	מאַלפּע די (ס)
month (12, 20)	חודש דער (חדשים) [כוידעש (כאַדאָשים)]
more	נאָך
more (than) (6)	מער (ווי)
morning: in the morning (2, 16)	אין דער פֿרי
Morocco (1)	מאַראָקאָ דאָס
mother (9)	מאַמע^ די (ס)
motivate (*v*) (10)	מאָטיווירן (מאָטיווירט)
motorcycle (21)	מאָטאָציקל דער (ען)
Mount Sinai (*SC*)	באַרג סיני דער [סיניי]
moustache (*pl*) (11)	וואָנצעס די
mouth (*SC*)	מויל דאָס (מײַלער)
movie theater (16)	קינאָ דער (ס)
Mr.	הער
Ms.	פֿרוי
much (6)	פֿיל; אַ סך [סאַך]
as much ... as	אַזוי פֿיל ... ווי
too much (*SC*)	צו פֿיל
how much (3)	וויפֿל
multiply (*v*)	מערן
museum (16)	מוזיי דער (ען)
mushroom (7, 13)	שוואָם דער (ען)
music (6)	מוזיק די
musician (10)	מוזיקער דער (ס) / מוזיקערין די (ס)
must (19)	מוזן (ער מוז)
my (7)	מײַן (מײַנע)

N

nail (*SC*)	**נאָגל** דער (נעגל)
naïve (9)	**נאַיִוו**
name (3)	**נאָמען** דער (נעמען)
what's your name? (*informal*) (1)	ווי הייסטו?
name: be named (*v*) (1)	**הייסן** (געהייסן)
napkin (13)	**סערוועטקע** די (ס)
narrow (7)	**שמאָל**
nation	**פֿאָלק** דאָס (פֿעלקער)
natural science (6)	**נאַטור־וויסנשאַפֿט** די
near (14)	**לעבן** [לעבם]
near (to) (1)	**נאָענט** (צו)
necessary	**נייטיק**
neck (*SC*)	**נאַקן** דער (ס)
need (*v*) (19)	**דאַרפֿן** (ער דאַרף)
nephew (9)	**פּלימעניק** דער (עס)
neuter (*gramm*)	**נייטראַל**
never (17)	**קיין מאָל נישט**
new (7)	**נײַ**
New Year (8)	**נײַיאָר** דער
newspaper (10)	**צײַטונג** די (ען)
nice (7, *CE*)	**שיין**
niece (9)	**פּלימעניצע** די (ס)
night (2)	**נאַכט** די (נעכט)
at night (2, 16)	בײַ נאַכט
nine (3)	**נײַן**
nineteen (3)	**נײַנצן**
ninety (3)	**נײַנציק**
Nisan (20)	**ניסן** [ניסן]
no (1)	**ניין**
no (*article*)	**קיין**
no one (19)	**קיינער** (...) **נישט**
noise (18)	**רעש** דער [ראַש]
noisemaker (18)	**גראַגער** דער (ס)
nominative (*gramm*) (9)	**נאָמינאַטיוו** דער (ן)
noodle (13)	**לאָקש** דער (ן)
noon (16)	**האַלבער טאָג**
north (1)	**צפֿון** [צאָפֿן]
North America (1)	**צפֿון־אַמעריקע** די
nose (*SC*)	**נאָז** די (נעזער)
not (2)	**נישט**
not any (6)	נישט קיין
notebook (5)	**העפֿט** די (ן)
nothing (15)	**גאָרנישט**
noun (8)	**סובסטאַנטיוו** דער (ן)
November (20)	**נאָוועמבער**
now (2)	**איצט**
number	**נומער** דער (ן)
numeral (3)	**צאָלוואָרט** דאָס (...ווערטער)
nut (13)	**נוס** (ניס)

O

October (20)	**אָקטאָבער**
of (1, 14)	**פֿון**
office (10)	**ביוראָ** דאָס (ען)
oil (13)	**בוימל** דער (ען)
old (7)	**אַלט**
I am ... years old (3)	איך בין אַלט ... יאָר
how old are you? (*informal*) (3)	ווי אַלט ביסטו?
older (than) (3)	**עלטער** (פֿון)
Omer, the 49-day period between Pesach and Shavuos (*SC*)	**עומר** דער [אוימער]
on (1, 14)	**אויף** [אַף]
one (3)	**איינס** (איין)
one (*impersonal pron*) (1)	**מען** (מע)
oneself (*reflexive pron*) (10)	**זיך**
onion (13)	**ציבעלע** די (ס)
only (17; 6)	**בלויז; נאָר**
open (*v*) (5)	**עפֿענען** (איך עפֿן, מיר עפֿענען)
opposite	**היפוך** דער (ים) [הייפעך (היפוכים)]
optimism	**אָפּטימיזם** דער
optimistic (9)	**אָפּטימיסטיש**
or (1)	**אָדער**
orange (color) (5)	**אָראַנזש** (אָראַנזשן, אָראַנזשענע)
orange (fruit) (13)	**מאַראַנץ** דער (ן)
order (22)	**סדר** דער (ים) [סיידער (סדאָרים)]
order (*v*) (10)	**באַשטעלן** (באַשטעלט)
organize (*v*) (10)	**אָרגאַניזירן** (אָרגאַניזירט)
original (9)	**אָריגינעל**
other (13)	**אַנדער**
one another	איינער דעם אַנדערן
our (7)	**אונדזער** (אונדזערע)
outside (*AB*, 20)	**אין דרויסן**
over (14)	**איבער**
own	**אייגן** (אייגענע)

P

p.m. (16)	**נ״מ** (נאָך מיטאָג)
page (*CE*)	**זײַט** די (ן)
pants (19)	**הויזן** די
paper (9, 13)	**פּאַפּיר** דאָס (ן)
parashah (section of the Torah) (*SC*)	**פּרשה** די (–יות) [פּאַרשע (ס)]
parents (9)	**עלטערן** די
pareve (neither dairy nor meat) (13)	**פּאַרעווע**
park (2, 16, *AB*)	**פּאַרק** דער (ן)

parrot (*AB*)	**פּאָפּוגײַ** דער (ען)
part	**טייל** דער (ן)
partner (9)	**פּאַרטנער** דער (ס) / **פּאַרטנערין** די (ס)
party (16)	**שׂימחה** די (–ות) [סימכע (ס)]
pass (*v*) (10)	**דערלאַנגען** (דערלאַנגט)
passenger (2)	**פּאַסאַזשיר** דער (ן)
past	**פֿאַרגאַנגען**
past tense (17)	פֿאַרגאַנגענע צײַט
patience	**געדולד** די
peaceful	**רויִק**
peach (13)	**פֿערשקע** די (ס)
peacock (17)	**פּאַווע** די (ס)
pear (*AB*, 11, 13)	**באַר** די (ן)
peasant (11)	**פּויער** דער (ים)
pen (5)	**פֿען** די (ען); **פֿעדער** די (ס)
pencil (*AB*, 5)	**בלײַער** דער (ס)
pepper (13)	**פֿעפֿער** דער
performance	**פֿאָרשטעלונג** די (ען)
perfume (*v*) (10)	**פּאַרפֿומירן** (פּאַרפֿומירט)
person (8, 11)	**מענטש** דער (ן)
Pesach (Passover) (22)	**פּסח** דער [פּייסעך]
Pharaoh (22)	**פּרעה** דער (ס) [פּאַרע]
philosophy (6)	**פֿילאָסאָפֿיע** די
photograph (*v*) (10)	**פֿאָטאָגראַפֿירן** (פֿאָטאָגראַפֿירט)
photographer (10)	**פֿאָטאָגראַף** דער (ן) / **פֿאָטאָגראַפֿין** די (ס)
physics (6)	**פֿיזיק** די
piano (14)	**פּיאַנע** די (ס)
pick (fruit) (*v*) (11)	**רײַסן** (געריסן)
pickle (13)	**זויערע אוגערקע** די (ס)
picture	**בילד** דאָס (ער)
piece	**שטיק** דאָס (ער)
pilot (2)	**פּילאָט** דער (ן) / **פּילאָטין** די (ס)
pineapple (13)	**אַנאַנאַס** דער (ן)
pink (5)	**ראָזעווע**
pious	**פֿרום**
pizza (13)	**פּיצע** די (ס)
place (16)	**אָרט** דער (ערטער)
place (*v*) (5, 13)	**לייגן**
plan (*v*) (10)	**פּלאַנירן** (פּלאַנירט)
plate (13)	**טעלער** דער (—)
play (16)	**פּיעסע** די (ס)
play (*v*) (2)	**שפּילן**
playing card	**קאָרט** די (ן)
pleasant	**אײַנגענעם**
please (*formal/informal*) (*lit.* be so good) (2)	**זײַ(ט) אַזוי גוט**
pleased to meet you (1)	**זייער אײַנגענעם**
pleasure	**פֿאַרגעניגן** דאָס (ס)
with the greatest pleasure (2)	מיטן גרעסטן פֿאַרגעניגן
plum (7, 13)	**פֿלוים** די (ען)
plural (*gramm*)	**מערצאָל** די (ן)
plus (3)	**פּלוס**
poem (*AB*, 2)	**ליד** דאָס (ער)
poet (*AB*)	**פּאָעט** דער (ן)
point to (*v*) (5)	**ווײַזן אויף** [אַף] (געוויזן)
Poland (1)	**פּוילן** דאָס
polenta (corn mush) (13)	**מאַמעליגע** די
Polish (1)	**פּויליש** דאָס
political science (6)	**פּאָליטיק** די
politics (6)	**פּאָליטיק** די
ponder (*v*)	**קלערן**
ponytail (11)	**לאָשיק־עקל** דאָס (עך)
poor thing! (2)	**נעבעך**
popcorn (*pl*) (16)	**קאָקאָשעס** די
porcelain (13)	**פּאָרצעלײַ** דאָס
porridge (esp. of buckwheat) (13)	**קאַשע** די (ס)
position (13)	**פּאָזיציע** די (ס)
possibility	**מעגלעכקייט** די (ן)
possible	**מעגלעך**
poster	**פּלאַקאַט** דער (ן)
pot (9)	**טעפּל** דאָס (עך)
potato (2)	**בולבע** די (ס)
pour (*v*) (10)	**גיסן** (געגאָסן)
pray (*v*) (8, 16)	**דאַווענען**
prayer	**תּפֿילה** די (–ות) [טפֿילע (ס)]
prayer book	**סידור** דער (ים) [סידער (סידורים)]
prayer book for the Days of Awe (8)	**מחזור** דער (ים) [מאַכזער (מאַכזוירים)]
predestine (*v*)	**באַשערן** (באַשערט)
prepare (*v*)	**גרייטן** (געגרייט)
preposition (1)	**פּרעפּאָזיציע** די (ס)
present (*v*) (10)	**פּרעזענטירן** (פּרעזענטירט)
presentation (6)	**רעפֿעראַט** דער (ן)
give a presentation (*v*) (6)	האַלטן אַ רעפֿעראַט
probably (6)	**מסתּמא** [מיסטאָמע]
problem	**פּראָבלעם** די (ען)
no problem	**נישקשה** [נישקאָשע]
profession (10)	**פּראָפֿעסיע** די (ס)
professor (1)	**פּראָפֿעסאָר** דער (ן) / **פּראָפֿעסאָרשע** די (ס)
pronoun (1)	**פּראָנאָם** דער (ען)
prophet	**נבֿיא** דער (ים) [נאָווי (נעוויִים)] / **נבֿיאה** די (–ות) [נעוויִע (ס)]
proud	**שטאָלץ**
psychology (6)	**פּסיכאָלאָגיע** די
puddle	**קאַלוזשע** די (ס)

Purim (18)	פּורים דער
Purim play (18)	פּורים־שפּיל די (ן)
purple (*invariable*) (5)	לילאַ
put (*v*) (13)	שטעלן
put away (*v*) (5)	אַוועק·לייגן (אַוועקגעלייגט)
put down (*v*) (5)	אַוועק·לייגן (אַוועקגעלייגט)
put in (into) (*v*) (5)	אַרײַנ·לייגן (אין) (אַרײַנגעלייגט)
put on (clothing) (*v*) (*SC*)	אָנ·טאָן (איך טו אָן, מיר טוען אָן; אָנגעטאָן)

Q

quarter	פֿערטל דאָס (עך)
a quarter past (nine) (16)	אַ פֿערטל נאָך (נײַן)
a quarter to (nine) (16)	אַ פֿערטל צו (נײַן)
queen	מלכּה די (–ות) [מאַלקע (ס)]
question (6)	פֿראַגע די (ס)
I have a question (*lit.* I want to ask something) (1)	איך וויל עפּעס פֿרעגן
The Four Questions (asked at the Passover seder) (22)	די פֿיר קשיות [קאַשעס]
question word (1)	פֿרעגוואָרט דאָס (...ווערטער)
quiet	שטיל
quiz (6)	אויספֿרעג דער (ן)
take a quiz (*v*) (6)	האַלטן אַן אויספֿרעג

R

radish (13)	רעטעכל דאָס (עך)
rail	רעלס דער (ן)
rain (20)	רעגן דער (ס)
it's raining (20)	עס גייט אַ רעגן
raisin (13)	ראָזשינקע די (ס)
rare	זעלטן (זעלטענע)
raspberry (13)	מאַלינע די (ס)
rather (2)	בעסער
read (*v*) (2)	לייענען
ready (*CE*)	גרייט
really (*CE*, 9)	טאַקע
reason	סיבה די (–ות) [סיבע (ס)]
receive (*v*) (15)	באַקומען (באַקומען)
recently (17)	לעצטנס
recognize (*v*)	דערקענען (דערקענט)
record (*v*) (10)	רעקאָרדירן (רעקאָרדירט)
red (5)	רויט
regards: my regards (to)... (19)	אַ גרוס...
rejoice (*v*)	פֿרייען זיך
relationship	באַציִונג די (ען)
relative (9)	קרובֿ דער (ים) [קאָרעוו (קרויווים)] / קרובֿה די (–ות) [קרויווע (ס)]
religion (6)	רעליגיע די
religious (9)	רעליגיעז
remember (*v*) (1)	דערמאָנען זיך; געדענקען (געדענקט)
repair (*v*)	פֿאַרריכטן (פֿאַרריכט / פֿאַרראָכטן)
repeat (another's words) (*v*) (*CE*)	נאָכ·זאָגן (נאָכגעזאָגט)
repeat (*v*) (*CE*)	איבער·חזרן [איבערכאַזערן] (איבערגעחזרט)
reside (*v*) (1)	וווינען
rest (4)	רו די
restaurant (16)	רעסטאָראַן דער (ען)
retired	אויף פּענסיע [אַף]
rewrite (*v*)	איבער·שרײַבן (איבערגעשריבן)
rice (13)	רײַז דער
rich (9)	רײַך
ride (*v*) (17)	רײַטן (איז געריטן)
right (direction)	רעכטס
(on the) right (7, 13)	(אויף) רעכטס
right (10)	גערעכט
you're right	דו ביסט גערעכט
river (17)	טײַך דער (ן)
road	וועג דער (ן)
rocking chair (14)	וויגשטול דער (ן)
Romania (1)	רומעניע די
Romanian (1)	רומעניש דאָס
roof (12)	דאַך דער (דעכער)
room (1)	צימער דער (ן)
roommate	מיטוווינער דער (ס) / מיטוווינערין די (ס)
rose (9)	רויז די (ן)
Rosh Hashanah (8)	ראָש־השנה דער [ראָשעשאָנע]
Rosh Hashanah greeting card (8)	לשנה־טובֿה די (–ות) [לעשאָנע־טויווע (ס)]
row	ריי די (ען)
rug (14)	טעפּעך דער (ער)
run (*v*) (2)	לויפֿן (איז געלאָפֿן)
run away (*v*)	אַנטלויפֿן (איז אַנטלאָפֿן)
Russia (1)	רוסלאַנד דאָס
Russian (1)	רוסיש דאָס

S

sad (7)	טרויעריק
sadness	טרויער דער
salmon (13)	לאַקס דער (ן)
salt (13)	זאַלץ די (ן)
salty (13)	זאַלציק
same	זעלבער
sandal (19)	סאַנדאַל דער (ן)
Saturday (2, 4)	שבת [שאַבעס]
saucer (13)	טעלערל דאָס (עך)
Saudi Arabia (1)	סאַוד־אַראַביע די

say (*v*) (1)	**זאָגן**
how does one say ... in Yiddish? (1)	ווי זאָגט מען ... אויף ייִדיש?
scarf (19)	**שאַל** די (ן)
school (16)	**שול** די (ן)
schoolwork (6)	**שוּלאַרבעט** די
scissors (5)	**שער** די (ן)
scroll (18)	**מגילה** די (–ות) [מעגילע (ס)]
sea	**ים** דער (ען) [יאַם (ען)]
search (for) (*v*)	**זוכן**
season (20)	**צײַט פֿון יאָר** די
seasoning (13)	**פּריפּראַווע** די (ס)
second	**צווייט**
secret	**סוד** דער (ות) [סאָד (סוידעס)]
secretary (10)	**סעקרעטאַר** דער (ן) / **סעקרעטאַרשע** די (ס)
seder (22)	**סדר** דער (ים) [סיידער (סדאָרים)]
hold or take part in a seder (*v*) (22)	פּראַווען אַ סדר
seder plate (for ritual food items) (22)	**קערה** די (–ות) [קײַרע (ס)]
see (*v*) (3)	**זען** (איך זע, מיר זעען; געזען)
sell (*v*) (10)	**פֿאַרקויפֿן** (פֿאַרקויפֿט)
send (*v*) (11)	**שיקן**
sentence (5)	**זאַץ** דער (ן)
separable verbal prefix (5)	**קאָנווערב** דער (ן)
September (20)	**סעפּטעמבער**
serious (8)	**ערנסט**
set (*v*) (13)	**זעצן**
set the table (*v*) (13)	גרייטן צום טיש
seven (3)	**זיבן** [זיבם]
seventeen (3)	**זיבעצן**
seventy (3)	**זיבעציק**
several	**עטלעכע**
sew (*v*) (10)	**נייען**
Shabbos (2, 4)	**שבת** דער (ים) [שאַבעס (שאַבאָסים)]
Shabbos candle (4)	**שבת־ליכט** דאָס (—)
shake (*v*) (12)	**שאָקלען** (איך שאָקל)
shalach monos (parcel of treats given to friends and neighbors on Purim) (18)	**שלח־מנות** דער [שאַלאַכמאָנעס]
Shavuos (*SC*)	**שבֿועות** דער [שווּעס]
shawl (19)	**שאַל** די (ן)
she (1)	**זי**
shelf (14)	**פּאָליצע** די (ס)
Shemini Atzereth (12)	**שמיני־עצרת** דער [שמינאַצערעס]
Shevat (20)	**שבֿט** [שוואַט]
shine (*v*)	**שײַנען**
the sun is shining (20)	עס שײַנט די זון
ship (21)	**שיף** די (ן)
shirt (19)	**העמד** דאָס (ער)
shock (*v*) (10)	**שאָקירן** (שאָקירט)
shoe (19)	**שוך** דער (שיך)
shoemaker (10)	**שוסטער** דער (ס) / **שוסטערקע** די (ס)
Shofar (ram's horn blown during the Days of Awe) (8)	**שופֿר** דער (ות) [שויפֿער (שויפֿרעס)]
blow shofar (*v*) (8)	בלאָזן שופֿר
shohet (ritual slaughterer) (11)	**שוחט** דער (ים) [שויכעט (שאָכטים)]
shopkeeper (10)	**קרעמער** דער (ס) / **קרעמערקע** די (ס)
shore	**ברעג** דער (ן)
short (7)	**קורץ**
shorts (19)	**קורצע הייזלעך**
should (19)	**זאָלן** (ער זאָל)
shoulder (*SC*)	**אַקסל** דער (ען)
show (*v*)	**װײַזן** (געוויזן)
shower (*SC*)	**שפּריץ** דער (ן)
sick (2)	**קראַנק**
side	**זײַט** די (ן)
side (of a family)	**צד** דער (צדדים) [צאַד (צדאָדים)]
side lock (11)	**פּאה** די (–ות) [פּייע (ס)]
Simchas Torah (12)	**שׂימחת־תּורה** דער [סימכעס־טוירע]
similar	**ענלעך**
simply (for no special reason)	**סתּם** [סטאַם]
sin (8)	**זינד** די (—)
sing (*v*) (2)	**זינגען** (געזונגען)
singer (3, 10)	**זינגער** דער (ס) / **זינגערין** די (ס)
singular (*gramm*)	**אייזצאָל** די (ן)
sink (*SC*)	**וואַשטיש** דער (ן)
sister (9)	**שוועסטער** די (—)
sit (*v*) (2, 13)	**זיצן** (איז געזעסן)
sit down (*v*) (*CE*)	**אַוועק·זעצן זיך** (אַוועקגעזעצט)
Sivan (20)	**סיוון** [סיוון]
six (3)	**זעקס**
sixteen (3)	**זעכצן**
sixty (3)	**זעכציק**
skirt (19)	**קליידל** דאָס (עך)
sky (20)	**הימל** דער (ען)
slaughter (*v*) (11)	**שעכטן** (געשאָכטן)
slave (22)	**שקלאַף** דער (ן)
sleep (*v*) (2)	**שלאָפֿן** (איז געשלאָפֿן)
slow (7)	**פּאַמעלעך**
sly	**כיטרע**
small (7)	**קליין**
smart (7)	**קלוג**
smell (*v*) (*SC*)	**שמעקן**
smooth (11)	**גלאַט**

snake (17)	**שלאַנג** די (ען)
sneeze (*v*) (*SC*)	**ניסן** (גענאָסן)
snow (20)	**שניי** דער (ען)
it is snowing (20)	עס פֿאַלט אַ שניי
snowflake (20)	**שנייעלע** דאָס (ך)
so (*adv*) (6)	**אַזוי׳**
so (*conj*) (16; *CE*)	**טאָ; איז...**
soap (*SC*)	**זייף** די (ן)
social science (6)	**סאָציאַ׳ל־וויסנשאַפֿט** די
sociology (6)	**סאָציאָלאָגיע** די
sock (19)	**זאָק** דער (ן)
sofa (14)	**סאָפֿע** די (ס)
soft (7)	**ווייך**
some	**עטלעכע**
someone (10)	**עמעצער**
someone (*acc/dat*)	עמעצן
something (19)	**עפּעס**
sometimes (9)	**אַ מאָל**
son (9)	**זון** דער (זין)
sonata	**סאָנאַטע** די (ס)
song (*AB*, 2)	**ליד** דאָס (ער)
soon (16)	**באַלד**
sorry (*formal/informal*) (2)	**זײַ(ט) מוחל**
so-so (2)	**נישקשה** [נישקאָשע]
sour (13)	**זויער**
sour cream (13)	**סמעטענע** די
south (1)	**דרום** [דאָרעם]
South America (1)	**דרום־אַמעריקע** די
Spain (1)	**שפּאַניע** די
Spanish (1)	**שפּאַניש** דאָס
speak (*v*) (1)	**רעדן**
spend time (*v*)	**פֿאַרברענגען** (פֿאַרברענגט / פֿאַרבראַכט)
spicy (13)	**פּיקאַנט**
spin (*v*) (15)	**דרייען**
spoon (13)	**לעפֿל** דער (—)
spring (20)	**פֿרילינג** דער (ען)
stand (*v*) (2, 13)	**שטיין** (איך שטיי, מיר שטייען; איז געשטאַנען)
stanza (15)	**סטראָפֿע** די (ס)
stapler (5)	**דרעטלער** דער (ס)
start (doing) (*v*) (5)	**אָנ·הייבן** (אָנגעהויבן)
state (1)	**שטאַט** דער (ן)
station	**סטאַנציע** די (ס)
stay (*v*) (17)	**בלײַבן** [בלײַבם] (איז געבליבן)
step... (relative) (9)	**שטיפֿ...**
stepfather (9)	**שטיפֿטאַטע^** דער (ס)
stepmother (9)	**שטיפֿמאַמע^** די (ס)
stick (11)	**שטעקן** דער (ס)
still	**נאָך; נאָך אַלץ**

stomach (*SC*)	**בויך** דער (בײַכער)
stop (doing) (*v*) (5)	**אויפֿ·הערן** [אוף] (אויפֿגעהערט)
store (7, 16)	**קראָם** די (ען)
storm (20)	**שטורעם** דער (ס)
it's stormy (20)	עס איז אַ שטורעם
story (15)	**דערציילונג** די (ען); **מעשׂה** די (–ות) [מײַסע (ס)]
straight (7)	**גלײַך**
strange	**מאָדנע**
stranger	**פֿרעמדער (מענטש)** דער
strawberry (13)	**טרוסקאַפֿקע** די (ס)
stream (17)	**וואַסערל** דאָס (עך)
street (1)	**גאַס** די (ן)
streetcar (21)	**טראַמווײַ** דער (ען)
stroll (16)	**שפּאַציר** דער (ן)
stroll (*v*) (16)	**שפּאַצירן** (שפּאַצירט)
strong (7)	**שטאַרק**
student (1)	**סטודענט** דער (ן) / **סטודענטקע** די (ס)
study (a subject) (*v*) (6)	**שטודירן** (שטודירט)
style	**מאָדע** די (ס)
in style	אין דער מאָדע
subject (of instruction) (6)	**לימוד** דער (ים) [לימעד (לימודים)]
subsequent (3)	**ווײַטערדיק**
subway (21)	**אונטערבאַן** די (ען)
such	**אַזאַ** (אַזעלכע)
suddenly (20)	**פּלוצלינג; מיט אַ מאָל**
sugar (13)	**צוקער** דער
suggest (*v*)	**פֿיר·לייגן** (פֿירגעלייגט)
suit (19)	**קאָסטיום** דער (ען)
suit (*v*)	**פּאַסן**
suitcase (19)	**טשעמאָדאַן** דער (ען)
sukkah (12)	**סוכּה** די (–ות) [סוקע (ס)]
sukkah covering (12)	**סכך** דער [סכאַך]
Sukkos (12)	**סוכּות** דער [סוקעס]
summer (20)	**זומער** דער (ן)
sun (20)	**זון** די (ען)
the sun is shining (20)	עס שײַנט די זון
Sunday (2)	**זונטיק**
sunglasses (19)	**זונברילן** די
supper (13)	**אָוונטברויט** דאָס (ן)
surname (3)	**פֿאַמיליע** די (ס)
sweater (19)	**סוועטער** דער (ס)
sweet (13)	**זיס**
swim (*v*) (10)	**שווימען** (איז געשווומען)
swimming trunks (19)	**שווימקעס** די
synagogue (16)	**שול** די (ן)

T

table (5) — **טיש** דער (ן)
  set the table (*v*) (13) — גרייטן צום טיש
tablecloth (13) — **טישטעך** דער (ער)
tailor (10) — **שנײַדער** דער (ס) / **שנײַדערין** די (ס)
take (*v*) (5) — **נעמען** (גענומען)
  take a quiz, exam (*v*) (5) — האַלטן אַן אויספֿרעג, עקזאַמען
take off (clothing) (*v*) (*SC*) — **אױס·טאָן** (איך טו אויס, מיר טוען אויס; אױסגעטאָן)
take out (from) (*v*) (5) — **אַרױס·נעמען** (פֿון) (אַרױסגענומען)
take place (*v*) (16) — **פֿאָר·קומען** (זי קומט פֿאָר, זיי קומען פֿאָר; איז פֿאָרגעקומען)
tall (7) — **הויך**
Tammuz (20) — **תּמוז** [טאַמעז]
tango — **טאַנגאָ** דער (ס)
tasty (13) — **געשמאַק**
taxi (21) — **טאַקסי** דער (ס)
tea (*AB*, 13) — **טיי** די (ען)
teach (*v*) (6) — **לערנען**
teacher (2, 5) — **לערער** דער (ס) / **לערערין** די (ס)
tear — **טרער** די (ן)
tear (*v*) (11) — **רײַסן** (געריסן)
teaspoon (13) — **לעפֿעלע** דאָס (ך)
telepathic (9) — **טעלעפּאַטיש**
telephone number (3) — **טעלעפֿאָן־נומער** דער (ן)
television (programming) (10) — **טעלעוויזיע** די
television set (14) — **טעלעוויזאָר** דער (טעלעוויזאָרן)
tell (a story) (*v*) — **דערציילן** (דערציילט)
ten (3) — **צען**
tense (*gramm*) (16) — **צײַט** די (ן)
  past tense (17) — פֿאַרגאַנגענע צײַט
Tevet (20) — **טבֿת** [טייװעס]
than — **ווי**
thank God (2) — **ברוך־השם** [באָרעכאַשעֹם]
thank you, thanks (2) — **אַ דאַנק**
  thank you very much — אַ גרויסן/שיינעם דאַנק
that (*conj*) (19) — **אַז**
  that is (to say) (9) — הייסט עס
that (*relative pron*) — **וואָס**
that (the other) — **יענער**
the (*f nom/acc; pl*) (1, 11, 13) — **די**
the (*m acc/dat; n dat*) (11, 13) — **דעם**
the (*m nom; f dat*) (1, 13) — **דער**
the (*n nom/acc*) (1, 11) — **דאָס**
theater (16) — **טעאַטער** דער (ס)
theater arts (6) — **דראַמאַטורגיע** די
their (7) — **זייער** (זייערע)
them (*acc/dat*) (11, 14) — **זיי**
then (19) — **דעמאָלט**
there — **דאָרטן**
  there is/are (6) — עס איז/זײַנען דאָ
  there isn't/aren't any ... (6) — עס איז/זײַנען נישטאָ קיין ...
  there (goes) (2) — אָט (גייט)
these — **די**
they (2) — **זיי**
thick (7) — **דיק**
thin (7) — **דין**
thing (17) — **זאַך** די (ן)
think (*v*) — **טראַכטן** (געטראַכט)
  I think so (6) — איך מיין אַז יאָ
  I don't think so (6) — איך מיין אַז ניין
  think that (*v*) (6) — מיינען אַז
thirteen (3) — **דרײַצן**
thirty (3) — **דרײַסיק**
this (*f; m; n*) — **די; דער; דאָס**
thought — **געדאַנק** דער (ען)
thousand (*alt.* one thousand) (3) — **טויזנט**
three (3) — **דרײַ**
through (14) — **דורך**
throw out (*v*) — **אַרױס·וואַרפֿן** (אַרױסגעוואָרפֿן)
thunder (20) — **דונער** דער (ן)
thunder (*v*) — **דונערן**
  it's thundering (20) — עס דונערט
Thursday (2) — **דאָנערשטיק**
ticket (16) — **בילעט** דער (ן)
tickle (*v*) — **קיצלען**
tie (19) — **קראַוואַט** דער (ן)
time (2, 16) — **צײַט** די (ן)
  (at) what time . . . (16) — וויפֿל אַ זייגער...
  what time is it? (16) — וויפֿל האַלט דער זייגער?
time (instance) — **מאָל** דאָס (—)
times — **מאָל**
  three times four (3) — דרײַ מאָל פֿיר
tired (2) — **מיד**
Tishri (20) — **תּשרי** [טישרע]
to (7, 14) — **צו; אין; אויף** [אַף]
  to the theater — אין טעאַטער
  to a concert — אויף אַ קאָנצערט
to (someone's house) (14) — **צו**
to (*with place name*) — **קיין**
today (4, 6) — **הײַנט**
together (3) — **צוזאַמען**
tomato (13) — **פּאָמידאָר** דער (ן)
tomorrow (6) — **מאָרגן**
tongue (*SC*) — **צונג** די (ען)

too (also) (7)	אויך
too (excessively) (7)	צו
tooth (*SC*)	צאָן דער (ציין)
toothbrush (*SC*)	צייִנבערשטל דאָס (עך)
Torah (Pentateuch)	תּורה די [טוירע]
Torah scroll (12)	ספֿר־תּורה דער (ספֿרי־...) [סייפֿער־טוירע (סיפֿרע־...)]
towel (19, *SC*)	האַנטעך דער (ער)
train (21)	באַן די (ען)
translation	איבערזעצונג די (ען)
tree (*AB*, 7, 17)	בוים דער (ביימער)
trickle (*v*) (17)	רינען (איז גערונען)
trip	נסיעה די (–ות) [נעסיִע (ס)]
trolley (21)	טראַמוויַ דער (ען)
true (*CE*)	אמת [עמעס]
try (*v*) (*CE*)	פּרוּוון
Tuesday (2)	דינסטיק
tulip (9)	טולפּאַן דער (ען)
Turkey (1)	טערקיַ די
turn	ריי די (ען)
turn (*v*) (15; 16)	דרייען; פֿאַרקערעווען זיך (איך פֿאַרקערעווע זיך, מיר פֿאַרקערעווען זיך; פֿאַרקערעוועט)
turtle (17)	טשערעפּאַכע די (ס)
twelve (3)	צוועלף
twenty (3)	צוואַנציק
two (3)	צוויי
tzimmes (sweet fruit or vegetable stew) (13)	צימעס דער (ן)

U

ugly (7)	מיאוס [מיִעס]
Ukraine (1)	אוקראַיִנע די
Ukrainian (1)	אוקראַיִניש דאָס
umbrella (20)	שירעם דער (ס)
uncle (9)	פֿעטער דער (ס)
under (14)	אונטער
underline (*v*)	אונטער·שטרײַכן (אונטערגעשטרײַכט / אונטערגעשטראָכן)
understand (*v*) (1)	פֿאַרשטיין (איך פֿאַרשטיי, מיר פֿאַרשטייען; פֿאַרשטאַנען)
undressed: get undressed (*v*) (*SC*)	אויס·טאָן זיך (איך טו זיך אויס, מיר טוען זיך אויס; אויסגעטאָן)
unfamiliar	פֿרעמד
United States (1)	פֿאַראייניקטע שטאַטן די
university (1)	אוניווערסיטעט די (ן)
until (16)	ביז
us (*acc/dat*) (11, 14)	אונדז
use (*v*) (5)	ניצן
useful (1)	נוציק
usually (2)	געווייִנטלעך
utensil	כּלי די (ם) [קײלע (קײלים)]

V

vacation (10)	וואַקאַציע די (ס)
vase (14)	וואַזע די (ס)
vegetable (13, *SC*)	גרינס דאָס (ן)
vehicle	פֿאָרמיטל דאָס (ען)
verb (1)	ווערב דער (ן)
very (1)	זייער
vest (19)	וועסט דער (ן)
vinegar (13)	עסיק דער
violin	פֿידל דער (ען)
visit (*v*)	קומען/זײַן צו גאַסט
vocabulary (2)	וואָקאַבולאַר דער (ן)
vodka	וואָדקע די (ס)
take a shot of vodka (*v*) (6)	אַרײַנכאַפּן אַ וואָדקע
voice (8)	קול דאָס (ער) [קאָל (קעלער)]
vomit (*v*) (*SC*)	ברעכן (געבראָכן)

W

wait (*v*) (15)	וואַרטן (געוואַרט)
waiter (10)	קעלנער דער (ס) / קעלנערין די (ס)
wake up (*v*) (*SC*)	אויפֿ·וואַכן [אוף] (אויפֿגעוואַכט); אויפֿ·כאַפּן זיך [אוף] (אויפֿגעכאַפּט)
wall (5)	וואַנט די (ווענט)
want (*v*) (19)	וועלן (ער וויל; געוואָלט)
wardrobe (14)	אַלמער דער (ס)
warm (20)	וואַרעם
wash (*v*) (*SC*)	וואַשן (געוואַשן)
water (*AB*, 11)	וואַסער דאָס (ן)
watermelon (13)	אַרבוז דער (ן)
way	וועג דער (ן)
we (2)	מיר
weak (7)	שוואַך
wear (*v*) (11)	טראָגן (געטראָגן)
weather (20)	וועטער דער (ן)
wedding (9)	חתונה די (–ות) [כאַסענע (ס)]; חופּה די (–ות) [כופּע (ס)]
wedding canopy	חופּה די (–ות) [כופּע (ס)]
Wednesday (2)	מיטוואָך
week (2, 4)	וואָך די (ן)
last week (17)	פֿאַרגאַנגענע וואָך
weekend (19)	סוף־וואָך דער (ן) [סאָף־...]
welcome: you're welcome (2)	נישטאָ פֿאַר וואָס
well (2)	גוט
well done!	יישר־כּוח [יאַשער־קויעך]
well (*interjection*) (2)	נו
well, all right (2)	נו, גוט

west (1)	**מערבֿ** [מײַרעװ]
wet (20)	**נאַס**
what (1)	**װאָס**
what a...	**סאַראַ...**
wheel	**ראָד** די (רעדער)
when	**װען; אַז**
where (1)	**װוּ**
which (1)	**װעלכער** (װעלכע, װעלכעס); **װאָסער** (װאָסערע)
while (SC)	**בשעת** [בעשאַ́ס]
whip (*v*) (11)	**שמײַסן** (געשמיסן)
white (5)	**װײַס**
who (1)	**װער**
whole (5)	**גאַנץ**
whom (11)	**װעמען**
whose (7)	**װעמענס**
why (5)	**פֿאַר װאָס**
wide (7)	**ברײט**
wife (9)	**װײַב** דאָס (ער); **פֿרוי** די (ען)
will (*future tense aux)* (21)	**װעל** (איך װעל, דו װעסט)
win (*v*) (15)	**געװינען** (געװוּנען); **אױ́ס·שפּילן** (אױ́סגעשפּילט)
wind (20)	**װינט** דער (ן)
it's windy (*lit.* a wind is blowing) (20)	עס בלאָזט אַ װינט
window (5)	**פֿענצטער** דער (—)
wine (4, 13)	**װײַן** דער (ען)
winter (20)	**װינטער** דער (ן)
wipe (*v*) (SC)	**אָ́פּ·װישן** (אָ́פּגעװישט)
wish (*v*) (8, 11)	**װינטשן** (געװוּנטשן)
with (2, 14)	**מיט**
without	**אָן**
wolf (17)	**װאָלף** דער (װעלף)
woman (9)	**װײַב** דאָס (ער); **פֿרוי** די (ען)
wonderful!	**אײַ־אײַ־אײַ́**
word (1)	**װאָרט** דאָס (װערטער)
work (10)	**אַרבעט** די (ן)
work (*v*) (*AB*, 4)	**אַ́רבעטן** (איך אַרבעט, ער אַרבעט; געאַרבעט)
worker (10)	**אַ́רבעטער** דער (ס) / **אַ́רבעטערין** די (ס)
world (6)	**װעלט** די (ן)
in the world	אויף דער װעלט
in the world to come (6)	אויף יענער װעלט
worry (6)	**זאָרג** די (ן)
worry (*v*)	**זאָרגן**
worse	**ערגער**
wow!	**אוּװאַ́!**
write (*v*) (1, 2)	**שרײַבן** [שרײַבם] (געשריבן)
writer (3, 10)	**שרײַבער** דער (ס) / **שרײַבערין** די (ס)

Y

yarmulke (11)	**יאַ́רמלקע** די (ס)
year (8)	**יאָר** דאָס (ן)
I am ... years old (3)	איך בין אַלט ... יאָר
yearn (for) (*v*)	**בענקען** (נאָך)
yellow (5)	**געל**
yes (1)	**יאָ**
yesterday (6)	**נעכטן**
yet (6)	**נאָך**
not yet	נאָך נישט
Yiddish (1)	**ייִדיש** דאָס
in Yiddish (*CE*)	אויף ייִדיש [אַף]
Yom Kippur ("day of atonement") (8)	**יום־כּיפּור** דער [יאָם־קיפּער]
you (*pl; sg formal acc/dat*) (11, 14)	**אײַך**
you (*pl; sg formal*) (2)	**איר**
you (*sg informal acc*) (11)	**דיך**
you (*sg informal dat*) (14)	**דיר**
you (*sg informal*) (1)	**דו**
young (7)	**יונג**
younger (than) (3)	**ייִנגער** (פֿון)
your (*pl; sg formal*) (7)	**אײַער** (אײַערע)
your (*sg informal*) (7)	**דײַן** (דײַנע)

Z

zero (3)	**נול**

INDEXES

Three indexes follow: Culture Index (page I1), Grammar Index (page I4), and Vocabulary Index (page I7). Song and film titles are included in the Culture Index.

The notation *n* following a page number indicates that the subject is treated in a note box on that page. The notation *r* indicates a reference page (Vocabulary Overview or Grammar Overview).

CULTURE INDEX

GRAMMAR INDEX

VOCABULARY INDEX

T

V

W

Y

CREDITS

Grateful acknowledgment is made for use of the following video stills, photographs, realia, and readings.

Page Number	Citation
12	Traditional folk lyrics: "Lomir ale in eynem."
43, 44, 55	World Outline Map. Maps of the World.
71	Traditional folk lyrics: "Bulbe."
83	Traditional folk lyrics: "Sholem-aleykhem."
84	Jacob Ben-Ami and Edgar Ulmer, directors, *Grine felder* (USA: Collective Film Producers, 1937), National Center for Jewish Film at Brandeis University, 1978, DVD.
103	S. Efron (Zalmen Yefroikin) and Yudel Mark, "Vos tut der tate," in *Yidishe kinder b'* (New York: Educational Department of the Workmen's Circle, 1961), 51.
105	S. N. Sokolov, P. P. Uvarov, A. F. Belavin, and V. A. Kamenyetski, "Velt-karte," in *Geografisher atlas* (Moscow: Tsentraler felker-farlag fun f.s.s.r., 1928), 22–23.
110	Sh. Berenstein, "Sholem-aleykhem," in *Magazin fun yudishe lider far dem yudishen folk* (Zhytomyr: Y. M. Baksht, 1869).
111	Traditional folk lyrics: "Melave-malke lid."
113	Isidor Kaufmann, *Friday Evening* (c. 1920), oil on canvas, The Jewish Museum, in Maurice Berger and Joan Rosenbaum, eds., *Masterworks of the Jewish Museum* (New York: The Jewish Museum, New York and Yale University Press, 2004), 139.
114	"Sholem aleykhem: ilustrirte byografye," in *Argentiner beymelekh* 20:213/14 (Buenos Aires: March–April 1959), 5.
139	Benjamin Harshav, "Moyshe Kulbak Taught at My School," interviewed by Christa Whitney in North Haven, CT (Yiddish Book Center: Wexler Oral History Project, March 18, 2013), <https://www.yiddishbookcenter.org/collections/oral-histories/excerpts/woh-ex-0002384/moyshe-kulbak-taught-my-school>.
182	Traditional folk lyrics: "Shoyn avek der nekhtn."
204	Traditional folk lyrics: "Hevl iz havolim."
208	Kadia Molodowsky, "Martsepanes," in *Martsepanes: mayselekh un lider far kinder un yugnt* (New York: Educational Committee of the Workmen's Circle and CYCO Publishing House, 1970), 8–10.
209	Joseph Berne, director, *Mirele efros* (USA: Credo Pictures, 1939), National Center for Jewish Film at Brandeis University, 1978, DVD.
212	The Williamsburg Art Company, Rosh Hashanah postcard (c. 1910), collection of Yeshiva University Museum, New York, NY.
215	Hayyim Schauss, "A vort tsu yomim-neroim," in *Dos yontif-bukh* (New York: Self-published, 1933), 77.
216–217	Zina Rabinowitz, "Leshone-toyves," in *Der liber yontef* (*Our Holidays*) (New York: Farlag matones, 1958), 29–31.
218	Shmuel Tsesler, "Leshone-toyve," in Yoysef Mlotek and Mates Olitski, *Yidishe kinder b'* (New York: Bildungs komitet fun arbeter-ring, 1975), 13.
220	L–R, "Jewish New Year's greeting card" and "A Jewish New Year's Greeting," from the Archives of the YIVO Institute for Jewish Research, New York, NY, <http://yivo1000towns.cjh.org/album_details.asp?SearchType=SysCollections&CollectionName=Jewish+Holidays&CollectionID=39>.
221	"Tkhine nokh kapores shlogn," in *Shas tekhine rav peninim* (New York: Hebrew Publishing Company, 1916), 219–220.
223	Alexander Vaisman, *A Shidekh* (1997), oil on canvas, private collection of the Vaisman family.

Page Number	Citation
224	New York Public Library, "Posters, Yiddish: Learn English, Tompkins Square, Oct. 1920" (1920), New York Public Library Archives, New York Public Library, New York, NY, shelf number at NYPL: MssArc RG10 5928, <https://digitalcollections.nypl.org/items/510d47da-e321-a3d9-e040-e00a18064a99>.
234	Kadia Molodowsky, "Efnt dem toyer," in *Yidishe kinder (mayselekh)* (New York: Central Committee of the Jewish Folk Schools of the Jewish National Workers Alliance and Poale Zion in the United States and Canada, 1945), 21–22.
237	Moyshe Kulbak, *Zelmenyaner*, in *Geklibene verk* (New York: Congress for Jewish Culture, 1953), 17–25.
253	M. M. Shaffir, "Yidish iz mayn mame," in *A stezhke* (Montreal: Published by the author, 1940), 100.
255	Mark Varshavski, "Di mekhutonim geyen," in *Yidishe folkslider* (Buenos Aires: Yoysef lifshits-fond baym kultur-kongres in argentine, 1958), 123-125.
257	Mani Leyb, "A morgnlid," in *Vunder iber vunder* (New York: Educational Department of the Workmen's Circle, 1930), 16.
268	Traditional folk lyrics: "Vos zhe vilstu."
274	Fyvush Finkel, "'Now there was an actor!'—Fyvush Finkel on Yiddish comic actor Ludwig Satz," interviewed by Christa Whitney in New York, NY (Yiddish Book Center: Wexler Oral History Project, October 23, 2014), <http://www.yiddishbookcenter.org/collections/oral-histories/excerpts/woh-ex-0004311/now-there-was-actor-fyvush-finkel-yiddish-comic-actor-ludwig-satz>.
280–281	Y. L. Peretz, "Etele," in *Far kleyne kinder: gezang un shpil*, vol. 1 (Vilna: Vilner farlag fun b. a. kletskin, 1925), 96.
287–288	Moyshe Nadir, "Mayn mishpokhe," in *Kind on keyt* (New York: International Workers Order, 1936), 6–8.
300–301	Traditional folk lyrics: "Shikt der har."
304	Sh. Anski, Sholem Aleichem, Kadia Molodowsky, and Rokhl Korn. From the Archives of the YIVO Institute for Jewish Research, New York, NY.
304	Mendele Moykher Sforim. Public Domain. Esther Kreitman. Photo courtesy of Hazel Karr.
309	Y. Y. Sigal, "A kholem vegn a kreml," in *Lider far yidishe kinder* (New York: Educational Department of the Workmen's Circle, 1961), 18.
325	Immanuel Olsvanger, *L'Chayim!* (New York: Schocken Books, 1949), 73.
331	Symcha Pietruszka, "Suke, sukes" and "Simkhes toyre," in *Yidishe folks-entsiklopedye*, vol. 2 (New York: Gilead Press, 1949), 418–421, 871–872.
332	Joseph Green and Conrad Tom, directors, *Mamele* (USA: Sphinx Film Corp., 1938), National Center for Jewish Film at Brandeis University, 2013, DVD.
333	Marc Chagall, opening illustration to chapter "Sukes," in Bella Chagall, *Brenendike likht* (New York: Folks-farlag bam idishn fraternaln folks-ordn, 1945), 89.
335	Bella Chagall, *Brenendike likht* (New York: Folks-farlag bam yidishn fraternaln folks-ordn, 1945), 96–97.
337	Abraham Reisen, "In suke," in *Naye verk* (Warsaw: Bikher far ale, 1911), 2:94–95.
339	Mark Varshavski, "Kinder, mir hobn simkhes-toyre," in *Yidishe folkslider* (Buenos Aires: Yoysef lifshits-fond baym kultur-kongres in argentine, 1958), 134-137.
342	Raphael Soyer, Dancing Lesson (1926), in *Self-Revealment: A Memoir* (New York: Maecenas Press–Random House, 1969), 57. © Estate of Raphael Soyer, courtesy of Forum Gallery, New York, NY.
343	Raphael Soyer, "Credo," in *100 hayntsaytike amerikaner yidishe moler un skulptorn (One Hundred Contemporary American Jewish Artists)* (New York: YKUF Art Section, 1947), 176.

Page Number	Citation
344	United States Census Bureau, "Awareness Poster, Yiddish—Form D-3289 (Y)" (November 2009), <https://www.census.gov/2010census/partners/pdf/Awareness_Poster_Yiddish.pdf>, accessed July 20, 2017.
356	Meir Charatz, "Dos bisele shpayz," in *In fremdn gan-eydn* (Tel Aviv: I. L. Peretz Publishing House, 1974), 71.
359	Isadore Lillian, "Gefilte Fish".
382	Sofia Palatnikova, interviewed by Dov-Ber Kerler and Jeffrey Veidlinger (AHEYM: The Archive of Historical and Ethnographic Yiddish Memories, Indiana University, July 17, 2002) <http://eviada.webhost.iu.edu/atm-playback.cfm?w=89&sn=MDV%20688&t=1754&sID=69&pID=162&sc=1&fbclid=IwAR3bdehVtju6s9wMu1YJPUJsVUMpGBXlUbAqmlJ3QrHaydDCY8517xQnyNs. 06:47–10:27>.
384, 385	Traditional folk lyrics: "Got hot bashafn himl mit erd."
394	Jacob Gordin, *Got, mensh un tayfel*, in *Yankev gordin's dramen*, vol. 1 (New York: Soyrkel fun yankev gordin's fraynt, 1911), 12.
396	Joseph Seiden, director, *Got, mentsh un tayvl* (USA: Aaron Productions, Inc., 1949), National Center for Jewish Film at Brandeis University, 1978, DVD.
416	Meir Charatz, "Un ot azoy," in *In fremdn gan-eydn* (Tel Aviv: I. L. Peretz Publishing House, 1974), 282.
418	Y. L. Cahan, "13. A mayse fun a bobetske mit a sakh kinderlekh: zibete mayse," in *Gezamlte ksovim, vol. 5 (yidishe folks-mayses)* (Vilna: YIVO, 1940), 49.
422, bottom left	Tsirl Waletzky, illustration to "Di mayse fun khanike," in Yoysef Mlotek and Mates Olitski, *Yidishe kinder b'* (New York: Bildungs komitet fun arbeter-ring, 1975), 39. Found as reprinted in *Lakat khomer-limud beyidish; khanuka ba; khanike kumt* (Tel Aviv: Misrad hakhinukh vehatarbut, 1986), 12.
422, bottom right	S. Efron (Zalmen Yefroikin) and Yudel Mark, *Yidishe kinder b'* (New York: Educational Department of the Workmen's Circle, 1961), 84.
422, top	Tsirl Waletzky, *Khanike* (New York: Shultsenter baym yidishn kultur-kongres, 1967), 2, 10.
423	Yoysef Mlotek and Mates Olitski, "Di mayse fun khanike," in *Yidishe kinder b'* (New York: Bildungs komitet fun arbeter-ring, 1975), 39–40.
423	Yudl Mark, *Di mayse fun khanike* (New York: Bildungs komitet fun arbiter-ring, 1946), 15–16.
426	Leon Elbe, "Tsum zeydn af latkes," in *Ingele ringele: di tshikave vunderlakhe geshikhte fun a ingele mit a ringele* (New York: Farlag matones, 1929), 60–65.
429	Mordkhe Rivesman, "Khanike, oy khanike," in Samuel Bugatch, ed., *Doyres zingen* (New York: Farband bikher farlag, 1961), 251.
431	A. Bulkin, "Dreydl-shpil," in *Ruike shpiln* (Vilna: Yidishe tsentrale shul-organizatsye, 1921), 33–34.
434	Stanisława Centnerszwerowa, *Pejzaż* [*Landscape*] (1917), oil on canvas, Muzeum Sztuki w Łodzi, Łódź, Poland.
436	Ester Levin, "Freylekhe geshikhte n' 2," in *Grininke beymelekh* 10:180 (Vilna: May 15, 1936), National Library of Israel, 319-320.
455	Advertisement for Tip-Top, *Undzer tribune* 8:3 (Mexico City: July 15, 1942), 15.
456–457	Advertisements for Idisher folks teater and Bibliotek fun der idisher yugnt-gezelshaft, *Meksikaner shriftn* 2:2 (Mexico City: 1937), 2.
461–462, A12	*Der nayester yudisher salon flirt* (Warsaw: B. Diamondstein, 1919), 4, 15, 18; <https://archive.org/details/dernayeseryudishoounse>.
469	Advertisement for Yidish-vokh 2016, email (Copake: Yugntruf, 2016).
469–470	"Shabes 8.20," in "Tsaytplan: yidish-vokh 2016" (Copake, NY: Yugntruf, August 20, 2016), 10.

Page Number	Citation
473–474	Fanni Levando, advertisement and "Bazukher-bukh," in *Vegetarish-dietisher kokhbukh: 400 shpayzn gemakht oysshlislekh fun grinsn* (Wilno: G. Kleckina, 1938), 232–234.
475	Shaul and Yitzhak Goskind, directors, *Dos yidishe lebn in bialistok* (Warsaw: Sektor Films, 1939), National Center for Jewish Film at Brandeis University, DVD.
517	Traditional folk lyrics: "Di mame iz gegangen."
519	Khaver-Paver, "Der hoz un a zunen shtral," in *Khaver-pavers mayselakh*, vol. 1 (*Mayzele ganef*) (New York: Farlag matones, 1925), 57–59.
525	Elimeylekh Lebenshul, "Minhogim un yontoyvim," in *Kobrin zamlbukh (an iberblik ibern yidishn kobrin)* (ed. Meylekh Glotser) (Buenos Aires: Bukh-komitet baym kobriner landslayt fareyn, 1951), 74.
525	Rokhl Leye Mletshkovitsh, "Mayn heym in velkher ikh bin oysgevaksn," in *Porisover yizker-bukh* (ed. Yekhiel Granatshteyn) (Tel Aviv: Irgun yoytsey porisov in yisroel, 1971), 242–243.
528	Ida Maze, "Purim-lid," in *Vaksn mayne kinderlekh: muter un kinder-lider* (Montreal: Self-published with the help of Kanader yidisher kongres, 1954), 172.
529	Fania Brantsovsky, "Purim at the Sofye Gurevich Shul," interviewed by Christa Whitney in Vilnius, Lithuania (Yiddish Book Center: Wexler Oral History Project, July 27, 2012), <http://www.yiddishbookcenter.org/collections/oral-histories/excerpts/woh-ex-0002446/purim-sofye-gurevich-school>.
530	Joseph Green and Jan Nowina-Przybylski, directors, *Der purim-shpiler* (Poland: Green-Film, 1937), National Center for Jewish Film at Brandeis University, DVD.
532–533	Louis Leon Ribak, "Credo," and painting *In mitn zumer (Midsummer)*, in *100 haynttsaytike amerikaner yidishe moler un skulptorn (One Hundred Contemporary American Jewish Artists)* (New York: YKUF Art Section, 1947), 152–153.
535	"Invitation to a Purim Ball" (Kołomyja, Second Polish Republic: Algemeyner profesyoneler fareyn "briderlekhkeyt," in kolomey, February 28, 1926). From the Archives of the YIVO Institute for Jewish Research, New York, NY, <http://polishjews.yivoarchives.org/archive/index.php?p=digitallibrary/digitalcontent&id=2294#>.
569	Traditional folk lyrics: "Yome, yome."
572	"Tayere idishe tekhter!" (2014), placard found posted in Williamsburg, New York, NY.
583	Meir Kharats, "S'iz fintster in gas," in *In fremdn gan-eydn* (Tel Aviv: I. L. Peretz Publishing House, 1974), 335.
588	Philip Krantz, "Di tsvelf mazoles," in *Himel un erd: astronomye far'n folk* (New York: Forverts, 1918), 42.
591–592	Elkhonen Indelman, "Mayn yidisher kalendar," in *Gut yontef kinder* (New York: Jewish Education Committee Press, 1958), 4–6.
599	Rivka Basman Ben-Hayim, "A vort," in *Liderheym* (Tel Aviv: Beys sholem-aleykhem, 2012), 17.
600	"New York harbor by moonlight" (Berlin: Souvenir Post Card Co., c. 1901-1907), The Miriam and Ira D. Wallach Division of Art, Prints and Photographs: Picture Collection, The New York Public Library, New York, NY, <https://digitalcollections.nypl.org/items/510d47e2-8d93-a3d9-e040-e00a18064a99>.
600	Anna Margolin, "Shlanke shifn," in *Lider* (New York: Orion Press,1929), 52.
607	Traditional folk lyrics: "Her nor, du sheyn meydele."
609–611	Abraham Hochman, *Di geheyme kraft, oder der shlisel tsu der nevue* (New York: Professor A. Hochman, 1909), 45–48, 54–71 (text), 7 (business card).
615	Traditional folk lyrics: "Zog zhe rebenyu."

Page Number	Citation
620	Traditional folk lyrics: "Shnirele-perele."
628	Samuel Zagat, "Gimpel beynish der shadkhn: vos der veter novi hot tsu ihm iz oykh shver tsu farshtehn," *Di warheit* (New York: March 21, 1914).
631	Moyshe-Leyb Halpern, "Di zun vet aruntergeyn," in *In nyu-york* (New York: Farlag matones, 1954), 156.
632	Ilya Motyleff and Sidney Goldin, directors, *Dem khazns zindl* (*The Cantor's Son*) (USA: Eron Pictures, 1937), National Center for Jewish Film at Brandeis University, DVD.
634-635	Itzik Manger, "Afn veg shteyt a boym," in *Lid un balade* (New York: Itsik-manger-komitet, 1952), 369–370.
640–641	Yoysef Mlotek and Mates Olitski, "Fun khumesh," in *Yidishe kinder b'* (New York: Bildungs komitet fun arbeter-ring, 1975), 88–89.
641–642	Symcha Pietruszka, "Peysekh" and "Seyder (peysekh baynakht)," in *Yidishe folks-entsiklopedye*, vol. 2 (New York: Gilead Press, 1949), 413–414, 580–582.
643–644	Shira Gorshman, "Peysekh," in *Yomtev inmitn vokh: roman, dertseylungen, un noveln, rayze-bilder* (Moscow: Farlag sovetski pisatel, 1984), 170–171.
646–647	Beyle Schaechter-Gottesman, "S'iz matse do," in *Fli mayn flishlang: kinderlider mit musik* (New York: League for Yiddish, 1999), 36–37.
649	Yudel Mark, translator, "Ma nishtano," in Mikhl Gelbart, Israel Jacob Schwartz, Hershl Novak, and Y. Levin, eds., *A naye hagode shel peysekh* (Philadelphia: Bildungs komitet fun arbeter ring, 1948), 7.
651	Elizabeth Elkin Weiss, *The Rabbi* (1973), graphite on paper, private collection of the Weiss family.
653	"Leshone toyve shifskarte" (New York: Hebrew Publishing Company, 1909). From the Archives of the YIVO Institute for Jewish Research, New York, NY.
671	Symcha Pietruszka, "Shvues," in *Yidishe folks-entsiklopedye*, vol. 2 (New York: Gilead Press, 1949), 799–800.
673	Mayer Kirshenblatt, Shavuot (1993), acrylic on canvas, in *They Called Me Mayer July: Painted Memories of a Jewish Childhood in Poland Before the Holocaust* (Berkeley: University of California Press, 2007), 283–284.

Every attempt to contact rights holders has been made; if there are any omissions, please contact us at education@yiddishbookcenter.org.